ETERNAL
PERSPECTIVES

ETERNAL
PERSPECTIVES
❧ A COLLECTION OF QUOTATIONS ❧
ON HEAVEN, THE NEW EARTH, AND LIFE AFTER DEATH

RANDY
ALCORN

Tyndale House Publishers, Inc.
Carol Stream, Illinois

Library of Congress Cataloging-in-Publication Data

Eternal perspectives : a collection of quotations on heaven, the new earth, and life after death / [compiled by] Randy Alcorn.
    p. cm.
    Includes bibliographical references (p.) and index.
    ISBN 978-1-4143-4557-4 (hc)
 1. Heaven—Christianity. 2. Future life—Christianity. I. Alcorn, Randy C.
    BT846.3.E825 2012
    236′.2—dc23   2011041690

It's only right that Nanci and I should dedicate a book named *Eternal Perspectives* to the wonderful staff, board members, and volunteers of Eternal Perspective Ministries, the nonprofit organization we launched in 1990, which by God's grace and their efforts continues to expand its Christ-centered impact: Brenda Abelein, Janet Albers, Lance Alcorn, Stephanie Anderson, Bryan Brown, Doreen Button, Amy Campbell, Kress Drew, Jay Echternach, Rebecca Ekstrom, Robin Green, Bonnie Hiestand, Mary Hunt, Linda Jeffries, Wendy Jeffries, Steve Keels, Dave Martin, Paul Martin, Sharon Misenhimer, Dwight Myers, Kathy Norquist, Bob Schilling, Sandi Swanson, and Sherie Way.

It's also only right that we should include the supporters of our ministry, some of whom for twenty-two years now have partnered with us so that together we might invest in eternity, to the glory of our Lord Jesus and in the celebration of his grace and kindness. Nanci and I wish to thank all of you for who you are and what you do. We are deeply grateful to God for each of you! We honor you for "your partnership in the gospel from the first day until now" (Philippians 1:5) because you have honored King Jesus. It is our privilege to serve him by your side.

Contents

Acknowledgments ix

Introduction. xi

Adventure: New Opportunities and Abilities 1

Anticipating and Longing for Heaven and
     the New Earth 13

Beauty 29

Bodies and Their Resurrection 37

Boredom 53

Bride of Christ 61

Children. 67

Choosing between Heaven and Hell. 73

Continuity of Personal Identity
     (from This Life to the Next). 87

Culture, Arts, and Technology on the New Earth . . 101

The Curse 117

Death. 127

Dream World or Reality? 145

Earth's Demolition and Renovation 161

Eating and Drinking 173

Eternity and Life after Death 183

Ethnicity and Diversity 197

Friends and Relationships. 205

Gender and Sexuality 219

Glory 225

God, and Our Relationship with Him 233
Heaven's Saints Seeing Events on Earth 251
Hell 257
Home. 287
Jesus. 299
Joy, Happiness, and Laughter. 311
Judgment and Justice 329
The Kingdom of Heaven 339
Knowledge, Learning, and Books. 351
Marriage and Family 363
New Earth: The Future Heaven 373
The New Jerusalem 391
Paradise: The Present Heaven. 407
Paths to Heaven and Hell. 417
Pets and Animals 427
Pilgrim Mentality. 443
Play, Sports, and Recreation 451
Preparing for Heaven 461
Redemption. 475
Reign of Christ and His People 491
Rest in Heaven. 505
Resurrection of the Universe. 513
Rewards and Treasures 531
Sinners No More, Forever Righteous 545
Thinking Heavenward 555
Time and Process in Heaven. 573
Uniting of Heaven and Earth 583
Work in Heaven. 595
Worship and Music 607

Notes 617
Index 653
About the Author. 657

Acknowledgments

Thanks to Doreen Button for helping me assemble many of these quotations from my research notes, articles, and books.

Thanks to Kathy Norquist for going through my selected quotations in search of problems that needed fixing.

Thanks to Bonnie Hiestand, Stephanie Anderson, and Bob Schilling for being available to help me find elusive bibliographic details on that last, harried sixteen-hour workday before the final book corrections had to be submitted. Special thanks to Bob who, when there was no other alternative, bravely left his computer to conduct a scholarly hands-on search in an actual seminary library (you know, the kind with books). His venture was a smashing success, leading to yet another great quotation and proving that there are still hidden treasures that can be found only in real, bound volumes beautifully positioned on shelves.

Finally, thanks to all my wonderful friends at Tyndale House, including Ron Beers, Carol Traver, Lisa Jackson, and Karen Watson, for agreeing to publish books I believe God has put on my heart, and Joan Hutcheson, who has tirelessly attended to so many of the details.

And thanks above all to Stephanie Voiland Rische, for being one of the finest, most patient, and most delightful editors I've ever had (and I've had some very good ones). Stephanie, it is an honor to work with you.

Introduction

In your presence there is fullness of joy; at your right
hand are pleasures forevermore.
PSALM 16:11, ESV

The sense that we will live forever somewhere has shaped every
civilization in human history. Australian Aborigines pictured
Heaven as a distant island beyond the western horizon. The early
Finns thought it was an island in the faraway east. Mexicans,
Peruvians, and Polynesians believed that they went to the sun or
the moon after death. Native Americans believed that in the afterlife their spirits would hunt the spirits of buffalo. Although various
depictions of the afterlife differ, the unifying testimony of the
human heart throughout history is belief in life after death. Anthro-
pological evidence suggests that every culture has a God-given,
innate sense of the eternal—that this world is not all there is.

But which beliefs are true? And which speculations are grounded
on solidly biblical concepts? In researching my book *Heaven*, I collected and read 150 books on the subject, and I've read another dozen
since writing it—nearly every book about Heaven I have ever been
able to locate. I underlined particularly significant portions of many

of these, but only a small amount of the most interesting material made it into that book or my other books on the subject, including *In Light of Eternity, 50 Days of Heaven, TouchPoints: Heaven, Heaven for Kids,* and *We Shall See God.* I've often regretted that great words of insight into Heaven and the New Earth have been left to sit unseen in hundreds of files in my computer!

Over the years I've received thousands of letters and had hundreds of conversations with people about the Heaven books. I find many people thirsty for more insight. This compilation of quotations is true to Scripture and, I believe, speaks to areas of great interest. Necessarily, some of these involve speculation, but I have tried not to include any that contradict what God has revealed in his Word. I don't agree with every aspect of the theologies or personal lives of those I quote from, but I do believe these quotations will help prepare God's children for the magnificent world our Savior and Lord is preparing for us.

The majority of quotations in this book are from other people. But because I've written a number of nonfiction books on Heaven, and I have scenes depicting Heaven in most of my novels, I have included passages from my own books that may prove enlightening or encouraging for readers. It's inevitable, since I've written all these books on Heaven and believe what I wrote (and know where to find it!), that there are a significant number of those quotes. I have deliberately chosen ones that supplement and expand on others' quotations. My greatest delight in assembling this book has not been in my own writing but in what I have discovered over many years of research in the writings of others. I am indebted first to God's Word and then to these many writers who helped me formulate my own insights.

Whether our hearts are heavy or light, whether recent days have brought us joy or sorrow or both, there is something soul stirring about contemplating what God has promised us and what Christ shed his blood and rose to guarantee us—eternal life with him and his people in a land of never-ending wonder.

As W. H. Griffith Thomas wrote, "The consideration of heaven is no mere spiritual luxury, no mere intellectual dissipation, no imaginative revelry, but is really and definitely practical and suitable . . . and has a real bearing on our daily life."[1]

I have always enjoyed reading books of well-chosen quotations on interesting subjects. I like the breadth, the variety, the joy of discovering a beautifully written or particularly insightful observation. I like writing that causes me to think about and to rethink positions I have taken for granted but that may not be accurate. I enjoy marking the page, writing notes in the margin, or highlighting the e-book, and I hope you'll find yourself doing the same with this volume.

If while reading a compilation of quotations I come periodically to something I don't much value, I console myself that I've wasted very little time reading it! You won't treasure everything equally in this volume, but I'm confident many entries will encourage and enrich you as you contemplate God's revealed promises concerning Heaven and the great and eternal world that will be our home, where we will live forever with him.

I am especially grateful to God for the opportunity to assemble this book because my many interactions with grieving, lonely, and hurting believers have prompted me to envision how some people will use it. They will pick it up and perhaps read just one quotation or page or section at a sitting, and they will smile, nod, weep, pray, and worship. They may underline it, read a quotation to a friend, e-mail it, or post a quotation on Facebook. They may copy it and place it somewhere prominent. God may use it to touch their hearts and comfort them, or to help them find joy and prepare for the world to come. I know how deeply God has spoken to me through many of the words in this book, and I am thrilled at the thought that he will do the same for others.

Whether you skip around this volume looking at topics of interest or work your way from cover to cover, I pray God will use it to help you set your mind above, where Christ is (Colossians 3:1-2). I pray your heart will testify more and more that you are a citizen of another world, of a better country, with a glorious King. And I pray you will joyfully cling to his promises that he will return to restore and remake a ruined Earth. He will bring his throne and Heaven itself down to it to set up his eternal Kingdom, where he will reign as King of kings. In that world, joy will be the air we breathe—may this book help us to inhale some of that joy here and now!

You'll notice *Eternal Perspectives* contains a number of quotations from Scripture directly following each new topic heading. That's because no other statements in this book, certainly not my own, are authoritative. Everything else of value in this book is derivative of and secondary to what God has done for us and promised us.

Quoting Scripture about Heaven and the New Earth raises an important issue and brings to mind a Christian leader who was visiting my office in 2003. He looked at the dozens of books and extensive notes scattered around the room and asked what I was writing. "A big book on Heaven," I said. He wrinkled his brow. "Well," he replied, "since Scripture says, 'No eye has seen, no ear has heard, no mind has conceived what God has prepared for those who love him,' what will you be talking about? Obviously, we can't know what God has prepared for us in Heaven." (He was referring to 1 Corinthians 2:9.)

I said to him what I always say: "You didn't complete the sentence. You also have to read verse 10. Here's how the complete sentence reads: 'No eye has seen, no ear has heard, no mind has conceived what God has prepared for those who love him—*but God has revealed it to us by his Spirit*'" (emphasis added). The context makes it clear that this revelation is God's Word (verse 13), which tells us what God has prepared for us. What we otherwise could not have known about Heaven, because we're unable to see it, God says *he has revealed to us through his Spirit*. This means that God has explained to us what Heaven and the New Earth are like. Not exhaustively, but accurately. God tells us about Heaven and the New Earth in his Word, not so we can shrug our shoulders and remain ignorant, but because he wants us to understand and anticipate what awaits us!

We cannot anticipate or desire what we cannot imagine. That's why, I believe, God has given us glimpses of Heaven in the Bible—to fire up our imaginations and kindle a desire for Heaven in our hearts.

And that's why Satan will always discourage our imaginations—or misdirect them to ethereal or misguided notions that violate Scripture. As long as the resurrected universe remains either undesirable or unimaginable to us, Satan succeeds in sabotaging our love for Heaven, which makes us more desperately attached to our current existence and more vulnerable to embracing a shortsighted rather than an eternal perspective.

Scripture provides us with a substantial amount of information, direct and indirect, about the world to come, with enough detail to help us envision it, but not so much as to make us think we can completely wrap our minds around it. I believe that God expects us to use our imaginations, even as we recognize their limitations and flaws. If God didn't want us to imagine what Heaven will be like, he wouldn't have told us as much about it as he has (or, conversely, he would have told us everything there was to know).

Rather than ignore our imaginations, I believe we should fuel them with Scripture, allowing them to step through the doors that Scripture opens. I did not come to the Bible with the same view of Heaven that I came away with. On the contrary, as a young Christian, and even as a young pastor, I viewed Heaven in many of the same stereotypical ways I now reject. It was only through years of scriptural study, meditation, and research on the subject that I came to the view of Heaven I now embrace.

Discussions of Heaven tend to be either hyper-imaginative or utterly unimaginative. Bible believers have tended toward the latter, yet both approaches are potentially dangerous. What we need are biblically inspired imaginations. Yes, there are things Scripture has not directly told us. As C. S. Lewis wrote, "Guesses, of course, only guesses. If they are not true, something better will be."[2] But there are many things God has told us in Scripture that do not require guesswork on our part. He has told us so we don't have to guess, but so we can imagine, in our mind's eye, what he has revealed to be true.

One of the distinctives of this book of quotations reflects my own personal convictions about a vital biblical doctrine that Bible-believing Christians have ignored—that of the New Earth and our eternal future as resurrected people living in a resurrected physical universe. If you're familiar with my books, you know the emphasis I put on this. You will find in this book perhaps a few hundred references to this exciting biblical teaching that you may never have seen before.

All the quotations I cite, of course, are subject to biblical scrutiny. I chose them because I found them inspirational, educational, or both. But apart from the Scripture itself, nothing in this book is authoritative. I encourage you to hold what I say up to God's Word to test it, as the book of Acts describes: "Now the Bereans were of more noble character than the Thessalonians, for they received the message with great eagerness and examined the Scriptures every day to see if what Paul said was true" (Acts 17:11).

The apostle Paul himself, under God's inspiration, wrote, "Test everything. Hold on to the good" (1 Thessalonians 5:21).

You will notice that I do not quote from any books involving near-death experiences or visions, in which people claim to have gone to Heaven or to Hell and personally observed it. The reason for this is simple—neither I nor this book's readers can be certain about those experiences. There just isn't any objective way to verify them.

I've read most of these books, and I realize that a number of these accounts come from sincere followers of Christ. But some of them contradict the others, and more seriously, they sometimes contradict Scripture itself. Now God can certainly give people experiences and visions without consulting me. But when someone says he or she died and went to Heaven and saw a rainbow-colored horse, for instance, though it may be interesting and that person is certain this really happened, I can't be so sure. So while I do not mean to dismiss all these accounts, and I know some readers might have wished me to include them, it seemed inappropriate to cite them in a book of this sort.

Counting the biblical passages, this book contains more than 1,500 quotations about Heaven and the New Earth. I encourage you to ask God's help in removing the blinders of preconceived ideas and becoming open to what Scripture teaches. Paul said, "Reflect on what I am saying, for the Lord will give you insight into all this" (2 Timothy 2:7). I encourage you to pray, "Open my eyes that I may see wonderful things in your law" (Psalm 119:18). What Scripture actually teaches us is far more wonderful than the tired stereotypes of Heaven that have long dominated not only popular culture but even the church.

For God's children, I pray that what you find in this book will help you draw closer to the Person who made you for himself and will deepen your desire for the place he is making for you. If you are not yet a child of God, I pray that what you find in this book will prompt you to turn to the Savior, who said, "This is eternal life: that they may know you, the only true God, and Jesus Christ, whom you have sent" (John 17:3).

Adventure: New Opportunities and Abilities

All these people died still believing what God had promised them. They did not receive what was promised, but they saw it all from a distance and welcomed it. They agreed that they were foreigners and nomads here on earth. Obviously people who say such things are looking forward to a country they can call their own. If they had longed for the country they came from, they could have gone back. But they were looking for a better place, a heavenly homeland. That is why God is not ashamed to be called their God, for he has prepared a city for them.

HEBREWS 11:13-16, NLT

The nations will fear the name of the LORD,
    all the kings of the earth will revere your glory.

For the LORD will rebuild Zion
  and appear in his glory.

PSALM 102:15-16

They will neither harm nor destroy
  on all my holy mountain,
for the earth will be full of the knowledge of the LORD
  as the waters cover the sea.

In that day the Root of Jesse will stand as a banner
for the peoples; the nations will rally to him, and his
place of rest will be glorious.

ISAIAH 11:9-10

I suspect that every saved soul in heaven is a great wonder, and that
heaven is a vast museum of wonders of grace and mercy—a palace of
miracles, in which everything will surprise everyone who gets there.[3]

Charles Spurgeon, "Feeble Faith Appealing to a Strong Savior"

Everyone raised his hand to pick the fruit he best liked the look of,
and then everyone paused for a second. This fruit was so beautiful
that each felt, "It can't be meant for me . . . surely we're not allowed
to pluck it."
  "It's all right," said Peter. ". . . I've a feeling we've got to the
country where everything is allowed."[4]

C. S. Lewis, *The Last Battle*

Aslan turned to them and said, "You do not yet look so happy as I
mean you to be."
  Lucy said, "We're so afraid of being sent away, Aslan. And you
have sent us back into our own world so often."
  "No fear of that," said Aslan. "Have you not guessed?"
  Their hearts leaped and a wild hope rose within them.

"There was a *real* railway accident," said Aslan softly. "Your father and mother and all of you are—as you used to call it in the ShadowLands—dead. The term is over: the holidays have begun. The dream is ended: this is the morning."

And as he spoke he no longer looked to them like a lion; but the things that began to happen after that were so great and beautiful that I cannot write them. And for us this is the end of all the stories, and we can most truly say that they all lived happily ever after. But for them it was only the beginning of the real story. All their life in this world and all their adventures in Narnia had only been the cover and the title page; now at last they were beginning Chapter One of the Great Story, which no one on earth has read; which goes on forever; in which every chapter is better than the one before.[5]

C. S. Lewis, *The Last Battle*

Something better awaits and beckons us all. We shall be "like the angels," which means not neutered, anaemic spirits, but full, free and liberated persons in whom all the possibilities of our God-given humanity will burst forth in undreamed-of fulfillment.[6]

Bruce Milne, *The Message of Heaven and Hell*

In the glimpses afforded of [Jesus'] life beyond resurrection we find . . . freedoms even further enhanced. At the physical level he can appear, disappear and then reappear at will (cf. John 20:19, 26; Luke 24:15, 31, 36, 51); at the moral and spiritual level there is a freedom from the awful burden of responsibility for the completion of his mission; at the relational level there is a new freedom to indwell and personally identify with all who belong to him. Such is the promise of the heavenly life—an existence of boundless freedoms.[7]

Bruce Milne, *The Message of Heaven and Hell*

We are partly "Heaven-blind" because the worldview our culture has adopted has made it hard to *see* supernatural colors.[8]

Daniel Brown, *What the Bible Reveals about Heaven*

Their souls being on fire with holy love, shall not be like a fire pent up, but like a flame uncovered and at liberty. Their spirits, being winged with love, shall have no weight upon them to hinder their flight. There shall be no lack of strength or activity, nor any lack of words with which to praise the Object of their affection. Nothing shall hinder them from communing with God, and praising and serving Him just as their love inclines them to do. Love naturally desires to express itself; and in heaven the love of the saints shall be at full liberty to express itself as it desires, whether it be towards God or to created beings.[9]

Jonathan Edwards, *Heaven: A World of Love*

In Heaven, as on earth, *each* of us will be or do something no one else will be or do as well. No one will be superfluous.[10]

Peter Kreeft, *Everything You Ever Wanted to Know about Heaven*

If it brings glory to God and increases our knowledge of Him, you will indeed be able to engage in some form of time travel.[11]

Larry Dick, *A Taste of Heaven*

We want to serve God more, but we have to sleep. We want to pray and study the Bible, but we grow weary. In Heaven, bodies will do whatever we want them to do. We will possess boundless energy with which to serve God.[12]

Steven J. Lawson, *Heaven Help Us!*

Actually, we will do many of the same things in Heaven that we did here on the earth—just perfectly.[13]

Steven J. Lawson, *Heaven Help Us!*

Look at the pictures of your deceased parents on your bedroom wall. Do you ever wonder, especially on their birthdays, where they are, and what they're doing?[14]

Arthur Roberts, *Exploring Heaven*

This voice of joy [in Heaven] is not like our old complaints, our impatient groans and sighs; nor this melodious praise like the scoffs and revilings, or the oaths and curses which we heard on earth. This body is not like that we had, nor this soul like the soul we had, nor this life like the life we lived. We have changed our place and state, our clothes and thoughts, our looks, language and company.

Before, a saint was weak and despised; so proud and peevish we could often scarce discern his graces; but now, how glorious is a saint! Where is now their body of sin, which wearied themselves and those about them? Where are now our different judgments, reproachful names, divided spirits, exasperated passions, strange looks, uncharitable censures? Now we are all of one judgment, of one name, of one heart, house and glory. O sweet reconciliation! Happy union! Now the Gospel shall no more be dishonored through our folly.

No more, my soul, shalt thou lament the sufferings of the saints or the church's ruins; nor mourn thy suffering friends, nor weep over their dying beds or their graves. Thou shalt never suffer thy old temptations from Satan, the world or thy own flesh. Thy pains and sickness are all cured; thy body shall no more burden thee with weakness and weariness; thy aching head and heart, thy hunger and thirst, thy sleep and labor are all gone.

O what a mighty change is this! from the dunghill to the throne! from persecuting sinners to praising saints! from a vile body to this which "shines as the brightness of the firmament!" from a sense of God's displeasure to the perfect enjoyment of him in love! from all my doubts and fears to this possession which puts me out of doubt! from all my fearful thoughts of death to this joyful life! Blessed change! Farewell sin and sorrow for ever; farewell my rocky, proud, unbelieving heart; my worldly, sensual, carnal heart; and welcome now my most holy, heavenly nature. Farewell repentance, faith and hope; and welcome love, and joy, and praise.[15]

Richard Baxter, *The Saints' Everlasting Rest*

Heaven is not a dream. Heaven is absolute reality. It is objective reality to us, not subjective. We don't make Heaven what it is, God does.

5

It is stable and very real. It unfolds with an orderly, yet spontaneous perfection. We do not skip frantically from one reality to another, back and forth, in and out, up and down as in a nightmare.

If the setting of a boat in water or a train is needed to fulfill God's desired experience, then it is so. In whatever setting God wishes to express Himself, there are no limitations to whatever He may choose.[16]

Drake Whitchurch, *Waking from Earth*

I do live expecting great things in the life that is ripening for me and all mine—when we shall have all the universe for our own, and be good merry helpful children in the great house of our father. . . . When we are all just as loving and unselfish as Jesus; when like him, our one thought of delight is that God is, and is what he is, . . . then, darling, you and I and all will have grand liberty wherewith Christ makes free—opening his hand to send us out like white doves to range the universe.[17]

George MacDonald, letter to his dying daughter

I haven't been cheated out of being a complete person—I'm just going through a forty-year delay, and God is with me even through that. Being "glorified"—I know the meaning of that now. It's the time, after my death here, when I'll be on my feet dancing.[18]

Joni Eareckson Tada

If Jesus' resurrected body is a clue, along with accounts of angels appearing to a host of other biblical worthies, I surmise that we will transport ourselves not only across but also through space—and with what by earth standards would seem incredible speed. Anyone who has envied a hawk's ability to soar or a whale's to dive can get enthusiastic about heavenly release from present limitations of mobility.[19]

Arthur Roberts, *Exploring Heaven*

These small and perishable bodies we now have were given to us as ponies are given to schoolboys. We must learn to manage: not that we may some day be free of horses altogether but that some day we may ride bare-back, confident and rejoicing, those greater mounts, those winged, shining and world-shaking horses which perhaps even now expect us with impatience, pawing and snorting in the King's stables. Not that the gallop would be of any value unless it were a gallop with the King; but how else—since He has retained His own charger— should we accompany Him?[20]

C. S. Lewis, *Miracles*

We shall not cease from exploration
And the end of all our exploring
Will be to arrive where we started
And know the place for the first time.[21]

T. S. Eliot, "Little Gidding"

As our minds expanded, we came to the realization that there were no limitations to that which we might do. Eternity gave us the opportunity to carry forward the grandest enterprises, reach the highest aspirations, and realize our loftiest ambitions. And ever before us there were new heights to surmount, new wonders to admire, new truths to comprehend, and fresh objects to call forth the powers of body and mind and soul.[22]

Walton Brown, *Home at Last*

Throughout eternity we will live full, truly human lives, exploring and managing God's creation to his glory. Fascinating vistas will unfold before us as we learn to serve God in a renewed universe.[23]

Edward Donnelly, *Biblical Teaching on the Doctrines of Heaven and Hell*

What will these glorified human beings be able to do in their trans- figured universe, on their transfigured earth? The simplest answer seems to be: whatever they wish. For according to an old theological dictum heaven will mean the satisfaction of every rational desire. And their transfigured cosmos will obviously be an "extension of heaven," wide open to whatever use the glorified men will wish to put it. It will be theirs to use and develop into an even better and better universe. There will be no conflicts, no enmities, no hatred, no wars, no property bounds, no segregation, no discrimination. There will be abundant space and abundant opportunity for everyone to do whatever he wishes and wherever he wishes. . . . Their beatific vision will make it impossible for them to be uncharitable, envious, jealous, avaricious, unjust.[24]

E. J. Fortman, *Everlasting Life after Death*

There will be new planets to develop, new principles to discover, new joys to experience. Every moment of eternity will be an adventure of discovery.[25]

Ray C. Stedman, "The City of Glory"

Imagine sitting around campfires on the New Earth, wide-eyed at the adventures recounted. Yes, I mean telling real stories around real campfires. Why not? After all, friendship, camaraderie, laughter, stories, and cozy campfires are all good gifts from God.[26]

Randy Alcorn, *Heaven*

On the New Earth we may experience adventures that make our current mountain climbs, surfing, skydiving, and upside-down roller coaster rides seem tame. Why do I say this? It's more than wishful thinking. It's an argument from design. We take pleasure in exhilarating experiences not because of sin but because *God wired us this way*. We weren't made to sit all day in dark rooms, watching actors pretend to live and athletes do what we can't.[27]

Randy Alcorn, *Heaven*

At 2:30 a.m., on November 19, 2002, I stood on our deck gazing up at the night sky. Above me was the Leonid meteor shower, the finest display of celestial fireworks until the year 2096. For someone who has enjoyed meteor showers since he was a kid, this was the celestial event of a lifetime.

There was only one problem: clouds covered the Oregon sky. Of the hundreds of streaking meteors above me, I couldn't see a single one. I felt like a blind man being told, "You're missing the most beautiful sunset of your lifetime. You'll never be able to see another like it."

Was I disappointed? Sure. After searching in vain for small cracks in the cloud cover, I went inside and wrote these paragraphs. I'm disappointed, but not disillusioned. Why? Because I did *not* miss the celestial event of my lifetime.

My lifetime is forever. My residence will be a new universe, with far more spectacular celestial wonders, and I'll have the ability to look through the clouds or rise above them.

During a spectacular meteor shower a few years earlier, I had stood on our deck watching a clear sky. Part of the fun was hearing oohs and aahs in the distance, from neighbors looking upward. Multiply these oohs and aahs by ten thousand times ten thousand, and it'll suggest our thunderous response to what our Father will do in the new heavens as we look upward from the New Earth.[28]

Randy Alcorn, *50 Days of Heaven*

Heaven will be deeply appreciated by the disabled, who will be liberated from ravaged bodies and minds, and by the sick and elderly who will be free from their pains and restrictions. They will walk and run and see and hear, some for the first time. Hymn writer Fanny Crosby said, "Don't pity me for my blindness, for the first face I ever see will be the face of my Lord Jesus."[29]

Randy Alcorn, *Money, Possessions, and Eternity*

In Heaven, we will be able to do as we wish and go where we wish, never wondering if our wishes are wrong!

Randy Alcorn, unpublished notes

Think of friends or family members who loved Jesus and are with him now. Picture them with you, walking together in this place. All of you have powerful bodies, stronger than those of an Olympic decathlete. You are laughing, playing, talking, and reminiscing. Now you see someone coming toward you. It's Jesus, with a big smile on his face. You fall to your knees in worship. He pulls you up and embraces you.

At last, you're with the person you were made for, in the place you were made for. Everywhere you go, there will be new people to meet, including Charles Spurgeon and his friends Charles Stanford and Hugh Stowell Brown. There will be new places to enjoy, new things to discover. What's that you smell? A feast? A party's ahead. And you're invited.[30]

Randy Alcorn, *We Shall See God*

One of the greatest things about Heaven is that we'll no longer have to battle our desires. They'll always be pure, attending to their proper objects. We'll enjoy food without gluttony and eating disorders. We'll express admiration and affection without lust, fornication, or betrayal. Those simply won't exist.[31]

Randy Alcorn, *Heaven*

Do you remember a time when you really felt good about yourself? Not in pride or arrogance, but when you sensed you honored God, helped the needy, were faithful, humble, and servant-hearted, like Jesus? Do you remember when you encouraged someone? when you experienced who you were meant to be? when you were running or swimming or working and felt you were strong enough to go on forever (even though later you could hardly get out of bed)? That was a little taste of who you'll be in Heaven.[32]

Randy Alcorn, *Heaven*

I believe the New Earth will offer us opportunities we wished for but never had. God's original plan was that human beings would live happy and fulfilling lives on Earth. If our current lives are our only chances at that, God's plan has been thwarted. Consider the injustice—many honest, faithful people never got to live fulfilling lives, while some dishonest and unfaithful people seemed to fare much better.[33]

Randy Alcorn, *Heaven*

Want to see the crossing of the Red Sea? Want to be there when Daniel's three friends emerge from the fiery furnace? It would be simple for God to open the door to the past.

Because God is not limited by time, he may choose to show us past events as if they were presently happening. We may be able to study history from a front-row seat.[34]

Randy Alcorn, *Heaven*

The term *perfect* is often misused when it describes our state in Heaven. I've heard it said, for instance, "We'll communicate perfectly, so we'll never be at a loss for words." I disagree. I expect we'll sometimes grasp for words to describe the wondrous things we'll experience. I expect I'll stand in speechless wonder at the glory of God. I'll be morally perfect, but that doesn't mean I'll be capable of doing anything and everything. (Adam and Eve were morally perfect, but that didn't mean they could automatically invent nuclear submarines or defy gravity. They were perfect yet finite, just as we will be.)[35]

Randy Alcorn, *Heaven*

Some people have a deep fear of public speaking, and they imagine that ruling means they'll be miserable, having to be "up front" and speak to groups. But the fear, anxiety, dread, and turmoil we associate with certain activities on the present Earth will be *gone* on the New Earth. If

God wants us to do something, we'll be wired and equipped to do it. Our service will not only bring him glory but also bring us joy.[36]

Randy Alcorn, *Heaven*

We all have dreams but often don't see them realized. We become discouraged and lose hope. But as Christ's apprentices, we must learn certain disciplines. Apprentices in training must work hard and study hard to prepare for the next test or challenge. Apprentices may wish for three weeks of vacation or more pay to pursue outside interests. But the Master may see that these would not lead to success. He may override his apprentices' desires in order that they might learn perspective and patience, which will serve them well in the future. While the young apprentices experience the death of their dreams, the Master is shaping them to dream greater dreams that they will one day live out on the New Earth with enhanced wisdom, skill, appreciation, and joy.[37]

Randy Alcorn, *Heaven*

Anticipating and Longing for Heaven and the New Earth

Hope deferred makes the heart sick,
> but a longing fulfilled is a tree of life.

Solomon, Proverbs 13:12

They were longing for a better country—a heavenly one. Therefore God is not ashamed to be called their God, for he has prepared a city for them.

Hebrews 11:16

We groan, longing to be clothed with our heavenly dwelling. . . . As long as we are at home in the body we are away from the Lord. . . . We . . . would prefer to be away from the body and at home with the Lord.

Paul, 2 Corinthians 5:2, 6, 8

According to His promise we are looking for new heavens and a new earth, in which righteousness dwells.

PETER, 2 PETER 3:13, NASB

The promises are the Christian's Magna Carta of liberty; they are the title deeds of his heavenly estate. Happy is he who knows how to read them well and call them all his own.[38]

Charles Spurgeon, "Obtaining Promises," Sermon 435

Christian, meditate much on heaven, it will help thee to press on, and to forget the toil of the way. This vale of tears is but the pathway to the better country: this world of woe is but the stepping-stone to a world of bliss. And, after death, what cometh? What wonder-world will open upon our astonished sight?[39]

Charles Spurgeon, *Morning and Evening*

A man on his deathbed turned to his physician and mumbled, "What is Heaven like, Doctor?" How could the physician describe Heaven in such brief moments? As his mind searched for an answer for his friend, the doctor heard his dog scratching at the door. "Can you hear my dog scratching at your door?" inquired the physician. The sick man assured him that he could. "Well," the doctor said, "Heaven must be like that. My dog does not know what is in this room. He only knows he wants to be with me. So it is with Heaven! Our Master is there. That is all we need to know!"[40]

James Jeremiah, *The Place Called Heaven*

To speak of "imagining heaven" does not imply or entail that heaven is a fictional notion, constructed by deliberately disregarding the harsher realities of the everyday world. It is to affirm the critical role of the God-given human capacity to construct and enter into mental pictures of divine reality, which are mediated through Scripture and the subsequent tradition of reflection and development. We are able to inhabit the mental images we create, and thence anticipate the delight of finally entering the greater reality to which they correspond.[41]

Alister McGrath, *A Brief History of Heaven*

One of the most disconcerting experiences which can come our way is to make a long journey, perhaps even to the other side of the world, and to discover on arrival that we have not been expected. The hotel reservation has not been made, or, even more devastating, the friendly home is all locked up and the warm welcome we have anticipated over the miles is not awaiting us, due to a mix-up of dates or the loss of a letter or e-mail. Heaven, however, is guaranteed not to disappoint. . . . We are expected.[42]

Bruce Milne, *The Message of Heaven and Hell*

One day when George MacDonald, the great Scottish preacher and writer, was talking with his son, the conversation turned to heaven and the prophet's version of the end of all things. "It seems too good to be true," the son said at one point. A smile crossed MacDonald's whiskered face. "Nay," he replied, "it is just so good it must be true."[43]

Larry Dixon, *Heaven: Thinking Now about Forever*

"When God wants to carry a point with his children," Emerson said, "he plants his argument into the instincts." Our deepest instinct is heaven. Heaven is the ache in our bones, the splinter in our heart.[44]

Mark Buchanan, *Things Unseen*

The man who is about to sail for Australia or New Zealand as a settler, is naturally anxious to know something about his future home, its climate, its employments, its inhabitants, its ways, its customs. All these are subjects of deep interest to him. You are leaving the land of your nativity, you are going to spend the rest of your life in a new hemisphere. It would be strange indeed if you did not desire information about your new abode. Now surely, if we hope to dwell for ever in that "better country, even a heavenly one," we ought to seek all the knowledge we can get about it. Before we go to our eternal home we should try to become acquainted with it.[45]

J. C. Ryle, *Heaven*

"Lying here on my bed, when I [missionary Adoniram Judson] could not talk, I have had such views of the loving condescension of Christ, and the glories of heaven, as I believe are seldom granted to mortal man. It is not because I shrink from death that I wish to live, neither is it because the ties that bind me here, though some of them are very sweet, bear any comparison with the drawings I at times feel toward heaven; but a few years would not be missed from my eternity of bliss, and I can well afford to spare them, both for your sake and for the sake of the poor Burmans [people he served].

"I am not tired of my work, neither am I tired of the world; yet when Christ calls me home, I shall go with the gladness of a boy bounding away from his school. Perhaps I feel something like the young bride, when she contemplates resigning the pleasant association of her childhood for a yet dearer home—though only a very little like her, for *there is no doubt resting on my future.*"

"Then death would not take you by surprise," I [Edward Judson, Adoniram's son] remarked, "if it should come even before you could get on board ship?"

"O, no," he said, "death will never take me by surprise—do not be afraid of that—I feel so strong in Christ. He has not led me so tenderly thus far, to forsake me at the very gate of heaven. No, no; I am willing to live a few years longer, if it should be so ordered; and if otherwise, I am willing and glad to die now. I leave myself entirely in the hands of God, to be disposed of according to His will."[46]

Edward Judson, *The Life of Adoniram Judson*

While Christians still accept heaven as an article of faith, their vigor in defining the nature of eternal life has much diminished. In spite of the current revival of religious interest in America and Europe, the desire to discuss the details of heavenly existence remains a low priority.[47]

Colleen McDannell and Bernhard Lang, *Heaven: A History*

When you speak of Heaven . . . let your face light up, let it be irradiated with a heavenly gleam, let your eyes shine with reflected glory. But when you speak of Hell—well, then your ordinary face will do.[48]

Charles Spurgeon

The seventeenth-century philosopher, mathematician, and theologian Blaise Pascal gave a reason for [the feeling that something is] missing. Do you miss, he asked, something you've never had? Do you grieve the absence of a third leg, or the loss of a second pair of eyes? No. We ache only when something we once knew, held, tasted, goes missing. We sorrow over the eyes or legs or arms we once had and then lost, not over those we have never had. So why is it that our heart feels this harrowing absence, this desolate sense of loss? What are we missing?[49]

Mark Buchanan, *Things Unseen*

Homesickness—this perpetual experience of missing something— usually gets misdiagnosed and so wrongly treated. . . . All our lives we take hold of the wrong thing, go to the wrong place, eat the wrong food. We drink too much, sleep too much, work too long, take too many vacations or too few—all in the faint hope that this will finally satisfy us and so silence the hunger within.

. . . Here is the surprise: God made us this way. He made us to yearn—to always be hungry for something we can't get, to always be missing something we can't find, to always be disappointed with what we receive, to always have an insatiable emptiness that no thing can fill and an untamable restlessness that no discovery can still. Yearning itself is healthy—a kind of compass inside us, pointing to True North.

It's not the wanting that corrupts us. What corrupts us is the wanting that's misplaced, set on the wrong thing. If we don't understand that—if we don't understand that God has set eternity in our hearts to make us heavenly-minded, we skew or subvert the yearning and scatter it in a thousand wrong directions.

But the cure for our yearning and our restlessness is not to keep getting more. . . . The cure is to yearn for the right thing, the Unseen Things.

. . . We are metaphysically handicapped. This is not so much a design flaw as a *designed* flaw, a glitch wired into the system, a planned obsolescence.

. . . This shaking, unslaked desire in me is a divining rod for streams of Living Water. . . . He put in me, in you, a homing device for heaven. We just won't *settle* for anything less.[50]

Mark Buchanan, *Things Unseen*

A Philadelphia law firm sent flowers to an associate in Baltimore upon the opening of its new offices. Through some mix-up, the ribbon that bedecked the floral piece read "Deepest Sympathy."

When the florist was informed of his mistake, he let out a cry of alarm. "Good heavens," he exclaimed, "then the flowers that went to the funeral said, "'Congratulations on your new location!'"

Heaven will be a wonderful new location.[51]

Steven J. Lawson, *Heaven Help Us!*

I had rather be in hell with Christ, than be in heaven without him.[52]

Martin Luther, quoted in *We Shall See God*

O my Lord Jesus Christ, if I could be in heaven without You, it would be a hell; and if I could be in hell, and have You still, it would be a heaven to me, for You are all the heaven I need.[53]

Samuel Rutherford, quoted in *Morning and Evening*

You want to go home. The instinct for heaven is just that: homesickness, ancient as night, urgent as daybreak. All your longings—for the place you grew up, for the taste of raspberry tarts that your mother once pulled hot from the oven, for that bend in the river where your father took you fishing as a child, where the water was dark and swirling and the caddis flies hovered in the deep shade—all these longings are a homesickness, a wanting in full what all these things only hint at, only prick you with. These are the things seen that conjure in our emotions the Things Unseen.[54]

Mark Buchanan, *Things Unseen*

Like Adam, we have all lost Paradise; and yet we carry Paradise around inside of us in the form of a longing for, almost a memory of, a blessedness that is no more, or the dream of blessedness that may someday be again.[55]

Frederick Buechner, *The Magnificent Defeat*

A real, almost palpable, yearning attends me. . . . My yearnings whisper, "There should be more." I sense that I was meant to be more . . . better, that I was meant to live in a world of beauty, justice, and love; that I have a capacity to love and be loved that even my deepest loves and friendships can't satisfy. I struggle to find ways to express it. All I know is that it feels like homesickness.[56]

Jean Fleming, *The Homesick Heart*

The sweetest thing in all my life has been the longing . . . to find the place where all the beauty came from . . . my country, the place where I ought to have been born. Do you think it all meant nothing, all the longing? The longing for home.[57]

Psyche, in *Till We Have Faces*, by C. S. Lewis

The human heart holds a secret. If we could read the language of our heart—an undeciphered hieroglyph etched in the deepest part of our being—we would find an implanted assurance of other realms.[58]

Jean Fleming, *The Homesick Heart*

In nature, everything moves in the direction of its hungers. In the spiritual world it is not otherwise. We gravitate toward our inward longing, provided of course that those longings are strong enough to move us.[59]

A. W. Tozer, *The Size of the Soul*

God does not create a longing or a hope without having a fulfilling reality ready for them. But our longing is our pledge, and blessed are the homesick, for they shall come home.[60]

Isak Dinesen, *Babette's Feast and Other Anecdotes of Destiny*

Creatures are not born with desires unless satisfaction for those desires exists. A baby feels hunger: well, there is such a thing as food. A duckling wants to swim: well, there is such a thing as water. Men feel sexual desire: well, there is such a thing as sex. If I find in myself a desire which no experience in this world can satisfy, the most probable explanation is that I was made for another world. If none of my earthly pleasures satisfy it, that does not prove that the universe is a fraud. Probably earthly pleasures were never meant to satisfy it, but only to arouse it, to suggest the real thing. If that is so, I must take care, on the one hand, never to despise, or be unthankful for, these earthly blessings, and on the other, never to mistake them for the something else of which they are only a kind of copy, or echo, or mirage. I must keep alive in myself the desire for my true country, which I shall not find till after death; I must never let it get snowed under or turned aside; I must make it the main object of life to press on to that other country and to help others to do the same.[61]

C. S. Lewis, *Mere Christianity*

For the power Thou hast given me to lay hold of things unseen: For the strong sense I have that this is not my home: For my restless heart which nothing finite can satisfy: I give Thee thanks, O God.[62]

John Baillie, *A Diary of Private Prayer*

Most of us find it very difficult to want "Heaven" at all—except in so far as "Heaven" means meeting again our friends who have died. One reason for this difficulty is that we have not been trained: our whole education tends to fix our minds on this world. Another reason is that when the real want for Heaven is present in us, we do not recognise it. Most people, if they had really learned to look into their own hearts, would know that they do want, and want acutely, something that cannot be had in this world. There are all sorts of things in this world that offer to give it to you, but they never quite keep their promise. . . . There was something we grasped at, in that first moment of longing, which just fades away in the reality.[63]

C. S. Lewis, *Mere Christianity*

God will see to it that the man who finds God in his earthly happiness and thanks him for it does not lack reminder that earthly things are transient, that it is good for him to attune his heart to what is eternal, and that sooner or later there will be times when he can say in all sincerity, "I wish I were home."[64]

Dietrich Bonhoeffer, *Letters and Papers from Prison*

Can you hear the sighing in the wind? Can you feel the heavy silence in the mountains? Can you sense the restless longing in the sea? Can you see it in the woeful eyes of an animal? Something's coming . . . something better.[65]

Joni Eareckson Tada, *Heaven: Your Real Home*

What can this incessant craving, and this impotence of attainment mean, unless there was once a happiness belonging to man, of which only the faintest traces remain, in that void which he attempts to fill with everything within his reach?[66]

Blaise Pascal, *Pensées*

The settled happiness and security which we all desire, God withholds from us by the very nature of the world: but joy, pleasure, and merriment He has scattered broadcast. We are never safe, but we have plenty of fun, and some ecstasy. It is not hard to see why. The security we crave would teach us to rest our hearts in this world and oppose an obstacle to our return to God: a few moments of happy love, a landscape, a symphony, a merry meeting with our friends, a bathe or a football match, have no such tendency. Our Father refreshes us on the journey with some pleasant inns, but will not encourage us to mistake them for home.[67]

C. S. Lewis, *The Problem of Pain*

We have come to a wretched emphasis in the Christian Church, so that when we talk about the future, we talk about "eschatology" instead of heaven.

Once more I repeat that Christians are living too much in the "present now"—and the anticipation of better things to come has almost died out of the Church of Christ.

We find ourselves so well-situated now that we don't really need any tomorrow's heaven. We don't need to hope—we have everything well enough now.[68]

A. W. Tozer, *The Quotable Tozer II*

The Christian optimism is based on the fact that we do *not* fit in to the world. I had tried to be happy by telling myself that man is an animal, like any other which sought its meat from God. But now I really was happy, for I had learnt that man is a monstrosity. I had been right in feeling all things as odd, for I myself was at once worse and better than all things. The optimist's pleasure was prosaic, for it dwelt on the naturalness of everything; the Christian pleasure was poetic, for it dwelt on the unnaturalness of everything in the light of the supernatural. The modern philosopher had told me again and again that I was in the right place, and I had still felt depressed even in acquiescence. But I had heard that I was in the *wrong* place, and my soul sang for joy, like a bird in spring. The knowledge found out and illuminated forgotten chambers in the dark house of infancy. I knew now why grass had always seemed to me as queer as the green beard of a giant, and why I could feel homesick at home.[69]

   G. K. Chesterton, *Orthodoxy*

Let us greet the day which assigns each of us to his own home, which snatches us from this place and sets us free from the snares of the world, and restores us to paradise and the kingdom. Anyone who has been in foreign lands longs to return to his own native land. . . . We regard paradise as our native land.[70]

   Cyprian, *Mortality*

To come to Thee is to come home from exile, to come to land out of the raging storm, to come to rest after long labour, to come to the goal of my desires and the summit of my wishes.[71]

   Charles Spurgeon, *Morning and Evening*

Our greatest affliction is not anxiety, or even guilt, but rather homesickness—a nostalgia or ineradicable yearning to be at home with God.[72]

   Donald Bloesch, *Theological Notebook*

We are afraid that heaven is a bribe, and that if we make it our goal we shall no longer be disinterested. It is not so. Heaven offers nothing that a mercenary soul can desire. It is safe to tell the pure in heart that they shall see God, for only the pure in heart want to.[73]

   C. S. Lewis, *The Problem of Pain*

If we take the imagery of Scripture seriously, if we believe that God will one day give us the Morning Star and cause us to put on the splendour of the sun, then we may surmise that both the ancient myths and the modern poetry, so false as history, may be very near the truth as prophecy. At present we are on the outside of the world, the wrong side of the door. We discern the freshness and purity of morning, but they do not make us fresh and pure. We cannot mingle with the splendours we see. But all the leaves of the New Testament are rustling with the rumour that it will not always be so. Some day, God willing, we shall get *in*.[74]

C. S. Lewis, *The Weight of Glory*

The world is booby-trapped. It's rigged for disappointment. On earth everything falls short of some hoped-for ideal. Everything good down here has a tragic brevity and a funny aftertaste to it. It all falls short and shortly falls apart. None of it possesses any ultimacy.

In response, we can become so cynical that we poison ourselves, so self-indulgent that we devour ourselves, so despairing that we collapse into ourselves. In fact, self-pity and self-indulgence, boredom and despair, envy and greed—such are only yearning gone sour. They are just the greasy residue that remains after yearning has gone unfulfilled too many times. A sadness like ash settles on our doings and our desires. We find trinkets to fiddle with, trivia to distract us. A once-burning zeal dwindles to a dry itch, and everything becomes a frantic attempt to get the passion back, or a plodding resignation to its death.[75]

Mark Buchanan, *Things Unseen*

The door on which we have been knocking all our lives will open at last. . . . Apparently, then, our lifelong nostalgia, our longing to be reunited with something in the universe from which we now feel cut off, to be on the inside of some door which we have always seen from the outside, is no mere neurotic fancy, but the truest index of our real situation. And to be at last summoned inside would be both glory and honour beyond all our merits and also the healing of that old ache.[76]

C. S. Lewis, *The Weight of Glory*

All of us are homesick for Eden.
We yearn to return to a land we've never known.
Deep is the need to go back to the garden,
A burning so strong, for a place we belong,
A place that we know is home.[77]

Claire Cloninger and Paul Smith

Here thou hast no abiding city; and wherever thou shalt be, thou art a stranger and a pilgrim; nor wilt thou ever have rest except thou be united with Christ.[78]

Thomas à Kempis, *The Imitation of Christ*

I may not long for death, but I surely long for heaven.[79]

Joseph Bayly, *A Voice in the Wilderness*

The youthful build their hopes upon the mists of dawn. The healthy launch their optimistic conquests under the fleeting smile of a noonday sun. Those who succeed enjoy the fickle favors of fortune for a while. But after youth has flown, health is gone, and earthly aspirations recede before the advancing shadows of senility and death, then, turning from the wreckage of our shattered dreams, we scan the farther banks of Jordan and long for home.[80]

E. X. Heatherley, *Our Heavenly Home*

People sometimes tell me that they dread the thought of endless days. But when I press them, what they truly dread is endless monotony and boredom and repetition of the same dull things over and over. Their human heart longs for freshness and newness and adventure, yet also longs for the familiar, the sense of being home. Heaven will fulfill not one longing, but both.

Randy Alcorn, unpublished notes

Nothing is more often misdiagnosed than our homesickness for Heaven. We think that what we want is sex, drugs, alcohol, a new job, a raise, a doctorate, a spouse, a large-screen television, a new car, a cabin in the woods, a condo in Hawaii. What we really want is the person we were made for, Jesus, and the place we were made for, Heaven. Nothing less can satisfy us.[81]

Randy Alcorn, *50 Days of Heaven*

Home is where friends come to visit us. Home is where we read and reflect and listen to the music we enjoy. It's where we putter and plant gardens and rest to gain strength for our tasks. Home is the place I inhale the wonderful aroma of strong rich coffee every morning. . . . Home is where Nanci fixes wonderful meals, including the world's best apple pie.

I realize it sounds like I'm romanticizing home. Yes, many people have had very bad experiences in their earthly homes. But the point is, our home in heaven is our real home. It will have all the good things about our earthly home, multiplied many times, but none of the bad.[82]

Randy Alcorn, *In Light of Eternity*

Nobody wants to leave a good party early. Christians faced with death often feel they're leaving the party before it's over. They have to go home early. They're disappointed, thinking of all they'll miss when they leave.

But the truth is, the real party is under way at home—precisely where they're going! They're not the ones missing the party; those of us left behind are. . . .

One by one, believers will disappear from the world. Those of us who are left behind will grieve that our loved ones have left home. In reality, however, our believing loved ones aren't leaving home, they're going home. They'll be home before us. We'll be arriving at the party a little later. Laughter and rejoicing—a party awaits us. Don't you want to join it?[83]

Randy Alcorn, *TouchPoints: Heaven*

We long for a return to Paradise—a perfect world, without the corruption of sin, where God walks with us and talks with us in the cool of the day. Because we're human beings, we desire something tangible and physical, something that will not fade away. And that is exactly what God promises us—a home that will not be destroyed, a kingdom that will not fade, a city with unshakable foundations, an incorruptible inheritance.[84]

Randy Alcorn, *Heaven*

Sometimes when we look at this world's breathtaking beauty—standing in a gorgeous place where the trees and flowers and rivers and mountains are wondrous—we feel a twinge of disappointment. Why? Because we know we're going to leave this behind. In consolation or self-rebuke, we might say, "This world is not my home." If we were honest, however, we might add, "But part of me sure wishes it were."[85]

Randy Alcorn, *Heaven*

After reading my novel *Deadline*, which portrays Heaven as a real and exciting place, a woman wrote me, "I've been a Christian since I was five. I'm married to a youth pastor. When I was seven, a teacher at my Christian school told me that when I got to Heaven I wouldn't know anyone or anything from Earth. I was terrified of dying. I was never told any different by anyone. . . . It's been really hard for me to advance in my Christian walk because of this fear of Heaven and eternal life."

Let those words sink in: "this *fear* of Heaven and eternal life." Referring to her recently transformed perspective, she said, "You don't know the weight that has been lifted off of me. . . . Now I can't wait to get to Heaven."[86]

Randy Alcorn, *We Shall See God*

When I see ocean fish in an aquarium, I enjoy watching them, but I feel as if something's wrong. They don't belong there. It's not their home. The fish weren't made for that little glass box; they were made for a great ocean.

I suppose the fish don't know any better, but I wonder if their instincts tell them that their true home is elsewhere. I know *our* instincts tell us that this fallen world isn't our home—we were made for someplace better.[87]

Randy Alcorn, *Heaven*

I've never been to Heaven, yet I miss it. Eden's in my blood. The best things of life are souvenirs from Eden, appetizers of the New Earth. There are just enough of them to keep us going but never enough to make us satisfied with the world as it is or ourselves as we are. We live between Eden and the New Earth, pulled toward what we once were and what we yet will be.[88]

Randy Alcorn, *We Shall See God*

Beauty

One thing have I asked of the LORD,
    that will I seek after:
that I may dwell in the house of the LORD
    all the days of my life,
to gaze upon the beauty of the LORD
    and to inquire in his temple.

DAVID, PSALM 27:4, ESV

The Mighty One, God, the LORD,
    speaks and summons the earth
    from the rising of the sun to the place where
        it sets.
From Zion, perfect in beauty,
    God shines forth.
Our God comes and will not be silent;
    a fire devours before him,
    and around him a tempest rages.

He summons the heavens above,
and the earth, that he may judge his people:
"Gather to me my consecrated ones,
who made a covenant with me by sacrifice."
And the heavens proclaim his righteousness,
for God himself is judge.

ASAPH, PSALM 50:1-6

This is what the LORD Almighty says: "In a little
while I will once more shake the heavens and the
earth, the sea and the dry land. I will shake all nations,
and the desired of all nations will come, and I will fill
this house with glory," says the LORD Almighty.

HAGGAI 2:6-7

Holy, holy, holy is the LORD Almighty;
the whole earth is full of his glory.

ISAIAH 6:3

O Lord,
I live as a fish in a vessel of water,
only enough to keep me alive,
but in heaven I shall swim in the ocean.
Here I have a little air in me to keep me breathing,
but there I shall have sweet and fresh gales;
Here I have a beam of sun to lighten my darkness,
a warm ray to keep me from freezing;
yonder I shall live in light and warmth for ever
Quicken my hunger and thirst after the realm above.[89]

The Valley of Vision: A Collection of Puritan Prayers and Devotions

Give me to know that heaven is all love,
   where the eye affects the heart,
   and the continual viewing of thy beauty
   keeps the soul in continual transports of delight.
Give me to know that heaven is all peace,
   where error, pride, rebellion, passion raise no head.
Give me to know that heaven is all joy,
   the end of believing, fasting, praying,
   mourning, humbling, watching, fearing, repining;
And lead me to it soon.[90]

The Valley of Vision: A Collection of Puritan Prayers and Devotions

How soon do earthly lovers come to an end of their discoveries of each other's beauty; how soon do they see all there is to be seen! But in Heaven there is with new beauties always being discovered.[91]

Jonathan Edwards, *Heaven: A World of Love*

In heaven 'tis the directly reverse of what 'tis on earth; for there, by length of time things become more and more youthful, that is, more vigorous, active, tender, and beautiful.[92]

Jonathan Edwards, *The Works of Jonathan Edwards: The Miscellanies*

The attributes of God are to be seen in the visible creation, but they are to be seen in a brighter and superior light in the new creation. There is not one of the attributes of God which has no illustration under God's revelation of his grace. You shall be happy in your whole being if you can fully rejoice in that which God creates.[93]

Charles Spurgeon, "God Rejoicing in the New Creation," Sermon 2211

The most tragic strain in human existence lies in the fact that the pleasure which we find in the things of this life, however good that pleasure may be in itself, is always taken away from us. The things for which men strive hardly ever turn out to be as satisfying as they expected, and in the rare cases in which they do, sooner or later they are snatched away. . . . For the Christian, all those partial, broken and fleeting perfections which he glimpses in the world around him, which wither in his grasp and are snatched away from him even while they wither, are found again, perfect, complete and lasting in the absolute beauty of God.[94]

Peter Toon, *Heaven and Hell: A Biblical and Theological Overview*

If there is a rush to see beautiful objects, grand and sublime sights, magnificent scenery, and the works of art, on account of the intense pleasure enjoyed through sense of sight, what shall we say of the exquisite pleasures in store for that sense in Heaven! Then again, reflect how very captivating, soothing, and enlivening is music. The ear revels in it, and pours into the soul torrents of harmony, which make her, for the time, altogether forget the outer world. So captivating is it that hours pass by unheeded, and she would almost fancy it is the echoes of angels' voices she hears. What, then, must heavenly harmony be, if our imperfect music is so delightful? Think, also, how exquisitely the odors of flowers, incense, and all manner of perfumery produce a soothing effect upon man, banishing cares, and infusing a new life into him. What must these pleasures be in Heaven?

The five senses of the human body are not mere accidental ornaments, which may or may not exist; they are essential to the integrity of its nature.[95]

Father J. Boudreau, *The Happiness of Heaven*

Earth's crammed with heaven, and every common bush afire with God; but only he who sees takes off his shoes—the rest sit round it and pluck blackberries.[96]

Elizabeth Barrett Browning, *Aurora Leigh*

All beauty in the world is either a memory of Paradise or a prophecy of the transfigured world.[97]

Nicholas Berdyaev, *The Divine and the Human*

Will our resurrection bodies require food or an equivalent energy source? I think so, for although greatly enhanced, we remain creatures of God, not ghostly apparitions. Will we need clothing? It's a beneficial social practice on earth, in my judgment (considering the alternative), and certainly practical, weather wise. It would be a nice convention to continue, in heaven, whether or not the climate requires it. As for jewelry and other accessories, I guess our yearning for beauty might lead to some such enjoyments. . . . Clothes are especially fulfilling for people who find artistic expression and satisfaction through designing or wearing them.[98]

Arthur Roberts, *Exploring Heaven*

The books or the music in which we thought the beauty was located will betray us if we trust to them; it was not in them, it only came through them, and what came through them was longing. These things the beauty, the memory of our own past are good images of what we really desire; but if they are mistaken for the thing itself they turn into dumb idols, breaking the hearts of their worshippers. For they are not the thing itself; they are only the scent of a flower we have not found, the echo of a tune we have not heard, news from a country we have not visited.[99]

C. S. Lewis, *Screwtape Proposes a Toast*

In glorified bodies we will enjoy a restored and improved Eden, a place of pristine beauty and unbroken fellowship. . . . The new heaven and earth will provide an environment conducive to the most precious values we now know—just and loving relationships, fellowship, beauty, and significant activity.[100]

Gordon Lewis and Bruce Demarest, *Integrative Theology*

God uses the mind as a living pallet that paints the color, shape, form and texture of His creation. Mind is a prism that breaks out and manifests God's perfect light onto the rich and glorious details of Heaven, all under God's command and control.[101]

Drake Whitchurch, *Waking from Earth*

The unquiet republic of the maze of planets, struggling fierce towards heaven's free wilderness.[102]

Percy Bysshe Shelley, "Prometheus Unbound"

We do not want merely to see beauty. . . . We want something else which can hardly be put into words—to be united with the beauty we see, to pass into it, to receive it into ourselves, to bathe in it, to become part of it.[103]

C. S. Lewis, *The Weight of Glory*

The beauty of the present world . . . has something about it of the beauty of a chalice, beautiful in itself but more hauntingly beautiful in what we know it's meant to be filled with. . . . When we read Romans 8, we find Paul affirming that the whole of creation is groaning in travail as it longs for its redemption. Creation is good, but it is not God. It is beautiful, but its beauty is at present transient. It is in pain, but that pain is taken into the very heart of God and becomes part of the pain of new birth. The beauty of creation, to which art responds and which it tries to express, imitate, and high-light, is not simply the beauty it possesses in itself but the beauty it possesses in view of what is promised to it: back to the chalice, the violin, the engagement ring. We are committed to describing the world not just as it should be, not just as it is, but as—by God's grace alone!—one day it will be.[104]

N. T. Wright, *Surprised by Hope*

It is virtually beyond our power to conceive of a future as consistently delightful as that which Christ is preparing for us. And who is to say what is possible with God?[105]

A. W. Tozer, *Born after Midnight*

If God hath made this world so fair
Where sin and death abound,
How beautiful beyond compare
Will paradise be found.[106]

James Montgomery, *The Poetical Works*

When I anticipate my first glimpse of Heaven, I remember the first time I went snorkeling. I saw countless fish of every shape, size, and color. And just when I thought I'd seen the most beautiful fish, along came another even more striking. Etched in my memory is a certain sound—the sound of a gasp going through my rubber snorkel as my eyes were opened to that breathtaking underwater world.

I imagine our first glimpse of Heaven will cause us to similarly gasp in amazement and delight. That first gasp will likely be followed by many more as we continually encounter new sights in that endlessly wonderful place.[107]

Randy Alcorn, *We Shall See God*

Everything God tells us suggests we will look back at the present Earth and conclude, creatively speaking, that God was just "warming up" and getting started.

Look at God's track record in creating natural wonders in this universe. On Mars, the volcano Olympus Mons rises 79,000 feet, nearly three times higher than Mount Everest. The base of Olympus Mons is 370 miles across and would cover the entire state of Nebraska. The Valles Marineris is a vast canyon that stretches one-sixth of the way around Mars. It's 2,800 miles long, 370 miles wide, and 4.5 miles deep. Hundreds of our Grand Canyons could fit inside it.

The New Earth may have far more spectacular features than these. Imagine what we might find on the new Mars or the new Saturn and Jupiter and their magnificent moons. I remember vividly the thrill of first seeing Saturn's rings through my new telescope when I was eleven years old. It exhilarated me and stirred my heart. Five years later, I heard the gospel for the first time and came to know

Jesus, but the wonders of the heavens helped lead me to God. How many times in the new universe will we be stunned by the awesomeness of God's creation?[108]

Randy Alcorn, *Heaven*

Compared to what he now beheld, the world he'd come from was a land of shadows, colorless and two-dimensional. This place was fresh and captivating, resonating with color and beauty. He could not only see and hear it, but feel and smell and taste it. Every hillside, every mountain, every waterfall, every frolicking animal in the fields seemed to beckon him to come join them, to come from the outside and plunge into the inside. This whole world had the feel of cool water on a blistering August afternoon. The light beckoned him to dive in with abandon, to come join the great adventure.

"I know what this is," Li Quan said.

"Tell me," said the Carpenter.

"It's the substance that casts all those shadows in the other world. The circles there are copies of the spheres here. The squares there are copies of the cubes here. The triangles there are copies of the pyramids here. Earth was a flatland. This is . . . well, the inside is bigger than the outside, isn't it? How many dimensions are there?"

"Far more than you have seen yet," the King said, laughing.

"This is the Place that defines and gives meaning to all places," Li Quan said. "I never imagined it would be like this."[109]

Li Quan and Jesus, in *Safely Home,* by Randy Alcorn

Bodies and Their Resurrection

See also Resurrection of the Universe.

> Your dead will live;
>   their bodies will rise.
> You who dwell in the dust,
>   wake up and shout for joy. . . .
>   The earth will give birth to her dead.

ISAIAH 26:19

> After my skin has been destroyed,
>   yet in my flesh I will see God;
> I myself will see him
>   with my own eyes—I, and not another.

JOB 19:26-27

Many of those whose bodies lie dead and buried will rise up, some to everlasting life and some to shame and everlasting disgrace.

AN ANGEL, DANIEL 12:2, NLT

Someone may ask, "How are the dead raised? With what kind of body will they come?" How foolish! What you sow does not come to life unless it dies. When you sow, you do not plant the body that will be, but just a seed. . . . But God gives it a body as he has determined, and to each kind of seed he gives its own body. All flesh is not the same: Men have one kind of flesh, animals have another, birds another and fish another. There are also heavenly bodies and there are earthly bodies; but the splendor of the heavenly bodies is one kind, and the splendor of the earthly bodies is another. . . .

So will it be with the resurrection of the dead. The body that is sown is perishable, it is raised imperishable; it is sown in dishonor, it is raised in glory; it is sown in weakness, it is raised in power; it is sown a natural body, it is raised a spiritual body.

If there is a natural body, there is also a spiritual body. . . . And just as we have borne the likeness of the earthly man, so shall we bear the likeness of the man from heaven.

I declare to you, brothers, that flesh and blood cannot inherit the kingdom of God, nor does the perishable inherit the imperishable. . . .

We will be changed. For the perishable must clothe itself with the imperishable, and the mortal with immortality. When the perishable has been clothed with the imperishable, and the mortal with immortality, then the saying that is written will come true: "Death has been swallowed up in victory."

Where, O death, is your victory?
　　Where, O death, is your sting?

Paul, 1 Corinthians 15:55

The Lord Jesus Christ . . . will transform our lowly
bodies so that they will be like his glorious body.

Paul, Philippians 3:20-21

Beloved, we are God's children now; it does not yet
appear what we shall be, but we know that when he
appears we shall be like him, for we shall see him
as he is.

John, 1 John 3:2, rsv

The self-same bodies of the dead which were laid in the grave, being
then again united to their souls forever, shall be raised up by the
power of Christ.

Westminster Larger Catechism

Thou wilt come to raise my body from the dust,
and re-unite it to my soul,
by a wonderful work of infinite power and love,
greater than that which bounds the ocean's waters,
ebbs and flows the tides,
keeps the stars in their courses,
and gives life to all creatures.[110]

The Valley of Vision: A Collection of Puritan Prayers and Devotions

This earthly body is slow and heavy in all its motions, listless and
soon tired with action. But our heavenly bodies shall be as fire; as
active and as nimble as our thoughts are.[111]

Benjamin Calamy, *Sermons Preached upon Several Occasions*
by Benjamin Calamy

Why does God go to all the trouble to dirty his hands, as it were, with our decaying, sin-stained flesh, in order to reestablish it as a resurrection body and clothe it with immortality? . . . Because his Son paid the price of death so that the Father's purpose for the material universe would be fulfilled, namely, that he would be glorified in it, including in our bodies forever and ever.[112]

John Piper, "What Happens When You Die?"

Resurrected bodies are not intended just to float in space, or to flit from cloud to cloud. They call for a *new earth* on which to live and to work, glorifying God. The doctrine of the resurrection of the body, in fact, makes no sense whatever apart from the doctrine of the new earth.[113]

Anthony Hoekema, "Heaven: Not Just an Eternal Day Off"

After the Resurrection, you must remember, we shall need a place to live in—a literal, material place of residence. For these bodies of ours will be alive as well as our spirits, and they will need a world to live in, a New Heaven and a New Earth. Christ is preparing a place not for disembodied spirits, for they are already before the throne of God perfectly blessed. No, a place for the entire personhood of his people, when spirit, soul, and body shall be again united and we as complete people shall receive the adoption—that is, the redemption of our bodies. Then the complete personhood of every believer shall be perfected in the glory of Christ.[114]

Charles Spurgeon, "A Prepared Place for a Prepared People," Sermon 2751

These bodies, given life by his Spirit who dwells in us and united to souls purified and refined, shall one day tread upon an Earth delivered from the Curse, and shall live beneath new heavens (Isaiah 65:17-19). Have they not new desires? They shall tread a New Earth, for they have new ways.[115]

Charles Spurgeon, "God Rejoicing in the New Creation," Sermon 2211

We will not be disembodied spirits in the world to come, but redeemed spirits, in redeemed bodies, in a redeemed universe.[116]

R. A. Torrey, *Heaven or Hell*

The resurrection of the body . . . declares that God will make good and bring to perfection the human project he began in the Garden of Eden.[117]

Timothy George, "Heavenly Bodies"

[The body] shall be of that size which it either had attained or should have attained in the flower of its youth, and shall enjoy the beauty that arises from preserving symmetry and proportion in all its members . . . overgrown and emaciated persons need not fear that they shall be in heaven of such a figure as they would not be even in this world if they could help it.[118]

Augustine, *The City of God*

[Paul] speaks of two sorts of body, the present one and the future one. He uses two key adjectives to describe these two bodies. Unfortunately, many translations get him radically wrong at this point, leading to the widespread supposition that for Paul the new body would be a spiritual body in the sense of a nonmaterial body, a body that in Jesus's case wouldn't have left an empty tomb behind it. It can be demonstrated in great detail, philologically and exegetically, that this is precisely not what Paul meant. The contrast he is making is not between what we would mean by a present physical body and what we would mean by a future spiritual one, but between a present body animated by the normal human soul and a future body animated by God's spirit.

And the point about the future body is that it will be incorruptible. The present flesh and blood is corruptible, doomed to decay and die. That's why Paul says, "Flesh and blood cannot inherit God's kingdom." The new body will be incorruptible. The entire chapter [1 Corinthians 15], one of Paul's longest sustained discussions and the vital climax of the whole letter, is about new creation, about the creator God remaking the creation, not abandoning it as Platonists of all sorts, including Gnostics, would have wanted.[119]

N. T. Wright, *Surprised by Hope*

The wife of old John Ryland asked: "Do you think," she said, "you will know me in heaven?" "Why," said he, "I know you here; and do you think I shall be a bigger fool in heaven than I am on earth?" The question is beyond dispute. We shall live in heaven with bodies and that decides the matter. We shall know each other in heaven: you may take that for a positive fact, and not mere fancy.

But now a word of warning. . . . If your bodies are to dwell in heaven, I beseech you take care of them. I do not mean to take care of what you eat and drink, and wherewithal you shall be clothed; but I mean, take care that you do not let your bodies be polluted by sin. If this throat is to warble forever with songs of glory, let not words of lust defile it; if these eyes are to see the King in his beauty, ever let this be your prayer: "Turn off my eyes from beholding vanities;" if these hands are to hold a palm-branch, O, let them never take a bribe, let them never seek after evil; if these feet are to walk the golden streets, let them not be swift after mischief; if this tongue is forever to talk of all he said and did, ah! let it not utter light and frothy things; and if this heart is to pulsate forever with bliss, I beseech you give it not unto strangers, neither let it wander after evil. If this body is to live forever, what care we ought to take of it; for our bodies are temples of the Holy Ghost, and they are members of the Lord Jesus.[120]

Charles Spurgeon, "The Resurrection of the Dead," Sermons 66–67

In his resurrected body Jesus talked with his disciples and ate with them, and yet he disappeared from their sight. Apparently he could accommodate to earthly dimensions and yet transcend them. The ascension that followed several weeks of appearances demonstrated that this transcendence was the norm—at least until, as he said, "in like manner I will return again." He left the believers' sphere of reality so the Spirit could extend his presence in a non-spatial way. So by analogy we surmise that our resurrection bodies retain self-conscious identities and recognizable configurations, but possess far more capabilities than our present earthly ones, including extra dimensional mobility.[121]

    Arthur Roberts, *Exploring Heaven*

Man, being a creature compounded of body and spirit, was designed for its highest happiness, and the perfection of its nature in this state of union, and not in a state of separation. And let it be observed, that when the body shall be raised from the grave, it shall not be such flesh and blood as we now wear, nor made up of such materials, as shall clog or obstruct the soul in any of its most vigorous and divine exercises; but it shall be a "spiritual body" (1 Corinthians 15:44), a body fitted to serve a holy and a glorified spirit in its actions and its enjoyments, and to render the spirit capable of some further excellencies, both of action and enjoyment, than it is naturally capable of without *a* body. What sort of qualities this new-raised body shall be endued with, in order to increase the excellency or the happiness of pious souls, *will* be, in a great measure, a mystery or a secret, till that blessed morning appears.[122]

    Isaac Watts, *The World to Come*

Christianity is not a platonic religion that regards material things as mere shadows of reality, which will be sloughed off as soon as possible. Not the mere immortality of the soul, but rather the resurrection of the body and the renewal of all creation is the hope of the Christian faith.[123]

    John Piper, *Future Grace*

We will almost certainly carry into eternity new senses—probably with coordination between them that is only hinted at here. Our senses of taste and smell work closely together, but our senses of touch and hearing have a different relationship. We coordinate information in our brain among all the senses, but can we imagine that it might feel good physically to enjoy a lovely cloud bank or shapely tree?

New concepts are going to delight our intellectual apprehension—which itself will be more acute with faculties now undreamed of. We repeat: eternity cannot exhaust infinity.[124]

T. W. Hunt and Melana Hunt Monroe, *From Heaven's View*

Pleasure has become almost a dirty word amongst some Christians today, probably because pleasure is so often self-indulgent and sensual in our society. In heaven there is fullness of joy and (physical) pleasures forever more. These pleasures must include the physical and material, for two of the greatest rewards in heaven will be a new and glorious physical body, and immortality.

Why would God give us physical bodies forever if there were not material rewards to enjoy forever with all of our physical senses?[125]

Larry Dick, *A Taste of Heaven*

Peter was made to walk on water in his old body. Imagine what Christ will enable you to do in your new one?[126]

Larry Dick, *A Taste of Heaven*

Howsoever perfect in form and feature anyone may be, there is always some deficiency; some member, organ, or feature is slightly distorted, imperfect, or out of proportion to the rest.

On the resurrection day, all these defects and blemishes disappear, and the human body is again, far more than in the beginning, a masterpiece of God's creative power, wisdom, and love.

Oh! with what rapturous delight will the soul reunite herself with that beautiful body, and make it her temple forever! It was the companion of her sorrows and her joys in this world. But it was, too, a body of sin and death, and she had, perhaps more than once, sighed and prayed to be delivered from it. But now that it is purified, beautified, and glorified, she re-enters it with joy, because it is become the fit companion of a beautified spirit. The fond mother meeting her long-lost child, and, in the joy of her heart, pressing it to her bosom, is a faint image of the joy which the soul will experience in the reunion with her glorified body.[127]

Father J. Boudreau, *The Happiness of Heaven*

Rising with the gift of impassibility does not mean that our bodies will be unfeeling as marble statues. It only means that they shall be free from the power of suffering; but that does not exclude the power of receiving pleasure. Glory does not destroy nature, but rather, it perfects nature.[128]

Father J. Boudreau, *The Happiness of Heaven*

Some of us that have struggled with accepting the bodies we have been given for earth may not be terribly enthralled with the idea of another one quite like it for eternity! . . . Paul uses the realm of nature to help us to grasp an infinitesimal part of the truth of it. He says our heavenly body will be as superior as the flower to the bulb! That's a good picture. Think of a daffodil bulb. Then think of the flower. Could there be any comparison between them? Yet both are unmistakably daffodil in nature. One belongs to the earth and is totally suitable for its environment. But the flower of the bulb dances in the fresh air and sunlight about the ground, totally suited to its environment.[129]

Jill Briscoe, *Heaven and Hell*

The body is the matter of the soul, and the soul is the form of the body . . . not a dispensable extra. The soul carries its body with it. When death separates the two, we have a freak, a monster, an obscenity. That is why we are terrified of ghosts and corpses, though both are harmless: they are the obscenely separated aspects of what belongs together as one. That is why Jesus wept at Lazarus' grave: not merely for His bereavement but for this cosmic obscenity (John 11:33-35). A soul without its body is not liberated. . . . It is empty.[130]

Peter Kreeft, *Everything You Ever Wanted to Know about Heaven*

Some scientists believe there may be ten or possibly eleven dimensions of space. We are reasonably at home in three of them—width, length, and height. Four if we include time. Other dimensions apparently are "curled-up" . . . meaning they elude direct detection. For humanity to function in other dimensions may require newly adapted bodies. Better software for new hardware.[131]

Arthur Roberts, *Exploring Heaven*

One of the few modern writers who has tried to help us with the task of *imagining* what the risen body might be like [is] C. S. Lewis. In a variety of places, but particularly in his remarkable book *The Great Divorce,* he manages to get us to envisage bodies that are more solid, more real, more substantial than our present ones. That is the task that 2 Corinthians in particular invites us to. These will be bodies of which the phrase "the weight of glory," taken from that letter (4:17), will be seen, felt, and known to be appropriate.

. . . An "immortal body" is something most people find so strange that they don't even pause to wonder if that's what Paul and the other early Christians were talking about. But it is.

There is a world of difference between this belief and a belief in an "immortal soul." Platonists believe that all humans have an immortal element within them, normally referred to as "soul." (Having praised C. S. Lewis, I should say that he seems to fall into this trap.) In the New Testament, however, immortality is something that only God possesses by nature and that he then shares, as a gift of grace rather than an innate possession, with his people.

Why will we be given new bodies? According to the early Christians, the purpose of this new body will be to rule wisely over God's new world.[132]

N. T. Wright, *Surprised by Hope*

[The resurrection of the body] is the Christian's brightest hope. Many believers make a mistake when they long to die and long for Heaven. Those things may be desirable, but they are not the ultimate for the saints. The saints in Heaven are perfectly free from sin and, so far as they are capable of it, are perfectly happy. But a disembodied spirit never can be perfect until it is reunited to its body.

God made man not pure spirit but body and spirit, and the spirit alone will never be content until it sees its physical frame raised to its own condition of holiness and glory.

Think not that our longings here below are not shared in by the saints in Heaven. They do not groan so far as any pain can be, but they long with greater intensity than you and I for the "adoption . . . the redemption of our bodies" (Romans 8:23).

People have said there is no faith in Heaven, and no hope. They know not what they say—in Heaven faith and hope have their fullest swing and their brightest sphere, for glorified saints believe in God's promise and hope for the resurrection of the body.[133]

Charles Spurgeon, "Creation's Groans and the Saints' Sighs," Sermon 788

I still can hardly believe it. I, with shriveled, bent fingers, atrophied muscles, gnarled knees, and no feeling from the shoulders down, will one day have a new body, light, bright, and clothed in righteousness—powerful and dazzling. Can you imagine the hope this gives someone spinal-cord injured like me? Or someone who is cerebral palsied, brain-injured, or who has multiple sclerosis?

Imagine the hope this gives someone who is manic-depressive. No other religion, no other philosophy promises new bodies, hearts, and minds. Only in the Gospel of Christ do hurting people find such incredible hope.[134]

Joni Eareckson Tada, *Heaven: Your Real Home*

In the new heavens and new earth, there will be a place and activities for our resurrection bodies, which will never grow old or become weak or ill. . . . We can expect that in the new heavens and new earth there will be a fully perfect earth that is once again "very good." And we can expect that we will have physical bodies that will once again be "very good" in God's sight, and that will function to fulfill the purposes for which he originally placed man on the earth.

For that reason, it should not strike us as surprising to find that some of the descriptions of life in heaven include features that are very much part of the physical or material creation that God has made. We shall *eat and drink* at "the marriage supper of the Lamb" (Revelation 19:9). Jesus will once again *drink wine* with his disciples in the heavenly kingdom (Luke 22:18). The "*river* of the water of life" will flow "from the throne of God and of the Lamb through the middle of the *street of the city*" (Revelation 22:1). The *tree of life* will bear "twelve kinds of fruit, yielding its fruit each month" (Revelation 22:2). There is no strong reason to say these expressions are merely symbolic, without any literal reference. Are symbolic banquets and symbolic wine and symbolic rivers and trees somehow superior to real banquets and real wine and real rivers and trees in God's eternal plan? These things are just some of the excellent features of the perfection and final goodness of the physical creation that God has made.[135]

Wayne Grudem, *Systematic Theology*

We once were told that each seven years our every cell is renewed. Now scientists claim it is every three years, and yet we do not lose identity. We are the same persons with the same individuality as we were twenty or fifty years ago, even though we do not have the same bodies molecularly. A person of fifty has worn out more than sixteen bodies but is still the same person.

If this renewal is so in our earthly span, why is it so difficult to believe that God has something better for us, a body suited for an eternal order?[136]

Charles Ferguson Ball, *Heaven*

The glorified body is not a different body, but a different form of the same body.[137]

Thomas Oden, *Life in the Spirit*

Possessing glorified bodies will be surpassingly wonderful when it happens, but it has not happened yet; and until it happens our departed Christian loved ones do *not* possess their promised resurrection-bodies of deathless beauty. . . . There are those who teach that Christian believers are clad in their resurrection bodies immediately after death.

. . . We must not confuse the present *intermediate* state of our departed Christian loved ones with their yet-future *ultimate* state after the second coming of Christ: (1) They have not yet gone to the city of pearly gates; (2) they have not yet received their final reward for service; and (3) they are not yet clothed with their resurrection bodies.[138]

J. Sidlow Baxter, *The Other Side of Death*

I said of this poor body, "You have not yet been newly created. The venom of the old serpent still taints you. But you shall yet be delivered. You shall rise again if you die and are buried, or you shall be changed if the Lord should suddenly come today. You, poor body, which drags me down to the dust in pain and sorrow, even you shall rise and be remade in the redemption of the body. For the new creation has begun in me, with God's down payment of his Spirit."

Oh beloved, can't you rejoice in this? I encourage you to do so. Rejoice in what God is doing in this new creation! Let your whole spirit be glad! Leap down, you waterfalls of joy! Overflow with gladness! Let loose the torrents of praise![139]

Charles Spurgeon, "God Rejoicing in the New Creation," Sermon 2211

However miserable, powerless and contemptible in life and death [our bodies are], Christ will at his coming render our bodies beautiful, pure, shining and worthy of honor, until they correspond to his own immortal, glorious body. Not like it as it hung on the cross or lay in the grave, bloodstained, livid and disgraced; but as it is now, glorified at the Father's right hand. We need not, then, be alarmed at the necessity of laying aside our earthly bodies; at being despoiled of the honor, righteousness and life adhering in them, to deliver it to the devouring power of death and the grave—something well calculated to terrify the enemies of Christ: but we may joyfully hope for and await his speedy coming to deliver us from this miserable, filthy pollution.[140]

Martin Luther, "Enemies of the Cross of Christ"

The resurrected Christ said, "Touch me and see; a ghost does not have flesh and bones, as you see I have" (Luke 24:39). He walked on Earth; we will walk on Earth. He occupied space; we will occupy space.[141]

Randy Alcorn, *Heaven*

Because we each have a physical body, we already have the single best reference point for envisioning a *new* body. It's like the new upgrade of my word processing software. When I heard there was an upgrade available, I didn't say, "I have no idea what it will be like." I knew that for the most part it would be like the old program, only better. Sure, it has some new features that I didn't expect, and I'm glad for them. But I certainly recognize it as the same program I've used for a decade.

Likewise, when we receive our resurrected bodies, we'll no doubt have some welcome surprises—maybe even some new features (though no glitches or programming errors)—but we'll certainly recognize our new bodies as being *ours*. God has given us working models to guide our imagination about what our new bodies will be like on the New Earth.[142]

Randy Alcorn, *Heaven*

Joni [Eareckson Tada] tells of speaking to a class of mentally handicapped Christians. They thought it was great when she said she was going to get a new body. But then she added, "And *you're* going to get new minds." The class broke out in cheers and applause. They knew just what they wanted—new minds.

My body and mind, for the moment, may be relatively healthy.

But as an insulin-dependent diabetic, I've known what it is for both my body and my mind to fail me. They suffer under the Curse enough that I too know just what I want—a new body and a new mind, without sin, suffering and incapacity. Every year that goes by, I long more to be a resurrected person and to live on the resurrected Earth, with my resurrected brothers and sisters, and above all, with my Lord—the resurrected Jesus.[143]

Randy Alcorn, *Heaven*

God designed us with five senses. They're part of what makes us human. Because God's original ideas are always good, our resurrection bodies will surely have these senses. And for all we know, they may have more.

Psalm 139:14: "Thank you for making me so wonderfully complex! Your workmanship is marvelous—how well I know it."

If our current bodies are so marvelous, as David recognizes, how much more will we praise God for the wonders of our resurrection bodies? Will our eyes be able to function alternately as telescopes and microscopes? Will our eyes be able to see new colors? Will our ears serve as sound-gathering disks? Will our sense of smell be far more acute, able to identify a favorite flower—or person—miles away, so we can follow the scent to the source?

Although we don't know the answers to these questions, it seems reasonable to suggest all of our resurrected senses will function at levels we've never known. On the New Earth, we'll continually be discovering, to our delight, what we never knew existed, what we've been missing all our lives. No joy is greater than the joy of discovery. The God who always surpasses our expectations will forever give us more of himself and his creation to discover.[144]

Randy Alcorn, *TouchPoints: Heaven*

Boredom

To me, living means living for Christ, and dying is even better. But if I live, I can do more fruitful work for Christ. So I really don't know which is better. I'm torn between two desires: I long to go and be with Christ, which would be far better for me.

PAUL, PHILIPPIANS 1:21-23, NLT

"They will proclaim my glory among the nations. And they will bring all your brothers, from all the nations, to my holy mountain in Jerusalem as an offering to the LORD—on horses, in chariots and wagons, and on mules and camels," says the LORD.

ISAIAH 66:19-20

You will show me the path of life;
> In Your presence is fullness of joy;
> At Your right hand are pleasures forevermore.

DAVID, PSALM 16:11, NKJV

It is surely a Satanic triumph of the first order to have taken the fascination out of a doctrine that must be either a fascinating lie or a fascinating fact. Even if people think of Heaven as a fascinating lie, they are at least fascinated with it, and that can spur further thinking, which can lead to belief. But if it's dull, it doesn't matter whether it's a dull lie or a dull truth. Dullness, not doubt, is the strongest enemy of faith, just as indifference, not hate, is the strongest enemy of love.[145]

Peter Kreeft, *Everything You Ever Wanted to Know about Heaven*

I don't believe in an afterlife, so I don't have to spend my whole life fearing hell, or fearing heaven even more. For whatever the tortures of hell, I think the boredom of heaven would be even worse.[146]

Isaac Asimov

[Miss Watson] went on and told me all about the good place. She said all a body would have to do there was go around all day long with a harp and sing, forever and ever. So I didn't think much of it. But I never said so. I asked her if she reckoned Tom Sawyer would go there, and she said not by a considerable sight. I was glad about that, because I wanted him and me to be together.[147]

Huck Finn, in *The Adventures of Huckleberry Finn,* by Mark Twain

I assume that you're like me: I can get itchy-skinned and scratchy-throated after an hour or so of church. I can get distracted and cranky when it goes too long. My feet ache, my backside numbs, my eyes glaze, my mind fogs, my belly growls. I find myself fighting back yawns, and then not fighting them back, letting them gape and roar, a signal to my oppressors: Let my people go.

And I'm the pastor.

Is heaven church forever?

The popular images we have of heaven only make it worse. A long tradition in art, both classical and pop, has depicted it as the playground of plump, porcelain-skinned cherubs, flitting about on stubby wings or lolling about on downy clouds, plucking harps, singing in sweet, trilling falsettos. Everything is soft, wispy, dainty, pastel, languid. And this is supposed to inspire us.

. . . I have an ambition. I want to recover something that has been almost completely buried under the accumulation of two thousand years of false ideas. I want to restore something that, from the tampering and mauling of countless hands, from the blowing and wheezing of countless pulpits, has been so damaged that it's unrecognizable. I want to render a true picture of heaven.

If we are going to become heavenly-minded, we need a vision of heaven worthy of the effort. If heaven is what the stereotypical portraits of it make it out to be—the chubby angels, the fluffy clouds, the chamber music, the endless church—I'm no more interested in it than Huck Finn is. The only thing that vision of heaven inspires is boredom—or, worse, dread.

Have any believers, anywhere, ever worked in a leprosarium or burned at the stake or been devoured by lions because images of doll-like cherubs danced in their heads?[148]

Mark Buchanan, *Things Unseen*

Nearly every Christian I have spoken with has some idea that eternity is an unending church service. . . . We have settled on an image of the never-ending sing-along in the sky, one great hymn after another, forever and ever, amen. And our heart sinks. *Forever and ever? That's it? That's the good news?* And then we sigh and feel guilty that we are not more "spiritual." We lose heart, and we turn once more to the present to find what life we can.[149]

John Eldredge, *The Journey of Desire*

When I was a boy, the thought of Heaven used to frighten me more than the thought of Hell. I pictured Heaven as a place where time would be perpetual Sundays, with perpetual services from which there would be no escape.[150]

David Lloyd George, British prime minister

Be assured of this: once in heaven, we shall never grow weary of seeing God's face, of beholding God's glory, of delighting in God's presence, of basking in God's love, of exploring God's immensities, or of engaging in God's holy worship and service.[151]

Richard Brooks, *The Doors of Heaven*

Our pictures of Heaven are dull, platitudinous and syrupy; therefore, so is our faith, our hope, and our love of Heaven.[152]

Peter Kreeft, *Everything You Ever Wanted to Know about Heaven*

Why won't we be bored in heaven? Because it's the one place where both impulses—to go beyond, to go home—are perfectly joined and totally satisfied. It's the one place where we're constantly discovering—where everything is always fresh and the possessing of a thing is as good as the pursuing of it—and yet where we are fully at home—where everything is as it ought to be and where we find, undiminished, that mysterious something we never found down here. . . . And this lifelong melancholy that hangs on us, this wishing we were someone else somewhere else, vanishes too. Our craving to go beyond is always and fully realized. Our yearning for home is once and for all fulfilled. The ahh! of deep satisfaction and the aha! of delighted surprise meet, and they kiss.[153]

Mark Buchanan, *Things Unseen*

I knew I should want to go to heaven, but I didn't. I would have said that I want to go to heaven when I die, but mainly, I just didn't want to go to hell. My problem was a badly warped theology. I knew that in heaven we would worship God forever. But the only model I had for worship was church, and frankly, I wasn't in love with church enough to want it to go on through ages of ages, world without end. My mental image was of Reverend Cant droning on for ever and ever.

Somewhere in the back of my mind, quite unconsciously, heaven was an extended, boring church service like those I had not yet learned to appreciate on earth—with this exception: that you never got to go home to the roast beef dinner. What a way to anticipate my eternal destiny. But then I read *The Great Divorce*. It awakened in me an appetite for something better than roast beef. It aroused a longing to inherit that for which I was created, for that which would fulfill my utmost longings and engender new longings and fulfill those too.

After reading *The Great Divorce*, for the first time in my life, I felt heaven to be both utterly real and utterly desirable.[154]

Wayne Martindale, *Journey to the Celestial City*

As a child, I feared heaven would be boring. I missed the point of gold streets and pearly gates. As a 10-year-old, what I really liked doing most was playing baseball, collecting fossils, and hunting frogs.

In the years that followed, the deaths of family members and friends have changed the way I think about heaven. But I still have questions. What will we do after enjoying long embraces, tears of laughter, and catching up? My mind still locks up like an overloaded computer when I try to weigh imponderable questions about a hereafter that will last forever.

Ironically, what gives me the most peace of mind is not cutting loose my imagination, but rather learning to trust. I find rest in the thought that God doesn't want us to know what He has planned for us. I wouldn't be surprised to hear such a God say something like, "If I told you, I'd have to take you." Or, based on the apostle Paul's experience, "If I told you how good it's going to be, I'd have to make life more difficult for you now."[155]

Mart De Haan, *Been Thinking About*

The literature of pilgrimage lavishes its attention on the journey to heaven and then becomes largely silent when the pilgrim finally arrives there, leaving us with the impression that what goes on there is beyond finite human understanding. Unless we realize that the technique being used is one of negation in which the absence of activity signals not poverty but a richness beyond our understanding, we can scarcely avoid sympathizing with people who try to render the Christian hope of heaven ridiculous by saying that *they* do not want to spend eternity playing harps.[156]

Wayne Martindale, *Journey to the Celestial City*

Gary Larson showed a common view of Heaven in one of his *Far Side* cartoons. In it a man with angel wings and a halo sits on a cloud, doing nothing, with no one nearby. He has the expression of someone stuck on a desert island, bored because he has absolutely nothing to do. A caption shows what he's thinking: "Wish I'd brought a magazine."[157]

Randy Alcorn, *Heaven for Kids*

Consider the old proverb, "Eat, drink, and be merry, for tomorrow we die." It assumes that the only earthly pleasures we'll ever enjoy must be obtained now. As Christians, we should indeed eat, drink, and be merry—and also sacrifice, suffer, and die—all to the glory of God. In doing so, we're preparing for an eternal life in which we will eat, drink, and be merry, but never again die. This present life, then, is not our last chance to eat, drink, and be merry—rather, it is the last time our eating, drinking, and merrymaking can be corrupted by sin, death, and the Curse.[158]

Randy Alcorn, *Heaven*

Our belief that Heaven will be boring betrays a heresy—that *God* is boring. There's no greater nonsense. What's true is that our desires for pleasure and the experience of joy come directly from God's hand. God designed and gave us our taste buds, adrenaline, sex drives, and the nerve endings that convey pleasure to our brains. Likewise, our imaginations and our capacity for joy and exhilaration were *made by the very God we accuse of being boring*! Do we imagine that we ourselves came up with the idea of fun?[159]

Randy Alcorn, *50 Days of Heaven*

[A] reason people assume Heaven is boring is that their Christian lives are boring. That's not God's fault; it's their own. God calls us to follow him in an adventure that should put us on life's edge. He's infinite in creativity, goodness, beauty, and power. If we're experiencing the invigorating stirrings of God's Spirit, trusting him to fill our lives with divine appointments, experiencing the childlike delights of his gracious daily kindnesses, then we'll know that God is exciting and Heaven is exhilarating. People who love God crave his companionship. To be in his presence will be the very opposite of boredom.[160]

Randy Alcorn, *Heaven*

We think of ourselves as fun-loving, and of God as a humorless killjoy. But we've got it backward. It's not God who's boring; it's us. Did we invent wit, humor, and laughter? No. God did. We'll never begin to exhaust God's sense of humor and his love for adventure. The real question is this: How could God not be bored with *us*?[161]

Randy Alcorn, *Heaven*

Satan need not convince us that Heaven doesn't exist. He need convince us only that Heaven is a place of boring, unearthly existence. If we believe that lie, we'll be robbed of our joy and anticipation, we'll set our minds on this life and not the next, and we won't be motivated to share our faith. Why should we share the "good news" that people can spend eternity in a boring, ghostly place even *we're* not looking forward to?[162]

Randy Alcorn, *TouchPoints: Heaven*

Most of us would love to spend the evening with a great author, musician, artist, or head of state. God is the master artist who created the universe, the inventor of music, the author and main character of the unfolding drama of redemption. Head of state? He's king of the entire universe. Yet if someone says, "I want to go to Heaven to be with God forever," others wonder, *Wouldn't that be boring?*

What are we thinking?[163]

Randy Alcorn, *Heaven*

In Heaven, we'll be at home with the God we love and who loves us wholeheartedly. Lovers don't bore each other. People who love God could never be bored in his presence.[164]

Randy Alcorn, *Heaven*

Bride of Christ

The Spirit and the bride say, "Come!" And let him who hears say, "Come!" Whoever is thirsty, let him come; and whoever wishes, let him take the free gift of the water of life.

JOHN, REVELATION 22:17

I saw a new heaven and a new earth, for the first heaven and the first earth had passed away, and there was no longer any sea. I saw the Holy City, the new Jerusalem, coming down out of heaven from God, prepared as a bride beautifully dressed for her husband.

JOHN, REVELATION 21:1-2

Can anything ever separate us from Christ's love? Does it mean he no longer loves us if we have trouble or calamity, or are persecuted, or hungry, or destitute, or in danger, or threatened with death? (As the Scriptures say, "For your sake we are killed every day; we are being slaughtered like sheep.") No, despite all these things, overwhelming victory is ours through Christ, who loved us.

And I am convinced that nothing can ever separate us from God's love. Neither death nor life, neither angels nor demons, neither our fears for today nor our worries about tomorrow—not even the powers of hell can separate us from God's love. No power in the sky above or in the earth below—indeed, nothing in all creation will ever be able to separate us from the love of God that is revealed in Christ Jesus our Lord.

PAUL, ROMANS 8:35-39, NLT

Blessed are those who are invited to the wedding supper of the Lamb!

THE ANGEL, REVELATION 19:9

God is most glorified in us when we are most satisfied in him.[165]

John Piper, *Desiring God*

As they increase in the knowledge of God and of the works of God, the more they will see of his excellency; and the more they see of his excellency . . . the more will they love him; and the more they love God, the more delight and happiness . . . will they have in him.[166]

Jonathan Edwards, *The Miscellanies*

In Jesus' day, the Jewish marriage custom required that the groom go to the bride's father and establish the price for gaining his bride. The father and the future husband sealed the covenant with a cup shared between them. The groom would then leave for a lengthy period, returning to his father's home where he prepared an apartment that would become their home.

Then, without announcement, when everything was finally ready and the wedding feast prepared, he would leave his father's home and walk through the streets of the town to receive his bride and take her home.

Needless to say, there was no time to prepare herself for that great celebration if she waited to hear the shouts in the streets. Given that her hope was fixed on that day, she had already prepared herself in anticipation of his coming for her.[167]

Joseph Stowell, *Eternity*

Do you find it odd to think of God as an enthralled lover? Do you feel awkward thinking of Jesus as a suitor intoxicated on love? If so, how else do you explain his actions? Did logic put God in a manger? Did common sense nail him to a cross?

. . . He came as a prince with his eye on the maiden, ready to battle even the dragon itself if that's what it took to win her hand. . . .

You are spoken for. You are engaged, set apart, called out, a holy bride. Forbidden waters hold nothing for you. You have been chosen for his castle. Don't settle for one-night stands in the arms of a stranger.

Be obsessed with your wedding date. Guard against forgetfulness. Be intolerant of memory lapses. Write yourself notes. Memorize verses. Do whatever you need to do to remember. Aim at what is in heaven. . . . Think only about the things in heaven (Colossians 3:1-2). You are engaged to royalty, and your Prince is coming to take you home.[168]

Max Lucado, *When Christ Comes*

The bride eyes not her garment,
*   But her dear bridegroom's face;*
I will not gaze at glory,
*   But on my King of grace;*
Not on the crown he giveth,
*   But on His pierced hand:*
The Lamb is all the glory
*   Of Immanuel's land.*[169]

Annie Ross Cousin, *Immanuel's Land*

Samuel Rutherford compares our experience in heaven with a bride's delight on her wedding day. What is it that thrills her most of all? Her dress? The flowers? The guests? None of these. "The bride taketh not, by a thousand degrees, so much delight in her wedding garment as she doth in her bridegroom; so we, in the life to come . . . shall not be so much affected with the glory that goeth about us, as with the bridegroom's joyful face and presence."[170]

Edward Donnelly, *Biblical Teaching on the Doctrines of Heaven and Hell*

[Cinderella] had to live with a wicked stepmother and stepsisters, but when she went to the ball she met a prince. And even though she had to go back to her hard existence for a while, her life was never the same because her prince didn't forget her. He came one day and took her away to his castle to be his bride.

. . . Even while you are ironing clothes and scrubbing floors, the Prince named Jesus Christ is coming back to get you someday and take you to be with Him forever.[171]

Tony Evans, *Tony Evans Speaks Out on Heaven and Hell*

The one-flesh marital union is a signpost pointing to our relationship with Christ as our bridegroom. Once we reach the destination, however, the signpost becomes unnecessary. That one marriage—our marriage to Christ—will be so completely satisfying that even the most wonderful earthly marriage couldn't be as fulfilling. Earthly marriage is a shadow, a copy, an echo, of the true and ultimate marriage. Once that ultimate marriage begins, at the Lamb's wedding feast, all the human marriages that pointed to it will have served their noble purpose and will be assimilated into the one great marriage they foreshadowed. The purpose of marriage is not to replace Heaven, but to prepare us for it.[172]

Randy Alcorn, *50 Days of Heaven*

It's only because of the Bridegroom's work that the chosen princess, the church, can enter the presence of her Lord. Yet her wedding dress is woven by her many acts of faithfulness while away from her Bridegroom on the fallen Earth. . . . Each prayer, each gift, each hour of fasting, each kindness to the needy—all these are the threads that have been woven together into this wedding dress. Her works have been empowered by the Spirit, and she has spent her life on Earth sewing her wedding dress for the day when she will be joined to her beloved Bridegroom.

This gives us a wonderful reason to remain here on this Earth, even though we long to be with our beloved Jesus. The wedding approaches, yet . . . part of us wants fewer days between now and the wedding, because we're so eager to be with our Beloved in our new home. But another part wants more days to better prepare for the wedding, to sew our dress by acts of faithful service to God.

The imagery is beautiful but potentially disturbing. A pure bride doesn't want to appear scantily clothed or dressed in rags at the altar before her beloved Bridegroom and a crowd of guests. But if she has been diligent to prepare, her dress will be substantial, beautiful, and complete.[173]

Randy Alcorn, *We Shall See God*

We aren't individual brides of Christ; we are collectively the bride of Christ. Christ is not a polygamist. He will be married to one bride, not millions. We belong to each other and need each other. We should guard not only our own purity, but each other's. We *are* our brother's keeper. . . . Because we will be part of a community of saints that constitutes the bride of Christ for eternity, and because we will worship and serve him together, to prepare properly for Heaven we must be part of a church now.[174]

Randy Alcorn, *Heaven*

Like a bride's dreams of sharing a home with her groom, our love for Heaven should be overflowing and contagious, like our love for God. The more I learn about God, the more excited I get about Heaven. The more I learn about Heaven, the more excited I get about God.

Randy Alcorn, notes

As the church, we're part of the ultimate Cinderella story—we'll be rescued from a home where we labor, often without appreciation or reward. One day we'll be taken into the arms of the Prince and whisked away to live in his palace.[175]

Randy Alcorn, *We Shall See God*

Children

From the lips of children and infants
    you have ordained praise.

DAVID, PSALM 8:2; JESUS, MATTHEW 21:16

Let the little children come to me, and do not hinder
them, for the kingdom of heaven belongs to such
as these.

JESUS, MATTHEW 19:14

Truly, I say to you, unless you turn and become like
children, you will never enter the kingdom of heaven.
Whoever humbles himself like this child is the greatest in the kingdom of heaven.

    Whoever receives one such child in my name
receives me, but whoever causes one of these little

ones who believe in me to sin, it would be better for
him to have a great millstone fastened around his neck
and to be drowned in the depth of the sea. . . .

See that you do not despise one of these little
ones. For I tell you that in heaven their angels always
see the face of my Father who is in heaven.

JESUS, MATTHEW 18:3-6, 10, ESV

Will our children be as we last saw them? I do not know nor can
I prove it from Scripture (for Scripture is silent at this point), but
I believe with all my heart that God will raise the little ones as such,
and that the mother's arms that have ached for them will have the
opportunity of holding them. The father's hand that never held the
little hand will be given that privilege. I believe that the little ones
will grow up in heaven in the care of their earthly parents . . . there
are no children in hell. . . . Referring to children Christ said, "Of
such is the kingdom of heaven."[176]

J. Vernon McGee, *Death of a Little Child*

It's not the crying, the helplessness, the messes, the immaturity of
children that we love. It's the unfeigned joy of life, the exuberance,
the inquisitiveness, the laughter, the spontaneous affection. In heaven
we will all be like that![177]

Larry Dick, *A Taste of Heaven*

Some ground the idea of the eternal blessedness of the infant upon
its *innocence*. We do no such thing. We believe that the infant fell in
the first Adam "for in Adam all died." . . . If infants be saved it is not
because of any natural innocence. They enter heaven by the very same
way that we do: they are received in the name of Christ.[178]

Charles Spurgeon, "Infant Salvation," Sermon 411

Should it not thrill any mother to know that the darling treasure taken from her bosom as a tiny infant will be seen again, not as an unopened bud, but as a full-bloomed rose in the garden of paradise?

What a reunion that will be![179]

J. Sidlow Baxter, *The Other Side of Death*

Infants compose a great part of the family of Christ, and . . . Jesus Christ is known to have had a love and amiableness towards the little ones. When they shouted in the temple, "Hosanna!" did he rebuke them? No; but rejoiced in their boyish shouts. "Out of the mouths of babes and sucklings hath God ordained strength," and does not that text seem to say that in heaven there shall be "perfect praise" rendered to God by multitudes of cherubs who were here on earth—your little ones fondled in your bosom—and then suddenly snatched away to heaven. I could not believe it of Jesus, that he would say to little children, "Depart, ye accursed, into everlasting fire in hell!" I cannot conceive it possible of him as the loving and tender one, that when he shall sit to judge all nations, he should put the little ones on the left hand, and should banish them for ever from his presence. Could he address them, and say to them, "I was an hungered, and ye gave me no meat; I was thirsty, and ye gave me no drink, sick, and in prison, and ye visited me not?" How *could* they do it? And if the main reason of damnation lie in sins of omission like there which it was not possible for them to commit, for want of power to perform the duty how, then, shall he condemn and cast them away?[180]

Charles Spurgeon, "Infant Salvation," Sermon 411

[To a woman whose godly daughter had died:] If sorrows could be diminished in proportion to the multitude of those who share in them, the spring of your tears would have been drawn almost dry, and the tide of grief have sunk low, by being divided into a thousand streams. But though this cannot afford perfect relief to your Ladyship, yet it must be some consolation to have been blessed with a daughter, whose removal from our world could give occasion for so general a mourning.

I confess, Madam, the wound which was made by such a smarting stroke is not to be healed in a day or two, reason permits some risings of the softer and kinder passions in such a season; it shows at least that our hearts are not marble, and reveals the tender ingredients that are moulded up in our frame; nor does religion permit us to be insensible when a God afflicts, though he doth it with the hand of a father and a friend. Nature and love are full of these sensibilities, and incline you to miss her presence in every place where she was wont to attend you, and where you rejoiced in her as one of your dearest blessings. She is taken away indeed from mortal sight, and to follow her remains to the grave, and, to dwell there, gives but a dark and melancholy view, till the great rising-day. Faith may ken the distant prospect, and exult in the sight of that glorious futurity.

Yet I think there is also a nearer relief, Madam, to your sorrows. By the virtues which shone in her life, you may trace the ascent of her spirit to the world of immortality and joy. Could your Ladyship keep the eye of your soul directed thither, you would find it an effectual balm for a heart that bleeds at the painful remembrance of her death. What could your Ladyship have asked as a higher favour of heaven, than to have born and trained up a child for that glorious inheritance, and to have her secured of the possession beyond all possible fear or danger of losing it?[181]

Isaac Watts, *The World to Come*

We sometimes feel that a life which was so brief was in vain, and that God has mocked us by giving us the little one and then by taking it away immediately. The child had no opportunity to perform a work, nor was there any time given to develop character. Let us remember, first of all, that the little one had an eternal spirit, and that it has gone into the presence of God where there will be an eternity to perform works and develop character. . . A brief life is not an incomplete life.[182]

J. Vernon McGee, *Death of a Little Child*

There are no such abnormalities as immortal babies. There is no such thing as everlasting childhood. . . . We simply must realize (thankfully so) that in heaven there is no perpetual suspension of growth, no permanent immaturity. All is progressive vitality.[183]

J. Sidlow Baxter, *The Other Side of Death*

The grace of God has sought out in the world the greatest sinners. It has not passed by the vilest of the vile. He who called himself the chief of sinners was a partaker of the love of Christ. All manner of sin and of blasphemy have been forgiven unto man. He has been able to save unto the uttermost them that come unto God by Christ, and does it seem consistent with such grace as this that it should pass by the myriads upon myriads of little ones, who wear the image of the earthy Adam, and never stamp upon them the image of the heavenly? I cannot conceive such a thing. He that has tasted and felt, and handled the grace of God, will, I think, shrink instinctively from any other doctrine than this, that infants dying such, are most assuredly saved.[184]

Charles Spurgeon, "Infant Salvation," Sermon 411

The gate is strait, but the Lord knows how to bring thousands through it without making it any wider, and we ought not to seek to shut any out by seeking to make it narrower. Oh! I do know that Christ will have the victory, and that as he is followed by streaming hosts, the black prince of hell will never be able to count so many followers in his dreary train as Christ in his resplendent triumph. And if so we *must* have the children saved; yea, brethren, if not so, we *must have them*, because we feel anyhow they must be numbered with the blessed, and dwell with Christ hereafter.[185]

Charles Spurgeon, "Infant Salvation," Sermon 411

On the New Earth many opportunities lost in this life will be wonderfully restored. Although it's not directly stated and I am therefore speculating, it's possible that parents whose hearts were broken through the death of their children will not only be reunited with them but will also experience the joy of seeing them grow up . . . in a perfect world.[186]

Randy Alcorn, *Heaven*

In Psalm 8:2, David says, "From the lips of children and infants you have ordained praise" (quoted by Jesus in Matthew 21:16). The inclusion of infants is significant because they would not be *conscious* of giving praise; it would have to be something instinctive. So, although children are sinners who need to be saved, God may well have a just way to cover them with Christ's blood so they go to Heaven when they die.[187]

Randy Alcorn, *Heaven*

If children do go to Heaven when they die, why doesn't God tell us that directly? It may be that he anticipates the twisted logic and rationalization it might foster in us. It might take from us the sense of urgency to see our children come to faith in Christ. It might cause us to be less concerned about the sacred God-given task of extending physical and financial help to the underprivileged and getting the gospel to children around the world. We must do what God has called us to do, which includes protecting, rescuing, feeding, evangelizing, and discipling children.[188]

Randy Alcorn, *Heaven*

Choosing between Heaven and Hell

You can enter God's Kingdom only through the
narrow gate. The highway to hell is broad, and its gate
is wide for the many who choose that way. But the
gateway to life is very narrow and the road is difficult,
and only a few ever find it.

Jesus, Matthew 7:13-14, nlt

The Lord isn't really being slow about his promise,
as some people think. No, he is being patient for your
sake. He does not want anyone to be destroyed, but
wants everyone to repent.

Peter, 2 Peter 3:9, nlt

Many of those whose bodies lie dead and buried will
rise up, some to everlasting life and some to shame
and everlasting disgrace.

An angel, Daniel 12:2, nlt

Not everyone who says to me, "Lord, Lord," will enter the kingdom of heaven, but only he who does the will of my Father who is in heaven. Many will say to me on that day, "Lord, Lord, did we not prophesy in your name, and in your name drive out demons and perform many miracles?" Then I will tell them plainly, "I never knew you. Away from me, you evildoers!"

JESUS, MATTHEW 7:21-23

Hell is the greatest compliment God has ever paid to the dignity of human freedom.[189]

G. K. Chesterton

No one who is ever in hell will be able to say to God, "You put me here," and no one who is in heaven will ever be able to say, "I put myself here."[190]

John Hannah

The entire New Testament is overshadowed by the certainty of a coming day of universal judgment, and by the problem thence arising: how may we sinners get right with God while there is yet time?[191]

J. I. Packer, *Knowing God*

Heaven is beautiful because it is the expression of that which is the perfection of beauty. And while that is true of heaven, I must also say that hell is the place of unrelieved, monstrous ugliness, because there is no perfection; there is only monstrous moral deformity. There is nothing beautiful in hell. And in heaven, of course, there is supreme beauty.

Earth lies halfway between. Earth knows ugliness and beauty; it's halfway between heaven and hell. And the inhabitants of earth must decide whether they are to seek the beauty of heaven or the monstrous, unrelieved ugliness of hell.[192]

A. W. Tozer, *The Attributes of God*

"Oh, Aslan," said Lucy. "Will you tell us how to get into your country from our world?"

"I shall be telling you all the time," said Aslan. "But I will not tell you how long or short the way will be; only that it lies across a river. But do not fear that, for I am the great Bridge Builder. And now come; I will open the door in the sky and send you to your own land." . . .

"Are—are you there too, Sir?" said Edmund.

"I am," said Aslan. "But there I have another name. You must learn to know me by that name."[193]

C. S. Lewis, *The Voyage of the Dawn Treader*

I have met no people who fully disbelieved in Hell and also had a living and life-giving belief in Heaven.[194]

C. S. Lewis, *Letters to Malcolm*

Even to one without religious commitment and theological convictions, it should be an unsettling thought that this world is attempting to chart its way through some of the most perilous waters in history, having now decided to ignore what was for nearly two millennia its fixed point of reference—its North Star. The certainty of judgment, the longing for heaven, the dread of hell: these are not prominent considerations in our modern discourse about the important matters of life. But they once were.[195]

A. J. Conyers, *The Eclipse of Heaven*

Hell is the absence of God, and God is the author of all the pleasures. . . . Heaven is that place where all that is and all that happens issues out of God's creative genius. . . . If we like the good things of earth, we will love heaven. God through Christ invented all the earthly pleasures, and He is the same one now preparing a place for us and will come again to receive us to Himself.[196]

Wayne Martindale, *Journey to the Celestial City*

The moral dissimilarity creates hell. For those beings who are morally dissimilar to God, hell is their final place. For those creatures who are morally similar to God, with some likeness to God, heaven is their place because their nature belongs there.[197]

 A. W. Tozer, *The Attributes of God*

All your life an unattainable ecstasy has hovered just beyond the grasp of your consciousness. The day is coming when you will wake to find, beyond all hope, that you have attained it, or else, that it was within your reach and you have lost it forever.[198]

 C. S. Lewis, *The Problem of Pain*

You will have met people who are so full of the spirit of Christ that any destiny other than heaven is unthinkable. These people also have many of the joys that will characterize heaven, even in the midst of earthly pain. You will also have met people who hate goodness: who prefer evil companions and evil acts, though it makes them wretched and miserable. When they do encounter good persons, they condemn them, perverting their reason by rationalizing evil and finding ways to blame the good or God or religion for their problems and the problems of the world. They already hate goodness because it implicitly condemns the evil they have chosen. They wouldn't like heaven if they could have it. They are, in a sense, already in hell, preferring darkness to light.[199]

 Wayne Martindale, *Journey to the Celestial City*

It is confessed that the doctrine of the resurrection of the dead at the last day, and the everlasting joys, and the eternal sorrows, that shall succeed it, as they are described in the New Testament, are a very awful sanction to the gospel of Christ, and carry in them such principles of hope and terror as should effectually discourage vice and irreligion, and become a powerful attractive to the practice of faith and love, and universal holiness.

But so corrupt and perverse are the inclinations of men in this fallen and degenerate world, and their passions are so much impressed and moved by things that are present or just at hand, that the joys of heaven, and the sorrows of hell, when set far beyond death and the grave at some vast unknown distance of time, would have but too little influence on their hearts and lives. And though these solemn and important events are never so certain in themselves, yet being looked upon as things a great way off, make too feeble an impression on the conscience, and their distance is much abused to give an indulgence to present sensualities.[200]

Isaac Watts, *The World to Come*

In 1952, young Florence Chadwick stepped into the waters of the Pacific Ocean off Catalina Island, determined to swim to the shore of mainland California. She'd already been the first woman to swim the English Channel both ways. The weather was foggy and chilly; she could hardly see the boats accompanying her. Still, she swam for fifteen hours. When she begged to be taken out of the water along the way, her mother, in a boat alongside, told her she was close and that she could make it. Finally, physically and emotionally exhausted, she stopped swimming and was pulled out. It wasn't until she was on the boat that she discovered the shore was less than half a mile away. At a news conference the next day she said, "All I could see was the fog. . . . I think if I could have seen the shore, I would have made it."[201]

C. J. Mahaney, "Loving the Church"

An Indiana cemetery has a tombstone, more than one hundred years old, with the following epitaph:

> *Pause, stranger, when you pass me by:*
> > *As you are now, so once was I.*
> *As I am now, so you will be.*
> > *So prepare for death and follow me.*

An unknown passerby scratched these additional words on the tombstone:

> *To follow you I'm not content,*
> *Until I know which way you went.*[202]

Ron Rhodes, *Heaven: The Undiscovered Country*

Perhaps some kind surviving friend may engrave my name with the number of my days, upon a plain funeral stone, without ornament and below envy: There shall my tomb stand among the rest as a fresh monument of the frailty of nature and the end of time. It is possible some friendly foot may now and then visit the place of my repose, and some tender eye may bedew the cold memorial with a tear: One or another of my old acquaintance may possibly attend there to learn the silent lecture of mortality from my grave stone, which my lips are now preaching aloud to the world: And if love and sorrow should reach so far, perhaps while his soul is melting in his eyelids, and his voice scarce finds an utterance, he will point with his finger, and show his companion the month and the day of my decease. O that solemn, that awful day, which shall finish my appointed time on earth, and put a full period to all the designs of my heart, and all the labours of my tongue and pen!

Think, O my soul, that while friends or strangers are engaged on that spot, and reading the date of thy departure hence, thou wilt be fixed under a decisive and unchangeable sentence, rejoicing in the rewards of time well-improved, or suffering the long sorrows which shall attend the abuse of it, in an unknown world of happiness or misery.[203]

Isaac Watts, *The World to Come*

What has been said on this subject may well awaken and alarm the unconverted. First, by putting them in mind of their misery, in that they have no portion or right in this world of love. You have heard what has been said of heaven, what kind of glory and blessedness is there, and how happy the saints and angels are in that world of perfect love. But consider that none of this belongs to you, if you are unconverted. When you hear of such things, you hear of that in which you have no share.[204]

Jonathan Edwards, *Heaven: A World of Love*

This life is the only time to prepare for dying, to get ready to stand before the Judge of the whole earth, and to secure our title to the heavenly blessedness.[205]

Isaac Watts, *The World to Come*

A dying man once gathered his four children around him. To each of the first three he simply said, "Good night." But then he turned to his fourth child and said, "Good-bye, Son."

The young man said, "Dad, you told the others good night. Why did you tell me good-bye?"

The dying man answered, "Because they are Christians, and I'll see them in the morning in heaven. But you have not come to Christ, and unless you do I'll never see you again."[206]

Tony Evans, *Tony Evans Speaks Out on Heaven and Hell*

Anybody other than Jesus Christ who gives you an opinion about death, heaven, and hell is giving you an uninformed opinion. So don't let anybody who hasn't been there tell you about eternity, because you can't afford to get this one wrong.[207]

Tony Evans, *Tony Evans Speaks Out on Heaven and Hell*

How, then, can you rest in such a predicament as you are in, and go about so carelessly from day to day, and so heedless and negligent of your precious, immortal souls? Consider seriously these things, and be wise for yourself, before it is too late; before your feet stumble on the dark mountains, and you fall into the world of wrath and hatred, where there is weeping, and wailing, and gnashing of teeth, with spiteful malice and rage against God, and Christ, and one another, and with horror and anguish of spirit forever.

Flee to the stronghold while you are prisoners of hope, before the door of hope is closed, and the agonies of the second death shall begin their work, and your eternal doom is sealed![208]

Jonathan Edwards, *Heaven: A World of Love*

What shall it profit you and me to study theories about a future state, if we know not on which side we shall be found at the last day?[209]

J. C. Ryle, *Heaven*

How could [a] man enjoy the meeting of true Christians in heaven who takes no pleasure in meeting true Christians on earth? Heaven is a prepared place for a prepared people. He that hopes to be gathered with saints in heaven while he only loves the gathering of sinners on earth is deceiving himself.[210]

J. C. Ryle, *Heaven*

There are only two kinds of people in the end: those who say to God, "Thy will be done," and those to whom God says, in the end, "*Thy will be done*." All that are in Hell, choose it. Without that self-choice there could be no Hell. No soul that seriously and constantly desires joy will ever miss it. Those who seek find. To those who knock it is opened.[211]

C. S. Lewis, *The Great Divorce*

Does God send us to hell? He doesn't have to. All sin gravitates there. There is a polarization between good and evil, light and darkness. God always attracts His creation, His beloved Hearts, and repels opposition or egotism and sin. There is no neutral zone where we can safely sit and just enjoy the ride. Every choice we make builds on this attraction to God or else repels us away.[212]

Drake Whitchurch, *Waking from Earth*

Every man who knocks on the door of a brothel is looking for God.[213]

G. K. Chesterton

No matter how wise a man may think himself, if he neglects to enquire as to the long, long journey which he must soon take on the other side of death he is a fool. That millions of people can treat the matter with jaunty indifference must be an astonishment to angels and demons.

While millions show little interest, others are deeply concerned but are misdirected, perplexed, or deceived by untrue teachings. Cults and "isms" spread plausible errors about life the other side of death, while many . . . evangelicals seem too busy with other issues to give truly biblical answers.[214]

J. Sidlow Baxter, *The Other Side of Death*

How a person dies is crucial to his state afterwards. If he enters death benefiting from the imputed righteousness of Christ, with his sins pardoned through the sin-offering of Christ, then at death that person enters life, a life of at-present unimaginable fulness and of glorious service. But if he dies trusting self-righteously to what he is and has done, then he faces God without God and without hope in the world.[215]

Paul Helm, *The Last Things*

A few years ago something unusual happened to a professional singer I know, named Ruthanna.

. . . Ruthanna and her husband were excited because she had been asked to sing at the wedding of a very rich man. The party after the wedding was held on the top two floors of the tallest skyscraper in Seattle. Waiters in tuxedos passed out wonderful food and drinks. The bride and groom cut a ribbon at the bottom of the stairs that led up to the top floor. Then they went up the stairs, and their guests followed.

At the top of the stairs stood a man with a big book open in front of him. . . . He would check his book and make sure the name was there before letting anyone in to the party.

When Ruthanna and her husband came to the door, she gave the man their names. "I am Ruthanna Metzgar and this is my husband, Roy."

He searched the names starting with the letter M. "I'm not finding it. Would you spell it, please?"

Ruthanna spelled her name slowly. After searching the book, the man said, "I'm sorry, but your name isn't here."

"There must be some mistake," Ruthanna replied. "I'm the singer. I sang for this wedding!"

The man answered, "It doesn't matter who you are or what you did. Without your name in the book, you can't come to the party."

He motioned to a waiter and said, "Show these people to the service elevator, please."

The Metzgars followed the waiter past beautifully decorated tables covered with food that looked really good. The other room was filling up with well-dressed people who were having the time of their lives.

The waiter led Ruthanna and Roy to the service elevator, ushered them in, and pushed G for the parking garage. . . . Quietly and sadly, they drove away. After a while Ruthanna's husband asked her what had happened.

"When the invitation arrived, I was busy," Ruthanna replied. "I never bothered to send the note back telling them I was coming. Besides, I was the singer. I thought I didn't have to respond to the invitation to go to the party."

Ruthanna started to cry. It was partly because she had missed the most amazing dinner party she'd ever had a chance to attend. But it was partly because she now had a little idea of what it will be like someday for people who stand before Christ and find their names are not written in the Lamb's Book of Life.[216]

Randy Alcorn, *Heaven for Kids*

It's of paramount importance to make sure you are going to Heaven, not Hell. The voice that whispers, "There's no hurry. Put this book down—you can always think about it later," is not God's voice. God says, "Now is the day of salvation" (2 Corinthians 6:2) and "Choose for yourselves this day whom you will serve" (Joshua 24:15).[217]

Randy Alcorn, *We Shall See God*

For those who know Christ, their place is Heaven. For those who do not know Christ, their place is Hell.[218]

Randy Alcorn, *Heaven*

There is no middle ground. Either you are a follower of Jesus or you are not.[219]

Randy Alcorn, *Heaven*

As human beings, we have a terminal disease called *mortality*. The current death rate is 100 percent. Unless Christ returns soon, we're all going to die. We don't like to think about death; yet, worldwide, 3 people die every second, 180 every minute, and nearly 11,000 every hour. If the Bible is right about what happens to us after death, it means that more than 250,000 people every day go either to Heaven or Hell.[220]

Randy Alcorn, *Heaven*

God loves us enough to tell us the truth. There are two eternal destinations, not one, and we must choose the right path if we are to go to Heaven. All roads do not lead to Heaven. Only one does: Jesus Christ.[221]

Randy Alcorn, *We Shall See God*

Satan has obvious motives for fueling our denial of eternal punishment: He wants unbelievers to reject Christ without fear; he wants Christians to be unmotivated to share Christ; and he wants God to receive less glory for the radical nature of Christ's redemptive work.[222]

Randy Alcorn, *Heaven*

The best of life on Earth is a glimpse of Heaven; the worst of life is a glimpse of Hell. For Christians, this present life is the closest they will come to Hell. For unbelievers, it is the closest they will come to Heaven.[223]

Randy Alcorn, *Heaven*

Earth leads directly into heaven, just as it leads directly into hell. Life here is a running start into one or the other. Heaven and hell are both retroactive to earth. . . . Earth is the in-between world touched both by heaven and hell, affording a choice between the two.[224]

Randy Alcorn, *In Light of Eternity*

Let me ask you: If you died today (and you may very well), what heritage have you left to your family, your church, your neighborhood, your community, your fellow workers or your classmates?

I didn't ask what kind of inheritance, but what kind of heritage?

There is entirely too much emphasis placed on the money we leave our families and entirely too little placed on the legacy or heritage we leave them. To some people "ready to die" means they have lots of life insurance and a will. People, that's not being ready to die! . . .

It only takes money to leave an inheritance. It takes character and spiritual vitality to leave a heritage.[225]

Randy Alcorn, "Death: Signing and Framing Your Life's Portrait"

A financial counselor will say, "You can't go back at age sixty-five and snap your fingers to compensate for forty years of poor planning."

But what's far more important is that you can't reach the end of your life, snap your fingers, and compensate for a lifetime of poor planning to meet God.[226]

Randy Alcorn, *The Law of Rewards*

The door of eternity swings on the hinges of our present lives.[227]

Randy Alcorn, *The Law of Rewards*

We can't do life here over again. There's no retaking the course once we've failed it. There's no improving a D to an A. No rescheduling the final exams. Death is the deadline. There's no extension.

A basketball game is over at the final buzzer. Shots taken late don't count. When the trumpet heralds Christ's return, our eternal future begins and our present opportunity ends. If we have failed by then to use our money, possessions, time, and energy for eternity, then we have failed—period.[228]

Randy Alcorn, *The Law of Rewards*

People who want to get to Florida don't simply get in the car and start driving, hoping the road they're on will somehow get them there. Instead, they look at a map and chart their course. They do this in advance, rather than waiting until they arrive at the wrong destination or discover they've spent three days driving the wrong direction. The goal of getting to Heaven is worthy of greater advance planning than we would give to any other journey, yet some people spend far more time preparing for a trip to Disney World.[229]

Randy Alcorn, *We Shall See God*

Continuity of Personal Identity (from This Life to the Next)

I myself will see him
>   with my own eyes—I, and not another.
>   How my heart yearns within me!

JOB 19:27

The days of the blameless are known to the LORD,
>   and their inheritance will endure forever.

DAVID, PSALM 37:18

They were startled and frightened and thought they saw a spirit. And [Jesus] said to them, "Why are you troubled, and why do doubts arise in your hearts? See my hands and my feet, that it is I myself. Touch me, and see. For a spirit does not have flesh and bones as you see that I have." And when he had said this, he showed them his hands and his feet.

LUKE 24:37-40, ESV

Let nothing move you as you busy yourselves in the Lord's work. Be sure that nothing you do for him is ever lost or ever wasted.

PAUL, 1 CORINTHIANS 15:58, PHILLIPS

Until you have given up your self to Him you will not have a real self.[230]

C. S. Lewis, *Mere Christianity*

When Scripture tells us that "we shall be changed," we must not imagine that we shall be changed into angels, or into some other nature different from the human. The change means a supernatural elevation and perfection of our whole nature, and not its destruction. The transition of change of the child into the man, neither changes nor destroys the faculties of his mind nor the senses of his body; neither does it create new powers or faculties which he had not before. His gradual growth into manhood only develops and perfects what the hand of God had placed in his nature on the day of His creation.[231]

Father J. Boudreau, *The Happiness of Heaven*

The life we now have as the persons we now are will continue in the universe in which we now exist.[232]

Dallas Willard, *The Divine Conspiracy*

Somewhere in my broken, paralyzed body is the seed of what I shall become. The paralysis makes what I am to become all the more grand when you contrast atrophied, useless legs against splendorous resurrected legs. I'm convinced that if there are mirrors in heaven (and why not?), the image I'll see will be unmistakably "Joni," although a much better, brighter Joni.[233]

Joni Eareckson Tada, *Heaven: Your Real Home*

The Jesus we meet after the resurrection is clearly the same person as the figure met in the Gospel records prior to his resurrection. . . . Luke makes the same point more directly by citing Jesus' words, "It is I myself!" (Luke 24:39).

This continuity of Jesus' personhood is also expressed in the moving encounters with individuals after the resurrection, which John sensitively records—Mary (20:10-18), Thomas (20:24-29) and Peter (21:15-22). In each case Jesus draws upon his previous knowledge of them, in Mary's case with the deeply moving recitation of her name, "Mary!" (20:16), reflecting a relationship of profoundest mutual understanding and awareness. In Thomas's case Jesus recites back to him his very conditions for belief, "Put your finger here . . ." (20:27), evoking Thomas's "My Lord and my God!", the personal "my" surely reflecting an assured confidence that the one before him is no other than the Jesus he knew and followed during his years as a disciple. With Peter the exchange is based upon the validity of John's excla-mation in 21:7, "It is the Lord!"—this is the Jesus we have followed through the years.

We can therefore conclude with conviction that life in the heav-enly world will preserve personal identity. There will be continuity of our personhood. . . . Our personhood is immortal. By God's faithful grace we shall endure eternally.[234]

Bruce Milne, *The Message of Heaven and Hell*

This life [according to philosopher Isaac Taylor, 1787–1865] functions as an "initiatory course" for heaven and thus trains us for the employ-ments of the future. . . . Neither the experience of death nor the judg-ment of God radically alters the character of the soul. What death does do is to make the human character—good or evil—sharper, more vivid, more intense. The life after death is actually more heightened than that before.

. . . When we think of heaven as the next stage of life then it only follows that we will utilize the skills learned on earth. All the "versatility, the sagacity, the calculation of chances, the patience and assiduity, the promptitude and facility" which we have developed to manage our earthly affairs will find scope in heaven. God will not permit his creatures to "stand aloof" and be "idle spectators of omnipotence."[235]

Colleen McDannell and Bernhard Lang, *Heaven: A History*

It is irrational to suppose we change our species. God does not rip up his handiwork as a mistake. . . . We would lose that by becoming angels just as much as by becoming apes. . . . The potency to become an adult oak is still there in a frozen acorn but not in a frozen tulip bulb.[236]

Peter Kreeft, *Everything You Ever Wanted to Know about Heaven*

What is it that marks each of us as the same individual at birth, as an adult, and in the resurrection? The adult is the same person as the child, despite all the change that goes on within the human body. Similarly, despite the transformation that will occur at resurrection, we know from Paul that we will still be the same person.[237]

Millard Erickson, *Christian Theology*

This issue [whether people will be resurrected at the age they died] caused the spilling of much theological ink, especially during the Middle Ages. . . . By the late thirteenth century, the church's emerging consensus was this: "As each person reaches their peak of perfection around the age of 30, they will be resurrected, as they would have appeared at that time—even if they never lived to reach that age." Peter Lombard's discussion of the matter is typical of his age: "A boy who dies immediately after being born will be resurrected in that form which he would have had if he had lived to the age of thirty."

The New Jerusalem will thus be populated by men and women as they would appear at the age of 30 . . . but with every blemish removed.[238]

Alister McGrath, *A Brief History of Heaven*

Human nature is deficient in a twofold manner: in one way because it has not yet obtained its ultimate perfection, and in a second way, because it has already receded from its ultimate perfection. Human nature is deficient in the first way in children, and in the second way in the aged. And therefore in each of these, human nature will be brought back by the resurrection to the state of its ultimate perfection, which is in the state of youth, toward which the movement of growth is terminated, and from which the movement of degeneration begins.[239]

Thomas Aquinas, *Summa Theologica*

Our DNA is programmed in such a way that, at a particular point, we reach optimal development from a functional perspective. For the most part, it appears that we reach this stage somewhere in our twenties and thirties. . . . If the blueprints for our glorified bodies are in the DNA, then it would stand to reason that our bodies will be resurrected at the optimal stage of development determined by our DNA.[240]

Hank Hanegraaff, *Resurrection*

No one in that company [in Heaven] struck me as being of any particular age. One gets glimpses, even in our country, of that which is ageless—heavy thought in the face of an infant, and frolic childhood in that of a very old man.[241]

C. S. Lewis, *The Great Divorce*

The heavenly inhabitants . . . remain in eternal youth.[242]

Jonathan Edwards, quarterly lecture November 1747

Many still wonder whether humans are transformed into angels in heaven. . . . A careful reading of Revelation shows no hints or direct statements that humans ever have that option or outcome. Humans in heaven are redeemed. Angels in heaven are unfallen and unredeemed. It would be no advancement to go from being redeemed to being unredeemed. No song in heaven, anticipated and recorded by John, has as one of its themes thanksgiving for being made angels! The idea of persons, whether infants or adults, becoming angels is traceable to mystic writings, fairy tales, and sentimental poems. It is not found in or founded on Scripture.[243]

John Gilmore, *Probing Heaven*

Do they mean that along with men certain structures and achievements will also be saved? Does the new world so build upon what we call a technical, political, or moral progress that those who are now in the service of the resurrection forces are gathering building materials for the glorified world? We know that the resurrection forces which are already active will later create the new world. But we ask: Will this be done with the results which are already attained?[244]

Hendrikus Berkhof, *Christ the Meaning of History*

Heaven is to earth as the butterfly is to the caterpillar.[245]

Peter Kreeft and Ronald Tacelli, *Handbook of Christian Apologetics*

The world into which we shall enter in the Parousia of Jesus Christ is . . . not another world; it is this world, this heaven, this earth; both, however, passed away and renewed. It is these forests, these fields, these cities, these streets, these people, that will be the scene of redemption.[246]

Edward Thurneysen

If we had reason to believe that our experience in heaven would be entirely different from all our experience here on earth, would it attract us?[247]

W. Graham Scroggie, *What about Heaven?*

Shall we know one another in Heaven? Shall we love and remember? . . . We are never told we shall, because, I expect, it was not necessary to say anything about this which our own hearts tell us. We do not need words. For if we think for a minute, we know. Would you be yourself if you did not love and remember? . . . We are told that we shall be like our Lord Jesus. Surely this does not mean in holiness only, but in everything; and does not He know and love and remember? He would not be Himself if He did not, and we should not be ourselves if we did not.[248]

Amy Carmichael, *Thou Givest . . . They Gather*

One of our church members asked me if we will know each other once we get to heaven. The answer is that we won't really know each other *until* we get to heaven. Why? Because we cannot fully know each other now. All I can know about other people is what I see and what they tell me. And that's not all there is to a person. But in heaven all the masks and the pretense will be removed, and we will know each other as God created us to be.[249]

Tony Evans, *Tony Evans Speaks Out on Heaven and Hell*

Every kingdom work, whether publicly performed or privately endeavoured, partakes of the kingdom's imperishable character. Every honest intention, every stumbling word of witness, every resistance of temptation, every motion of repentance, every gesture of concern, every routine engagement, every motion of worship, every struggle towards obedience, every mumbled prayer, everything, literally, which flows out of our faith-relationship with the Ever-Living One, will find its place in the ever-living heavenly order which will dawn at his coming.[250]

Bruce Milne, *The Message of Heaven and Hell*

The Lord does not forsake the work of his hands. In faithfulness he upholds his creation order. Even the great crisis that will come on the world at Christ's return will not annihilate God's creation or our cultural development of it. The new heaven and the new earth the Lord has promised will be a continuation, purified by fire, of the creation we now know. There is no reason to believe that the cultural dimensions of earthly reality (except insofar as they are involved in sin) will be absent from the new, glorified earth that is promised. In fact, the biblical indications point in the opposite direction. Describing the new earth as the new Jerusalem, John writes that "The kings of the earth will bring their splendor into it. . . . The glory and the honor of the nations will be brought into it" (Revelation 21:24, 26). This very likely refers to the cultural treasures of mankind which will be purified by passing through the fires of judgment, like gold in a crucible.[251]

Albert Wolters, *Creation Regained*

The life beyond is represented by Jesus as being indissolubly united with the present world. The two worlds are not separate apart, but they are the upper and lower hemispheres of a perfectly rounded whole. . . . The Christian lives the eternal life in the midst of time. The whole of his earthly life . . . opens into the eternal; it is possessed by the eternal; eternity is in his heart, and in every passing moment; he is as much in eternity as he ever can be. Having entered upon the eternal life here and now; having begun the practice of it, all that the future can possibly bring will simply be a continuation and enlargement of what is already possessed.[252]

James Campbell, *Heaven Opened*

Although earthly *family* relationships will be superseded, my dear mother will always be the same person. I myself will always be the *same person.* For the Christian, death neither obliterates human identity nor submerges the individual distinctives of human personality. Those traits and characteristics which are individually peculiar to you and me will not only reappear yonder but will be refined and accentuated. All the unlovely will have been eliminated, and every loveable feature will be retained, emphasized, sublimated. As there have been special loves here, so will there continue to be in that higher life.[253]

J. Sidlow Baxter, *The Other Side of Death*

The patriarchs are mentioned by their names; and so it is clear they are known: they are not three anonymous bodies, but Abraham, Isaac, and Jacob.

Many enquire, "Shall we know our friends in heaven?" Why should we not? The saints in heaven are never spoken of in Scripture as moving about anonymously; but their names are spoken of as written in the book of life. Why is this? . . .

Concerning those that have gone before us, we gather from this whole text that they are not lost. We know where they are. Neither have they lost anything, for they are what they were, and more. Abraham has about him still everything that is Abrahamic; he is Abraham still. And Isaac has everything about him that properly belongs to Isaac. And Jacob has all about him that makes him God's Israel.

These good men have lost nothing that really pertained to their individuality, nothing that made them precious in the sight of the Lord. They have gained infinitely. They are Abraham and Isaac and Jacob now at their best, or rather they are waiting till the trumpet of the Resurrection shall sound when their bodies also shall be united to their spirits, and then Abraham, and Isaac and Jacob will be *completely* Abraham, Isaac and Jacob, world without end.

As Abraham is not lost to Isaac nor to Jacob nor to God nor to himself, so are our beloved ones by no means lost to us. We are by no means deprived of our dear ones by their death: they *are*; they are themselves; and they are ours still.[254]

Charles Spurgeon, "Departed Saints Yet Living," Sermon 1863

If an endless field of human knowledge and of human ability is now being formed by all that takes place in order to make the visible world and material nature subject to us, and if we know that this dominion of ours over nature will be complete in eternity, we may conclude that the knowledge and dominion we have gained over nature here can and will be of continued significance, even in the Kingdom of glory.[255]

Abraham Kuyper, *De Gemeene Gratie*

Your capacity for happiness in heaven is shaped by the development and refinement and depth of your capacity on earth. What we do now is not discarded once we enter eternity. What we learn now is not erased in heaven. Nothing in Scripture leads us to believe that everyone will be instantaneously, equally, and exhaustively educated at the inauguration of our heavenly existence. What we experience in joy and understanding and insight now is not destroyed, but is the foundation on which all our eternal experience and growth is based.[256]

Sam Storms, "Heaven: The Eternal Increase of Joy"

We, whose "names are written in heaven" (Luke 10:20) and to whom new heavenly names have already been assigned (Cf. Revelation 2:17), shall stand as *individuals* before an *Individual* when we render our final account (Cf. 2 Corinthians 5:10).

. . . The entire doctrinal structure of the Bible, including God's redemptive plan and His prophetic program, assumes the persistence of our discernible identities. . . . For instance, there will be recognition and differentiation when the righteous dead are raised from among the wicked at our Lord's return. This will happen when Jesus judges "every man" according to his works . . . when he assigns twelve special thrones to the apostles in the New Jerusalem.[257]

E. X. Heatherley, *Our Heavenly Home*

No introductions were necessary when Peter, James and John came face to face with Moses and Elijah on "the holy mount." They recognized the heavenly visitants on sight! Likewise . . . the "rich man" in Hades knew and called Abraham by name, though he had never seen him while on earth. If living humans have been known to recognize departed saints, and if a sinner in perdition has been able to identify the soul of a righteous man he never saw before, we shall undoubtedly know more, far more, when we are glorified, than now—not less than mortals on earth and the lost in hell![258]

E. X. Heatherley, *Our Heavenly Home*

The former things shall not be remembered [Isaiah 43:18]. Some refer these words to heaven and earth; as if he had said that henceforth they shall have no celebrity and no name. But I choose rather to refer them to the former times; for he means that the joy at being restored shall be so great that they shall no longer remember their miseries. . . . Not that God wished the first deliverance to be set aside or blotted out of the hearts of believers; but because by comparison the one brought a kind of forgetfulness over the other, just as the sun, when he rises, deprives the stars of their brightness.[259]

John Calvin, *Commentary on the Book of the Prophet Isaiah*

You said that the Lord declared plainly that those who shall obtain the resurrection shall then be as the angels. You brought this objection: The angels, being without flesh, are on this account in the utmost happiness and glory. We must then, as we are to be made equal to the angels, be like them stripped of flesh, and be angels. But you overlooked this, my excellent friend, that He who created and set in order the universe out of nothing, ordained the nature of immortal beings to be distributed not only among angels and ministers, but also among principalities, and thrones, and powers. For the race of angels is one, and that of principalities and powers another; because immortal beings are not all of one order, and constitution, and tribe, and family, but there are differences of race and tribe. And neither do the cherubim, departing from their own nature, assume the form of angels; nor, again, do angels assume the form of the others. For they cannot be anything but what they are and have been made. Moreover, man also having been appointed by the original order of things to inhabit the world, and to rule over all that is in it, when he is immortal, will never be changed from being a man into the form either of angels or any other; for neither do angels undergo a change from their original form to another. For Christ at His coming did not proclaim that the human nature should, when it is immortal, be remoulded or transformed into another nature, but into what it was before the fall. For each one among created things must remain in its own proper place, that none may be wanting to any, but all may be full.[260]

Methodius, *The Discourse on the Resurrection*

When I became a Christian as a high school student, I became a new person, yet I was still the same person I'd always been. My mother saw a lot of changes, but she still recognized me. She said, "Good morning, Randy," not "Who are *you*?" I was still Randy Alcorn, though a substantially transformed Randy Alcorn. My dog never growled at me—he knew who I was.

Likewise, this same Randy (who is now very different) will undergo another change at death. And I will undergo yet *another* change at the resurrection. But through all the changes *I will still be who I was and who I am*. There will be continuity from this life to the next.[261]

Randy Alcorn, *50 Days of Heaven*

Strangely, though Jesus in his resurrected body proclaimed, "I am not a ghost" (Luke 24:39, NLT), countless Christians think they will be ghosts in the eternal Heaven. I know this because I've talked with many of them. They think they'll be disembodied spirits, or wraiths. The magnificent, cosmos-shaking victory of Christ's resurrection— by definition a physical triumph over physical death in a physical world—escapes them. If Jesus had been a ghost, if *we* would be ghosts, then *redemption wouldn't have been accomplished*.

On the other hand, though the doors were locked, Christ suddenly appeared in the room where the disciples were gathered (John 20:19). Christ's body could be touched and clung to and could consume food, yet it could apparently "materialize" as well. How is this possible? Could it be that a resurrection body is structured in such a way as to allow its molecules to pass through solid materials or to suddenly become visible or invisible? Though we know that Christ could do these things, we're not explicitly told we'll be able to. It may be that some aspects of his resurrection body are unique because of his divine nature.

We won't be angels, but we'll be *with* angels—and that'll be far better.[262]

Randy Alcorn, *Heaven*

Music is easily carried over to a new world, unless sound and time and instruments and hearing are essentially different. So while the pages of some of Bach's and Handel's compositions will crumble or burn, the compositions themselves will presumably reside in memories. While a great painting will presumably burn, the capacity to create a greater painting will endure and be multiplied.

Randy Alcorn, unpublished notes

We are not simply told there will be lasting reward in Heaven for temporal service for Christ on earth. We are told that the service itself is eternal—it is gold that endures the fire. Works that will go on into Heaven. Does this suggest that they will be the actual, tangible basis on which whatever we do in Heaven will be built? Will a child's story written out of love for Jesus literally survive this world either in Heaven's handwriting or the child's own? Will a chair fashioned for Jesus be immune to the fire, not just the reward for building the chair? Will certain works of art, literature and music survive either literally (on the canvas and paper they were written on), or in substance (being re-created or enacted) in Heaven?

Randy Alcorn, unpublished notes

When we get in the car, we turn on our favorite music and head home to barbecue with friends, watch a ball game, play golf, ride bikes, work in the garden, or curl up with a cup of coffee and a good book. We do these things not because we are sinners but because we are *people*. We will still be people when we die and go to Heaven. This isn't a disappointing reality—it's God's plan. He made us as we are—except the sin part, which has nothing to do with friends, eating, sports, gardening, or reading.[263]

Randy Alcorn, *50 Days of Heaven*

You will be *you* in Heaven. Who else would you be? If Bob, a man on Earth, is no longer Bob when he gets to Heaven, then, in fact, Bob did not go to Heaven. If we weren't ourselves in the afterlife, then we couldn't be held accountable for what we did in this life. . . . We'll be ourselves without the sin—meaning that we'll be the best we can be.[264]

Randy Alcorn, *TouchPoints: Heaven*

My father lived through the Great Depression. He told me stories of sleeping outside in the cold, covered only with newspaper. Dad first told me these stories *fifty years* after the fact. He'd been able to sleep inside for half a century, but he vividly remembered the hard times. Suppose someone had said to him, "You can't appreciate having a warm fire and a warm bed unless there's the threat of sleeping out in the cold tonight." He'd say, "You think I'll ever forget those days?" His memories didn't make him miserable; they made him grateful.

After our bodily resurrection, we'll still remember the darkness and dangers of this life. We'll contrast our past experiences with the light and safety of the New Earth, and we'll be profoundly grateful.[265]

Randy Alcorn, *Heaven*

Culture, Arts, and Technology
on the New Earth

The LORD said to Moses, "See, I have chosen Bezalel
son of Uri . . . and I have filled him with the Spirit
of God, with skill, ability and knowledge in all kinds
of crafts—to make artistic designs for work in gold,
silver and bronze, to cut and set stones, to work
in wood, and to engage in all kinds of craftsmanship. Moreover, I have appointed Oholiab son of
Ahisamach, of the tribe of Dan, to help him. Also
I have given skill to all the craftsmen to make everything I have commanded you."

EXODUS 31:1-6

I will sing to the LORD all my life;
    I will sing praise to my God as long as I live.

PSALM 104:33

We will sing with stringed instruments
all the days of our lives
        in the temple of the LORD.

ISAIAH 38:20

I will build you up again
        and you will be rebuilt, O Virgin Israel.
Again you will take up your tambourines
        and go out to dance with the joyful.
Again you will plant vineyards
        on the hills of Samaria;
the farmers will plant them
        and enjoy their fruit.

GOD, JEREMIAH 31:4-5

Jesus did many other things as well. If every one of
them were written down, I suppose that even the
whole world would not have room for the books that
would be written.

JOHN 21:25

The city does not need the sun or the moon to shine
on it, for the glory of God gives it light, and the Lamb
is its lamp. The nations will walk by its light, and the
kings of the earth will bring their splendor into it. On
no day will its gates ever be shut, for there will be no
night there. The glory and honor of the nations will
be brought into it.

JOHN, REVELATION 21:23-26

My dear brothers, stand firm. Let nothing move you. Always give yourselves fully to the work of the Lord, because you know that your labor in the Lord is not in vain.

PAUL, 1 CORINTHIANS 15:58

In the beginning man was given the so-called cultural mandate— the command to rule over the earth and to develop a God-glorifying culture. Because of man's fall into sin, that cultural mandate has never been carried out in the way God intended. Only on the new earth will it be perfectly and sinlessly fulfilled. Only then shall we be able to rule the earth properly.[266]

Anthony Hoekema, "Heaven: Not Just an Eternal Day Off"

Some people may find it difficult to envision drama or literature without plots involving villainy, deceit, violence, or adultery. . . . Such fears are understandable, because it is difficult to see beyond the horizon of our experience. These questions reflect an inadequate vision of resurrected life. Consider comedy that makes you laugh but not at the expense of another. Reflect upon poetry that brings tears to your eyes, paintings that put you in raptures, music that gives you goose bumps, . . . Do our aesthetic adventures depend upon sin for flavor? I think not. In heaven, as on earth, effective drama portrays a triumph of good over evil. I daresay the vastness and the openness of the renewed cosmos offers adventures adequate for epic tales, just as it provides raw material for the visual arts, for painting, for sculpture, for architecture.[267]

Arthur Roberts, *Exploring Heaven*

God may ultimately choose not to preserve this book or that building, but he will spare enough authors and architects to re-create the best of whatever is lost.[268]

Michael Wittmer, *Heaven Is a Place on Earth*

When you painted on earth . . . it was because you caught glimpses of Heaven in the earthly landscape.[269]

The Spirit, in *The Great Divorce,* by C. S. Lewis

The rise of human civilization hints at a coming splendor. Civilization has brought health and safety. It has brought freedom from toil and provided creative enjoyment to millions of persons. How much more, freed from the curse of sin, will civilization flourish! Heaven will provide for urban as well as pastoral living. . . . Already the city of man is probing the galaxies. Already it has catalogued the human genome. . . . With the curse of sin gone, apocalypses past, surely human beings in heaven will become active stewards of the Lord in completing or extending the universe of things and ideas. . . . Civilization is not old; it has barely begun![270]

Arthur Roberts, *Exploring Heaven*

We have a creative task in the world. We must shape things in ways for which there is sometimes no clear direction. This is why imagination is not just a feature of the arts; it is a feature of human life itself. Without imagination, without experimentation, without openness to new questions and new possibilities, there can be no science and no technology. We are not challenging God when we do this, at least not when we do it in humility and faith. We are not stealing fire from the gods. We are taking up our responsibility before God to shape what he has placed in our hands.[271]

Paul Marshall, *Heaven Is Not My Home*

Part of God's plan for the earth is that it be filled and subdued by humankind, that its latent possibilities be unlocked and actualized in human history and civilization. A good deal of that development has already taken place, though it is distorted by humanity's sinfulness.

We must choose *restoration* rather than *repristination.* It would be a profound mistake to attempt to go back to the original stage of the earth's development, to the sort of world exemplified by the garden of Eden. From a cultural point of view, that situation was primitive and undeveloped. It preceded Jabal, Jubal, and Tubal Cain (sons of Lamech), for example, who introduced a number of historical advances (animal husbandry, music making, metalworking) that contributed significantly to the furtherance of civilization (Genesis 4:20-22). It is doubtful whether Adam and Eve were acquainted with the wheel; it is certain that they had not yet discovered how to make textiles (Genesis 3:21) or bake bricks (Genesis 11:3). . . . Repristination would entail the *cultural* return to the garden of Eden, a return that would turn back the historical clock.[272]

Albert Wolters, *Creation Regained*

Salvation in Jesus Christ, conceived in the broad creational sense, means a restoration of culture and society in their present stage of development. That restoration will not necessarily oppose literacy or urbanization or industrialization or the internal combustion engine, although these historical developments have led to their own distortions or evils. Instead, the coming of the kingdom of God demands that these developments be reformed, that they be made answerable to their creational structure, and that they be subjected to the ordinances of the Creator.

Biblical religion is historically progressive, not reactionary. It views the whole course of history as a movement from a garden to a city, and it fundamentally affirms that movement. Once again, the kingdom of God claims *all* of creation, not only in all its departments, but also in all its stages of development.[273]

Albert Wolters, *Creation Regained*

Scientists, teachers, artisans, farmers, merchants, and artists require a social structure to find personal fulfillment and to contribute value to others. The word *commonwealth* conveys this idea. Heaven will be a wealth of people from every cultural and linguistic group, with diverse traditions and customs. With a cosmos freed from sin and with inhabitants guided by the twin goals of truth and love, human beings can become fully co-creators with God.[274]

Arthur Roberts, *Exploring Heaven*

Life in the new creation will not be a repristination of all things—a going back to the way things were at the beginning. Rather, life in the new creation will be a restoration of all things—involving the removal of every sinful impurity and the retaining of all that is holy and good. Were the new creation to exclude the diversity of the nations and the glory of the kings of the earth, it would be impoverished rather than enriched, historically regressive and reactionary rather than progressive. To express the point in the form of a question: is it likely that the music of Bach and Mozart, the painting of Rembrandt, the writing of Shakespeare, the discoveries of science, etc., will be altogether lost upon life in the new creation?[275]

Albert Wolters, *Creation Regained*

Everything which authentically reflects the God of truth, all that is of abiding worth from within the national stories and the cultural inheritance of the world's peoples, will find its place in the New Jerusalem. This will hardly surprise us if we have drunk at the wells of human culture and have experienced the deepening of sensitivity, broadening of understanding and enlargement of heart and mind which such engagement can promote.

The one who is Lord of the whole of life was never going to bring us at the end into an eternal existence of mental constriction, or of emotional and creative impoverishment. Creativity will surely be valued, for such an anticipation must be in keeping with the nature of him who set the morning stars a-singing when he created them at the beginning, and whose joyful, uninhibited cry echoes across the battlements of the new creation. "See, I am making everything new!"

In other words, the "glory and honour of the nations" will only provide a starting point. What creative possibilities await us in the unfolding of the eternal ages no present imagination can begin to unravel. And since we are going to a heaven of, among other things, unprecedented cultural creativity, what authentication this gives to the worthwhileness of all such endeavour in the present. In this, too, we may dare to believe, "[our] labour in the Lord is not in vain" (1 Corinthians 15:58).[276]

Bruce Milne, *The Message of Heaven and Hell*

What we need is not to be rescued from the world, not to cease being human, not to stop caring for the world, not to stop shaping human culture. What we need is the power to do these things according to the will of God. We, as well as the rest of creation, need to be redeemed.[277]

Paul Marshall, *Heaven Is Not My Home*

Every legitimate and excellent fruit of human culture will be carried into and contribute to the splendour of life in the new creation. Rather than the new creation being a radically new beginning, in which the excellent and noble fruits of humankind's fulfillment of the cultural mandate are wholly discarded—the new creation will benefit from, and be immensely enriched by, its receiving of these fruits.[278]

Cornelius Venema, *The Promise of the Future*

Nothing of the diversity of the nations and peoples, their cultural products, languages, arts, sciences, literature, and technology—so far as these are good and excellent—will be lost upon life in the new creation.[279]

Cornelius Venema, *The Promise of the Future*

[Critiquing what Paul Marshall calls "lifeboat theology":] It is as if the creation were the *Titanic*, and now that we've hit the iceberg of sin, there's nothing left for us to do but get ourselves into lifeboats. The ship is sinking rapidly, God has given up on it and is concerned only with the survival of his people. Any effort we make to salvage God's creation amounts to rearranging the deck chairs. Instead, some say, our sole task is to get into the lifeboats, to keep them afloat, to pluck drowning victims out of the water, and to sail on until we get to heaven where all will be well.

[Proposing the alternative of "ark theology":] Noah's ark saved not only people, but it preserved God's other creatures as well. The ark looked not to flee but to return to the land and begin again. Once the flood subsided, *everyone and everything was intended to return again to restore the earth.*[280]

Paul Marshall, *Heaven Is Not My Home*

Kings in those days were more than political rulers; they were the representatives and bearers of the cultures of the nations over which they ruled. John is here speaking [in Revelation 21:24] about the cultural and artistic contributions of various national groups which shall then have made their home in the new Jerusalem. . . . [I]n the life to come various types of people will retain their unique gifts. These gifts will develop and mature in a sinless way, and will be used to produce new cultural products to the everlasting glory of God's name. . . .

The fact that not only kings but nations are mentioned implies that the various cultural contributions of different ethnic groups will then no longer be in competition with each other, but will harmoniously enrich life in the Holy City. Christ, who is the lamp of that city, will then draw all these cultural products into his service, for the glory of his Father.[281]

Anthony Hoekema, "Heaven: Not Just an Eternal Day Off"

How might we expect [Paul] to finish such a chapter [1 Corinthians 15]? By saying, "Therefore, since you have such a great hope, sit back and relax because you know God's got a great future in store for you"? No. Instead, he says, "Therefore, my beloved ones, be steadfast, immovable, always abounding in the work of the Lord, because you know that in the Lord your labour is not in vain."

What does he mean? How does believing in the future resurrection lead to getting on with the work in the present? Quite straightforwardly. The point of the resurrection, as Paul has been arguing throughout the letter, is that *the present bodily life is not valueless just because it will die.* God will raise it to new life. What you do with your body in the present matters because God has a great future in store for it. And if this applies to ethics, as in 1 Corinthians 6, it certainly also applies to various vocations to which God's people are called. What you *do* in the present—by painting, preaching, singing, sewing, praying, teaching, building hospitals, digging wells, campaigning for justice, writing poems, caring for the needy, loving your neighbor as yourself—*will last into God's future.* These activities are not simply ways of making the present life a little less beastly, a little more bearable, until the day when we leave it behind altogether (as the hymn so mistakenly puts it, "Until that day when all the blest to endless rest are called away"). They are part of what we may call *building for God's kingdom.*

It's no good falling back into the tired old split-level world where some people believe in evangelism in terms of saving souls for a timeless eternity and other people believe in mission in terms of working for justice, peace, and hope in the present world. That great divide has nothing to do with Jesus and the New Testament and everything to do with the silent enslavement of many Christians (both conservative and radical) to the Platonic ideology of the Enlightenment. Once we get the resurrection straight, we can and must get mission straight.[282]

N. T. Wright, *Surprised by Hope*

The possibilities that now rise before us boggle the mind. Will there be 'better Beethovens' on the new earth? . . . better Rembrandts, better Raphaels? Shall we read better poetry, better drama, and better prose? Will scientists continue to advance in technological achievement, will geologists continue to dig out the treasures of the earth, and will architects continue to build imposing and attractive structures? Will there be exciting new adventures in space travel? . . . Our culture will glorify God in ways that surpass our most fantastic dreams.[283]

Anthony Hoekema, "Heaven: Not Just an Eternal Day Off"

At Christ's return, the earth will be healed from sin's wounds. These include not only toxic waste and chemical pollution but also cultural and moral pollution. The healing of wounds implies the return to an original condition. If our new bodies will look enough like the old bodies to be recognizable, doesn't this suggest that the New Earth will look enough like the old Earth for us to recognize it?

. . . The New Earth will still be just as much Earth as the new us will still be us. Our resurrection bodies will have our eyes, ears, mouth, and nose. Like Christ's body, ours will maintain their distinguishing features. If our new bodies will so closely correspond to the present ones, won't the New Earth just as closely correspond to the present one? Will there be a New Mount Saint Helens and New Himalayas and a New Alaska under the new northern lights? Will there be a New Bermuda, a New Canada, a New Australia?

. . . My understanding of Scripture suggests that the New Earth will include not only resurrected geographical locations but also resurrected cultures. The kings of the nations will bring their tribute, splendor, and glory into the New Jerusalem (Revelation 21:24, 26). There will be not one nation but many. This reference gives us biblical basis to suppose that the best culture, history, art, music, and the languages of the old Earth will be redeemed, purified, and carried over to the New Earth.

Surely these kings and cultures who bring their "splendor" and "glory" into the new world won't start from scratch. They'll bring into the new world a national and personal history, an ethnic identity, and a wealth of customs, art forms, and knowledge. All these will be purified, but that leaves plenty of room for distinctive cultural celebrations, holidays, meals, sports, and many customs.[284]

Randy Alcorn, *Heaven*

In Daniel's vision of the Messiah's return to Earth, "He was given authority, honor, and royal power over all the nations of the world, so that people of every race and nation and language would obey him" (Daniel 7:14, NLT). There's a direct continuity between the kingdoms of the old Earth and God's eternal Kingdom on the New Earth. Earthly kingdoms will not be destroyed but "handed over" to God's people: "Then the sovereignty, power and greatness of the kingdoms under the whole heaven will be handed over to the saints" (Daniel 7:27).

Surely the greatness of the nations that will be handed over to God's people cannot be restricted only to those nations existing at Christ's return. Indeed, most of the nations Daniel speaks of—including Babylon, Medo-Persia, and Rome—faded away long ago. But in the sweeping breadth of his redemptive work, I believe that God will resurrect not only modern nations but also ancient ones, including, for instance, Babylon and Rome. I think it's likely we'll not merely meet the redeemed people of ancient civilizations but also walk among redeemed civilizations. Are ancient Assyrians, Sumerians, Phoenicians, Babylonians, and Greeks among God's redeemed? We know they are, for no nation, past or present, is excluded from "every tribe and language and people and nation" (Revelation 7:9). In Heaven, God has determined to have representatives from *every* tribe, people group, and culture.

Because Scripture explicitly tells us that resurrected nations will be part of the New Earth, I think there's every reason to believe we'll see a resurrected Egypt, Rome, India, and China, as well as resurrected cultures of every part of ancient Africa, South America, North America, Australia, Asia, and Europe, including small cultures about which we presently know very little.

I interpret "every tribe and language and people and nation" literally. God chose people in even predominantly pagan nations and reached them by sending men and women or angels, dreams, and visions. What people groups will be worshiping Christ on the New Earth? Celts, Goths, Huns, Lombards, Saxons, Vikings, Serbs, Croats, Slovenes, Canaanites, Hittites, Phoenicians, Sumerians, Assyrians,

Persians, Mongols, Malaysians, Aztecs, Mayans, Incas—and countless other civilizations, ancient and modern. Representatives of nations and cultures that no longer exist today will be raised, to God's glory, in a purified form that includes whatever pleased God and excludes whatever didn't.

Do you have a special interest in Europe of the Middle Ages? Then perhaps you'll enjoy developing relationships with those who lived in that era. Perhaps on the New Earth you'll live in a beautified version of their culture. (We shouldn't assume that all ancient people would embrace every modern convenience, even when given the choice.)

. . . I believe we have more than just biblical *permission* to imagine resurrected races, tribes, and nations living together on the New Earth; we have a biblical *mandate* to do so. So close your eyes and imagine those ancient civilizations. Not just what they were, but what they yet will be.[285]

Randy Alcorn, *Heaven*

Some people expect the New Earth to be a return to Eden, with no technology or the accomplishments of civilization. But that doesn't fit the biblical picture of the great city, the New Jerusalem. Nor is it logical. Would we expect on the New Earth a literal reinvention of the wheel?[286]

Randy Alcorn, *Heaven*

The first person Scripture describes as "filled with the Spirit" wasn't a prophet or priest; he was a craftsman, "with skill, ability and knowledge in all kinds of crafts—to make artistic designs . . . and to engage in all kinds of craftsmanship" (Exodus 31:1-3).

God gifted and called Bezalel to be a skilled laborer, a master craftsman, a God-glorifying artist. Bezalel and Oholiab were not only to create works of art but also to train apprentices to do so. The gifting and calling were from God: "He has filled them with skill to do all kinds of work as craftsmen, designers, embroiderers in blue, purple and scarlet yarn and fine linen, and weavers—all of them master craftsmen and designers" (Exodus 35:35).

If you don't believe craftsmanship will be an important part of the New Earth, read Exodus 25–40. God tells his people in exquisite detail how to sew clothing, what colors to use, how to construct the furniture for the Ark of the Covenant and Tabernacle, what stones to put on the high priest's breastplate, and so on.

The Master Designer goes into great detail in his instructions for building the Tabernacle: the veil and curtain, the Ark of the Covenant, the table, the lampstand, the altar of burnt offerings, the courtyard, the incense altar, the washbasin, the priests' clothing. The design, precision, and beauty of these things tell us about God, ourselves, and the culture of the New Earth. Those who imagine that spirituality is something ethereal and invisible—unrelated to our physical skills, creativity, and cultural development—fail to understand Scripture. God's instructions and his delight in the gifts he imparts to people to accomplish these tasks make clear what we should expect in Heaven: greater works of craftsmanship and construction, unhindered by sin and death.

It wasn't an accident that Jesus was born into a carpenter's family. Carpenters are makers. God is a maker. He'll never cease being a maker. God made us, his image-bearers, to be makers. We'll never cease to be makers. When we die, we won't leave behind our creativity, but only what hinders our ability to honor God through what we create.[287]

Randy Alcorn, *Heaven*

In the movie *Babette's Feast*, a Parisian chef is forced to leave her home through the misfortunes of war. Babette ends up in a windswept Danish coastal village, working as a maid for two women who lead a small, austere Christian sect that frowns on such worldly things as gourmet cooking. Babette grows to love these elderly sisters. When she comes into a large sum of money, she spends it all on giving a single dinner party for the sisters and their friends. It's a picture of God's extravagant grace. Babette realizes that she'll never again be able to afford to give such a gift or to prepare such a meal. One of the sisters is a talented singer who had little opportunity to use her gift. Touched by Babette's generosity, she consoles her: "I feel, Babette, that this is not the end. In Paradise you will be the great artist that God meant you to be! . . . Ah, how you will enchant the angels!"[288]

Randy Alcorn, *50 Days of Heaven*

If mankind had never sinned, would we have invented the wheel and created machinery? Certainly. On the New Earth, shouldn't we expect machinery made for the good of mankind and the glory of God? On the New Earth people might invent machinery that could take us to the far ends of the New Milky Way, to other galaxies and beyond. Why not? Is this notion more unthinkable than it once was to imagine sailing a ship across an ocean or flying a plane across the world or landing a spacecraft on the moon? Because people in this fallen world have extended their dominion beyond our current Earth, might we not expect people on the New Earth to extend their Christ-exalting reach into the new universe? . . . From the night I first saw Andromeda's galaxy, I've wanted to go there. I now think it's likely I will.[289]

Randy Alcorn, *Heaven*

Will the new planets be mere ornaments, or does God intend for us to reach them one day? Even under the Curse, we've been able to explore the moon, and we have the technology to land on Mars. What will we be able to accomplish for God's glory when we have resurrected minds, unlimited resources, complete scientific cooperation, and no more death?[290]

Randy Alcorn, *Heaven*

I want to be part of a group that explores the vast reaches of the new cosmos. When my fellow explorers and I return home to Earth, the capital planet, and enter the gates of the capital city, we'll gather for food and drinks, and catch up on our stories. I'll listen to your stories; maybe you'll listen to mine. Perhaps I'll write about great planets of star systems far away. I'll tell how my explorations deepened my love for Jesus. And you'll play or sing for me the music of praise you composed while I was gone. I'll marvel at its beauty, and I'll see Jesus in it and in you. Maybe I'll write a book about the Omega galaxy, while you'll write one about the music of the heart. We'll exchange manuscripts, stimulate new insights, and draw each other closer to God.[291]

Randy Alcorn, *Heaven*

In this world, even under the Curse, human imagination and skill have produced some remarkable works. The statues of Easter Island. Stonehenge. . . . The Golden Gate Bridge. Baseball. Heart transplants. Prenatal surgery. Microwave ovens. DVDs. The space shuttle. Chocolate ice cream. Pecan pie. Sports cars. It's a list that never ends.

With the resources God will lavishly give us on the New Earth, what will we be able to accomplish together? When we think about this, we should be like children anticipating Christmas—sneaking out of bed to see what's under the Christmas tree. . . .

Angels could have maintained the world as God created it. But it takes God's image-bearers to develop, expand, and enrich the earth. That is culture.[292]

Randy Alcorn, *Heaven*

This reigning, expanding, culture-enriching purpose of God for mankind on Earth was never revoked or abandoned. It has only been interrupted and twisted by the Fall. But neither Satan nor sin is able to thwart God's purposes. Christ's redemptive work will ultimately restore, enhance, and expand God's original plan.[293]

Randy Alcorn, *Heaven*

The Curse

[God] said to the woman,

"I will sharpen the pain of your pregnancy,
   and in pain you will give birth.
And you will desire to control your husband,
   but he will rule over you."

And to the man he said,

"Since you listened to your wife and ate from the tree
   whose fruit I commanded you not to eat,
the ground is cursed because of you.
   All your life you will struggle to scratch a living
      from it.
It will grow thorns and thistles for you,
   though you will eat of its grains.
By the sweat of your brow
   will you have food to eat

until you return to the ground
    from which you were made.
For you were made from dust,
    and to dust you will return."

GOD, GENESIS 3:16-19, NLT

I will put enmity
    between you and the woman,
    and between your offspring and hers;
he will crush your head,
    and you will strike his heel.

GOD, GENESIS 3:15

Instead of the thorn shall come up the cypress tree,
    and instead of the brier shall come up the
        myrtle tree.

GOD, ISAIAH 55:13, NKJV

All have sinned and fall short of the glory of God.

PAUL, ROMANS 3:23

Anyone who has died has been freed from sin.

PAUL, ROMANS 6:7

The creation waits in eager expectation for the sons of God to be revealed. For the creation was subjected to frustration, not by its own choice, but by the will of the one who subjected it, in hope that the creation itself will be liberated from its bondage to decay and brought into the glorious freedom of the children of God.

We know that the whole creation has been groaning as in the pains of childbirth right up to the present time. Not only so, but we ourselves, who have the first-fruits of the Spirit, groan inwardly as we wait eagerly for our adoption as sons, the redemption of our bodies.

PAUL, ROMANS 8:19-23

Christ redeemed us from the curse of the law by becoming a curse for us.

PAUL, GALATIANS 3:13, ESV

No longer will there be any curse.

JOHN, REVELATION 22:3

There is no element and no part of the world which is being touched, as it were, with a sense of its present misery, that does not intensely hope for a resurrection.[294]

John Calvin, *Commentary on Romans*

The Earth in ruins reveals a magnificence which shows the sign of a royal founder and an extraordinary purpose. Creation glows with a thousand beauties even in its present fallen condition, yet clearly enough it is not as when it came from the Maker's hand—the slime of the serpent is on it all—this is not the world which God pronounced to be "very good." . . .

It is a sad, sad world. Thorns and thistles it brings forth, not from its soil alone, but from all that comes of it. Earth wears upon her brow, like the mark of Cain, the brand of transgression.

If there were no future to this world as well as to ourselves, we might be glad to escape from it, counting it to be nothing better than a huge penal colony, from which it would be a thousand mercies for both body and soul to be liberated.

At this present time, the groaning and anguish which are general throughout creation are deeply felt among the sons of men. There is a general wail among nations and peoples. You can hear it in the streets of the city. May God in mercy put his hand to the helm of the ship and steer her safely. . . .

These are to us the promises of the coming glory. If you have the Spirit of God in your soul, you may rejoice over it as the pledge and token of the fullness of bliss and perfection that "God has prepared for those who love him."[295]

Charles Spurgeon, "Creation's Groans and the Saints' Sighs," Sermon 788

No more let sins and sorrows grow
Nor thorns infest the ground;
He comes to make His blessings flow
Far as the Curse is found.

Isaac Watts, "Joy to the World"

[God] hangs on to his fallen original creation and salvages it. He refuses to abandon the work of his hands—in fact, he sacrifices his own Son to save his original project. Humankind, which has botched its original mandate and the whole creation along with it, is given another chance in Christ; we are reinstated as God's managers on earth. The original good creation is to be restored.[296]

Albert Wolters, *Creation Regained*

Whatever sin has touched and polluted, God will redeem and cleanse. If redemption does not go as far as the curse of sin, then God has failed. Whatever the extent of the consequences of sin, so must the extent of redemption be.[297]

Steven J. Lawson, *Heaven Help Us!*

Ever since God expelled Adam and Eve from the garden, we have lived in an unnatural environment—a world in which we were not designed to live. We were built to enjoy a garden without weeds, relationships without friction, fellowship without distance. But something is wrong and we know it, both within our world and within ourselves. Deep inside we sense we're out of the nest, always ending the day in a motel room and never at home.[298]

Larry Crabb

Because of man's fall into sin, a curse was pronounced over this creation. God now sent his Son into this world to redeem that creation from the results of sin. The work of Christ, therefore, is not just to save certain individuals, not even to save an innumerable throng of blood-bought people. The total work of Christ is nothing less than to redeem this entire creation from the effects of sin. That purpose will not be accomplished until God has ushered in the new earth, until Paradise Lost has become Paradise Regained.[299]

Anthony Hoekema, *The Bible and the Future*

Never forget that when we are dealing with any pleasure in its healthy and normal and satisfying form, we are, in a sense, on the Enemy's ground. I know we have won many a soul through pleasure. All the same, it is His invention, not ours. He made the pleasures: all our research so far has not enabled us to produce one. All we can do is to encourage the humans to take the pleasures which our Enemy has produced, at times, or in ways, or in degrees, which He has forbidden. Hence we always try to work away from the natural condition of any pleasure to that in which it is least natural, least redolent of its Maker, and least pleasurable. An ever increasing craving for an ever diminishing pleasure is the formula.[300]

The demon Wormwood, in *The Screwtape Letters*, by C. S. Lewis

Redemption in Jesus Christ reaches just as far as the fall. The horizon of creation is at the same time the horizon of sin and of salvation. To conceive of either the fall or Christ's deliverance as encompassing less than the whole of creation is to compromise the biblical teaching of the radical nature of the fall and the cosmic scope of redemption.[301]

Albert Wolters, *Creation Regained*

No longer are we in danger of substituting a visionary life in the future for the actual life of the present, or of shunning the world instead of improving it; or of making religion a preparation for heaven, instead of the practice of right living on earth. The danger is all on the other side. This world is too much with us; Heaven, too little. . . . Over-worldliness, not other-worldliness is the besetting sin of the times.[302]

James Campbell, *Heaven Opened*

Our present powers over nature have been severely limited. We are spoiled children whose Father has taken away their dangerous toys. Imagine the chaos the world would be if it were inhabited by a billion evil magicians, each trying to be its own God. . . . Before the power of union with nature can be restored, union with God must be restored.[303]

Peter Kreeft, *Everything You Ever Wanted to Know about Heaven*

In Genesis we see the first Paradise closed. In Revelation we see the new Paradise opened. In Genesis we find the entrance of human sin. In Revelation we see the exclusion of human sin. In Genesis the curse was imposed. In Revelation the curse is removed. In Genesis access to the tree of life was disinherited. In Revelation access to the tree of life is reinherited. In Genesis we see the beginning of sorrow and death. In Revelation we see the end of sorrow and death. In Genesis man's dominion is broken. In Revelation we see man's dominion restored. In Genesis we see the evil triumph of Satan. In Revelation we see the ultimate triumph of the Lamb. In Genesis, God's walk with man was interrupted. In Revelation, God's walk with man resumes. In Genesis we see Paradise lost. In Revelation we see Paradise regained.[304]

Steven J. Lawson, *Heaven Help Us!*

The fall affects the whole range of earthly creation. . . . Sin is a parasite on, and not a part of, creation; and . . . to the degree that it affects the whole earth, sin profanes all things, making them "worldly," "secular," "earthly." Consequently, every area of the created world cries out for redemption and the coming of the kingdom of God.[305]

Albert Wolters, *Creation Regained*

The curse which fell upon the ground was not eternal; thorns and thistles pass away. God will bless the earth for Christ's sake even as once he cursed it for man's sake.

"Your will be done in earth, as it is in heaven." *It was so once.* Perfect obedience to the heavenly upon this earth will only be a return to the good old times which ended at the gate of Eden. There was a day when no gulf was dug between earth and heaven; there was scarcely a boundary line, for the God of heaven walked in Paradise with Adam. All things on earth were then pure, and true, and happy. It was the garden of the Lord.

Alas, that the trail of the serpent has now defiled everything. . . .

The Lord is king: and he has never left the throne. As it was in the beginning so shall it be yet again. . . .

"Your will be done in earth, as it is in heaven." *It will be so at the last.* . . . There is to be "a new heaven and a new earth, where righteousness dwells." This creation which now "groans and travails in pain," in sympathy with man, is to be brought forth from its bondage into the glorious liberty of the children of God.[306]

Charles Spurgeon, "A Heavenly Pattern for Our Earthly Life," Sermon 1778

We would not judge the possibilities of automobiles merely by a survey of those we find in the junkyard or the possibilities of plant life by considering only plants that have been starved of necessary nutrients.

The human body was made to be the vehicle of human personality ruling the earth for God and through his power. Withdrawn from that function by loss of its connection with God, the body is caught in the inevitable state of corruption in which we find it now. And with this loss came the loss of the power required to fulfill their role as God's rulers over the earth.[307]

Dallas Willard, *The Spirit of the Disciplines*

"There shall no longer be any curse" (Revelation 22:3). The hope, the promise, the anticipation of this verse is inexpressible—it is weighty, thick with promise and joy. Let your imagination go where this verse leads you. Write it down, post it on your refrigerator and dashboard and bathroom mirror.

Randy Alcorn, unpublished notes

The most beautiful person you've ever seen is under the Curse, a shadow of the beauty that once characterized humanity. If we saw Adam and Eve as they were in Eden, they would likely take our breath away. If they would have seen us as we are now, they likely would have been filled with shock and pity.[308]

Randy Alcorn, *Heaven*

We've never seen men and women as they were intended to be. We've never seen animals the way they were before the Fall. We see only marred remnants of what once was.

Likewise, we've never seen nature unchained and undiminished. We've only seen it cursed and decaying. Yet even now we see a great deal that pleases and excites us, moving our hearts to worship.

If the "wrong side" of Heaven can be so beautiful, what will the right side look like? If the smoking remains are so stunning, what will Earth look like when it's resurrected and made new, restored to the original?[309]

Randy Alcorn, *Heaven*

Our greatest deliverance in Heaven will be from ourselves. Our deceit, corruption, self-righteousness, self-sufficiency, hypocrisy—all will be gone forever.[310]

Randy Alcorn, *We Shall See God*

In Heaven we won't just be better than we are now—we'll be better than Adam and Eve were before they fell. Our resurrection bodies may be very much like their bodies were before the Fall, but we'll be a redeemed humanity with knowledge of God, including his grace, far exceeding theirs.[311]

Randy Alcorn, *Heaven*

Do you ever sense creation's restlessness? Do you hear groaning in the cold night wind? Do you feel the forest's loneliness, the ocean's agitation? Do you hear longing in the cries of whales? Do you see blood and pain in the eyes of wild animals, or the mixture of pleasure and pain in the eyes of your pets? Despite vestiges of beauty and joy, something on this earth is terribly wrong. Not only God's creatures but even inanimate objects seem to feel it. But there's also hope, visible in springtime after a hard winter.[312]

Randy Alcorn, *Heaven*

God will remove the parasite without killing the patient.[313]

Randy Alcorn, *Heaven*

Isn't it reasonable to suppose that the pristine conditions of God's original creation were such that stellar energy would be replenished, planets would not fall out of orbit, and humans and animals would not die? What if God intended that our dominion over the earth would ultimately extend to the entire physical universe? Then we would not be surprised to see the entire creation come under the Curse, because it would all be under our stewardship.[314]

Randy Alcorn, *50 Days of Heaven*

Earth cannot be delivered from the Curse by being destroyed. It can be delivered only by being *resurrected*.[315]

Randy Alcorn, *We Shall See God*

We will expect less of this life, and enjoy it more, when we remind ourselves that it is not the best, that something far better is coming—something bought by the blood of God.

Randy Alcorn, notes

Astronomy has been my hobby since childhood. Years before I came to know Christ, I was fascinated by the violent collisions of galaxies, explosions of stars, and implosions into neutron stars and black holes. The second law of thermodynamics, entropy, tells us that all things deteriorate. This means that everything was once in a better condition than it is now. Children and stars can both be born, but both ultimately become engaged in a downward spiral. Even the remotest parts of the universe reveal vast realms of fiery destruction. On the one hand, these cataclysms declare God's greatness. On the other hand, they reflect something that is out of order on a massive scale.

It seems possible that even the second law of thermodynamics (at least as it is popularly understood) may have been the product of mankind's fall. If true, it demonstrates the mind-boggling extent of the Curse. The most remote galaxy, the most distant quasar, was somehow shaken by mankind's sin.[316]

Randy Alcorn, *Heaven*

The Curse is real, but *temporary.* Jesus will reverse the Curse. Earth won't merely be put out of its misery; Christ will infuse it with a far greater life. Then, at last, it will become all God intended it to be.[317]

Randy Alcorn, *If God Is Good . . .*

Death

See now that I myself am He!
    There is no god besides me.
I put to death and I bring to life,
    I have wounded and I will heal,
    and no one can deliver out of my hand.

GOD, DEUTERONOMY 32:39

The waves of death swirled about me;
    the torrents of destruction overwhelmed me.
The cords of the grave coiled around me;
    the snares of death confronted me.
In my distress I called to the LORD;
    I called out to my God.
From his temple he heard my voice;
    my cry came to his ears.

DAVID, 2 SAMUEL 22:5-7

The dust returns to the ground it came from,
    and the spirit returns to God who gave it.

SOLOMON, ECCLESIASTES 12:7

Man does not know his time.

SOLOMON, ECCLESIASTES 9:12, ESV

I know you will bring me down to death,
    to the place appointed for all the living.

JOB 30:23

O LORD, make me know my end
        and what is the measure of my days;
        let me know how fleeting I am!
Behold, you have made my days a few handbreadths,
        and my lifetime is as nothing before you.
Surely all mankind stands as a mere breath!

DAVID, PSALM 39:4-5, ESV

Teach us to number our days
    that we may get a heart of wisdom.

MOSES, PSALM 90:12, ESV

Why, you do not even know what will happen tomorrow. What is your life? You are a mist that appears for
a little while and then vanishes.

JAMES 4:14

The LORD is my Shepherd; I shall not want. He maketh
me to lie down in green pastures: he leadeth me beside
the still waters. He restoreth my soul: he leadeth me
in the paths of righteousness for his name's sake. Yea,

though I walk through the valley of the shadow of death,
I will fear no evil: for thou art with me; thy rod and thy
staff they comfort me. Thou preparest a table before
me in the presence of mine enemies: thou anointest my
head with oil; my cup runneth over. Surely goodness and
mercy shall follow me all the days of my life: and I will
dwell in the house of the LORD for ever.

DAVID, PSALM 23, KJV

He will swallow up on this mountain
    the covering that is cast over all peoples,
    the veil that is spread over all nations.
    He will swallow up death forever;
and the Lord GOD will wipe away tears from all faces,
    and the reproach of his people he will take away
        from all the earth,
    for the LORD has spoken.

ISAIAH 25:7-8, ESV

Sin came into the world through one man, and death
through sin. . . . But the free gift is not like the trespass.
For if many died through one man's trespass, much more
have the grace of God and the free gift by the grace of
that one man Jesus Christ abounded for many. . . . For
if, because of one man's trespass, death reigned through
that one man, much more will those who receive the
abundance of grace and the free gift of righteousness
reign in life through the one man Jesus Christ.

PAUL, ROMANS 5:12, 15, 17, ESV

[Christ] must reign until he has put all his enemies
under his feet. The last enemy to be destroyed is death.

PAUL, 1 CORINTHIANS 15:25-26

Where, O death, is your victory?
Where, O death, is your sting?

PAUL, 1 CORINTHIANS 15:55

By [Christ's] death he might destroy him who holds the power of death—that is, the devil—and free those who all their lives were held in slavery by their fear of death.

HEBREWS 2:14-15

There will be no more death or mourning or crying or pain, for the old order of things has passed away.

JESUS, REVELATION 21:4

May I view things in the mirror of eternity,
waiting for the coming of my Lord,
listening for the last trumpet call,
hastening unto the new heaven and earth. . . .
May I speak each word as if my last word,
and walk each step as my final one.
If my life should end today, let this be my best day.[318]

The Valley of Vision: A Collection of Puritan Prayers and Devotions

Supreme Ruler of the visible and invisible worlds,
. . . May I be daily more and more conformed to thee,
with the meekness and calmness of the Lamb in my soul,
and a feeling sense of the felicity of heaven,
where I long to join angels free from imperfections,
where in me the image of my adored Saviour will be com-
pletely restored,
so that I may be fit for his enjoyments and employments.
I am not afraid to look the king of terrors in the face,
For I know I shall be drawn, not driven, out of the world.[319]

The Valley of Vision: A Collection of Puritan Prayers and Devotions

It ought to be the business of every day to prepare for our last day.[320]

Matthew Henry, "Directions for Daily Communication with God"

My knowledge of that life is small,
  The eye of faith is dim,
But it's enough that Christ knows all,
  And I shall be with him.[321]

Richard Baxter

H. S. Laird's father, a Christ-loving man, lay dying. His son sat at his bedside and asked, "Dad, how do you feel?" His father replied: "Son, I feel like a little boy on Christmas Eve."[322]

Jack MacArthur, adapted from *Exploring in the Next World*

Though the Witch knew the Deep Magic, there is a magic deeper still which she did not know. Her knowledge goes back only to the dawn of time. But if she could have looked a little further back, into the stillness and the darkness before Time dawned . . . she would have known that when a willing victim who had committed no treachery was killed in a traitor's stead, the Table would crack and Death itself would start working backwards.[323]

C. S. Lewis, *The Lion, the Witch and the Wardrobe*

I'm standing on the seashore. A ship at my side spreads her white sails to the morning breeze and starts for the blue ocean. She's an object of beauty and strength and I stand and watch her until, at length, she hangs like a speck of white cloud just where the sea and the sky come down to mingle with each other. And then I hear someone at my side saying, "There, she's gone."

Gone where? Gone from my sight, that is all. She is just as large in mast and hull and spar as she was when she left my side. And just as able to bear her load of living freight to the place of destination. Her diminished size is in *me*, not in her.

And just at the moment when someone at my side says, "There, she's gone," there are other eyes watching her coming, and there are other voices ready to take up the glad shout, "Here she comes!" And that is dying.[324]

Source uncertain

Soon you will read in the newspaper that I am dead. Don't believe it for a moment. I will be more alive than ever before. . . . Earth recedes. . . . Heaven opens before me![325]

D. L. Moody, on his deathbed

> *I once scorned ev'ry fearful thought of death,*
> *When it was but the end of pulse and breath,*
> *But now my eyes have seen that past the pain*
> *There is a world that's waiting to be claimed.*
> *Earthmaker, Holy, let me now depart,*
> *For living's such a temporary art.*
> *And dying is but getting dressed for God,*
> *Our graves are merely doorways cut in sod.*[326]

Calvin Miller, *The Divine Symphony*

We can banish all fear of being absorbed into the "All" which Buddhism holds before us, or reincarnated in some other life form as in the post-mortem prospect of Hinduism. . . . The self with which we were endowed by the Creator in his gift of life to us, the self whose worth was secured forever in the self-substitution of God for us on the cross, *that self* will endure into eternity. Death cannot destroy us.[327]

Bruce Milne, *The Message of Heaven and Hell*

> *Since One, for Love, Died on a tree*
> *And, in the stony Tomb was lain,*
> *Behold, I show a mystery:*
> *All sepulchers are sealed in vain!*[328]

John Richard Moreland, *A Blue Wave Breaking*

We preach that it is wonderful to be a Christian, that Heaven is to be gained and Hell shunned. Then when one of our loved ones dies, we act as if it were all a lie. Our actions say that this world is better than the next, that death is a tragedy, and we ask querulously in our unbelief, Why? Why? Why?

We feel that Heaven is bearable, all right, when one has sucked dry all the pleasures of earth. We feel that, only after old age has come upon us, when life is a burden, when health has failed, when we are in the way and our children don't want us, then perhaps we should be resigned to go to Heaven. Subconsciously we look upon Heaven as a scrapheap for the worn-out and useless, a kind of old people's home—better than nothing but not as good as this world, with youth, health and prosperity.

Shame on us! When we weep and lament at the death of our loved ones, we often make void our testimony, cast reflection upon the Bible and irreverence on Heaven.

For the Christian, death is not a tragedy but a glorious promotion—not the sad end, but the glorious beginning.

. . . However much we miss our loved ones when they fall asleep, let us remember that our mourning is selfish. There is rejoicing in Heaven. Not one in that blessed land would, if he could, return to the decaying form he left, to live out the life he had planned, to see the happiest future he could imagine on this earth. . . . "Blessed are the dead which die in the Lord from henceforth."[329]

John Rice, *Bible Facts about Heaven*

When I die, I shall change my place but not my company.[330]

John Preston, cited in *The Doors of Heaven*

Oh, God, this is the end; for me the beginning of life.[331]

Dietrich Bonhoeffer, just before he was hanged by the Nazis

There shall be a second death, but over us it shall have no power. Do you understand the beauty of the picture? As if we might walk through the flames of Hell and they should have no power to devour us, any more than when Shadrach, Meshach, and Abednego paced with ease over the hot coals of Nebuchadnezzar's seven-times heated furnace.

Death may bend his bow and fit the arrow to the string. But we laugh at you, oh death! And you, oh Hell, we will despise! For over both of you enemies of mankind we shall be more than conquerors through him who loved us (Romans 8:37). We shall stand invulnerable and invincible, defying and laughing to scorn our every foe. And all this because we are washed from sin and covered with a spotless righteousness. . . .

Brothers and sisters, lift up your heads. Contending with sin and cast down with doubts, lift up your heads and wipe the tears from your eyes. There are days coming, the likes of which angels have not seen, but you shall see them.[332]

Charles Spurgeon, "The First Resurrection," Sermon 391

Here in this world,
He bids us come;
there in the next,
He shall bid us welcome.[333]

John Donne

The best grieving is the rollercoaster ride that takes our emotions up with happy memories, down with the vacant feeling of loss and around with awkwardly decreasing feelings of disorientation and disbelief. Grieving is as much about us as it is about the one who died.[334]

Daniel Brown, *What the Bible Reveals about Heaven*

Death entered the realm of mankind when the first person elected not to follow God's instructions for how to live. Adam and Eve were fooled into believing that God was trying to deny them something that would make life better for them than what He had already arranged.[335]

Daniel Brown, *What the Bible Reveals about Heaven*

Death, carefully pondered, resolutely faced, actually loses its grip on us, its deadlock on our imaginations. It can wholly reawaken holy wonder. We learn to cherish those things we often take for granted: lying beneath a huge sky alongside a child, searching out shapes in clouds; the taste of freshly picked carrots with the dirt only brushed off; the prickly, tickling feel of cat's whiskers on your leg; the sound of rain plinking down metal pipes at night. And the things we often seek after desperately—recognition for a contract deal, more money, a holiday on a luxury cruiser, five minutes alone with *that* woman—become to us nothing, detritus underfoot, smoke in the eyes.[336]

Mark Buchanan, *Things Unseen*

The gate of death is the gate of exit; the gate of Heaven is the gate of entrance; but these two are so close together that as the one shuts, the other opens. When a ripened saint was getting near the end of life's journey, his friends said, "He is lying at the gate of death." He himself said, "I am lying at the gate of Heaven." Both were correct, for to the dying Christian the two gates are practically one.[337]

James Campbell, *Heaven Opened*

I am bowed down and could best express myself in a flood of tears as I survey the line of graves so newly dug. The Master is gathering the ripest of his fruit, and well does he deserve them. His own dear hand is putting his apples of gold into his baskets of silver, and as we see that it is the Lord, we are bewildered no longer.

His word, as it comes before us in the text [John 14:1-2], calms and quiets our spirits. It dries our tears and calls us to rejoicing as we hear our heavenly Bridegroom praying, "Father, I desire that they also, whom you have given me, may be with me where I am, to see my glory." We understand why the dearest and best are going. We see in whose hand is held the magnet which attracts them to the skies. One by one they must depart from this lowland country to dwell above, in the palace of the King, for Jesus is drawing them to himself.

Our dear babes go home because "he will gather the lambs in his arms; he will carry them in his bosom" (Isaiah 40:11). And our ripe saints go home because the Beloved comes into his garden to gather lilies. These words of our Lord Jesus explain the continual home-going. They are the answer to the riddle which we call death.[338]

Charles Spurgeon, "Why They Leave Us," Sermon 1892

Life is real, life is earnest,
And the grave is not its goal:
"Dust thou art, to dust returnest,"
Was not spoken of the soul.[339]

Henry Wadsworth Longfellow, "A Psalm of Life"

Most people think we are in the land of the living on our way to the land of the dying. But actually, we are in the land of the dying on our way to the land of the living. . . . Death is a conjunction, not a period. . . . Death is a conjunction followed by a destination.[340]

Tony Evans, *Tony Evans Speaks Out on Heaven and Hell*

Death, our "last enemy" (1 Corinthians 15:26), has through the work of Christ become our friend. Our most dreaded opponent has become for us the servant who opens the door to heavenly bliss. Death for the Christian is therefore not the end but a glorious new beginning.[341]

Anthony Hoekema, *The Bible and the Future*

Death. It is the most misunderstood part of life. It is not a great sleep but a great awakening. It is that moment when we awake, rub our eyes, and see things at last the way God has seen them all along.[342]

Ken Gire, *Instructive Moments with the Savior*

We consider it strange that Christians claim to believe that heaven—being present with God—is so wonderful, and yet act as if going there were the greatest tragedy.

We believe that death will someday be destroyed, but it is still a painful experience which all of us must face. We believe that some Christians may have idealistic views of deathbed rapture and be unprepared for this enemy's grim violence. God has not promised His children an easy death or deathbed visions of glory. He has promised an open door beyond.[343]

Joseph Bayly, *When a Child Dies*

The moment you come into this world you are beginning to go out of it.[344]

Martyn Lloyd-Jones, *Romans: The Final Perseverance of the Saints*

When a Christian dies, it's not a time to despair, but a time to trust. Just as the seed is buried and the material wrapping decomposes, so our fleshly body will be buried and will decompose. But just as the buried seed sprouts new life, so our body will blossom into a new body. As Jesus said, "Unless a grain of wheat falls into the earth and dies, it remains a single grain of wheat; but if it dies, it brings a good harvest" (John 12:24, Phillips).

What have you done today to avoid death? Likely a lot.

Why the effort? Because you are worried about staying alive. That won't be a worry in heaven.

Heaven has no planes that I know of. If it does, they don't crash. But if they crash, no one dies. So you don't have to worry.[345]

Max Lucado, *When Christ Comes*

God says . . . regarding our body: "Let's finish with the one you have, and then I have a surprise."[346]

Max Lucado, *When Christ Comes*

Facing death is central both to the character of Christian experience and to Christian witness. What gives death its poignancy and its seriousness is not only that it is the parting of friends but that it heralds the judgment. It brings to a close that one life on earth the character of which will irrevocably fix the life beyond the grave.[347]

Paul Helm, *The Last Things*

How monotonously alike all the great tyrants and conquerors have been: how gloriously different are the saints. . . . Nothing in you that has not died will ever be raised from the dead. Look for yourself, and you will find in the long run only hatred, loneliness, despair, rage, ruin, and decay. But look for Christ and you will find Him, and with Him everything else thrown in.[348]

C. S. Lewis, *Mere Christianity*

We have not lost our dear ones who have departed from this life, but have merely sent them ahead of us, so we also shall depart and shall come to that life where they will be more than ever dear as they will be better known to us, and where we shall love them without fear of parting.[349]

Augustine, letter to Lady Italica

All of us who enjoy God are also enjoying each other in Him.[350]

Augustine, *On the Christian Doctrine*

Sleep, like death, is a temporary experience and ends in a great awakening. I think the image of sleep is used for death so often in Scripture because sleep and death are both universal experiences. . . . When I've worked hard, I look forward to lying down in a refreshing sleep. I don't fear sleep or try to avoid it; I embrace it. We close our eyes in anticipation of a new day. For the Christian, death is falling asleep to all we have known in this realm and waking up in Christ's presence.

Death is also compared to *taking down a tent*. Our present bodies are our temporary dwelling places. . . . The assurance of the Christian is that when this earthly tent is destroyed, "we have a building from God, an eternal house in heaven, not built by human hands" (2 Corinthians 5:1). Death is the first step in a wonderful process that will eventually bring us a permanent, glorified body that will never age or decay or require a wheelchair.[351]

Douglas Connelly, *The Promise of Heaven*

The Bible is completely silent about the experiences . . . people had while they were dead—no mention of tunnels, soft lights or any other of the near-death happenings some people today claim to have. When people come back to life in the Bible, they do so not to tell about what it was like to die but to be testimonies of God's glory. The point is not what death is like but what God is like.[352]

Daniel Brown, *What the Bible Reveals about Heaven*

Birth is such an excellent analogy for death. As surely as a newborn baby "dies" from the womb-world into this world, so will our passing from life on Earth be a birth into another. . . . Babies do not cease to exist when they pass down the birth canal; they just don't live in the womb any longer. The person in the womb becomes the person who lives in the world. The person in the world becomes the person who lives in Heaven.[353]

Daniel Brown, *What the Bible Reveals about Heaven*

Death is deliverance to life beyond your imagining. . . . The death incident is merely a passage from earth life, from the womb that has contained you until now, into the marvelous newness of heaven life. You'll go through a dark tunnel, you may experience pain—just as you did when you were born a baby—but beyond the tunnel is heaven. I promise you, you'll enjoy heaven.[354]

Joseph Bayly, *A Voice in the Wilderness*

[C. S. Lewis, five months before he died, writing to a woman who feared her coming death:] Can you not see death as a friend and deliverer? . . . What is there to be afraid of? . . . Your sins are confessed. . . . Has this world been so kind to you that you should leave with regret? There are better things ahead than any we leave behind. . . . Our Lord says to you, "Peace, child, peace. Relax. Let go. I will catch you. Do you trust me so little?" . . . Of course, this may not be the end. Then make it a good rehearsal.

Yours (and like you, a tired traveler, near the journey's end), C. S. Lewis.[355]

C. S. Lewis, *Letters to an American Lady*

The tension that the Christian experiences as he faces the grave is the tension between faith—his faith in the promises of God that he will conquer death—and sight, what he presently sees of death and its destructive effects. He does not see the glory, for he has no first-hand experience of the resurrected, glorified life, and yet he believes. All he sees is what is passing, not the reality to which faith clings. Faith is stretched because the bridge between faith and sight is not yet spanned. Faith is not yet turned into sight. . . .

The record of the ways in which God has kept his promises to his people supports the belief that what he has promised to do in the future, namely to bring the believer through death, he will be able to carry out. So that the hope of deliverance through death is not wishful thinking.[356]

Paul Helm, *The Last Things*

Why should we start and fear to die?
What timorous worms we mortals are!
Death is the gate of endless joy,
And yet we dread to enter there.
The pains, the groans, and dying strife,
Fright our approaching souls away;
We still shrink back again to life,
Fond of our prison and our clay.[357]

Isaac Watts, *An Arrangement of the Psalms, Hymns, and Spiritual Songs of Isaac Watts*

With the promises of God so distinct and beautiful, it is unbecoming that a Christian should make such a fearful thing of death. The fact that we Christians do display a neurosis about dying indicates that we are not where we ought to be spiritually. If we had actually reached a place of such spiritual commitment that the wonders of heaven were so close that we longed for the illuminating Presence of our Lord, we would not go into such a fearful and frantic performance every time we find something wrong with our physical frame.

I do not think that a genuine, committed Christian ever ought to be afraid to die. We do not have to be because Jesus promised that He would prepare a proper place for all of those who are born again, raised up out of the agony and stress of this world through the blood of the everlasting covenant into that bright and gracious world above.[358]

A. W. Tozer, *The Attributes of God*

The longest way must have its close—the gloomiest night will wear on to a morning. An eternal, inexorable lapse of moments is ever hurrying the day of the evil to an eternal night, and the night of the just to an eternal day. We have walked with our humble friend thus far in the valley of slavery; first through flowery fields of ease and indulgence, then through heart-breaking separations from all that man holds dear. Again, we have waited with him in a sunny island, where generous hands concealed his chains with flowers; and, lastly, we have followed him when the last ray of earthly hope went out in night, and seen how, in the blackness of earthly darkness, the firmament of the unseen has blazed with stars of new and significant lustre.[359]

Harriet Beecher Stowe, *Uncle Tom's Cabin*

Death is like a great ocean, and we are on this shore seeing people depart. But every ocean has two shores, and every person we see depart is seen as arriving on that other shore. Death is not the end.

Just as birth was our ticket to this world, so death is our ticket to the next. It is less of an end than a beginning. If I told you today I would move you from the slums to a beautiful country estate, you would not focus on the life you were ending but the life you were beginning.[360]

Randy Alcorn, "Death: Signing and Framing Your Life's Portrait"

Jesus came to deliver us from the fear of death, "so that by his death he might destroy him who holds the power of death—that is, the devil—and free those who all their lives were held in slavery by their fear of death" (Hebrews 2:14-15).

In light of the coming resurrection of the dead, the apostle Paul asks, "Where, O death, is your victory? Where, O death, is your sting?" (1 Corinthians 15:55).[361]

Randy Alcorn, *We Shall See God*

Talking about death won't bring it a moment sooner. But it will give us opportunity to prepare for what lies ahead. If life's greatest certainty is death, wouldn't it be foolish not to prepare for what lies beyond this life? Any life that leaves us unprepared for death is a wasted life.[362]

Randy Alcorn, *The Law of Rewards*

"You will not die" is the world's oldest lie. Universalism is its oldest heresy. An airbrush, a facelift and lipstick don't make it any more true.

Randy Alcorn, unpublished notes

What do we gain if we pretend mortality isn't a fact of life? It's neither morbid nor inappropriate to speak of it. Denial of truth—not truth itself—is the breeding ground for anxiety. One of the greatest gifts you can bestow on your loved ones is the honest anticipation of reunion in the better world, the one for which we were made.

Randy Alcorn, notes

Death, though a curse in itself, was also the only way out from under the Curse—and only because God had prepared a way to defeat death and restore mankind's relationship with him.[363]

Randy Alcorn, *50 Days of Heaven*

Death is an abnormal condition because it tears apart what God created and joined together. God originally designed bodies to last as long as our souls, and that's exactly what He'll give us in the resurrection.[364]

Randy Alcorn, *Heaven*

When five-year-old Emily Kimball was hospitalized and heard she was going to die, she started to cry. Even though she loved Jesus and wanted to be with him, she didn't want to leave her family behind. Then her mother had an inspired idea. She asked Emily to step through a doorway into another room, and she closed the door behind her. One at a time, the entire family started coming through the door to join her. Her mother explained that this was how it would be. Emily would be the first to go through death's door into Heaven. Eventually, the rest of the family would follow, probably one by one, joining her on the other side. Emily understood.

The analogy would have been even more complete if someone representing Jesus had been in the room to greet her—along with departed loved ones and Bible characters and angels.[365]

Randy Alcorn, *50 Days of Heaven*

Dream World or Reality?

Christ did not enter a man-made sanctuary that was only a copy of the true one; he entered heaven itself.

Hebrews 9:24

I looked and in heaven the temple, that is, the tabernacle of the Testimony, was opened. Out of the temple came the seven angels with the seven plagues. They were dressed in clean, shining linen and wore golden sashes around their chests. Then one of the four living creatures gave to the seven angels seven golden bowls filled with the wrath of God, who lives for ever and ever. And the temple was filled with smoke from the glory of God and from his power, and no one could enter the temple until the seven plagues of the seven angels were completed.

John, Revelation 15:5-8

We speak wisdom among those who are mature, yet not the wisdom of this age, nor of the rulers of this age, who are coming to nothing. But we speak the wisdom of God in a mystery, the hidden wisdom which God ordained before the ages for our glory, which none of the rulers of this age knew; for had they known, they would not have crucified the Lord of glory.

But as it is written:

"Eye has not seen, nor ear heard,
Nor have entered into the heart of man
The things which God has prepared for those who
            love Him."

But God has revealed them to us through His Spirit. For the Spirit searches all things, yes, the deep things of God. For what man knows the things of a man except the spirit of the man which is in him? Even so no one knows the things of God except the Spirit of God. Now we have received, not the spirit of the world, but the Spirit who is from God, that we might know the things that have been freely given to us by God.

These things we also speak, not in words which man's wisdom teaches but which the Holy Spirit teaches, comparing spiritual things with spiritual. But the natural man does not receive the things of the Spirit of God, for they are foolishness to him; nor can he know them, because they are spiritually discerned. But he who is spiritual judges all things, yet he himself is rightly judged by no one. For "who has known the mind of the LORD that he may instruct Him?" But we have the mind of Christ.

PAUL, 1 CORINTHIANS 2:5-16, NKJV

"I asked Reverend Dobson about Heaven and he said it was like Abraham Lincoln's goodness living after him."

"And why didn't you like it?"

"Well, don't you see? It amounts to saying there isn't any Heaven at all."

"I don't see that it amounts to that. What do you want Heaven to be?"

"Well, I don't know. I want it to be something. I thought he'd tell me what it was."[366]

John Updike, "Pigeon Feathers"

The heaven to which they have gone is not only an inward experience or subjective condition of blessedness; it is a *place*. As the sun is everywhere present in our solar system by the light and heat which it diffuses—besides the one place where it concentratedly is—so, and much more so, God is everywhere immanent throughout the universe, while yet there is one place, inconceivable as yet to our finite minds, where apparently his throne and presence are ineffably concentrated. That place is heaven in the supreme sense.[367]

J. Sidlow Baxter, *The Other Side of Death*

Although fundamentalists would discard the suggestion that heaven no longer is an active part of their belief system, eternal life has become an unknown place or a state of vague identity. Conservative Christians confront rationalized religion with a heightened sense of faith, religious feeling, and community, but they do not return to the rich heavenly images of previous generations. The drama of the future is decidedly this-worldly; it occurs during the period before and during the millennium, not in a heavenly world.[368]

Colleen McDannell and Bernhard Lang, *Heaven: A History*

Heaven is not a state of mind. Heaven is reality itself. All that is fully real is Heavenly. For all that can be shaken will be shaken and only the unshakable remains.[369]

The Teacher, in *The Great Divorce*, by C. S. Lewis

We shall in the future world see the material forms of the new heavens and the new earth in such a way that we shall most distinctly recognize God everywhere present and governing all things, material as well as spiritual.[370]

Augustine, *The City of God*

Every personality is either local, universal, or extinct. Therefore, any "heaven" occupied by resurrected bodies is bound to be an actual locality, not merely some kind of theoretical state existing within an indefinable void.

Our heavenly home is neither some sort of nebulous "state" without a setting, nor merely an isolated region in the sky. It is a spiritually-conditioned cosmos having no frontiers and no forbidden bounds, save only that it excludes the abysmal prison of the damned.[371]

E. X. Heatherley, *Our Heavenly Home*

Where we will spend eternity, is part of the new cosmos; but it is a place as real and substantial as any location on Earth today. Heaven is not a state of mind or an altered consciousness to be accessed through meditation, hypnosis, drugs or mental discipline. Heaven is not a mystical oneness with the cosmos, a collective memory of the race or a featureless idea like beauty or truth. Heaven is not in your mind or wherever and whatever you want it to be.[372]

Daniel Brown, *What the Bible Reveals about Heaven*

Three serious arguments, however, commend and make credible heaven as a place. First, God is said to have created heaven as well as earth. How could God have created something that can't be located? The second reason . . . Christ ascended with a resurrection body. How can a body that was tangible, that took up space, not exist in a heavenly place? Third, there are specific texts, both in the Old Testament and in the New Testament, which speak of heaven as a place. Isaiah 57:15 (NASB) says, of God, ". . . I dwell on a high and holy place. . . ." Jesus' statement regarding preparing a "place" (John 14:1, 2) would make him utter a malapropism, using the wrong word.[373]

John Gilmore, *Probing Heaven*

Viewing heaven as the abode of souls, not bodies, sounds attractive. Especially when it comes to logistics. No need to puzzle about where to put everyone, what a new body would look like, whether there's sex in heaven, and whether other forms of life continue (horses, maybe, but not flies?), and how a God who is spirit can sit upon a throne.[374]

Arthur Roberts, *Exploring Heaven*

When Aslan said you could never go back to Narnia, he meant the Narnia you were thinking of. But that was not the real Narnia. That had a beginning and an end. It was only a shadow or a copy of the real Narnia, which has always been here and always will be here: just as our own world, England and all, is only a shadow or copy of something in Aslan's real world.

. . . All of the old Narnia that mattered, all the dear creatures, have been drawn into the real Narnia through the Door. And of course it is different; as different as a real thing is from a shadow or as waking life is from a dream.[375]

Lord Digory, in *The Last Battle*, by C. S. Lewis

The idea of heaven as a place is also the easiest sense in which to understand Jesus' promise, "I go to prepare a *place* for you" (John 14:2 [KJV]). He speaks quite clearly of going from his existence in this world back to the Father, and then returning again: "And when I go and prepare a *place* for you, I will come again and will take you to myself, that *where I am* you may be also" (John 14:3).[376]

Wayne Grudem, *Systematic Theology*

Make no mistake: if He rose at all
    it was as His body;
    if the cells' dissolution did not reverse, the molecules
    reknit, the amino acids rekindle,
    the Church will fall.
It was not as the flowers,
    each soft Spring recurrent;
    it was not as His Spirit in the mouths and fuddled
    eyes of the eleven apostles;
    it was as His Flesh: ours.
The same hinged thumbs and toes,
    the same valved heart
    that—pierced—died, withered, paused, and then
    regathered out of enduring Might
    new strength to enclose.
Let us not mock God with metaphor,
    analogy, sidestepping transcendence;
    making of the event a parable, a sign painted in the
    faded credulity of earlier ages:
    let us walk through the door.
The stone is rolled back, not papier-mache,
    not a stone in a story,
    but the vast rock of materiality that in the slow
    grinding of time will eclipse for each of us
    the wide light of day.
And if we will have an angel at the tomb,
    make it a real angel,
    weighty with Max Planck's quanta, vivid with hair,
    opaque in the dawn light, robed in real linen
    spun on a definite loom.

Let us not seek to make it less monstrous,
> *for our own convenience, our own sense of beauty,*
> *lest, awakened in one unthinkable hour, we are*
> *embarrassed by the miracle,*
> *and crushed by remonstrance.*[377]

John Updike, "Seven Stanzas at Easter"

Christianity holds that we do not *create* Heaven because we desperately want it to be true, but that Heaven exists because it is part of ultimate reality. Belief in Heaven is not escapism from a sinful world, but realism, for our beliefs conform to the way things really are. That is why C. S. Lewis makes the seemingly audacious statement that "it is more important that heaven should exist than that any of us should reach it."[378]

Barry Morrow, *Heaven Observed*

Life after death, for many Christians, means existing only in the memory of their families and of God. Scientific, philosophical, and theological skepticism has nullified the modern heaven and replaced it with teachings that are minimalist, meager, and dry.[379]

Colleen McDannell and Bernhard Lang, *Heaven: A History*

Make no mistake about it, Heaven is a *real* place. It is not a state of mind. Not a figment of man's imagination. Not a philosophical concept. Not a religious abstraction. Not a sentimental dream. Not the medieval fancy of an ancient scientist. Not the worn-out superstition of a liberal theologian. It's an actual place. A location far more real than where you presently live. . . . It is a *real* place where God lives. It is the *real* place from which Christ came into this world. And is the *real* place to which Christ returned at His ascension—*really*.[380]

Steven J. Lawson, *Heaven Help Us!*

Suppose we *have* only dreamed, or made up, all those things—trees and grass and sun and moon and stars and Aslan himself. Suppose we have. Then all I can say is that . . . the made-up things seem a good deal more important than the real ones. Suppose this black pit of a kingdom of yours *is* the only world. Well, it strikes me as a pretty poor one. And that's a funny thing, when you come to think of it. We're just babies making up a game, if you're right. But four babies playing a game can make a play-world which licks your real world hollow.[381]

Puddleglum, in *The Silver Chair,* by C. S. Lewis

We are very shy nowadays of even mentioning heaven. We are afraid of the jeer about "pie in the sky," and of being told that we are trying to "escape" from the duty of making a happy world here and now into dreams of a happy world elsewhere. But either there is "pie in the sky" or there is not. If there is not, then Christianity is false, for this doctrine is woven into its whole fabric. If there is, then this truth, like any other, must be faced, whether it is useful at political meetings or no. Again, we are afraid that heaven is a bribe, and that if we make it our goal we shall no longer be disinterested. It is not so. Heaven offers nothing that a mercenary soul can desire. It is safe to tell the pure in heart that they shall see God, for only the pure in heart want to. There are rewards that do not sully motives. A man's love for a woman is not mercenary because he wants to marry her, nor his love for poetry mercenary because he wants to read it, nor his love of exercise less disinterested because he wants to run and leap and walk. Love, by definition, seeks to enjoy its object.

You may think that there is another reason for our silence about heaven—namely, that we do not really desire it. But that may be an illusion. What I am now going to say is merely an opinion of my own without the slightest authority, which I submit to the judgment of better Christians and better scholars than myself. There have been times when I think we do not desire heaven but more often I find myself wondering whether, in our heart of hearts, we have ever desired anything else.[382]

C. S. Lewis, *The Problem of Pain*

The goal and end of a person's calling does not terminate in this life, but it makes sense only in the light of the life to come. His calling in this life is part of God's heavenly calling, the call that leads to heaven. While the Christian, in being called by grace, already has eternal life, such life will fully be realized, blossom and bear fruit, only in the life to come. And the Christian's daily work, intrinsically satisfying and worthwhile as it may be, will also find its fulfillment through the formation of character, and perhaps even in some of the products of human culture, in the city of the New Jerusalem, the new heaven and new earth wherein dwells righteousness.

There are, then, two basic extremes to be avoided. One is to think of this life as a shadow, as not real; to belittle and devalue it to the point where it is not worth living. The other mistake is to think that the present life is everything. The basic fact about the present life is that it is important and valuable in all its aspects because it leads to the world to come.[383]

Paul Helm, *The Last Things*

Clearly the earth is a *place* that exists at a certain location in our space-time universe, but can heaven also be thought of as a *place* that can be joined to the earth?

. . . "As they were looking on, he was lifted up, and a cloud took him out of their sight" (Acts 1:9; cf. Luke 24:51: "While he blessed them, he parted from them"). The angels exclaimed, "This Jesus, who was taken up from you *into heaven*, will come in the same way as you saw him go into heaven" (Acts 1:11). It is hard to imagine how the fact of Jesus' ascension to a *place* could be taught more clearly.

[Stephen, in Acts 7:55-56,] did not see mere symbols of a state of existence. It seems rather that his eyes were opened to see a spiritual dimension of reality which God has hidden from us in this present age, a dimension which nonetheless really does exist in our space/time universe, and within which Jesus now lives in his physical resurrection body, waiting even now for the time when he will return to earth. Moreover, the fact that we will have resurrection bodies like Christ's resurrection body indicates that heaven will be a place, for in such physical bodies (made perfect, never to become weak or die again), we will inhabit a specific place at a specific time, just as Jesus now does in his resurrection body.

. . . These texts [including John 14:2, 3] lead us to conclude that heaven is even now a place—though one whose location is now unknown to us and whose existence is now unable to be perceived by our natural senses. It is this place of God's dwelling that will be somehow made new at the time of the final judgment and will be joined to a renewed earth.[384]

Wayne Grudem, *Systematic Theology*

The idea of the human Jesus now being in heaven, in his thoroughly embodied risen state, comes as a shock to many people, including many Christians. Sometimes this is because many people think that Jesus, having been divine, stopped being divine and became human, and then, having been human for a while, stopped being human and went back to being divine (at least, that's what many people think Christians are supposed to believe). More often it's because our culture is so used to the Platonic idea that heaven is, by definition, a place of "spiritual," nonmaterial reality so that the idea of a solid body being not only present but also thoroughly at home there seems like a category mistake. The ascension invites us to rethink all this; and, after all, why did we suppose we knew what heaven was? Only because our culture has suggested things to us. Part of Christian belief is to find out what's true about Jesus and let that challenge our culture.[385]

N. T. Wright, *Surprised by Hope*

This is the point at which we modern Westerners are called to make a huge leap of the imagination. We have been buying our mental furniture for so long in Plato's factory that we have come to take for granted a basic ontological contrast between "spirit" in the sense of something immaterial and "matter" in the sense of something material, solid, physical. . . .

What Paul is asking us to imagine is that there will be a new mode of physicality, which stands in relation to our present body as our present body does to a ghost. It will be as much more real, more firmed up, more *bodily*, than our present body as our present body is more substantial, more touchable, than a disembodied spirit. We sometimes speak of someone who's been very ill as being a shadow of their former self. If Paul is right, a Christian in the present life is a mere shadow of his or her *future* self, the self that person will be when the body that God has waiting in his heavenly storeroom is brought out, already made to measure, and put on over the present one—or over the self that will still exist after bodily death. This is where one of the great Easter hymns gets it exactly right:

> *O how glorious and resplendent*
> *Fragile body, shall thou be,*
> *When endued with so much beauty,*
> *Full of health, and strong, and free!*
> *Full of vigour, full of pleasure,*
> *That shall last eternally.*[386]

N. T. Wright, *Surprised by Hope*

I am not concerned in that question, whether human souls separated from their bodies have any other corporeal vehicle to which they are united, or by which, they act during the intermediate state between death and the resurrection. All that I propose to maintain here, is, that that period or interval is not a *state of sleep*, or utter unconsciousness and inactivity: And, whether it be united to a vehicle [temporary body] or no, I call it still the Separate State, because it is a state of the soul's separation from this body, which is united to it in the present life.[387]

Isaac Watts, *The World to Come*

Future existence is not a purely spiritual existence; it demands a life in a body, and in a material universe.[388]

W. Graham Scroggie, *What about Heaven?*

Our happiness is not designed to be complete till the soul and body are united in a state of Perfection and glory: And this happiness was conferred early on those two favourites of heaven [Enoch and Elijah].[389]

Isaac Watts, *The World to Come*

Every belief that would make our resurrection bodies less physical than Adam's and Eve's, or that makes the New Earth less earthly than the original Earth, essentially credits Satan with a victory over God by suggesting that Satan has permanently marred God's original intention, design, and creation.[390]

Randy Alcorn, *Heaven*

The present Heaven is normally invisible to those living on Earth. But this doesn't mean it isn't physical. And even if it isn't physical, that doesn't mean it isn't real. . . . When Stephen was being stoned because of his faith in Christ, he "looked up to heaven and saw the glory of God, and Jesus standing at the right hand of God. 'Look,' he said, 'I see heaven open and the Son of Man standing at the right hand of God'" (Acts 7:55-56). Scripture tells us that Stephen did not dream this but actually *saw* it. God didn't create a vision for Stephen in order to make Heaven *appear* physical. Rather, he allowed Stephen to see an intermediate Heaven that *was* (and is) physical.[391]

Randy Alcorn, *50 Days of Heaven*

After reading one of my books, a missionary wrote to me, deeply troubled that I thought Heaven might be a physical place. In our correspondence, no matter how many Scripture passages I pointed to, it didn't matter. He'd always been taught that Heaven was "spiritual" and therefore not physical. To suggest otherwise was, in his mind, to commit heresy. . . . He seemed convinced that if Heaven *were* physical, it would be less sacred and special. He viewed physical and spiritual as opposites. When I asked him to demonstrate from Scripture why Heaven cannot be a physical place, he told me the answer was very simple: because "God is spirit" (John 4:24). He believed that verse settled the question once and for all.

But saying that God is spirit is very different from saying that Heaven is spirit. Heaven, after all, is not the same as God. God created Heaven; therefore, he did not always dwell there. . . . If we are to draw inferences about the nature of Heaven, we shouldn't derive them from the nature of God. After all, he is a one-of-a-kind being who is infinite, existing outside of space and time. Rather, we should base our deductions on the nature of humanity. It's no problem for the infinite God to dwell wherever mankind dwells. The question is whether finite humans can exist as God does—outside of space and time. I'm not certain we can. But I am certain that *if* we can, it is only as a temporary aberration that will be permanently corrected by our bodily resurrection in preparation for life on the New Earth.[392]

Randy Alcorn, *Heaven*

If Christ's body in the present Heaven has physical properties, it stands to reason that others in Heaven might have physical forms as well, even if only temporary ones. It also makes sense that other aspects of the present Heaven would have physical properties—so that, for example, when Christ is seen standing at the right hand of God (Acts 7:56), he is actually standing on something.[393]

Randy Alcorn, *Heaven*

If we know there is physical substance in Heaven (namely, Christ's body), can we not also assume that other references to physical objects in Heaven, including physical forms and clothing, are literal rather than figurative?[394]

Randy Alcorn, *TouchPoints: Heaven*

Because ethereal notions of Heaven have largely gone unchallenged, we often think of Heaven as less real and less substantial than life here and now. (Hence, we don't think of Heaven as a place where people will hug, and certainly not in *these* bodies.) But in Heaven we won't be shadow people living in shadowlands—to borrow C. S. Lewis's imagery. Instead, we'll be fully alive and fully physical in a fully physical universe.[395]

Randy Alcorn, *Heaven*

We use the term *eternal life* without thinking what it means. *Life* is an earthly existence in which we work, rest, play, and relate to one another in ways that include using our creative gifts to enrich culture and then enjoy it. Yet we have redefined *eternal life* to mean an off-Earth existence stripped of the defining properties of what we know life to be. Eternal life means enjoying forever the finest moments of life on Earth the way they were intended. Since in Heaven we'll finally experience life at its best, it would be more accurate to call our present existence the *beforelife* rather than to call what follows the *afterlife.*[396]

Randy Alcorn, *We Shall See God*

Understanding and anticipating the physical nature of the New Earth corrects a multitude of errors. It frees us to love, without guilt, the world that God has made, while saying no to that world corrupted by our sin. It reminds us that God himself gave us the earth, gave us a *love* for the earth, and will give us the New Earth.[397]

Randy Alcorn, *50 Days of Heaven*

Is Heaven mere metaphor? According to many poets and modern thinkers, yes. According to the Bible, absolutely not.

Randy Alcorn, unpublished notes

I remember the morning a pastor came to see me. His teenage son Kevin, who was also his best friend, had died four months earlier.

As the pastor sat in my office, he opened his hand to reveal a beautiful reddish, polished stone. I'd never seen anything like it. He said it was jasper, which I recognized as a stone that will make up the walls of the New Jerusalem (Revelation 21:18). The stone was a reminder of his son Kevin and of the assurance that he and his son will live together again in a glorious city with jasper walls.

The pastor insisted I keep the jasper stone. He said, "I want you to know I'm praying for you as you write your book about Heaven. And I want you to have this stone to remind you of Heaven's reality."

I often look at the stone and hold it in my hand. The more I do, the more beautiful it becomes. It's not ghostly; it's solid and substantial—just like the place that awaits us.[398]

Randy Alcorn, *Heaven*

We do not desire to eat gravel. Why? Because God did not design us to eat gravel. Trying to develop an appetite for a disembodied existence in a non-physical Heaven is like trying to develop an appetite for gravel. No matter how sincere we are, and no matter how hard we try, it's not going to work. Nor should it.

Our desires correspond precisely to God's plans. It's not that we want something, so we engage in wishful thinking that what we want exists. It's the opposite—the reason we want it is precisely because God has planned for it to exist. As we'll see, resurrected people living in a resurrected universe isn't our idea—it's *God*'s.[399]

Randy Alcorn, *Heaven*

God does not want us to pretend there's a Heaven because that would make us feel better. The Bible is not about our feelings. It is about raw, objective truth—reality. We should not believe in Heaven because it gives us hope but only because it is real—as real as the Christ who promises it and has gone before us to prepare it for us.

Randy Alcorn, unpublished notes

An interpretive approach that makes everything symbolic also makes everything subjective. It will never allow us to break free of our assumptions and see what the Bible really says about Heaven, our bodily resurrection, and life on the New Earth. . . . The river going through the New Jerusalem becomes God's grace, the tree becomes Christ, the city walls become security. Or the river becomes Christ, the tree God's grace, and the city walls God's omnipotence. . . . But if the text can be said to mean *everything*, it ceases to mean *anything*. One cannot have serious interpretive discussions with those who interpret all references to the New Earth figuratively. Why? Because as soon as you cite a passage depicting anything tangible, they will dismiss it by saying, "You can't take that literally."[400]

Randy Alcorn, *Heaven*

Earth's Demolition and Renovation

The wilderness and the wasteland shall be glad for
them, and the desert shall rejoice and blossom as
the rose.

Isaiah 35:1, NKJV

This is what the Sovereign Lord says: On the day I
cleanse you from all your sins, I will resettle your towns,
and the ruins will be rebuilt. The desolate land will be
cultivated instead of lying desolate in the sight of all
who pass through it. They will say, "This land that was
laid waste has become like the garden of Eden; the cities
that were lying in ruins, desolate and destroyed, are
now fortified and inhabited." Then the nations around
you that remain will know that I the Lord have rebuilt
what was destroyed and have replanted what was desolate. I the Lord have spoken, and I will do it.

God, Ezekiel 36:33-36

The earth is the LORD's, and everything in it, the world, and all who live in it.

DAVID, PSALM 24:1

The glory of the LORD fills the whole earth.

GOD, NUMBERS 14:21

The man who makes me his refuge will inherit the land [earth] and possess my holy mountain.

GOD, ISAIAH 57:13

This world in its present form is passing away.

PAUL, 1 CORINTHIANS 7:31

At the renewal of all things, when the Son of Man sits on his glorious throne, you who have followed me will also sit on twelve thrones, judging the twelve tribes of Israel.

JESUS, MATTHEW 19:28

[Christ] must remain in heaven until the time comes for God to restore everything, as he promised long ago through his holy prophets.

PETER, ACTS 3:21

God was pleased to have all his fullness dwell in him [Christ], and through him to reconcile to himself all things, whether things on earth or things in heaven, by making peace through his blood, shed on the cross.

PAUL, COLOSSIANS 1:19-20

Behold, I will create new heavens and a new earth.

GOD, ISAIAH 65:17

I saw a new heaven and a new earth, for the first heaven and the first earth had passed away.

JOHN, REVELATION 21:1

The Lord isn't really being slow about his promise, as some people think. No, he is being patient for your sake. He does not want anyone to be destroyed, but wants everyone to repent. But the day of the Lord will come as unexpectedly as a thief. Then the heavens will pass away with a terrible noise, and the very elements themselves will disappear in fire, and the earth and everything on it will be found to deserve judgment.

Since everything around us is going to be destroyed like this, what holy and godly lives you should live, looking forward to the day of God and hurrying it along. On that day, he will set the heavens on fire, and the elements will melt away in the flames. But we are looking forward to the new heavens and new earth he has promised, a world filled with God's righteousness.

And so, dear friends, while you are waiting for these things to happen, make every effort to be found living peaceful lives that are pure and blameless in his sight.

And remember, our Lord's patience gives people time to be saved.

PETER, 2 PETER 3:9-15, NLT

What a spectacle is that fast approaching advent of our Lord! . . . What exultation of the angelic hosts! What glory of the rising saints! What kingdom of the righteous that will follow! What city of New Jerusalem! Yes, and there are other sights: that last day of judgment, with its eternal issues; that day unlooked for by the nations, the theme of their derision, when the world gray with age, and all its many products, shall be consumed in one great flame.[401]

Tertullian, *The Shows*

Neither is the substance nor the essence of the creation annihilated (for faithful and true is he who has established it), but "the form of the world passes away" [1 Corinthians 7:31]; that is, those things among which transgression has occurred, because man has grown old in them.[402]

Irenaeus, *Against Heresies*

God promises that the glory of his people will demand a glorious creation to live in. So the fallen creation will obtain the very freedom from futility and evil and pain that the church is given. So when God makes all things new, he makes us new spiritually and morally, he makes us new physically, and then he makes the whole creation new so that our environment fits our perfected spirits and bodies.[403]

John Piper, "Behold, I Make All Things New"

If the form of the world passes away, it is by no means an annihilation or destruction of their material substance that is shown to take place, but a kind of change of quality and a transformation of appearance.[404]

Origen, *First Principles*

In his redemptive activity, God does not destroy the works of his hands, but cleanses them from sin and perfects them, so that they may finally reach the goal for which he created them. Applied to the problem at hand, this principle means that the new earth to which we look forward will not be totally different from the present one, but will be a renewal and glorification of the earth on which we now live.[405]

Anthony Hoekema, *The Bible and the Future*

According to Scripture the present world will neither continue forever nor will it be destroyed and replaced by a totally new one. Instead it will be cleansed of sin and re-created, reborn, renewed, made whole. While the kingdom of God is first planted spiritually in human hearts, the future blessedness is not to be spiritualized. Biblical hope, rooted in incarnation and resurrection, is creational, this-worldly, visible, physical, bodily hope. The rebirth of human beings is completed in the glorious rebirth of all creation, the New Jerusalem whose architect and builder is God himself.[406]

Herman Bavinck, *The Last Things*

We believe that the present physical mass of the universe is to be changed anew into something better. We believe that this will not come to pass until the number of elect humans has reached its final total, and the blessed city . . . has been brought to completion; also that, after the completion of the city, the renewal will follow without delay.[407]

Anselm, *Why God Became Man*

The dwelling should befit the dweller. But the world was made to be man's dwelling; therefore, it should be fitting for man. Now, man will be renewed; therefore, the world will be likewise. . . . Now man has some likeness to the universe by which he is called "a little world." Thus, man loves the whole world naturally and consequently desires its good. Therefore, so that man's desire is satisfied, the universe must also be made better.[408]

Thomas Aquinas, *Summa Theologica*

Of the elements of the world I shall only say this one thing, that they are to be consumed, only that they may be renovated, their substance remaining the same, as it may be easily gathered from Romans 8:21, and from other passages.[409]

John Calvin, *Commentaries on the Catholic Epistles*

The elements will not be removed but changed. For we expect not other heavens and another earth, but new heavens and a new earth.[410]

William Ames (Amesius), *Medullas Theologiae*

God's design was perfectly to restore all the ruins of the fall . . . by his Son; and therefore we read of the *restitution of all things* (Acts 3:19-21). . . .

Man's *soul* was ruined by the fall; the image of God was defaced; man's nature was corrupted, and he became dead in sin. The design of God was, to restore the soul of man to life and the divine image in conversion, to carry on the change in sanctification, and to perfect it in glory.

Man's *body* was ruined; by the fall it became subject to death. The design of God was, to restore it from this ruin. . . .

The *world* was ruined, as to man, as effectually as if it had been reduced to *chaos* again; all heaven and earth were overthrown. But the design of God was, to restore all, and as it were to create a new heaven and a new earth (Isaiah 65:17; 2 Peter 3:13).

The work by which this was to be done, was begun immediately after the fall, and so is carried on till all is finished, when the whole world, heaven and earth, shall be restored.[411]

Jonathan Edwards, *Works of Jonathan Edwards*

The destruction here foretold is not annihilation. (a.) The world is to be burned up; but combustion is not a destruction of substance. It is merely a change of state or condition. (b.) The destruction of the world by water and its destruction by fire are analogous events; the former was not annihilation, therefore, the second is not. (c.) The destruction spoken of is elsewhere called a regeneration (Matthew 19:28); a restoration (Acts 3:21); a deliverance from the bondage of corruption (Romans 8:21). . . . (d.) There is no evidence either from Scripture or experience, that any substance has ever been annihilated. If force is motion, it may cease; but cessation of motion is not annihilation, and the common idea in our day, among scientists, is that no force is ever lost; it is, as they say, only transformed.[412]

Charles Hodge, *Systematic Theology*

Will earth simply be renewed, or will it be completely destroyed and replaced by another earth, newly created by God? Some passages appear to speak of an entire new creation: The author of Hebrews (quoting Psalm 102) tells us of the heavens and earth, "They will perish, but you remain; they will all grow old like a garment, like a mantle you will roll them up, and they will be changed" (Hebrews 1:11-12). Later he tells us that God has promised, "Yet once more I will shake not only the earth but also the heaven," a shaking so severe as to involve "the removal of what is shaken . . . in order that what cannot be shaken may remain" (Hebrews 12:26-27). Peter says, "The day of the Lord will come like a thief, and then the heavens will pass away with a loud noise, and the elements will be dissolved with fire, and the earth and all the works that are upon it will be burned up" (2 Peter 3:10). A similar picture is found in Revelation, where John says, "From his presence earth and sky fled away, and no place was found for them" (Revelation 20:11). Moreover, John says, "Then I saw a new heaven and a new earth; for the first heaven and the first earth had passed away, and the sea was no more" (Revelation 21:1).

Within the Protestant world, there has been disagreement as to whether the earth is to be destroyed completely and replaced, or just changed and renewed. . . . It is difficult to think that God would entirely annihilate his original creation, thereby seeming to give the devil the last word and scrapping the creation that was originally "very good" (Genesis 1:31). The passages above [that] speak of shaking and removing the earth and of the first earth passing away may simply refer to its existence in its present form, not its very existence itself, and even 2 Peter 3:10, which speaks of the elements dissolving and the earth and the works on it being burned up, may not be speaking of the earth as a planet but rather the surface things on the earth (that is, much of the ground and the things on the ground).[413]

Wayne Grudem, *Systematic Theology*

It is not satisfactory to say that the universe will be utterly destroyed, and sea and air and sky will be no longer. For the whole world will be deluged with fire from heaven, and burnt for the purpose of purification and renewal; it will not, however, come to complete ruin and corruption. For if it were better for the world not to be than to be, why did God, in making the world, take the worse course? But God did not work in vain, or do that which was worst. God therefore ordered the creation with a view to its existence and continuance, as also the *Book of Wisdom* confirms, saying, "For God created all things that they might have their being; and the generations of the world were healthful, and there is no poison of destruction in them." And Paul clearly testifies this, saying, "For the earnest expectation of the creature waiteth for the manifestation of the sons of God. For the creature was made subject to vanity, not willingly, but by reason of him that subjected the same in hope: because the creature itself also shall be delivered from the bondage of corruption into the glorious liberty of the children of God." For the creation was made subject to vanity, he says, and he expects that it will be set free from such servitude, as he intends to call this world by the name of creation. For it is not what is unseen but what is seen that is subject to corruption.

The creation, then, after being restored to a better and more seemly state, remains, rejoicing and exulting over the children of God at the resurrection; for whose sake it now groans and travails, waiting itself also for our redemption from the corruption of the body.

. . . "Thus saith the Lord that created the heaven, it is He who prepared the earth and created it, He determined it; He created it not in vain, but formed it to be inhabited." For in reality God did not establish the universe in vain, or to no purpose but destruction, as those weak-minded men say, but to exist, and be inhabited, and continue. Wherefore the earth and the heaven must exist again after the conflagration and shaking of all things.[414]

Methodius, *The Discourse on the Resurrection*

If our opponents say, How then is it, if the universe be not destroyed, that the Lord says that "heaven and earth shall pass away;" and the prophet, that "the heaven shall perish as smoke, and the earth shall grow old as a garment;" we answer, because it is usual for the Scriptures to call the change of the world from its present condition to a better and more glorious one, destruction; as its earlier form is lost in the change of all things to a state of greater splendour. . . . We may expect that the creation will pass away, as if it were to perish in the burning, in order that it may be renewed, not however that it will be destroyed, that we who are renewed may dwell in a renewed world without taste of sorrow; according as it is said, "When Thou lettest Thy breath go forth, they shall be made, and Thou shalt renew the face of the earth"; God henceforth providing for the due temperature of that which surrounds it. For as the earth is to exist after the present age, there must be by all means inhabitants for it, who shall no longer be liable to death, nor shall marry, nor beget children, but live in all happiness, like the angels, without change or decay. Wherefore it is silly to discuss in what way of life our bodies will then exist, if there is no longer air, nor earth, nor anything else.[415]

Methodius, *The Discourse on the Resurrection*

In Revelation 21–22 . . . it is not we who go to heaven, it is heaven that comes to earth; indeed, it is the church itself, the heavenly Jerusalem, that comes down to earth. This is the ultimate rejection of all types of Gnosticism, of every worldview that sees the final goal as the separation of the world from God, of the physical from the spiritual, of earth from heaven. It is the final answer to the Lord's Prayer, that God's kingdom will come and his will be done on earth as in heaven. It is what Paul is talking about in Ephesians 1:10, that God's design, and promise, was to sum up all things in Christ, things both in heaven and on earth. It is the final fulfillment, in richly symbolic imagery, of the promise of Genesis 1, that the creation of male and female would together reflect God's image in the world. And it is the final accomplishment of God's great design, to defeat and abolish death forever—which can only mean the rescue of creation from its present plight of decay.

Heaven and earth, it seems, are not after all poles apart, needing to be separated forever when all the children of heaven have been rescued from this wicked earth. . . .

What is promised in this passage, then, is what Isaiah foresaw: a new heaven and a new earth replacing the old heaven and the old earth, which were bound to decay. This doesn't mean, as I have stressed throughout, that God will wipe the slate clean and start again. . . . As in Romans and 1 Corinthians, the living God will dwell with and among his people, filling the city with his life and love and pouring out grace and healing in the river of life that flows from the city out to the nations. There is a sign here of the future project that awaits the redeemed in God's eventual new world. So far from sitting on clouds playing harps, as people often imagine, the redeemed people of God in the new world will be the agents of his love going out in new ways, to accomplish new creative tasks, to celebrate and extend the glory of his love.[416]

N. T. Wright, *Surprised by Hope*

God will one day change our bodies and make them fit for our souls, and then he will change this world itself. It is no speculation to say that we look for new heavens and a New Earth where righteousness dwells, and that there will come a time when "the lion shall eat straw like the ox" and "the leopard shall lie down with the young goat" (Isaiah 11:6-7).

We expect to see this world that is now so full of sin to be turned into a paradise, a garden of God. We believe that the Tabernacle of God will be among men, that he will dwell among them and they shall see his face, and his name shall be on their foreheads. We expect to see the New Jerusalem descend out of Heaven from God.

In this very place, where sin has triumphed, we expect that grace will much more abound.[417]

Charles Spurgeon, "Creation's Groans and the Saints' Sighs," Sermon 788

Reconcile. Redeem. Restore. Recover. Return. Renew. Regenerate. Resurrect. Each of these biblical words begins with the *re-* prefix, suggesting a return to an original condition that was ruined or lost. For example, *redemption* means to buy back what was formerly owned. Similarly, *reconciliation* means the restoration or re-establishment of a prior friendship or unity. *Renewal* means to make new again, restoring to an original state. *Resurrection* means becoming physically alive again, after death.

These words emphasize that God always sees us in light of what he intended us to be, and he always seeks to *restore us* to that design. Likewise, he sees the earth in terms of what he intended it to be, and he seeks to restore it to its original design.[418]

Randy Alcorn, *50 Days of Heaven*

"The earth is the LORD's, and everything in it, the world, and all who live in it" (Psalm 24:1). God has never surrendered his title deed to the earth. He owns it—and he will not relinquish it to his enemies. In fact, Scripture tells us that "the reason the Son of God appeared was to destroy the devil's work" (1 John 3:8).

Note that it says Christ came not to destroy the *world* (which is *his* world) but to destroy the devil's *works*, which are to twist and pervert and ruin the world God made. Redemption will forever destroy the work of the devil by removing his hold on creation and by reversing the consequences. Far from destroying the world, God's plan is to *keep it from being destroyed* by Satan. God's plan is to remove the destruction that has already been inflicted on it. His plan is to redeem the world. God placed mankind on Earth to fill it, rule it, and develop it to God's glory. But that plan has never been fulfilled. Should we therefore conclude that God's plan was ill-conceived, thwarted, or abandoned? No. These conclusions do not fit the character of an all-knowing, all-wise, sovereign God. Second Peter 3 does *not* teach that God will destroy the earth and then be done with it. Rather, it promises that God will renew Heaven *and* Earth.

God is not some hapless inventor whose creation failed. He has a masterful plan, and he will *not* surrender us *or* the earth to the trash heap.[419]

Randy Alcorn, *50 Days of Heaven*

In Revelation 21:1, the Greek word *kainos*, translated "new" in the term *New Earth*, means new "in the sense that what is old has become obsolete, and should be replaced by what is new. In such a case the new is, as a rule, superior in kind to the old."

Paul uses the same word, *kainos*, when he speaks of a believer in Christ becoming "a new creation" (2 Corinthians 5:17). The believer is still the same person as before, but he or she has been made new. Likewise, the New Earth will be the same as the old Earth, but made new.

In our resurrection, God may gather the scattered DNA and atoms and molecules of our dead and decayed bodies. In the earth's resurrection, he will regather all he needs of the scorched and disfigured Earth. As our old bodies will be raised to new bodies, so the old Earth will be raised to become the New Earth.

So, will the earth be *destroyed* or *renewed*? The answer is *both*—but the destruction will be temporal and partial, whereas the renewal will be eternal and complete.[420]

Randy Alcorn, *50 Days of Heaven*

Eating and Drinking

I will not drink of this fruit of the vine from now on until that day when I drink it anew with you in my Father's kingdom.

JESUS, MATTHEW 26:29

I confer on you a kingdom, just as my Father conferred one on me, so that you may eat and drink at my table in my kingdom.

JESUS, LUKE 22:29-30

Blessed are those who are invited to the wedding supper of the Lamb!

THE ANGEL, REVELATION 19:9

On this mountain the LORD Almighty will prepare a feast of rich food for all peoples, a banquet of aged wine—the best of meats and the finest of wines.

ISAIAH 25:6

When he had said this, he showed them his hands and feet. And while they still did not believe it because of joy and amazement, he asked them, "Do you have anything here to eat?" They gave him a piece of broiled fish, and he took it and ate it in their presence.

TWO MEN ON EMMAUS ROAD, LUKE 24:40-43

We are witnesses of everything he did in the country of the Jews and in Jerusalem. They killed him by hanging him on a tree, but God raised him from the dead on the third day and caused him to be seen. He was not seen by all the people, but by witnesses whom God had already chosen—by us who ate and drank with him after he rose from the dead. He commanded us to preach to the people and to testify that he is the one whom God appointed as judge of the living and the dead. All the prophets testify about him that everyone who believes in him receives forgiveness of sins through his name.

PETER, ACTS 10:39-43

Blessed is the man who will eat at the feast in the kingdom of God.

JESUS, LUKE 14:15

To him who overcomes, I will give the right to eat from the tree of life, which is in the paradise of God.

JESUS, REVELATION 2:7

John Bradford, being martyred at the stake at Smithfield in 1555, was able to say to John Leaf, the young man being burned with him: "Be of good comfort, brother; for we shall have a merry supper with the Lord this night."[421]

Richard Brooks, *The Doors of Heaven*

Celebration, holy days (holidays) of fellowshipping and feasting together is a vibrant part of heaven. It is very much associated with *joy* and *rejoicing* in the Bible. Food, conversation, singing, shouting, praise, nature, music, thankfulness, rewards, prayer and people, are all associated with *rejoicing* in heaven. This is how we will celebrate together. The feasts of the Old Testament went on for days. Imagine how long the parties in heaven will last![422]

Larry Dick, *A Taste of Heaven*

Food is not a necessity in Heaven, but a simple enjoyment, an expression of God's artistic nature, another facet of His infinite beauty and variety.[423]

Drake Whitchurch, *Waking from Earth*

When Jesus talked about the future, he pictured it most often as a party! Jesus was criticized regularly during his earthly ministry for having too much fun. The uptight religious people called Jesus a drunkard and a friend of low-class sinners. Even the followers of John the Baptizer were scandalized that Jesus didn't require his disciples to put on sad faces and skip meals. Jesus enjoyed banquets and parties on earth because they reminded him so much of heaven—and because they provided wonderful opportunities to teach people how the social rules will change when Jesus is in charge.[424]

Douglas Connelly, *The Promise of Heaven*

If we consider to what end God created foods, we shall find that he wished not only to provide for our necessities, but also for our pleasure and recreation. . . . With herbs, trees and fruits, besides the various uses he gives us of them, it was his will to rejoice our sight by their beauty, and to give us yet another pleasure in their odours.[425]

John Calvin, *Institutes of the Christian Religion*

One day while eating in the home of a Pharisee, Jesus said to his host, "When you give a luncheon or dinner, . . . invite the poor, the crippled, the lame, the blind, and you will be blessed. Although they cannot repay you, you will be repaid at the resurrection of the righteous" (Luke 14:12-14). When Jesus made this reference to the resurrection of the dead, a man at the same dinner said to him, "Blessed is the man who will eat at the feast in the kingdom of God" (Luke 14:15). Since they were eating together at the time, the obvious meaning of "eat" and "feast" is literal. If the man who said this was wrong to envision literal eating after the bodily resurrection, Jesus had every opportunity to correct him. But he didn't. In fact, he built on the man's words to tell a story about someone who prepared a banquet and invited many guests (Luke 14:16-24).

Clearly, both the man and Jesus were talking about actual eating at actual banquets, like the one they were at. One translation has the man at the dinner state, "What a privilege it would be to have a share in the Kingdom of God!" (Luke 14:15, NLT). But the Greek words do not mean "have a share in" the Kingdom; they mean "eat" in the Kingdom!

I don't always take the Bible literally. Scripture contains many figures of speech. But it's incorrect to assume that because some figures of speech are used to describe Heaven, all that the Bible says about Heaven, therefore, is figurative. When we're told we'll have resurrection bodies like Christ's and that he ate in his resurrection body, why should we assume he was speaking figuratively when he refers to tables, banquets, and eating and drinking in his Kingdom?

. . . We're commanded, "Glorify God in your body" (1 Corinthians 6:20, NKJV). What will we do for eternity? Glorify God in our bodies. We're told, "Whether you eat or drink or whatever you do, do it all for the glory of God" (1 Corinthians 10:31). What will we do for eternity? Eat, drink, and do all to the glory of God.

An evangelical author tells us, "In Heaven, Scripture indicates that we shall neither eat nor drink." But Scripture tells us no such thing. In fact, it couldn't show more clearly that we will eat and drink on the New Earth.[426]

Randy Alcorn, *Heaven*

Only two people lived before the Fall. This means only two people have ever eaten food at its best, with their capacity to taste at its best.

The great wine Christ made and served at the wedding of Cana was a foretaste of that best of wines he will provide for us on the New Earth. Even in this cursed world, Scripture is filled with more feasts than fasts. Who created our taste buds? Who determined what we like and what we don't? God did. The food we eat is from God's hand. Our resurrected bodies will have resurrected taste buds. We can trust that the food we eat on the New Earth, some of it familiar and some of it brand-new, will taste better than anything we've ever eaten here.

Food isn't just functional. We could get nourishment, after all, by mixing everything together in a blender, with no regard to color or texture or taste. Food is also for our enjoyment—not only its consumption but also its preparation and presentation. Shouldn't we expect boundless creativity in these as well? (If you've seen the marvelous movie *Babette's Feast*, you know what I mean.)[427]

Randy Alcorn, *Heaven*

If we take literally the earthly depictions of life on the New Earth, we can make a direct connection between our current lives and our future in Heaven. When I'm eating with people here, enjoying food and friendship, it's a bridge to when I'll be eating there, enjoying food and friendship at the banquet table God has prepared for us (Revelation 19:9). This isn't making a blind leap into a shadowy afterlife; it's just taking a few natural steps in the light Scripture has given us.[428]

Randy Alcorn, *We Shall See God*

We won't "need" fine meals; we don't *need* them now. But we enjoy them now for the same reason we'll enjoy them then—because God made us to enjoy them and to glorify him as we eat and drink (1 Corinthians 10:31).[429]

Randy Alcorn, *Heaven*

Consider the facts. God made coffee. Coffee grows on Earth, which God made for mankind, put under our management, and filled with resources for our use. When God evaluated his creation, he deemed coffee trees, along with all else, to be "very good." Many people throughout history have enjoyed coffee—even in a fallen world where neither coffee nor our taste buds are at their best.

God tells us that he "richly provides us with everything for our enjoyment" (1 Timothy 6:17). Does "everything" include coffee? Paul also says, "For everything God created is good, and nothing is to be rejected if it is received with thanksgiving, because it is consecrated by the word of God and prayer" (1 Timothy 4:4-5). Again, does "everything" include coffee?

Given these biblical perspectives—and realizing that caffeine addiction or anything else that's unhealthy simply won't exist on the New Earth—can you think of any persuasive reason why coffee trees and coffee drinking wouldn't be part of the resurrected Earth?

Will the New Earth have fewer resources for human enjoyment than Eden did or than the world under the Curse offers? If you're tempted to say, "But in Heaven our minds will be on spiritual things, not coffee," your Christoplatonism detector should go off. It's fine if you don't like coffee, but to suggest that coffee is inherently unspiritual is . . . well, heresy. It directly contradicts the Scriptures just cited. God made the physical and spiritual realms not to oppose each other but to be united in bringing glory to him.

On the New Earth, we will "drink . . . from the spring of the water of life" (Revelation 21:6). God will prepare for us "a banquet of aged wine . . . the finest of wines" (Isaiah 25:6). Not only will we drink water and wine, we'll eat from fruit trees (Revelation 22:2), and there's every reason to believe we'll drink juice made from the twelve fruits from the tree of life. So, along with drinking water, wine, and fruit juice, is there any reason to suppose we wouldn't drink coffee or tea? Can you imagine drinking coffee or tea with Jesus on the New Earth? If you can't, why not? [430]

Randy Alcorn, *Heaven*

If for health reasons you shouldn't drink coffee now, then don't. But aside from personal preference, the only compelling reason for not having coffee in Heaven would be if coffee were sinful or harmful. But it won't be. If drinking coffee would be unspiritual on the New Earth, then it must be unspiritual now. . . .

Those who for reasons of allergies, weight problems, or addictions can't regularly consume peanuts, chocolate, coffee, and wine—and countless other foods and drinks—may look forward to enjoying them on the New Earth. To be free from sin, death, and bondage on the New Earth will mean that we'll enjoy more pleasures, not fewer. And the God who delights in our pleasures will be glorified in our grateful praise. [431]

Randy Alcorn, *Heaven*

Imagine mealtimes full of stories, laughter, and joy without fear of insensitivity, inappropriate behavior, anger, gossip, lust, jealousy, hurt feelings, or anything that eclipses joy. That will be Heaven. [432]

Randy Alcorn, *Heaven*

Strangely . . . many people . . . believe we won't eat or drink in the eternal Heaven. They assume the biblical language about eating and drinking and banquets is figurative and that we will eat only "in a spiritual sense." But how does one eat in a spiritual sense? And why is there a need to look for a spiritual sense when resurrected people in actual bodies will live on a resurrected Earth? [433]

Randy Alcorn, *Heaven*

You and I have never eaten food in a world untouched by the Fall and the Curse. The palate and taste buds were injured in the Fall, as were all food sources. The best-tasting food we've ever eaten wasn't nearly as good as it must have tasted in Eden or as it will on the New Earth.

The person who's eaten the widest variety of meals on Earth still hasn't tasted countless others. How many special dishes will you discover on the New Earth? As yet, you may not have tasted your favorite meal—and if you have, it didn't taste as good as it will there. The best meals you'll ever eat are all still ahead of you on the New Earth.

If it seems trivial or unspiritual to anticipate such things, remember that it's God who promises that on the New Earth we will sit at tables, at banquets and feasts, and enjoy the finest foods and drinks. And to top it off, our Father promises that he *himself* will prepare for us the finest foods (Isaiah 25:6).

Don't you think he *wants* us to look forward to eating at his table?[434]

Randy Alcorn, *Heaven*

When we think of Heaven as unearthly, our present lives seem unspiritual, like they don't matter. When we grasp the reality of the New Earth, our present, earthly lives suddenly matter. Conversations with loved ones matter. The taste of food matters. Work, leisure, creativity, and intellectual stimulation matter. Rivers and trees and flowers matter. Laughter matters. Service matters. Why? *Because they are eternal.*

Life on Earth matters not because it's the only life we have, but precisely because it isn't—it's the beginning of a life that will continue without end. It's the precursor of life on the New Earth. Eternal life doesn't begin when we die—it has already begun. Life is not, as Macbeth supposed, "a tale told by an idiot, full of sound and fury, signifying nothing." Informed by the doctrines of creation, redemption, resurrection, and the New Earth, our present lives take on greater importance, infusing us with purpose. Understanding Heaven doesn't just tell us *what* to do, but *why*. What God tells us about our future lives enables us to interpret our past and serve him in our present.

Consider the old proverb, "Eat, drink, and be merry, for tomorrow we die." It assumes that the only earthly pleasures we'll ever enjoy must be obtained now. As Christians, we should indeed eat, drink, and be merry—and also sacrifice, suffer, and die—all to the glory of God. In doing so, we're preparing for an eternal life in which we will eat, drink, and be merry, but never again die. This present life, then, is not our last chance to eat, drink, and be merry—rather, it is the last time our eating, drinking, and merrymaking can be corrupted by sin, death, and the Curse.

We need to stop acting as if Heaven were a myth, an impossible dream, a relentlessly dull meeting, or an unimportant distraction from real life. We need to see Heaven for what it is: the realm we're made for. If we do, we'll embrace it with contagious joy, excitement, and anticipation.[435]

Randy Alcorn, *Heaven*

Thinking of Heaven will motivate us to live each day in profound thankfulness to God: "Therefore, since we are receiving a kingdom that cannot be shaken, let us be thankful, and so worship God acceptably with reverence and awe" (Hebrews 12:28).

In *Perelandra*, C. S. Lewis's protagonist says of his friend Ransom, who has recently returned from another planet, "A man who has been in another world does not come back unchanged." A man who gives sustained thought to another world—the Heaven where Christ is and the resurrected Earth where we will live forever with him—also does not remain unchanged. He becomes a new person. He'll no longer fill his stomach with stale leftovers and scraps fallen to a dirty kitchen floor. He smells the banquet being prepared for him. He won't spoil his appetite. He knows what his mouth is watering for.[436]

Randy Alcorn, *Heaven*

Eternity and Life after Death

He has made everything beautiful in its time. He has also set eternity in the hearts of men; yet they cannot fathom what God has done from beginning to end.

SOLOMON, ECCLESIASTES 3:11

To the end that my tongue and my heart and everything glorious within me may sing praise to You and not be silent. O Lord my God, I will give thanks to You forever.

DAVID, PSALM 30:12, AMP

Multitudes who sleep in the dust of the earth will awake: some to everlasting life, others to shame and everlasting contempt.

AN ANGEL, DANIEL 12:2

[The angel] replied, "Go your way, Daniel, because the words are closed up and sealed until the time of the end. Many will be purified, made spotless and refined, but the wicked will continue to be wicked. None of the wicked will understand, but those who are wise will understand. . . . As for you, go your way till the end. You will rest, and then at the end of the days you will rise to receive your allotted inheritance."

THE ANGEL, DANIEL 12:9-10, 13

[The Father] has caused us to be born again to a living hope through the resurrection of Jesus Christ from the dead, to an inheritance that is imperishable, undefiled, and unfading, kept in heaven for you.

PETER, 1 PETER 1:3-4, ESV

There is nothing heroic about our passing, leaving families and friends, but then, death is never heroic and it is never kind. Death is never artistic, always much more likely to be crude and messy and humiliating.

The preacher who once stood with strength and keenness to preach the living Word of God to dying men is now in his bed, his cheeks hollow and his eyes staring, for death is slipping its chilly hand over that earthly tabernacle.

The singer whose gifts have been used to glorify God and to remind men and women of the beauty of heaven above is now hoarse, dry-lipped, whispering only a half-spoken word before death comes.

But, brethren, this is not the end. I thank God that I know that this is not all there is. My whole everlasting being, my entire personality—all that I have and all that I am are cast out on the promises of God that there is another chapter!

At the close of every obituary of His believing children, God adds the word *henceforth!* After every biography, God adds the word *henceforth!* There will be a tomorrow and this is the reason for Christian joy.[437]

A. W. **Tozer**, *Who Put Jesus on the Cross?*

I may not see you many more times, but, Mountain, I shall be alive when you are gone; and, River, I shall be alive when you cease running toward the sea; and Stars, I shall be alive when you have fallen from your sockets in the great down-pulling of the material universe.[438]

W. B. Hinson

Our Creator would never have made such lovely days, and have given us the deep hearts to enjoy them, above and beyond all thought, unless we were meant to be immortal.[439]

Nathaniel Hawthorne, *The Old Manse*

The best is yet to be.[440]

John Wesley, *Wesley Bicentennial*

The man who has met God is not looking for something—he has found it. He is not searching for light—upon him the Light has already shined!

. . . He may hear the tin whistle starting every new parade, but he will be cautious. He is waiting for a trumpet note that will call him away from the hurly-burly and set in motion a series of events that will result at last in a new heaven and a new earth.

He can afford to wait![441]

A. W. Tozer, *The Attributes of God*

Appreciation of heaven is frequently highest among those nearing death. . . . John Bradford (1510–1555), less than five months before his fiery departure from life for preaching the gospel in violent times, wrote to a friend of the glories of heaven he anticipated:

I am assured that though I want here, I have riches there; though I hunger here, I shall have fullness there; though I faint here, I shall be refreshed there; and though I be accounted here as a dead man, I shall there live in perpetual glory.

That is the city promised to the captives whom Christ shall make free; that is the kingdom assured to them whom Christ shall crown; there is the light that shall never go out; there is the health that shall never be impaired; there is the glory that shall never be defaced; there is the life that shall taste no death; and there is the portion that passes all the world's preferment. There is the world that shall never wax worse; there is every want supplied freely without money; there is no danger, but happiness, and honour, and singing, and praise and thanksgiving unto the heavenly Jehovah, "to him that sits on the throne," "to the lamb" that here was led to the slaughter that now "reigns"; with whom I "shall reign" after I have run this comfortless race through this miserable earthly vale.[442]

John Bradford, "A Sweet Contemplation of Heaven and Heavenly Things"

Those texts where man is represented as one being, may be explained with very great ease, considering man as made up of two distinct substances, body and spirit united into one personal agent. . . . But the several texts where the soul and body are so strongly and plainly distinguished . . . there is no possible way of representing these Scriptures but by supposing a Separate State of existence for souls after the body is dead.[443]

Isaac Watts, *The World to Come*

To question the fact of conscious, personal existence after death is . . . to fly in the face of the cumulative evidence of the written Word of God, an authority of sufficient veracity for Jesus Christ, the only sinless mind in history, and the supreme authority on spiritual life and destiny, to stake his own life upon its truth. To deny the life to come is to pit ourselves and our woefully limited understanding against the massive twin authorities of the God-inspired Scriptures and the undeviating conviction of Jesus Christ.[444]

Bruce Milne, *The Message of Heaven and Hell*

"It is finished," said our blessed Lord on the cross: "It is finished," may every one of his followers say at the hour of death, and at the end of time: My sins and follies, my distresses and my sufferings, are finished for ever, and the mighty angel swears to it, that the *time* of those evils is *no longer*: They are vanished, and shall never return. O happy souls, who have been so wise to count the short and uncertain number of your days on earth, as to make an early provision for a removal to heaven. Blest are you above all the powers of present thought and language. Days, and months, and years, and all these short and painful periods of time, shall be swallowed up in a long and blissful eternity; the stream of time which has run between the banks of this mortal life, and bore you along amidst many dangerous rocks of temptation, fear and sorrow, shall launch you out into the ocean of pleasures which have no period: Those felicities must be everlasting, for duration has no limit there.[445]

Isaac Watts, *The World to Come*

The public will eagerly buy up thin books on near-death experiences but never give the Scriptures second thought.

Are near-death encounters superior to scriptural teaching?

Hans Küng noted that of the 150 cases of dying persons investigated by the American physician, R. A. Moody, not a single individual really died. What bearing does this have on the value of what is said? It pointed up that dying is not death. Dying is the way out of life, death is the "destination."

This distinction reduces the impact of the testimonies, because no one has actually returned from the dead to tell what the other side is like.

Near-death reports aren't near enough to heaven to warrant basing beliefs on them.[446]

John Gilmore, *Probing Heaven*

A remarkable thing in connection with the disembodied spirits who are said to send communications from the unseen realm through spiritualistic mediums, is that with hardly an exception, they never speak of having seen Jesus. Their attitude regarding Him is unaccountable except on the ground that they are not in Heaven, but in some lower sphere; for since Jesus is Heaven's chief attraction they could not miss seeing and hearing about Him. If they were really in the place where Jesus is, their reports would be full of Him.[447]

James Campbell, *Heaven Opened*

The day thou fearest as the last is the birthday of eternity.[448]

Seneca, "Consolations Against Death"

I could not picture someone in Heaven. I had seen pictures of the state of Virginia, and I knew where it was on a map. Mike had bearings in my mind when he was still alive, but once he died, I had a hard time imagining where he was. Nothing in my life experience allowed me to mentally frame existence beyond the grave. So, in a weird way, Mike disappeared like someone who gets lost in a big crowd of people. I guessed he was out there or "up there" somewhere, but I could not put it all together in my mind. Believing in Heaven is not the same as being able to visualize it.[449]

Daniel Brown, *What the Bible Reveals about Heaven*

Twentieth-century religious visions, near-death experiences, imaginative literature or poetry, and spiritualist accounts continue to describe the existence of life in the other world. Life after death is still life and so a mother's voice may still be recognized, a heavenly field will blossom with flowers, a warm and loving God will greet each new arrival.[450]

Colleen McDannell and Bernhard Lang, *Heaven: A History*

The Heaven into which our loved ones have gone bends very low, and draws us up to itself. Across the narrow boundary line that separates it from us we wistfully look, anticipating with joy the time when we shall pass over; and while we turn with renewed zeal to our tasks that await us here, life is never the same to us again. It is henceforth inseparably connected with the hereafter.[451]

James Campbell, *Heaven Opened*

At the age of eighty-three I asked myself what I knew about the home of God, and I was truly shocked to admit I knew very little. . . . The best brochure about eternity is the Bible. Yet because people are too busy to read the Scriptures, they remain ignorant of details they urgently need to know. . . . Increasing age and the fact that I shall soon be making my own pilgrimage, have begotten within my soul an intense desire to explore this fascinating subject.[452]

Ivor Powell, *Heaven: My Father's Country*

When you know the truth about what happens to you after you die, and you believe it, and you are satisfied with all that God will be for you in the ages to come, that truth makes you free indeed. Free from the short, shallow, suicidal pleasures of sin, and free for the sacrifices of mission and ministry that cause people to give glory to our Father in heaven.[453]

John Piper, *Future Grace*

People are the only things that will last for eternity. Everything else stops at the border.[454]

Joseph Stowell, *Eternity*

The "life after death" which is the Christian's concern has a definite shape and character. It is a personal entrance into the presence of God to receive the reward of the deeds done in the body, the final verdict.[455]

W. Graham Scroggie, *What about Heaven?*

Life, says the Apostle, is not in spite of death, but by means of it.[456]

W. Graham Scroggie, *What about Heaven?*

The world, beautiful as it is, is not enough. The beauty itself doesn't satisfy. It promises satisfaction that, mirage-like, it can't provide. Yet the beauty is a mimetic clue, both echo and foretaste, of Things Unseen, an enigmatic hint of Elsewhere which we puzzle over but rarely decipher. He has set eternity in the hearts of men; yet they cannot fathom what God has done. He is everywhere baiting us, prodding, luring us. He is playing hide-and-seek with heaven and earth, strewing clues all around, brushing the commonplace with the scent of Things Unseen.

Making us always wish for more, and always coming up short.[457]

Mark Buchanan, *Things Unseen*

The perspective on life you get from the graveyard is a good one. . . . But it's not the best one. That perspective comes from the eternal city. . . . "We cannot," Timothy Jones writes, "live rightly until we aim past life. Eternity provides the only goal that makes ultimate sense of our lives."[458]

Mark Buchanan, *Things Unseen*

The most striking characteristic that distinguished the early Christians from their pagan neighbours was their *hope*. When Saint Paul described the pagan as "having no hope," it was no mere rhetorical flourish, but plain truth. The world of ancient Greek and Roman civilization was a world of fascinating beauty. It could boast of splendid courage, high intellectual power, and superb loveliness of poetry and art; but in spite of all the grandeur and charm it was a world without hope. . . . Old age was dreaded as the threshold leading out into the dark and cold. . . . Over that classical civilization death reigned as king of terrors. . . . Now by the resurrection of Christ the king of terrors had been dethroned. Unlike their pagan neighbours the early Christians were men and women of hope. . . . A new dimension had been given to their lives—the dimension of the future, of eternal life.[459]

Bruce Milne, *The Message of Heaven and Hell*

Would Paul ever have said, "to die is gain," if from the moment of his demise he was to lie in the stark oblivion of soul-sleep for an indeterminate duration? What possible "gain" could it have been, to leave his Spirit-filled ministry, his rich communion with Christ, his bringing of thousands to know the Savior, his founding of churches around the world, his teaching of believers, his inspired letter-writing for the guidance and edification of the Christian assemblies? As 2 Corinthians 12:1-4 tells us, Paul had been "caught up" by the Holy Spirit and given more than a glimpse of what awaits the Christian on the other side of death; and *that* is what he has in mind when he exults, "To die is *gain*"![460]

    J. Sidlow Baxter, *The Other Side of Death*

I meet many faithful Christians who, in spite of their faith, are deeply disappointed in how their lives have turned out. Sometimes it is simply a matter of how they experience aging, which they take to mean they no longer have a future. But often, due to circumstances or wrongful decisions and actions by others, what they had hoped to accomplish in life they did not. They painfully puzzle over what they may have done wrong, or over whether God has really been with them.

    Much of the distress of these good people comes from a failure to realize that their life lies before them. That they are coming to the end of their present life, life "in the flesh," is of little significance. What is of significance is the kind of person they have become. Circumstances and other people are not in control of an individual's character or of the life that lies endlessly before us in the kingdom of God.[461]

    Dallas Willard, *The Divine Conspiracy*

As for those who have fallen asleep in Jesus, we need not fret or trouble ourselves about them. When children go upstairs to bed, do their elder brothers and sisters, who sit up later, gather together, and cry because the other children have fallen asleep? Ah, no! They feel that they have not lost them, and they expect to meet again in the morning; and so do we!

Therefore, let us not weep and lament to excess concerning the dear ones who are fallen asleep in Christ, for all is well with them. They are at rest: shall we weep about that? They are enjoying their eternal triumph: shall we weep about that? They are as full of bliss as they can possibly be: shall we weep about that? If any of your sons and daughters were taken away from you to be made into kings and queens in a foreign land, you might shed a tear or two at parting, but you would say, "It is for their good; let them go."[462]

Charles Spurgeon, "Fallen Asleep," Sermon 2659

Did you ever notice, concerning Job's children, that when God gave him twice as much substance as he had before, he gave him only the same number of children as he formerly had? The Lord gave him twice as much gold, and twice as much of all sorts of property, but he only gave him the exact number of children that he had before. Why did he not give the patriarch double the number of children as well as twice the number of cattle? Why, because God reckoned the first ones as being his still. . . . In the same way, consider your friends who are asleep in Christ as still yours—not a single one lost.[463]

Charles Spurgeon, "Fallen Asleep," Sermon 2659

What we long for is not just living forever. What resonates deep in our hearts is a sincere expectation of someday enjoying a life of perpetual good and bounty. That is not a fanciful pipe dream! It is a foreshadowing of Heaven.

. . . In our desire to know more about the place where we will spend eternity, we are like kids anticipating a great summer vacation.[464]

Daniel Brown, *What the Bible Reveals about Heaven*

Eternal life is not just a life that goes on without end. It is a quality of life that directly corresponds with all that has been in God's heart for us since the beginning of the cosmos. It is life with nothing missing and nothing wrong. It is life without fear, pain, disappointment or shame. There will be no pride or envy, hate or confusion, no regret or disorder.[465]

Daniel Brown, *What the Bible Reveals about Heaven*

Scripture teaches that, upon death, the soul leaves the body and goes into the spirit world to await the resurrection. In his parable concerning the rich man and Lazarus, Jesus describes the horrors of judgment in the afterlife, rather than the horrors of karmic debt in another life. . . . In sharp contrast to a world-view in which humanity perfects itself through an endless cycle of birth and rebirth, the Christian world-view maintains that we are vicariously perfected by the righteousness of Christ. Thus, salvation is not based on what we do, but rather on what Christ has done.[466]

Hank Hanegraaff, *Resurrection*

Rather than a series of bodies that die, resurrection makes alive forever the same body that died. Rather than seeing personhood as a soul in a body, resurrection sees each human being as a soul-body unity. While reincarnation is a process of perfection, resurrection is a perfected state. Reincarnation is an intermediate state, while the soul longs to be disembodied and absorbed in God; but, resurrection is an ultimate state, in which the whole person, body and soul, enjoys the goodness of God.[467]

Norman Geisler, *Baker Encyclopedia of Christian Apologetics*

We often feel as if grace had done its utmost when it has carried us safely through the desert, and set us down at the gate of the kingdom. We feel as if, when grace has landed us there, it has done all for us that we are to expect.

But God's thoughts are not our thoughts. He does exceeding abundantly above all we ask or think. It is just when we reach the threshold of the prepared heavenly city, that grace meets us in new and more abundant measures, presenting us with the recompense of the reward.

The love that shall meet us then to bid us welcome to the many mansions, shall be love beyond what we were here able to comprehend. . . .

It was grace which on earth said to us, "Come unto Me, and I will give you rest"; and it will be grace, in all its exceeding riches, that will hereafter say to us, "Come, you who are blessed of my Father, inherit the kingdom prepared for you from the foundation of the world."[468]

Horatius Bonar, "The God of Grace"

"An overwhelming majority of Americans continue to believe that there is life after death and that heaven and hell exist," according to a Barna Research Group poll. But what people actually believe about Heaven and Hell varies widely. A Barna spokesman said, "They're cutting and pasting religious views from a variety of different sources—television, movies, conversations with their friends." The result is a highly subjective theology of the afterlife, disconnected from the biblical doctrine of Heaven.[469]

Randy Alcorn, *Heaven*

Many books and programs these days talk about messages from the spirit realm, supposedly from people who've died and now speak through channelers or mediums. They claim to have come from Heaven to interact with loved ones, yet they almost never talk about God or express wonder at seeing Jesus. But no one who had actually been in Heaven would neglect to mention what Scripture shows to be Heaven's main focus: God himself. If you had spent an evening dining with a king, you wouldn't come back and talk about the wall hangings and place settings; you'd talk about the king. When Heaven was revealed to the apostle John, he recorded the details, but first and foremost, from beginning to end, he kept talking about Jesus.[470]

Randy Alcorn, *50 Days of Heaven*

God uses suffering and impending death to unfasten us from this earth and to set our minds on what lies beyond. I've lost people close to me. (Actually, I haven't *lost* them, because I know where they are—rather, I've lost *contact* with them.) I've spent a lot of time talking to people who've been diagnosed with terminal diseases. These people, and their loved ones, have a sudden and insatiable interest in the afterlife. Most people live unprepared for death. But those who are wise will go to a reliable source to investigate what's on the other side. And if they discover that the choices they make during their brief stay in this world will matter in the world to come, they'll want to adjust those choices accordingly.[471]

Randy Alcorn, *Heaven*

Without an eternal perspective, without understanding the reality that the best is yet to come, we assume that people who die young, who are handicapped, who aren't healthy, who don't get married, or who don't _____ [fill in the blank] will inevitably miss out on the best life has to offer. But the theology underlying those assumptions is fatally flawed. We're presuming that our present Earth, bodies, culture, relationships, and lives are superior to those of the New Earth.

What are we thinking?[472]

Randy Alcorn, *Heaven*

I don't look back nostalgically at wonderful moments in my life, wistfully thinking the best days are behind me. I look at them as foretastes of an eternity of better things. The buds of this life's greatest moments don't shrivel and die; they blossom into greater moments, each to be treasured, none to be lost. Everything done in dependence on God will bear fruit for eternity. This life need not be wasted. In small and often unnoticed acts of service to Christ, we can invest this life in eternity, where today's faithfulness will forever pay rich dividends.

"Thanks, Lord, that the best is yet to be." That's my prayer. God will one day clear away sin, death, and sorrow, as surely as builders clear away debris so they can begin new construction.[473]

Randy Alcorn, *Heaven*

We don't want to live as some other kind of creatures in some other world. What we want is to be sinless, healthy people living on Earth, but without war, conflict, disease, disappointment, and death. We want to live in the kind of world where our dreams, the deepest longings of our hearts, really do come true.

That is exactly what God's Word promises us.

Our failure to grasp this hurts us in countless ways. We become discouraged, supposing that if we're handicapped, we'll never know the joy of running in a meadow or the pleasure of swimming. Or if we aren't married—or don't have a good marriage—we'll never know the joy of marriage.

On the New Earth, in perfect bodies, we'll run through meadows and swim in lakes. We'll have the most exciting and fulfilling marriage there's ever been, a marriage so glorious and complete there will be no purpose for another. Jesus himself will be our bridegroom!

The smartest person God ever created in this world may never have learned to read because he or she had no opportunity. The most musically gifted person may never have touched a musical instrument. The greatest athlete may never have competed in a game. The sport you're best at may be a sport you've never tried, your favorite hobby one you've never thought of. Living under the Curse means we miss countless opportunities. The reversing of the Curse, and the resurrection of our bodies and our Earth, mean we'll regain lost opportunities and inherit many more besides.[474]

Randy Alcorn, *Heaven*

Ethnicity and Diversity

From one man he made every nation of men, that they should inhabit the whole earth; and he determined the times set for them and the exact places where they should live.

PAUL, ACTS 17:26

As my vision continued that night, I saw someone like a son of man coming with the clouds of heaven. He approached the Ancient One and was led into his presence. He was given authority, honor, and sovereignty over all the nations of the world, so that people of every race and nation and language would obey him. His rule is eternal—it will never end. His kingdom will never be destroyed.

DANIEL 7:13-14, NLT

Your blood has ransomed people for God from every tribe and language and people and nation. And you have caused them to become a kingdom of priests for our God. And they will reign on the earth.

JOHN, REVELATION 5:9-10, NLT

We hear them declaring the wonders of God in our own tongues!

THE CROWD AT PENTECOST, ACTS 2:11

Those who are unwilling to accept those who "are not our kind" will have a lot of trouble in heaven, since some from every tribe and nation will be there.[475]

Joseph Stowell, *Eternity*

One of the greatest characteristics of our modern culture is our egalitarian mindset, the desire for everybody to be equal. If this were the case in heaven, it likely would be terribly dull. Can you imagine what it would be like to have no heroes, no role models for your children, and only yourself to look up to? The modern fixation on equality is perhaps one of the greatest blind spots of modernity.[476]

Barry Morrow, *Heaven Observed*

If He had no use for all these differences, I do not see why He should have created more souls than one.[477]

C. S. Lewis, *The Problem of Pain*

Heaven consummates and celebrates the original unity of humanity, which racial conflicts have obscured. Scripture asserts our common origin. "Beneath the fact of racial sin lies the fact of racial unity." Heaven elevates the unity of mankind under God never realized on earth.[478]

John Gilmore, *Probing Heaven*

Heaven is heaven because of its permanent unity, tranquility, and harmony. The kind of unity heaven will reserve and enhance will be the kind in which diversities are allowed, recognized, matured, perfected, and cleansed of jealousies, of bitterness, and of pride. The unity is perfect; these differences are not done away. . . . Inequality yields variety and helps banish dullness. A long distance driver, before whom the road is flat, fights tedium. An even road can be boring. Universal equality can be supremely dull.[479]

John Gilmore, *Probing Heaven*

There is no one human individual or group who can fully bear or manifest all that is involved in the image of God, so that there is a sense in which that image is collectively possessed. The image of God is, as it were, parceled out among the peoples of the earth. By looking at different individuals and groups we get glimpses of different aspects of the full image of God.

Indeed, linguistic, racial, and national boundaries have provided the framework for a variety of cultural social experiments involving the human spirit. When the end of history arrives, then, there *is* something to be gathered in—diverse cultural riches to be brought into the Heavenly City. That which has been parceled out in human history must now be collected for the glory of the creator.[480]

Richard Mouw, *When the Kings Come Marching In*

Nothing of the diversity of the nations and peoples, their cultural products, languages, arts, sciences, literature, and technology—so far as these are good and excellent—will be lost upon life in the new creation.[481]

Cornelius Venema, *The Promise of the Future*

I believe there will be more in heaven than in hell. If you ask me why I think so, I answer, because Christ in everything is to have the preeminence (Colossians 1:18), and I cannot conceive how he could

have the preeminence if there are to be more in the dominions
of Satan than in paradise.

Moreover, it is said there is to be a multitude that no man can
number in heaven (Revelation 7:9). I have never read that there is
to be a multitude that no man can number in hell.

I rejoice to know that the souls of all infants, as soon as they die,
speed their way to paradise. Think what a multitude there is of them!
And then there are the just and the redeemed of all nations up till
now. And there are better times coming, when the religion of Christ
shall be universal. And in the thousand years of the great millennial
state there will be enough saved to make up all the deficiencies of the
thousands of years that have gone before.

Charles Spurgeon, "Heavenly Worship," Sermon 110

The saints are like so many vessels of different sizes cast into a sea of
happiness where every vessel is full: this is eternal life, for a man ever
to have his capacity filled. But after all 'tis left to God's sovereign pleasure, 'tis his prerogative to determine the largeness of the vessel.[482]

Jonathan Edwards

It is even possible—in my own thinking it is quite likely—that
throughout eternity we will be aware of who we are and where we
have come from—aware not only of our individual personality traits
but also of our cultural, ethnic, and racial identities. It may be that
the exchange of those cultural gifts which have been forged under the
pressures of sinful historical development will not be a single event
but an ongoing dialogue in the continuing life of the Heavenly City.
Perhaps the fully sanctified *exploration* of "the glory and the honor of
the nations" is a process that will only begin as we enter the gates of
the City. The Lord has assembled together Scots and Swedes, Iranians
and Navajos, and has addressed them, saying: "Once you were no-
people, but now you are my-people."[483]

Richard Mouw, *When the Kings Come Marching In*

As the Lamb of God he will draw all of the goods, artifacts, and instruments of culture to himself; the kings of the earth will return their authority and power to the Lamb who sits upon the throne; Jesus is the one whose blood has purchased a multi-national community, composed of people from every tribe and tongue and nation. His redemptive ministry, *as* the ministry of the Lamb, is cosmic in scope.[484]

Richard Mouw, *When the Kings Come Marching In*

Part of the central achievement of the incarnation, which is then celebrated in the resurrection and ascension, is that heaven and earth are now joined together with an unbreakable bond and that we too are by rights citizens of both together. We can, if we choose, screen out the heavenly dimension and live as flatlanders, materialists. If we do that, we will be buying in to a system that will go bad, and will wither and die, because earth gets its vital life from heaven.

But if we focus our attention on the heavenly dimension, all sorts of positive and practical results will follow. In Colossians 3:11 Paul sees the unity of the church across cultural and ethnic boundaries as one of the first of these results. In the passage that follows, he lists all kinds of other things that ought to appear in the life of anyone who really sets his or her mind on the world that is now Jesus' primary home, the world that is designed to heal and restore our present one. In each case what he's talking about is *actual current physical reality, shot through now with the life of heaven.*

The created order, which God has begun to redeem in the resurrection of Jesus, is a world in which heaven and earth are designed not to be separated but to come together. In that coming together, the "very good" that God spoke over creation at the beginning will be enhanced, not abolished. The New Testament never imagines that when the new heavens and new earth arrive, God will say, in effect, "Well, that first creation wasn't so good after all, was it? Aren't you glad we've got rid of all that space, time and matter?" Rather, we must envisage a world in which the present creation, which we think of in those three dimensions, is enhanced, taken up into God's larger purposes, no doubt, but certainly not abandoned.[485]

N. T. Wright, *Surprised by Hope*

"To him that overcometh will I give . . . a white stone, and in the stone a new name written, which no man knoweth saving he that receiveth it" (Revelation 2:17). What can be more a man's own than this new name which even in eternity remains a secret between God and him? And what shall we take this secrecy to mean? Surely, that each of the redeemed shall forever know and praise some one aspect of the divine beauty better than any other creature can. Why else were individuals created, but that God, loving all infinitely, should love each differently? . . . If all experienced God in the same way and returned Him an identical worship, the song of the Church triumphant would have no symphony, it would be like an orchestra in which all the instruments played the same note. . . . Heaven is a city, and a Body, because the blessed remain eternally different: a society, because each has something to tell all the others—fresh and ever fresh news of the "My God" whom each finds in Him whom all praise as "Our God."[486]

C. S. Lewis, *The Problem of Pain*

Racism is not only an injustice toward men, but a rejection of God's own character—it is our liking only certain things about God and rejecting others.

Randy Alcorn, unpublished notes

Like the current earthly Jerusalem, the New Jerusalem will be a melting pot of ethnic diversity. But unlike the current city, the groups in the New Jerusalem will be united by their common worship of King Jesus. They will delight in each other's differences, never resent or be frightened by them.[487]

Randy Alcorn, *Heaven*

All people are equal in worth, but they differ in gifting and perfor-mance. God is the creator of diversity, and diversity means "inequality" of gifting (1 Corinthians 12:14-20). Because God promises to reward people differently according to their differing levels of faithfulness in this life, we should not expect equality of possessions and positions in Heaven.

If everyone were equal in Heaven in all respects, it would mean we'd have no role models, no heroes, no one to look up to, no thrill of hearing wise words from someone we deeply admire. I'm not equal to Hudson Taylor, Susanna Wesley, George Mueller, or C. S. Lewis. I want to follow their examples, but I don't need to be their equals.[488]

Randy Alcorn, *Heaven*

We live in a culture that worships equality, but we err when we reduce equality to sameness. It's illogical to assume everyone in Heaven will be able to compose a concerto with equal skill or be able to throw a ball as far as everyone else. In a perfect world, Adam was bigger and stron-ger than Eve, and Eve had beauty, sensitivities, and abilities Adam didn't. In other words, diversity—not conformity—characterizes a perfect world.[489]

Randy Alcorn, *Heaven*

Tribes, peoples, and nations will all make their own particular contri-bution to the enrichment of life in the New Jerusalem (Revelation 5:9; 7:9; 21:24-26). Daniel prophesied that the Messiah would be "given dominion and glory and a kingdom, that all peoples, nations, and lan-guages should serve him" (Daniel 7:14, ESV). Just as the church's diver-sity of gifts serves the good of others (1 Corinthians 12:7-11), so our diversity will serve everyone's good in the new universe.

Consider what it will be like to see the Masai of Kenya, the Dinka of Sudan, the Hmong, Athabaskans, Tibetans, Aucans, Icelanders, Macedonians, Moldovans, Moroccans, and Peruvians. Hundreds of nations, thousands of people groups will gather to worship Christ. And many national and cultural distinctives, untouched by sin, will continue to the glory of God.[490]

Randy Alcorn, *Heaven*

In Heaven will Cambodians place their hands together and bow their heads in greeting? Will Kenyans dance to their distinctive drumbeats? Will Argentineans love soccer? Will Cubans speak Spanish and Britons speak English and Brazilians speak Portuguese? Why wouldn't they?

We won't be omniscient, so it's doubtful we'll know all languages. But certainly we could learn them much faster. Those of us who aren't naturally gifted in languages may be amazed at our abilities. Language experts, including translators, may see their skills pick up where they left off and further develop at unprecedented rates. They'll have eternity to learn as many languages as they wish.

What purpose will different languages serve on the New Earth? Knowing a language is part of understanding who people are and what their culture is like. All that, on the New Earth, to the glory of God.[491]

Randy Alcorn, *Heaven*

Will we have ethnic and national identities? Yes. Hundreds of nations, thousands of people groups will gather to worship Christ. And many national and cultural distinctives, untouched by sin, will continue to the glory of God. The kings and leaders of nations will be united because they share the King's righteousness; and they, with him, will rejoice in their differences as a tribute to his creativity and multi-faceted character.[492]

Randy Alcorn, *TouchPoints: Heaven*

There's no reason to believe we'll all be equally tall or strong or that we'll have the same gifts, talents, or intellectual capacities. If we all had the same gifts, they wouldn't be special. If you can do some things better than I can, and I than you, then we'll have something to offer each other.[493]

Randy Alcorn, *Heaven*

Friends and Relationships

See also Marriage and Family.

I always thank God for you because of his grace given you in Christ Jesus.

Paul, 1 Corinthians 1:4

What is our hope, our joy, or the crown in which we will glory in the presence of our Lord Jesus when he comes? Is it not you? Indeed, you are our glory and joy.

Paul, 1 Thessalonians 2:19-20

You long to see us, just as we also long to see you. . . . How can we thank God enough for you in return for all the joy we have in the presence of our God because of you? Night and day we pray most earnestly that we may see you again.

Paul, 1 Thessalonians 3:6, 9-10

The Lord himself will descend from heaven with
a cry of command, with the voice of an archangel,
and with the sound of the trumpet of God. And
the dead in Christ will rise first. Then we who
are alive, who are left, will be caught up together
with them in the clouds to meet the Lord in the
air, and so we [together] will always be with the
Lord. Therefore encourage one another with
these words.

PAUL, 1 THESSALONIANS 4:16-18, ESV

Relationships are the only things you can take with you into
heaven.[494]

Larry Dick, *A Taste of Heaven*

No one dies finished. There is never enough time to do and to be all
that we can, even all that we should. Our lives are incomplete in all
three of their essential relationships: (1) to ourselves, (2) to others,
and (3) to God.[495]

Peter Kreeft, *Everything You Ever Wanted to Know about Heaven*

Our communication will be perfect. . . . In eternity, not only will we
say it right, but our fellow royals will hear what we are saying.[496]

T. W. Hunt and Melana Hunt Monroe, *From Heaven's View*

We can sit for hours listening to the interesting conversation of a
learned man. . . . If these pleasures are so exquisite here below, where,
after all, the wisest know so little, what shall we say of those same
pleasures in Heaven?[497]

Father J. Boudreau, *The Happiness of Heaven*

Heaven will be no strange place to us when we get there. We shall not be depressed by the cold, shy, chilly feeling that we know nothing of our companions. We shall feel at home.[498]

    J. C. Ryle, *Heaven*

All the misunderstandings, hasty judgments, disappointments, resentments and hurts of the past that can happen in even the best of relationships, will be forgiven and forgotten. There will only be unconditional love and ecstatic joy at seeing each other again.

    Records, detailed records, are kept in heaven on every person and family. You will be able to accurately trace your ancestry back to Noah and Adam. More than this, you will have the opportunity to meet and spend time with your ancestors that made it into heaven. What a fascinating experience to hear and see firsthand how God has worked down through the generations to you![499]

    Larry Dick, *A Taste of Heaven*

Social life can tear families apart as well as to knit them together. . . . In heaven nobody has to prove worth by denigrating a neighbor, ridiculing another person, or betraying a friend.[500]

    Arthur Roberts, *Exploring Heaven*

You'll be able to go down to the corner of Gold Street and Silver Boulevard, run into Abraham, and ask him a few questions. David can tell you the story of how he killed Goliath. You can ask Jonah what it felt like to be swallowed by a fish and live inside of it for three days.[501]

    Tony Evans, *Tony Evans Speaks Out on Heaven and Hell*

I have often thought I should love to see Isaiah, and as soon as I get to Heaven, I would like to ask for him, because he spoke more of Jesus Christ than all the rest.

    I am sure I should want to find out good George Whitefield—

he who so continually preached to the people and wore himself out with a more than angelic zeal.

Oh yes! We shall have choice company in Heaven when we get there. There will be no distinction of learned and unlearned, clergy and laity, but we shall walk freely among one another. We shall feel that we are family.[502]

Charles Spurgeon, "Heaven and Hell," Sermons 39, 40

I know that Christ is all in all; and that it is the presence of God that makes Heaven to be heaven. But yet it much sweetens the thoughts of that place to me that there are there such a multitude of my most dear and precious friends in Christ.[503]

Richard Baxter, *The Practical Works of Richard Baxter*

Since paradise is far better than this earth, we can be sure our knowledge there will not be less than it is here but greater. If we know our loved ones down here on earth, undoubtedly we shall know them more completely up there, in a most profound fellowship of love.[504]

Steven Waterhouse, *Not by Bread Alone*

All the truly great and good, all the pure and holy and excellent from this world, and it may be from every part of the universe, are constantly tending toward heaven. As the streams tend to the ocean, so all these are tending to the great ocean of infinite purity and bliss. The progress of time does but bear them on to its blessedness; and us, if we are holy, to be united to them there. Every gem which death rudely tears away from us here is a glorious jewel forever shining there.[505]

Jonathan Edwards, *Heaven: A World of Love*

Every Christian friend that goes before us from this world is a ransomed spirit waiting to welcome us in heaven. There will be the infant of days that we have lost below, through grace to be found above. There the Christian father, and mother, and wife, and child, and friend, with whom we shall renew the holy fellowship of the saints, which was interrupted by death here, but shall be commenced again in the upper sanctuary, and then shall never end. There we shall have companionship with the patriarchs and fathers and saints of the Old and New Testaments, and those of whom the world was not worthy. . . . And there, above all, we shall enjoy and dwell with God the Father, whom we have loved with all our hearts on earth; and with Jesus Christ, our beloved Savior, who has always been to us the chief among ten thousands, and altogether lovely; and with the Holy Spirit, our Sanctifier, and Guide, and Comforter; and shall be filled with all the fullness of the Godhead forever![506]

Jonathan Edwards, *Heaven: A World of Love*

Alas for him who never sees
The stars shine through his cypress-trees!
Who, hopeless, lays his dead away,
Nor looks to see the breaking day
Across the mournful marbles play!
Who hath not learned in hours of faith
The truth to flesh and sense unknown,
That Life is ever lord of Death
And Love can never lose its own.[507]

John Greenleaf Whittier, "Snow Bound"

If we have known one another here, we shall know one another there. I have dear departed friends up there, and it is always a sweet thought to me, that when I shall put my foot, as I hope I may, upon the threshold of heaven, there will come my sisters and brothers to clasp me by the hand and say, "Yes, my loved one, at last you are here."

Dear relatives that have been separated, you will meet again in heaven. One of you has lost a mother—she is gone above; and if you follow the track of Jesus, you shall meet her there. . . .

We shall recognize our friends: husband, you will know your

wife again. Mother, you will know those dear babes of yours—you marked their features when they lay panting and gasping for breath. You know how you hung over their graves when the cold sod was sprinkled over them, and it was said, "Earth to earth. Dust to dust, and ashes to ashes." But you shall hear those beloved voices again: you shall hear those sweet voices once more; you shall yet know that those whom you loved have been loved by God.[508]

Charles Spurgeon, "Heaven and Hell," Sermons 39, 40

There shall be no wall of separation in heaven to keep the saints divided, nor shall they be hindered from the full and complete enjoyment of each other's love by distance of habitation; for they shall all be together, as one family, in their heavenly Father's house. Nor shall there be any lack of full acquaintance to hinder the greatest possible intimacy; and much less shall there be any misunderstanding between them, or misinterpreting things that are said or done by each other. There shall be no disharmony through difference of disposition, or manners, or circumstances, or from various opinions, interests, feelings or alliances. But all shall be united in the same interest, and all alike allied to the same Savior, and all employed in the same business, serving and glorifying the same God.

And in heaven all shall not only be related one to another, but they shall be each other's, and belong to each other.[509]

Jonathan Edwards, *Heaven: A World of Love*

Oh, I reckon on meeting David, whose Psalms have so often cheered my soul! I long to meet with Martin Luther and Calvin, and to have the power of seeing such men as Whitfield and Wesley, and walking and talking with them in the golden streets. Yes, Heaven would scarcely be so full of charms in the prospect if there were not the full conviction in our minds that we should know the saints and feast with them.

Charles Spurgeon, "The New Wine of the Kingdom," Sermon 3526

We know that Heaven would scarce be Heaven at all if we were to be but solitary isolated spirits amongst a crowd of others whom we did not know or love. We know that the next world and this world come from the same God who is the same always. We know that in this world He has bound us up in groups, knowing and loving and sympathizing with each other. Unless His method utterly changes He must do the same hereafter. And we have seen what a prophecy of recognition lies deep in the very fibers of that nature which God has implanted in us. If we shall not know one another, why is there this undying memory of departed ones, the aching void that is never filled on earth? The lower animals lose their young and in a few days forget them. But the poor, human mother never forgets. When her head is bowed with age, when she has forgotten nearly all else on earth, you can bring the tears into her eyes by mentioning the child that died in her arms forty years ago. Did God implant that divine love in her only to disappoint it? God forbid! A thousand times, no. In that world the mother shall meet her child, and the lonely widow shall meet her husband, and they shall learn fully the love of God in that rapturous meeting with Christ's benediction resting on them.

I know there are further questions rising in our hearts. Will our dear ones remember us? Will they, in all the years of progress, have grown too good and great for fellowship with us? There is no specific answer save what we can infer from the boundless goodness and kindness of God. Since he does not forget us we may be sure they will not forget us. Since His superior greatness and holiness does not put Him beyond our reach, we may be sure that theirs will not—their growth will be mainly a growth of love which will only bring them closer to us for ever and ever.[510]

J. Paterson-Smyth, *The Gospel of the Hereafter*

The joys we find in companionship of noble, unselfish, thoughtful people here give only the faintest conception of the joys of heaven's companionships.[511]

R. A. Torrey, *Heaven or Hell*

There would be no point in these words of consolation [in 1 Thessalonians 4:14-18] if they did not imply the mutual recognition of saints. The hope with which he cheers wearied Christians is the hope of meeting their beloved friends again. . . . But in the moment that we who are saved shall meet our several friends in heaven, we shall at once know them, and they will at once know us.[512]

J. C. Ryle, *Heaven*

Absent friends and friends gone on the last long journey stand once more together, bright with an immortal glow, and like the disciples who saw their Master floating in the clouds above them, we say, "Lord, it is good to be here!" How fair the wife, the husband, the absent mother, the grey-haired father, the manly son, the bright-eyed daughter! Seen in the actual present, all have some fault, some flaw; but absent, we see them in their permanent and better selves. Of our distant home we remember not one dark day, not one servile care, nothing but the echo of its holy hymns and the radiance of its brightest days—of our father, not one hasty word, but only the fullness of his manly vigour and noble tenderness—and of our mother, nothing of mortal weakness, but a glorified form of love—of our brother, not one teasing, provoking word of brotherly freedom, but the proud beauty of his noblest hours—of our sister, our child, only what is fairest and sweetest.

This is to life the true ideal, the calm glass wherein looking, we shall see that, whatever defects cling to us, they are not, after all, permanent, and that we are tending to something nobler than we yet are: it is "the earnest of our inheritance until the redemption of the purchased possession." In the resurrection we shall see our friends for ever as we see them in these clairvoyant hours.[513]

Harriet Beecher Stowe, *The Minister's Wooing*

There is undoubtedly an inconceivably pure, sweet, and fervent love between the saints in glory. . . .

For all shall have as much love as they desire, and as great manifestations of love as they can bear. And in this manner, all shall be fully satisfied. And where there is perfect satisfaction, there can be no reason for envy. And there will be no temptation for any to envy those that are above them in glory, on account of the latter being lifted up with pride; for there will be no pride in heaven.[514]

Jonathan Edwards, *Heaven: A World of Love*

In heaven this desire of love, or this fondness for being loved, will never fail of being satisfied. No inhabitants of that blessed world will ever be grieved with the thought that they are slighted by those that they love, or that their love is not fully and fondly returned.[515]

Jonathan Edwards, *Heaven: A World of Love*

Such is the love of every saint to every other saint, that it makes the glory which he sees other saints enjoy, as it were, his very own. He so rejoices that they enjoy such glory that it is in some respects as if he himself enjoyed it in his own personal experience (see 1 Corinthians 12:26).

There shall be none there to tempt any to dislike or hatred; no busybodies, or malicious adversaries, to make intentional misrepresentations, or create misunderstandings, or spread abroad any evil reports, but every being and every thing shall combine to promote love, and the full enjoyment of love. Heaven itself, the place of habitation, is a garden of pleasures, a heavenly paradise, fitted in all respects for an abode of heavenly love; a place where they may have sweet society and perfect enjoyment of each other's love. None are unsocial or distant from each other. The petty distinctions of this world do not draw lines in the society of heaven, but all meet in the equality of holiness and of holy love.[516]

Jonathan Edwards, *Heaven: A World of Love*

All shall enjoy each other in perfect prosperity and riches, and honor, without any sickness, or grief, or persecution, or sorrow, or any

enemy to molest them, or any busybody to create jealousy or misunderstanding, or mar the perfect, and holy, and blessed peace that
reigns in heaven![517]

Jonathan Edwards, *Heaven: A World of Love*

How happy is that love, in which there is an eternal progress in all
these things; wherein new beauties are continually discovered, and
more and more loveliness, and in which we shall forever increase in
beauty ourselves; where we shall be made capable of finding out and
giving, and shall receive, more and more endearing expressions of love
forever: our union will become more close, and communication more
intimate.[518]

Jonathan Edwards, *The Miscellanies*

Paul says to his friends in Thessalonica, "We loved you so much"
and "You had become so dear to us," then speaks of his "intense
longing" to be with them (1 Thessalonians 2:8, 17). In fact, Paul
anticipates his ongoing relationship with the Thessalonians as part
of his heavenly reward: "What is our hope, our joy, or the crown
in which we will glory in the presence of our Lord Jesus when he
comes? Is it not you? Indeed, you are our glory and joy" (1 Thessalonians 2:19-20).

Isn't this emphatic proof that it's appropriate for us to deeply love
people and look forward to being with them in Heaven? Paul sees no
contradiction in referring to both Christ and his friends as his hope
and joy and crown in Heaven.

Paul then asks, "How can we thank God enough for you in
return for all the joy we have in the presence of our God because of
you?" (3:9). The joy he takes in his friends doesn't compete with his
joy in God—it's part of it. Paul thanks God for his friends. Whenever
we're moved to thank God for people, we're experiencing exactly what
he intended.

Paul also says to the Thessalonians, "You long to see us, just as
we also long to see you. . . . How can we thank God enough for you

in return for all the joy we have in the presence of our God because of you? Night and day we pray most earnestly that we may see you again" (3:6, 9-10). Paul finds joy in God's presence because of other Christians. He anticipates the day "when our Lord Jesus comes with all his holy ones" (3:13). He looks forward to being with Jesus *and* his people.

Paul tells the Thessalonians that we'll be reunited with believing family and friends in Heaven: "Brothers, we do not want you to be ignorant about those who fall asleep, or to grieve like the rest of men, who have no hope. . . . God will bring with Jesus those who have fallen asleep in him. . . . We who are still alive and are left will be caught up together with them. . . . And so we will be with the Lord forever. Therefore encourage each other with these words" (4:13-14, 17-18). Our source of comfort isn't only that we'll be with the Lord in Heaven but also that we'll be with each other.[519]

Randy Alcorn, *Heaven*

We'll experience all the best of human relationships, with none of the worst. The burdens and tragedies of life will be lifted from us. We'll be free of what displeases God and damages relationships. No abortion clinics or psychiatric wards. No missing children. No rape or abuse. No drug rehabilitation centers. No bigotry, muggings, or killings. No worry, depression, or economic downturns. No wars. No unemployment. No anguish over failure and mis-+communication. No pretense or wearing masks. No cliques. No hidden agendas, backroom deals, betrayals, secret ambitions, plots, or schemes.[520]

Randy Alcorn, *Heaven*

One of the things I'm looking forward to in Heaven is meeting people I've known only by phone and e-mail. For those friends I rarely see, we'll finally have time and access to enjoy each other's company.

I want to spend time again with the people who had an influence on me as a young Christian. I don't know how many of my ancestors were Christians. Perhaps not many. But I can't wait to meet the ones who were and to hear their stories.

I'm eager to meet the young women our family supported in the Dominican Republic. I want to talk to some Cambodian pastors and Chinese house church members who received Bibles from the ministries we gave to. What will it be like to meet the Sudanese people our church helped rescue from slavery and oppression? I want to thank them for their faith and example.

I want to spend time with my handicapped friends and watch them enjoy the freedom of new bodies and minds. I look forward to sharp intellectual exchanges with those who finished their course on Earth with Alzheimer's. (Maybe I'll be one of them.)

I want to spend time with the martyrs, some of whose stories I've read. Most of them didn't know each other on Earth, but Revelation 6:9-11 portrays them as close-knit in Heaven.

We'll surely have many new relationships, some based on common interests, experiences, and histories on Earth. If you have a special interest in first-century Rome, perhaps you'll enjoy developing relationships with those who lived in that place and time.

We'll talk with angels who saw the earth created and who watched their comrades rebel. We'll meet angels who guarded and served us while we were on Earth. Don't you look forward to asking them questions?

If our conversations would be limited only to the earth's past, we might run the reservoir dry after fifty thousand years. But the beauty is that Heaven will bring as many new developments as Earth ever did, and eventually far more. We won't *begin* to run out of things to think about or talk about. The reservoir won't run dry. It will be replenished daily, forever expanding.[521]

Randy Alcorn, *Heaven*

Perhaps you're disappointed that you've never had the friendships you long for. In Heaven, you'll have much closer relationships with people you already know, but it's also possible that you haven't yet met the closest friends you'll ever have. Perhaps it will be someone seated next to you at the first great feast. After all, the God who orchestrates friendships will be in charge of the seating arrangements.[522]

Randy Alcorn, *50 Days of Heaven*

Gender and Sexuality

God created man in his own image,
    in the image of God he created him;
    male and female he created them.

GENESIS 1:27

Under the apple tree I roused you;
    there your mother conceived you,
    there she who was in labor gave you birth.
Place me like a seal over your heart,
    like a seal on your arm;
    for love is as strong as death,
    its jealousy unyielding as the grave.
It burns like blazing fire,
    like a mighty flame.
Many waters cannot quench love;
    rivers cannot sweep it away.

If one were to give
    all the wealth of one's house for love,
    it would be utterly scorned.

THE SHULAMMITE BRIDE, SONG OF SONGS 8:5-7

I think our present outlook might be like that of a small boy who, on being told that the sexual act was the highest bodily pleasure should immediately ask whether you ate chocolates at the same time. On receiving the answer "No," he might regard absence of chocolates as the chief characteristic of sexuality. In vain would you tell him that the reason why lovers in their carnal raptures don't bother about chocolates is that they have something better to think of. The boy knows chocolate: he does not know the positive thing that excludes it. We are in the same position. We know the sexual life; we do not know, except in glimpses, the other thing which, in Heaven, will leave no room for it.[523]

    C. S. Lewis, *Miracles*

The counterfeit phrase "having sex" (meaning "intercourse") was minted only recently. Of course a nun "has sex": she is female. . . . The significance of the linguistic change is that we have trivialized sex into a thing to do rather than a quality of our inner being. . . . If sexuality is part of our inner essence, then it follows that there is sexuality in Heaven, whether or not we "have sex" and whether or not we have sexually distinct social roles in Heaven.[524]

    Peter Kreeft, *Everything You Ever Wanted to Know about Heaven*

In Heaven . . . all earthly perversions of the true sexuality are overcome, especially the master perversion, selfishness. The highest pleasure always comes in self-forgetfulness. Self always spoils its own pleasure. Pleasure is like light; if you grab at it, you miss it; if you try to bottle it, you get only darkness; if you let it pass, you catch the glory. The self has a built-in, God-imagining design of self-fulfillment by self-forgetfulness, pleasure through unselfishness, ecstasy by *ekstasis*, "standing-outside-the-self." This is not the self-conscious self-sacrifice of the do-gooder but the spontaneous, unconscious generosity of the lover.[525]

Peter Kreeft, *Everything You Ever Wanted to Know about Heaven*

Gender is not an arbitrary description of humans. It is not a distinction we have created, but it is part of reality. . . .

Without gender we do not exist. There is no such being as a neuter person. . . . Humans can be neutered, but there is no transformation into a new or third sex. There are only two sexes.

. . . Did God create sexual differences from what he was in himself? Were these sexual dissimilarities replicas of what he was in himself or were they specially created categories? When Scripture says man is made in God's image, does his image include one gender, no gender, or both genders?[526]

John Gilmore, *Probing Heaven*

In the most important and obvious sense there is certainly sex [gender] in Heaven simply because there are human beings in Heaven. . . . Even if sex were *not* spiritual, there would be sex in Heaven because of the resurrection of the body. The body is not a mistake to be unmade or a prison cell to be freed from, but a divine work of art designed to show forth the soul as the soul is to show forth God, in splendor and glory and overflow of generous superfluity.[527]

Peter Kreeft, *Everything You Ever Wanted to Know about Heaven*

"They will neither marry nor be given in marriage; they will be like the angels" [Mark 12:25]. This statement has been commonly understood to imply a non-physical, non-sexual and hence purely "spiritual" existence in heaven. It has also contributed to a rather disapproving view of sexual passion, even within the marriage covenant.

. . . The love for our brothers and sisters within the family of God which will be perfected in heaven surely ought not to be anticipated as a passionless, anaemic business. It will be purged of all sinful, selfish elements and will no longer, as Jesus implies, express itself in genital sexual intimacy. However, the idea that in heaven our love for those of the other gender, as for those of our own gender, will be immeasurably richer, deeper and mutually more satisfying than anything we can know here on earth is surely a biblically grounded anticipation.[528]

Bruce Milne, *The Message of Heaven and Hell*

Since there are bodies in Heaven, able to eat and be touched, like Christ's resurrection body (John 20:27), there is the *possibility* of physical intercourse.

. . . This spiritual intercourse with God is the ecstasy hinted at in all earthly intercourse, physical or spiritual. It is the ultimate reason why sexual passion is so strong, so different from other passions, so heavy with suggestions of profound meanings that just elude our grasp. No mere practical needs account for it. No mere animal drive explains it. . . . And human sexuality is a foretaste of that self-giving, that losing and finding the self, that oneness-in-manyness that is the heart of the life and joy of the Trinity. That is what we long for; that is why we tremble to stand outside ourselves in the other, to give our whole selves, body and soul: because we are images of God the sexual being.

And this earthly love is so passionate because Heaven is full of passion, of energy and dynamism.[529]

Peter Kreeft, *Everything You Ever Wanted to Know about Heaven*

The God who gave us the wonder, excitement, fulfillment and ecstasy of physical union within marriage is more than able to replace and exceed the joy of this gift in heaven. Since there is no procreation in heaven, our glorified new bodies may not need the same hormonal drives, anyway. Yes, sex is a very powerful drive now, but despite what our current pop culture would have us believe, the spiritual drive in man is really the one which longs most to be satisfied.[530]

Larry Dick, *A Taste of Heaven*

What is no longer needed for biological purposes may be expected to survive for splendor. Sexuality is the instrument both of virginity and of conjugal virtue; neither men nor women will be asked to throw away weapons they have used victoriously. It is the beaten and the fugitives who throw away their swords. The conquerors sheathe theirs and retain them. "Trans-sexual" would be a better word than "sexless" for the heavenly life.[531]

C. S. Lewis, *Miracles*

Because sex was designed to be part of a marriage relationship, marriage and sex logically belong together. Because we're told by Jesus in Matthew 22 that humans won't be married to each other, and sex is intended for marriage, then logically we won't be engaging in sex.[532]

Randy Alcorn, *Heaven*

Some people try to prove there will be no gender in Heaven by citing Paul's statement that in Christ there is neither "male nor female" (Galatians 3:28). But Paul refers to something that's already true on Earth: the equality of men and women in Christ. The issue isn't the obliteration of sexuality (you don't lose your gender at conversion).

Was Jesus genderless after his resurrection? Of course not. No one mistook him for a woman—or as androgynous. He's referred to with male pronouns.

We'll never be genderless because human bodies aren't genderless. The point of the resurrection is that we will have real human bodies essentially linked to our original ones. Gender is a God-created aspect of humanity.[533]

Randy Alcorn, *Heaven*

"I am still a man here, and everyone I see is clearly male or female, more distinctly in fact than on earth. I had thought perhaps there would be no gender here. I had read that we would all be . . . like angels, like you."

Zyor looked surprised.

"You are like us in that you do not marry and bear children here. But as for your being a man, what else would you be? Elyon may unmake what men make, but he does not unmake what he makes. He made you male, as he made your mother and wife and daughters female. Gender is not merely a component of your being to be added in or extracted and discarded. It is an essential part of who you are."[534]

Finney and Zyor, in *Deadline*, by Randy Alcorn

Glory

"O Lord, open his eyes so he may see." Then the Lord opened the servant's eyes, and he looked and saw the hills full of horses and chariots of fire all around Elisha.

2 Kings 6:17

Stephen, full of the Holy Spirit, looked up to heaven and saw the glory of God, and Jesus standing at the right hand of God. "Look," he said, "I see heaven open and the Son of Man standing at the right hand of God."

Luke, Acts 7:55-56

The Spirit himself testifies with our spirit that we are God's children. Now if we are children, then we are heirs—heirs of God and co-heirs with Christ, if indeed we share in his sufferings in order that we may also share in his glory.

PAUL, ROMANS 8:16-17

Our present sufferings are not worth comparing with the glory that will be revealed in us.

PAUL, ROMANS 8:18

Our light and momentary troubles are achieving for us an eternal glory that far outweighs them all.

PAUL, 2 CORINTHIANS 4:17

Rejoice that you participate in the sufferings of Christ, so that you may be overjoyed when his glory is revealed.

PETER, 1 PETER 4:13

Splendor and majesty are before him;
    strength and joy in his dwelling place.
Ascribe to the LORD, O families of nations,
    ascribe to the LORD glory and strength,
      ascribe to the LORD the glory due his name.
Bring an offering and come before him;
    worship the LORD in the splendor of his holiness.

DAVID, 1 CHRONICLES 16:27-29

Father, I want those you have given me to be with me where I am, and to see my glory, the glory you have given me because you loved me before the creation of the world.

JESUS, JOHN 17:24

Lord of all being,
There is one thing that deserves my greatest care,
 that calls forth my ardent desires,
That is, that I may answer the great end for which I am made—
 to glorify thee who hast given me being,
 and to do all the good I can for my fellow men;
Verily, life is not worth having
 if it be not improved for this noble purpose.[535]

The Valley of Vision: A Collection of Puritan Prayers and Devotions

The picture of our Lamb-Shepherd leading us "to living fountains of waters" has the sure sense of him continually showing fresh delights to his redeemed and glorified flock, such that even in heaven (far from us having arrived and "that being it") he will be leading us on and on, deeper and deeper, higher and higher in spiritual ecstasies that we cannot yet even begin to imagine. Even in heaven we shall be going from glory to glory. Our God and Saviour is inexhaustible![536]

Richard Brooks, *The Doors of Heaven*

The other world is an undiscovered country. . . . We are sure of Heaven when we are sure of God. . . . We know that the One who has done "exceedingly abundantly above all that we are able to ask or think" will not disappoint the hope which He has kindled within our hearts, but will fill us with a glad surprise when we behold the greatness and the glory of the inheritance which He has reserved for us above.[537]

James Campbell, *Heaven Opened*

Wherever the inhabitants of that blessed world shall turn their eyes, they shall see nothing but dignity, and beauty, and glory.

And in heaven, shall be all those objects that the saints have set their hearts upon, and which they have loved above all things while in this world.[538]

Jonathan Edwards, *Heaven: A World of Love*

Heaven is not like winning the pools or the Grand Lottery, a way of satisfying one's wildest dreams, it is the privilege of beholding the glory of Christ. And only those who are related to Christ here, united to him by faith, will find heaven a pleasant or a congenial place to be. For if a person despises Christ and his teaching here, what reason is there to think that he will enjoy and be captivated by the presence of the glorified Christ?[539]

Paul Helm, *The Last Things*

Compare . . . the excellencies of heaven with those glorious *works of creation* which our eyes now behold. What wisdom, power and goodness are manifested therein! How does the majesty of the Creator shine in this fabric of the world! "His works are great, sought out of all them that have pleasure therein." What divine skill in forming the bodies of men or beasts! What excellency in every plant! What beauty in flowers! What variety and usefulness in herbs, plants, fruits and minerals! What wonders are contained in the earth and its inhabitants; the ocean of waters, with its motions and dimensions; and the constant succession of spring and autumn, of summer and winter! Think, then, "If these things, which are but servants to sinful man, are so full of mysterious worth, what is that place where God himself dwells, and which is prepared for just men made perfect with Christ!"

What glory is there in the least of yonder stars! What a vast resplendent body is yonder moon, and every planet! What an inconceivable glory has the sun! But all this is nothing to the glory of heaven. Yonder sun must there be laid aside as useless. Yonder sun is but darkness to the lustre of my Father's house. I shall myself be as glorious as that sun. This whole earth is but my Father's footstool. This thunder is nothing to his dreadful voice. These winds are nothing to the breath of his mouth. If the "sending rain, and making the sun to rise on the just and on the unjust," be so wonderful, how much more wonderful and glorious will that Sun be which must shine on none but saints and angels?[540]

Richard Baxter, *The Saints' Everlasting Rest*

Dark providences, never understood before, will then be clearly seen, and all that puzzles us now will become plain to us in the light of the Lamb. . . . Oh! what a manifestation! All this proceeds from the exalted Lamb. Whatever there may be of effulgent splendour, Jesus shall be the centre and soul of it all. Oh! to be present and to see Him in His own light, the King of kings, and Lord of lords![541]

Charles Spurgeon, *Morning and Evening*

I am assured that though I want here, I have riches there; though I hunger here, I shall have fullness there; though I faint here, I shall be refreshed there; and though I be accounted here as a dead man, I shall there live in perpetual glory.[542]

John Bradford, *Writings of John Bradford*

The architecture of Heaven is theocentric, designed for one thing— to reflect and magnify the brilliant glory of God.

Talk about a light show! Here is God's laser show, showing off His glory for all the universe to see. No wonder the angels cover their faces.[543]

Steven J. Lawson, *Heaven Help Us!*

Everything will be glorified, even nature itself. And that seems to me to be the biblical teaching about the eternal state: that what we call heaven is life in this perfect world as God intended humanity to live it. When he put Adam in Paradise at the beginning, Adam fell, and all fell with him, but men and women are meant to live in the body, and will live in a glorified body in a glorified world, and God will be with them.[544]

Martyn Lloyd-Jones, *Great Doctrines of the Bible*

The hope which these teachings of Paul conjures up is thus not an uncertain hope. The believer does not hope against hope. He does not hope against all the odds, or against all the evidence. Such a hope would be hopeless. Rather, what is hoped for, union with Christ in glory, is certain. It is guaranteed by the eternal purpose of God, and by the resurrection and glorification of Christ in time. Why then is it *hope*? Simply because what is hoped for is future. . . . The believer rejoices in hope of the glory of God (Romans 5:2).[545]

Paul Helm, *The Last Things*

In this world it doth not yet appear what we shall be. God's people are a hidden people, but when Christ receives His people into heaven, He will touch them with the wand of His own love, and change them into the image of His manifested glory. They were poor and wretched, but what a transformation! They were stained with sin, but one touch of His finger, and they are bright as the sun, and clear as crystal.[546]

Charles Spurgeon, *Morning and Evening*

Most of us think of heaven as a state of alleviation—the final taking away of our burdens and sorrows. God did not design heaven to be a mere negative (a negation of our earthly problems) but to be rather a positive state of assumption. In eternity future, we will become fully absorbed in and reflective of unimaginable glory.

Even in our present negativism we would not boast, "I don't have a bad cold right now." We do not brag about negatives. When we "graduate," we will take into eternity future what we have been *becoming*—in our nature, in our attributes, and in our glory. The difference in our being or our nature will not be in kind but in degree. On that magnificent occasion we will take all our accumulated glories into the presence of Christ to share glory with Him forever.[547]

T. W. Hunt and Melana Hunt Monroe, *From Heaven's View*

There is a moving story which comes out of the persecution of the Christians in the third and fourth centuries. One aged saint had spent many years in a dark and gloomy dungeon, bound by a great ball and chain. When the emperor Constantine ascended the throne, thousands of Christians were released from imprisonment, and among them this old man. Desiring to recompense him for his years of misery, the emperor commanded that the ball and chain be weighed and the old man given the equivalent weight in gold. Thus, the greater the weight of his chain, the greater was his reward when release came. But the reality Paul speaks of [in 2 Corinthians 4:17] is even greater than this. He says the weight of glory will be beyond all comparison. The Greek expression is, literally, "abundance upon abundance." It is such an abundance that it constitutes a great "weight." We speak of the "weight of responsibility" not always as a burden but often as a challenge. Here is the great challenge of a weight of glory, offering indescribable opportunity to those for whom it is prepared.[548]

Ray C. Stedman, *Authentic Christianity*

Heaven purifies our daily walk. The holy, sinless environment of Heaven calls us to live by the same standard of personal holiness. The hope of Heaven cleans out our hearts of inbred worldliness and alleviates sinful living. . . . Heaven heals our broken hearts. Paul said that the deepest pains of our wounded hearts are not worthy to be compared with the glories to come (Romans 8:18). How true! The more we gaze into Heaven, the more clearly we understand that our present trials pale in comparison to the glory that awaits us.[549]

Steven J. Lawson, *Heaven Help Us!*

Our glory as lesser kings and queens will serve to magnify his greater glory as the King of kings. We won't absorb and keep the glory given us, but we will reflect it and emanate it toward its proper object: Christ himself. This is evident in the fact that God's worshiping children will "lay their crowns before the throne" (Revelation 4:10).[550]

Randy Alcorn, *Heaven*

God's glory will be the air we breathe, which will make us want to breathe deeper. In the new universe, we'll never be able to travel far enough to leave God's presence. Wherever we go, God will be there. However great the wonders of Heaven, God himself is Heaven's greatest prize.[551]

Randy Alcorn, *50 Days of Heaven*

What will we do for eternity? Eat, drink, and do all to the glory of God.[552]

Randy Alcorn, *Heaven*

As a Christian, the day I die will be the best day I've ever lived. But it won't be the best day I ever *will* live. Resurrection day will be far better. And the first day on the New Earth—that will be one *big* step for mankind, one giant leap for God's glory.[553]

Randy Alcorn, *TouchPoints: Heaven*

God, and Our Relationship with Him

God so loved the world that he gave his one and only Son, that whoever believes in him shall not perish but have eternal life.

JOHN 3:16

Whom have I in heaven but you? And earth has nothing I desire besides you. My flesh and my heart may fail, but God is the strength of my heart and my portion forever.

ASAPH, PSALM 73:25-26

One thing I ask of the LORD, this is what I seek: that I may dwell in the house of the LORD all the days of my life, to gaze upon the beauty of the LORD and to seek him in his temple.

DAVID, PSALM 27:4

Without holiness no one will see the Lord.

HEBREWS 12:14

Blessed are the pure in heart, for they will see God.

JESUS, MATTHEW 5:8

O God, you are my God, earnestly I seek you; my soul thirsts for you, my body longs for you, in a dry and weary land where there is no water.

DAVID, PSALM 63:1

No longer will a man teach his neighbor, or a man his brother, saying, "Know the LORD," because they will all know me, from the least of them to the greatest.

GOD, JEREMIAH 31:34

I will put my dwelling place among you, and I will not abhor you. I will walk among you and be your God, and you will be my people.

GOD, LEVITICUS 26:11-12

My dwelling place will be with them; I will be their God, and they will be my people.

GOD, EZEKIEL 37:27

God has said: "I will live with them and walk among them, and I will be their God, and they will be my people."

PAUL, 2 CORINTHIANS 6:16

I heard a loud voice from the throne saying, "Behold, the dwelling place of God is with man. He will dwell with them, and they will be his people, and God himself will be with them as their God. . . . They will see his face, and his name will be on their foreheads."

JOHN, REVELATION 21:3; 22:4, ESV

They feast on the abundance of your house; you give them drink from your river of delights. For with you is the fountain of life.

DAVID, PSALM 36:8-9

To regain her lost power, the church must see Heaven opened and have a transforming vision of God. . . . Not the utilitarian God who is having a run of popularity today, whose chief claim to men's attention is His ability to bring them success in their various undertakings.

. . . The God we must learn to know is the Majesty in the heavens.[554]

A. W. Tozer, *The Knowledge of the Holy*

God himself is the great good which they are brought to the possession and enjoyment of by redemption. He is the highest good, and the sum of all that good which Christ purchased. . . . The redeemed will indeed enjoy other things . . . but that which they shall enjoy in the angels, or each other, or in anything else whatsoever, that will yield them delight and happiness, will be what will be seen of God in them.[555]

Jonathan Edwards, *The Sermons of Jonathan Edwards*

Conversion is like stepping across the chimney piece out of a Looking-Glass world, where everything is an absurd caricature, into the real world God made; and then begins the delicious process of exploring it limitlessly.[556]

Evelyn Waugh

I am going to him whom my soul hath loved, or rather hath loved me with an everlasting love; which is the whole ground of all my consolation. The passage is very irksome and wearisome through strong pain of various sorts which are all issued in an intermitting fever. . . . I am leaving the ship of the church in a storm, but while the great Pilot is in it the loss of a poor under-rower will be inconsiderable. Live and pray and hope and wait patiently and do not despair; the promise stands invincible that he will never leave thee nor forsake thee.[557]

John Owen

The glorified see God's face more clearly because there are no idols to stand between him and them. Our idolatrous love of worldly things is a chief cause of our knowing so little of spiritual things. One cannot fill his life cup from the pools of Earth and yet have room in it for the crystal streams of Heaven. But they have no idols there in Heaven—nothing to occupy the heart, no rival for the Lord Jesus. He reigns supreme within their spirits, and therefore they see his face.[558]

Charles Spurgeon, "The Heaven of Heaven," Sermon 824

[The follower of Jesus] desires to be nearer perfection, and more like those who are in heaven. And this is one reason why he longs to be in heaven, that he may be perfectly holy. And the great principle which leads him thus to struggle, is love. It is not only fear; but it is love to God, and love to Christ, and love to holiness. Love is a holy fire within him, and, like any other flame which is in a degree pent up, it will and does struggle for liberty; and this its struggling is the struggle for holiness.[559]

Jonathan Edwards, *Heaven: A World of Love*

Man's chief end is to glorify God, and to enjoy him forever.

Westminster Shorter Catechism

The kingdom must not be understood as merely the salvation of certain individuals or even as the reign of God in the hearts of his people; it means nothing less than the reign of God over his entire created universe. . . . The kingdom is not man's upward climb to perfection but God's breaking into human history to establish his reign and to advance his purposes.[560]

Anthony Hoekema, *The Bible and the Future*

If the goodness, beauty, and wonder of creatures are so delightful to the human mind, the fountainhead of God's own goodness (compared with the trickles of goodness found in creatures) will draw excited human minds entirely to itself.[561]

Thomas Aquinas, *Summa contra Gentiles*

When the Bible defines eternal life, it is not in terms of location or duration but in terms of relationship with God: "This is eternal life, that they may know Thee, the only true God, and Jesus Christ whom Thou hast sent" (John 17:3).[562]

Daniel Brown, *What the Bible Reveals about Heaven*

It is not a smooth and easy way, neither will your weather be fair and pleasant; but whosoever hath seen the invisible God and the fair City, makes no reckoning of losses or crosses.[563]

Samuel Rutherford, *Letters of Samuel Rutherford*

It is the presence of God that gives bliss to moral creatures and the absence of God that brings everlasting woe to moral creatures.[564]

A. W. Tozer, *The Attributes of God*

God is the highest good of the reasonable creature, and the enjoyment of him is the only happiness with which our souls can be satisfied. To go to heaven fully to enjoy God, is infinitely better than the most pleasant accommodations here. Fathers and mothers, husbands, wives, children, or the company of earthly friends, are but shadows. But the enjoyment of God is the substance. These are but scattered beams, but God is the sun. These are but streams, but God is the fountain. These are but drops, but God is the ocean.[565]

Jonathan Edwards, "The Christian Pilgrim"

We may ignore, but we can nowhere evade, the presence of God. The world is crowded with Him. He walks everywhere, incognito.[566]

C. S. Lewis, *Letters to Malcolm*

The saints in heaven love God for His own sake, and each other for God's sake, and for the sake of the relation that they have to Him, and the image of God that is upon them. All their love is pure and holy.[567]

Jonathan Edwards, *Heaven: A World of Love*

How can we preserve both free will and sinlessness in Heaven? . . . God is our model and solution: we solve this pseudo problem in the same way God does. He is both free and sinless.

. . . We will be free to be the true selves God designed us to be, free to be determined by God. This determination does not remove our freedom but *is* our freedom.[568]

Peter Kreeft, *Everything You Ever Wanted to Know about Heaven*

All Heaven—angels and saints alike—fall down like cut timber before God in utter humility and submission. . . . They are knocked flat on their faces by His regal splendor. . . . Any time someone is in God's presence, whether on earth or in Heaven, they *always* react this way. Why? They've seen the glory of God, that's why![569]

Steven J. Lawson, *Heaven Help Us!*

More important than all the physical beauty of the heavenly city, more important than the fellowship we will enjoy eternally with all God's people from all nations and all periods in history, more important than our freedom from pain and sorrow and physical suffering, and more important than our reigning over God's kingdom—more important by far than any of these will be the fact that we will be in the presence of God and enjoying unhindered fellowship with him.[570]

Wayne Grudem, *Systematic Theology*

God is a God of inestimable beauty and glory. . . . A God of precise order, structure, and majesty. A God of accessibility and openness. . . . A God of unimaginable . . . grandeur and lavishness. . . . We can tell what God is like simply by walking through His house.[571]

Steven J. Lawson, *Heaven Help Us!*

All our inferiorities, complexes, and painful memories will be erased when God Himself wipes the tears from our eyes. Any action of God is total; imagine *God* cleaning your tear-stained face! We repeat: if God does anything, how "done" is it?[572]

T. W. Hunt and Melana Hunt Monroe, *From Heaven's View*

In the Bible God is not an afterthought, a personification perhaps of an existent physical reality. At least the first verse of Genesis guards against all possible errors; if "God in the beginning created the Heaven" God cannot have emerged from Heaven. An equally unacceptable notion is also destroyed by the preamble of creation: the God of Heaven is not confined to Heaven, as if he were only there but nowhere else. The God who created Heaven is also the God who created Earth and who performs his works in every part of the universe. The primary relationship between God and Heaven, therefore, is that of Creator and Creation, of Maker and Work. . . . God is the subject and Heaven the object in creation; thus God is "God of Heaven" because Heaven is God's Heaven, and not because he is Heaven's god. Therefore he is essentially known and worshipped as "one above the Heavens."[573]

Ulrich Simon, *Heaven in the Christian Tradition*

We will constantly be more amazed with God, more in love with God, and thus ever more relishing his presence and our relationship with him. Our experience of God will never reach its consummation. We will never finally arrive, as if upon reaching a peak we discover there is nothing beyond. Our experience of God will never become stale. It will deepen and develop, intensify and amplify, unfold and increase, broaden and balloon.[574]

Sam Storms, "Heaven: The Eternal Increase of Joy"

God's throne, God's river, God's tree, God's service, God's face, God's seal, God's reign: such are the features of the life of the people of God in the coming Holy City. . . . It is life totally centered on God. That is the deepest and most glorious prospect imaginable, for there is no reality comparable to the triune God, the ever-blessed Father. . . .
In the end we were made by God and made for him, and in knowing him to ever-deepening degree lies the realization of all our dreams and desires. To that heaven will introduce us, and upon that limitless journey it will set our first steps. The return of the Lord, and the dawning of heaven, is where that journey will begin.[575]

Bruce Milne, *The Message of Heaven and Hell*

The reason why we have no ease of heart or soul [is that] we are seeking our rest in trivial things which cannot satisfy, and not seeking to know God, almighty, all-wise, all-good. . . . We shall never cease wanting and longing until we possess Him in fullness and joy. Then we shall have no further wants. Meanwhile His will is that we go on knowing and loving until we are perfected in heaven. . . . The more clearly the soul sees the blessed face by grace and love, the more it longs to see it in its fullness.[576]

Julian of Norwich, *Revelations of Divine Love*

Abraham, Isaac, and Jacob have long been enjoying happiness, and shall enjoy it throughout eternity. . . . God is not the God of the short-lived, who are so speedily dead; but he is the living God of an immortal race, whose present is but a dark passage into a bright future which can never end.[577]

Charles Spurgeon, "Departed Saints Yet Living," Sermon 1863

How great shall be that felicity, which shall be tainted with no evil, which shall lack no good, and which shall afford leisure for the praises of God, who shall be all in all! . . . True peace shall be there, where no one shall suffer opposition either from himself or any other. God Himself, who is the Author of virtue, shall there be its reward; for, as there is nothing greater or better, He has promised Himself. What else was meant by His word through the prophet, "I will be your God, and ye shall be my people," than, I shall be their satisfaction, I shall be all that men honorably desire,—life, and health, and nourishment, and plenty, and glory, and honor, and peace, and all good things? This, too, is the right interpretation of the saying of the apostle, "That God may be all in all." He shall be the end of our desires who shall be seen without end, loved without cloy, praised without weariness. This outgoing of affection, this employment, shall certainly be, like eternal life itself, common to all.[578]

Augustine, *The City of God*

God is the fountain of love, as the sun is the fountain of light. And therefore the glorious presence of God in heaven, fills heaven with love, as the sun, placed in the midst of the visible heavens in a clear day, fills the world with light. . . . He is a full and over-flowing, an inexhaustible fountain of love. And in that He is an unchangeable and eternal being, He is an unchangeable and eternal fountain of love. . . . And there this glorious fountain forever flows forth in streams, yea, in rivers of love and delight, and these rivers swell, as it were, to an ocean of love, in which the souls of the ransomed may bathe with the sweetest enjoyment, and their hearts, as it were, be deluged with love, and that forever![579]

Jonathan Edwards, *Heaven: A World of Love*

God will be so known by us, and shall be so much before us, that we shall see Him by the spirit in ourselves, in one another, in Himself, in the new heavens and the new earth, in every created thing which shall then exist; and also by the body we shall see Him in every body which the keen vision of the eye of the spiritual body shall reach.[580]

Augustine, *The City of God*

In Heaven people don't *try* to listen to God or even *try* to do what is right. All being is a natural spontaneous connection to God from within our Heart.

In Heaven we choose not to have an alternative to God.[581]

Drake Whitchurch, *Waking from Earth*

A sense of need continues to be a feature of the relationship with God in heaven. This need is not the need for forgiveness or deliverance from the power of sin, as here on earth. Rather, it is a need fostered by our new closeness to God, and with that our new capacity to desire him. . . . Heaven will both satisfy and dissatisfy us. . . . Having found God, or, better, having been at last so overwhelmingly found by him, we will yearn for him as we never have before. To know God and to thirst to know him more and more is the paradox of heaven.[582]

Bruce Milne, *The Message of Heaven and Hell*

It is one of the heaviest trials of a true Christian upon earth that he meets so few people who are entirely of one mind with him about religion. How often in society he finds himself obliged to hold his tongue and say nothing, and to hear and see many things which make his heart ache, and send him back to his own home heavy and depressed!

It is a rare privilege to meet two or three occasionally to whom he can open his heart, and with whom he can speak freely, without fear of giving offence or being misunderstood.

But there will be an end of this stage of things in the kingdom of heaven. Those who are saved will find none there who have not been led by the same Spirit, and gone through the same experience as themselves.

There will not be a man or woman there who has not felt deeply the burden of sin, mourned over it, confessed it, fought with it, and tried to crucify it.

There will not be man or woman there who has not fled to Christ by faith, cast the whole weight of their soul upon Him, and rejoiced in Him as their Redeemer.

There will not be a man or woman there who has not delighted in the Word of God, poured out their soul in prayer at the throne of grace, and striven to live a holy life.[583]

J. C. Ryle, *Heaven*

To see the face of God, to look into his eyes without shame or trace of fear, is the ultimate height of redemption. The invitation of the writer to the Hebrews on the basis of Christ's perfect sacrifice, "Let us draw near to God . . ." (Hebrews 10:22), finds here its final realization. . . . That seeing of the face of God to which the psalmists had aspired (Psalms 11:7; 27:4; 42:2) and of which the prophets had dreamed (Isaiah 52:8; 60:2; Zechariah 9:14) is now realized. We will live, at last, *coram Deo*, "before the face of God," as Luther put it.

Helen Keller, after a lifetime of blindness, was once asked what she would do if, for just one day, the power of sight were restored to her. She replied, "I should call to me all my dear friends and look long into their faces." What a prospect for every child of God, to be called into the presence of the dearest Friend of our lives, whom we have here known by faith and not by sight, and there to look, and look, for ever.[584]

Bruce Milne, *The Message of Heaven and Hell*

The text says they "shall see his face"; by which I understand two things: first, that they shall literally and physically, with their risen bodies, actually look into the face of Jesus; and secondly, that spiritually their mental faculties shall be enlarged, so that they shall be enabled to look into the very heart, and soul, and character of Christ, so as to understand him, his work, his love, his all in all, as they never understood him before.

They shall literally, I say, see his face, for Christ is no phantom; and in heaven though divine, and therefore spiritual, he is still a man, and therefore material like ourselves. The very flesh and blood that suffered upon Calvary is in heaven; the hand that was pierced with the nail now at this moment grasps the scepter of all worlds; that very head which was bowed down with anguish is now crowned with a royal diadem; and the face that was so marred is the very face which beams resplendent amidst the thrones of heaven. Into that selfsame countenance we shall be permitted to gaze. O what a sight!

We shall see and know even as we are known; and amongst the great things that we shall know will be this greatest of all, that we shall know Christ: we shall know the heights, and depths, and lengths, and breadths of the love of Christ that *exceeds* knowledge.

In the blessed vision the saints see Jesus, and they see him clearly. We may also remark that *they see him always;* for when the text says "They shall see his face," it implies that they never at any time are without the sight. Never for a moment do they unlock their arm from the arm of their Beloved. They are not as we are—sometimes near the throne, and others afar off by backslidings; sometimes hot with love, and others cold with indifference; sometimes bright as seraphs, and others dull as clods—but forever and ever they are in closest association with the Master, for "they shall see his face." They surely see his face the more clearly because all the clouds of care are gone from them.[585]

Charles Spurgeon, "The Heaven of Heaven," Sermon 824

Some of you while sitting here to-day have been trying to lift up your minds to heavenly contemplation, but you cannot; the business has gone so wrong this week; the children have vexed you so much; sickness has been in the house so sorely; you yourself feel in your body quite out of order for devotion—these enemies break your peace.

Now they are vexed by none of these things in heaven, and therefore they can see their Master's face. They are not cumbered with Martha's cares; they still occupy Mary's seat at his feet. When shall you and I have laid aside the farm, and the merchandise, and the marrying, and the burying, which come so fast upon each other's heels, and when shall we be forever with the Lord. . . .

Life is but a moment: how short it will appear in eternity. Even here hope perceives it to be brief; and though impatience counts it long, yet faith corrects her, and reminds her that one hour with God will make the longest life to seem but a point of time, a mere nothing, a watch in the night, a thing that was and was not, that has come and gone.[586]

Charles Spurgeon, "The Heaven of Heaven," Sermon 824

Without question, the most marvelous thing of all about heaven—heaven's supreme delight—will be unbroken fellowship with God Himself.

The closer we draw to the Lord Jesus and the more we set our hearts and minds on heavenly glories above, the better prepared we shall be for heaven's perfection. Fellowship won't mean sitting at the feet of Jesus and fighting back boredom while everyone else is enraptured. No. Fellowship will be the best of what earthly friendship merely hinted at.

. . . Heaven's Wedding Supper of the Lamb will be the perfect party. The Father has been sending out invitations and people have been RSVP-ing through the ages. Jesus has gone ahead to hang the streamers, prepare the feast, and make our mansion ready. And like any party, what will make it sweet is the fellowship.

Fellowship with our glorious Savior and with our friends and family.[587]

Joni Eareckson Tada, *Heaven: Your Real Home*

The joy of heavenly love shall never be interrupted or trifled by jealousy. Heavenly lovers will have no doubt of the love of each other. They shall have no fear that the declarations and professions of love are hypocritical; but shall be perfectly satisfied of the sincerity and strength of each other's affection, as much as if there were a window in every breast, so that everything in the heart could be seen. There shall be no such thing as flattery or insincerity in heaven, but there perfect sincerity shall reign through all in all. Everyone will be just what he seems to be, and will really have all the love that he seems to have. It will not be as in this world, where comparatively few things are what they seem to be, and where professions are often made lightly and without meaning. But there, every expression of love shall come from the bottom of the heart, and all that is professed shall be really and truly felt.

The saints shall know that God loves them, and they shall never doubt the greatness of His love, and they shall have no doubt of the love of all their fellow inhabitants in heaven.[588]

Jonathan Edwards, *Heaven: A World of Love*

Matthew 5:8 says, "Blessed are the pure in heart, for they shall see God." The Greek verb translated "see" *(horao)* speaks of a future continuous reality in an environment where we are continually [seeing] God. Kings of the ancient Orient secluded themselves from their people. To have an audience with a king was a rare privilege. Believers, however, will forever see the King of kings![589]

John MacArthur, *Heaven: Selected Scriptures*

God wants to please you. He is pleased when you are His child, when you're surrendered, when your will is His will and His will is yours, when you are not in rebellion and not seeking your own will. God loves to please His people.

Did you ever see a father bringing gifts to his children? Did you ever see a lover bringing gifts to his bride? He wants to please the people He loves, and the people that love Him. The idea that God must always make you miserable is not a biblical idea at all. Jesus Christ knew God and He suffered from the irritations and persecutions of the world, the bitterness of their polluted hearts. They made it hard for Him. But He was pleased with God and God was pleased with Him. "This is my beloved Son, in whom I am well pleased" (Matthew 3:17). "Well done, thou good and faithful servant" (Matthew 25:21). God can say that now to His people.

God isn't pleased by your being miserable. He will make you miserable if you won't obey, but if you're surrendered and obedient, the goodness of God has so wrought through Jesus Christ that now He wants to please you. And He wants to answer your prayers so you will be happy in Him. . . .

Did you ever stop to think that God is going to be as pleased to have you with Him in heaven as you are to be there?[590]

A. W. Tozer, *The Attributes of God*

We'll worship Jesus as the Almighty and bow to him in reverence, yet we'll never sense his disapproval in Heaven—because we'll never disappoint him. He'll never be unhappy with us. We'll be able to relax fully—the other shoe will never drop. No skeletons will fall out of our closets. Christ bore every one of our sins. He paid the ultimate price so we would be forever free from sin—and the fear of sin.

All barriers between us and him will be gone forever. He will be our best friend there.[591]

Randy Alcorn, *We Shall See God*

God and Satan are not equal opposites. Likewise, Hell is not Heaven's equal opposite. Just as God has no equal as a person, Heaven has no equal as a place.[592]

Randy Alcorn, *Heaven*

If you had the opportunity to spend the evening with any person who's ever lived, whom would you choose? . . .

Is Jesus the first person you would choose? Who is more beautiful, talented, knowledgeable, fascinating, and interesting than he?

The good news is, *he chose you*. If you're a Christian, you'll be with him for eternity.[593]

Randy Alcorn, *Heaven*

God isn't displeased when we enjoy a good meal, marital sex, a football game, a cozy fire, or a good book. He's not up in Heaven frowning at us and saying, "Stop it—you should only find joy in me." This would be as foreign to God's nature as our heavenly Father as it would be to mine as an earthly father if I gave my daughters a Christmas gift and started pouting because they enjoyed it too much. No, I gave the gift to bring joy to them and to me—if they didn't take pleasure in it, I'd be disappointed. Their pleasure in my gift to them draws them closer to me. I am *delighted* that they enjoy the gift.[594]

Randy Alcorn, *Heaven*

Might we walk with Jesus (not just spiritually, but also physically) while millions of others are also walking with him? Might we not be able to touch his hand or embrace him or spend a long afternoon privately conversing with him—not just with his spirit, but his whole person?

It may defy our logic, but God is capable of doing far more than we imagine. Being with Christ is the very heart of Heaven, so we should be confident that we will have unhindered access to him.[595]

Randy Alcorn, *Heaven*

The King stepped from the great city, just outside the gate, and put his hand on my shoulder. I was aware of no one and nothing but him. I saw before me an aged, weathered King, thoughtful guardian of an empire. But I also saw a virile Warrior-Prince primed for battle, eager to mount his steed and march in conquest. His eyes were keen as sharpened swords yet deep as wells, full of the memories of the old and the dreams of the young.[596]

Nick Seagrave, in *Edge of Eternity*, by Randy Alcorn

We may imagine we want a thousand different things, but God is the one we really long for. His presence brings satisfaction; his absence brings thirst and longing. *Our longing for Heaven is a longing for God*—a longing that involves not only our inner beings, but our bodies as well. Being with God is the heart and soul of Heaven. Every other heavenly pleasure will derive from and be secondary to his presence. God's greatest gift to us is, and always will be, himself.[597]

Randy Alcorn, *Heaven*

Going to Heaven without God would be like a bride going on her honeymoon without her groom. A Heaven without God would be like a palace without a king. If there's no king, there's no palace. If there's no God, there's no Heaven.[598]

Randy Alcorn, *Heaven*

Have you known people who couldn't be boring if they tried? Some people are just fascinating. It seems I could listen to them forever. But not really. Eventually, I'd feel as if I'd gotten enough. But we can never get enough of God. There's no end to what he knows, no end to what he can do, no end to who he is. He is mesmerizing to the depths of his being, and those depths will never be exhausted. No wonder those in Heaven always redirect their eyes to him—they don't want to miss anything.[599]

Randy Alcorn, *Heaven*

Heaven's Saints Seeing Events on Earth

"I tell you the truth, if anyone keeps my word, he will never see death." At this the Jews exclaimed, "Now we know that you are demon-possessed! Abraham died and so did the prophets, yet you say that if anyone keeps your word, he will never taste death. Are you greater than our father Abraham? He died, and so did the prophets. Who do you think you are?" . . . "Your father Abraham rejoiced at the thought of seeing my day; he saw it and was glad." "You are not yet fifty years old," the Jews said to him, "and you have seen Abraham!" "I tell you the truth," Jesus answered, "before Abraham was born, I am!"

JOHN 8:51-53, 56-58

There is rejoicing in the presence of the angels of God over one sinner who repents.

JESUS, LUKE 15:10

Brothers, we do not want you to be ignorant about those who fall asleep, or to grieve like the rest of men, who have no hope.

PAUL, 1 THESSALONIANS 4:13

When [the Lamb] opened the fifth seal, I saw under the altar the souls of those who had been slain because of the word of God and the testimony they had maintained. They called out in a loud voice, "How long, Sovereign Lord, holy and true, until you judge the inhabitants of the earth and avenge our blood?" Then each of them was given a white robe, and they were told to wait a little longer, until the number of their fellow servants and brothers who were to be killed as they had been was completed.

JOHN, REVELATION 6:9-11

Since we are surrounded by such a great cloud of witnesses, let us throw off everything that hinders and the sin that so easily entangles, and let us run with perseverance the race marked out for us. Let us fix our eyes on Jesus, the author and perfecter of our faith, who for the joy set before him he endured the cross, scorning its shame, and sat down at the right hand of the throne of God.

HEBREWS 12:1-2

When Moses and Elijah appeared with our Lord Jesus on the Mount of Transfiguration, it soon became evident that *they* had been watching developments on earth and were able to talk familiarly about them. Is not the same inferable of Christians who are now yonder? Though they are lost to our sight, are we lost to *theirs*?

"For it seems to me that God has put us apostles on display at the end of the procession, like men condemned to die in the arena. We have been made a spectacle to the whole universe, to angels as well as men" (1 Corinthians 4:9, NIV).

That word *spectacle* in the Greek is *theatron*, a place for public shows, a theater for the performance of drama before spectators. It is an arresting figure. Perhaps the common saying, "All the world's a stage," is truer than many think. Paul says that he and his fellow-apostles were like actors on a theater stage, and the spectators were not only men here on earth, but angels and other realms.

. . . If angels and others in those non-earthly spheres are witnesses of what goes on here, are not our departed Christian loved ones observers also?

How long did it take Moses and Elijah to travel from wherever they were in the unseen realm to join our Lord on that mountain summit? Perhaps the heaven, or the part of it, where our translated Christian brethren are is not as far from this planet as we have traditionally assumed. I think it should be both challenging and comforting to us that those who have gone *there* still see us who are left *here*.

. . . Like all other created beings, they are finite and therefore can be in only one place at any given instant. If they are *there*, in the heavenly paradise, they cannot be simultaneously *here* in the vicinity of earth. Nevertheless, there certainly is *movement* to and from in that spirit-realm. Scripture makes repeatedly clear that the sinless *angels* have often come from there to here with communications for men. May it not be, also, that the indefinable sphere of holy rest where the departed saints are reaches nearer to this old earth (as before suggested) than we have hitherto thought?[600]

J. Sidlow Baxter, *The Other Side of Death*

The martyrs in Heaven know that God hasn't yet brought judgment on their persecutors (Revelation 6:9-11). This suggests the inhabitants of Paradise can see what's happening on Earth, at least to some extent. In Revelation 18:20, when Babylon is brought down, an angel points to events happening on Earth and says, "Rejoice over her, O heaven! Rejoice, saints and apostles and prophets! God has judged her for the way she treated you." That the angel specifically addresses people living in Heaven indicates that they are aware of what's happening on Earth.

Further, there is "the roar of a great multitude in heaven shouting: 'Hallelujah!'" and praising God for specific events of judgment that have just taken place on Earth (Revelation 19:1-5). Again, the saints in Heaven are clearly observing what is happening.[601]

Randy Alcorn, *50 Days of Heaven*

Because Heaven's saints will return with Christ to set up his Kingdom on Earth (Revelation 19:11-14), it's hard to imagine that they would be ignorant of the culmination of human history. The depiction of saints in Heaven as blissfully unaware of what is happening on Earth seems inconceivable. After all, God and his angels (and the saints themselves) are about to return for the ultimate battle in the history of the universe, after which Christ will be crowned King. People on Earth may be oblivious to Heaven, but people in Heaven are *not* oblivious to Earth.

When King Saul wrongly appealed to the witch of Endor to call the prophet Samuel back from the afterlife, the medium was terrified when God actually sent him. But Samuel remembered what Saul had done before Samuel died, and he was aware of what had happened since (1 Samuel 28:3-8, 16-19). Though God could have briefed Samuel on all this, it seems likely the prophet knew these things simply because those in Heaven are aware of what happens on Earth.

. . . Christ said, "There is rejoicing in the presence of the angels of God over one sinner who repents" (Luke 15:10). Notice it does not speak of rejoicing *by* the angels but *in the presence* of angels. Who is doing this rejoicing in Heaven? Logically, it would include God, but also the saints in Heaven, who would deeply appreciate the wonder of human conversion—especially the conversion of those they knew and loved on Earth.

If people in Heaven rejoice over conversions on Earth, then obviously *they must be aware of what is happening on Earth*—and not just generally, but specifically, down to the details of individuals coming to faith in Christ.[602]

Randy Alcorn, *50 Days of Heaven*

Many assume that people in Heaven must not be aware of anything on Earth or else they wouldn't be happy. But people in Heaven are not frail beings whose joy can be preserved only by shielding them from what's really going on in the universe!

Happiness in Heaven is not based on ignorance, but on perspective. Those in the presence of Christ will share God's perspective. God is full of joy, despite his awareness of what's happening on Earth, and despite his displeasure with certain things on Earth. Surely God's happiness is the prevailing mood of Heaven. We should not assume that happiness in Heaven is contingent upon ignorance concerning Earth![603]

Randy Alcorn, *50 Days of Heaven*

Hell

The Son of Man will send out his angels, and they
will weed out of his kingdom everything that causes
sin and all who do evil. They will throw them into the
fiery furnace. . . . Then the righteous will shine like
the sun in the kingdom of their Father.

JESUS, MATTHEW 13:41-43

Woe to you who are well fed now, for you will go
hungry. Woe to you who laugh now, for you will
mourn and weep.

JESUS, LUKE 6:25

What good is it for a man to gain the whole world,
yet forfeit his soul? Or what can a man give in
exchange for his soul?

JESUS, MARK 8:36-37

Depart from me, you who are cursed, into the eternal fire prepared for the devil and his angels.

JESUS, MATTHEW 25:41

Enter through the narrow gate. For wide is the gate and broad is the road that leads to destruction, and many enter through it. But small is the gate and narrow the road that leads to life, and only a few find it.

JESUS, MATTHEW 7:13-14

He will come with his mighty angels, in flaming fire, bringing judgment on those who don't know God and on those who refuse to obey the Good News of our Lord Jesus. They will be punished with eternal destruction, forever separated from the Lord and from his glorious power.

PAUL, 2 THESSALONIANS 1:7-9, NLT

Who then is the faithful and wise servant, whom the master has put in charge of the servants in his household to give them their food at the proper time? It will be good for that servant whose master finds him doing so when he returns. I tell you the truth, he will put him in charge of all his possessions. But suppose that servant is wicked and says to himself, "My master is staying away a long time," and he then begins to beat his fellow servants and to eat and drink with drunkards. The master of that servant will come on a day when he does not expect him and at an hour he is not aware of. He will cut him to pieces and assign him a place with the hypocrites, where there will be weeping and gnashing of teeth.

JESUS, MATTHEW 24:45-51

I am the way and the truth and the life. No one comes to the Father except through me.

JESUS, JOHN 14:6

They will be punished with everlasting destruction and shut out from the presence of the Lord and from the majesty of his power.

PAUL, 2 THESSALONIANS 1:9

The sinners in Zion are terrified; trembling grips the godless: "Who of us can dwell with the consuming fire? Who of us can dwell with everlasting burning?"

ISAIAH 33:14

It is better for you to enter the kingdom of God with one eye than with two eyes to be thrown into hell, where "their worm does not die and the fire is not quenched."

JESUS, MARK 9:47-48, ESV

I tell you, many will come from east and west and recline at table with Abraham, Isaac, and Jacob in the kingdom of heaven, while the sons of the kingdom will be thrown into the outer darkness. In that place there will be weeping and gnashing of teeth.

JESUS, MATTHEW 8:11-12, ESV

I sat in class as a boy of eighteen and heard Dr. Torrey lecture on the future destiny of unbelievers. . . . He said, "In conclusion, two things are certain. First, the more closely men walk with God and the more devoted they become to His service, the more likely they are to believe this doctrine. Many men tell us they love their fellow men too much to believe this doctrine; but the men who show their love in more practical ways than sentimental protestations about it, the men who show their love for their fellow men as Jesus Christ showed His, by laying down their lives for them, *they believe it, even as Jesus Christ Himself believed it.*

"Second, men who accept a loose doctrine regarding the ultimate penalty of Sin (Restorationism or Universalism or Annihilationism) lose their power for God. They may be very clever at argument and zealous in proselytizing, but they are poor at soul-saving. They are seldom found beseeching men to be reconciled to God. They are more likely to be found trying to upset the faith of those already won by the efforts of others, than winning men who have no faith at all. If you really believe the doctrine of endless, conscious torment of the impenitent, and the doctrine really gets hold of you, you will work as you never worked before for the salvation of the lost. If you in any way abate this doctrine, it will abate your zeal."[604]

R. A. Torrey

I hold gnashing of teeth to be the extremest pain that shall follow an evil conscience; that is, despair; namely, to know that one everlastingly must be separated from God. What hell is, we know not; only this we know, that there is such a sure and certain place.[605]

Martin Luther, *The Familiar Discourses of Dr. Martin Luther*

There are few things stressed more strongly in the Bible than the reality of God's work as Judge.[606]

J. I. Packer, *Knowing God*

God's anger was seen to be not a passion, but a principle—the eternal hatred of wrong, which corresponds with the eternal love of right, and which is only another aspect of love. The magnetic needle swings on its delicate axis; it attracts at one end; it repels at the other.[607]

A. T. Pierson, *Many Infallible Proofs*

The vague and tenuous hope that God is too kind to punish the ungodly has become a deadly opiate for the consciences of millions. It hushes their fears and allows them to practice all pleasant forms of iniquity while death draws every day nearer and the command to repent goes unheeded.[608]

A. W. Tozer, *The Knowledge of the Holy*

Sinner, you have heard us speak of the resurrection of the righteous. To you the word *resurrection* has no music. There is no flash of joy in your spirit when you hear that the dead shall rise again. But, oh, I pray you lend me your ear while I assure you in God's name that you shall rise. Not only shall your soul live—you have perhaps become so brutish that you forget you have a soul—but your body itself shall live.

Those eyes that have been full of lust shall see sights of horror. Those ears which have listened to the temptations of the evil one shall hear the thunders of the Day of Judgment. Those very feet that lead you to the worthless pleasures shall attempt but utterly fail to sustain you when Christ shall sit in judgment.

Don't think that when your body is put into the soil you will be done with it. It has been partner with your soul in sin. It shall share with your soul in punishment. [God] is able to "destroy both soul and body in hell" (Matthew 10:28).[609]

Charles Spurgeon, "The First Resurrection," Sermon 391

May God grant that it may be a place which you shall never see and whose dread you shall never feel. When you die, sinner, flight from Hell becomes impossible. You are lost then, eternally. Oh, while yet you are on praying ground, I pray you, think on your end. Think! Think! This warning may be the last you shall ever hear. . . .

Believe on Christ and you shall be saved. Trust him and all the horrors of the future shall have no power over you. Oh, that today some of you may trust my Master for the first time in your lives. This done, you need not curiously inquire what the future shall be, but you may sit down calmly and say, "Come when it will, my soul is on the Rock of ages. It fears no ill; it fears no tempest; it defies all pain. Come quickly! Come quickly! Even so, come quickly, Lord Jesus."[610]

Charles Spurgeon, "The First Resurrection," Sermon 391

His wrath is not an impetuous and changeable passion, but an eternal and unchangeable principle.[611]

A. T. Pierson, *Many Infallible Proofs*

I am the way into the city of woe.
 I am the way to a forsaken people.
 I am the way to eternal sorrow.
Sacred justice moved my architect.
 I was raised here by divine omnipotence,
 Primordial love and ultimate intelligence.
Only those elements time cannot wear
 Were made before me, and beyond time I stand.
 Abandon all hope ye who enter here.[612]

Dante Alighieri, "The Gate of Hell," *The Inferno*

[In my vision of Hell] I felt a fire within my soul the nature of which I am utterly incapable of describing. My bodily sufferings were so intolerable that, though in my life I have endured the severest sufferings . . . none of them is of the smallest account by comparison . . . to say nothing of the knowledge that they would be endless and never-ceasing. And even these are nothing by comparison with the agony of my soul . . . accompanied by such hopeless and distressing misery, that I cannot too forcibly describe it. To say that it is as if the soul were continually being torn from the body is very little, for that would mean that one's life was being taken by another; whereas in this case it is the soul itself that is tearing itself to pieces. . . . I felt, I think, as if I were being both burned and dismembered; and I repeat that that interior fire and despair are the worst things of all.

In that pestilential spot, where I was quite powerless to hope for comfort, it was impossible to sit or lie, for there was no room to do so. I had been put in this place which looked like a hole in the wall, and those very walls, so terrible to the sight, bore down upon me and completely stifled me. There was no light and everything was in the blackest darkness. . . . Although there was no light, it was possible to see everything the sight of which can cause affliction. . . . I was terrified by all this, and, though it happened nearly six years ago, I still am as I write: even as I sit here, fear seems to be depriving my body of its natural warmth. I . . . give thanks to the Lord, Who, as I now believe, has delivered me from such terrible and never-ending torments.[613]

Teresa of Avila, *The Life of Teresa of Jesus*

It doesn't matter how small the sins are provided that their cumulative effect is to edge the man away from the Light and out into the Nothing. Murder is no better than cards if cards can do the trick. Indeed the safest road to Hell is the gradual one—the gentle slope, soft underfoot, without sudden turnings, without milestones, without signposts.[614]

The demon Wormwood, in *The Screwtape Letters*, by C. S. Lewis

Oh the dreadful state of sinful creatures, who continue in such obstinacy, who waste away the means of grace and the seasons of hope, week after week, and month after month, till the day of grace and hope is for ever at an end with them! Hopeless creatures! Under the power and the plague of sin, under the wrath and curse, of a God, under the eternal displeasure of Jesus who was once the minister of his Father's love; and they must abide under all this wretchedness through a long eternity, and in the land of everlasting despair.[615]

Isaac Watts, *The World to Come*

If there be one thing in hell worse than another, it will be seeing the saints in heaven. Oh, to think of seeing my mother in heaven while

I am cast out! Oh, sinner, to see thy brother in heaven—he who was rocked in the selfsame cradle . . . yet thou art cast out. And, husband, there is your wife in heaven, and you are among the damned. And do you see your father? Your child is before the throne, and you—accursed of God and of man—are in hell. Oh, the hell of hells will be to see our friends in heaven, and ourselves lost.

Charles Spurgeon, "The Sin of Unbelief," Sermon 3

The hell of hells will be the thought that it is forever. You will look up on the throne of God, and it shall be written, "Forever!" When the damned jingle the burning irons of their torments, they shall say, "Forever!" When they howl, echo cries, "Forever!"

Charles Spurgeon, "Paul's First Prayer," Sermon 16

Think lightly of hell, and you will think lightly of the cross. Think little of the sufferings of lost souls, and you will soon think little of the Savior who delivers you from them.

Charles Spurgeon, "Future Punishment a Fearful Thing," Sermon 682

I greatly fear that the denial of the eternity of future punishment is one wave of an incoming sea of infidelity. Deny the awful character of the desert of sin, and the substitutionary work of Christ will soon follow. Indeed we have living proofs of this at this day, and we shall see many more before long. The new teaching eats as doth a canker. It speaks fair, but in its heart there is a deadly enmity to the gospel itself, and the sooner this is seen to be so the better for the church of God.

Charles Spurgeon, "Purging Out the Leaven," Sermon 965

If we could hear the wailings of the pit for a moment, we should earnestly entreat that we might never hear them again.

Charles Spurgeon, "Compassion for Souls," Sermon 974

I can personally bear witness to the way in which the solemn Word of the Lord makes my whole soul to tremble to its center. . . . O Beloved, I am not sorry that you tremble before the refining fire of sacred Truth. I should be much distressed if you did not.

God's searching Word makes man tremble—so does the Word when it is in the form of a threat. Believe me, dear friends, the Word of God about the doom of sinners is very dreadful. Hence, there are some that try to pare them down and cut the solemn meaning out of them. And then they say, "I could not rest comfortably if I believed the orthodox doctrine about the ruin of man." Most true, but what right have we to rest comfortably?

What grounds or reason can there be why we ever should have a comfortable thought with regard to the doom of those who refuse the Savior? If with that dreadful doom before us which Holy Scripture threatens to ungodly men we do grow far too indifferent, to what will the Church of God come when it has torn out the doctrine from the Bible and given it up?

He who seeks comfort at the expense of Truth will be a fool for his pains. Blessed in the end will that man be who can endure the Word of the Lord, when it is all thunder and flaming fire—and does not rebel against it, but bows before it.

If it makes you tremble, it was meant to make you tremble. If a sermon concerning the future punishment of sin does not make the hearer tremble, it is clear that it is not of God. For Hell is not a thing to talk about without trembling. My inmost desire is to feel more and more the overwhelming power of Jehovah's judgment against sin so that I may preach with all the deeper solemnity the danger of the impenitent and with tears and trembling may beseech them to be reconciled.

Charles Spurgeon, "Trembling at the Word of the Lord," Sermon 2071

Let us never arraign God before our bar. It is a horrible thing for any man ever to say, "Well, if God acts like that, I do not see the justice of it." How dare you even hint that the Judge of all the earth is not just? He hath said, "I will have mercy on whom I will have mercy, and I will have compassion on whom I will have compassion;" so do not you say, "It cannot be so." Is it so written in God's Word? Then it is so just because it is there.

If God has said anything, it is not right for you to ask for an explanation of his reason for saying it, or to summon him to your judgment-seat. What impertinence is this! He must always do right; he cannot do wrong.

Some have staggered over the doctrine of eternal punishment, because they could not see how that could be consistent with God's goodness. I have only one question to ask concerning that: Does God reveal it in the Scriptures? Then I believe it, and leave to him the vindication of his own consistency.

I am sure that he will not inflict a pain upon any creature which that creature does not deserve, that he will never cause any sorrow or misery which is not absolutely necessary, and that he will glorify himself by doing the right, the loving, the kind thing, in the end. If we do not see it to be so, it will be nonetheless so because we are blind.

Charles Spurgeon, "The Way of Wisdom," Sermon 2862

The doctrine of Christ's vicarious atonement logically stands or falls with that of eternal punishment.[616]

William Shedd, *The Doctrine of Endless Punishment*

There seems to be a kind of conspiracy . . . to forget, or to conceal, where the doctrine of hell comes from. The doctrine of hell is not a device of "mediaeval priestcraft" for frightening people into giving money to the church: it is Christ's deliberate judgment on sin. . . . We cannot repudiate Hell without altogether repudiating Christ.[617]

Dorothy Sayers, *Introductory Papers on Dante*

God the Father (who now pleads with mankind to accept the reconciliation that Christ's death secured for all) and God the Son (our appointed Judge, who wept over Jerusalem) will in a final judgment express wrath and administer justice against rebellious humans. God's holy righteousness will hereby be revealed; God will be doing the right thing, vindicating himself at last against all who have defied him. . . . God will judge justly, and all angels, saints, and martyrs will praise him for it. So it seems inescapable that we shall, with them, approve the judgment of persons—rebels—whom we have known and loved.[618]

J. I. Packer, "Hell's Final Enigma"

The New Testament always conceives of this eternal punishment as consisting of an agonizing knowledge of one's own ill desert, of God's displeasure, of the good that one has lost, and of the irrevocable fixed state in which one now finds oneself. The doctrine of eternal punishment was taught in the synagogue even before our Lord took it up and enforced it in the Gospels. All the language that strikes terror into our hearts—weeping and gnashing of teeth, outer darkness, the worm, the fire, gehenna, the great gulf fixed—is all directly taken from our Lord's teaching. It is from Jesus Christ that we learn the doctrine of eternal punishment.[619]

J. I. Packer, *Your Father Loves You*

Not one smile from the face of God for ever, not one glimpse of love or mercy in his countenance, not one word of grace from Jesus Christ who was once the chief messenger of the grace of God, not one favourable regard from all the holy saints and angels; but the fire and brimstone burn without end, "and the smoke of this their torment will ascend for ever and ever before the throne of God and the Lamb." Oh—please—none of mine.

Who knows how keen and bitter will be the agonies of an awakened conscience, and the vengeance of provoked God in that world of misery? How will you cry out, "O what a wretch have I been to renounce all the advices of a Compassionate father, when he would have persuaded me to improve the time of youth and health! Alas, I turned a deaf ear to his advice, and now time is lost, and my hopes of mercy for ever perished. How have I treated with ridicule among my vain companions the compassionate and pious counsels of my aged parents who laboured for my salvation? How have I scorned the tender admonitions of a mother, and wasted that time in sinning and sensuality which should have been spent in prayer and devotion? And God turns a deaf ear to my cries now, and is regardless of all my groanings."

This sort of anguish of spirit with loud and cutting complaints would destroy life itself, and these inward terrors would sting their souls to death, if there could be any such thing as dying there. Such sighs and sobs and bitter agonies would break their hearts, and dissolve their being, if the heart could break, or the being could be dissolved: But immortality is their dreadful portion, immortality of sorrows to punish their wicked and willful abuse of time, and that waste of the means of grace they were guilty of in their mortal state.[620]

Isaac Watts, *The World to Come*

In the long run the answer to all those who object to the doctrine of hell is itself a question: "What are you asking God to do?" To wipe out their past sins and, at all costs, to give them a fresh start, smoothing every difficulty and offering every miraculous help? But He has done so, on Calvary. To forgive them? They will not be forgiven. To leave them alone? Alas, I am afraid that is what He does.[621]

C. S. Lewis, *The Problem of Pain*

If God is supremely just, and just in a sense which is recognizable as just by his human creatures, and if hell exists because it is ordained by God, then hell must be just.[622]

Paul Helm, *The Last Things*

Hell is not in the Bible for us to debate it or to reject it. It is there so that we might escape from it! Hence the urgency of needing to "flee from the wrath to come" (Matthew 3:7).[623]

Richard Brooks, *The Doors of Heaven*

If you don't want God, you don't get His heaven.[624]

Tony Evans, *Tony Evans Speaks Out on Heaven and Hell*

Earth, I think, will not be found by anyone to be in the end a very distinct place. I think earth, if chosen instead of Heaven, will turn out to have been, all along, only a region in Hell: and earth, if put second to Heaven, to have been from the beginning a part of Heaven itself.[625]

C. S. Lewis, *The Great Divorce*

Hell is oneself,
Hell is alone, the other figures in it
Merely projections.[626]

T. S. Eliot, *The Cocktail Party*

Which way I fly is Hell; myself am Hell;
And in the lowest deep a lower deep
Still threat'ning to devour me opens wide,
To which the Hell I suffer seems a Heav'n.[627]

John Milton, *Paradise Lost*

I fear my natural tenderness might warp me aside from the rules and the demands of strict justice, and the wise and holy government of the great God.

But as I confine myself almost entirely to the revelation of Scripture in all my searches into the things of revealed religion and Christianity, I am constrained to forget or to lay aside that softness and tenderness of animal nature which might lead me astray, and to follow the unerring dictates of the word of God.

The Scripture frequently, and in the plainest and strongest manner, asserts the everlasting punishment of sinners in hell; and that by all the methods of expression which are used in Scripture to signify, an everlasting continuance.

. . . I must confess here, if it were possible for the great and blessed God any other way to vindicate his own eternal and unchangeable hatred of sin, the inflexible justice of his government, the wisdom of his severe threatenings, and the veracity of his predictions, if it were also possible for him, without this terrible execution, to vindicate the veracity, sincerity, and wisdom of the Prophets and Apostles, and Jesus Christ his Son, the greatest and chiefest of his divine messengers; and then, if the blessed God should at any time, in a consistence with his glorious and incomprehensible perfections, release those wretched creatures from their acute pains and long imprisonment in hell, either with a design of the utter destruction of their beings by annihilation, or to put them into some unknown world, upon a new foot of trial, I think I ought cheerfully and joyfully to accept this appointment of God, for the good of millions of my fellow-creatures, and add my joys and praises to all the song: and triumphs of the heavenly world in the day, of such a divine and glorious release of these prisoners.

But I feel myself under a necessity of confessing, that I am utterly unable to solve these difficulties according to the discoveries of the New Testament, which must be my constant rule of faith, and hope, and expectation, with regard to myself and others. I have read the strongest and best writers on the other side, yet after all my studies I have not been able to find any way how these difficulties may be removed, and how the divine perfections, and the conduct of God in his Word, may be fairly vindicated without the establishment of this doctrine, as awful and formidable as it is.[628]

Isaac Watts, *The World to Come*

If you could think of a prison, if you could think of a place where all hope and mercy had fled, then you would be thinking of hell. If you could think of a place where all moral wisdom was absent, all holiness gone and all goodness absent, where there was no justice, mercy, love, kindness, grace, tenderness or charity, but only multiplied monstrous fullness of unholiness, moral folly, hate, cruelty and injustice—then you would think of hell.[629]

A. W. Tozer, *The Attributes of God*

People worry about whether there is fire in hell or not. I have no reason not to believe it; what the Bible says I take as the truth. I would not hesitate to refer to the fires of hell, for the Scripture talks about the "lake of fire" (Revelation 20:14-15). But if there were no fire in hell, if hell were a habitable country, it still would be the ugliest country in the universe, the most shockingly deformed place that is known in the creation because there is none of the perfection of beauty. Only God is absolutely perfect.[630]

A. W. Tozer, *The Attributes of God*

John Greenleaf Whittier wrote that the saddest of all human words are "It might have been." In hell, every regret will be eternally remembered.

. . . Worm of hell gnaws away at the life of the condemned person. But the difference is that this gnawing never stops because the life it is gnawing on is never consumed. And the gnawing is highly personalized, "their worm," because each person's level of regret will be unique to that person's life. This is the unending mental torment of hell—the churning of regret over lost opportunities for salvation, poor choices made in life, and the condemnation of others whom the lost person loved. The rich man agonized for his brothers.

. . . Imagine having eternity to remember the things you would give anything to forget.[631]

Tony Evans, *Tony Evans Speaks Out on Heaven and Hell*

Picture an alcoholic who can't get a drink, an addict who can't get a fix, or a greedy person whose greed will never be satisfied, and you have a picture of hell.

Some people think hell will have a purifying effect on sinners, who will realize the error of their ways and become repentant. But I don't see that in the Bible.

The sin nature of those in hell will cry out eternally for fulfillment—only there will be none. The worm will not die.[632]

Tony Evans, *Tony Evans Speaks Out on Heaven and Hell*

The rejection of the idea of everlasting punishment springs not from creation but from rebellion.

. . . The question is not whether Ingersoll or anyone else dislikes, hates, despises, and defies the doctrine of hell but whether God in his Word has revealed it.[633]

William Hendriksen, *The Bible on the Life Hereafter*

The very fires of Hell are the love and joy of God experienced as wrath and torment by the soul that hates the light and its purifying fire.[634]

Peter Kreeft, *Everything You Ever Wanted to Know about Heaven*

Hell is certainly the most unpopular of all Christian doctrines. It scandalizes almost all non-Christians. How shall we judge it? By counting heads? The democracy of truth is, of course, nonsense, both in principle (it is the facts that make an idea true, not the number of people who believe it) and in practice (most great truths were discovered by those who swam against the stream). As a matter of fact, even democracy supports Hell if only we extend the franchise to the dead by tradition.[635]

Peter Kreeft, *Everything You Ever Wanted to Know about Heaven*

Dishonesty is often used to justify the modernist's disbelief in Hell. "It inspires servile fear rather than genuine love." . . . But even if it does, that does not prove it isn't *true.* "This is a gun pointed at your head" inspires servile fear, but it may be true nevertheless.[636]

Peter Kreeft, *Everything You Ever Wanted to Know about Heaven*

If in a God-created universe "all that is, is good," then either Hell is not, or Hell is good.

Answer: In one sense, Hell is not, as blindness is not. They exist, but only as privations. Darkness is not a thing, like light, but the absence of a thing. The joylessness, purposelessness and meaninglessness of Hell are not positive being, but the absence of joy, purpose, and meaning.

In another sense, Hell is good. . . . God would not tolerate hell unless it were proper, and best, and just, and even consonant with His love. . . . The answer to the question "If God is love how can there be Hell?" is that only because God is love can there be Hell! God's love created the highest creatures, free creatures, creatures who were also creatures of their own destinies, and some of them created Hell.

God did not have to create free creatures. . . . But love plays dangerous games.[637]

Peter Kreeft, *Everything You Ever Wanted to Know about Heaven*

It is true that justice without love is hardness of heart; but love without justice is softness of head. We usually have a "straw man" concept of justice as mere legalism. . . .

If love is reduced to kindness and justice to sameness, of course God could not allow Hell.[638]

Peter Kreeft, *Everything You Ever Wanted to Know about Heaven*

If there is no hell, God is not just. If there is no punishment of sin, heaven is apathetic toward the rapists and pillagers and mass murderers of society. If there is no hell, God is blind toward the victims and has turned his back on those who pray for relief. If there is no wrath toward evil, then God is not love, for love hates that which is evil.[639]

Max Lucado, *When Christ Comes*

Hell is not a place of corruption, a diabolical society, a community out of God's reach. It is where corruption is impeccably punished, punished according to strict justice. In this sense God reigns in hell as he reigns in heaven. Nothing which is not in accordance with strict justice will be permitted to enter there. So that we can be satisfied, at the outset, that whatever happens in hell is just; no-one can or will justifiably complain about hell or the fate of its inhabitants.[640]

Paul Helm, *The Last Things*

Why should any be lost, if God could save all?

. . . Is hell, the endurance of everlasting punishment for sin, in some sense the triumph of evil? Some are ready to assert this, and to argue that since it is inconceivable that evil could triumph in God's universe there cannot be a hell. On such a view hell is the triumph of evil, because evil natures, that is, unregenerated, untransformed human natures, will remain for all time. And so a universe which was, at the beginning, created all-good, will remain for ever less than all good, since it will contain evil people.

. . . If pain *per se* is an evil, then hell is the triumph of evil. But if, on the other hand, hell is a just place, because none suffer there except those who deserve to suffer, and none suffer more, nor less, than they deserve, then hell is not evil.

. . . Far from being an anomaly, or the triumph of evil, hell demonstrates the justice of God in a public, unmistakable way.[641]

Paul Helm, *The Last Things*

Hell is not the result of the petulant temper of a capricious and unstable God, but of his strict and exact justice.

So hell is a place of pain, but not of defiance or resistance. It is not a demonic colony which has gained unilateral independence from God. Because there is full recognition of God's justice, God's character is vindicated, and hence glorified, even by those who in this life have defied him and who suffer for it.[642]

Paul Helm, *The Last Things*

The purpose of the New Testament in emphasizing, as it does, the fact of hell, is not sadistic. Hell is not revealed so that perverted people can gloat over the thought of suffering. Hell is revealed in order to warn men and women. We are told about the wrath to come and urged to flee from it (Matthew 3:7). We are told that there will be no escape if we neglect so great salvation (Hebrews 2:3). Such passages as these show that hell is not a fiction invented by priests to keep the people quiet, but that it is plain fact.[643]

Paul Helm, *The Last Things*

"Mas'r Haley was mighty oneasy, and that he couldn't sit in his cheer no ways, but was a walkin' and stalkin' to the winders and through the porch."

"Sarves him right!" said Aunt Chloe, indignantly. "He'll get wus nor oneasy, one of these days, if he don't mend his ways. *His* master'll be sending for him, and then see how he'll look!"

"He'll go to torment, and no mistake," said little Jake.

"He desarves it!" said Aunt Chloe grimly; "he's broke a many, many, many hearts,—I tell ye all!" she said, stopping with a fork uplifted in her hands; "it's like what Mas'r George reads in Revelations,—souls a callin' under the altar! and a callin' on the Lord for vengeance on sich!—and by and by the Lord he'll hear 'em—so he will!"

Aunt Chloe, who was much revered in the kitchen, was listened to with open mouth; and the dinner being now fairly sent in, the whole kitchen was at leisure to gossip with her, and to listen to her remarks.

"Sich 'll be burnt up forever, and no mistake; won't ther?" said Andy.

"I'd be glad to see it, I'll be boun'," said little Jake. . . .

"Pray for them that 'spitefully use you, the good book says," says Tom.

"Pray for 'em!" said Aunt Chloe; "Lor, it's too tough! I can't pray for 'em."

"It's natur, Chloe, and natur's strong," said Tom, "but the Lord's grace is stronger; besides you oughter think what an awful state a poor crittur's soul's in that'll do them ar things,—you oughter thank God that you an't *like* him, Chloe. I'm sure I'd rather be sold, ten thousand times over, than to have all that ar poor crittur's got to answer for."[644]

Harriet Beecher Stowe, *Uncle Tom's Cabin*

It seems likely that the damned will have a very limited ability to move from place to place, a very limited access to the wide expanse of the universe. In our view they will be very lonely creatures, sharing the loneliness of Satan, the Great Prince of Loneliness. Just what they will be in their own view, in their own minds, we do not know. We can only wonder and wish they had chosen God.[645]

E. J. Fortman, *Everlasting Life after Death*

The one principle of Hell is—"I am my own!"[646]

George MacDonald, "Kingship"

[In hell] sinners go on sinning and receiving the recompense of their sin, refusing, always refusing, to bend the knee.[647]

D. A. Carson, *How Long, O Lord?*

Although God is the misery of hell as he is the joy of heaven, the damned souls contribute to their own misery and not to one another's relief. They have no more friends in hell than they have in heaven. Instead of the damned being comforted in each other's company, it is probable that they will be as coals or brands in the fire that heat and burn one another. . . . Edwards says that so far from other wicked persons being a comfort, they will "greatly augment" each other's misery and torment as they detest, hate, and condemn one another. If, as George Bernard Shaw and others have claimed, all the interesting people will be in hell, they will have no interest in one another except to torture. . . . In hell misery hates company.[648]

John Gerstner, *Jonathan Edwards on Heaven and Hell*

When you look forward, you shall see a long forever, a boundless duration before you, which will swallow up your thoughts, and amaze your soul; and you will absolutely despair of ever having any deliverance, any end, any mitigation, any rest at all; you will know certainly that you must wear out long ages, millions of millions of ages, in wrestling and conflicting with this almighty merciless vengeance; and then you will have so done, when so many ages have actually been spent by you in this manner, you will know that all is

but a point to what remains. . . . For, who knows the power
of God's anger?[649]

Jonathan Edwards, "Sinners in the Hands of an Angry God"

John Blanchard tells of an occasion when Francis Schaeffer was visibly
moved by the thought of hell. In his chalet in Switzerland he was
explaining Scripture to a group of young people. Intelligent and
inquisitive, they admired their teacher's unique ability to relate God's
Word to contemporary culture. Various topics were covered, until
eventually a young man asked, "Dr. Schaeffer, what about those who
have never heard the gospel?" They waited expectantly for the inci-
sively brilliant answer. But Schaeffer did not speak. Instead, he bowed
his head and wept.[650]

Edward Donnelly, *Biblical Teaching on the Doctrines of Heaven and Hell*

In comparison with heaven, hell is like a tiny cavern submerged in
a shoreless sea—an isolated penal dungeon lost in the bottomless
depths of a boundless universe.[651]

E. X. Heatherley, *Our Heavenly Home*

The truth is, that the saints in heaven have no "loved ones" in hell—
or none, at least, who are still esteemed as such. They doubtless have
many *former* friends and relatives there. But since death terminates all
purely temporal relationships, allowing only spiritual bonds to persist,
the problem vanishes when it is considered from the heavenly point
of view.[652]

E. X. Heatherley, *Our Heavenly Home*

Like it or not, the doctrine of hell is a part of the warp and woof of
the Christian message, part of its very fabric. It cannot be cut out
without causing all the remainder to unravel.[653]

Paul Helm, *The Last Things*

The doctrine of hell is an integral part of the Christian faith, and where the general acceptance by a community of the system of Christian belief fades then so will belief in hell.[654]

Paul Helm, *The Last Things*

Little needs to be said about the absurdity of suggesting that the Creator should suffer more than the cumulative sufferings of all of mankind, if there were no hell to save us from. Without hell, there is no need for salvation. Without salvation, there is no need for a sacrifice. And without sacrifice, there is no need for a Savior.[655]

Hank Hanegraaff, *Resurrection*

The whole difficulty of understanding Hell is that the thing to be understood is so nearly Nothing. But ye'll have had experiences . . . it begins with a grumbling mood, and yourself still distinct from it: perhaps criticising it. And yourself, in a dark hour, may will that mood, embrace it. Ye can repent and come out of it again. But there may come a day when you can do that no longer. Then there will be no *you* left to criticise the mood, nor even to enjoy it, but just the grumble itself going on forever like a machine.[656]

The Teacher, in *The Great Divorce*, by C. S. Lewis

People who choose to believe there's no afterlife seem to have something in common with one another. They like to blame the God they claim doesn't exist for banishing them to a hell they claim doesn't exist.

If you knew someone hated you—and perhaps encouraged others to shun you—because of some wrong he imagined you had committed against him, is it likely you would ask him to be your roommate? Suppose he came to you and apologized for casting blame your direction and you forgave him and the two of you became good friends? When you found out he needed to leave his apartment in a few weeks, you'd probably be happy to clean up one of your extra rooms, and hang a new shower curtain in the spare bath to prepare for his arrival.

That's a little like what God has done for us. He's preparing the "forever Heaven"—the New Earth—for those of us who have claimed His work on our behalf; freely forgiving us for treating Him as less than Lord.

Those who still want nothing to do with Him will get what they've spent their life on Earth preparing for: eternity away from His presence.

Doreen Button, personal note

It's long-term results we seek. Tactics count only insofar as they produce the desired impact on Fletcher—reality distortion, moral failure, thoughts and actions displeasing to the Enemy. Whatever sends them to hell, we support. Whatever draws them toward heaven, we oppose.[657]

The demon Foulgrin, in *Lord Foulgrin's Letters*, by Randy Alcorn

In a sense, none of our loved ones will be in Hell—only some whom we *once* loved. Our love for our companions in Heaven will be directly linked to God, the central object of our love. We will see him in them. We will not love those in Hell because when we see Jesus as he is, we will love only—and will only want to love—whoever and whatever pleases and glorifies and reflects him.

What we loved in those who died without Christ was God's beauty we once saw in them. When God forever withdraws from them, I think it's likely they'll no longer bear his image and no longer reflect his beauty. Without God, they'll be stripped of all the qualities we loved. Therefore, paradoxically, they will not truly be the people we loved. I can't prove biblically what I've just stated, but it rings true, even if the thought now seems horrifying.[658]

Randy Alcorn, *TouchPoints: Heaven*

Because God is fair, hell won't be the same for everyone. The severity of punishment will vary with the degree of truth known and the nature and number of sins committed. This concept is foreign to most Christians, but is clearly taught in Scripture (Matthew 11:20-24; Luke 20:45-47; Romans 2:3-5). This is no consolation, however, since the "best" of hell will still be hell—eternal exclusion from the presence of God and the soothing light of his grace.[659]

Randy Alcorn, *Money, Possessions, and Eternity*

As Heaven is an eternal manifestation of God's grace, Hell is an eternal manifestation of God's justice.

Randy Alcorn, unpublished notes

We must not believe Satan's lie that it's unloving to speak to people about Hell. The most basic truth is that there are only two possible destinations after death: Heaven and Hell. Each is just as real and just as eternal as the other. Unless and until we surrender our lives to Jesus Christ, we're headed for Hell. . . . Would we think it unloving if a doctor told us we had a potentially fatal cancer? And would the doctor not tell us if the cancer could be eradicated? Why then do we not tell unsaved people about the cancer of sin and evil and how the inevitable penalty of eternal destruction can be avoided by the atoning sacrifice of Jesus Christ?[660]

Randy Alcorn, *Heaven*

If we understood Hell even the slightest bit, none of us would ever say, "Go to Hell." It's far too easy to go to Hell. It requires no navigational adjustments. We were born with our autopilot set toward Hell. It is nothing to take lightly—Hell is the single greatest tragedy in the universe.[661]

Randy Alcorn, *We Shall See God*

If we understood God's nature and ours, we would be shocked not that some people could go to Hell (where else would sinners go?), but that any would be permitted into Heaven. Unholy as we are, we are disqualified from saying that infinite holiness doesn't demand everlasting punishment. By denying the endlessness of Hell, we minimize Christ's work on the cross.[662]

Randy Alcorn, *Heaven*

Many people imagine that it is civilized, humane, and compassionate to deny the existence of an eternal Hell. But in fact, it is arrogant that we, as creatures, would dare to make such an assumption in opposition to what God the Creator has clearly revealed in His Word.[663]

Randy Alcorn, *We Shall See God*

Hell will be agonizingly dull, small, and insignificant, without company, purpose, or accomplishment. It will not have its own stories; it will merely be a footnote on history, a crack in the pavement. As the new universe moves gloriously onward, Hell and its occupants will exist in utter inactivity and insignificance, an eternal non-life of regret and—perhaps—diminishing personhood.[664]

Randy Alcorn, *Heaven*

Many books deny Hell. Some embrace universalism, the belief that all people will ultimately be saved. Some consider Hell to be the invention of wild-eyed prophets obsessed with wrath. They argue that Christians should take the higher road of Christ's love. But this perspective overlooks a conspicuous reality: *In the Bible, Jesus says more than anyone else about Hell.*[665]

Randy Alcorn, *Heaven*

Those who assume their religious activities will get them to Heaven have a terrible surprise ahead.[666]

Randy Alcorn, *Heaven*

Because God is the source of all good, and Hell is the absence of God, Hell must also be the absence of all good.[667]

Randy Alcorn, *Heaven*

Of this we may be absolutely certain: Hell will have no power over Heaven; none of Hell's misery will ever veto any of Heaven's joy.[668]

Randy Alcorn, *Heaven*

Many believe this life is all there is. Their philosophy? "You go around only once, so grab for whatever you can."

If you're a child of God, you do *not* just go around once on Earth. This one earthly life is not all there is. You get another—one far better and without end. You'll inhabit the New Earth! You'll live with the God you cherish and the people you love as an undying person on an undying Earth. Those who go to Hell are the ones who go around only once here.[669]

Randy Alcorn, *We Shall See God*

[Gregory Lowell, Doc, had departed his body.] He realized in a flash of insight he had been wrong all those years in thinking that life ended with death. He had not ceased to exist. Indeed, the very idea of a person ceasing to exist was suddenly ludicrous. Upon death, people merely relocated from one place to another.

A sickening feeling of foreboding gripped him; he was unprepared for this realm. And it was now too late to prepare.

Doc knew instinctively that whatever lay ahead of him would never end. This truth was self-evident. He felt embarrassed and foolish he had ever thought otherwise.

How could I have been so deceived?

Yet even as he asked the question, he knew he had willingly deceived himself because of how he did not want to live and what he did not want to believe.

What had Finney told him? "The reason you don't want to

believe in a Creator is because then you'd have to believe in a Judge—and you don't want to think you'll be held accountable for how you've lived. But there is, and you will be."

This irritated him before, and it irritated him now. Who was Finney to preach to him?

Doc looked around uneasily, trying to get his bearings. Where were the others? He could see or hear no one. A flood of proud and confident words from the past rushed over him. The party where he said, "I'd rather be in hell with intelligent people than in heaven with a bunch of Christians." The times he'd quoted Mark Twain—"It's heaven for atmosphere and hell for company." His retort to Finney—"I'd rather be anywhere with anyone than to be with a herd of narrow-minded fundamentalists and their narrow-minded God.". . .

"You're a fool," he'd said to Finney. . . . "I didn't ask for anyone to go to the cross. I pay my own way. I don't want your religion; it's a pacifier for fools. And I don't want any part of your God." . . .

"I'd rather be judged a fool by you for the moment, than be judged a fool by God for eternity." Finney's eyes pleaded with him. "Doc, don't say you'd rather pay your own way. You may get your wish. It's called hell. God not being there is what will make it hell."

Doc shivered as the scenario played itself out in his mind. . . . *How could God do this to me? If God was a God of love, he would offer me a way out.*

He would not allow himself to realize God's love had indeed made a way out, and at immense cost to himself. Or to realize this way had been explained to him many times, by one of his best friends and others as well. He had rejected the way. He wanted another way, a way that would not force him to confess to wrongdoing. A way that would compliment him, not accuse him. A way that didn't require him to crawl on his knees like a sniveling beggar. He would find his own way. He always had before.

Yet even as he said this to himself, he sensed the ropes slipping through his hands. Verses of the Bible he had tried to ignore, thrust upon him by Finney, flashed back into his mind. Jesus said, "I am the way, the truth and the life—no man comes to the Father but by me."

No other way. "Neither is there any other name under heaven given among men, whereby we must be saved." No other way. It was God's way or none.

Then none it will be, he had decided, thinking himself brave.

He felt burning. A fury welled up inside him. Anger and bitterness, unfocused hostility, frustration leading him to lash out. But there was no one to lash out at. No one to cower in fear at the power of the great athlete, the scholar, the renowned doctor, the skilled surgeon.

The pain began to sink in deeper, creating a desperate desire for relief. It was a pain far worse than any he had ever felt before. . . . This was only the first hour of hell, and there was no calendar to check off the days until the sentence was finished. How could he endure even a day, much less an eternal night? How long would tomorrow be? He could not bear the thought of it.

Doc thirsted for help, but not redemption. He hungered for hope, but not righteousness. He longed for friendship, but not with those who followed God. He could see in his mind's eye Dante's sign that hung over the entrance to hell's inferno. "Abandon all hope ye who enter here."

Where were the great people Twain said would inhabit hell? There were no great people here. No people at all, or perhaps many, but not one he could see or hear. No company of the damned with whom to commiserate and strategize an escape, like in all the prison movies. Commiseration is the one desirable element of suffering, and hell had nothing desirable to offer. No camaraderie. No family. No sports, no music, no movies. Utter and complete boredom, with nothing to distract him from his own agony.

Suddenly he heard a sound, a terrible sound, so awful it proved him wrong when he'd thought that any sound would be welcome. It was an almost human sound, but more like an animal writhing in agony. A sound of moaning building to a horrible scream. It went on and on, torturing him, its only consolation the fact that someone or something else must be here with him.

He realized the terrible truth—the scream was his. . . .

He determined to end his life, but didn't know how. He had no tool with which to inflict harm on himself, nor did this body, though capable of great suffering, seem capable of being harmed. It was like a bush that burned but was not consumed.

Thirst without water to quench it. Hunger without food to satisfy it. Loneliness without company to assuage it. There was no God here. He'd gotten his wish. On earth he'd managed to reject God while still getting in on so many of the blessings and provisions of God. But it was now clear, excruciatingly clear, the absence of God meant the absence of all good.

There was no laughter. There could be no laughter where there was no hope. The awful realization descended on him that there was no storyline here. No opening scene, no developing plot, no climax, no resolution. No character development. No travel, no movement. Only constant nothingness, going nowhere.

This was Doc Lowell's first day in hell. And he knew, despite every protestation erupting from within him, that every day would be the same, and of his days here there could be no end. Excruciating and eternal. Hell was heaven refused.

No sleep. No escape. No relief. No end. Questions pointed their mocking bony fingers at him. Why had he been so sure about what he did not know? Why had he been so stubborn, insisting on being his own god, living by his own rules? He'd been a fool, and would remain one, for all eternity.

No, no, no! I am not a fool. Finney was the fool. It was Finney. Not me. Not me! Not ME![670]

Randy Alcorn, *Deadline*

Home

They will build houses and dwell in them; they will plant vineyards and eat their fruit.

God, Isaiah 65:21

They were longing for a better country—a heavenly one. Therefore God is not ashamed to be called their God, for he has prepared a city for them.

Hebrews 11:16

Our citizenship is in heaven, and from it we await a Savior, the Lord Jesus Christ, who will transform our lowly body to be like his glorious body.

Paul, Philippians 3:20-21, ESV

Whether we are at home or away, we make it our aim to please him.

Paul, 2 Corinthians 5:9, ESV

In my Father's house are many rooms; if it were not
so, I would have told you. I am going there to prepare
a place for you. And if I go and prepare a place for
you, I will come back and take you to be with me that
you also may be where I am.

JESUS, JOHN 14:2-3

Since heaven is here pictured as the Father's house, it is more natural
to think of "dwelling-places" within a house as rooms or suites. . . .
The simplest explanation is best: my Father's house refers to heaven,
and in heaven are many rooms, many dwelling-places. The point is
not the lavishness of each apartment, but the fact that such ample
provision has been made that there is more than enough space for
every one of Jesus' disciples to join him in his Father's home.[671]

D. A. Carson, *The Gospel according to John*

There is a dear old friend of mine, now in Heaven. When he came to
this church one Sunday, I said to him, "Our old friend so-and-so has
gone home." The one to whom I spoke was an old man himself, one
of our most gracious elders, and he looked at me in a most significant
way, and his eyes twinkled as he said, "He could not do better, dear
Pastor. He could not do better. And you and I will do the same thing
one of these days. We also shall go home!"

Our aged friend has himself gone home since that time, and now
I say of him, "He could not have done better." Why, that is where
good children always go at night—home. . . .

But as for those who have fallen asleep in Jesus, we need not fret
or trouble ourselves about them. When children go upstairs to bed,
do their elder brothers and sisters, who sit up later, gather together
and cry because the other children have fallen asleep? Ah, no! They
feel that they have not lost them, and they expect to meet again in
the morning; and so do we![672]

Charles Spurgeon, "Fallen Asleep," Sermon 2659

If He had no use for all these differences, I do not see why He should have created more souls than one. . . . Your soul has a curious shape because it is a hollow made to fit a particular swelling in the infinite contours of the divine substance, or a key to unlock one of the doors in the house with many mansions. For it is not humanity in the abstract that is to be saved, but you—you, the individual reader, John Stubbs or Janet Smith. . . . Your place in heaven will seem to be made for you and you alone, because you were made for it—made for it stitch by stitch as a glove is made for a hand.[673]

C. S. Lewis, *The Problem of Pain*

Home, as we all know, is the place where we are generally loved for our own sakes, and not for our gifts or possessions; the place where we are loved to the end, never forgotten, and always welcome. This is one idea of heaven. Believers are in a strange land and at school in this life. In the life to come they will be at home.[674]

J. C. Ryle, *Heaven*

The Christian is a person with two homes, two addresses, two pieces of "real estate" to which he or she has title of ownership. One is our earthly domicile, that space where we live and which we can in some degree and in some sense claim as "ours." The other is beyond the curtain of our mortality, finally revealed in the glory of the parousia, our "eternal inheritance" which is our "eternal home."[675]

Bruce Milne, *The Message of Heaven and Hell*

A fear of making the future inheritance seem too material has led many to spiritualize away the very truths which lead us to look upon it as our home. Christ assured His disciples that He went to prepare mansions for them in the Father's house.[676]

Ellen G. White, *The Great Controversy*

We are born with two impulses. These jostle each other from womb to grave. They make us constantly restless, anxious, weary, cranky.

The first impulse is *to go beyond*. It is to capture some virgin newness, some pristine creation—to fling out wide to the horizons, make a stomach-fluttering leap into the unknown. We seek novelty. We hunger for new beginnings. We crave discovery, conquest, adventure—to find that which has never yet been seen. . . .

The second impulse is *to go home*. It is to recapture some unspoiled origins, some unchanging sameness—to dig back down to the bedrock, curl back into the womb. We cherish the familiar. We long for the way we were. We seek safety, domesticity, serenity— to find again that which we've lost.[677]

Mark Buchanan, *Things Unseen*

How the sea lion came to the barren lands, no one could remember. It all seemed so very long ago. So long, in fact, it appeared as though he had always been there. Not that he belonged in such an arid place. How could that be? He was, after all, a sea lion. But as you know, once you have lived so long in a certain spot, no matter how odd, you come to think of it as home.[678]

John Eldredge, *The Journey of Desire*

What if Earth
Be but the shadow of Heav'n, and things therein
Each to other like, more than on Earth is thought?[679]

John Milton, *Paradise Lost*

This world is our home: we are made to live here. It has been devastated by sin, but God plans to put it right. Hence, we look forward with joy to newly restored bodies and to living in a newly restored heaven and earth. We can love this world because it is God's, and it will be healed, becoming at last what God intended from the beginning.[680]

Paul Marshall, *Heaven Is Not My Home*

Faith is, in the end, a kind of homesickness—for a home we have never visited but have never stopped longing for.[681]

Philip Yancey, *Disappointment with God*

The entrance of the greater world is wide and sure, and they who see the straitness and the painfulness from which they have been delivered must wonder exceedingly as they are received into those large rooms with joy and immortality.[682]

Amy Carmichael

"In my Father's house are many rooms. . . . I am going there to prepare a place for you." *Place* is singular, but *rooms* is plural. This suggests Jesus has in mind for each of us an individual dwelling that's a smaller part of the larger place. This place will be home to us in the most unique sense.

The term *room* is cozy and intimate. The terms *house* or *estate* suggest spaciousness. That's Heaven: a place both spacious and intimate. Some of us enjoy coziness, being in a private space. Others enjoy a large, wide-open space. Most of us enjoy both—and the New Earth will offer both.

Heaven isn't likely to have lots of identical residences. God loves diversity, and he tailor-makes his children *and* his provisions for them. When we see the particular place he's prepared for us—not just for mankind in general but for us in particular—we'll rejoice to see our ideal home.[683]

Randy Alcorn, *Heaven*

Our true home in Heaven will have all the good things about our earthly homes, multiplied many times, but *none of the bad.*

The world says, "You can never go home again." It means that while we were gone, home changed and so did we. Our old house may have been destroyed or sold, been renovated or become run-down. In contrast, when this life is over—and particularly when we arrive on the New Earth—God's children will truly be able to come home for the very first time. Because our home in Heaven will never burn, flood, or be blown away, we'll never have to wonder whether home will still be there when we return. The new heavens and New Earth will never disappear. They'll give a wonderful permanence to the word *home*.[684]

Randy Alcorn, *Heaven*

I live in Oregon. When I've flown home from overseas and landed in New York, I feel I've come "home," meaning I'm in my home country. Then when I land in Oregon, I'm more home. When I come to my hometown, everything looks familiar. Finally, when I arrive at my house, I'm really home. But even there I have a special room or two. Scripture's various terms—*New Earth, country, city, place,* and *rooms*—involve such shades of meaning to the word *home.*

Nanci and I love our home. When we're gone long enough, we miss it. It's not just the place we miss, of course—it's family, friends, neighbors, church. Yet the place offers the comfort of the routine, the feel of the bed, the books on the shelf. It's not fancy, but it's home. When our daughters were young, our family spent two months overseas visiting missionaries in six different countries. It was a wonderful adventure, but three days before the trip ended, our hearts turned a corner, and home was all we could think of.

Our love for home, our yearning for it, is a glimmer of our longing for our true home.

A passage in Isaiah starts "Behold, I will create new heavens and a new earth" and ends with "They will neither harm nor destroy on all my holy mountain" (Isaiah 65:17-25). In between is a verse that appears to refer to life on the New Earth: "They will build houses and dwell in them; they will plant vineyards and eat their fruit" (Isaiah 65:21). This involves not only houses but land. (Some argue that because the previous verse appears to speak of death, this must refer only to the Millennium.)

The New Earth's citizens will build, plant, and eat, as human beings on Earth always have. Like Adam and Eve in Eden, we'll inherit a place that God has prepared for us. But we'll be free to build on it and develop it as we see fit, to God's glory.[685]

Randy Alcorn, *Heaven*

I believe Scripture teaches that on the New Earth we'll open our homes to guests. I base this on Christ's words in Luke 16.

After speaking of the shrewd servant's desire to use earthly resources so that "people will welcome me into their houses" (v. 4), Jesus told his followers to "use worldly wealth to gain friends" (v. 9). Jesus instructed them to use their earthly resources to gain friends by making a difference in their lives on Earth. The reason? "So that when it [life on Earth] is gone, you will be welcomed into eternal dwellings" (v. 9).

Our "friends" in Heaven appear to be those whose lives we've touched on Earth and who now have their own "eternal dwellings." Luke 16:9 seems to say these "eternal dwellings" of our friends are places where we'll stay and enjoy companionship—second homes to us as we move about the Kingdom.

Because many people mistakenly believe that Heaven won't be earthlike, it never occurs to them to take this passage literally. They think "eternal dwellings" is a general reference to Heaven. But surely Christ isn't saying we'll enter Heaven because we used our money wisely. In the parable, the eternal dwellings are Heaven's equivalent to the private homes that the shrewd servant could stay in on Earth.

Do I believe Jesus is suggesting we'll actually share lodging, meals, and fellowship with friends in God's Kingdom? Yes. I'm aware that some readers will think this far-fetched. But that's only because when we think of Heaven, we don't think of resurrected people living on a resurrected Earth, living in dwelling places, and eating and fellowshiping together. But isn't that exactly what Scripture teaches us? [686]

Randy Alcorn, *Heaven*

She stared at the Cosmic Center, intoxicated by his character. This was her only king. This her only kingdom. The character of God defined the landscape of heaven. The Carpenter had prepared a place all right. What a place! . . .

"You have already learned much here, have you not?"

"Yes," Dani said. "For one thing, I've learned why my country never felt like home to me. . . . And given all the injustice and suffering, who would want it to be? I never fit in there, Torel. Sometimes I thought it was because of my skin color. Now I realize it was because of the God-shaped emptiness within me, the void that could only be filled by being in his presence. By being here. . . .

"While on earth I kept hearing heaven's music," Dani said, "but it was elusive, more like an echo. All that clatter, all those competing sounds, all the television programs and ringing phones and traffic and voices drowned out Elyon's music. Sometimes I'd dance to the wrong beat, march to the wrong anthem. I was never made for that place. I was made for this one."

The wild rush of Joy, the rapture of discovery overwhelmed her. . . .

She remembered the rough sketches she used to make before starting to paint. "Mount Hood, Niagara Falls, the Grand Canyon, the Oregon Coast, all those places on earth were only rough sketches of this place. The best parts of the old world were sneak previews of this one. Like little foretastes, like licking the spoon from Mama's beef stew an hour before supper." She smiled at her mother and grabbed her hand.

"I'm home," she shouted, first hugging her mother, then grabbing the angel's hands and dancing in a circle, turning around and around and around, taking pleasure in his unfamiliarity and awkwardness at the dance, while her mother clapped a beat. "Did you hear me, Torel? I'm really home!"[687]

Dani and Torel, in *Dominion,* by Randy Alcorn

If we follow through with the construction and residence imagery Scripture itself employs, then all believers are engaged in a sort of eternal building project, the results of which may vary widely. If we imagine angels employed by Jesus in our heavenly building projects, we might envision ourselves asking, "Why isn't my house larger than this?" Their response? "We did the best we could with what you sent us."[688]

Randy Alcorn, *The Law of Rewards*

The saying goes, "This world is not our home." We should qualify that to say "This world—as it now is, under the Curse—is not our home." But we should also add, "This world—as it will be, delivered from the Curse—will be our home."

Randy Alcorn, notes

Eventually they arrived on a world more beautiful than Dani could fathom—cascading waterfalls, rainbows of a hundred colors, mountain peaks five times higher than any on earth. Oceans with blue-green water, and waves crashing upon rocks the size of mountains. Grassy meadows, fields of multicolored flowers—colors she had never seen before. This place seemed somehow familiar to her, yet how could it, since it was like nothing she'd ever seen? Still, she felt profoundly at home.

"Why hasn't anyone told me of this place until now? I'd think it would be the talk of heaven!"

The Carpenter smiled at her. "They did not tell you because they do not know of it. They've never been here."

"What do you mean?"

"You are the first to visit this world."

"No," she said, then her face flushed. "How could that be?"

"This is yours. As your father once built you that tree house, I fashioned this place just for you."

. . . "This is all for me?"

"Yes," the Carpenter said. "Do you like it?"

"Oh, I love it. And I haven't even begun to explore it! Thank you. Oh, thank you." She hugged him tight. He took delight in her delight.

"This is not the ultimate place I have prepared for you, my daughter. But it is a pleasant beginning, isn't it?"[689]

Jesus and Dani, in *Dominion*, by Randy Alcorn

In Heaven, what kind of a place can we expect our Lord to have prepared for us? . . . I think we can expect to find the best place ever made by anyone, for anyone, in the history of the universe. The God who commends hospitality will not be outdone in his hospitality to us. . . .

Jesus is the carpenter from Nazareth. He knows how to build. He's had experience building entire worlds (billions of them, throughout the universe). He's also an expert at *repairing* what has been damaged—whether people or worlds. He does not consider his creation disposable. This damaged creation cries out to be repaired, and it is his plan to repair it. He's going to remodel the old Earth on a grand scale. How great will be the resurrected planet that he calls the New Earth—the one he says will be our home . . . and *his*.

When you're traveling late at night and you don't know where you're going to stay, nothing's more discouraging than finding a No Vacancy sign. There's no such sign in Heaven. If we've made our reservations by accepting God's gift in Christ, then Heaven is wide open to us. Jesus knew what it was like to have no vacancy in the inn and to sleep in a barn. On the New Earth, he'll have plenty of room for all of us.[690]

Randy Alcorn, *Heaven*

"How long, O Lord?" the voices of millions cried out.

"Because of the oppression of the weak and the groaning of the needy, I will now arise," said the King. "I will rescue them."

The King stood in front of his throne. His eyes—and all those across the heavens—were fixed now on a young locksmith from Pushan, who languished in prison, dying of tuberculosis, coughing up blood. As Li Shen's life faded, the King gripped the hilt of the sword, then unsheathed it. He lifted it up, stretching out his arm. He whistled to a white stallion, a creature unlike any other. It flew to him, dancing and snorting, rising up on its back legs, eager to run to battle. The King, shining with the brilliance of a thousand quasars, mounted his great steed.

All heaven watched the young man breathe his last at the feet of his tormentors. At that moment the Warrior-King, eyes wet and white-hot, cried out with a voice that shook heaven and earth: *"No longer!"*

Michael threw his arm forward, the hosts of heaven shouted, and millions of horses gathered, mounted by warriors of every tribe, nation, and tongue. Eternity's door swung open on its hinges. Out of one realm and into another rode an army like there had never been.

"The time has come," roared the King. "Rescue my people! Destroy my enemies!" The Morning Star, who had once come as Lamb, now returned as Lion, with ten thousand galaxies forming the train of his imperial robe.

A mighty army appeared from the distant reaches of the cosmos, progressing across billions of stars and planets. Vast hordes of warriors moved past Orion's nebula in an explosion of colors. The army advanced toward earth in rumbling cadence. Without saddle or bridle, they rode great white Thoroughbreds, proud stallions that seemed to know their mission as well as they knew their riders. Some of the mounts pulled chariots of fire, streaking like meteors across the sky.

A legion of angels gathered in formation in back of and to the sides of the Commander. Not far behind him were twelve men and, following them, a great company of martyrs, warriors whose hands moved to the hilts of their swords, the fire of righteousness in their eyes exploding into infernos.

. . . Streams of red-hot molten rock spewed from mountains across the broken planet. A bright red river of heat and light burned through trees and stone, consuming all in its path. Earthquakes and tidal waves and floods assaulted the cities. A tormented earth exacted revenge on the fallen stewards who had caused its ruin. The world heaved and moaned in destruction—or was it rebirth?

"Deliver us!" cried scattered bands of fugitives, strangers, and pilgrims—those whose home had never been on earth, those of whom the world was not worthy.

On the dark planet, kingdoms of men dissolved into ruin. Like a scythe clearing a path, earthquakes brought down rows of skyscrapers. Stock exchanges crumbled. Businesses burned. All whose hope and refuge was earth . . . in an instant became homeless.

Then I saw heaven opened, and a white horse was standing there. And the one sitting on the horse was named Faithful and True. For he judges fairly and then goes to war. His eyes were bright like flames of fire, and on his head were many crowns. A name was written on him, and only he knew what it meant. He was clothed with a robe dipped in blood, and his title was the Word of God. The armies of heaven, dressed in pure white linen, followed him on white horses. From his mouth came a sharp sword, and with it he struck down the nations. He ruled them with an iron rod, and he trod the winepress of the fierce wrath of almighty God. On his robe and thigh was written this title: King of kings and Lord of lords.[691]

Randy Alcorn, *Safely Home*

Jesus

The sun will no more be your light by day, nor will the brightness of the moon shine on you, for the LORD will be your everlasting light, and your God will be your glory. Your sun will never set again, and your moon will wane no more; the LORD will be your everlasting light, and your days of sorrow will end.

GOD, ISAIAH 60:19-20

Rejoice greatly. . . . See, your king comes to you, righteous and having salvation, gentle and riding on a donkey, on a colt, the foal of a donkey. . . . He will proclaim peace to the nations. His rule will extend from sea to sea and from the River to the ends of the earth.

GOD, ZECHARIAH 9:9-10

I am the light of the world. Whoever follows me will never walk in darkness, but will have the light of life.

JESUS, JOHN 8:12

By a single offering [himself] he has perfected for all time those who are being sanctified.

HEBREWS 10:14, ESV

The Son of Man did not come to be served, but to serve, and to give his life as a ransom for many.

JESUS, MATTHEW 20:28

Father, I want those you have given me to be with me where I am, and to see my glory, the glory you have given me because you loved me before the creation of the world.

JESUS, JOHN 17:24

By him [Jesus] all things were created: things in heaven and on earth, visible and invisible, whether thrones or powers or rulers or authorities; all things were created by him and for him. He is before all things, and in him all things hold together. And he is the head of the body, the church; he is the beginning and the firstborn from among the dead, so that in everything he might have the supremacy. For God was pleased to have all his fullness dwell in him, and through him to reconcile to himself all things, whether things on earth or things in heaven, by making peace through his blood, shed on the cross.

PAUL, COLOSSIANS 1:16-20

Who shall separate us from the love of Christ? . . .
Neither death nor life, neither angels nor demons,
neither the present nor the future, nor any powers,
neither height nor depth, nor anything else in all creation, will be able to separate us from the love of God
that is in Christ Jesus our Lord.

PAUL, ROMANS 8:35, 38-39

We have confidence to enter the Most Holy Place
by the blood of Jesus.

HEBREWS 10:19

Let us . . . with confidence draw near to the throne
of grace.

HEBREWS 4:16, ESV

To him who loves us and has freed us from our sins
by his blood, and has made us to be a kingdom and
priests to serve his God and Father—to him be glory
and power for ever and ever! Amen.

Look, he is coming with the clouds,
and every eye will see him,
even those who pierced him;
and all the peoples of the earth will mourn
because of him.

So shall it be! Amen.

"I am the Alpha and the Omega," says the Lord
God, "who is, and who was, and who is to come,
the Almighty."

JOHN, REVELATION 1:5-8

I wept and wept because no one was found who was worthy to open the scroll or look inside. Then one of the elders said to me, "Do not weep! See, the Lion of the tribe of Judah, the Root of David, has triumphed. He is able to open the scroll and its seven seals." Then I saw a Lamb, looking as if it had been slain, standing in the center of the throne, encircled by the four living creatures and the elders. . . . He came and took the scroll from the right hand of him who sat on the throne. And when he had taken it, the four living creatures and the twenty-four elders fell down before the Lamb. . . . And they sang a new song: "You are worthy to take the scroll and to open its seals, because you were slain, and with your blood you purchased men for God from every tribe and language and people and nation."

JOHN, REVELATION 5:4-9

The Lamb at the center of the throne will be their shepherd; he will lead them to springs of living water.

AN ELDER, REVELATION 7:17

Here I am! I stand at the door and knock. If anyone hears my voice and opens the door, I will come in and eat with him, and he with me.

JESUS, REVELATION 3:20

Thy main plan, and the end of thy will
is to make Christ glorious and beloved in heaven where
he is now ascended,
where one day all the elect will behold his glory and love
and glorify him forever.
Though here I love him but little,
may this be my portion at last.

In this world thou hast given me a beginning,
*   one day it will be perfected in the realm above.*[692]

The Valley of Vision: A Collection of Puritan Prayers and Devotions

When I am afraid of evils to come, comfort me by showing me
*   that in myself I am a dying, condemned wretch,*
*   but that in Christ I am reconciled, made alive, and satisfied;*
*   that I am feeble and unable to do any good,*
*   but that in him I can do all things;*
*   that what I now have in Christ is mine in part,*
*   but shortly I shall have it perfectly in heaven.*[693]

The Valley of Vision: A Collection of Puritan Prayers and Devotions

When the people of God reach heaven, they will see Jesus Christ, God and man, with their bodily eyes, as He will never lay aside the human nature. They will behold that glorious blessed body, which is personally united to the divine nature, and exalted above principalities and powers and every name that is named. There we shall see, with our eyes, that very body which was born of Mary at Bethlehem, and crucified at Jerusalem between two thieves: the blessed head that was crowned with thorns; the face that was spit upon; the hands and feet that were nailed to the cross; all shining with inconceivable glory.[694]

Thomas Boston, *Human Nature in Its Fourfold State*

The resurrection of Jesus is much more than a conclusive argument for life after death, but it is also that. If Jesus rose from the dead, then there is no room for doubt that death is not the end of our journey. If Jesus truly rose, then there is for every person a heaven to embrace and a hell to shun.[695]

Bruce Milne, *The Message of Heaven and Hell*

[Christ's resurrection] is not a matter of a "spirit appearance," but the utterly unprecedented, unique, world-transforming, heaven-anticipating, sovereign action of the Creator in the first installment of remaking the world.[696]

Bruce Milne, *The Message of Heaven and Hell*

There is not one inch in the entire area of our human life about which Christ, who is Sovereign of all, does not cry out, "Mine!"[697]

Abraham Kuyper, *Abraham Kuyper: A Centennial Reader*

One of the clearest features of Jesus' activity in the records of his ministry after Easter is his solicitous care for his disciples. . . .

It is perhaps his ministry to the individual, however, which is so indicative of the "heavenly communality." His interactions with Mary Magdalene (John 20:10-18), Thomas (20:24-29) and Peter (21:15-22) are replete with such profound and understanding sensitivity and loving concern that one is almost drawn to argue that the experience of the cross brought Jesus even closer to those whom he has drawn to himself over the years of his public ministry. . . . We may note the astonishing degree and depth of his mutual care and commitment.[698]

Bruce Milne, *The Message of Heaven and Hell*

The merits of Jesus are enough! We are going to heaven on the merits of another—there is no question about that. We will get in because another went out on our behalf. We will live because another died. We will be with God because another was rejected from the presence of God in the terror of the crucifixion. We go to heaven on the merits of another.[699]

A. W. Tozer, *The Quotable Tozer II*

The whole outlook of mankind might be changed if we could all believe that we dwell under a friendly sky and that the God of heaven, though exalted in power and majesty, is eager to be friends with us.[700]

A. W. Tozer, *The Knowledge of the Holy*

What shall we do in heaven? Not lounge around but worship, work, think, and communicate, enjoying activity, beauty, people, and God. First and foremost, however, we shall see and love Jesus, our Savior, Master, and Friend.[701]

J. I. Packer, *Your Father Loves You*

I bear my testimony that there is no joy to be found in all this world like that of sweet communion with Christ! I would barter all else there is of Heaven for that! Indeed, that *is* heaven! As for the harps of gold, and the streets like clear glass, and the songs of seraphs, and the shouts of the redeemed—one could very well give all these up, counting them as a drop in a bucket—if we might forever live in fellowship and communion with Jesus.[702]

Charles Spurgeon, "Bringing the King Back," Sermon 808

Oh, to think of heaven without Christ! It is the same thing as thinking of hell. Heaven without Christ! It is day without the sun, existing without life, feasting without food, seeing without light. It involves a contradiction in terms. Heaven without Christ! Absurd. It is the sea without water, the earth without its fields, the heavens without their stars. There cannot be a heaven without Christ. He is the sum total of bliss, the fountain from which heaven flows, the element of which heaven is composed. Christ is heaven and heaven is Christ.[703]

Charles Spurgeon, "Forever with the Lord," Sermon 1136

Since it is God's will that you should outlive me, remember our friendship. It was useful to God's church and its fruits await us in heaven. I do not want you to tire yourself on my account. I draw my breath with difficulty and expect each moment to breathe my last. It is enough I live and die for Christ, who is to all his followers a gain both in life and in death.[704]

John Calvin, letter written to a friend the day Calvin died (May 27, 1564)

"This is the solution to the world's problems? A lowly lamb? A weak, submissive sheep?" Precisely. The answer to man's problems is the Lamb of God—Jesus Christ. The Lion-Lamb. The Sovereign Savior. What a combination of meekness and majesty![705]

Steven J. Lawson, *Heaven Help Us!*

Mr. Standfast, just before death: "I am going now to see that head that was crowned with thorns and that face that was spat upon for me. I have formerly lived by hearsay and faith, but now I go where I shall live by sight and shall be with him in whose company I delight myself."[706]

John Bunyan, *The Pilgrim's Progress*

His appearance from heaven will not only be the last event of the old order but also the first of the new order; further, by this appearance he will complete God's work in the old age in order to become the Center of the new age. In, through, by, and with him the End will be the Beginning and the Last will be the First.
AMEN. COME, LORD JESUS.[707]

Peter Toon, *Heaven and Hell*

Heaven enters wherever Christ enters, even in this life.[708]

C. S. Lewis, *Letters of C. S. Lewis to Arthur Greeves*

When we look into the face of our Lord and he looks back at us with infinite love, we will see in him the fulfillment of everything that we know to be good and right and desirable in the universe. In the face of God we will see the fulfillment of all the longing we have ever had to know perfect love, peace, and joy, and to know truth and justice, holiness and wisdom, goodness and power, and glory and beauty.[709]

Wayne Grudem, *Systematic Theology*

Between the rivers of Eden, which watered the whole earth, and the river of life above, beautiful and clear as crystal, flows the stream from His side, His blood which He shed for sinners on the cross.

Between the trees of the first and of the second Paradise there stands, silent and sublime, that other tree, the tree of shame, the accursed tree of the cross, upon which Christ once hung. From this cross God stretches out His hand to the lost wanderer in the wilderness, longing to bring him back for ever from his own ways to the heavenly homeland. With his origins in Eden and longing for Eden, the sinner may find his place of rest at the cross. . . . Through him the redeeming powers of the Most High were to be morally revealed. The end . . . was to be nothing less than glory to God in the highest, peace on earth, and good will towards men.

At the coming of the new heaven and the new earth everything capable of redemption will have been redeemed.[710]

Erich Sauer, *The King of the Earth*

At the doorway into life stood a shining being of natural radiance, but with the brightness of a million klieg lights. The radiance threatened to blind her, but somehow her new eyes could endure it. This was more than a man, yet clearly a man. She knew at once who it was. He who had been from eternity past, he who had left his home in heaven to make one here for her. He who spun the galaxies into being with a single snap of his fingers, who was the light that illumined darkness with a million colors, who turned midnight into sunrise. . . .

"Welcome, my little one!" He smiled broadly, the smile teeming with approval. "Well done, my good and faithful servant. Enter into the kingdom prepared for you. Enter into the joy of your Lord!"

He hugged her tight and she hugged him back, clutching on to his back, then grasping his shoulders. She didn't know how long it lasted. These same arms had hugged her before, somehow—she recognized their character and strength—but she enjoyed the embrace now as she'd never dreamed she could enjoy any embrace. It was complete, utterly encompassing, a wall of protection no force in the universe could break through. His was the embrace she was made for. He was the Bridegroom, the object of all longing, the fulfillment of all dreams.

"My sweet Jesus," she said. . . .

"Your hand." She looked at the other. "Both hands. And your feet." He allowed her to contemplate what she saw.

These were the hands of a Carpenter who cut wood and made things, including universes and angels and every person who had ever lived. These same hands once hauled heavy lumber up a long lonely hill. These same hands and feet were once nailed to that lumber in the Shadowlands, in the most terrible moment from the dawn of time. The wound that healed all wounds could make them temporary only by making itself eternal. Hands and feet of the only innocent man became forever scarred so that no guilty one would have to bear his own scars.

She saw his pain. An ancient pain that was the doorway to eternal pleasures. Understanding rushed upon her and penetrated her mind as the howling wind had penetrated every crack in her bedroom in that old ramshackle Mississippi home. She wept again, dropping to his marred feet and caressing them with her hands. He put his fingers under her chin and turned her eyes up toward his.

"For you," he said to her, "I would do it all again."

. . . They talked long, just the two of them, without hurry and without distraction. A circle of people surrounded them, waiting for them to finish. But she did not want to finish. She was held captive by one face.[711]

Jesus and Dani, in *Dominion,* by Randy Alcorn

Desire is a signpost pointing to Heaven. Every longing for better health is a longing for the perfect bodies we'll have on the New Earth. Every longing for romance is a longing for the ultimate romance with

Christ. Every thirst for beauty is a thirst for Christ. Every taste of joy is but a foretaste of a greater and more vibrant joy than can be found on Earth now.[712]

Randy Alcorn, *We Shall See God*

Joy, Happiness, and Laughter

There is rejoicing in the presence of the angels of God over one sinner who repents.

JESUS, LUKE 15:10

The LORD will comfort Zion; he will comfort all her waste places. And her wilderness He will make like Eden, and her desert like the garden of the LORD; joy and gladness will be found in her, thanksgiving and sound of a melody.

ISAIAH 51:3, NASB

Blessed are you who hunger now, for you will be satisfied. Blessed are you who weep now, for you will laugh. Blessed are you when men hate you, when they exclude you and insult you. . . . Rejoice in that day and leap for joy, because great is your reward in heaven.

JESUS, LUKE 6:21-23

Hear the word of the LORD, O nations;
    proclaim it in distant coastlands:
"He who scattered Israel will gather them
    and will watch over his flock like a shepherd."
For the LORD will ransom Jacob
    and redeem them from the hand of those
        stronger than they.
They will come and shout for joy on the heights
        of Zion;
    they will rejoice in the bounty of the LORD—
    the grain, the new wine and the oil,
    the young of the flocks and herds.
They will be like a well-watered garden,
    and they will sorrow no more.
Then maidens will dance and be glad,
    young men and old as well.
    I will turn their mourning into gladness;
    I will give them comfort and joy instead
        of sorrow.

GOD, JEREMIAH 31:10-13

Thou art preparing joy for me and me for joy;
    I pray for joy, wait for joy, long for joy;
        give me more than I could hold, desire, or think of.
    Measure thou to me my times and degrees of joy,
        at my work, business, duties.
If I weep at night, give me joy in the morning.
Let me rest in the thought of thy love,
    pardon for sin, my title to heaven,
    my future unspotted state.
I am an unworthy recipient of thy grace. . . .
Let my heart leap towards the eternal sabbath,
    where the work of redemption, sanctification,
    preservation, glorification is finished and perfected
        for ever,

> *where thou wilt rejoice over me with joy.*
> *There is no joy like the joy of heaven,*
> *for in that state are no sad divisions,*
> *unchristian quarrels, contentions, evil designs,*
> *weariness, hunger, cold, sadness, sin,*
> *suffering, persecutions, toils of duty.*
> *O healthful place where none are sick!*
> *O happy land where all are kings!*
> *O holy assembly where all are priests!*
> *How free a state where none are servants except to thee!*
> *Bring me speedily to the land of joy.*[713]

The Valley of Vision: A Collection of Puritan Prayers and Devotions

Earth has no sorrow that Heaven cannot heal.

Thomas Moore, "Come, Ye Disconsolate"

There was the blue sky overhead, and grassy country spreading as far as he could see in every direction. . . . "It seems, then," said Tirian, smiling himself, "that the Stable seen from within and the Stable seen from without are two different places."

"Yes," said the Lord Digory. "Its inside is bigger than its outside."

"Yes," said Queen Lucy. "In our world too, a Stable once had something inside it that was bigger than our whole world."

It was the first time she had spoken. . . . She was drinking everything in even more deeply than the others. She had been too happy to speak.[714]

C. S. Lewis, *The Last Battle*

We must, therefore, be on our guard against any view of Heaven which would make its principal happiness come from creatures. We must ever remember that no creature, either here or hereafter, can give perfect happiness to man. Wherefore, in our meditations on Heaven, we must beware of making its chief happiness consist in delightful music, social intercourse with the saints, or in the pleasures enjoyed through the glorified senses, however pure and refined we may imagine them to be. This then, is the first error to be avoided, and with much care; not only because it is untrue, but also because it lowers the beatitude of Heaven, which consists essentially in the vision, love and enjoyment of God Himself.

The second error to be avoided consists in placing the whole happiness of man so completely and exclusively in the Beatific Vision that neither the resurrection of the body with its glorious gifts, nor the communion of saints, nor heavenly music, nor any other creature, can increase the happiness already enjoyed by the soul in the possession of God.[715]

Father J. Boudreau, *The Happiness of Heaven*

Then shall I see, and hear, and know
All I desired or wished below;
And every power find sweet employ
In that eternal world of joy.[716]

Isaac Watts, "Psalm 92:1, Sweet Is the Work of God My King"

In this world, we receive a portion of our light from the moon, but that light is still from the sun, because the moon has no light on her own. She is a mere reflector, or instrument by which, during the night, the sun conveys to us a portion of his light. So, in Heaven, God is the only source of happiness and joy, and no creature is or can be a source of happiness independently of Him. But He can and does make use of creatures to adorn, perfect, and complete the happiness of the whole man.[717]

Father J. Boudreau, *The Happiness of Heaven*

Think of this, ye mortals, who crave after human love. You desire to love and to be loved. Love is the sunshine of your lives. But, do what you will, it can never give you perfect happiness here below; for when you have, at last, succeeded in possessing the object after which you so ardently sighed, you discover in it imperfections which you had not suspected before; and these lessen your happiness. But suppose, even, that you are of the few who are as happy as they expected to be—how long will your blessedness last? A few years, at most. Then, death, with a merciless hand, tears away from you the objects of your love. Is not this the end of all earthly happiness?

Look up to Heaven, and there see the blessed in the presence of God. They are as happy today in their love as they were hundreds of years ago; and when millions of ages have rolled by, they shall still possess the object of their love, which is the eternal God.[718]

Father J. Boudreau, *The Happiness of Heaven*

The enjoyment of God is the only happiness with which our souls can be satisfied. To go to heaven, fully to enjoy God, is infinitely better than the most pleasant accommodations here. Fathers and mothers, husbands, wives, or children, or the company of earthly friends, are but shadows; but God is the substance. These are but scattered beams, but God is the sun. These are but streams. But God is the ocean.[719]

Jonathan Edwards, "The Christian Pilgrim"

What can this incessant craving, and this impotence of attainment mean, unless there was once a happiness belonging to man, of which only the faintest traces remain, in that void which he attempts to fill with everything within his reach?[720]

Blaise Pascal, *Pensées*

God destines us for an end beyond the grasp of reason.[721]

Thomas Aquinas, *Summa Theologica*

No one can live without delight, and that is why a man deprived of spiritual joy goes over to carnal pleasures.[722]

Thomas Aquinas, *Summa Theologica*

When the followers of Jesus Christ lose their interest in heaven they will no longer be happy Christians, and when they are no longer happy Christians they cannot be a powerful force in a sad and sinful world. It may be said with certainty that Christians who have lost their enthusiasm about the Savior's promises of heaven-to-come have also stopped being effective in Christian life and witness in this world.[723]

A. W. Tozer, *The Quotable Tozer II*

Find your joy where God would have you find it, namely, in that part of your nature which is new. Rejoice in the new principles, the new promises, the new covenant, and the blood of the new covenant which are yours—all of them. The Kingdom of God is within you; rejoice in it.

Find your joy in the new creation of God as you see it in others. The angels rejoice over one sinner who repents (Luke 15:10); surely you and I ought to do so! Try and do good, and bring others to Christ. And when a soul shows signs of turning to its God, let that be your joy.

"Be glad and rejoice *forever*." As long as you live, there will be something in the new creation that shall be to you a fresh joy and delight. Heaven will only enlarge this same joy. Be glad forever, because God will ever be creating something fresh in which you may be glad.

It may be said of the joy we ought to feel that it is a joy God intended for us: "Behold, I create Jerusalem to be a joy, and her people to be a gladness" (Isaiah 65:18). He has made the new city, the new people, the new world to be a source of joy.

We ought to be glad and rejoice forever in that which God creates. Ours is a heritage of joy and peace. My dear brothers and sisters, if anybody in the world ought to be happy, we are the people.

How large our obligations! How boundless our privileges! How brilliant our hopes![724]

Charles Spurgeon, "God Rejoicing in the New Creation," Sermon 2211

become a precept? Then we will gladly enough obey, and our heart shall dance for joy.[738]

Charles Spurgeon, "God Rejoicing in the New Creation," Sermon 2211

Joy fills and overflows heaven now. Jesus said that laughter replaces tears in heaven. He contrasted the sadness of time with the joy of eternity (Luke 6:21). Joy bubbled up when Christ threw down Satan in his first coming (Revelation 12:12; John 12:31), and rejoicing erupts over each sinner whose life is changed (Luke 15:5-7, 9, 10, 32).[739]

John Gilmore, *Probing Heaven*

The humor of heaven will be vastly improved over earth, made infinite both in variety, use, and amount. There humor will not be hollow, harsh, or dirty. There put-down jokes will not be directed against others. . . . God has originated all good things, including good humor. He has always had a sense of humor. His creation is proof of it.[740]

John Gilmore, *Probing Heaven*

The angels know what the joys of heaven are, and therefore, they rejoice over one sinner who repents.[741]

Charles Spurgeon, "The Sympathy of the Two Worlds," Sermon 203

Since heaven is going to be such a celebration, maybe we should work at bringing a little more spontaneous joy into our gatherings with other Christians right now. . . . We've practiced crabbiness so long that we've forgotten how to enjoy the bountiful goodness of God. You might start a real revolution at your church or in your small group or at the next fellowship dinner if you just smile—or laugh out loud![742]

Douglas Connelly, *The Promise of Heaven*

What a pleasure is there in the heavenly kingdom, without fear of death; and how lofty and perpetual a happiness with eternity of living![743]

Cyprian, "Treatise VII: On the Morality"

What is the essence of heaven? . . . In their beatific vision, love and enjoyment of the triune god. For the three divine persons have an infinitely perfect vision and love and enjoyment of the divine essence and of one another. And in this infinite knowing, loving and enjoying lies the very life of the triune God, the very essence of their endless and infinite happiness. If the blessed are to be endlessly and supremely happy, then, they must share in the very life of the triune God, in the divine life that makes Them endlessly and infinitely happy.[744]

    E. J. Fortman, *Everlasting Life after Death*

Not one heart is there that is not full of love, and not a solitary inhabitant that is not beloved by all the others. And as all are lovely, so all see each other's loveliness with full contentment and delight. Every soul goes out in love to every other; and among all the blessed inhabitants, love is mutual, and full, and eternal.[745]

    Jonathan Edwards, *Heaven: A World of Love*

The inhabitants of heaven shall all know that they will continue in the perfect enjoyment of each other's love forever.

    They shall be in no fear of any end to this happiness, or of any abatement from its fullness and blessedness, or that they shall ever be weary of its exercises and expressions, or overindulged with its enjoyments, or that the beloved objects shall ever grow old or disagreeable, so that their love shall at last die away.[746]

    Jonathan Edwards, *Heaven: A World of Love*

All in heaven shall flourish in immortal youth and freshness. In that glorious place, age will not diminish anyone's beauty or vigor; and love shall abide in every one's heart, as a living spring perpetually springing up in the soul, or as a flame that never dies away.

    Everything in the heavenly world shall contribute to the joy of the saints, and every joy of heaven shall be eternal.[747]

    Jonathan Edwards, *Heaven: A World of Love*

Heaven is not simply about the reality or experience of joy, but its *eternal increase*. The blessedness of the beauty of heaven is progressive, incremental, and incessantly expansive.

The happiness of heaven is not like the steady, placid state of a mountain lake where barely a ripple disturbs the tranquility of its water. Heaven is more akin to the surging, swelling waves of the Mississippi at flood stage.[748]

Sam Storms, "Heaven: The Eternal Increase of Joy"

Hardly anything will bring you more joy than to see other saints with greater rewards than you, experiencing greater glory than you, given greater authority than you! . . . You will then delight only in delighting in the delight of others. Their achievement will be your greatest joy. Their success will be your highest happiness.[749]

Sam Storms, "Heaven: The Eternal Increase of Joy"

To love someone is to desire their greatest joy. As their joy increases, so too does yours in them. If their joy did not increase, neither would yours.[750]

Sam Storms, "Heaven: The Eternal Increase of Joy"

All aspects of our "perfection" in heaven admit of degrees precisely because we are and always will be finite. Whatever is finite has boundaries and boundaries, by definition, are capable of being exceeded and extended. Knowledge that is perfect and free from error is not necessarily comprehensive. Our happiness will be perfect in that it will be entirely free from trouble and trial and evil, but that perfection, as strange as it may sound, is always subject to improvement.[751]

Sam Storms, "Heaven, the Eternal Increase of Joy"

I send you a rose, which ought to please you extremely, seeing what a rarity it is at this season. And with the rose you must accept its thorns, which represent the bitter suffering of our Lord, while the green leaves represent the hope we may entertain, that through the same sacred passion we, having passed through the darkness of this short winter of our mortal life, may attain to the brightness and felicity of an eternal spring in Heaven.[752]

Galileo Galilei

I am sure that our Lord is looking for heavenly minded Christians. His Word encourages us to trust Him with such a singleness of purpose that He is able to deliver us from the fear of death and uncertainties of tomorrow. I believe He is up there preparing me a mansion—"He is fixing up a mansion which shall forever stand; for my stay shall not be transient in that happy, happy land!"

Read again what John said about his vision of the future to come:

"And I saw a new heaven and a new earth. . . ." (Revelation 1:1-4)

It is just too bad that we have relegated this passage to be read mostly at funeral services. The man who was reporting this was on his way to the New Jerusalem!

. . . Ah, the people of God ought to be the happiest people in all the wide world! People should be coming to us constantly and asking the source of our joy and delight—redeemed by the blood of the Lamb, our yesterdays behind us, our sin under the blood forever and a day, to be remembered against us no more forever. God is our Father, Christ is our Brother, the Holy Spirit our Advocate and Comforter. Our Brother has gone to the Father's house to prepare a place for us, leaving with us the promise that He will come again!

Don't send Moses, Lord, don't send Moses! He broke the tablets of stone.

Don't send Elijah for me, Lord! I am afraid of Elijah—he called down fire from heaven.

Don't send Paul, Lord! He is so learned that I feel like a little boy when I read his epistles.

Oh Lord Jesus, come Yourself! I am not afraid of You. You took the little children as lambs to Your fold. You forgave the woman taken in adultery. You healed the timid woman who reached out in the crowd to touch You. We are not afraid of You!

Even so, come, Lord Jesus!

Come quickly!⁷⁵³

A. W. Tozer, *Who Put Jesus on the Cross?*

We know that people in Heaven have a range of feelings—all good ones. We're told of banquets, feasts, and singing. Remember, God assures those who mourn now, "You will laugh" (Luke 6:21, NIV). Laughter is an emotional response. Feasting, singing, and rejoicing involve feelings. Our present emotions are bent by sin, but they will be straightened forever when God removes the Curse.

Just two verses after Jesus promises, "You will laugh," he tells us precisely when the promise will be fulfilled: "Rejoice in that day and leap for joy, because great is your reward in heaven" (Luke 6:23, NIV).

Jesus doesn't say, "If you weep now, soon things on Earth will take a better turn, and then you'll laugh." Things won't always take a better turn on Earth. Just as our reward will come in Heaven, laughter (itself one of our rewards) will come in Heaven, compensating for our present sorrow. Yet by God's grace, we can laugh on Earth now, getting a head start on Heaven's laughter.

God won't only wipe away all our tears; he'll also fill our hearts with joy and our mouths with laughter. And just as laughter itself will be redeemed, so our emotions will be free at last of all sin, ill will, and lack of perspective.

If you are experiencing hard times that leave you physically and emotionally frail or drained, take heart.⁷⁵⁴

Randy Alcorn, *We Shall See God*

Great humor comes from great wit. And Heaven will be full of great wit! There is nothing like the laughter of old friends . . . and new ones. And that will be Heaven. Heaven will have the unexpected and challenges that require ingenuity. Do we seriously believe Adam and Eve always knew what would happen next, were always prepared with an answer in advance? No, they were finite, as are we, and as we will always be. Finite creatures must always laugh at themselves and their limitations and lack of what only their Creator has, just as we laugh at animals good-naturedly when they don't get it, and rejoice with them if and when they figure it out. And God will laugh and rejoice with us.

Randy Alcorn, unpublished notes

The best carefree moments on Earth bring laughter. And if we can laugh hard now—in a world full of poverty, disease, and disasters— then surely what awaits us in Heaven is far greater laughter.

One of Satan's great lies is that God—and goodness—is joyless and humorless, while Satan—and evil—bring pleasure and satisfaction. In fact, it's Satan who's humorless. Sin didn't bring him joy; it forever stripped him of joy. In contrast, envision Jesus with his disciples. If you cannot picture Jesus teasing them and laughing with them, you need to reevaluate your theology of Creation and Incarnation. We need a biblical theology of humor that prepares us for an eternity of celebration, spontaneous laughter, and overflowing joy.[755]

Randy Alcorn, *50 Days of Heaven*

Two jars can both be full, but the one with greater capacity contains more. Likewise, all of us will be full of joy in heaven, but some may have more joy because their capacity for joy will be larger, having been stretched through trusting God in this life.[756]

Randy Alcorn, *The Law of Rewards*

When I speak . . . of the multifaceted joys of the resurrected life in the new universe, some readers may think, *But our eyes should be on the giver, not the gift; we must focus on God, not on Heaven.* This approach sounds spiritual, but it erroneously divorces our experience of God from life, relationships, and the world. . . . All secondary joys are *derivative* in nature. They cannot be separated from God. Flowers are beautiful for one reason—God is beautiful. Rainbows are stunning because God is stunning. Puppies are delightful because God is delightful. Sports are fun because God is fun. Study is rewarding because God is rewarding. Work is fulfilling because God is fulfilling.

Ironically, some people who are the most determined to avoid the sacrilege of putting things before God miss a thousand daily opportunities to thank him, praise him, and draw near to him.[757]

Randy Alcorn, *Heaven*

Perhaps God will offer us a choice, in keeping with our service for him on Earth, of where we might want to serve him on the New Earth. In any case, we can be certain that we'll do something we enjoy, because on the New Earth we'll want what God wants. [Our highest calling will be to enjoy him and all he has for us.][758]

Randy Alcorn, *50 Days of Heaven*

Judgment and Justice

When the Son of Man comes in his glory, and all the angels with him, he will sit on his throne in heavenly glory. All the nations will be gathered before him, and he will separate the people one from another as a shepherd separates the sheep from the goats. He will put the sheep on his right and the goats on his left.

Then the King will say to those on his right, "Come, you who are blessed by my Father; take your inheritance, the kingdom prepared for you since the creation of the world. For I was hungry and you gave me something to eat, I was thirsty and you gave me something to drink, I was a stranger and you invited me in, I needed clothes and you clothed me, I was sick and you looked after me, I was in prison and you came to visit me."

Then the righteous will answer him, "Lord, when did we see you hungry and feed you, or thirsty and give you something to drink? When did we see you a stranger and invite you in, or needing clothes and clothe you? When did we see you sick or in prison and go to visit you?"

The King will reply, "I tell you the truth, whatever you did for one of the least of these brothers of mine, you did for me."

JESUS, MATTHEW 25:31-40

The righteous will never be uprooted, but the wicked will not remain in the land.

SOLOMON, PROVERBS 10:30

We make it our goal to please him, whether we are at home in the body or away from it. For we must all appear before the judgment seat of Christ, that each one may receive what is due him for the things done while in the body, whether good or bad.

PAUL, 2 CORINTHIANS 5:9-10

"I . . . am about to come and gather all nations and tongues, and they will come and see my glory. . . . As the new heavens and the new earth that I make will endure before me," declares the LORD, "so will your name and descendants endure. From one New Moon to another and from one Sabbath to another, all mankind will come and bow down before me," says the LORD. "And they will go out and look upon the dead bodies of those who rebelled against me; their worm will not die, nor will their fire be quenched, and they will be loathsome to all mankind."

GOD, ISAIAH 66:18, 22-24

If God did not spare angels when they sinned, but sent them to hell, putting them into gloomy dungeons to be held for judgment; if he did not spare the ancient world when he brought the flood on its ungodly people, but protected Noah, a preacher of righteousness, and seven others; if he condemned the cities of Sodom and Gomorrah by burning them to ashes, and made them an example of what is going to happen to the ungodly; and if he rescued Lot, a righteous man, who was distressed by the filthy lives of lawless men (for that righteous man, living among them day after day, was tormented in his righteous soul by the lawless deeds he saw and heard)—if this is so, then the Lord knows how to rescue godly men from trials and to hold the unrighteous for the day of judgment, while continuing their punishment.

PETER, 2 PETER 2:4-9

Rejoice over [Babylon], O heaven! Rejoice, saints and apostles and prophets! God has judged her for the way she treated you.

REVELATION 18:20

The devil, who deceived them, was thrown into the lake of burning sulfur, where the beast and the false prophet had been thrown. They will be tormented day and night for ever and ever. Then I saw a great white throne and him who was seated on it. Earth and sky fled from his presence, and there was no place for them. And I saw the dead, great and small, standing before the throne, and books were opened. Another book was opened, which is the book of life. The dead were judged according to what they had done as recorded in the books. The sea gave up the dead that

were in it, and death and Hades gave up the dead that
were in them, and each person was judged according
to what he had done.

JOHN, REVELATION 20:10-13

Hell is a place of justice, where punishment is dispensed not in accordance with the warped and partial and ignorant procedures of human society, but immaculately, in accordance with the standards of him who is supremely just. There will be no cause for complaint. Every mouth will be stopped, not forcibly but by the recognition of the justice of the proceedings.[759]

Paul Helm, *The Last Things*

The Day of the Lord is a terrifying thing, filled with "destruction from the Almighty" and "fury and burning anger." It will be "a day of clouds, a time of doom," a "great and terrible day" when "the sun will be turned to darkness, and the moon into blood." But we should not forget that this judgment from God against the earth is part of His gracious plan on behalf of His children—those who want His will and His way. . . . His judgment upon the world is for our sakes, to give us relief, not more to worry about.[760]

Daniel Brown, *What the Bible Reveals about Heaven*

Judgment is making haste towards us; months and days of divine patience are flying swift away, and the last great day is just at hand: Then we must give an account of "all that has been done in the body whether it has been good or evil." And what a dismal and distressing surprise will it be to have the Judge come upon us in a blaze of glory and terror, while we have no good account to give at his demand? And yet this is the very end and design of all our time, which is lengthened out to us on this side of the grave, and of all the advantages that we have enjoyed in this life, that we may be ready to render up our account with joy to the Judge of all the earth.[761]

Isaac Watts, *The World to Come*

Never before nor ever again will there transpire a judgment where the relevant evidence is even remotely as comprehensive. This point is worth underlining when accusations of unfairness are raised concerning God's judgment. The final judgment will be the only judgment in all of time and history which is *truly fair*.[762]

Bruce Milne, *The Message of Heaven and Hell*

Cups of cold water given in his name are noted and treasured by this Judge, who understands and knows all. Nor will he overlook that care for others which finds its deepest expression in the ministry of prayer.[763]

Bruce Milne, *The Message of Heaven and Hell*

According to Revelation 18:5 and 20:12, God is not going to trust individual memories, nor the memories of our friends. (We conveniently forget what is distasteful.) . . . When the Lord judges in unerring justice there will be no memory gaps, no missing minutes of tape, no erasures . . . no sudden forgetfulness and no shredding of hateful thoughts. We shall see our deeds as God has seen them. The day of cover-up will be over. The masks will come off.[764]

John Gilmore, *Probing Heaven*

If actual suffering is lacking, then so is punishment. Let us be clear on this: *punishment entails suffering.* And suffering necessarily entails consciousness. . . . A critical point to make about the punishment described in Matthew 25:46 is that it is said to be *eternal.* There is no way that annihilationism or an extinction of consciousness can be forced into that passage.[765]

Thomas Ice and Timothy J. Demy, *What the Bible Says about Heaven and Eternity*

God takes no pleasure in the death of the wicked yet His holiness demands He judge sin and sinners. At the Great White Throne judgment you will experience only a great satisfaction at the justice of God in dealing with even your own relatives that reject His salvation.[766]

Larry Dick, *A Taste of Heaven*

Men will be judged on the basis of the light they had, not on the basis of a light they never saw. The person in the remote jungle who never heard of Jesus is judged differently than the person who is only a broadcast or open Bible away from the gospel.[767]

Max Lucado, *When Christ Comes*

Judgment is so woven into the ministry of Christ that his teaching would be severely distorted if all references to it were eliminated. The teaching of Christ on judgment is thus not an appendix to the good news of the gospel, an afterthought, but (strangely perhaps) it is part of the very texture of the good news.[768]

Paul Helm, *The Last Things*

While it may appear that the love and grace of God which are so prominent in the preaching of the good news of the gospel exclude the justice and righteousness of God, this is an illusion.

So divine justice requires the punishment of sin because it is sin, and the same divine justice is central to the gospel of the love of God because it is through divine justice being satisfied that the love and grace of God come undeservedly to the ungodly.[769]

Paul Helm, *The Last Things*

In that day, every inward working of the human soul will be discovered—every appetite, passion, inclination, and affection, with all the various combinations of them and every temper and disposition that constitutes the whole complex character of each individual. Who was righteous, who was unrighteous, and in what degree every action, or person, or character was either good or evil will be seen clearly and infallibly.[770]

John Wesley, *The Nature of Salvation*

The Christian doctrine of the last judgment reminds us that the universe we live in is not a physical accident, the result of mere random collisions of atoms, but that behind the apparently random is the hand of God, and more than this, that the order of divine providence is a moral order, that all our thoughts and actions count morally, and that we shall all give an account of them in a final way.[771]

Paul Helm, *The Last Things*

Christ says that at the last judgment "many that are first shall be last; and the last shall be first" (Mark 10:31). This overturning of expectations is not due to divine whimsy or irrationality, but to the fact that the judge of all the hearts of men will judge according to truth. Because of this, many confident expectations will be overturned. Many seemingly pious people will be rejected while many that are seemingly impious will be received.[772]

Paul Helm, *The Last Things*

One day God will expose all frauds. Those whose "place in history" was revered. Those whose cover-up succeeded.[773]

R. T. Kendall, *When God Says "Well Done!"*

What the Christian doctrine of judgment presupposes is that a person's eternal relation to God will be determined wholly by his past at the time of the judgment. God will reach back into a person's life, to retrieve buried memories and half-forgotten desires, and he will bring these to an accurate and utterly faithful assessment at the bar of divine justice. Every secret thing will be taken into account and a verdict passed accordingly. Such justice, *retrospective* in its scope, assesses all human action and the springs of such action, in accordance with the divine law, whether that law is revealed in Scripture or known through the conscience (Romans 2:15).

Divine justice is thus dispensed in accordance with what a person was and is, and not with what he may become or will become. Such justice is therefore to be distinguished from pains and penalties inflicted in order to produce better behaviour. The Bible has a place for such pains and penalties in what it teaches about divine chastisement (Hebrews 12:5-11), the aim of which is to improve and to renew. But judgment has no such aim. When judgment is pronounced there is no opportunity for improvement. Those who are filthy must be filthy still (Revelation 22:11). Such judgment is in accordance with justice.[774]

Paul Helm, *The Last Things*

No-one who is involved in the final judgment will have cause to exult or complain at a miscarriage of justice. No-one will be able to say that his case was not thoroughly looked into, or that the judge had an imperfect grasp of the law, or that the jury was corrupt. For the judgment of God is according to truth, exhaustive and unerring. God the judge is just in all his ways (Psalm 145:17).[775]

Paul Helm, *The Last Things*

The only natural argument of any weight, for the immortality of the soul, takes its rise from this observation, that justice is not extended to the good, nor executed upon the bad, man in this life; and that, as the Governor of the world is just, man must live hereafter to be judged.[776]

Jonathan Edwards, *Miscellaneous Observations on Important Theological Subjects*

It is a most unreasonable thing to suppose that there should be no future punishment, to suppose that God who had made man a rational creature, able to know his duty, and sensible that he is deserving punishment when he does it not; should let man alone, and let him live as he will, and never punish him for his sins, and never make any difference between the good and the bad; that he should make the world of mankind and then let it alone, and let men live all their days in wickedness, in adultery, murder, robbery, and persecution, and the like, and suffer them to live in prosperity, and never punish them; that he should suffer them to prosper in the world far beyond many good men, and never punish them hereafter.[777]

Jonathan Edwards, "Sermon VII on Romans 2:8-9"

If in this life only we had hope, we were of all men most miserable (1 Corinthians 15:19). But here is the comfort and patience of the Saints: they wait for another world, and they know it is a just thing with God, to give them rest after their labors (2 Thessalonians 1:9) and a crown after their combat (2 Timothy 4:8) and after their long pilgrimage, and everlasting habitation (2 Corinthians 5:1). Be patient, saith the apostle, and settle your hearts for the coming of the Lord draweth near (James 5:7). When they that have sown in tears shall reap in joy (Psalm 126:5; James 5:7; Hebrews 10:36).

. . . We should always live in expectation of the Lord Jesus in the Clouds, with oil in our lamps, prepared for His coming. Blessed is that servant whom his master when he cometh shall find so doing: he shall say unto him, Well done good and faithful servant, enter into thy Master's joy (Luke 12:43; Matthew 25:21).[778]

James Ussher, *A Body of Divinity*

God's Word treats the judgment of believers with great sobriety. It does not portray it as a meaningless formality, going through the motions before we get on to the real business of heavenly bliss. Rather, Scripture presents it as a monumental event in which things of eternal significance are brought to light and things of eternal consequence are put into effect.[779]

Randy Alcorn, *The Law of Rewards*

A man went to visit the caretaker of a large estate that had an absentee owner. Noticing how meticulously the caretaker performed every chore, the visitor asked him, "When do you expect the owner to return?" The caretaker's reply: "Today, of course."

Like soldiers ready at any moment for a barracks inspection, the servants are constantly aware this could be the day of the master's return. If they knew the day or hour of that return, they could waste time. They might "borrow" some of the master's money, figuring to replace it before he comes back. When they cease to expect the master's return, embezzlement or squandering become great temptations. But the stewards know that the master is a man of his word. He will keep his promise to return. The servants must live each day as if it were the day of the master's return. One day it will be.

Our death is equivalent to the master's return, for it marks the day our earthly service ends. Our service record "freezes" into its final form, to be evaluated as such by our Master at the judgment.[780]

Randy Alcorn, *Money, Possessions, and Eternity*

In the day that we stand before our Master and Maker, it will not matter how many people on earth knew our name, how many called us great, and how many considered us fools. It will not matter whether schools and hospitals were named after us, whether our estate was large or small, whether our funeral drew ten thousand or no one. It will not matter what the newspapers or history books said or didn't say. What will matter is one thing and one thing only—what the Master thinks of us.[781]

Randy Alcorn, *Money, Possessions, and Eternity*

We'll never question God's justice, wondering how he could send good people to Hell. Rather, we'll be overwhelmed with his grace, marveling at what he did to send bad people to Heaven. (We will no longer have any illusion that fallen people are good without Christ.)[782]

Randy Alcorn, *Heaven*

The Kingdom of Heaven

My kingdom is not of this world. . . . You are right in saying I am a king. In fact, for this reason I was born, and for this I came into the world.

JESUS, JOHN 18:36-37

At the renewal of all things, when the Son of Man sits on his glorious throne, you who have followed me will also sit on twelve thrones, judging the twelve tribes of Israel.

JESUS, MATTHEW 19:28

The seventh angel sounded his trumpet, and there were loud voices in heaven, which said:

"The kingdom of the world has become
    the kingdom of our Lord and of his Christ,
and he will reign for ever and ever."

And the twenty-four elders, who were seated on their thrones before God, fell on their faces and worshiped God, saying:

"We give thanks to you, Lord God Almighty,
     the One who is and who was,
because you have taken your great power
     and have begun to reign.
The nations were angry;
     and your wrath has come.
The time has come for judging the dead,
     and for rewarding your servants the prophets
and your saints and those who reverence your name,
     both small and great—
and for destroying those who destroy the earth."

Then God's temple in heaven was opened, and within his temple was seen the ark of his covenant. And there came flashes of lightning, rumblings, peals of thunder, an earthquake and a great hailstorm.

JOHN, REVELATION 11:15-19

He shall see the labor of His soul, and be satisfied.
     By His knowledge My righteous Servant shall
          justify many,
     For He shall bear their iniquities.
     Therefore I will divide Him a portion with the
          great,
     And He shall divide the spoil with the strong,
     Because He poured out His soul unto death,
     And He was numbered with the transgressors,
     And He bore the sin of many,
     And made intercession for the transgressors.

GOD, ISAIAH 53:11-12, NKJV

The LORD will be king over all the earth. On that day there will be one LORD—his name alone will be worshiped.

GOD, ZECHARIAH 14:9, NLT

There before me was one like a son of man, coming with the clouds of heaven. He approached the Ancient of Days and was led into his presence. He was given authority, glory and sovereign power; all peoples, nations and men of every language worshiped him. His dominion is an everlasting dominion that will not pass away, and his kingdom is one that will never be destroyed.

DANIEL 7:13-14

Rejoice greatly, O Daughter of Zion!
    Shout, Daughter of Jerusalem!
See, your king comes to you,
    righteous and having salvation,
    gentle and riding on a donkey,
    on a colt, the foal of a donkey.
I will take away the chariots from Ephraim
    and the war-horses from Jerusalem,
    and the battle bow will be broken.
He will proclaim peace to the nations.
    His rule will extend from sea to sea
    and from the River to the ends of the earth.

ORACLE, ZECHARIAH 9:9-10

The righteous will shine like the sun in the kingdom of their Father.

JESUS, MATTHEW 13:43

I confer on you a kingdom, just as my Father conferred one on me, so that you may eat and drink at
my table in my kingdom.

Jesus, Luke 22:29-30

Do not be afraid, little flock, for your Father has been
pleased to give you the kingdom.

Jesus, Luke 12:32

Blessed are the poor in spirit, for theirs is the kingdom of heaven. . . . Blessed are the meek, for they
will inherit the earth. . . . Blessed are those who are
persecuted because of righteousness, for theirs is the
kingdom of heaven.

Jesus, Matthew 5:3, 5, 10

As in Adam all die, so in Christ all will be made alive.
But each in his own turn: Christ, the firstfruits; then,
when he comes, those who belong to him. Then the
end will come, when he hands over the kingdom to
God the Father after he has destroyed all dominion,
authority and power. For he must reign until he has
put all his enemies under his feet.

Paul, 1 Corinthians 15:22-25

Come, you who are blessed by my Father; take your
inheritance, the kingdom prepared for you since the
creation of the world.

Jesus, Matthew 25:34

The central thing for Jesus and the apostles, and for the Bible as a
whole, is *the final triumph and eternal reign of God.* Whatever our

individual prospects may be, and however confidently we may affirm our personal hope of life after death, *the future is finally the future of God*, envisaged as the return in glory of his Son, the messianic King Jesus, the overthrow of all God's enemies and the arrival of the kingdom of God in its fullness—the "new heaven and earth of righteousness." "Going to," or "being in," heaven means our participation in *that*.[783]

Bruce Milne, *The Message of Heaven and Hell*

Over and over again the Scriptures make this plain: the political power which has been so corrupted and twisted in the hands and hearts of sinful rulers must be returned to its rightful source.[784]

Richard Mouw, *When the Kings Come Marching In*

The signs of the times reveal that the great victory of Christ has been won, and that therefore the decisive change in history has occurred. They reveal that God is at work in the world, busy fulfilling his promises and bringing to realization the final consummation of redemption. They reveal the central meaning of history: the Lord rules, and is working out his purposes.[785]

Anthony Hoekema, *The Bible and the Future*

The truth about our Christian destiny will be reinstated when we return to biblical language about "entering the Kingdom," "inheriting the Kingdom," "inheriting the earth" (Matthew 5:5), "reigning as kings on the earth" (Revelation 5:10), "reigning with the Messiah for a thousand years" (Revelation 20:1-6). . . . The tragedy of man is of kingship lost. The goal of man is kingship regained in association with the great King Messiah who has pioneered the way to victory over the world.[786]

Anthony Buzzard, *Our Fathers Who Aren't in Heaven*

We cannot understand biblical revelation, human history, or the events of our own lives if we don't grasp God's plan for the new heavens and New Earth. . . . [Christ's] redemption acquires the significance of an all-inclusive divine drama, of a cosmic struggle . . . the goal of which is to bring back the entire created cosmos under God's dominion and rule.[787]

Herman Ridderbos, *Paul and Jesus*

We must see [history] as moving toward the goal of a finally restored and glorified universe.[788]

Anthony Hoekema, *The Bible and the Future*

You can be certain you won't regret any sacrifice you made for the kingdom. The hours of service for Christ? You won't regret them. The money you gave? You'd give it a thousand times over. The times you helped the poor and loved the lost? You'd do it again.

. . . You'd change the diapers, fix the cars, prepare the lessons, repair the roofs. One look into the faces of the ones you love, and you'd do it all again.[789]

Max Lucado, *When Christ Comes*

Despite all their disappointments, the faithful never abandoned hope in God's covenants with Abraham and David, guaranteeing a final restoration and liberation under the reign of the promised Prince Messiah.

Since the dawn of history the faithful have awaited the coming of the one who was to be empowered to reverse the tragedy which had befallen Adam and Eve and the human race as a whole. This was the King Messiah, God's legal agent, imbued with the divine Spirit, who would triumph over the spiritual powers of darkness that had enslaved mankind's first parents and their descendants ever since. . . .

Using Jesus as His human agent, the Second Adam, God was beginning to reassert His authority and recover rebel province earth from the clutches of the Devil. In the words of the beloved Apostle, Jesus was commissioned to "unravel the work of the Devil" (1 John 3:8). Peter captured the essence of the work of Jesus the Messiah with these words: "You know of Jesus of Nazareth, how God anointed Him with the Holy Spirit and with power, and how He went about doing good, and healing all who were oppressed by the Devil, for God was with Him" (Acts 10:38).[790]

Anthony Buzzard, *Our Fathers Who Aren't in Heaven*

The Kingdom of God, then, is an empire ruled by the king of Israel enthroned in Jerusalem. This definition will throw a flood of light on what Jesus meant by the Good News about the Kingdom of God. The Hebrew term "Kingdom of the Lord" reappears in Revelation 11:15, where, at the seventh trumpet blast, the power of present political states is to be transferred to the "Kingdom of our Lord and of His Christ."[791]

Anthony Buzzard, *Our Fathers Who Aren't in Heaven*

After nearly two thousand years of uncomprehending Gentile opposition, the promise to Abraham of progeny, blessing, greatness, and land must be reinstated in the churches' teaching as the coherent and unifying theme of biblical faith in God and Christ and the essential core of the Christian Gospel about the Kingdom of God.

In the words of Jesus: "Many will come from the north, south, east and west and sit down with Abraham, Isaac, Jacob and all the prophets at the banquet table in the Kingdom of God" (Matthew 8:11; Luke 13:28, 29). Together as members of the Messianic community drawn from all colors and races they will "rule as kings *upon the earth*" (Revelation 5:10), which is what Jesus meant by "inheriting the earth." In so speaking Jesus was simply echoing the ancient promise to the faithful that God would "exalt them to inherit the land" (Psalm 37:34). Jesus is clearly a prophet of restoration, seeing Himself as the agent of God commissioned to head up the divine operation for the rescue of man from the tyranny and deception of the Devil.

The writer to the Hebrews spoke of attaining the "future inhabited earth" (Hebrews 2:5). . . . The time is coming when "the saints possess the Kingdom" and "all nations serve and obey them" (Daniel 7:22, 27).[792]

Anthony Buzzard, *Our Fathers Who Aren't in Heaven*

To snatch saved souls away to a disembodied heaven would destroy the whole point. God is to become king of the whole world at last. And he will do this not by declaring that the inner dynamic of creation (that it be ruled by humans) was a mistake, nor by declaring that the inner dynamic of his covenant (that Israel would be the means of saving the nations) was a failure, but rather by fulfilling them both.[793]

N. T. Wright, *Surprised by Hope*

The Kingdom of God (or Kingdom of Heaven, which is a synonym) has as its primary definition, especially in Matthew, Mark and Luke, a world empire, centered in Jerusalem, administered by the Messiah and the saints. It is the goal of the entire divine purpose and the objective placed before every Christian believer. The outcome of history is the restoration of Eden under a new divine rule. The Kingdom of God has nothing to do with the present movements designed to reform society, however well intentioned. Much less is it to be a Kingdom *in* heaven as a place for departed souls at death. Nor should the Kingdom of God be reduced to a synonym for the Church. The equation of the Kingdom with the Church has caused untold confusion.[794]

Anthony Buzzard, *Our Fathers Who Aren't in Heaven*

Everything in the Gospels points to the idea that life in the Kingdom of God in the Age to Come will be life on the earth—life transformed by the Kingdom of God when His people enter in their full blessing (Matthew 19:28).[795]

George Ladd, *A Theology of the New Testament*

We shall dwell in glorified bodies on the glorified earth. This is one of the great Christian doctrines that has been *almost entirely forgotten and ignored.* Unfortunately the Christian Church—I speak generally—*does not believe this,* and therefore does not teach it. It has lost its hope, and this explains why it spends most of its time in trying to improve life in this world, in preaching politics. . . . But something remarkable is going to be true of us according to the Apostle Paul in 1 Corinthians 6:1-3: "Dare any of you having a matter against another, go to law against the unjust and not before the Saints? Do you not know that the Saints shall rule the world?" . . . *This is Christianity. This is the truth by which the New Testament Church lived.* It was because of this that they were not afraid of their persecutors. . . . This was the secret of their endurance, their patience and their triumphing over everything that was set against them.[796]

Anthony Buzzard, *Our Fathers Who Aren't in Heaven*

While the writings of the Apostles concentrate on the development of the Church as the leaders-in-training of the coming Messianic era, there is no evidence that New Testament Christians had abandoned the "Jewish picture" of the Messiah as coming governor of a renewed world order. How could they when the Scriptures which Jesus endorsed had painted such a vivid picture of the Messiah's future intervention in world affairs? Based on the biblical hope, which Jesus never discounted, the Jews pray three times daily that "speedily the world will be perfected under the Kingdom of the Almighty. . . . Let all the inhabitants of the world perceive and know that unto Thee every knee must bow, every tongue must swear . . . and let them all accept the yoke of Your Kingdom."[797]

Anthony Buzzard, *Our Fathers Who Aren't in Heaven*

What shall be the estate of the Elect in Heaven? They shall be unspeakably and everlastingly blessed and glorious in body and soul; being freed from all imperfections and infirmities, yea from such Graces as imply imperfection, as Faith, Hope, Repentance, etc.

endued with perfect Wisdom and Holiness, possessed with all the pleasures that are at the right hand of God, seated as princes in Thrones of majesty, crowned, with Crowns of Glory, possessing the new Heaven and Earth wherein dwelleth Righteousness, beholding and being filled with the fruition of the glorious presence of God, and of the Lamb, Jesus Christ, in the company of innumerable Angels and holy Saints, as the Scripture phrases are.

What shall follow this? Christ shall deliver up that dispensatory kingdom (which He received for the subduing of His enemies and accomplishing the salvation of His church) unto God the Father, and God shall be all in all for all eternity.[798]

James Ussher, *A Body of Divinity*

Consider this prophetic statement: "The kingdom of the world has become the kingdom of our Lord and of his Christ, and he will reign for ever and ever" (Revelation 11:15). It doesn't say that Christ will destroy this world's kingdom. It doesn't even say he'll replace this world's kingdom. No, the kingdom of this world will actually *become* the Kingdom of Christ. God won't obliterate earthly kingdoms but will *transform them into his own.* And it's that new earthly kingdom (joined then to God's heavenly Kingdom) over which "he will reign for ever and ever."

This is a revolutionary viewpoint, standing in stark contrast to the prevalent myth that God's Kingdom will demolish and replace the kingdoms of Earth rather than cleanse, redeem, and resurrect them into his eternal Kingdom. This brings us back again to that remarkable statement about the New Jerusalem: "The nations will walk by its light, and the kings of the earth will bring their splendor into it. On no day will its gates ever be shut. . . . The glory and honor of the nations will be brought into it" (Revelation 21:24-26).[799]

Randy Alcorn, *Heaven*

On prophecy, there is a difference between being right and being orthodox. While eschatology itself is essential, in the sense that it's at the heart of God's plan, it is not essential that we understand in detail how the future will fall together. The cornerstone of all eschatology—required for orthodoxy—is a belief in the second coming of Christ. His physical return to this earth. The second cornerstone is belief in Heaven, the eternal Kingdom of the new heavens and New Earth, where God makes all things right, eliminates sin and suffering, reverses the Curse and ushers in an eternity forever changed by the redemptive work of Christ. The details of the Tribulation and the Millennium are matters worth discussing, but Bible-believing people can and do have widely divergent understandings. Since this book concerns both the present heavenly state and the eternal heaven to come, the reader's beliefs about the Tribulation are not significant to it and beliefs about the Millennium are secondary.

Randy Alcorn, unpublished notes

Under God's covenant with Israel, the people never looked for the Messiah to reign in Heaven. That would be nothing new, because God already reigns in Heaven. Establishing God's Kingdom was never about an immaterial spirit realm. It always concerned the one place in the universe made for mankind, the one place where God's reign has been disputed: Earth.[800]

Randy Alcorn, *Heaven*

Knowledge, Learning, and Books

The LORD gives wisdom, and from his mouth come
knowledge and understanding.

SOLOMON, PROVERBS 2:6

Grow in the grace and knowledge of our Lord and
Savior Jesus Christ. To him be glory both now and
forever! Amen.

PETER, 2 PETER 3:18

Instruct a wise man and he will be wiser still; teach
a righteous man and he will add to his learning.

SOLOMON, PROVERBS 9:9

Now we see but a poor reflection as in a mirror; then we shall see face to face. Now I know in part; then I shall know fully, even as I am fully known.

PAUL, 1 CORINTHIANS 13:12

[God] raised us up with him and seated us with him in the heavenly places in Christ Jesus, so that in the coming ages he might show the immeasurable riches of his grace in kindness toward us in Christ Jesus.

PAUL, EPHESIANS 2:6-7, ESV

There are more things in heaven and earth, Horatio,
Than are dreamt of in your philosophy.

Shakespeare, *Hamlet,* Act I, Scene V

We cannot believe that those who are in the Lord's presence can ever again be sad, but this does not mean that in order to be joyful they must be ignorant.[801]

W. Graham Scroggie, *What about Heaven?*

Knowledge is a source of the most exquisite pleasures.

If it is so in this world, where the curse of sin has darkened the mind, and where knowledge is so limited, and so mingled with error and doubt, what shall we say of those pleasures in Heaven? There the intellect of man receives a supernatural light; it is elevated far above itself by the light of glory.[802]

Father J. Boudreau, *The Happiness of Heaven*

I would have no fault of mine deprive me of the smallest degree of fruition. I can say, then, that if I were asked whether I should prefer to endure all the trials in the world until the world itself ends, and afterwards to gain a little more glory, or to have no trials and attain to one degree less of glory, I should answer that I would most gladly accept all the trials in exchange for a little more fruition in the understanding of the wonders of God, for I see that he who understands Him best loves and praises Him best.[803]

Teresa of Avila, autobiography

We will probably not be stuck with the ages we had when we left earth, but in heaven we will all be babes in knowledge—ready, eager, and able to learn as never before.[804]

John Gilmore, *Probing Heaven*

Heaven is not going to be the cessation of school. If anything it will be graduate school for everyone, including those who were the learning disabled on earth![805]

John Gilmore, *Probing Heaven*

According to Scripture, when the soul enters heaven it continues to live. It does not just remain everlastingly in a fixed position. It does not simply "stay put." It lives more abundantly than ever before. Now to live means to think, to have fellowship, to see and hear, to rejoice, etc. Now, it would seem to me, for finite beings, in a state of sinlessness, such living spells progress. Is it at all probable that we shall think and not advance in knowledge? That we shall have fellowship—and what a fellowship!—and not make progress in love? That we shall see and hear the glories of heaven and not become enriched in our experience of heavenly joy?

. . . Just as the "perfect" Christ-child was the one who "advanced in wisdom and stature, and in favor with God and men," so it may well be in heaven.[806]

William Hendriksen, *The Bible on the Life Hereafter*

In the Fall, a curtain was lowered, which has caused us to "see through a glass darkly," but in Heaven that curtain will be lifted, and "I shall know, even as I am known" [1 Corinthians 13:12]. One of the great joys of heaven will be that of taking all the time necessary to unravel all the mysteries about God, about man, and about the universe.[807]

Don Baker, *Heaven: A Glimpse of Your Future Home*

A friend of mine asked a question, "Do you think we shall go to school in heaven?" . . . If the saints are to reign with Christ, do you think they will need special training to be prepared for any emergency which may arise? For example, supposing I were asked to rule over a city, or two, or ten, what would I know about that kind of job? Surely the Lord would not expect anyone to do something for which he was not qualified. So there must be a place where the saints will be taught what they need to know.[808]

Ivor Powell, *Heaven: My Father's Country*

Since God is infinite, and in Him are all treasures of wisdom, we would throughout eternity be ever searching, ever learning, yet would never exhaust the riches of His wisdom, His goodness, or His power.[809]

Walton Brown, *Home at Last*

Since God is infinite and we can never exhaust his greatness (Psalm 145:3), and since we are finite creatures who will never equal God's knowledge or be omniscient, we may expect that for all eternity we will be able to go on learning more about God and about his relationship to his creation. In this way we will continue the process of learning that was begun in this life, in which a life "fully pleasing to him" is one that includes continually "increasing in the knowledge of God" (Colossians 1:10).[810]

Wayne Grudem, *Systematic Theology*

First Corinthians 13:12 does not say that we will be omniscient or know everything (Paul could have said we will know all things, *ta panta*, if he had wished to do so), but, rightly translated, simply says that we will know in a fuller or more intensive way, "even as we have been known," that is, without any error or misconceptions in our knowledge.[811]

Wayne Grudem, *Systematic Theology*

The Christian is the really free man—he is free to have imagination. This too is our heritage. The Christian is the one whose imagination should fly beyond the stars.[812]

Francis Schaeffer, *Art and the Bible*

The life of Heaven is one of intellectual pleasure. . . . [The intellect] is purified, strengthened, enlarged, and enabled to see God as He is in His very essence. It is enabled to contemplate, face to face, Him who is the first essential Truth. It gazes undazzled upon the first infinite beauty, wisdom, and goodness, from whom flow all limited wisdom, beauty, and goodness found in creatures. Who can fathom the exquisite pleasures of the human intellect when it thus sees all truth as it is in itself![813]

Father J. Boudreau, *The Happiness of Heaven*

We remember the great delight with which he [Martin Luther] recounted the course, the counsels, the perils and escapes of the prophets, and the learning with which he discoursed on all the ages of the Church, thereby showing that he was inflamed by no ordinary passion for these wonderful men. Now he embraces them and rejoices to hear them speak and to speak to them in turn. Now they hail him gladly as a companion, and thank God with him for having gathered and preserved the Church.[814]

Philip Melanchthon's memorial address about his departed friend Martin Luther, 1546

Our first and last wisdom in Heaven is Socratic, just as it is on earth: to know how little we know. If there is no end of the need for humility in the moral order (the saint is the one humble enough not to think he is a saint), the same is true of the intellectual order (the wise man is the one humble enough to know he has no wisdom) . . . by Heavenly standards all of us, even in Heaven, are children. And by the standard of the *infinite*, inexhaustible perfection of God, we remain children forever. Happy children, fulfilled children, but children.[815]

Peter Kreeft, *Everything You Ever Wanted to Know about Heaven*

For a long time it has been a bright anticipation of mine, that in Heaven, I would be able to study the Bible with far greater light, and with better help than it is possible for me to get here. It seems to me that the study of His Word will be one of the great joys of the redeemed in Glory.[816]

Judson Palmer, "The Child of God between Death and the Resurrection"

They could have Halls of Science, of Art, of Literature, Mathematics, where all man's achievements of the past would be on record, where they could study these, absorb them, and be drawn to expand them further and further in innumerable directions. They could have Halls of Music where they could see and study all the great achievements men have made in composition, in instrumentation, in orchestration, in singing . . . and be drawn to expand these, one in this way, another in that way.[817]

E. J. Fortman, *Everlasting Life after Death*

I beg you, my dearest brother, to live among these books to meditate on them, to know nothing else, to seek nothing else. Does not this seem to you to be a little bit of heaven here on earth? . . . Let us learn upon earth that knowledge which will continue with us in Heaven.[818]

Jerome, a letter to the church

My friend said, "I don't see why there shouldn't be books in Heaven. But you will find that your library in Heaven contains only some of the books you had on earth." "Which?" I asked. "The ones you gave away or lent." "I hope the lent ones won't still have all the borrowers' dirty thumb marks," said I. "Oh yes they will," said he. "But just as the wounds of the martyrs will have turned into beauties, so you will find that the thumb-marks have turned into beautiful illuminated capitals or exquisite marginal woodcuts."[819]

C. S. Lewis, *God in the Dock*

The first humans lived in process, as God ordained them to. Adam knew more a week after he was created than he did on his first day.

Nothing is wrong with process and the limitations it implies. Jesus "grew in wisdom and stature" (Luke 2:52). Jesus "learned obedience" (Hebrews 5:8). Growing and learning cannot be bad; the sinless Son of God experienced them. They are simply part of being human.

Unless we cease to be human after our resurrection, we will go on growing and learning. If anything, sin makes us less human. When the parasite of sin is removed, full humanity will be restored—and improved.

The sense of wonder among Heaven's inhabitants shows Heaven is not stagnant but fresh and stimulating, suggesting an ever-deepening appreciation of God's greatness (Revelation 4–6). Heaven's riches are rooted in Heaven's God. We will find in Heaven a continual progression of stimulating discovery and fresh learning as we keep grasping more of God.

In *Hamlet*, Shakespeare called what lies beyond death "the undiscover'd country." It's a country we yearn to discover—and by Christ's grace, we will.[820]

Randy Alcorn, *Heaven*

Will our knowledge and skills vary? Will some people in Heaven have greater knowledge and specialized abilities than others? Why not? Scripture shows there will be differences in Heaven. We will be individuals, each with our own memories and God-given gifts. Some of our knowledge will overlap, but not all. We'll be learners forever. God doesn't want us to stop learning. What he wants to stop is what prevents us from learning.[821]

Randy Alcorn, *TouchPoints: Heaven*

God alone is omniscient. When we die, we'll see things far more clearly, and we'll know much more than we do now, but we'll *never* know everything.[822]

Randy Alcorn, *Heaven*

Paul, in Ephesians 2:7, unveils one of God's purposes in his redemptive work: "in order that in the coming ages he might show the incomparable riches of his grace and his kindness to us in Christ Jesus." The word translated *show* means "to reveal." The phrase *in the coming ages* clearly indicates that this will be a progressive, ongoing revelation, in which we learn more and more, about God's grace and kindness in Christ. We will never stop learning about Him and his qualities and affection for us.

I often learn new things about my wife, daughters, and closest friends, even though I've known them for many years. If I can always be learning something new about finite, limited human beings, how much more will I be learning about Jesus in the ages to come? None of us will ever begin to exhaust his depths.

Jesus said to his disciples, "Learn from me" (Matthew 11:29). On the New Earth we'll have the privilege of sitting at Jesus' feet as Mary did, walking with him over the countryside as his disciples did, and always learning from him. In Heaven, we'll continually learn new things about God, going ever deeper in our understanding.[823]

Randy Alcorn, *50 Days of Heaven*

Think of what it will be like to discuss science with Isaac Newton, Michael Faraday, and Thomas Edison or to discuss mathematics with Pascal. Imagine long talks with Malcolm Muggeridge or Francis

Schaeffer. Think of reading and discussing the writings of C. S. Lewis, J. R. R. Tolkien, G. K. Chesterton, or Dorothy Sayers with the authors themselves. How would you like to talk about the power of fiction at a roundtable with John Milton, Daniel Defoe, Victor Hugo, Fyodor Dostoyevsky, Leo Tolstoy, and Flannery O'Connor?

How about discussing God's attributes with Stephen Charnock, A. W. Pink, A. W. Tozer, and J. I. Packer? Or talking theology with Augustine, Aquinas, Calvin, and Luther? Then, when differences arise, why not invite Jesus in to clear things up?

Imagine discussing the sermons of George Whitefield, Jonathan Edwards, Charles Finney, and Charles Spurgeon with the preachers themselves. Or sitting down to hear insights on family and prayer from Susanna Wesley. Or talking about faith with George Mueller or Bill Bright, then listening to their stories. You could cover the Civil War era with Abraham Lincoln and Harriet Beecher Stowe. Or the history of missions with William Carey, Amy Carmichael, Lottie Moon, or Hudson and Maria Taylor. You could discuss ministry ideas with Brother Andrew, George Verwer, Luis Palau, Billy Graham, Joni Eareckson Tada, Chuck Colson, or Elisabeth Elliot.

We'll contemplate God's person and works, talking long over dinner and tea, on walks and in living rooms, by rivers and fires. Intellectual curiosity isn't part of the Curse—it is God's blessing on his image-bearers. He made us with fertile, curious minds so that we might seek truth and find him, our greatest source of pleasure. In Heaven our intellectual curiosity will surely surface—and be satisfied—only to surface and be satisfied again and again.[824]

Randy Alcorn, *Heaven*

There's so much to discover in this universe, but we have so little time and opportunity to do it. The list of books I haven't read, music I've never heard, and places I haven't been is unending. There's much more to know. I look forward to discovering new things in Heaven— forever. And at the end of each day I'll have the same amount of time left as I did the day before![825]

Randy Alcorn, *Heaven*

Will there be books in Heaven? We know that sixty-six books, those that comprise the Bible, will be in Heaven—"Your Word, O Lord, is eternal; it stands firm in the heavens" (Psalm 119:89). Jesus said, "Heaven and earth will pass away, but my words will never pass away" (Matthew 24:35). Presumably, we will read, study, contemplate, and discuss God's Word.

There are also other books in Heaven: "I saw the dead, great and small, standing before the throne, and books were opened. Another book was opened, which is the book of life. The dead were judged according to what they had done as recorded in the books" (Revelation 20:12).

What are these books? They appear to contain documentation of everything ever done by anyone on earth. To say the least, they must be extensive.

. . . Other passages describe a scroll in Heaven. Jesus opens a great scroll (Revelation 5:1, 5), and an angel holds a little scroll (Revelation 10:2). The psalm writer David said, "Record my lament; list my tears on your scroll—are they not in your record?" (Psalm 56:8). He asked that his tears be kept in Heaven's permanent record.

Malachi 3:16-18 is a remarkable passage that tells us God documents the faithful deeds of his children on Earth: "Then those who feared the Lord talked with each other, and the Lord listened and heard. A scroll of remembrance was written in his presence concerning those who feared the Lord and honored his name. 'They will be mine,' says the Lord Almighty, 'in the day when I make up my treasured possession. I will spare them, just as in compassion a man spares his son who serves him. And you will again see the distinction between the righteous and the wicked, between those who serve God and those who do not.'"

God is proud of his people for fearing him and honoring his name, and he promises that all will see the differences between those who serve him and those who don't. Those distinctions are preserved in this scroll in Heaven.

The king often had scribes record the deeds of his subjects so that he could remember and properly reward his subjects' good deeds

(Esther 6:1-11). While God needs no reminder, he makes a permanent record so that the entire universe will one day know his justification for rewarding the righteous and punishing the wicked.

There's no hint that God will destroy any or all of the books and
scrolls presently in Heaven. It's likely that these records of the faithful
works of God's people on Earth will be periodically read throughout
the ages.[826]

Randy Alcorn, *Heaven*

I believe that on the New Earth, we'll also read books, new and old,
written by people. Because we'll have strong intellects, great curiosity,
and unlimited time, it's likely that books will have a *greater* role in our
lives in Heaven than they do now. The libraries of the New Earth, I
imagine, will be fantastic.

We'll have no lack of resources to study and understand. . . .
Will we search for information and do research on the New Earth?
Why not?

. . . Every biblical genealogy is a testimony to God's interest in
history, heritage, and the unfolding of events on Earth. Will God lose
interest in Earth? Will we? No. The New Earth's history includes that
of the old Earth. But a new history will be built and recorded, a new
civilization, wondrous beyond imagination. And we who know the
King will all be part of it.

Books are part of culture. I expect many new books, great
books, will be written on the New Earth. But I also believe that some
books will endure from the old Earth. Any book that contains false-
hood and dishonors God will have no place in Heaven. But what
about great books, nonfiction and fiction? Will we find A. W. Tozer's
The Knowledge of the Holy, J. I. Packer's *Knowing God*, John Piper's
Desiring God, John Bunyan's *Pilgrim's Progress*, and the sermons of
Charles Spurgeon on the New Earth? I'll be amazed if we don't find
them there, just as I'll be amazed if no one sings John Newton's
"Amazing Grace" in Heaven.

Perhaps those of us who are writers will go back to some of our
published works and rewrite them in light of the perspective we'll

gain. Maybe we'll look at our other books and realize they're no longer important—and some of them never were. The New Earth, I think, will confirm many things I've written in this book. It will completely dismantle others. "What was I thinking?" I'll ask myself. (If I knew which parts those were right now, I'd cut them out!) And I'll marvel at how much better the New Earth is than I ever imagined.[827]

Randy Alcorn, *Heaven*

Marriage and Family

See also Friends and Relationships.

It is not good for the man to be alone. I will make a helper suitable for him.

GOD, GENESIS 2:18

In the resurrection, therefore, of the seven, whose wife will she be? For they all had her.

THE SADUCCEES, MATTHEW 22:28, ESV

You are wrong, because you know neither the Scriptures nor the power of God. For in the resurrection they neither marry nor are given in marriage, but are like angels in heaven.

JESUS, MATTHEW 22:29-30

Husbands, love your wives, just as Christ loved the church and gave himself up for her to make her holy, cleansing her by the washing with water through the word, and to present her to himself as a radiant church, without stain or wrinkle or any other blemish, but holy and blameless. In this same way, husbands ought to love their wives as their own bodies. He who loves his wife loves himself. After all, no one ever hated his own body, but he feeds and cares for it, just as Christ does the church—for we are members of his body. "For this reason a man will leave his father and mother and be united to his wife, and the two will become one flesh." This is a profound mystery—but I am talking about Christ and the church. However, each one of you also must love his wife as he loves himself, and the wife must respect her husband.

PAUL, EPHESIANS 5:25-33

[In Heaven] I shall be near thee
dwell with my family
stand in thy presence chamber,
be an heir of thy kingdom,
as the spouse of Christ,
as a member of his body,
one with him who is with thee,
and exercise all my powers of body and soul
in the enjoyment of thee.[828]

The Valley of Vision: A Collection of Puritan Prayers and Devotions

The purpose of marriage is not to replace Heaven, but to prepare us for it.[829]

Drake Whitchurch, *Waking from Earth*

You will be exponentially closer to your spouse in Heaven than the happiest day of your marriage here. Your relationship will be far more meaningful there because there will be no misunderstandings. No hurt feelings. No selfishness. No impatience. Just perfect love.[830]

Steven J. Lawson, *Heaven Help Us!*

On the marble cross erected over his wife's grave, Charles Kingsley had these words inscribed, "We have loved, we love, we shall love." After the death of his wife, Browning wrote in her New Testament the words of Dante, "Thus I believe, thus I affirm, thus I am certain it is, that from this life I shall pass to another better, where the lady lives of whom my soul was enamoured." "We are agreed," says John Fiske, "that the life beyond the grave would be a delusion and a cruel mockery without the continuance of the tender household affections which alone make the present life worth living."[831]

James Campbell, *Heaven Opened*

"I comfort myself with the hope that we'll know the thing there, that maybe we're but tryin' to believe here. But at any rate you have proved well that you and me's one, Robert. Now we know from Scripture that the Master came to make forever one, of them that was two. And we know also that he conquered Death. So he would never let Death make the one that he had make one into two again. There's no reason to think it! For all I know, what looks like a goin' away may be a comin' nearer. And there may be ways of comin' nearer to one another up yonder that we know nothing about down here." . . .

"Hoot, Janet! You know there's neither marryin' or givin' in marriage, there."

"Who was sayin' anything about marryin' or givin' in marriage, Robert? Is that to say that you and me's to be no more to one another than other folk? We wouldn't say, now would we, that just 'cause marriage is not the way of the country, there's to be nothing better in the place of it!"[832]

Janet and Robert, in *Sir Gibbie,* by George MacDonald

I have just heard, to my great surprise, that I have but a few days to live. It may be that before this reaches you, I shall have entered the palace. Don't trouble to write. We shall meet in the morning.[833]

F. B. Meyer, letter to a friend a few days before his death

A great multitude of dear ones is there expecting us; a vast and mighty crowd of parents, brothers, and children, secure now of their own safety, anxious yet for our salvation, long that we may come to their right and embrace them, to that joy which will be common to us and to them.[834]

Bede the Venerable, All Saints Day sermon

Those whom you laid in the grave with many tears are in good keeping: you will yet see them again with joy. Believe it, think it, rest on it. It is all true.[835]

J. C. Ryle, *Heaven*

If a man could mount to heaven and survey the mighty universe, his admiration of its beauties would be much diminished unless he had some one to share in his pleasure.[836]

Cicero, *De Amicitia*

We were made for God. Only by being in some respect like Him, only by being a manifestation of His beauty, lovingkindness, wisdom or goodness, has any earthly Beloved excited our love. It is not that we have loved them too much, but that we did not quite understand what we were loving. It is not that we shall be asked to turn from them, so dearly familiar, to a Stranger. When we see the face of God we shall know that we have always known it. He has been a party to, has made, sustained and moved moment by moment within, all our earthly experiences of innocent love. All that was true love in them was, even on earth, far more His than ours, and ours only because His. In Heaven there will be no anguish and no duty of turning away from our earthly Beloveds. First, because we shall have turned already; from the portraits to the Original, from the rivulets to the Fountain, from the creatures he made lovable to Love Himself. But secondly, because we shall find them all in Him. By loving Him more than them we shall love them more than we now do.[837]

C. S. Lewis, *The Four Loves*

I once heard a woman make this foolish statement, after losing her husband to death, "If John isn't in heaven, then I don't want to be there either." Why is that foolish? Because she is putting John before God. God will be there: . . . God's first commandment in the Decalog is, "You shall have no other gods before me" (Exodus 20:3).[838]

Chuck McGowen, *Let's Talk about Heaven*

If I knew that never again would I recognize that beloved one with whom I spent more than thirty-nine years here on earth, my anticipation of heaven would much abate. To say that we shall be with Christ and that that will be enough, is to claim that there we shall be without the social instincts and affections which mean so much to us here. . . . Life beyond cannot mean impoverishment, but the enhancement and enrichment of life as we have known it here at its best.[839]

W. Graham Scroggie, *What about Heaven?*

Jesus said the institution of human marriage would end, having fulfilled its purpose. But he never hinted that deep relationships between married people would end. In our lives here, two people can be business partners, tennis partners, or pinochle partners. But when they're no longer partners, it doesn't mean their friendship ends. The relationship built during one kind of partnership often carries over to a permanent friendship after the partnership has ended. I expect that to be true on the New Earth for family members and friends who stood by each other here.[840]

Randy Alcorn, *Heaven*

The joy of marriage in Heaven will be far greater because of the character and love of our bridegroom. I rejoice for Nanci and for myself that we'll both be married to the most wonderful person in the universe. He's already the one we love most—there is no competition. On Earth, the closer we draw to Christ, the closer we draw to each other. Surely the same will be true in Heaven. What an honor it'll be to know that God chose us for each other on this old Earth so that we might have a foretaste of life with him on the New Earth. I fully expect that Nanci will remain my closest friend besides Jesus himself. And I expect other family relationships not to be lost, but to be deepened and enriched.[841]

Randy Alcorn, *50 Days of Heaven*

"At the resurrection people will neither marry nor be given in marriage; they will be like the angels in heaven" (Matthew 22:30).

There's a great deal of misunderstanding about this passage. A woman wrote me, "I struggle with the idea that there won't be marriage in heaven. I believe I'll really miss it."

But the Bible does *not* teach there will be no marriage in Heaven. In fact, it makes it clear there *will* be marriage in Heaven. What it says, in Ephesians 5:31-32, is that there will be *one* marriage, between Christ and his bride—and we'll all be part of it.[842]

Randy Alcorn, *50 Days of Heaven*

Here on Earth we long for a perfect marriage. That's exactly what we'll have—a perfect marriage with Christ. My wife, Nanci, is my best friend and my closest sister in Christ. Will we become more distant in the new world? Of course not—we'll become closer, I'm convinced.

The God who said, "It is not good for the man to be alone" (Genesis 2:18) is the giver and blesser of our relationships. Life on this earth matters. What we do here touches strings that reverberate for all eternity. Nothing will take away from the fact that Nanci and I are marriage partners here and that we invest so much of our lives in each other, serving Christ together. I fully expect no one besides

God will understand me better on the New Earth, and there's nobody whose company I'll seek and enjoy more than Nanci's.

People with good marriages are each other's best friends. There's no reason to believe they won't still be best friends in Heaven.[843]

Randy Alcorn, *Heaven*

People have told me we shouldn't long for Heaven and reunion with loved ones, only for God. If that were true, God would condemn rather than commend his people who "were longing for a better country— a heavenly one" (Hebrews 11:16). King David saw no contradiction between seeking God the person and seeking Heaven the place. The two were inseparable: "One thing have I asked of the LORD, that will I seek after: that I may dwell in the house of the LORD all the days of my life, to gaze upon the beauty of the LORD and to inquire in his temple" (Psalm 27:4, ESV). Notice that David says he seeks "one thing"—to be in God's magnificent place and to be with God's magnificent person.

. . . God is the source of all joy—all other joys are secondary and derivative. They come from him, find their meaning in him, and cannot be divorced from him. Likewise, while Christ is our primary treasure, he encourages us to store up other treasures in Heaven (Matthew 6:19-21).

Christ is Heaven's center of gravity, but we don't diminish his importance by enjoying natural wonders, angels, or people. On the contrary, we'll exalt him and draw closer to him as we enjoy all he created.[844]

Randy Alcorn, *Heaven*

I suggest the possibility that in Heaven we'll see people as we most remember them on earth. So I'll see my parents as older, and they'll see me as younger. I'll see my children as younger, and they'll see me as older. I don't mean that physical forms will actually change but that the resurrection body will convey the real person we have known, and we will see each other through different eyes.[845]

Randy Alcorn, *Heaven*

Jesus said, "Blessed are you who hunger now, for you will be satisfied. Blessed are you who weep now, for you will laugh. Blessed are you when men hate you, when they exclude you and insult you. . . . Rejoice in that day and leap for joy, because great is your reward in heaven" (Luke 6:21-23).

Heaven offers more than comfort; it offers *compensation*. Perhaps in some way on the New Earth, the wives and children of the five missionaries killed by the Auca Indians will receive "comp time" with their loved ones. Consider the millions of Christians who've suffered and died in prison because of their faith, who were snatched away from their families, deprived of opportunities they craved with children and parents and spouses. Wouldn't it be just like Jesus to reward them on the New Earth with opportunities to do the very things they missed—and far better things as well?

. . . In the same way that the hungry will fill up in Heaven and those who weep will laugh, will those who suffer tragedy experience a compensating victory? Maybe on the New Earth my friend Greg will experience a greater but not dissimilar form of the joy he'd have had on this earth if he had not died as a teenager, impaled on a fence post. Maybe all my mom missed because she died before our daughters became adults will be hers in Heaven. She was a faithful servant of God and loved her granddaughters, who were very young when she died. I think God allowed my mom to watch them get married and become mothers, but one day she'll do more than watch them. I think it's likely that when they're together on the New Earth, she'll enjoy all the time she missed with them—and they with her. Maybe those who lost infants to miscarriage and disease and accidents will be given make-up time with them in the new world.

If a father dies before his daughter's wedding and if he and she are Christians, then he'll be there for his daughter's ultimate wedding—to Christ. They will experience a far greater joy on the New Earth than the joy they could have experienced on the old Earth if he had lived longer. If he died before she became an accomplished pianist, he may hear her now from Heaven, but he'll hear her play far better on the New Earth—and she'll see him watching her, delight on his face. If he never lived to see his believing son play basketball, he'll not only see him play on Earth but also play with him on the New Earth. And his children will enjoy the pleasure of seeing the look of utter approval on their father's face . . . and their Father's face.

. . . For those who know God, this sentiment is biblical. He's a God who redeems lost opportunities—especially those lost through our faithful service. I believe that once the Curse is lifted and death is forever reversed, we may live out many of the "could have beens" taken from us on this old Earth.

I think it's probable that two friends who always dreamed of going to a special place, but never managed to, will be able to go to that very place on the New Earth. And the man who couldn't get out of his wheelchair to go biking with his son will never lack that opportunity again.[846]

Randy Alcorn, *Heaven*

New Earth: The Future Heaven

Look! I am creating new heavens and a new earth,
    and no one will even think about the old ones
        anymore.
Be glad; rejoice forever in my creation!
    And look! I will create Jerusalem as a place
        of happiness.
    Her people will be a source of joy.
I will rejoice over Jerusalem
    and delight in my people.
And the sound of weeping and crying
    will be heard in it no more.

No longer will babies die when only a few days old.
    No longer will adults die before they have lived
        a full life.

No longer will people be considered old at one
      hundred!
    Only the cursed will die that young!
In those days people will live in the houses they build
    and eat the fruit of their own vineyards.
Unlike the past, invaders will not take their houses
    and confiscate their vineyards.
For my people will live as long as trees,
    and my chosen ones will have time to enjoy their
      hard-won gains.
They will not work in vain,
    and their children will not be doomed to
      misfortune.
For they are people blessed by the LORD,
    and their children, too, will be blessed.
I will answer them before they even call to me.
      While they are still talking about their needs,
      I will go ahead and answer their prayers!
The wolf and the lamb will feed together.
      The lion will eat hay like a cow.
      But the snakes will eat dust.
In those days no one will be hurt or destroyed on my
      holy mountain.
      I, the LORD, have spoken!

GOD, ISAIAH 65:17-25, NLT

"As the new heavens and the new earth that I make
will endure before me," declares the LORD, "so will
your name and descendants endure. . . . All mankind
will come and bow down before me," says the LORD.

ISAIAH 66:22-23

The LORD will comfort Zion; he will comfort all her
waste places. And her wilderness He will make like

Eden, and her desert like the garden of the LORD; joy and gladness will be found in her, thanksgiving and sound of a melody.

GOD, ISAIAH 51:3, NASB

He himself shall dwell in prosperity, and his descendants shall inherit the earth.

DAVID, PSALM 25:13, NKJV

According to his promise we are waiting for new heavens and a new earth in which righteousness dwells.

PETER, 2 PETER 3:13, ESV

I saw a new heaven and a new earth. . . . And I heard a loud voice from the throne saying, "Now the dwelling of God is with men, and he will live with them. They will be his people, and God himself will be with them and be their God. He will wipe every tear from their eyes. There will be no more death or mourning or crying or pain, for the old order of things has passed away." He who was seated on the throne said, "I am making everything new!" Then he said, "Write this down, for these words are trustworthy and true."

JOHN, REVELATION 21:1, 3-5

"I bet there isn't a country like this anywhere in our world. Look at the colours! You couldn't get a blue like the blue on those mountains in our world."

"Is it not Aslan's country?" said Tirian. . . .

"Those hills," said Lucy, "the nice woody ones and the blue ones behind—aren't they very like the southern border of Narnia?"

"Like!" cried Edmund after a moment's silence. "Why, they're exactly like . . ."

"And yet they're not like," said Lucy. . . . "They're more . . . more . . ."

"More like the real thing," said the Lord Digory softly.[847]

C. S. Lewis, *The Last Battle*

God will make the new earth his dwelling place. . . . Heaven and earth will then no longer be separated as they are now, but they will be one. But to leave the new earth out of consideration when we think of the final state of believers is greatly to impoverish biblical teaching about the life to come.[848]

Anthony Hoekema, *The Bible and the Future*

Our destiny is an earthly one: a new earth, an earth redeemed and transfigured. An earth reunited with heaven, but an earth, nevertheless.[849]

Paul Marshall, *Heaven Is Not My Home*

Christianity must yet triumph in a renovated earth, and with the returned Messiah as universal king, or fail. There is no third alternative.[850]

Anthony Buzzard, *Our Fathers Who Aren't in Heaven*

The very geography of the Promised Land, standing astride one of the great trade routes of the ancient world and without clear and secure natural boundaries, made it constantly vulnerable to enemy attack. It was an inherently insecure inheritance, as any history of the last thirty years in the Middle East will confirm.

At the domestic level, insecurity is no less a fact of life, as Jesus noted when contrasting the heavenly inheritance with the earthly. "Do not store up for yourselves treasures on earth, where moth and rust destroy, and where thieves break in and steal." . . . Our heavenly inheritance is finally invulnerable.[851]

Bruce Milne, *The Message of Heaven and Hell*

Prophecies of this nature [e.g., Isaiah 35:1; 51:3; 55:13; Ezekiel 36:35] should be understood as descriptions of the new earth, which God will bring into existence after Christ comes again—a new earth which will last, not just for a thousand years, but forever. . . . Keeping the doctrine of the new earth in mind . . . will open up the meaning of large portions of Old Testament prophetic literature in surprisingly new ways.[852]

Anthony Hoekema, *The Bible and the Future*

God's glory will fill and permeate the entire new Heaven—not just one centralized place. Thus, wherever we go in Heaven, we will be in the immediate presence of the full glory of God.[853]

Steven J. Lawson, *Heaven Help Us!*

There will be nothing unclean around us. We will live in a world spiritually clean from the pollution of all sin. . . . No abortion clinics, no divorce courts, no brothels, no bankruptcy courts, no psychiatric wards, and no treatment centers. . . . No pornography, no dial-a-porn, no teen suicide . . . no drive-by shootings, no racial tensions, and no prejudice.

There will be no misunderstandings, no injustice, no depression, no hurtful words, no gossip, no hurt feelings, no worry, no emptiness, and no child abuse.

There will be no wars, no financial worries . . . no heart monitors, no rust, no perplexing questions, no false teachers, no financial shortages, no hurricanes, no bad habits, no decay, no locks.

We will never need to confess sin. Never need to apologize again. Never need to straighten out a strained relationship. Never have to resist Satan again. Never have to resist temptation.

Never![854]

Steven J. Lawson, *Heaven Help Us!*

If a man would be alone, let him look at the stars. The rays that come from those heavenly worlds, will separate between him and what he touches. One might think the atmosphere was made transparent with this design, to give man, in the heavenly bodies, the perpetual presence of the sublime. Seen in the streets of cities, how great they are! If the stars should appear one night in a thousand years, how would men believe and adore; and preserve for many generations the remembrance of the city of God which had been shown! But every night come out these envoys of beauty, and light the universe with their admonishing smile.[855]

Ralph Waldo Emerson, "Nature"

The "new heaven and the new earth" mentioned in Revelation 21:1 are not newly created and never having existed before, but new in contrast with old, different from what heaven and earth (Genesis 1:1) formerly were. . . . The teaching of the entire Scripture is to the effect that God's plans are never defeated, that he does not replace but restore.

He who made Paradise for Adam will make heaven and earth new, far beyond Paradise, in the consummation.[856]

R. C. H. Lenski, *The Interpretation of St. Paul's Epistle to the Romans*

In ancient Palestine, a river was always a welcome place of comfort, rest, refreshment, and sustenance. It meant cool water to dry mouths parched by the arid desert. Imagine the joy of a weary traveler in the hot wilderness who came upon a crystal-clear, cool river! That will be our constant delight in Heaven after years of weary traveling in this wilderness of sin. Our tired bodies and burdened souls will be refreshed to the fullest.[857]

Steven J. Lawson, *Heaven Help Us!*

Contrary to popular opinion, the Christian hope is not that someday all believers get to die and go to heaven.

. . . Christians long for the fulfillment of Emmanuel. . . . We don't hope merely for the day when we go to live with God, but ultimately for that final day when God comes to live with us.

. . . Our God calls himself "Emmanuel," which means "God with us." Unfortunately, many Christians read this name backwards, as if Emmanuel means "us with God." If we think "us with God," we tend to imagine that the goal of life is to leave this planet and live forever with him in heaven.[858]

Michael Wittmer, *Heaven Is a Place on Earth*

We are earthlings. We were made to live here. This world is our home.

For too long, many evangelical Christians have mistakenly believed that the goal of life is to escape the bounds of earth.

. . . Heaven is merely the first leg of a journey that is round-trip.[859]

Michael Wittmer, *Heaven Is a Place on Earth*

New creation is the dominating notion of biblical theology because new creation is the goal or purpose of God's redemptive-historical plan; new creation is the logical main point of Scripture.[860]

Greg Beale, "The Eschatological Conception of New Testament Theology"

After sifting through centuries of opinions on heaven from within the Judeo-Christian tradition, Colleen McDannell and Bernhard Lang concluded that most views of heaven fall within one of two categories: either a theocentric model of heaven in which God and the individual's relationship with God are stressed or an anthropocentric model of heaven in which human ties (friends, family, community) play a greater role. Whereas the former model seems to be vague, mystical, and idealistic, the latter model has an optimistic and more positive view of the world, and projects the better qualities of social and physical life into heaven.

... They didn't see a third or moderating model, a model which was both theocentric and anthropocentric at the same time. .... Theocentric heaven does not exclude new uses on a new earth and physical activity. They found this true in late Augustine, in Luther and Calvin, and in Isaac Watts.

... The biblical theme of "new heaven and new earth" requires a magnificent full-scale active life in the habitation, use, and governing of the new earth by those who are part of the blissful eternal state.[861]

John Gilmore, *Probing Heaven*

If God is going to make for these glorified sons and daughters a "new heaven and a new earth," He obviously expects them to use them.

And this "new heaven and new earth" will not be just planet earth and its telluric atmosphere, but the entire cosmos with all its galactic systems so transformed by God as to fit the final condition of his glorified sons and daughters.[862]

E. J. Fortman, *Everlasting Life after Death*

Both in 2 Peter 3:13 and in Revelation 21:1 the Greek word used to designate the newness of the new cosmos is not *neos* but *kainos*. The word *neos* means new in time or origin, whereas the word *kainos* means new in nature or in quality. The expression *ouranon kainon kai gen kainen* ("a new heaven and a new earth," Revelation 21:1) means, therefore, not the emergence of a cosmos totally other than the present one, but the creation of a universe which, though it has been gloriously renewed, stands in continuity with the present one.[863]

Anthony Hoekema, *The Bible and the Future*

What will happen to planet earth? Will it and its atmosphere continue to exist? Will it still have mountains and valleys and plains, fields and meadows, rivers and lakes and seas and oceans? Breathtaking dawns and glorious sunsets and moonbeams dancing on its waters at night? Its whispering and roaring winds, its springtime rains and its winter snows? Will it continue to have plants and animals, forests, gardens, flowers, fruit-trees, birds and fish and animals of all kinds? Some theologians seem to say No. Glorified sons and daughters of God will have no need of all this. They will be intent on higher things. . . .

But most likely they are wrong. For planet earth was the dwelling place of the Incarnate Son of God, of the Word made flesh, of the Redeemer of mankind and of the world. He was born at Bethlehem, He lived at Nazareth, He walked the roads of Palestine, loved its hills and valleys, its flowers and trees, the birds of the air, the fish of the rivers and seas, the sheep that browsed on the hillsides. Will He permit all this to be just a memory? Will He not want it to go on throughout eternity but transformed so as to befit glorified men? Will he not want it to be the same and yet different, just as His risen body is the same and yet different? If plants and animals shared in man's fall, will He not want them to share in man's redemption and glory? If plants and animals were meant to be man's companions and joy in the past, why not in the future?[864]

E. J. **Fortman**, *Everlasting Life after Death*

The world into which we shall enter in the Parousia of Jesus Christ is . . . not another world; it is this world, this heaven, this earth; both, however, passed away and renewed. It is these forests, these fields, these cities, these streets, these people, that will be the scene of redemption.[865]

J. A. **Schep**, *The Nature of the Resurrection Body*

Since there are real men, so must there also be a real establishment (*plantationem*), that they vanish not away among non-existent things, but progress among those which have an actual existence. For neither is the substance nor the essence of the creation annihilated (for faithful and true is He who has established it), but "the *fashion* of the world passeth away;" that is, those things among which transgression has occurred, since man has grown old in them. . . . But when this [present] fashion [of things] passes away, and man has been renewed, and flourishes in an incorruptible state, so as to preclude the possibility of becoming old, [then] there shall be the new heaven and the new earth, in which the new man shall remain [continually], always holding fresh converse with God. And since (*or*, that) these things shall ever continue without end, Isaiah declares, "For as the new heavens and the new earth which I do make, continue in my sight, saith the LORD, so shall your seed and your name remain." And as the presbyters say, Then those who are deemed worthy of an abode in heaven shall go there, others shall enjoy the delights of paradise, and others shall possess the splendour of the city; for everywhere the Saviour shall be seen according as they who see Him shall be worthy.[866]

Irenaeus, *Against Heresies*

The general tenor of prophecy and the analogy of the divine dealings point unmistakably to this earth purified and renewed, and *not to the heavens* in any ordinary sense of the term, as the eternal habitation of the blessed.[867]

Henry Alford, *Greek New Testament*

The hills and valleys of Heaven will be to those you now experience not as a copy is to an original, nor as a substitute is to the genuine article, but as the flower to the root, or the diamond to the coal.[868]

C. S. Lewis, *Letters to Malcolm*

It is as hard to explain how this sunlit land was different from the old Narnia, as it would be to tell you how the fruits of that country taste. Perhaps you will get some idea of it, if you think like this. You may have been in a room in which there was a window that looked out on a lovely bay of the sea or a green valley that wound away among mountains. And in the wall of that room opposite to the window there may have been a looking glass. And as you turned away from the window you suddenly caught sight of that sea or that valley, all over again, in the looking glass. And the sea in the mirror, or the valley in the mirror, were in one sense just the same as the real ones; yet at the same time they were somehow different—deeper, more wonderful, more like places in a story: in a story you have never heard but very much want to know. The difference between the old Narnia and the new Narnia was like that. The new one was a deeper country; every rock and flower and blade of grass looked as if it meant more. I can't describe it any better than that; if you ever get there, you will know what I mean.

It was the Unicorn who summed up what everyone was feeling. He stamped his right forefoot on the ground and neighed and then cried,

"I have come home at last! This is my real country! I belong here. This is the land I have been looking for all my life, though I never knew it till now. The reason why we loved the old Narnia is that it sometimes looked a little like this. . . . Come further up, come further in!"[869]

C. S. Lewis, *The Last Battle*

"Why!" exclaimed Peter. "It's England. And that's the house itself—Professor Kirke's old home in the country where all our adventures began!"

"I thought that house had been destroyed," said Edmund.

"So it was," said the Faun. "But you are now looking at the England within England, the real England just as this is the real Narnia. And in that inner England no good thing is destroyed."[870]

C. S. Lewis, *The Last Battle*

Heaven, as the eternal home of the divine Man and of all the redeemed members of the human race, must necessarily be thoroughly human in its structure, conditions, and activities. Its joys and activities must all be rational, moral, emotional, voluntary and active. There must be the exercise of all the faculties, the gratification of all tastes, the development of all talent capacities, the realization of all ideals. The reason, the intellectual curiosity, the imagination, the aesthetic instincts, the holy affections, the social affinities, the inexhaustible resources of strength and power native to the human soul must all find in heaven exercise and satisfaction. Then there must always be a goal of endeavor before us, ever future. . . . Heaven will prove the consummate flower and fruit of the whole creation and of all the history of the universe.[871]

A. A. Hodge, *Evangelical Theology*

Don't run away with the idea that when I speak of the resurrection of the body I mean merely that the blessed dead will have excellent memories of their sensuous experiences on earth. I mean it the other way round; that memory as we know it is a dim foretaste, a mirage even, of a power which the soul, or rather Christ in the soul . . . will exercise hereafter. It need no longer . . . be private to the soul in which it occurs. I can now communicate to you the fields of my boyhood— they are building-estates today—only imperfectly, by words. Perhaps the day is coming when I can take you for a walk through them.[872]

C. S. Lewis, *Letters to Malcolm*

When we shall have plunged into a very bath of joy, we shall have found the delights even of communion on earth to have been but the dipping of the finger in the cup, but the dipping of the bread in the dish, whereas heaven itself shall be the participation of the whole of the joy, and not the mere foretaste of it.

Here we sometimes enter into the portico of happiness, there we shall go into the presence chamber of the King, here we look over the hedge and see the flowers in heaven's garden, there we shall walk between the beds of bliss, and pluck fresh flowers at each step; here we just look and see the sunlight of heaven in the distance, like the lamps of the thousand-gated cities shining afar off, but there we shall see them in all their blaze of splendor, here we listen to the whisperings of heaven's melody, borne by winds from afar; but there, entranced, amidst the grand oratorio of the blessed, we shall join in the everlasting hallelujah to the great Messiah, the God, the I AM.[873]

Charles Spurgeon, "Heavenly Rest," Sermon 133

Nonsense is made of the New Testament scheme, and God's unfolding Plan for world history, when it is proposed that the Christian destiny is to be enjoyed in a location removed from the earth. This destroys at a blow the promises given to Abraham and the faithful that they are to inherit the land and the world. There is no resolution of the original failure of man to carry out the divine mandate to rule the world if, in fact, the world never experiences the restoration of divine rule. The Christian faith is permanently frustrated when hope for the restoration of peace on earth is denied. The substitution of "heaven" in popular preaching perpetuates a notion which confuses Bible readers and renders meaningless the whole hope of the prophets (based on the covenant) that the world is going to enjoy an unparalleled era of blessing and international peace under the just rule of the Messiah and the resurrected faithful.[874]

Anthony Buzzard, *Our Fathers Who Aren't in Heaven*

The restoration of the Church shall be of such a nature that it shall last for ever. Many might be afraid that it would be ruined a second time; and therefore [Isaiah] declares that henceforth, after having been restored by God, its condition shall be permanent. Accordingly, he mentions here two benefits of surpassing excellence, restoration and eternity. When he speaks of "new heavens" and a "new earth," he looks to the reign of Christ, by whom all things have been renewed, as the Apostle teaches in the Epistle to the Hebrews. Now the design of this newness is, that the condition of the Church may always continue to be prosperous and happy. What is old tends to decay; what is restored and renewed must be of longer continuance.[875]

John Calvin, *Commentary on the Book of the Prophet Isaiah*

We believe that the material substance of the world must be renewed and that this will not take place until the number of the elect is completed and that happy kingdom be made perfect and that after its completion there will be no more change.[876]

Anselm, *Why the God-Man?*

Many Christians grow up assuming that whenever the New Testament speaks of heaven it refers to the place to which the saved will go after death. In Matthew's gospel, Jesus' sayings in the other gospels about the "kingdom of God" are rendered as "kingdom of heaven"; since many read Matthew first, when they find Jesus talking about entering the "kingdom of heaven," they have their assumptions confirmed and suppose that he is indeed talking about how to go to heaven when you die, which is certainly not what either Jesus or Matthew had in mind. Many mental pictures have grown up around this and are now assumed to be what the Bible teaches or what Christians believe. (A healthy corrective is found in a series of books by Randy Alcorn, principally *Heaven*. Alcorn comes from a tradition that might easily have lapsed into Shriver-type platitudes, but his study of scripture has led him to a far more robust and biblical view—even though he still uses the word *heaven* when what he emphatically talks about throughout is the new heavens and new earth.)[877]

N. T. Wright, *Surprised by Hope*

Some would argue that the New Earth shouldn't be called Heaven. But it seems clear to me that if God's special dwelling place is by definition Heaven, and we're told that "the dwelling of God" will be with mankind on Earth, then Heaven and the New Earth will be essentially the same place. We're told that "the throne of God and of the Lamb" is in the New Jerusalem, which is brought down to the New Earth (Revelation 22:1). Again, it seems clear that wherever God dwells with his people and sits on his throne would be called Heaven.[878]

Randy Alcorn, *Heaven*

If we want to know what the ultimate Heaven, our eternal home, will be like, the best place to start is by looking around us. We shouldn't close our eyes and try to imagine the unimaginable. We should open our eyes, because the present Earth is as much a valid reference point for envisioning the New Earth as our present bodies are a valid reference point for envisioning our new bodies. After all, we're living on

the remnants of a perfect world, as the remnants of a perfect humanity. We shouldn't read into the New Earth anything that's wrong
with this one, but can we not imagine what it would be like to be
unhindered by disease and death? Can we not envision natural beauty
untainted by destruction?

The idea of the New Earth as a physical place isn't an invention of short-sighted human imagination. Rather, it's the invention
of a transcendent God, who made physical human beings to live on
a physical Earth, and who chose to become a man himself on that
same Earth. He did this that he might redeem mankind and Earth.
Why? In order to glorify himself and enjoy forever the company of
men and women in a world he's made for us.[879]

Randy Alcorn, *Heaven*

Some people have never thought about Heaven's weather because
they don't think of Heaven as a real place, certainly not an earthly
one. Or they assume the New Earth will have bright sunshine, no
clouds, no rain . . . forever. Lightning, thunder, rain, and snow all
declare God's greatness. Is there any reason to conclude such things
will not be a part of the New Earth?

Of course, no one will die or be hurt by such weather. No one
will perish in a flood or be killed by lightning, just as no one will
drown in the river of life. Nature, including variations in climate, will
be a source of joy and pleasure, not destruction. If we stand amazed
now at the wonders of God's great creation, we'll be far more amazed
at the greater wonders of that greater creation.[880]

Randy Alcorn, *TouchPoints: Heaven*

Home is where we're with the ones we love. Heaven will be just like
that. We'll be with people we love, and we'll love no one more than
Jesus. . . . Because we've already lived on Earth, I think it will seem
from the first that we're coming home. Because we once lived on
Earth, the New Earth will strike us as very familiar.[881]

Randy Alcorn, *Heaven*

When Scripture speaks of a "new song," do we imagine something that is wordless, silent, or without rhythm? Of course not. Why? Because *it wouldn't be a song.*

If I promised you a new car, would you say, "If it's new, it probably won't have an engine, a transmission, doors, wheels, windows, or upholstery"? No, you'd never make such assumptions. Why? Because if a new car didn't have these things, *it wouldn't be a car.*

Likewise, when Scripture speaks of a new Earth, we can expect that it will be a far better version of the old Earth, but *it will truly be Earth.*[882]

Randy Alcorn, *50 Days of Heaven*

Eden was the absence of all Curse but the New Earth will be the presence of all blessing.

Randy Alcorn, unpublished notes

Many assume heaven will be unearthlike. But why do we think this? God designed earth for human beings. And every description of heaven includes references to earthly things—eating and traveling and animals and water and trees and fruits and a city and gates and streets.

The Bible speaks of the new heavens and the new earth—not a nonheavens and nonearth! "New" does not mean fundamentally different, but vastly superior.

The new earth will be a far better version of this earth. That's why we can anticipate it. That's why if we think of heaven as a place where disembodied spirits float around—which is never depicted in the Bible—we can't get excited about it. It's not a nonearth we long for—it's a new earth. And we long not for a nonbody but for a new body (2 Corinthians 5:1-4).

The promise of new heavens and new earth is introduced in Isaiah 65–66. John tells us after "the first heaven and first earth passed away" he saw a "new heaven and a new earth" and the holy city coming down out of heaven from God (Revelation 21:1-2). Peter speaks of the earth being burned, followed by a "new heavens and a new earth in which righteousness dwells" (2 Peter 3:10-13).

I understand this not as the absolute destruction of the planet, but the scorching of the surface and everything on it. It's as if an artist wiped paint away and started a new and better painting, but on the same canvas. As our resurrection bodies will be a superior recreation of our old ones, so the new earth will be the old earth liberated from sin and decay (Romans 8:19-22), radically and beautifully transformed.

Our beloved, Jesus, and our home, heaven. What a person. What a place. (What more could we possibly ask for?)[883]

Randy Alcorn, *In Light of Eternity*

Everything changes when we grasp that all we love about the old Earth will be ours on the New Earth—either in the same form or another. Once we understand this, we won't regret leaving all the wonders of the world we've seen or mourn not having seen its countless other wonders. Why? Because *we will yet be able to see them.*

God is no more done with the earth than he's done with us.[884]

Randy Alcorn, *Heaven*

Have you ever bought an economy ticket for a flight but because of overbooking or some other reason been upgraded to first class? Did you regret the upgrade? Did you spend your time wondering, *What am I missing out on by not being in the back of the plane?*

You go from little legroom to lots of legroom, from an adequate chair to a comfortable one, maybe even one with a footrest. Rather than just a sandwich, you get a meal, on real plates. The flight attendants keep filling your cup, give you a great dessert, and offer a hot hand towel. In other words, it's not just that the bad things about economy seats are minimized; it's that all the good things are made better.

The upgrade from the old Earth to the New Earth will be vastly superior to that from economy to first class. (It may feel more like an upgrade to first class from the baggage hold.) Gone will be sin, the Curse, death, and suffering. In every way we will recognize that the New Earth is better—in no sense could it ever be worse.[885]

Randy Alcorn, *Heaven*

The New Jerusalem

The glory of Lebanon will come to you, the pine,
the fir and the cypress together. . . . The sons of your
oppressors will come bowing before you; all who
despise you will bow down at your feet and will call
you the City of the LORD. . . . I will make you the
everlasting pride and the joy of all generations. . . .
I will make peace your governor and righteousness
your ruler. No longer will violence be heard in your
land, nor ruin or destruction within your borders, but
you will call your walls Salvation and your gates Praise.

GOD, ISAIAH 60:13-15, 18

As a bridegroom rejoices over his bride, so will your
God rejoice over you. . . . You who call on the LORD,
give yourselves no rest, and give him no rest till he

establishes Jerusalem and makes her the praise of
the earth. . . . Pass through, pass through the gates!
Prepare the way for the people. . . . Raise a banner for
the nations.

ISAIAH 62:5-7, 10

I will extend peace to her like a river, and the wealth
of nations like a flooding stream.

GOD, ISAIAH 66:12

[Abraham] was looking forward to the city with foundations, whose architect and builder is God.

HEBREWS 11:10

You have come to Mount Zion, to the heavenly Jerusalem, the city of the living God. You have come to
thousands upon thousands of angels in joyful assembly,
to the church of the firstborn, whose names are written in heaven. You have come to God, the judge of all
men, to the spirits of righteous men made perfect.

HEBREWS 12:22-23

We do not have an enduring city, but we are looking
for the city that is to come.

HEBREWS 13:14

I saw a new heaven and a new earth, for the first
heaven and the first earth had passed away. . . . I saw
the Holy City, the new Jerusalem, coming down out
of heaven from God.

JOHN, REVELATION 21:1-2

He carried me away in the Spirit to a mountain great and high, and showed me the Holy City, Jerusalem, coming down out of heaven from God. It shone with the glory of God, and its brilliance was like that of a very precious jewel, like a jasper, clear as crystal. It had a great, high wall with twelve gates, and with twelve angels at the gates. On the gates were written the names of the twelve tribes of Israel. There were three gates on the east, three on the north, three on the south and three on the west. The wall of the city had twelve foundations, and on them were the names of the twelve apostles of the Lamb.

The angel who talked with me had a measuring rod of gold to measure the city, its gates and its walls. The city was laid out like a square, as long as it was wide. He measured the city with the rod and found it to be 12,000 stadia in length, and as wide and high as it is long. He measured its wall and it was 144 cubits thick, by man's measurement, which the angel was using. The wall was made of jasper, and the city of pure gold, as pure as glass. The foundations of the city walls were decorated with every kind of precious stone. The first foundation was jasper, the second sapphire, the third chalcedony, the fourth emerald, the fifth sardonyx, the sixth carnelian, the seventh chrysolite, the eighth beryl, the ninth topaz, the tenth chrysoprase, the eleventh jacinth, and the twelfth amethyst. The twelve gates were twelve pearls, each gate made of a single pearl. The great street of the city was of pure gold, like transparent glass.

I did not see a temple in the city, because the Lord God Almighty and the Lamb are its temple. The city does not need the sun or the moon to shine on it, for the glory of God gives it light, and the Lamb is its lamp.

JOHN, REVELATION 21:10-23

The nations will walk by its light, and the kings of the earth will bring their splendor into it. On no day will its gates ever be shut. . . . The glory and honor of the nations will be brought into it.

JOHN, REVELATION 21:24-26

Nothing impure will ever enter [the city], nor will anyone who does what is shameful or deceitful, but only those whose names are written in the Lamb's book of life.

JOHN, REVELATION 21:27

The angel showed me the river of the water of life, as clear as crystal, flowing from the throne of God and of the Lamb down the middle of the great street of the city. On each side of the river stood the tree of life, bearing twelve crops of fruit, yielding its fruit every month. And the leaves of the tree are for the healing of the nations.

JOHN, REVELATION 22:1-2

No longer will there be any curse. The throne of God and of the Lamb will be in the city, and his servants will serve him.

JOHN, REVELATION 22:3

Blessed are those who . . . may go through the gates into the city.

JESUS, REVELATION 22:14

I am groaning with inexpressible groaning on my wanderer's path, and remembering Jerusalem with my heart lifted up towards it—Jerusalem my homeland, Jerusalem my mother.[886]

Augustine, *Confessions*

The "new Jerusalem" . . . does not remain in a "heaven" far off in space, but it comes down to the renewed earth; there the redeemed will spend eternity in resurrection bodies. So heaven and earth, now separated, will then be merged: the new earth will also be heaven, since God will dwell there with his people. Glorified believers, in other words, will continue to be in heaven while they are inhabiting the new earth.[887]

Anthony Hoekema, "Heaven: Not Just an Eternal Day Off"

In this heavenly city you will all be able to physically enjoy God's presence and glory and talk with Him face to face. Imagine having a daily pass to the Oval Office or Buckingham Palace? Well in this city you get a daily pass and free audience with the King of Kings and Lord of Lords, the Creator of the universe. Wow![888]

Larry Dick, *A Taste of Heaven*

Picture an area in the western United States between the Pacific Coast and the Mississippi River, roughly the distance from Los Angeles to Saint Louis. Or New York to Denver.

. . . God can never be accused of skimping or economizing . . . seven-million-foot height of the city. . . . This statement by John— "according to human measurements"—means this description is to be taken quite literally.

That's 2,250,000 square miles, on the ground. Then 1,500 miles up from there! Hang on! Are you ready for this? That's 3,375,000,000 cubic miles, enough room to comfortably accommodate 100,000 billion people!

It has been estimated that approximately thirty billion people have lived in the long history of the world. Even if everyone who ever lived was saved—which is not the case—that would still allow each person 200 square miles on the ground alone. . . . There will be plenty of room for everyone who makes it to Heaven.

And that's just in the city![889]

Steven J. Lawson, *Heaven Help Us!*

From the opposite standpoints of the Christian world, from different quarters of human life and character, through various expressions of their common faith and hope, through diverse modes of conversion, through different portions of the Holy Scripture will the weary travelers enter the Heavenly City and meet each other—"not without surprise"—on the shores of the same river of life.[890]

   D. L. Moody, *Heaven*

God also helps us understand that heaven is a particular place by showing us its capital—what we might call "downtown heaven."[891]

   Tony Evans, *Tony Evans Speaks Out on Heaven and Hell*

The gates of pearl were not an artistic whim, but had a theological purpose. They represented the Pearl of Great Price, a figure from the Gospels, which pointed to Jesus Christ.[892]

   John Gilmore, *Probing Heaven*

What do we count most valuable on earth?
Gold. Men live for gold, kill for it.
But in heaven gold is so plentiful
that they pave the streets with it.[893]

   F. B. Meyer

The term "tree of life" is collective, just like "avenue" and "river." The idea is not that there is just one single tree. No, there is an entire park: whole rows of trees alongside the river; hence, between the river and the avenue. And this is true with respect to all the avenues of the city. Hence, the city is just full of parks, Revelation 2:7. Observe, therefore, this wonderful truth: the city is full of rivers of life. It is also full of parks containing trees of life. These trees, moreover, are full of fruit.[894]

   William Hendriksen, *More than Conquerers*

I thought, if heaven's a city I'm not so sure I want to spend forever there.

The next morning changed my perspective. I pulled back the drapes of my seventeenth floor Buckhead hotel room and gazed out of the huge bay window at a cloudless blue sky above a rolling carpet of dark green. I never realized Atlanta had so many trees. Away to the south, in the center of my vision, a bright and beautiful city hovered between tree and sky. Its tall buildings shimmered, white and spotless in the early morning sunlight.

Then it hit me. What if this city really was spotlessly clean? What if it was a city where there was no fear of getting mugged, ripped off, or blown apart, a city where you could never be lost or even ignored? Imagine a city where everyone was kind and helpful, happy, honest, morally pure, and a relative![895]

Larry Dick, *A Taste of Heaven*

The new Jerusalem is a city of light—the light which is the glory of God. Therefore, it is a city of color. That's because color is actually nothing more than dissected light. Where there is no light, there is no color. . . . Because of His bright shining presence—so bright that there will be no need for the sun—all of this color will be flooding out of the new Jerusalem and illuminating the entire universe.

. . . Each gate tower is carved from a single, huge pearl. Why did God choose pearl? Perhaps because the beauty of a pearl comes from the pain of an oyster. It is beauty born out of pain. . . . The oyster relieves its pain by covering the irritating grain of sand with a soft, lustrous solution that hardens into a beautiful, growing pearl. The more pain the oyster endures, the more layers of luster, and the larger the pearl becomes.

What a picture of salvation! . . . "All other precious gems are metals or stones, but a pearl is a gem formed within the oyster—the only one formed by living flesh. . . . The pearl, we might say, is the answer of the oyster to that which injured it."

. . . How like God it is to build the gates of the new Jerusalem of pearl. . . . What gigantic suffering is symbolized by those gates of pearl! Throughout the endless ages we shall be reminded by those pearly gates of the immensity of the sufferings of Christ.[896]

Steven J. Lawson, *Heaven Help Us!*

I see the future of heaven as blending the natural and artificial according to Divine blueprint. Gone will be the coarse brutality of primitive eons. Gone the sophisticated brutality of technological society. Present will be the glories of the primitive, the great forests, the pure streams, the stillness of an Arctic night, the sonorous cadence of crickets on a summer evening, the beauty of sunsets over the prairie. Present will be structures more beautiful and functional than medieval cathedrals or modern towers. Heaven is depicted biblically as the city of God, with verdant, healing trees lining streets of transparent beauty.[897]

Arthur Roberts, *Exploring Heaven*

Everything is gone that ever made Jerusalem, like all cities, torn apart, dangerous, heartbreaking, seamy. You walk the streets in peace now. Small children play unattended in the parks. No stranger goes by whom you can't imagine a fast friend. The city has become what those who loved it always dreamed and what in their dreams she always was. The new Jerusalem. That seems to be the secret of Heaven. The new Chicago, Leningrad, Hiroshima, Beirut. The new bus driver, hot-dog man, seamstress, hairdresser. The new you, me, everybody.[898]

Frederick Buechner

We speak and sing of the pearly gates, the golden street, the jasper walls, and we like to imagine those as being descriptive of the heaven to which our departed Christian loved ones have gone. But where do those ideas about the pearly gates and golden street and jasper walls come from? They are from the last two chapters of the Bible, namely chapters 21 and 22. Yet those two chapters do not describe heaven, as is generally supposed; they refer to a respendent city of the future which is yet to be set up on this earth.

Therefore that future city must not be equated with heaven. No, it comes *down* from heaven, which means that it is not identical with heaven.[899]

J. Sidlow Baxter, *The Other Side of Death*

If the "New Jerusalem" has more than symbolic reality, why should it not have it in the "Holy Land"? Why should it not throughout eternity be where "Old Jerusalem" was, where our Redeemer taught, suffered, died that we might live a life of glory and happiness throughout the endless reaches of eternity? . . . What better site could there be for this eternal cosmic religious center than *Old Jerusalem*?[900]

E. J. Fortman, *Everlasting Life after Death*

O happy souls, that keep themselves awake to God in the midst of this dreaming world! Happy indeed, when our Lord shall call us out of these dusky regions, and we shall answer his call with holy joy, and spring upward to the inheritance of the saints in light! Then all the seasons of darkness, and slumbering, will be finished for ever; there is no need of laborious watchfulness in that world. . . . There is no want of the sun-beams to make their day-light, or to irradiate that city; the glory of God enlightens it with divine splendors, and the Lamb is the light thereof: No inhabitant can sleep under such an united blaze of grace and glory: No faintings of nature, no languors or weariness are found in all that vital climate; every citizen is for ever awake and busy under the beams of that glorious day; zeal, and love, and joy, are the springs of their eternal activity, and there is no night there.[901]

Isaac Watts, *The World to Come*

How delightful is it to me to behold and study those inferior works of creation! What a beautiful fabric do we here dwell in; the floor so dressed with herbs, and flowers, and trees, and watered with springs and rivers; the roof so widely expanded, so admirably adorned! What wonders do sun, moon and stars, seas and winds, contain! And hath

God prepared such a house for corruptible flesh, for a soul imprisoned? and doth he bestow so many millions of wonders upon his enemies? O what a dwelling must that be which he prepares for his dearly beloved children! and how will the glory of the New Jerusalem exceed all the present glory of earth! Arise then, O my soul, in thy contemplation, and let thy thoughts of that glory as far exceed in sweetness thy thoughts of the excellencies below! Fear not to go out of this body and this world, when thou must make so happy a change: but say, as one did when he was dying, "I am glad and even leap for joy, that the time is come, in which that mighty Jehovah, whose majesty in my search of nature I have admired, whose goodness I have adored, whom by faith I have desired and panted after, will now show himself to me face to face."[902]

Richard Baxter, *The Saints' Everlasting Rest*

Only the Christian church in the midst of all the world religions is able to proclaim the Bible's good news that God, the Creator and Redeemer, will bring a new order into being!

Indeed, it is the only good news available to a fallen race today—the news that God has promised a new order that is to be of eternal duration and infused with eternal life.

How amazing!

It is a promise from God of a new order to be based upon the qualities which are the exact opposite of man's universal blight—temporality and mortality!

God promises the qualities of perfection and eternity which cannot now be found in mankind anywhere on this earth.

What a prospect!

We are instructed that this new order, at God's bidding, will finally show itself in the new heaven and the new earth. It will show itself in the city that is to come down as a bride adorned for her husband.

The Word of God tells us that all of this provision for the redeemed has the quality of eternal duration.

It is not going to come just to go again. It is not to be temporal.

It is a new order that will come to stay.

It is not going to come subject to death. It is not to be mortal. It is a new order that will come to live and remain forever![903]

A. W. Tozer, *The Tozer Pulpit*

I wish you now to observe that we are linked with the creation. Adam in this world was in liberty, perfect liberty; nothing confined him; paradise was exactly fitted to be his seat. There were no wild beasts to rend him, no rough winds to cause him injury, no blighting heats to bring him harm; but in this present world everything is contrary to us.

Ungodly men prosper well enough in this world, they root themselves, and spread themselves like green bay trees: it is their native soil; but the Christian needs the hothouse of grace to keep himself alive at all—and out in the world he is like some strange foreign bird, native of a warm and sultry clime, that being let loose here under our wintry skies is ready to perish.

Now, God will one day change our bodies and make them fit for our souls, and then he will change this world itself. It is no speculation to say that we look for new heavens and a new earth where righteousness dwells; and that there will come a time when the lion shall eat straw like an ox, and the leopard shall lie down with the kid.

We expect to see this world that is now so full of sin to be turned into a paradise, a garden of God. We believe that the tabernacle of God will be among men, that he will dwell among them, and they shall see his face, and his name shall be on their foreheads. We expect to see the New Jerusalem descend out of heaven from God.

In this very place, where sin has triumphed, we expect that grace will much more abound.[904]

Charles Spurgeon, "Creation's Groans and the Saints' Sighs," Sermon 788

Since God will dwell on the New Earth with his people, and the thrones of both Father and Son will be there, we might view the New Earth as Heaven central, or Heaven's capital planet, with New Jerusalem its capital city.

Randy Alcorn, notes

Heaven's capital city will be filled with visual magnificence. "It shone with the glory of God, and its brilliance was like that of a very precious jewel, like a jasper, clear as crystal" (Revelation 21:11). John describes the opulence: "The wall was made of jasper, and the city of pure gold, as pure as glass. The foundations of the city walls were decorated with every kind of precious stone" (Revelation 21:18-19). John names twelve stones, eight of which correspond to the stones of the high priest's breastplate (Exodus 28–29).

The precious stones and gold represent incredible wealth, suggestive of the exorbitant riches of God's splendor.

John describes a natural wonder in the center of the New Jerusalem: "The river of the water of life, as clear as crystal, flowing from the throne of God and of the Lamb down the middle of the great street of the city" (Revelation 22:1-2). Why is water important? Because the city is a center of human life and water is an essential part of life. Ghosts don't need water, but human bodies do. We all know what it's like to be thirsty, but John was writing to people who lived in a bone-dry climate, who would have grasped the wonder of constantly available fresh water, pure and uncontaminated, able to satisfy the deepest thirst.

On the New Earth, we won't have to leave the city to find natural beauty. It will be incorporated into the city, with the river of life at its center. The river flows down the main street, most likely splitting into countless smaller streams that flow throughout the rest of the city. Can you picture people talking and laughing beside this river, sticking their hands and faces into the water and drinking?

After John describes the river of life, he mentions another striking feature: "On each side of the river stood the tree of life, bearing twelve crops of fruit, yielding its fruit every month. And the leaves of the tree are for the healing of the nations" (Revelation 22:2). It appears human beings may draw their strength and vitality through eating of this tree. The tree will produce not one crop but twelve. The newness and freshness of Heaven is demonstrated in the monthly yield of fruit. The fruit is not merely to be admired but consumed:

"To him who overcomes, I will grant to eat of the tree of life which is in the Paradise of God" (Revelation 2:7, NASB).[905]

Randy Alcorn, *Heaven*

[What kind of a view will we have in this city?] In describing the New Earth, John speaks of "a mountain great and high" (Revelation 21:10). . . . We know that the New Earth will have at least one mountain, and we can assume it has hundreds or thousands of them.

[And what will we find if we leave the city?] The New Earth's waterfalls may dwarf Niagara—or the New Niagara Falls may dwarf the one we know now. We'll find rock formations more spectacular than Yosemite's, peaks that overshadow the Himalayas, and forests deeper and richer than anything we see in my beloved Pacific Northwest.[906]

Randy Alcorn, *Heaven*

When the kings of the nations bring treasures into the city, is it possible that one purpose will be to give tribute to the King and another to exchange treasures with other people groups? Might they then bring back to their own people the cultural splendors, including discoveries and inventions, of other nations? Even now, honest trade brings benefit and pleasure to both parties.

People trade and engage in business for reasons besides survival. It's possible that business as we know it could be replaced by a social structure centered on creating, giving, and receiving. An artist might create a beautiful work and simply give it away for someone's delight, just as Christ freely gives of himself. Jesus said it's "more blessed to give than to receive" (Acts 20:35), so the joy of giving someone else a cultural treasure would exceed even the joy of receiving one.

Whether you work in a bookstore, bakery, or school, don't you experience joy in using your knowledge, skills, services, and products to help and please others? Sure, it's good and often necessary to earn money too, but that isn't the ultimate joy. If we dismiss the likelihood of business and commerce on the New Earth, we send the wrong message: that business and commerce are part of the Curse, inherently unspiritual or unimportant to God. On the contrary, God's Word tells us, "Whatever you do, work at it with all your heart, as working for the Lord, not for men, since you know that you will receive an inheritance from the Lord as a reward. It is the Lord Christ you are serving" (Colossians 3:23-24). We work for him on the present Earth, and we will work for him on the New Earth.[907]

Randy Alcorn, *Heaven*

The city's open gates are a great equalizer. There's no elitism in Heaven; everyone will have access because of Christ's blood. His death is the admission ticket to every nook and cranny of the New Jerusalem. People won't have to prove their worth or buy their way through the gates. All people will have access to the city's parks, museums, restaurants, libraries, concerts—anything and everything the city has to offer. Nobody will have to peek over the fence or look longingly through the windows.[908]

Randy Alcorn, *Heaven*

Presumably, there will be many other cities [in addition to the New Jerusalem] on the New Earth, such as those Jesus mentions in the stewardship parables, where he says that in the Kingdom some will rule over five cities and some over ten (Luke 19:17, 19). The kings of nations who bring their treasures into the New Jerusalem (Revelation 21:4) must come from and return to somewhere. Likely, they will come from other settlements beyond the New Jerusalem.[909]

Randy Alcorn, *50 Days of Heaven*

Adam was formed from the dust of the earth, forever establishing our connection to the earth (Genesis 2:7). Just as we are made *from* the earth, so too we are made *for* the earth. But, you may object, Jesus said he was going to prepare a place for us and would take us there to live with him forever (John 14:2-3). Yes. But *what is that place?*

Revelation 21 makes it clear—it's the New Earth. That's where the New Jerusalem will reside when it comes down out of Heaven. Only *then* will we be truly home.[910]

Randy Alcorn, *Heaven*

This city will have all the advantages we associate with earthly cities but none of the disadvantages. The city will be filled with natural wonders, magnificent architecture, thriving culture—but it will have no crime, pollution, sirens, traffic fatalities, garbage, or homelessness. It will truly be Heaven on Earth.[911]

Randy Alcorn, *TouchPoints: Heaven*

The Artist's fingerprints will be seen everywhere in the great city. Every feature speaks of his attributes. The priceless stones speak of his beauty and grandeur. The open gates speak of his accessibility. All who wish to come to him at his throne may do so at any time. We can learn a lot about people by walking through their houses. The whole universe will be God's house—and the New Jerusalem will be his living room. God will delight to share with us the glories of his capital city—and ours.[912]

Randy Alcorn, *Heaven*

Buildings on the scale of the New Jerusalem reflect extensive cultural advancement. Human builders will learn from God's design, just as Leonardo da Vinci learned by studying the form and flight of birds while working on his flying machine. What will clear-thinking human beings—unhindered by sin and the barriers that separate us—be able to design and build? What would Galileo, da Vinci, Edison, or Einstein achieve if they could live even a thousand years unhindered by the Curse? What will we achieve when we have resurrected bodies with resurrected minds, working together forever?

Some researchers suggest that we now use only 10 percent of our brainpower. Adam and Eve could likely use 100 percent of theirs— and their brainpower was probably far greater than ours. (Contrary to evolutionary assumptions, according to Scripture, mankind's greatest capacity was in the past.) On the New Earth, God's gifts to us will never be lost to age, death, pettiness, insecurity, or laziness. Undistracted and undiminished by sin and the demands of survival, mankind will create and innovate at unprecedented levels, to God's eternal glory.[913]

Randy Alcorn, *Heaven*

As I read Revelation 21–22, I'm struck with how the Elven paradise [in Tolkien's Lord of the Rings trilogy] reflects the Edenic elements of the New Jerusalem—rivers, trees, fruits, and mountains—while the Dwarves' view of beauty reflects the vast detailed architecture and precious stones of Heaven's capital. Which kind of beauty is better? We needn't choose between them. The New Earth will be filled with both. Whatever God's people create is also God's creation, for it is he who shapes and gifts and empowers us to create.

It's likely that our tastes will differ enough that some of us will prefer to gather in the main streets and auditoriums for the great cultural events, while others will want to withdraw to feed ducks on a lake or to leave the city with their companions to pursue adventures in some undeveloped place. Wherever we go and whatever we do, we'll never leave the presence of the King. For although he dwells especially in the New Jerusalem, he will yet be fully present in the far reaches of the New Universe—in which every subatomic particle will shout his glory.[914]

Randy Alcorn, *Heaven*

Paradise: The Present Heaven

I assure you, today you will be with me in paradise.

Jesus, Luke 23:43, nlt

I know a man in Christ who fourteen years ago was
caught up to the third heaven—whether in the body
or out of the body I do not know, God knows. And
I know that this man was caught up into paradise—
whether in the body or out of the body I do not
know, God knows— and he heard things that cannot
be told, which man may not utter.

Paul, 2 Corinthians 12:2-4, esv

He who has an ear, let him hear what the Spirit says
to the churches. To him who overcomes, I will give
the right to eat from the tree of life, which is in the
paradise of God.

God, Revelation 2:7

Thy presence makes our Paradise, and where Thou art is Heaven.[915]

John Milton

Keep me walking steadfastly towards the country of everlasting
  delights, that paradise-land which is my true inheritance.
Support me by the strength of heaven that I may never turn back,
  or desire false pleasures that wilt and disappear into nothing.
As I pursue my heavenly journey by thy grace
  let me be known as a man with no aim
  but that of a burning desire for thee,
  and the good and salvation of my fellow men.[916]

The Valley of Vision: A Collection of Puritan Prayers and Devotions

We who have gone through the day of sadness, shall enjoy together that day of gladness.[917]

Richard Baxter, *The Saints' Everlasting Rest*

The emphasis on the present heaven is clearly rest, cessation from earth's battles and comforts from earth's sufferings. The future heaven is centered more on activity and expansion, serving Christ and reigning with Him. The scope is much larger, the great city with its twelve gates, people coming and going, nations to rule. In other words, the emphasis in the present heaven is on the absence of earth's negatives, while in the future heaven it is the presence of earth's positives, magnified many times through the power and glory of resurrected bodies on a resurrected Earth, free at last from sin and shame and all that would hinder both joy and achievement.[918]

René Pache, *The Future Life*

The idea of a walled garden, enclosing a carefully cultivated area of exquisite plants and animals, was the most powerful symbol of paradise available to the human imagination, mingling the images of the beauty of nature with the orderliness of human construction. . . . The whole of human history is thus enfolded in the subtle interplay of sorrow over a lost paradise, and the hope of its final restoration.[919]

Alister McGrath, *A Brief History of Heaven*

We often wonder what things are of primal interest to our loved ones who have passed within the veil. Are they concerned mainly about our health, or our happiness, or our success in business? No; these are to them subordinate interests. What they are chiefly concerned about is our spiritual welfare. They want to know if we have turned to the Lord; if we have grown in grace; if we have kept our good name untarnished; if we have increased in usefulness to others. Especially do they want to know if their prayers have been answered in the repentance of those for whose eternal fellowship they can never cease to yearn.[920]

James Campbell, *Heaven Opened*

Must I indeed believe: that the redeemed in heaven are experiencing fullness of joy, pleasures forevermore while they sleep? that they behold God's face in righteousness and are satisfied with beholding his form while they sleep? that they sit down with Abraham, Isaac, and Jacob in their sleep? that the rich man, immediately after death, was in torments, cried, and pleaded all in his sleep? that Lazarus (the one referred to in the parable) was comforted in his sleep?[921]

William Hendriksen, *The Bible on the Life Hereafter*

We may be sure that all the saints and heroes of God cluster around the banisters of Heaven and gaze with the deepest concern upon us who are left here to run our race! . . . Since the grandstand of Glory is filled with so many eager observers, we should lay aside every sin and the besetting sin of unbelief and look to Jesus to complete (finish) our faith, and we should run our race with patience.

These sainted millions have run their race; they have fought their fight; they have finished their course. Now they watch on the sidelines as we take our places. . . . Let us run a good race!

Heavenly saints know what goes on there on earth. They know as Jesus knows. They see, not through a glass darkly, but face to face. God has no secrets from His beloved who are entered into His presence and rejoice in His courts.[922]

John Rice, *Bible Facts about Heaven*

We must stress, however, that the state of the believer in paradise, though far better than his present earthly state, is still imperfect. There is an important event still to take place which will complete his eternal bliss, and that is the resurrection of the body and its reunion with the soul or spirit at Christ's second coming. Therefore all the righteous now in paradise are waiting for their resurrection bodies.[923]

Spiros Zodhiates, *Life after Death*

Without holiness on earth, we shall never be prepared to enjoy heaven. Heaven is a holy place, the Lord of heaven is a holy being, the angels are holy creatures. Holiness is written on everything in heaven. . . . How shall we ever be at home and happy in heaven if we die unholy?[924]

J. C. Ryle, *Holiness*

Pagan fables of paradise were dim and distorted recollections of Eden.[925]

Alister McGrath, *A Brief History of Heaven*

Imagine, if you can, what it must be to live in a state of such inwrought holiness that no selfish thought, no unkind or impure motive, no wrong desire, ever clouds the mind; where no anxiety ever disturbs one's deep heart-rest; where no temptation ever shoots its gilded but poisoned arrows; where no suffering or sorrow ever rends one's spirit; and where no jarring discord of any kind ever sounds amid the deep, rich harmonies of a sinless society. That is where our departed Christian loved ones are. Not only are they themselves in heaven; they have heaven in themselves.[926]

J. Sidlow Baxter, *The Other Side of Death*

Not only shall we be in heaven, but heaven will be in *us*. Our perfected happiness will spring from perfected holiness. Our moral and spiritual nature will be in faultless harmony with that exquisite environment.

Have you ever tried to imagine what it will be like to have a mind that is radiant light with no darkness at all?—with never a selfish thought, never a wish that is not translucently pure, never a motive toward others that is not transparently sincere, never a fleck of envy or jealousy or resentment or unholy desire or competitiveness; never a tremor of doubt, never a wisp of fear, or flutter of pride, or whiff of self-assertiveness?[927]

J. Sidlow Baxter, *The Other Side of Death*

Would it not spoil the bliss of heaven for them if they saw us amid the troubles which hurt us here on earth? We may answer that question by asking another. Does it spoil heaven for our Lord Jesus as *he* sees those troubles which afflict us? Is it not a consolation to us Christians that he *does* see and know and care? The fact is, of course, that the Lord Jesus sees those troubles differently from the way we ourselves do.

How often, when grievous trouble fells us, we gasp, "Why has this come upon me?" . . . Not so our Lord Jesus. He sees it in the context of an educative divine process leading to rich reward. Similarly, our fellow-believers who are now with him yonder see things no longer in *our* short-sighted way, but in larger light and fuller comprehension. They see our earthly troubles as part of the "all things" which "work together" for our eternal good (Romans 8:28).[928]

J. Sidlow Baxter, *The Other Side of Death*

If we only had a glimpse of the glory of paradise to which the faithful dead have gone, we would never desire their return to earth.[929]

Steven Waterhouse, *Not by Bread Alone*

Our Christian relatives and friends now in heaven see our troubles on earth as differently from our earthly obscurity as radiant morn is different from murky dusk. They see our present adversities in true perspective as parts of a process leading to an infinite compensation.[930]

J. Sidlow Baxter, *The Other Side of Death*

Along with him, yonder, all his people who have joined him there are exercising *their* now-elevated priesthood as his privileged cointercessors, interceding for us who are still on earth. With far superior intelligence and mental illumination than they had while in the flesh, they continually intercede for you and me during our pilgrimage from here to there. Did you hear that, you who have been bereaved of dear ones and have wondered why God took them? Your treasured one yonder is thinking of you, loving you, praying for you; *praying* for you continually with such enlightened understanding that every such intercession is answered with a divine "Yes," and registers itself in sustenance and blessing which come to you daily. When the final consummation breaks upon us we shall find that their prayers in heaven on our behalf have brought far more blessing to us than if they had lingered longer on earth. Incidentally, what we are here saying may explain why deaths are permitted which seem inexplicable to us. What we have mistaken for strange unkindness on God's part may have been designed for our lasting blessing.[931]

J. Sidlow Baxter, *The Other Side of Death*

Many believers make a mistake when they long to die and long for heaven. Those things may be desirable, but they are not the ultimate for the saints. The saints in heaven are perfectly free from sin, and, so far as they are capable of it, they are perfectly happy; but a disembodied spirit never can be perfect until it is reunited to its body.

God made man not pure spirit, but body and spirit, and the spirit alone will never be content until it sees its corporeal frame raised to its own condition of holiness and glory.

Think not that our longings here below are not shared in by the saints in heaven. They do not groan, so far as any pain can be, but they long with greater intensity than you and I long, for the "adoption . . . the redemption of the body."

People have said there is no faith in heaven, and no hope; they know not what they say—in heaven faith and hope have their fullest swing and their brightest sphere, for glorified saints believe in God's promise, and hope for the resurrection of the body.

The apostle tells us that "they without us cannot be made perfect"; that is, until our bodies are raised, theirs cannot be raised, until we get our adoption day, neither can they get theirs.

The Spirit says Come, and the bride says Come—not the bride on earth only, but the bride in heaven says the same, bidding the happy day speed on when the trumpet shall sound, and the dead shall be raised incorruptible, and we shall be changed.

For it is true, beloved, the bodies that have turned into dust will rise again, the fabric which has been destroyed by the worm shall start into a nobler being, and you and I, though the worm devour this body, shall in our flesh behold our God.[932]

Charles Spurgeon, "Creation's Groans and the Saints' Sighs," Sermon 788

To suppose the church above, which has passed through its course of faith and obedience in afflictions, tribulations, and persecutions, to be ignorant of the state of the church here below in general, and unconcerned about it, to be without desires of its success, deliverance, and prosperity, unto the glory of Christ, is to lay them asleep in a senseless state, without the exercise of any grace, or any interest in the glory of God. And if they cry for vengeance on the obdurate persecuting world, Revelation 6:10, shall we suppose they have no consideration nor knowledge of the state of the church suffering the same things which they did themselves? And, to put it out of question, they are minded of it in the next verse by Christ himself (6:11).[933]

John Owen, *The Works of John Owen*

You are going now, said they, to the paradise of God,
wherein you shall see the tree of life, and eat of the never-fading fruit
thereof;
and when you come there, you shall have white robes given to you,
And your walk and talk shall be every day with the King,
Even all the days of eternity.[934]

John Bunyan, *The Pilgrim's Progress*

Scripture teaches that those who die will go to a real place, either the present Heaven or the present Hell, as conscious human beings with memory of their lives and relationships on Earth. Those in Hell will live in misery, hopelessness, and apparent isolation, while those in Heaven will live in comfort, joy, and rich relationship with God and others.[935]

Randy Alcorn, *Heaven*

Paradise was not generally understood as mere allegory, with a metaphorical or spiritual meaning, but as an actual physical place where God and his people lived together, surrounded by physical beauty, enjoying great pleasures and happiness.[936]

Randy Alcorn, *Heaven*

Will we be with the Lord forever? Absolutely. Will we always be with him in exactly the same place that Heaven is now? No.

In the intermediate Heaven, we'll be in Christ's presence, and we'll be joyful, but we'll be looking forward to our bodily resurrection and permanent relocation to the New Earth.[937]

Randy Alcorn, *TouchPoints: Heaven*

Let me suggest an analogy to illustrate the difference between the intermediate Heaven and the eternal Heaven. Suppose you live in a homeless shelter in Miami. One day you inherit a beautiful house in Santa Barbara, California, fully furnished, on a gorgeous hillside overlooking the ocean. With the home comes a wonderful job doing something you've always wanted to do. Not only that, but you'll also be near close family members who moved from Miami many years ago.

On your flight to Santa Barbara, you'll change planes in Denver, where you'll spend an afternoon. Some other family members, whom you haven't seen in years, will meet you at the Denver airport and board the plane with you to Santa Barbara, where they have inherited their own beautiful houses on another part of the same vast estate. . . .

When you talk to your friends in Miami about where you're going to live, would you focus on Denver? No. You might not even mention Denver, even though you will be a Denver-dweller for several hours. . . .

Similarly, the Heaven we will go to when we die, the intermediate Heaven, is a temporary dwelling place. It's a wonderfully nice place (much better than the Denver airport!), but it's still a stop along the way to our final destination: the New Earth. It will be great to see friends and family in the present Heaven whom we haven't seen for a while. But like us, they will be looking forward to the resurrection, after which we will actually live on the estate that God is preparing for us.

Another analogy is more precise. . . . Imagine leaving the homeless shelter in Miami and flying to the intermediate location, Denver, and then turning around and *going back* to your city of origin, which has been completely renovated—a New Miami. In this New Miami, you would no longer live in a homeless shelter but in a beautiful house in a glorious pollution-free, crime-free, sin-free city. So you would end up living not in a new home but in *a radically improved version of your old home*.[938]

Randy Alcorn, *50 Days of Heaven*

The present Heaven and the eternal Heaven are not the same. We can be assured there will be no sorrow on the New Earth, our eternal home. But though the present Heaven is a far happier place than Earth under the Curse, Scripture doesn't state there can be no sorrow there. At the same time, people in Heaven are not frail beings whose joy can only be preserved by shielding them from what's really going on in the universe. Happiness in Heaven is not based on ignorance but on perspective. Those who live in the presence of Christ find great joy in worshiping God and living as righteous beings in rich fellowship in a sinless environment. And because God is continuously at work on Earth, the saints watching from Heaven have a great deal to praise him for, including God's drawing people on Earth to himself (Luke 15:7, 10). But those in the present Heaven are also looking forward to Christ's return, their bodily resurrection, the final judgment, and the fashioning of the New Earth from the ruins of the old.[939]

Randy Alcorn, *Heaven*

When God sent Jesus to die, it was for our bodies as well as our spirits. He came to redeem not just "the breath of life" (spirit) but also "the dust of the ground" (body). When we die, it isn't that our real self goes to the present Heaven and our fake self goes to the grave; it's that part of us goes to the present Heaven and part goes to the grave to await our bodily resurrection. We will never be all that God intended for us to be until body and spirit are again joined in resurrection.[940]

Randy Alcorn, *Heaven*

Paths to Heaven and Hell

"Do not let your hearts be troubled. Trust in God; trust also in me. In my Father's house are many rooms; if it were not so, I would have told you. I am going there to prepare a place for you. And if I go and prepare a place for you, I will come back and take you to be with me that you also may be where I am. You know the way to the place where I am going."

Thomas said to him, "Lord, we don't know where you are going, so how can we know the way?"

Jesus answered, "I am the way and the truth and the life. No one comes to the Father except through me."

JESUS AND THOMAS, JOHN 14:1-6

Watch out for false prophets. They come to you in sheep's clothing, but inwardly they are ferocious wolves. By their fruit you will recognize them. Do people pick grapes from thornbushes, or figs from thistles? Likewise every good tree bears good fruit, but a bad tree bears bad fruit. A good tree cannot bear bad fruit, and a bad tree cannot bear good fruit. Every tree that does not bear good fruit is cut down and thrown into the fire. Thus, by their fruit you will recognize them.

Not everyone who says to me, "Lord, Lord," will enter the kingdom of heaven, but only he who does the will of my Father who is in heaven. Many will say to me on that day, "Lord, Lord, did we not prophesy in your name, and in your name drive out demons and perform many miracles?" Then I will tell them plainly, "I never knew you. Away from me, you evildoers!"

JESUS, MATTHEW 7:15-23

The devil, who deceived them, was thrown into the lake of burning sulfur, where the beast and the false prophet had been thrown. They will be tormented day and night for ever and ever. Then I saw a great white throne and him who was seated on it. Earth and sky fled from his presence, and there was no place for them. And I saw the dead, great and small, standing before the throne, and books were opened. Another book was opened, which is the book of life. The dead were judged according to what they had done as recorded in the books. The sea gave up the dead that were in it, and death and Hades gave up the dead that were in them, and each person was judged according to what he had done. Then death and Hades were thrown into the lake of fire. The lake of fire is the second death. If anyone's name was not found written in the book of life, he was thrown into the lake of fire.

JOHN, REVELATION 20:10-15

Evildoers shall be cut off; but those who wait on the
LORD, they shall inherit the earth. . . . The meek shall
inherit the earth, and shall delight themselves in the
abundance of peace. . . . For those blessed by Him
shall inherit the earth, but those cursed by Him shall
be cut off.

DAVID, PSALM 37:9, 11, 22, NKJV

I want to know one thing:
the way to heaven—how to land safe on that happy shore.
God Himself has condescended to teach the way;
for this very end He came from heaven.
He has written it down in a book. Oh, give me that book!
At any price give me the book of God!
I have it—here is knowledge enough for me.
Let me be a man of one book
Here, then, I am, far from the busy ways of men.
I sit down alone; only God is here.
In His presence I open and read His book
that I may find the way to heaven.[941]

John Wesley, *Sermons on Several Occasions*

We do not stray into the blessedness of heaven. We prepare for it,
and for it we are prepared. Heaven gets into us before we get into it.
We are counting on a future life of joy and gladness, but have we
ever tasted its joy and gladness here—the joy of the forgiven? We
hope to meet our loved ones whom we have loved and lost a while,
but do we trust the Christ they trusted and love the Lord they loved?

There are very few people who do not hope to enter the gates
of that celestial city when this brief life is ended. The question is, are
they on the right road?[942]

Charles Ferguson Ball, *Heaven*

How to get to Heaven is the question that has burdened men's hearts in every clime and every age since Adam sinned. Every heathen religion has its heaven of some kind, a place of blessedness hereafter, to be earnestly desired and sought for. Whether it is called "The Happy Hunting Ground" or "Nirvana" or something else, men long for Heaven.

To make sure of gaining Heaven men have brought gifts to witch doctors, made sacrifices to their gods, paid money to priests and tortured themselves with unspeakable pains. Men have offered their sons into the fiery iron arms of Moloch; women have thrown their babies to the crocodiles of the Ganges River, hoping to gain heaven.

Pilgrims have traversed burning deserts to bow at Mecca; crusaders have fought their way to Jerusalem to gain the assurance of peace and forgiveness hereafter. The fasting vigils of monks in their cells, the deeds of penitents who climbed stone stairs on bare knees and the millions of prayers, Ave Marias or Paternosters counted on rosary beads have been with a hope of gaining Heaven.

Men seek a way to Heaven in the waters of baptism, in the confessional box or in the bread and wine of the Lord's Supper. They seek Heaven by lodge rites, by giving gifts to the poor, by righteous deeds. Every human heart longs to make sure of blessedness and peace and happiness hereafter. Christian Scientists . . . call Jesus "the Way-shower." Jesus is not the Way-shower; He is the Way.

Jesus Himself is the only way. He is the "strait gate," the "narrow way." Every other way leads to destruction.

Jesus repeatedly said that He is the way to salvation, the way to Heaven. He said in John 7:37 [emphasis added], "If any man thirst, let him come unto *me*, and drink." He said in Matthew 11:28 [emphasis added], "Come unto *me*, all ye that labour and are heavy laden, and I will give you rest." True rest, true salvation, true forgiveness are not found by membership in a church nor by baptism nor by righteous living. They are found only in Christ.

If you have Christ, you have the way to heaven.[943]

John Rice, *Bible Facts about Heaven*

The soul that has wasted away all its time given for repentance and prayer, is, at the moment of death, left under everlasting hardness of heart; and whatsoever enmity against God and godliness was found in the heart in this world is increased in the world to come, when all manner of softening means and mercies are ever at an end.

. . . Fallen angels are sealed up under misery because there is no door of hope opened for them. But in this life there is hope for the worst of sinful men: There is the word of grace and hope calling them in the gospel; there is the voice of divine mercy sounding in the sanctuary, and blessed are they that hear the joyful sound: But if we turn the deaf ear to the voice of God and his Son, and to all the tender and compassionate entreaties of a dying Saviour, hope is hastening to its period. This very angel will shortly swear, that this joyful sound shall be heard no longer.

He comes now to the door of our hearts, he sues there for admittance, Open unto me and receive me as your Saviour and your Lord, give me and my gospel free admission, and I will come in and bestow upon you the riches of my grace and all thy salvation: Open your hearts to me with the holy desires and humble submission of penitence, and receive the blessings of righteousness, and pardon, and eternal life.[944]

Isaac Watts, *The World to Come*

"From paradise to paradise," such is the path of mankind according to God's all-loving plan. Created for life and prosperity, for peace and joy, man longs to return to the gates of his homeland. But between the gates of the first and of the second Paradise stands the Mediator, the Man from heaven, "the man Christ Jesus" (1 Timothy 2:5), the Saviour of the world.

Between the garden of the first and of the second Paradise there lies another, that quiet garden, the garden of Gethsemane, where in sternest struggle for you and me Jesus sought the face of His Father.[945]

Erich Sauer, *The King of the Earth*

We get in because Christ paid the admission price. It is as simple as that. . . . God does not let us in because he is impressed with our generosity, sincerity, notoriety, or ingenuity. We get in because Christ repossessed us through his death.[946]

John Gilmore, *Probing Heaven*

Keep me walking steadfastly towards the country of everlasting
    delights, that paradise-land which is my true inheritance.
Support me by the strength of heaven that I may never turn back,
    or desire false pleasures that wilt and disappear into nothing.
As I pursue my heavenly journey by thy grace
    let me be known as a man with no aim
    but that of a burning desire for thee,
    and the good and salvation of my fellow men.[947]

The Valley of Vision: A Collection of Puritan Prayers and Devotions

May I travel miry paths with a life pure from spot or stain. In needful transactions let my affection be in heaven, and my love soar upwards in flames of fire, my gaze fixed on unseen things, my eyes open to the emptiness, fragility, mockery of earth and its vanities. May I view all things in the mirror of eternity, waiting for the coming of my Lord, listening for the last trumpet call, *hastening* unto the new heaven and earth. Order this day all my communications according to Thy wisdom, and to the gain of mutual good. Forbid that I should not be profited or made profitable. May I speak each word as if my last word, and walk each step as my final one. If my life should end today, let this be my best day.[948]

The Valley of Vision: A Collection of Puritan Prayers and Devotions

In prayer I am lifted above the frowns and flatteries of life, and taste heavenly joys; entering into the eternal world I can give myself to Thee with all my heart, to be Thine for ever.[949]

The Valley of Vision: A Collection of Puritan Prayers and Devotions

It is Heaven and Hell that put bite into the Christian vision of life on earth, just as playing for high stakes puts bite into a game or a war or a courtship. Hell is part of the vision too: the height of the mountain is appreciated from the depth of the valley, and for winning to be high drama, losing must be possible. For salvation to be "good news," there must be "bad news" to be saved from. If all of life's roads lead to the same place, it makes no ultimate difference which road we choose. But if they lead to opposite places, to infinite bliss or infinite misery, unimaginable glory or unimaginable tragedy . . . then life is a life-or-death affair, a razor's edge, and our choice of roads is infinitely important.[950]

Peter Kreeft, *Everything You Ever Wanted to Know about Heaven*

It is sheer imperialism to insist that only one man-made road up the divine mountain is the right road and all others are wrong. But Christ does not claim to be a man who became God but God become Man. "No one has ascended into heaven but he who descended from heaven, the Son of man" (John 3:13). Christianity claims to be the road God made down, not the road we made up. That's why the "One Way" claim is necessary: because we are only repeating the message God gave us—we are mailmen, not authors.

It makes sense for God to make just one road. He starts from unity, from the top of the mountain. We start from diversity, from the bottom. Diverse human religions are indeed equal: equally failures.[951]

Peter Kreeft, *Everything You Ever Wanted to Know about Heaven*

One wonders why those who believe in the ultimate universal reconciliation of all men to God are so anxious to spread their theory. Undoubtedly it is a comfort to sinners who have no wish to repent now. But they are doing tremendous harm to them by deluding them with the false hope that they can refuse to obey Christ's command to "Repent" now (Matthew 4:17), and be given another chance to do it hereafter. Any theory that encourages men to continue in their sin is not of God.

. . . Leniency toward a Hitler or a Herod is a second crime against those whom they tortured and killed. There is no justice at all in the belief that the only punishment of the wicked will be limited to what they suffer during their earthly lifetime. Did Hitler really pay for his crimes against humanity? His suffering was nothing compared to the suffering he spread and the tortures he imposed. Anyone who rejects the doctrine of future eternal punishment is merely encouraging the perpetuation of evil here and now. He who is not afraid of the retribution of eternity curses God and kicks others around with impunity.

. . . Those who believe and propagate the theory of universal reconciliation today are not saying anything new; they are just repeating the lie of the devil in the Garden of Eden.

If God is going to be so kind as to forgive everybody in the future, why not do it now? Does God's mercy preclude punishing the unrepentant?

. . . How many people could we trust to obey the laws if they knew they would not be punished for disobeying them? How many people would tell the truth in a courtroom if they were not afraid of being penalized for perjury? Those who preach the final salvation of all, whether they died in unbelief or not, should consider the chaos into which this world would be plunged if this doctrine were to apply generally here on earth. Our sense of justice rejects it. Why should not God's sense of justice preclude it also?

If there were no future punishment, then those who die in a state of wickedness would really be better off and happier than the righteous who have renounced their own selfish wills in order to do God's will on earth, or than those who have sacrificed and suffered for Christ's service. The wicked men of Noah's day would really have had a greater reward than Noah, because they perished in the flood and escaped the difficulties and sorrows of life, and would be eternally reconciled to God. What did they lose? Nothing, since they would then have gone to heaven, or would eventually go there. Then Judas would not have done so badly when he committed suicide. He would have put an end to his torments, while those of the disciples would have continued because of persecution. Such a faith justifies and encourages not only suicide but also murder; for killing someone would literally liberate him from the troubles of earth, while liberating him to eventual eternal bliss. And the murderer himself would have nothing to lose in the end.

Such a doctrine also makes repentance and a holy life completely unnecessary. . . . If the sinner by right can enter heaven and enjoy its privileges as much as the believer, in spite of the fact that he made no effort to prepare for it by believing in and following Christ in this life, he would really be better off than the believer. . . . If heaven is assured to us, no matter what we do, why subject ourselves to the spiritual disciplines enjoined by the Word of God?

What, actually, is the difference between atheism and this theory of the ultimate reconciliation of all men to God? As far as it affects men's eternal destiny, none, since even the atheist, despite his unbelief, would one day go to live with God in whom he avowedly disbelieved. In fact, this theory, if true, would be worse than atheism, because it promises not only exemption from future punishment but also eternal bliss for the unrepentant sinner. . . . How could there be greater encouragement to a life of crime and debauchery than such a belief?[952]

Spiros Zodhiates, *Life after Death*

The world is full of people who (insofar as they think about it at all) imagine that they are going to heaven. They have no fears to the contrary, and are quite confident in the matter. Year in and year out funerals take place at which ministers (who should know better) pronounce firmly and confidently about this one and that one having arrived safely in heaven when, frankly such firmness and confidence (in many cases) is without any clear ground.[953]

Richard Brooks, *The Doors of Heaven*

Heaven's administration has strict immigration laws.[954]

Ivor Powell, *Heaven: My Father's Country*

To enter heaven as we are, and for heaven to remain heaven in the process, is a moral impossibility. Nothing that defiles can enter heaven (Revelation 21:27) and so the idea that death marks a natural and inevitable transition to the bliss of heaven, a bliss which awaits us all, is a deep and deadly mistake.[955]

Paul Helm, *The Last Things*

Judging by what's said at most funerals, you'd think nearly *everyone's* going to Heaven, wouldn't you? But Jesus made it clear that most people are *not* going to Heaven: "Small is the gate and narrow the road that leads to life, and only a few find it." We dare not "wait and see" when it comes to what's on the other side of death. We shouldn't just cross our fingers and hope that our names are written in the Book of Life (Revelation 21:27). We can know, we *should* know, before we die. And because we may die at any time, we need to know *now*— not next month or next year.[956]

Randy Alcorn, *Heaven*

If I wish to fly from Portland to North Carolina I can get there a number of ways. I can fly through Denver, Minneapolis, Chicago, Detroit, Salt Lake City, Dallas, or Atlanta. But if I want to arrive in Heaven, I cannot go through Buddha, Mohammed, or Moses. I can only go through Jesus.

Randy Alcorn, unpublished notes

Christ offers to everyone the gift of forgiveness, salvation, and eternal life: "Let the one who is thirsty come; and let the one who wishes take the free gift of the water of life" (Revelation 22:17). This is a text Spurgeon often quoted, and one each of us should ponder carefully.

This gospel gift, offered to us by God's sovereign grace, cannot be worked for, earned, or achieved in any sense. It's not dependent on our merit or effort, but solely on Christ's generous and sufficient sacrifice on our behalf.

God's greatest gift is himself. We don't need just salvation; we need Jesus, the Savior. It is the person, God, who graciously gives us the place, Heaven. A place purchased by his blood.[957]

Randy Alcorn, *We Shall See God*

Pets and Animals

"I now establish my covenant with you and with your descendants after you and with every living creature that was with you—the birds, the livestock and all the wild animals, all those that came out of the ark with you—every living creature on earth. . . . Never again will there be a flood to destroy the earth."

And God said, "This is the sign of the covenant I am making between me and you and every living creature with you, a covenant for all generations to come. . . . I will remember my covenant between me and you and all living creatures of every kind. . . . Whenever the rainbow appears in the clouds, I will see it and remember the everlasting covenant between God and all living creatures of every kind on the earth." . . .

God said to Noah, "This is the sign of the covenant I have established between me and all life on the earth."

God, Genesis 9:9-12, 15-17

Do you give the horse his strength? . . . Do you make him leap like a locust? . . . He paws fiercely, rejoicing in his strength. . . . He laughs at fear, afraid of nothing.

GOD, JOB 39:19-22

Wild animals and all cattle, small creatures and flying birds, kings of the earth and all nations, you princes and all rulers on earth, young men and maidens, old men and children. Let them praise the name of the LORD, for his name alone is exalted; his splendor is above the earth and the heavens.

PSALM 148:10-13

The creation itself will be liberated from its bondage to decay and brought into the glorious freedom of the children of God. We know that the whole creation has been groaning as in the pains of childbirth. . . . We ourselves . . . groan inwardly as we wait eagerly for . . . the redemption of our bodies.

PAUL, ROMANS 8:21-23

All flesh will see the salvation of God.

ISAIAH, QUOTED IN LUKE 3:6, NASB

In that day the wolf and the lamb will live together;
    the leopard will lie down with the baby goat.
The calf and the yearling will be safe with the lion,
    and a little child will lead them all.
The cow will graze near the bear.
    The cub and the calf will lie down together.
    The lion will eat hay like a cow.
The baby will play safely near the hole of a cobra.

Yes, a little child will put its hand in a nest of
    deadly snakes without harm.
Nothing will hurt or destroy in all my holy mountain,
    for as the waters fill the sea,
      so the earth will be filled with people who know
        the Lord.

GOD, ISAIAH 11:6-9, NLT

The wolf and the lamb will feed together, and the lion
will eat straw like the ox. . . . They will neither harm
nor destroy.

GOD, ISAIAH 65:25

Day and night they never stop saying: "Holy, holy,
holy is the Lord God Almighty, who was, and is, and
is to come." . . . The living creatures give glory, honor
and thanks to him who sits on the throne.

JOHN, REVELATION 4:8-9

Behold, I am making all things new.

JESUS, REVELATION 21:5, ESV

All the animals of the forest are mine, and I own the
cattle on a thousand hills. I know every bird on the
mountains, and all the animals of the field are mine.

GOD, PSALM 50:10-11, NLT

The godly care for their animals.

SOLOMON, PROVERBS 12:10, NLT

I heard every creature in heaven and on earth and
under the earth and on the sea, and all that is in them,
singing: "To him who sits on the throne and to the
Lamb be praise and honor and glory and power, for
ever and ever!"

JOHN, REVELATION 5:13

Something better remains after death for these poor creatures
[animals]. . . . [They] shall one day be delivered from this bondage
of corruption, and shall then receive an ample amends for all their
present sufferings.[958]

John Wesley, "The General Deliverance"

Are there animals in Heaven? The simplest answer is: Why not? How
irrational is the prejudice that would allow plants (green fields and
flowers) but not animals into Heaven!
. . . Animals belong in the "new earth" as much as trees.[959]

Peter Kreeft, *Everything You Ever Wanted to Know about Heaven*

Would the same animals be in Heaven as on earth? "Is my dead cat
in Heaven?" Again, why not? God can raise up the very grass; why
not cats? Though the blessed have better things to do than play with
pets, the better does not exclude the lesser. We were meant from the
beginning to have stewardship over the animals. We have not fulfilled
that divine plan yet on earth; therefore it seems likely that the right
relationship with animals will be part of Heaven: proper "petship."
And what better place to begin than with already petted pets?[960]

Peter Kreeft, *Everything You Ever Wanted to Know about Heaven*

It seems to me possible that certain animals may have an immortality,
not in themselves, but in the immortality of their masters. . . . Very
few animals indeed, in their wild state, attain to a "self" or ego. But if
any do, and if it is agreeable to the goodness of God that they should

live again, their immortality would also be related to man—not, this time, to individual masters, but to humanity.[961]

C. S. Lewis, *The Problem of Pain*

Why did the animals [in Eden] have a wonderful life? Because Man's Fate Determines The Animals' Fate.

After Adam and Eve ate of the tree of knowledge of good and evil, they were all cursed and the whole environment changed. In Genesis 3:17-19 man is cursed, and in Genesis 3:14 the animals are cursed. Death entered in, affecting not only mankind, but all animals as well. Adam is expelled from the Garden of Eden (Genesis 3:23). Death is now a part of life. The animals did not sin; man sinned. Why were the animals cursed? Because Man's Fate Determines the Animals' Fate.

God told Noah to build an ark. God told Noah to take two of every kind of animal and seven of every clean animal, and put them in the ark. These animals are saved with Noah and his family. Why are the animals saved also? Because Man's Fate Determines The Animals' Fate.

God established a covenant with Noah and the animals. He promised never to destroy man and the animals in a flood again. In Genesis Chapter 9, God repeatedly states that the covenant includes every fowl, the cattle, and every living creature. Why were the animals included in the covenant? Because Man's Fate Determines the Animals' Fate.[962]

Niki Behrikis Shanahan, *There Is Eternal Life for Animals*

Is it so unthinkable that God might answer the prayer of a human by re-creating a much-loved pet in the new earth, simply because we ask Him to?

. . . If He can resurrect the dead, then surely He can bring a tiny dog back to life. The Lord loves people and animals, and He definitely answers prayer.[963]

Steve Wohlberg, *Will My Pet Go to Heaven?*

Man suffers justly, the creatures unjustly. Our restoration is pure grace, that of the creature world is simple justice.[964]

R. C. H. Lenski, *The Interpretation of St. Paul's Epistle to the Romans*

It wasn't until the advent of seventeenth-century Enlightenment . . . that the existence of animal souls was even questioned in Western civilization. Throughout the history of the church, the classic understanding of living things has included the doctrine that animals, as well as humans, have souls.[965]

Gary Habermas and J. P. Moreland, *Beyond Death*

Every dog, cat, bird, horse, dolphin—or any other creature—was actually thoughtfully designed, purposefully planned, and uniquely created by the very same One who ultimately gave His life on a splintery cross! In other words, all animals are *really Jesus Christ's animals.* He made them, He loves them, and they're His pets, too. "For every beast of the forest *is Mine*, and the cattle on a thousand hills, I know all the birds of the mountains, And the wild beasts of the field *are Mine*" (Psalm 50:10, 11, italics added).[966]

Steve Wohlberg, *Will My Pet Go to Heaven?*

If God brings our pets back to life, it wouldn't surprise me. It would be just like Him. It would be totally in keeping with His generous character. . . . Exorbitant. Excessive. Extravagant in grace after grace. Of all the dazzling discoveries and ecstatic pleasures heaven will hold for us, the potential of seeing Scrappy would be pure whimsy— utterly, joyfully, surprisingly superfluous. . . . Heaven is going to be a place that will refract and reflect in as many ways as possible the goodness and joy of our great God, who delights in lavishing love on His children.[967]

Joni Eareckson Tada, *Holiness in Hidden Places*

And as I knelt beside the brook
To drink eternal life, I took
A glance across the golden grass,
And saw my dog, old Blackie, fast
As she could come. She leaped the stream—
Almost—and what a happy gleam
Was in her eye. I knelt to drink,
And knew that I was on the brink
Of endless joy. And everywhere
I turned I saw a wonder there.
And all that's left is joy,
And endless ages to employ
The mind and heart, and understand,
And love the sovereign Lord who planned
That it should take eternity
To lavish all his grace on me.[968]

John Piper, *Future Grace*

[Upon seeing in heaven a woman of unbearable beauty:]

"Is it? . . . Is it?" I whispered to my guide.

"Not at all," said he. "It's someone ye'll never have heard of. Her name on earth was Sarah Smith.". . .

"She seems to be . . . well, a person of particular importance?"

"Aye. She is one of the great ones. Ye have heard that fame in this country and fame on earth are two quite different things."

"And who are these gigantic people . . . look! They're like emeralds . . . who are dancing and throwing flowers before her?"

"Haven't you read Milton? A thousand liveried angels lackey her."

"And who are all these young men and women on each side?"

"They are her sons and daughters."

"She must have had a very large family, Sir."

"Every young man or boy that met her became her son—even if it was only the boy that brought meat to her back door. Every girl that met her was her daughter."

"Isn't that a bit hard on their own parents?"

"No. There are those that steal other people's children. But her motherhood was of a different kind. Those on whom it fell went back to their natural parents loving them more. Few men looked on her without becoming, in a certain fashion, her lovers. But it was the kind of love that made them not less true, but truer, to their own wives."

"And how . . . But Hullo! What are all these animals? A cat—two cats—dozens of cats. And all those dogs . . . why, I can't count them. And the birds. And the Horses."

"They are her beasts."

"Did she keep a sort of zoo? I mean this is a bit too much."

"Every beast or bird that came near her had a place in her love. In her they became themselves. And now the abundance of life she has in Christ from the Father flows over into them."[969]

The Teacher and the Traveler, in *The Great Divorce*, by C. S. Lewis

"Behold, I am the Lord, the God of all flesh. Is there anything too hard for Me?" (Jeremiah 32:27). If God wants to re-create in the new world some of the animals from this old world, it's an easy task. Besides, by then He will have already accomplished something much more dramatic—the resurrection of all the dead human beings.[970]

Steve Wohlberg, *Will My Pet Go to Heaven?*

Will "the creature," will even the brute creation, always remain in this deplorable condition? God forbid that we should affirm this; yea, or even entertain such a thought! . . . The whole brute creation will then, undoubtedly, be restored, not only to the vigour, strength, and swiftness which they had at their creation, but to a far higher degree of each than they ever enjoyed. They will be restored, not only to that measure of understanding which they had in paradise, but to a degree of it as much higher than that. . . .

And with their beauty their happiness will return. . . . In the new earth, as well as in the new heavens, there will be nothing to give pain, but everything that the wisdom and goodness of God can create to give happiness. As a recompense for what they [animals] once suffered

. . . they shall enjoy happiness suited to their state, without alloy, without interruption, and without end. . . . What, if it should then please the all-wise, the all-gracious Creator to raise them higher in the scale of beings? What, if it should please him . . . to make them . . . capable of knowing and loving and enjoying the Author of their being?[971]

John Wesley, "The General Deliverance," Sermon 60

Isaiah 11:6-9 speaks of a coming glorious era on Earth when animals will live in tranquility with each other and with people, neither harming nor destroying one another, for the earth will be filled with the knowledge of the Lord, and restored to its harmony with God.

Some interpreters contend that this passage speaks only of the Millennium, but . . . Isaiah anticipates an *eternal* Kingdom of God on Earth. Isaiah 65:17 and 66:22 specifically speak of the New Earth. Sandwiched between them is a reference very similar to that in Isaiah 11: "'The wolf and the lamb will feed together, and the lion will eat straw like the ox. . . . They will neither harm nor destroy on all my holy mountain,' says the LORD" (65:25).

When will there be *no more harm* on the earth? Not on the old Earth or even in the Millennium, which will end in rebellion and warfare, but on the New Earth, where there will be no more sin, death, or suffering (Revelation 21:4). These descriptions of animals peacefully inhabiting the earth *may* have application to a millennial kingdom on the old Earth, but their primary reference appears to be to God's eternal Kingdom, where mankind and animals will enjoy a redeemed Earth.[972]

Randy Alcorn, *Heaven*

"And all flesh will see the salvation of God" (Luke 3:6, NASB). The Greek word translated "flesh" is *sarx*. Some Bible versions translate this as "all people" or "all mankind," but the word is more inclusive. "All flesh" includes animals. They too will behold and benefit from Christ's redemptive work.[973]

Randy Alcorn, *Heaven*

Our resurrection, the redemption of our bodies, will bring deliverance not only to us *but also to the rest of creation, which has been groaning in its suffering.* This seems to indicate that on the New Earth, after mankind's resurrection, animals who once suffered on the old Earth will join God's children in glorious freedom from death and decay.[974]

Randy Alcorn, *Heaven*

One of the most revealing Old Testament pictures of God's redemptive work is the Flood and Noah's ark. When God saved people from the destruction of the Flood, he also took great care to save the animals, the people's companions and helpers. . . .

After the Flood, God made a covenant with Noah, and in that new covenant God included animals. Notice the repeated emphasis on animals:

God said to Noah and his sons:

"I now establish my covenant with you and with your descendants after you and *with every living creature* that was with you—*the birds, the livestock and all the wild animals,* all those that came out of the ark with you—*every living creature* on earth. . . . Never again will there be a flood to destroy the earth." And God said, "This is the sign of the covenant I am making between me and you and *every living creature* with you, a covenant for all generations to come. . . . I will remember my covenant between me and you and *all living creatures of every kind.* . . . Whenever the rainbow appears in the clouds, I will see it and remember the everlasting covenant between God and *all living creatures of every kind* on the earth." So God said to Noah, "This is the sign of the covenant I have established between me and *all life on the earth*." (Genesis 9:9-17, emphasis added)

God's plan for a renewed Earth after the Flood emphatically involved animals. Wouldn't we expect his plan for a renewed Earth after the future judgment to likewise include animals? If the rescue of mankind in the ark is a picture of redemption, doesn't the rescue of the animals in the ark also anticipate their restoration as part of God's redemptive purposes?[975]

Randy Alcorn, *Heaven*

God created us to be stewards of animals. He says, "the godly are concerned for the welfare of their animals" (Proverbs 12:10, NLT). We are caretakers for the animals, but they belong to God, not us (Psalm 50:10-11).

Some people regard emotional attachment to animals as a modern development. But many cultures' historical records demonstrate otherwise. The prophet Nathan spoke to King David of the poor man who had a little lamb "who shared his food, drank from his cup and even slept in his arms. It was like a daughter to him" (2 Samuel 12:3). There's no suggestion this man's affection for his pet was inappropriate. David, unaware the story was told to expose his own sin, angrily responded that the man who stole that precious pet deserved to die.

We needn't speculate how God might populate a perfect Earth. He populated Eden with animals, under the rule of people. God doesn't make mistakes. There's every reason to believe he'll restore this self-proclaimed "very good" arrangement on the New Earth. We should expect the New Earth to be a place where we'll fulfill our calling to be faithful rulers and stewards of animals.

God directed Adam to name the animals (Genesis 2:19-20). The process of naming involved a personal relationship with the name-bearer. Note that Adam wasn't instructed to name the plants, only his wife and the animals, indicating their special relationship.

Eden was perfect. But without animals Eden wouldn't be Eden. The New Earth is the new Eden—Paradise regained, with the Curse of the first Adam reversed, transformed into the blessing of the second Adam (Romans 5:14-15). Would God take away from us in Heaven what he gave, for delight and companionship and help, to Adam and Eve in Eden? Would he revoke his decision to put animals with people, under their care? Since he'll fashion the New Earth with renewed people, wouldn't we expect him also to include renewed animals?[976]

Randy Alcorn, *Heaven*

Christ proclaims from his throne on the New Earth: "Behold, I am making all things new" (Revelation 21:5, NASB). It's not just people who will be renewed, but the earth and everything in it. Do "all things" include animals? Of course. Horses, cats, dogs, deer, dolphins, and squirrels—as well as the inanimate creation—will be beneficiaries of Christ's death and resurrection. Christ's emphasis isn't on making new things, but on making old things new. It's not about inventing the unfamiliar, but restoring and enhancing the familiar. Jesus seems to be saying, "I'll take all I made the first time, including people and nature and animals and the earth itself, and bring them back as new, fresh, and indestructible." . . .

If God created on the New Earth human beings who had never before existed—rather than resurrecting people who had lived on the old Earth—would it fulfill the promise in Romans 8 of redemption, deliverance, and resurrection? No. Why? For the passage to be fulfilled, those redeemed and resurrected into the new world *must be the same ones who suffered in the old world.* Otherwise, their longing for redemption would go unmet.

As mankind goes, so go the animals. If we take to its logical conclusion the parallel that Paul makes between humans and animals groaning, then *at least some of those animals who suffered on the old Earth must be made whole on the New Earth.*[977]

Randy Alcorn, *50 Days of Heaven*

When God breathed a spirit into Adam's body, which was made from the earth, Adam became *nephesh*, a "living being" (Genesis 2:7). Remarkably, the same word, *nephesh*, is used for animals, just as it is for people—*both* are given God's breath of life (Genesis 1:30; 2:7; 6:17; 7:15, 22).[978]

Randy Alcorn, *50 Days of Heaven*

We know animals will be on the New Earth, which is a redeemed and renewed old Earth, in which animals had a prominent role. People will be resurrected to inhabit this world. As we saw, Romans 8:21-23 assumes animals as part of a suffering creation eagerly awaiting deliverance through humanity's resurrection. This seems to require that some animals who lived, suffered, and died on the old Earth must be made whole on the New Earth. Wouldn't some of those likely be our pets?[979]

Randy Alcorn, *Heaven*

The word translated "living creatures" is normally translated "animals." Somehow we have failed to grasp that the "living creatures" who cry out "Holy, holy, holy" are *animals*—living, breathing, intelligent and articulate *animals* who dwell in God's presence, worshiping and praising him. They preexisted and are greater than the animals we know. Perhaps they're the prototype creatures of Heaven after whom God designed Earth's animals. But even though they're highly intelligent and expressive, they're still animals; that's what Scripture calls them.[980]

Randy Alcorn, *Heaven*

Humorist Will Rogers said, "If there are no dogs in heaven, then when I die I want to go where they went." This statement was, of course, based on sentiment, not theology. However, it reflects something biblical: a God-given affection for animals. . . .

That's why the question of whether pets will be in Heaven is not, as some assume, stupid. Animals aren't nearly as valuable as people, but God is their Maker and has touched many people's lives through them. It would be simple for him to re-create a pet in Heaven if he wants to. He's the *giver* of all good gifts, not the *taker* of them. If it would please us to have a pet restored to the New Earth, that may be sufficient reason.[981]

Randy Alcorn, *Heaven*

Second Peter 3:5-7 draws a direct parallel between God's past judgment of the earth with water and his future judgment with fire. Mankind was judged in the Flood, but *God didn't limit his rescue to people;*

he also rescued representatives of every animal species to populate the earth. This is a powerful picture of what Romans 8 states: mankind and animals and all creation are linked together not only in curse and judgment but also in blessing and deliverance. Shouldn't we expect the same in the coming judgment by fire?

Since we know God will fashion the New Earth with renewed people and renewed features of ground and water and trees and fruit, shouldn't we expect him also to include renewed animals?

The burden of proof falls not on the assumption that animals *will* be part of God's New Earth, but on the assumption that they *won't*. Would God withhold from us on the New Earth what he gave to Adam and Eve in Eden for delight, companionship, and help? Would he revoke his decision to put animals on Earth with people, placing them under our care and rule? Or will he follow through on his original design?[982]

Randy Alcorn, *50 Days of Heaven*

Even if we didn't have the prophets speaking of a world in which animals no longer devour each other, and even if Romans 8 didn't talk of the nonhuman creation also benefiting from humanity's redemption, a strong case could be made for God re-creating animals on the New Earth. Personally, I can't think of a single passage of Scripture that would preclude this. Who created animals in the first place? Who designed their beauty, and made their unique and endearing and sometimes spectacular qualities? Who created us to appreciate and be delighted by those qualities? The connection between people and animals is God-designed. It existed before sin—why would it not exist after sin? It is God-created, God-honoring, "very good" and inspires our delight and heartfelt gratitude to God. There is every reason to expect to see animals on the redeemed world, God's New Earth.

Randy Alcorn, unpublished notes

Someone wrote to me, "My children are hoping extinct animals will be in Heaven, maybe even dinosaurs." . . . Were dinosaurs part of

God's original creation of a perfect animal world? Certainly. Will the restoration of Earth and the redemption of God's creation be complete enough to bring back extinct animals?[983]

Randy Alcorn, *Heaven*

Imagine Jurassic Park with all of the awesome majesty of those huge creatures but none of their violence and hostility. Imagine riding a brontosaurus—or flying on the back of a pterodactyl. Unless God made a mistake when he originally created them—and clearly he didn't— why *wouldn't* he include them when he makes "all things new"?[984]

Randy Alcorn, *TouchPoints: Heaven*

Pilgrim Mentality

Dear friends, I warn you as "temporary residents and
foreigners" to keep away from worldly desires that
wage war against your very souls. Be careful to live
properly among your unbelieving neighbors. Then
even if they accuse you of doing wrong, they will see
your honorable behavior, and they will give honor to
God when he judges the world.

PETER, 1 PETER 2:11-12, NLT

Hear my prayer, O LORD!
    Listen to my cries for help!
    Don't ignore my tears.
For I am your guest—
    a traveler passing through,
    as my ancestors were before me.

DAVID, PSALM 39:12, NLT

All these people were still living by faith when they
died. They did not receive the things promised; they
only saw them and welcomed them from a distance.
And they admitted that they were aliens and strangers
on earth. People who say such things show that they
are looking for a country of their own. . . . They were
longing for a better country—a heavenly one. . . .
[God] has prepared a city for them.

HEBREWS 11:13-14, 16

If any righteous man among the Christians passes from this world,
they rejoice and offer thanks to God, and they escort his body with
songs and thanksgiving as if he were setting out from one place to
another nearby.[985]

Aristides, *Apology*, ca.124 CE

*Assure us that we shall at last enter Immanuel's land
where none is ever sick, and the sun will always shine.*[986]
The Valley of Vision: A Collection of Puritan Prayers and Devotions

He is no fool who gives what he cannot keep to gain what he cannot
lose.[987]

Jim Elliot

The bliss of heaven! Have you grasped this? Do you have a clear sense
of what this bliss excludes and of what it includes? Do you bless God
and give him all the glory for it? Do you live every day of your Christian life in anticipation of the prospect of it, while, even now, you
are pressing on to know Christ? Is your present Christian life, seeking
to live near to God, a sort of "rough draft" of the life of full communion with God that you look forward to above?[988]

Richard Brooks, *The Doors of Heaven*

As distant lands beyond the sea,
    When friends go hence, draw nigh,
So heaven, when friends have hither gone,
    Draws nearer from the sky.

And as those lands the dearer grow
    When friends are long away,
So heaven itself, through loved ones dead,
    Grows dearer day by day.

Heaven is not far from those who see
    With the pure spirit's sight,
But near, and in the very hearts
    Of those who see aright.

Hymn, author unknown

Every Christian faces a paradox in this life: that of resting in the Lord, but of experiencing a continual restlessness. This present world is a restless place for the true Christian to live in, because it is not our resting place. Heaven is. Here (to use the language of Hebrews 11) we are like strangers in a foreign country, living in tents. And what is the point and nature of tents? They are temporary. You set them up and you take them down. They are designed for those who are on the move. And Christians are on the move. . . .

Does a traveller settle down to take his permanent rest while he is still "on the way"? No! He presses on to the journey's end, and then he rests.[989]

Richard Brooks, *The Doors of Heaven*

Life here is a "tent" existence, as contrasted with the heavenly life in a "building." Being a tent-maker by trade (Acts 18:3), this image would have been an obvious one for the apostle [Paul]. Two points are made by this metaphor. First, tents are exposed to storms and other external forces. They provide no great security, as every camper has learned. By the same measure, life here is vulnerable, subject to chance and change. By contrast, our heavenly life is secure, like a solid building, impervious to storm or other threatening external forces. Life in a tent is transient. Its appeal lies precisely in its ability to be moved around easily. It is the form of residence of the traveler and the pilgrim.

. . . The last call will come, the final tent site will be abandoned, and our pilgrimage will be over. By contrast, the heavenly life is rooted and permanent. We are "settled" in the "building not built by human hands," in that home which Jesus went through death and resurrection to prepare for us (John 14:1-2).[990]

Bruce Milne, *The Message of Heaven and Hell*

We are pilgrims, not hobos. A pilgrim has a home, a destination. In redemption God saves us from our wanderings, and gathers us into a land (Psalm 107:1-9).[991]

David Chilton, *Paradise Restored*

When a Christian realizes his citizenship is in heaven, he begins acting as a responsible citizen of earth. He invests wisely in relationships because he knows they're eternal. His conversations, goals, and motives become pure and honest because he realizes these will have a bearing on everlasting reward. He gives generously of time, money, and talent because he's laying up treasure for eternity. He spreads the good news of Christ because he longs to fill heaven's ranks with his friends and neighbors. All this serves the pilgrim well not only in heaven, but on earth; for it serves everyone around him.[992]

Joni Eareckson Tada, *Heaven: Your Real Home*

Discipleship training that lacks a clear view of preparation for eternity has little more than a "buck up and do good for Jesus" feel to it. The fact that we already belong to heaven and that our lives on earth are a pilgrimage toward heaven is rarely, if ever, taught. Yet that is what adds weight, meaning, and motivation to the process of sanctification. It is the reason Scripture calls us to "set [our] minds on things above" (Colossians 3:2).[993]

    Joseph Stowell, *Eternity*

As long as people were taught the idea . . . that our true home is elsewhere, there was a certain satisfaction in the answer itself. For centuries, the idea that this world is not, by itself, our home—emotionally, spiritually, or even socially—was a compelling idea because it was enormously convincing. It unlocked a secret about human existence that seemed to fit what everyone already sensed about human suffering, human aspiration, and the desire to express life in self-giving love. Neither the flame of persecution nor the ever-present danger of disease or war could extinguish this new lease on life. . . . Poverty was still painful but not hopeless. Illness might end in death, but death was not the absolute end. Life took on a creative and vibrant energy because it was harnessed to an overall purpose.[994]

    A. J. Conyers, *The Eclipse of Heaven*

I have been impressed afresh with the truth that all of life here is but a preparation for, a pilgrimage toward, and an investment in heaven.[995]

    Joseph Stowell, *Eternity*

We, as heaven-bound pilgrims, are the real homeless ones on this planet.[996]

    Joseph Stowell, *Eternity*

If I am misunderstood, maligned, or marginalized—physically or mentally persecuted because I am fully committed to the virtues and practices of righteousness and accurately reflect my place in the kingdom—then I will not be shaken. Because I have the confidence that though they may take everything from me here, the kingdom of heaven will be ultimately mine.[997]

    Joseph Stowell, *Eternity*

Let no one apologize for the powerful emphasis Christianity lays upon the doctrine of the world to come. Right there lies its immense superiority to everything else within the whole sphere of human thought or experience. When Christ arose from death and ascended into heaven He established forever three important facts; namely, that this world has been condemned to ultimate dissolution, that the human spirit persists beyond the grave and that there is indeed a world to come. . . .

The church is constantly being tempted to accept this world as her home, and sometimes she has listened to the blandishments of those who would woo her away and use her for their own ends. But if she is wise she will consider that she stands in the valley between the mountain peaks of eternity past and eternity to come. The past is gone forever and the present is passing as swift as the shadow on the sun dial of Ahaz. Even if the earth should continue a million years, not one of us could stay to enjoy it. We do well to think of the long tomorrow.[998]

A. W. Tozer, "The World to Come"

Let us recollect the frail tenure upon which we hold our *temporal mercies*. If we would remember that all the trees of earth are marked for the woodman's axe, we should not be so ready to build our nests in them.[999]

Charles Spurgeon, *Morning and Evening*

Christian: "We are going to Mount Zion."

Then Atheist fell into very great laughter.

Christian: "What's the meaning of your laughter?"

Atheist: "I laugh to see what ignorant persons you are, to take up on you so tedious a journey, and yet are like to have nothing but your travel for your pains. . . . There is not such a place as you dream of in all this world."

Hopeful: "What! No Mount Zion! Did we not see from the Delectable Mountains the Gate of the City? . . . Now do I rejoice in the hope of the Glory of God."

So they turned away from the man; and he, laughing at them, went his way.[1000]

John Bunyan, *The Pilgrim's Progress*

We pilgrims walk the tightrope between earth and heaven, feeling trapped in time, yet with eternity beating in our hearts. Our unsatisfied sense of exile is not to be solved or fixed while here on earth. Our pain and longings make sure we will never be content, and that's good; it is to our benefit that we do not grow comfortable in a world destined for decay.[1001]

Joni Eareckson Tada, *Heaven: Your Real Home*

The general tendency in the literature of pilgrimage is ascetic. We are given to understand how arduous the Christian life is, and how self-denying pilgrims must be as they avoid this thing, shun that one, and deny themselves the pleasures of life. But Jesus calls His disciples to enjoyment and pleasure as well as self-denial. The journey to heaven requires affirmation of God's gifts as well as a rejection of their per-versions. Heaven itself is a place of pleasure and as such sanctifies all legitimate pleasure. Taking our cue from Milton's marvelous portrayal of life in Paradise, we can say that one of the prerequisites for attaining heaven is a creaturely delight in the gifts that God has given to console pilgrims on their earthly pilgrimage.[1002]

Wayne Martindale, *Journey to the Celestial City*

When you're on a long airplane flight, you naturally socialize, eat, read, pray, sleep, and maybe talk about where you're going. But what would you think if a passenger in the window seat hung curtains over the window, taped photographs to the seat in front of him, and put up wall hangings? You'd think, *Hey, it's not that long of a trip. Once we get to the destination, what you're doing won't matter.*[1003]

Randy Alcorn, *The Law of Rewards*

One need not forgo power because he hates power. He may forgo it now precisely because he wants it in a better world. Jesus didn't tell his disciples they shouldn't want to be great, but that they could become great in the next world by being a servant in this one (Mark 10:42-44). Likewise, one does not forgo possessions here because he hates possessions, but because he wants them in another world. Jesus didn't tell his disciples they shouldn't want to be rich. Rather, he told them they could become rich in the next world by giving away riches in this one (Matthew 6:19-21).[1004]

Randy Alcorn, *Money, Possessions, and Eternity*

A wealthy plantation owner invited John Wesley to his home. The two rode their horses all day, seeing just a fraction of all the man owned. At the end of the day the plantation owner proudly asked, "Well, Mr. Wesley, what do you think?" After a moment's silence, Wesley replied, "I think you're going to have a hard time leaving all this."[1005]

Randy Alcorn, *Money, Possessions, and Eternity*

Following Christ is a call not to *abstain* from gratification but (sometimes) to *delay* gratification. More to the point, it's a call to *pursue* the gratification that will last. It's finding our joy in Christ, rather than seeking joy in the things of this world. Heaven, the place of eternal gratification and fulfillment, should be our polestar, reminding us where we are and which direction we need to go.[1006]

Randy Alcorn, *50 Days of Heaven*

A man who gives sustained thought to another world—the Heaven where Christ is and the resurrected Earth where we will live forever with him—also does not remain unchanged. He becomes a new person. He'll no longer fill his stomach with stale leftovers and scraps fallen to a dirty kitchen floor. He smells the banquet being prepared for him. He won't spoil his appetite. He knows what his mouth is watering for.[1007]

Randy Alcorn, *Heaven*

Play, Sports, and Recreation

This is what the LORD says: "I will return to Zion and dwell in Jerusalem. Then Jerusalem will be called the City of Truth, and the mountain of the LORD Almighty will be called the Holy Mountain."

This is what the LORD Almighty says: "Once again men and women of ripe old age will sit in the streets of Jerusalem, each with cane in hand because of his age. The city streets will be filled with boys and girls playing there."

ZECHARIAH 8:3-5

The mountains yield food for him [God's great creature behemoth] where all the wild beasts play.

GOD, JOB 40:20, ESV

Here is the sea, great and wide, which teems with creatures innumerable, living things both small and great. There go the ships, and Leviathan, which you formed to play in it.

Psalm 104:25-26, esv

The nursing child shall play over the hole of the cobra, and the weaned child shall put his hand on the adder's den. They shall not hurt or destroy in all my holy mountain; for the earth shall be full of the knowledge of the Lord as the waters cover the sea.

Isaiah 11:8-9

Swarms of living creatures will live wherever the river flows. There will be large numbers of fish, because this water flows there and makes the salt water fresh; so where the river flows everything will live. Fishermen will stand along the shore; from En Gedi to En Eglaim there will be places for spreading nets. The fish will be of many kinds—like the fish of the Great Sea.

Ezekiel 47:9-10

Do you not know that in a race all the runners run, but only one gets the prize? Run in such a way as to get the prize. Everyone who competes in the games goes into strict training. They do it to get a crown that will not last, but we do it to get a crown that will last forever. Therefore I do not run like a man running aimlessly; I do not fight like a man beating the air. No, I beat my body and make it my slave so that after I have preached to others, I myself will not be disqualified for the prize.

Paul, 1 Corinthians 9:24-27

If anyone competes as an athlete, he does not receive
the victor's crown unless he competes according to
the rules.

PAUL, 2 TIMOTHY 2:5

God plays. God creates playing. And man should play if he is to live
as humanly as possible and to know reality, since it is created by God's
playfulness.[1008]

Thomas Aquinas, *Summa Theologica*

Absent the misery of poverty or wealth, freed from infirmity,
restricted from petty jealousies and sinful pride, and with lots of
time on our hands, why shouldn't heaven be a wonderful place to
play? As children of God, guilt-free persons take each day as a gift.
They are playful in the best sense of that word. . . . The rhythms of
life now stave off monotony. How much more in heaven! With resurrection bodies, a renewed cosmos and a society free from sin, enjoyment won't fade. It's the weight of sin that jades the spirit and wearies
the body. Heaven, as Paul said, is "an eternal weight of glory." We
won't get bored there! The line between work and play is blurred
whenever, and wherever, the burden of sin has been lifted.[1009]

Arthur Roberts, *Exploring Heaven*

Play is one of our highest callings as Christians. So much else in our
lives is properly taken in doing *things—things we do to change things,
things we do in order that something else may happen.* But in play we
are not seeking to change anything, nor are we seeking something
beyond. We are simply being at home in the world and at peace
with God.

It's not the activity itself that makes the difference between work
and play, or even rest. It's the spirit in which we engage in them.[1010]

Paul Marshall, *Heaven Is Not My Home*

When I play a game well, I have for that limited period of time an experience of the body's resurrection. For there is no hint of a dualism between mind and body with either of them trying to oppress or bully the other. I bring to the game my total undivided self.[1011]

H. A. Williams, *True Resurrection*

The prophet [Ezekiel] was convinced there would be excellent fishing during the reign of Christ. He indicated that "fishers" would stand along the banks of the rivers, and conditions would be excellent. . . . That they possess immortal bodies presents no problem, for even the Savior after His resurrection ate a piece of broiled fish.[1012]

Ivor Powell, *Heaven: My Father's Country*

Dance and game *are* frivolous, unimportant down here; for "down here" is not their natural place. Here, they are a moment's rest from the life we were placed here to live. But in this world everything is upside down. That which, if it could be prolonged here, would be a truancy, is likest that which in a better country is the End of Ends. Joy is the serious business of Heaven.[1013]

C. S. Lewis, *The Joyful Christian*

[Liddell explaining to his sister that God had called him to missions work in China, but also to compete in the Olympics:] God made me fast, and when I run I feel His pleasure. . . . To give up running would be to hold Him in contempt.[1014]

Eric Liddell, in *Chariots of Fire*

I'm looking forward to long walks with good friends, shared meals without rushing, and endless laughter at no one's expense.

I'm anticipating meaningful work with plenty of time for reading, photography, fishing, and community service. For occasional entertainment I haven't written off stadiums and ballparks. If my hunch is right, competition between friends will be healthy in heaven.

I'm wondering if there might even be hockey without fights, soccer without brawls, and basketball playoffs where losing well is valued as much as winning. There may even be a safe form of boxing and NASCAR.

Frivolous speculation? Maybe. Insulting to God? I hope not. I'm trying to imagine a heaven that builds on the good we know while leaving behind the evil.[1015]

Mart De Haan, *Been Thinking About*

"And the sea was no more." Scarcely could we rejoice at the thought of losing the glorious old ocean. The new heavens and the New Earth are none the fairer to our imagination, if, indeed, there is literally to be no great and wide sea, with its gleaming waves and shelly shores.

Is not the text to be read as a metaphor, tinged with the prejudice with which the Eastern mind universally regarded the sea in the olden times? A real physical world without a sea is mournful to imagine; it would be an iron ring without the sapphire which made it precious.

There must be a spiritual meaning here. In the new dispensation there will be no division—the sea separates nations and separates peoples from each other. To John in Patmos the deep waters were like prison walls, shutting him out from his brethren and his work; there shall be no such barriers in the world to come. Leagues of rolling waves lie between us and many a kinsman whom tonight we prayerfully remember, but in the bright world to which we go, there shall be unbroken fellowship for all the redeemed family. In this sense there shall be no more sea.[1016]

Charles Spurgeon, *Morning and Evening*

When we read about no more seas, we think of God's doing away with the oceans that cover most of his beloved Earth. We think there will be no more surfing, tide pools, snorkeling, and fun on the beach, and there will be no more wonderful sea creatures.

When Revelation 21:1 says that "the sea was no more," we must try to understand *sea* in exactly the way the writer and his readers of the book of Revelation would have understood it. To the great majority of them, the sea was devoid of the romantic properties many of us associate with it. Rather, the sea consisted of those vast, icy, treacherous, stormy waters that separated families, destroyed ships, and drowned loved ones. The sea was chaos. It posed a constant threat, with its great creatures that swallowed up seafarers and its salt waters that poisoned people on the open sea who craved fresh water. With that understanding, "no more sea" was a reassuring prospect! . . .

It was God who created the seas (Genesis 1:9-10). Like everything else he made, they were very good (Genesis 1:31). But the Curse had a devastating effect on creation, including the ocean waters.

Even if Revelation 21:1 is a literal promise of "no more ocean," this doesn't necessarily mean the absence of large bodies of water. Revelation tells us a great river flows right through the capital city (22:1-2). How much more water will there be outside the city? Flowing rivers go somewhere. Some of the world's lakes are huge and sealike, so theoretically the New Earth could have even larger lakes. Huge lakes could, in effect, be freshwater oceans.

Ezekiel 47 speaks of the water flowing from the Temple, which parallels the water flowing from the Messiah's throne on the New Earth (Revelation 22). Ezekiel says, "I saw a great number of trees on each side of the river" (47:7, NIV). Then he is told, "This water flows toward the eastern region and goes down into the Arabah, where it enters the Dead Sea. When it empties into the sea, the salty water there becomes fresh. Swarms of living creatures will live wherever the river flows. There will be large numbers of fish, because this water flows there and makes the salt water fresh; so where the river flows everything will live" (Ezekiel 47:8-9, NIV).

Ezekiel 47 goes on to say, "Fruit trees of all kinds will grow on both banks of the river. Their leaves will not wither, nor will their fruit fail. Every month they will bear fruit, because the water from the sanctuary flows to them. Their fruit will serve for food and their leaves for healing" (verse 12). This promise is applied directly to the New Earth in Revelation 22:2. Since this is clearly a New Earth passage, it appears that the reference to "no more sea" in Revelation 21 may simply mean "no more sea as we now know it."[1017]

Randy Alcorn, *We Shall See God*

Just as we can look forward to cultural endeavors such as art, drama, and music on the New Earth, we can assume that we'll also enjoy sports there. According to the principle of continuity, we should expect the New Earth to be characterized by familiar, earthly (though uncorrupted) things.

Scripture compares the Christian life to athletic competitions (1 Corinthians 9:24, 27; 2 Timothy 2:5). Because sports aren't inherently sinful, we have every reason to believe that the same activities, games, skills, and interests we enjoy here will be available on the New Earth, with many new ones we haven't thought of. (Your favorite sport in Heaven may be one you've never heard of or one that hasn't yet been invented.) Sports and our enjoyment of them aren't a result of the Fall. I have no doubt that sinless people would have invented athletics, with probably more variations than we have today. Sports suit our minds and our bodies. They're an expression of our God-designed humanity.

What kinds of new sports and activities might we engage in on the New Earth? The possibilities are limitless. Perhaps we'll participate in sports that were once too risky. And just as we might have stimulating conversations with theologians and writers in Heaven, we might also have the opportunity to play our favorite sports with some of our favorite sports heroes. How would you like to, in your resurrection body, play golf with Payne Stewart or play basketball with David Robinson? How would you like to play catch with Andy Pettitte or go for a run with Jesse Owens or Eric Liddell?[1018]

Randy Alcorn, *Heaven*

Skydiving without a parachute? Maybe, maybe not. Scuba diving without an air tank? I hope so. Will we be able to tolerate diving to depths of hundreds of feet without special equipment? We know that our resurrection bodies will be superior. Won't it be fantastic to test their limits?

Those who know God and believe his promise of bodily resurrection can dream great dreams.

One day we will *live* those dreams.[1019]

Randy Alcorn, *Heaven*

People have told me, "But there can't be athletics in Heaven because competition brings out the worst in people." It's true that some people's sin spills over during athletic competition. But in Heaven, there will be no worst in us to bring out. People further object: "But in sports, someone has to lose. And in Heaven no one could lose." Who says so? I've thoroughly enjoyed many tennis matches and ten-kilometer races that I've lost. Losing a game isn't evil. It's not part of the Curse. To say that "everyone would have to win in Heaven" underestimates the nature of resurrected humanity.[1020]

Randy Alcorn, *Heaven*

Someone told me nobody would enjoy playing golf in Heaven because it would get boring always hitting holes in one. But why assume everyone's skills will be equal and incapable of further development? Just as our minds will grow in knowledge, our resurrection bodies can develop greater skills.[1021]

Randy Alcorn, *Heaven*

Have you ever imagined what it would be like to walk the earth with Jesus, as the disciples did? If you know Christ, you *will* have that opportunity—on the New Earth. Whatever we will do with Jesus, we'll be doing with the second member of the triune God. What will it be like to run beside God, laugh with God, discuss a book with God, sing and climb and swim and play catch with God? . . . The infinitely fascinating God is by far the most important and most interesting person we'll ever meet in Heaven.[1022]

Randy Alcorn, *50 Days of Heaven*

I love playing tennis and riding my bike and snorkeling in clear waters, as the physical person God has made me. I love the coziness of sitting next to Nanci on the couch in front of the fireplace, blanket over us and dog snuggled next to us.

These experiences are not Heaven—but they are little glimpses and *foretastes* of Heaven. What we love about this life are the things that resonate with the life God made us for. The things we love are not merely the best this life has to offer—they are previews of the greater life to come.[1023]

Randy Alcorn, *50 Days of Heaven*

Preparing for Heaven

Since everything around us is going to be destroyed like this, what holy and godly lives you should live, looking forward to the day of God and hurrying it along. On that day, he will set the heavens on fire, and the elements will melt away in the flames. But we are looking forward to the new heavens and new earth he has promised, a world filled with God's righteousness. And so, dear friends, while you are waiting for these things to happen, make every effort to be found living peaceful lives that are pure and blameless in his sight.

PETER, 2 PETER 3:11-14, NLT

You, brothers, are not in darkness so that this day should surprise you like a thief. You are all sons of the light and sons of the day. We do not belong to the night or to the darkness. So then, let us not be like others, who are asleep, but let us be alert and self-controlled. For those who sleep, sleep at night, and those who get drunk, get drunk at night. But since we belong to the day, let us be self-controlled, putting on faith and love as a breastplate, and the hope of salvation as a helmet. For God did not appoint us to suffer wrath but to receive salvation through our Lord Jesus Christ. He died for us so that, whether we are awake or asleep, we may live together with him. Therefore encourage one another and build each other up, just as in fact you are doing.

PAUL, 1 THESSALONIANS 5:4-11

What good is it for a man to gain the whole world, yet forfeit his soul? Or what can a man give in exchange for his soul?

JESUS, MARK 8:36-37

Look here, you who say, "Today or tomorrow we are going to a certain town and will stay there a year. We will do business there and make a profit." How do you know what your life will be like tomorrow? Your life is like the morning fog—it's here a little while, then it's gone. What you ought to say is, "If the Lord wants us to, we will live and do this or that." Otherwise you are boasting about your own plans, and all such boasting is evil. Remember, it is sin to know what you ought to do and then not do it.

JAMES 4:13-17, NLT

Until the day of life dawns above
let there be unrestrained fellowship with Jesus;
Until fruition comes, may I enjoy the earnest of my inheritance
and the firstfruits of the Spirit;

Until I finish my course with joy may I pursue it with diligence,
in every part display the resources of the Christian,
and adorn the doctrine of thee my God in all things.[1024]

The Valley of Vision: A Collection of Puritan Prayers and Devotions

Only one life, 'twill soon be past; only what's done for Christ will last.

C. T. Studd, "Only One Life"

It becomes us to spend this life only as a journey toward heaven . . .
to which we should subordinate all other concerns of life. Why
should we labor for or set our hearts on anything else, but that
which is our proper end and true happiness?[1025]

Jonathan Edwards, "The Christian Pilgrim"

Oh, Christian brethren, what is our light affliction
When compared to such an eternity as this?
Shame on us if we murmur and complain and turn back,
With such a heaven before our eyes![1026]

J. C. Ryle, "Home at Last"

Christianity asserts that every individual human being is going to live
for ever, and this must be either true or false. Now there are a good
many things which would not be worth bothering about if I were
going to live only seventy years, but which I had better bother about
very seriously if I am going to live for ever. Perhaps my bad temper
or my jealousy are gradually getting worse—so gradually that the
increase in seventy years will not be very noticeable. But it might be
absolute hell in a million years: in fact, if Christianity is true, Hell is
the precisely correct technical term for what it would be.[1027]

C. S. Lewis, *Mere Christianity*

We all believe, or have believed at some time, that there is one special
person who would be our perfect mate. It is not a false belief, but a

very ill-timed belief, because this perfect mate can only be found in Heaven. On earth, we are supposed to be learning how our sin is ruining perfect relationships, not trying to engage in one.

. . . If we see that earth is really a school to prepare us for the blissful experience of Heaven, then all the pressure of trying to find a perfect marriage on earth will disappear.[1028]

Drake Whitchurch, *Waking from Earth*

Heaven does not merely occur after earthly life ends, it comes on account of the earthly life. "What a man sows, that shall he also reap" is an important biblical truth.[1029]

Paul Helm, *The Last Things*

Set to work in good earnest to live a holy life; for it is by so doing that we deserve the highest powers of enjoyment. A few days of labor and struggle, and then, the undisturbed possession and enjoyment of God Himself, and of His beautiful and pure creatures, forever! This is what is in store for them that practice virtue and persevere unto the end.[1030]

Father J. Boudreau, *The Happiness of Heaven*

The one who heeds—or obeys—the word of God is the one who is ready for Heaven. It's not the one who has spiritual "goose bumps" about Heaven. . . . Nor the one who shouts the loudest or jumps the highest about the Second Coming.[1031]

Steven J. Lawson, *Heaven Help Us!*

We have at our fingertips experiences and offerings available only to kings in previous eras. Offered "heaven now," we give up the ultimate quest in pursuit of that which can be immediately consumed, be it a service, product, or pseudo-religious experience. Consumerism has all the distinguishing traits of outright paganism—we need to see it for what it really is.[1032]

Alan Hirsch, *The Forgotten Ways*

Live in Christ, die in Christ, and the flesh need not fear death.[1033]

John Knox

We prepare for many things in our lives. We study and train for our daily work and even for our leisure activities. We plan the important events of marriage, home, and family. Some even plan dinner parties or short vacations with almost military precision. Yet few people today, even among those of us who are unreservedly Christians, prepare to die. If anything, the reverse is the case. Many of us prefer not to think or speak about the prospect of death.[1034]

Chuck McGowen, *Let's Talk about Heaven*

Those who have cultivated a genuine heavenly-mindedness—who have named and nurtured the human longing for Elsewhere and Otherwise—have been people who have worked and prayed the most passionately, courageously, tirelessly, and unswervingly for the kingdom to come on earth as it is in heaven.[1035]

Mark Buchanan, *Things Unseen*

For three things I thank God every day of my life: thanks that he has vouchsafed me knowledge of his works; deep thanks that he has set in my darkness the lamp of faith; deep, deepest thanks that I have another life to look forward to—a life joyous with light and flowers and heavenly song.[1036]

Helen Keller

Be content to pass through all difficulties in the way to heaven. Though the path is before you, and you may walk in it if you desire, yet it is a way that is ascending, and filled with many difficulties and obstacles.

Be willing, then, to undergo the labor, and meet the toil, and overcome the difficulty. What is it all in comparison with the sweet rest that is at your journey's end? Be willing to resist all the natural inclination of flesh and blood, which is downward, and press onward and upward to the prize. At every step it will be easier and easier to ascend; and the higher your ascent, the more will you be cheered by the glorious prospect before you, and by a nearer view of that heavenly city where, in a little while, you shall forever be at rest.[1037]

Jonathan Edwards, *Heaven: A World of Love*

I do not know a more beautiful sight to be seen on Earth than a man who has served his Lord many years and who, having grown gray in service, feels that he must soon be called home. He is rejoicing in the firstfruits of the Spirit which he has obtained, but he is panting after the full harvest of the Spirit which is guaranteed to him. It is a pleasant and precious thing to so wait and to so hope. . . .

Cast your arms around the Cross of Christ, and give up your heart to God. Then, come what may, "neither death nor life, nor angels nor rulers, nor things present nor things to come, nor powers, nor height nor depth, nor anything else in all creation, will be able to separate us from the love of God in Christ Jesus our Lord" (Romans 8:38-39).

While you shall for a while sigh for more of Heaven, you will soon come to the dwelling places of happiness where sighing and sorrow shall flee away.[1038]

Charles Spurgeon, "Creation's Groans and the Saints' Sighs," Sermon 788

The story is told of a very rich woman who went to heaven, only to find out that her gardener had a bigger house than she did. She wasn't too happy about it, so she asked how that could be. The answer was, "We just used the material you sent up."[1039]

Tony Evans, *Tony Evans Speaks Out on Heaven and Hell*

No man would find it difficult to die who died every day. He would have practiced it so often, that he would only have to die but once more like the singer who has been through his rehearsals, and is perfect in his part, and has but to pour forth the notes once for all, and have done. Happy are they who every morning go down to Jordan's bank, and wade into the stream in fellowship with Christ, dying in the Lord's death, being crucified on his cross, and raised in his resurrection.[1040]

Charles Spurgeon, "Dying Daily," Sermon 828

A man came to my home seeking help. He desired to make his last will and testament. . . . He was bewildered when I casually asked, "How much will you have?" He stared at me, and replied, "Parson, don't be silly. I'll be dead."

"Of course you'll be dead, but when a man travels overseas he makes provision that he will not arrive penniless. . . . You have carefully arranged that each member of your family will inherit something, but what will you possess in the next world?" His reply was instantaneous and startling, "Good God, I never thought of that!"[1041]

Ivor Powell, *Heaven: My Father's Country*

Most of the emphasis in Christianity is on becoming happier here, healed here, more blessed here, and more fulfilled here.

. . . Without heaven in clear view our Christianity fails to have a heavenward compulsion pulling us closer to God, closer to eternity, closer to home. It tends to become instead self-serving entertainment or a therapeutic center. A heavenless church seeks to satisfy longings and needs here rather than serving and sacrificing here with a view to satisfaction there.[1042]

Joseph Stowell, *Eternity*

Since the separate soul returns to God who gave it, it is of vast importance that we be then prepared to come before him.

Some of us here would be mightily afraid of appearing before a prince, or a great and honourable person in an undress; but for our souls in a naked state, or in a garment of sinful pollution, to be surprised by the great and holy God, to be set on a sudden in his presence, what terror is contained in this thought! Now the watchful Christian hath this blessedness, that he is Washed from his defilements in the blood of the Lamb, "he is clothed with the robe of righteousness, and the garments of salvation" (Isaiah 61:10). He is prepared to appear before a God of infinite holiness without terror, for he is made like him, he bears his image, he appears as one of his children, and he is not afraid to see his Father.[1043]

Isaac Watts, *The World to Come*

A span of a life is nothing. But the man who lives that span, he is something. He can fill that tiny span with meaning so its quality is immeasurable, though its quantity may be insignificant. . . . A man must fill his life with meaning, meaning is not automatically given to life. It is hard work to fill one's life with meaning. . . . A life filled with meaning is worthy of rest. I want to be worthy of rest when I am no longer here. Do you understand what I am saying?[1044]

David Malter to his son Reuven, in *The Chosen*, by Chaim Potok

Perhaps it would be a good exercise for each of us to ask ourselves: Really, how many cities could I now govern under God? If, for example, Baltimore or Liverpool were turned over to me, with power to do what I want with it, how would things turn out? An honest answer to this question might do much to prepare us for our eternal future in this universe.[1045]

Dallas Willard, *The Divine Conspiracy*

You're heaven-bent. You eagerly await a Savior who, in turn, eagerly awaits you. There's a huge company with you, cheering every move you and your Savior make closer to each other.

He pours out grace for you to finish the race. He pours out more grace when you stumble, grow weary, fall down, lose heart. He stands at the head of the course and, while all the saints who have gone before line the roadway and cheer riotously, He stretches out His arms wide in exuberant welcome, exultant congregation.[1046]

Mark Buchanan, *Things Unseen*

You won't last long here. Think about what will become of you in another world. You are here today and gone tomorrow; we should plan every word and action as though we were going to die today; the person who thinks about his own death and daily prepares to die will be blessed.[1047]

Thomas à Kempis, *The Imitation of Christ*

Though the resurrection life will be mind-blowing beyond description, it is nevertheless true that we are learning how to handle the resurrection body by the way we handle our present body now. Though resurrection will be something new, it will not be entirely new; even though it will be strange, it won't be that strange.[1048]

Ray C. Stedman, *Authentic Christianity*

T. S. Eliot's observation, "I had far rather walk, as I do, in daily terror of eternity, than feel that this was only a children's game in which all the contestants would get equally worthless prizes in the end." Eliot's profound statement suggests that there is a seriousness to this life and that it is possible to win as well as to lose.[1049]

Barry Morrow, *Heaven Observed*

When we mourn the death of friends who were prepared for an early summons, let their preparation be our support. Blessed be God they were not found sleeping! While we drop our tears upon the grave of any young Christian who was awake and alive to God, that blessedness which Christ himself pronounces upon them, is a sweet cordial to mingle with our bitter sorrows, and will greatly assist to dry up the spring of them. The idea of their piety, and their approbation in the sight of God, is a balm to heal the wound, and give present ease to the heartache.[1050]

Isaac Watts, *The World to Come*

One time when a master died, a slave expressed doubt about the master's heavenly arrival. When asked why, he said, "When Massa go north, or go on a long journey to the springs, he talked about it for a long time and got ready. I never heard him talking about going to heaven. I never saw him get ready to go."[1051]

John Gilmore, *Probing Heaven*

Cultivate, then, your hope, dearly beloved. Make it to shine so plainly in you that your minister may hear of your hopefulness and joy, cause observers to take note of it because you speak of heaven and act as though you really expected to go there. Make the world know that you have a hope of heaven . . . that you are a believer in eternal glory and that you hope to be where Jesus is.[1052]

Charles Spurgeon, "The Hope Laid Up in Heaven," Sermon 1438

Just as a seasoned master enjoys a piece of art much more than a fledgling amateur possibly can, a saint who has been faithful under wholesome discipline in the school of Christian experience will be capable of more delight and richer achievements than one who has made a habit of "skipping classes" and "breaking the rules."[1053]

E. X. Heatherley, *Our Heavenly Home*

It is a serious thing to live in a society of possible gods and goddesses, to remember that the dullest and most uninteresting person you can talk to may one day be a creature which, if you saw it now, you would be strongly tempted to worship, or else a horror and a corruption such as you now meet, if at all, only in a nightmare. All day long we are, in some degree, helping each other to one or the other of these destinations. It is in the light of these overwhelming possibilities, it is with the awe and the circumspection proper to them, that we should conduct all our dealings with one another, all friendships, all loves, all play, all politics. There are no *ordinary* people. You have never talked to a mere mortal. Nations, cultures, arts, civilizations—these are mortal, and their life is to ours as the life of a gnat. But it is immortals whom we joke with, work with, marry, snub, and exploit—immortal horrors or everlasting splendours.[1054]

C. S. Lewis, *The Weight of Glory*

What will last for eternity? Not your car, house, degrees, trophies, or business. What will last for eternity is every service to the needy, every dollar given to feed the hungry, every cup of cold water given to the thirsty, every investment in missions, every prayer for the needy, every effort invested in evangelism, and every moment spent caring for precious children—including rocking them to sleep and changing their diapers. The Bible says we'll reap in eternity what we've planted in this life (Galatians 6:7-8).

. . . After all, if we really believe we're going to live forever in a realm where Christ is the center who brings us joy, and that righteous living will mean happiness for all, why wouldn't we choose to get a head start on Heaven through Christ-centered righteous living now?[1055]

Randy Alcorn, *Heaven*

We know Christ will say to some (but not all) believers, "Well done, good and faithful servant!" (Matthew 25:21). Not "Well said" or "Well believed" but "Well done." What separates the sheep from the goats is what they did and didn't do with their God-entrusted resources of time, money, and possessions.[1056]

Randy Alcorn, *The Law of Rewards*

Death gives rise to the question of life. Don Quixote tells his friend Sancho that as a dying soldier lay in his arms his eyes asked a question. Sancho asks, was the question "Why am I dying?" No, Don Quixote replies, it was the question "Why was I living?"[1057]

Randy Alcorn, "Death: Signing and Framing Your Life's Portrait"

What you do with your resources in this life is your autobiography. The book you've written with the pen of faith and the ink of works will go into eternity unedited, to be seen and read as is by the angels, the redeemed, and God himself. When we view today in light of the long tomorrow, the little choices become tremendously important. Whether I read my Bible today, pray, go to church, share my faith, and give my money—actions graciously empowered not by my flesh but by his Spirit—is of eternal consequence, not only for other souls, but for mine.[1058]

Randy Alcorn, *The Law of Rewards*

From childhood most of us learn to shut out our "true country," to stifle our thirst for the eternal, replacing it with the pursuit of the temporal. This is how we who were created to be spiritual end up being such accomplished materialists. But when we live with eternity in view, we'll do many things differently, and those we do the same will be done with transformed perspective—not only teaching and preaching and witnessing, but also washing dishes and pruning trees and repairing carburetors. Almost any honest activity—whether building a shed, driving a bus, or caring for a patient—can be an eternal contribution to people, an investment in God's eternal plan.[1059]

Randy Alcorn, *Money, Possessions, and Eternity*

The people who change lives are the ones who point us away from the world's short-term perspective to God's long-term perspective. Life on earth is a dot, a brief window of opportunity; life in Heaven (and ultimately on the New Earth) is a line going out from that dot for eternity. If we're smart, we'll live not for the dot, but for the line.

Randy Alcorn, notes

Giving is a giant lever positioned on the fulcrum of this world, allowing us to move mountains in the next world. Because we give, eternity will be different—for others and for us. . . . Giving doesn't strip me of vested interests; rather, it shifts my vested interests from earth to heaven—from self to God.

Of course, money isn't all I can give. Time, wisdom, and expertise are wonderful gifts. Giving in any form breaks affluenza's fever. Giving breaks me free from the gravitational hold of money and possessions. Giving shifts me to a new center of gravity—heaven.[1060]

Randy Alcorn, *The Treasure Principle*

If my wedding date is on the calendar, and I'm thinking of the person I'm going to marry, I shouldn't be an easy target for seduction. Likewise, when I've meditated on Heaven, sin is terribly unappealing. It's when my mind drifts from Heaven that sin seems attractive. Thinking of Heaven leads inevitably to pursuing holiness. Our high tolerance for sin testifies of our failure to prepare for Heaven.

Heaven should affect our activities and ambitions, our recreation and friendships, and the way we spend our money and time. If I believe I'll spend eternity in a world of unending beauty and adventure, will I be content to spend all my evenings staring at game shows, sitcoms, and ball games? Even if I keep my eyes off of impurities, how much time will I want to invest in what doesn't matter?

To be Heaven-oriented is to be goal-oriented in the best sense.[1061]

Randy Alcorn, *Heaven*

Redemption

Now that you have been set free from sin and have become slaves to God, the benefit you reap leads to holiness, and the result is eternal life. For the wages of sin is death, but the gift of God is eternal life in Christ Jesus our Lord.

PAUL, ROMANS 6:22-23

This is how God fulfilled what he had foretold through all the prophets, saying that his Christ would suffer. Repent, then, and turn to God, so that your sins may be wiped out, that times of refreshing may come from the Lord, and that he may send the Christ, who has been appointed for you—even Jesus. He must remain in heaven until the time comes for God to restore everything, as he promised long ago through his holy prophets.

PETER, ACTS 3:18-21

[God] made known to us the mystery of his will according to his good pleasure, which he purposed in Christ, . . . to bring all things in heaven and on earth together under one head, even Christ.

PAUL, EPHESIANS 1:9-10

The Spirit of the Sovereign LORD is on me, because the LORD has anointed me to preach good news to the poor. He has sent me to bind up the brokenhearted, to proclaim freedom for the captives and release from darkness for the prisoners.

ISAIAH 61:1

I am the Alpha and the Omega, the Beginning and the End. To him who is thirsty I will give to drink without cost from the spring of the water of life.

THE ONE SEATED ON THE THRONE, REVELATION 21:6

I write these things to you who believe in the name of the Son of God so that you may know that you have eternal life.

JOHN, 1 JOHN 5:13

God made him [Christ] who had no sin to be sin for us, so that in him we might become the righteousness of God.

PAUL, 2 CORINTHIANS 5:21

Salvation is found in no one else [but Jesus], for there is no other name under heaven given to men by which we must be saved.

PETER, ACTS 4:12

The LORD is compassionate and merciful,
> slow to get angry and filled with unfailing love.

He will not constantly accuse us,
> nor remain angry forever.

He does not punish us for all our sins;
> he does not deal harshly with us, as we deserve.

For his unfailing love toward those who fear him
> is as great as the height of the heavens above the
> > earth.

He has removed our sins as far from us
> as the east is from the west.

The LORD is like a father to his children,
> tender and compassionate to those who fear him.

For he knows how weak we are;
> he remembers we are only dust.

Our days on earth are like grass;
> like wildflowers, we bloom and die.

DAVID, PSALM 103:8-15, NLT

We are made right with God by placing our faith in Jesus Christ. And this is true for everyone who believes, no matter who we are. For everyone has sinned; we all fall short of God's glorious standard. Yet God, with undeserved kindness, declares that we are righteous. He did this through Christ Jesus when he freed us from the penalty for our sins. For God presented Jesus as the sacrifice for sin. People are made right with God when they believe that Jesus sacrificed his life, shedding his blood. This sacrifice shows that God was being fair when he held back and did not punish those who sinned in times past, for he was looking ahead and including them in what he would do in this present time. God did this to demonstrate his righteousness, for he himself is fair and just, and

he declares sinners to be right in his sight when they
believe in Jesus.

PAUL, ROMANS 3:22-26, NLT

The creation itself will be liberated from its bondage
to decay and brought into the glorious freedom of the
children of God. We know that the whole creation has
been groaning as in the pains of childbirth. . . . We
ourselves . . . groan inwardly as we wait eagerly for . . .
the redemption of our bodies.

PAUL, ROMANS 8:21-23

[The early Christians] believed that God was going to do for the
whole cosmos what he had done for Jesus at Easter.[1062]

N. T. Wright, *Surprised by Hope*

When Paul says, "We are citizens of heaven," he doesn't at all mean
that when we're done with this life we'll be going off to live in heaven.
What he means is that the savior, the Lord, Jesus the King—all of
those were of course imperial titles—will come *from* heaven *to* earth,
to change the present situation and state of his people. The key word
here is *transform*: "He will transform our present humble bodies to be
like his glorious body." Jesus will not declare that present physicality
is redundant and can be scrapped. Nor will he simply improve it, perhaps by speeding up its evolutionary cycle. In a great act of power—
the same power that accomplished Jesus' own resurrection, as Paul
says in Ephesians 1:19-20—he will *change* the present body into the
one that corresponds in kind to his own as part of his work of bringing all things into subjection to himself. Philippians 3, though it is
primarily speaking of human resurrection, indicates that this will take
place within the context of God's victorious transformation of the
whole cosmos.[1063]

N. T. Wright, *Surprised by Hope*

Maybe in heaven all our losses are not forgotten. Maybe they're returned. Maybe all the broken and strewn parts of ourselves come back, more alive and connected than they've ever been. But regardless of that, this one thing is true: Heaven is where our inescapable sense of loss and incompleteness is overcome. It is the one thing large enough to answer our deepest longings and console our deepest griefs. Our hunger for perfect justice and perfect mercy and perfect joy and perfect peace—all is met there.

Maybe, just maybe, the sorrow is not forgotten, or bathed in the light of perfect understanding. Maybe all of it, every last shred of it, is redeemed, given back.[1064]

Mark Buchanan, *Things Unseen*

Some will not be redeemed. There is no doctrine which I would more willingly remove from Christianity than this, if it lay in my power. But it has the full support of Scripture and, specially, of our Lord's own words; it has always been held by Christendom; and it has the support of reason. If a game is played, it must be possible to lose it. If the happiness of a creature lies in self-surrender, no one can make that surrender but himself . . . and he may refuse. I would pay any price to be able to say truthfully, "All will be saved." But my reason retorts, "Without their will, or with it?" If I say, "Without their will," I at once perceive a contradiction; how can the supreme voluntary act of self-surrender be involuntary? If I say, "With their will," my reason replies, "How if they *will not* give in?"[1065]

C. S. Lewis, *The Problem of Pain*

Why does God go to all the trouble to dirty his hands, as it were, with our decaying, sin-stained flesh, in order to reestablish it as a resurrection body and clothe it with immortality? . . . Because his Son paid the price of death so that the Father's purpose for the material universe would be fulfilled, namely, that he would be glorified in it, including in our bodies forever and ever.[1066]

John Piper, "What Happens When You Die?"

We need a clear understanding of the doctrine of the new earth, therefore, in order to see God's redemptive program in cosmic dimensions. We need to realize that God will not be satisfied until the entire universe has been purged of all the results of man's fall.[1067]

Anthony Hoekema, *The Bible and the Future*

Redemption is not a matter of an addition of a spiritual or supernatural dimension to creaturely life that was lacking before; rather, it is a matter of bringing new life and vitality to what was there all along. . . . The only thing redemption adds that is not included in the creation is the remedy for sin, and that remedy is brought in solely for the purpose of recovering a sinless creation. . . . Grace *restores* nature, making it whole once more.[1068]

Albert Wolters, *Creation Regained*

Why do we not know the country whose citizens we are? Because we have wandered so far away that we have forgotten it. But the Lord Christ, the king of the land, came down to us, and drove forgetfulness from our heart. God took to Himself our flesh so that He might be our way back.[1069]

Augustine

Genesis 1 and 2 speak of the good creation and mankind's task within it; Genesis 3 tells the story of the fall and its consequences. The importance of this sequence lies in the fact that there is no corruption of the earth before the fall—an unstained creation *is* possible. The good creation precedes, and is therefore distinct from, the fall and its effects. Evil cannot be blamed on the good creation, but only on the fall. . . . Evil is *not* inherent in the human condition: there once was a completely good creation and there will be again; hence, the restoration of creation is not impossible. Nothing in the world ought to be despaired of. Hope is grounded in the constant availability and the insistent presence of the good creation, even in those situations in which it is being terribly violated.[1070]

Albert Wolters, *Creation Regained*

The redemption achieved by Jesus Christ is *cosmic* in the sense that it restores the whole creation.

. . . Redemption means *restoration*—that is, the return to the goodness of an originally unscathed creation and not merely the addition of something supracreational. . . . This restoration affects the *whole* of creational life and not merely some limited area within it.

It is quite striking that virtually all of the basic words describing salvation in the Bible imply a *return* to an originally good state or situation. . . . To redeem is to "buy free," literally to "buy back," and the image it evokes is that of a kidnapping. A free person has been seized and is being held for ransom. Someone else pays the ransom on behalf of the captive and thus "buys back" his or her original freedom. The point of redemption is to free the prisoner from bondage, to give back the freedom he or she once enjoyed. Something similar can be said about *reconciliation*, in which, again, the prefix *re-* indicates going back to an original state. Here the image is that of friends who have fallen out, or former allies who have declared war on one another. They have become reconciled and return to their original friendship and alliance. Another salvation word beginning with *re-* is *renewal*—in fact Paul uses the comparable prefix *ana-* to coin the Greek word *anakainosis* when he speaks of "the *renewal* of your mind" in Romans 12:2. Literally, this word means "a making new again." What was once brand new but has gotten worse for wear is now renovated, brought back to its former newness. . . . Finally, the key biblical concept of "regeneration" implies a return to life after the entrance of death. All these terms suggest a *restoration* of some good thing that was spoiled or lost.[1071]

Albert Wolters, *Creation Regained*

For whatever reason God chose to make man as he is—limited and suffering and subject to sorrows and death—God had the honesty and the courage to take his own medicine. Whatever game he is playing with his creation, he has kept his own rules and played fair. He can exact nothing from man that he has not exacted from himself. He has himself gone through the whole of human experience, from the trivial irritations of family life and the cramping restrictions of hard work and lack of money to the worst horrors of pain and humiliation, defeat, despair, and death. When he was a man, he played the man. He was born in poverty and died in disgrace and thought it well worthwhile.[1072]

Dorothy Sayers, "The Greatest Drama Ever Staged"

Billions of people were seated on a great plain before God's throne. Most shrank back, while some crowded to the front, raising angry voices.

"Can God judge us? How can He know about suffering?" snapped one woman, ripping a sleeve to reveal a tattooed number from a Nazi concentration camp. "We endured terror . . . beatings . . . torture . . . death!"

Similar sufferers expressed their complaints against God for the evil and suffering he had permitted. What did God know of weeping, hunger and hatred? God leads a sheltered life in Heaven, they said.

Someone from Hiroshima, people born deformed, others murdered, each sent forward a leader. They concluded that before God could judge them, He should be sentenced to live on earth as a man to endure the suffering they had endured. Then they pronounced a sentence:

Let him be born a Jew. Let the legitimacy of his birth be doubted. Let his close friends betray him. Let him face false charges. Let a prejudiced jury try him and a cowardly judge convict him. Let him be tortured. Let him be utterly alone. Then, bloody and forsaken, let him die.

The room grew silent after the sentence against God had been pronounced. No one moved, and a weight fell on each face.

For suddenly, all knew that God already had served his sentence.

God's Son bore no guilt of his own; he bore ours. In his love for us, God self-imposed the sentence of death on our behalf. One thing we must never say about God—that he doesn't understand what it means to be abandoned utterly, suffer terribly, and die miserably.[1073]

John Stott, *The Cross of Christ*

What humanity needs is not the promise of a scientific immortality, but compassionate pity in this life and infinite mercy on the Day of Judgment.[1074]

Joseph Conrad, *Notes on Life and Letters*

In the unimaginable wonder of his grace, he himself grasped that fiery sword of wrath, plunged it at the cross into his own heart, and extinguished it there. He did this for us, foolish, sinning rebels.[1075]

Bruce Milne, *The Message of Heaven and Hell*

"And he that is athirst, let him come: he that will, let him take the water of life freely." Cf. Isaiah 55:1; Revelation 7:16, 17; 21:6. The emphasis is on the word *freely*! Glorious sovereign grace! Love to God, so touching and tender, addressed here to all those who have been made conscious of the need of living water. Let them not hesitate. Let them come. Let them take. It costs nothing. It costs *them* nothing! He paid the price. Hence, let them come, take, drink![1076]

William Hendriksen, *More than Conquerors*

Pascal, as no other, plotted humanity's story in these terms when he referred to man as a king who has lost his crown. "All the miseries of man prove his grandeur; they are the miseries of a dethroned monarch."

Redemption reverses this tragic abdication. In Christ we have begun again to experience a degree of mastery. In Christ we can even be referred to as "seated . . . with him in the heavenly realms" (Ephesians 2:6). With the coming of the heavenly order the restoration is complete. Humanity will again raise their heads and stand tall in God's presence, and in his world. The wretch will ascend the throne. The rebel will reign. The condemned will be crowned.[1077]

Bruce Milne, *The Message of Heaven and Hell*

"My will, not thine, be done," changed Paradise into a desert; "Thy will, not mine, be done," changed the desert back again into Paradise.[1078]

James Campbell, *Heaven Opened*

Christ accomplished down here the work which the Father also gave Him to do as the Son of *Man*. As *man* He once wore the crown of thorns, which the soil, unredeemed and under the curse, yielded Him, and as *man* He will on the day of cosmic regeneration (Matthew 19:28), as the Head of His body, reign with all His saints over the same soil—now redeemed and free from the curse. The *Divine* Redeemer became *man* and as such redeemed mankind, the ruler of the earth, and bound him to Himself in an eternal, inseparable oneness, and *thus* at the same time effected the redemption of the earth. This is the way discovered by grace.[1079]

Erich Sauer, *The King of the Earth*

The biblical idea of redemption always included the earth. Hebrew thought saw an essential unity between man and nature. . . . The Old Testament nowhere holds forth the hope of a bodiless, nonmaterial, purely "spiritual" redemption as did Greek thought. The earth is the divinely ordained scene of human existence. . . . There is an interrelation of nature with the moral life of man; therefore the earth must also share in God's final redemption.[1080]

Anthony Hoekema, *The Bible and the Future*

Oscar Cullmann uses a well-known figure: the Christian believer lives between D-day and V-day. D-day was the first coming of Christ, when the enemy was decisively defeated; V-day is the Second Coming of Christ, when the enemy shall totally and finally surrender.[1081]

Anthony Hoekema, *The Bible and The Future*

The devil will shrink back in defeat. The angels will step forward in awe. And we saints will stand tall in God's grace. As we see how much he has forgiven us, we will see how much he loves us. And we will worship him.[1082]

Max Lucado, *When Christ Comes*

What we need is *not* to be rescued from the world, not to cease being human, not to stop caring for the world, not to stop shaping human culture. What we need is the power to do these things according to the will of God. We, as well as the rest of creation, need to be redeemed. . . .

The Bible is the story of how sin has been, is being, and will be overcome through Jesus Christ. It is the story of how humankind has been, is being, and will be redeemed and restored to fellowship with God. The creatures God has made to love and rule and steward the earth will be redeemed.[1083]

Paul Marshall, *Heaven Is Not My Home*

Creation is to be redeemed; that is, space is to be redeemed, time is to be redeemed, and matter is to be redeemed. God said "very good" over his space-time-and-matter creation, and though the redeeming of this world from its present corruption and decay will mean trans-formations we cannot imagine, the one thing we can be sure of is that this redeeming of creation will not mean that God will say, of space, time and matter, "Oh, well, nice try, good while it lasted but obvi-ously gone bad, so let's drop it and go for a nonspatiotemporal, non-material world instead."[1084]

N. T. Wright, *Surprised by Hope*

Salvation is "re-creation"—not to imply that God scraps his earlier creation and in Jesus Christ makes a new one, but rather to suggest that he hangs on to his fallen original creation and salvages it. He refuses to abandon the work of his hands—in fact he sacrifices his own Son to save his original project. Humankind, which has botched its original mandate and the whole creation along with it, is given another chance in Christ; we are reinstated as God's managers on earth. The original good creation is to be restored.

The practical implications of that intention are legion. Marriage should not be avoided by Christians, but sanctified. Emotions should not be repressed, but purified. Sexuality is not simply to be shunned, but redeemed. Politics should not be declared off-limits, but reformed. Art ought not to be pronounced worldly, but claimed for Christ. Business must no longer be relegated to the secular world, but must be made to conform again to God-honoring standards.

Redemption is not a matter of an addition of a spiritual or supernatural dimension to creaturely life that was lacking before; rather, it is a matter of bringing new life and vitality to what was there all along.[1085]

Albert Wolters, *Creation Regained*

It is *all* of creation that is included in the scope of Christ's redemption: that scope is truly cosmic. Through Christ, God determined "to reconcile to himself *all* things," writes Paul (Colossians 1:20 [emphasis added]), and the words he uses (*ta panta*) preclude any narrow or personalistic understanding of the reconciliation he has in mind. It may seem strange to us that the apostle uses the word *reconcile* in this connection, when he has more than human beings in mind, but this usage simply confirms what we have learned about the scope of the fall: "all things" are drawn into the mutiny of the human race and its enmity toward God, and their strained relations with the Creator must be "patched up," brought once more into harmony with him. The scope of redemption is as great as that of the fall; it embraces creation as a whole. . . . Therefore in principle his redemption also removes all of sin's effects. . . . If the whole creation is affected by the fall, then the whole creation is also reclaimed in Christ.[1086]

Albert Wolters, *Creation Regained*

It is particularly striking that all of Jesus' miracles (with the one exception of the cursing of the fig tree) are miracles of *restoration*—restoration to health, restoration to life, restoration to freedom from demonic possession. Jesus' miracles provide us with a sample of the meaning of redemption: a freeing of creation from the shackles of sin and evil and a reinstatement of creaturely living as intended by God.

. . . Jesus . . . said to her, "Woman, you are set free from your infirmity" (Luke 13:12), and the woman immediately straightened up. This healing was at the same time a confrontation of the liberating King with the enslaving usurper, for Jesus himself adds that the woman was one "whom Satan has kept bound for eighteen long years" (v. 16). . . . "Go back and report to John what you hear and see: The blind receive sight, the lame walk, those who have leprosy are cured, the deaf hear, the dead are raised, and good news is preached to the poor" (Matthew 11:4-5). The healing, restoring work of Christ marks the invasion of the kingdom into the fallen creation.[1087]

Albert Wolters, *Creation Regained*

Even after the fall, the destiny and the redemption of the earth remain indissolubly united with the existence and development of the human race. The redemption of the earth is, in spite of all, still bound up with man. Creation nevertheless still waits for the revealing of the glory of the sons of God. Even though its liberation may in many respects come along other lines than might have been the case had man not sinned; yet the basic thought remains, that *man* is the instrument for the redemption of the earthly creation. And because this remains God's way and goal, there can be a new heaven and a new earth only . . . after the completion and conclusion of the history of human redemption (Revelation 21 and 22; cf. 20:11-15).

For all that it would not be right to regard man as the sole object of Christ's saving work. For great and mighty as is the redemption the Lord has brought to man, it goes inconceivably far beyond it. It is true that man stands at the centre of God's purposes of salvation, and it has indeed pleased Him to crystallize in man the mighty thoughts of His loving decrees, so that without man's history of salvation there would be no history of salvation at all; but for all that man is in no way justified in regarding himself as the *only* goal of the redeeming activity of Christ.[1088]

Erich Sauer, *The King of the Earth*

The Old Testament tells us that at the end of the world the world will not be destroyed but transformed into "new heavens and a new earth" with the whole universe sharing man's redemption. The New Testament also says this "world" of ours will "pass away" and then there will be a "new heaven and a new earth." By "world" it seems to mean our entire cosmos, not just planet earth, and by "new heavens and a new earth" it seems to mean a "new cosmos," not just planet earth. And by "pass away" it does not seem to mean that the world will be annihilated but rather that it will be transformed from its present condition to a condition that will befit terminal man.[1089]

E. J. Fortman, *Everlasting Life after Death*

You may think that you don't deserve forgiveness after all you've done. That's exactly right. *No one* deserves forgiveness. If we deserved it, we wouldn't need it. That's the point of grace. On the cross, Jesus experienced the Hell we deserve, so that for eternity we can experience the Heaven we don't deserve.[1090]

Randy Alcorn, *Heaven*

When we die, we face judgment, sometimes called the judgment of faith. The outcome of this judgment determines whether we go to the present Heaven or the present Hell. This initial judgment depends not on our works but on our faith, which itself is called a gift of God. It is not about what we've done during our lives but about what

Christ has done for us. If we have accepted Christ's atoning death for us, then when God judges us after we die, he sees his Son's sacrifice for us, not our sin. Salvation is a free gift, to which we can contribute absolutely nothing. We have only to humbly receive the gift.[1091]

Randy Alcorn, *TouchPoints: Heaven*

The world as it was, and the world as it will be, is exceedingly good. The world *as it is now*, inhabited by humanity *as we are now*, is twisted. But this is a temporary condition, with an eternal remedy: Christ's redemptive work.[1092]

Randy Alcorn, *Heaven*

If God had wanted to consign us to Hell and start over, he could have. He could have made a new Adam and Eve and sent the old ones to Hell. But he didn't. Instead, he chose to redeem what he started with—the heavens, Earth, and mankind—to bring them back to his original purpose. God is the ultimate salvage artist. He loves to restore things to their original condition—and make them even better.[1093]

Randy Alcorn, *Heaven*

Satan hates the New Heaven and the New Earth as much as a deposed dictator hates the new nation and the new government that replace his. Satan cannot keep Christ from defeating him, but he can persuade us that Christ's victory is only partial, that God will abandon his original plan for mankind and for the Earth.[1094]

Randy Alcorn, *We Shall See God*

Reign of Christ and His People

Of the increase of [Messiah's] government and peace
there will be no end.

GOD, ISAIAH 9:7

You gave them charge of everything you made,
putting all things under their authority.

DAVID, PSALM 8:6, NLT

In the time of those [earthly] kings, the God of
heaven will set up a kingdom [on earth] that will
never be destroyed. . . . It will crush all those kingdoms and bring them to an end, but it will itself
endure forever.

DANIEL 2:44

He [the Son of Man, Messiah] was given authority, glory and sovereign power; all peoples, nations and men of every language worshiped him. His dominion is an everlasting dominion that will not pass away, and his kingdom is one that will never be destroyed.

DANIEL 7:14

The saints of the Most High will receive the kingdom and will possess it forever—yes, forever and ever.

ONE LIKE A SON OF MAN, DANIEL 7:18

The sovereignty, power and greatness of the kingdoms under the whole heaven [i.e. on earth] will be handed over to the saints, the people of the Most High. His kingdom will be an everlasting kingdom, and all rulers will worship and obey him.

THE ANCIENT OF DAYS, DANIEL 7:27

Fear not, little flock, for it is your Father's good pleasure to give you the kingdom.

JESUS, LUKE 12:32, ESV

I assign to you, as my Father assigned to me, a kingdom, that you may eat and drink at my table in my kingdom and sit on thrones judging the twelve tribes of Israel.

JESUS, LUKE 22:29-30, ESV

Whoever can be trusted with very little can also be trusted with much.

JESUS, LUKE 16:10

Do you not know that the saints will judge the world? . . . Do you not know that we are to judge angels? How much more, then, matters pertaining to this life!

PAUL, 1 CORINTHIANS 6:2-3, ESV

He will rule from sea to sea and from the River to the ends of the earth. . . . All kings will bow down to him and all nations will serve him.

SOLOMON, PSALM 72:8, 11

I will preserve You and give You as a covenant to the people, to restore the earth, to cause them to inherit the desolate heritages.

GOD, ISAIAH 49:8, NKJV

You made [mankind] ruler over the works of your hands; you put everything under his feet.

DAVID, PSALM 8:6

To the one who conquers, I will grant him to sit with me on my throne, as I also conquered and sat down with my Father on his throne.

SOMEONE LIKE A SON OF MAN, REVELATION 3:21, ESV

You are worthy to take the scroll and to open its seals, because you were slain, and with your blood you purchased men for God from every tribe and language and people and nation. You have made them to be a kingdom and priests to serve our God, and they will reign on the earth.

THE FOUR LIVING CREATURES AND THE TWENTY-FOUR ELDERS, REVELATION 5:9-10

In the messianic kingdom the martyrs will reclaim the world as the possession which was denied to them by their persecutors. In the creation in which they endured servitude, they will eventually reign.[1095]

Irenaeus, *Against Heresies*

Can you imagine living in a society where everyone is so happy with leadership decisions, they rejoice and celebrate? Can you imagine a world where no one ever again complains about government? Yes, it's possible! It's predicted. It's prepared. It's the kingdom of heaven. And it's real![1096]

Larry Dick, *A Taste of Heaven*

William Penn once observed that the best system of government fails if people are bad and the worst works if people are good. In heaven bad people can't sabotage the system.[1097]

Arthur Roberts, *Exploring Heaven*

Our liveliness in all duties, our enduring of tribulation, our honoring of God, the vigor of our love, thankfulness, and all our graces, yea, the very being of our religion and Christianity, depend on the believing, serious thoughts of our rest [heaven].[1098]

Richard Baxter, *The Saints' Everlasting Rest*

An obedient response to the Good News about the Kingdom obviously entails an understanding of the meaning of the word "Kingdom." . . . What, then, is this Good News? A number of fundamental texts from the Hebrew Bible lie behind Jesus' use of the term "Kingdom of God." On these the expectation of the Kingdom of God is built. We must insist that the Good News embraced information about a coming world government, with Jesus as its chief executive, and how we must respond by preparing ourselves for its arrival.

That the hope of a new political order on earth was very much alive when Jesus began to preach is clear. In the light of the mass of other Messianic material in the Hebrew Bible it is in no way surprising that first-century Jews eagerly expected an era of national glory, to be realized in the Kingdom of the promised Messiah.[1099]

Anthony Buzzard, *Our Fathers Who Aren't in Heaven*

Humankind's job description is clearly stated. We were *not* designed just to live in mystic communion with our Maker, as is so often suggested. Rather, we were created *to govern the earth* with all living things—and to that specific end we were made in the divine likeness.[1100]

Dallas Willard, *The Spirit of the Disciplines*

God is the original; we are the organic image, the living copy. We do not rightly speak of God as King by projecting onto him regal imagery because we think it is fitting for God. Rather, bowing before God who has dominion is proper, for man as king over creation, is the image of kingship; God, the true king, is the reality that casts the image of the earthly king.[1101]

A. B. Caneday, "Veiled Glory"

Political structure adequate for the commonwealth of heaven may require local and regional officials to make decisions about energy distribution and recycling, development projects, educational, artistic, and communication facilities and staffing, intergalactic explorations, and scientific investigation. . . . Governance will certainly come easier among people whose resurrection bodies preclude sinful motivations.[1102]

Arthur Roberts, *Exploring Heaven*

Forget those images about lounging around playing harps. There will be work to do and we shall relish doing it. All the skills and talents we have put to God's service in this present life—and perhaps too the interests and likings we gave up because they conflicted with our vocation—will be enhanced and ennobled and given back to us to be exercised to his glory. This is perhaps the most mysterious, and least explored, aspect of the resurrection life. But there are several promises in the New Testament about God's people "reigning," and these cannot just be empty words. If, as we have already seen, the biblical view of God's future is of the renewal of the entire cosmos, there will be plenty to be done, entire new projects to undertake. In terms of the vision of original creation in Genesis 1 and 2, the garden will need to be tended once more and the animals renamed. These are only images, of course, but like all other future-oriented language they serve as true signposts to a larger reality—a reality to which most Christians give little or no thought.

The new body will be a gift of God's grace and love. However, there are several passages in the New Testament, not least in the words of Jesus himself, that speak of God's future blessings in terms of *reward* (a further answer, in other words, to the question why). Many Christians find this uncomfortable. We have been taught that we are justified by faith, not works, and, somehow, the very idea of being a Christian for what we will get out of it is distasteful.

But the image of reward in the New Testament doesn't work like that. It isn't a matter of calculation, of doing a difficult job in order to be paid a wage. It is much more like working at a friendship or a marriage in order to enjoy the other person's company more fully. It is more like practicing golf in order that we can go out on the course and hit the ball in the right direction. It is more like learning German or Greek so that we can read some of the great poets and philosophers who wrote in those languages. The "reward" is *organizationally connected to the activity,* not some kind of arbitrary pat on the back, otherwise unrelated to the work that was done. And it is always far in abundance beyond any sense of direct or equivalent payment. The reward of being able to read and enjoy Homer for the rest of your life is way beyond any kind of one-for-one payment for the slog of learning Greek. . . . All this relates directly to what Paul says in 1 Corinthians 15:58: the resurrection means that what you do in the present, in working hard for the gospel, is not wasted. It is not in vain. It will be completed, will have its fulfillment, in God's future.[1103]

N. T. Wright, *Surprised by Hope*

496

[Regarding "The Master will say, 'Well done, good and faithful servant. You have been faithful over a little; I will set you over much. Enter into the joy of your master'" (Matthew 25:23, ESV):] That "joy" is, of course, the creation and care of what is good, in all its dimensions. A place in God's creative order has been reserved for each one of us from before the beginnings of cosmic existence. His plan is for us to develop, as apprentices to Jesus, to the point where we can take our place in the ongoing creativity of the universe.[1104]

Dallas Willard, *The Divine Conspiracy*

God has a disposition to communicate himself, to spread abroad his own fullness. His purpose was for his goodness to over-spill his own Being, as it were. He chose to create the heavens and the earth so that his glory could come pouring out from himself in abundance. He brought a physical reality into existence in order that it might experience his glory and be filled with it and reflect it—every atom, every second, every part and moment of creation. He made human beings in his own image to reflect his glory, and he placed them in a perfect environment which also reflected it.[1105]

Jonathan Edwards, "The End for Which God Created the World"

Tragically, humanity failed to fulfill its calling as God's vice-regents. Instead we have tumbled down to the dust from which we were taken and groveled on the earth instead of reaching to the skies.[1106]

Bruce Milne, *The Message of Heaven and Hell*

These words ["let them have dominion," in Genesis 1:26] plainly declare the vocation of the human race to rule. They also call him to progressive growth in culture. Far from being something in conflict with God, cultural achievements are an essential attribute of the nobility of man as he possessed it in Paradise. Inventions and discoveries, the sciences and the arts, refinement and ennobling, in short, the advance of the human mind, are throughout the will of God. They are the taking possession of the earth by the royal human race (Genesis 1:28), the performance of a commission, imposed by the Creator, by God's ennobled servants, a God-appointed ruler's service for the blessing of this earthly realm.[1107]

Erich Sauer, *The King of the Earth*

The basic undertone of all that is revealed in the Apocalypse concerning the activities of heaven may be summed up in this one word: *throne*.[1108]

Wilbur Smith, *The Biblical Doctrine of Heaven*

[Regarding "joint heirs with Christ," Romans 8:17:] The boundless realms of his Father's universe are Christ's by prescriptive right. As "heir of all things," he is the sole proprietor of the vast creation of God, and he has admitted us to claim the whole as ours, by virtue of that deed of joint-heirship which the Lord hath ratified with his chosen people.

The golden streets of paradise, the pearly gates, the river of life, the transcendent bliss, and the unutterable glory, are, by our blessed Lord, made over to us for our everlasting possession. All that he has he shares with his people. The crown royal he has placed upon the head of his Church, appointing her a kingdom, and calling her sons a royal priesthood, a generation of priests and kings. He uncrowned himself that we might have a coronation of glory; he would not sit upon his own throne until he had procured a place upon it for all who overcome by his blood.

Crown the head and the whole body shares the honour. Behold here the reward of every Christian conqueror! Christ's throne, crown, sceptre, palace, treasure, robes, heritage, are yours. . . . Christ deems his happiness completed by his people sharing it. "The glory which thou gavest me have I given them." "These things have I spoken unto you, that my joy might remain in you, and that your joy might be full." The smiles of his Father are all the sweeter to him, because his people share them. The honours of his kingdom are more pleasing, because his people appear with him in glory.

More valuable to him are his conquests, since they have taught his people to overcome. He delights in his throne, because on it there is a place for them. He rejoices in his royal robes, since over them his skirts are spread. He delights the more in his joy, because he calls them to enter into it.[1109]

Charles Spurgeon, *Morning and Evening*

The saints that are highest in glory will be the lowest in humbleness of mind, for their superior humility is part of their superior holiness. Though all are perfectly free from pride, yet, as some will have greater degrees of divine knowledge than others, and larger capacities to see more of the divine perfections, so they will see more of their own comparative littleness and nothingness, and therefore will be lowest and most abased in humility. . . . And the superior in glory will be so far from slighting those that are inferior, that they will have most abundant love to them. . . . No envy, or malice, or revenge, or contempt, or selfishness shall ever enter there, but all such feelings shall be kept as far away as sin is from holiness, and as hell is from heaven![1110]

Jonathan Edwards, *Heaven: A World of Love*

Those that have a lower station in glory than others, suffer no lessening of their own happiness by seeing others above them in glory. On the contrary, all the members of that blessed society rejoice in each other's happiness, for the love of benevolence is perfect in them all. Every one has not only a sincere, but a perfect goodwill to every other. Sincere and strong love is greatly gratified and delighted in the prosperity of the beloved object; and if the love be perfect, the greater the prosperity of the beloved is, as it were, the food of love, and therefore the greater that prosperity, the more richly is love feasted.[1111]

Jonathan Edwards, *Heaven: A World of Love*

When the author of Hebrews says that we do "not yet" see everything in subjection to man (Hebrews 2:8), he implies that all things will eventually be subject to us, under the kingship of the man Christ Jesus. . . . This will fulfill God's original plan to have everything in the world subject to the human beings that he had made. In this sense, then, we will "inherit the earth" (Matthew 5:5) and reign over it as God originally intended.[1112]

Wayne Grudem, *Systematic Theology*

[Commenting on Isaiah 9:7: "Of the increase of his government . . . there will be no end."] Christ's government of the New Earth and the new universe will be ever-expanding. How could that be? . . . There are two ways in which a government can increase: (1) by expanding into previously ungoverned territories; or (2) by creating new territories (an option not available to us as humans). . . . Perhaps it will always increase because the new universe, though still finite, may be so vast that what Christ creates in a moment will never be exhaustively known by finite beings. From what we know of our current universe, with billions of galaxies containing millions of billions of stars and untold planets, this is certainly possible.[1113]

Randy Alcorn, *Heaven*

Bible-believing Jews in the first century were not foolish to think that the Messiah would be King of the earth. They were wrong about the Messiah's identity when they rejected Christ, and they were wrong to overlook his need to come as a suffering servant to redeem the world; but they were right to believe that the Messiah would forever rule the earth. He will!

Prior to Christ's return, his Kingdom will be intermingled with the world's cultures (Matthew 13:24-30). But his followers will be growing in character and proving their readiness to rule. Through adversity and opportunity, as well as in their artistic and cultural accomplishments, they will be groomed for their leadership roles in Christ's eternal Kingdom. Their society-transforming creative skills will be put on prominent display in the new universe, where they will "shine like the sun in the kingdom of their Father" (Matthew 13:43).[1114]

Randy Alcorn, *Heaven*

Because I teach on the subject of redeemed humanity ruling the earth, I've had many opportunities to observe people's responses. Often they're surprised to learn that we will reign in eternity over lands, cities, and nations. Many are skeptical—it's a foreign concept that seems fanciful. Nothing demonstrates how far we've distanced ourselves from our biblical calling like our lack of knowledge about our destiny to rule the earth. Why are we so surprised, when it is spoken of throughout the Old Testament and repeatedly reaffirmed in the New Testament?

Because crowns are the primary symbol of ruling, every mention of crowns as rewards is a reference to our ruling with Christ. In his parables, Jesus speaks of our ruling over cities (Luke 19:17). Paul addresses the subject of Christians ruling as if it were Theology 101: "Do you not know that the saints will judge the world? . . . Do you not know that we will judge angels?" (1 Corinthians 6:2-3). The form of the verb in this question implies that we won't simply judge them a single time but will continually rule them.

If Paul speaks of this future reality as if it were something every child should know, why is it so foreign to Christians today? Elsewhere he says, "If we endure, we will also reign with him" (2 Timothy 2:12). God's decree that his servants will "reign for ever and ever" on the New Earth (Revelation 22:5) is a direct fulfillment of the commission he gave to Adam and Eve: "Be fruitful and increase in number; fill the earth and subdue it. Rule over the fish of the sea and the birds of the air and over every living creature that moves on the ground" (Genesis 1:28). This mandate is confirmed by David: "You put us in charge of everything you made, giving us authority over all things" (Psalm 8:6, NLT).

When we consider that mankind's reign on the earth is introduced in the first chapters of the Bible, mentioned throughout the Old Testament, discussed by Jesus in the Gospels, by Paul in the Epistles, and repeated by John in the Bible's final chapters, it is remarkable that we would fail to see it.[1115]

Randy Alcorn, *Heaven*

The government of the New Earth won't be a democracy. It won't be majority rule, and it won't be driven by opinion polls. Instead, every citizen of Heaven will have an appointed role, one that fulfills him or her and contributes to the whole. No one will "fall through the cracks" in God's Kingdom. No one will feel worthless or insignificant.

When I write and speak on this subject, people often respond, "But I don't *want* to rule. That's not my idea of Heaven."

Well, it's *God's* idea of Heaven.

. . . We've been conditioned to associate governing with self-promoting arrogance, corruption, inequality, and inefficiency. But these are perversions, not inherent properties of leadership. Ruling involves responsibility—perhaps that's why some people don't look forward to it. Some live in anticipation of retirement, when responsibilities will be removed. Why would they want to take on an eternal task of governing? But what they think they want now and what they'll really want as resurrected beings—with strong bodies and minds in a society untouched by sin—may be quite different.[1116]

Randy Alcorn, *Heaven*

God is grooming us for leadership. He's watching to see how we demonstrate our faithfulness. He does that through his apprenticeship program, one that prepares us for Heaven. Christ is not simply preparing a place for us; he is preparing us for that place.[1117]

Randy Alcorn, *Heaven*

All the wrongs done on Earth by tyrants will be a thing of the past. No more persecution and injustice. The Earth that was first put under mankind's dominion and was twisted by the Fall will be redeemed, restored, and put under the righteous rule of a redeemed and restored mankind.

If the Bible made no other reference to believers ruling over an earthly kingdom, and it has plenty, the emphatic message of Daniel 7 would suffice: *The saints of God will rule the earth forever.*[1118]

Randy Alcorn, *Heaven*

The "country of their own" spoken of in Hebrews 11 is a real country, with a real capital city, the New Jerusalem. It is an actual place where these "aliens and strangers on earth" will ultimately live in actual bodies. If the promises that God made to them were promises on Earth and regarding Earth (and certainly they were), then the heavenly "country of their own" must ultimately include Earth. The fulfillment of these prophecies requires exactly what Scripture elsewhere promises—a resurrection of God's people and God's Earth.

What thrilled these expectant believers was not that God would rule in *Heaven*—he already did. What fueled their hope in the hardest of times was that one day God would rule on *Earth*; that he would forever remove sin, death, suffering, poverty, and heartache. They believed the Messiah would come to Earth, and in doing so bring Heaven to Earth.[1119]

Randy Alcorn, *50 Days of Heaven*

I once gave one of my books to a delightful hotel bellman in Atlanta. . . . He said he'd been praying for our group, which was holding a conference at the hotel. Later I gave him a little gift— a rough wooden cross. He seemed stunned, overwhelmed. With tears in his eyes he said, "You didn't need to do that. I'm only a bellman."

The moment he said it, God spoke to me. This brother had spent his life serving. . . . It will likely be someone like him I'll have the privilege of serving under in God's Kingdom. He was "only a bellman" who spoke with warmth and love, who served, who quietly prayed in the background for the success of a conference in his hotel. I saw Jesus in that bellman, and there was no "only" about him.

Who will be the kings of the New Earth? I think that bellman will be one of them. And I'll be honored to carry his bags.[1120]

Randy Alcorn, *We Shall See God*

Rest in Heaven

If Joshua had given them rest, God would not have spoken of another day later on. So then, there remains a Sabbath rest for the people of God, for whoever has entered God's rest has also rested from his works as God did from his. Let us therefore strive to enter that rest, so that no one may fall by the same sort of disobedience.

HEBREWS 4:8-11, ESV

I heard a voice from heaven say, "Write: Blessed are the dead who die in the Lord from now on." "Yes," says the Spirit, "they will rest from their labor, for their deeds will follow them."

JOHN, REVELATION 14:13

Lord Jesus, . . .
Love brought thee from heaven to earth,
from earth to the cross,
from the cross to the grave. . . .
Thy infinite love is a mystery of mysteries,
and my eternal rest lies
in the eternal enjoyment of it.[1121]

The Valley of Vision: A Collection of Puritan Prayers and Devotions

It is a proper distinction to make in saying that we shall rest from our "labours" but not from all our "works." Heaven is not (and never will be) a place of idleness.[1122]

Richard Brooks, *The Doors of Heaven*

There is a pass in Scotland called Glencoe, which supplies a beautiful illustration of what heaven will be to the man who comes to Christ. The road through Glencoe carries the traveler up a long and steep ascent, with many a little winding and many a little turn in its course. But when the top of the pass is reached, a stone is seen by the wayside, with these simple words engraven on it: "Rest, and be thankful."[1123]

J. C. Ryle, *The Upper Room*

Christian, this is a rest after thine own heart; it contains all that thy heart can wish; that which thou longest, prayest, labourest for, there thou shalt find it all. . . . Desire what thou canst, and ask what thou wilt, as a Christian, and it shall be given thee, not only to half the kingdom, but to the enjoyment both of kingdom and King. This is a life of desire and prayer, but that is a life of satisfaction and enjoyment. This rest is very suitable to the saints' necessities also, as well as to their natures and desires. It contains whatsoever they truly wanted. . . . It was Christ and perfect holiness which they most needed, and with these shall they be supplied.[1124]

Richard Baxter, *The Saints' Everlasting Rest*

Nineteenth-century ministers did not find it contradictory to support the notion that heaven was a place of rest *and* activity. Rest, for them, meant activity free from strain, fatigue, or alienation. They did not say that in heaven the saints alternated between periods of rest and activity. Rather the ministers equated rest *with* activity. . . . David Gregg clarified that the biblical symbol of the "many mansions" referred to homes crowded with employments, fellowship, and pleasures. "A home is a busy place," he elaborated; "the whole man and the whole woman find play there."[1125]

Colleen McDannell and Bernhard Lang, *Heaven: A History*

When I can read my title clear
To mansions in the skies,
I'll bid farewell to ev'ry fear,
And wipe my weeping eyes.

Should earth against my soul engage,
And fiery darts be hurled,
Then I can smile at Satan's rage,
And face a frowning world.

Let cares, like a wild deluge come,
And storms of sorrow fall!
May I but safely reach my home,
My God, my heav'n, my all.

There shall I bathe my weary soul
In seas of heav'nly rest,
And not a wave of trouble roll
Across my peaceful breast.[1126]

Isaac Watts, "The Hope of Heaven Our Support under Trials on Earth"

Dad can never lay down the burden of making a living. There are clothes to buy, rent to pay, mouths to feed, tuition to pay. Many a mother has an unceasing round of duties—no forty-hour week for her. She has no office hours—no time to be sick, no time for vacation, no time for study, no time to rest.

Let every tired and overburdened Christian rejoice in the comforting fact that one day he shall rest from his labors while his work goes on. Rest is part of the wonderful gain of one who dies in the Lord.

Hard labor is part of the curse put on mankind because of sin. The thorns and briars in the field, the travail and sorrow of motherhood, all the bread which mankind must eat in the sweat of his face and by unceasing labor are the fruit of sin. When God reaches down and takes one of His children out of this world of sin, then he is done with toil and finds rest from his labor.[1127]

John Rice, *Bible Facts about Heaven*

An old theologian once said, "Who chides a servant for taking away the first course of a feast when the second consists of far greater delicacies?" Who then can regret that this present world passes away when he sees that an eternal world of joy is coming? The first course is grace, but the second is glory, and that is as much better as the fruit is better than the blossom.[1128]

Charles Spurgeon, *Feathers for Arrows*

Heaven is defined as rest, not so much from work but from the worries and pressures of work that we have become so used to in a fallen world today. In heaven there will be plenty of time for celebration, relaxation and simply "chewing the fat" with others.[1129]

Larry Dick, *A Taste of Heaven*

God had completed His work. It was finished. So He rested and blessed the seventh day making it Holy and special forever. We are to keep it holy and special also, for our own benefit as much as for pleasing God. When we make it different from the work-a-day world, when we take time to rest and thank God for His blessings we are reminded life will be different one day. There is hope. There is heaven.[1130]

Larry Dick, *A Taste of Heaven*

If there be so certain and glorious a rest for the saints, why is there no more industrious seeking after it? One would think, if a man did once hear of such unspeakable glory to be obtained, and believed what he heard to be true, he should be transported with the vehemency of his desire after it, and should almost forget to eat and drink, and should care for nothing else, and speak of and inquire after nothing else, but how to get this treasure. And yet people who hear of it daily, and profess to believe it as a fundamental article of their faith, do as little mind it, or labour for it, as if they had never heard of any such thing, or did not believe one word they hear.[1131]

Richard Baxter, *The Saints' Everlasting Rest*

Heaven is rest not from work but from opposition, from the exhausting effort that comes from fighting against those powers and forces which would, if they could, stifle the life of God in the soul. The rest of heaven is not the rest of something that has wound itself down to stillness; it is rest from endurance against evil. Such a stand is no longer necessary in heaven, because in heaven there is no evil against which to endure, no remaining sinful nature in the believer, no world organised in opposition to God, no devil.[1132]

Paul Helm, *The Last Things*

In heaven life will follow a rhythm of activity and rest. This will keep eternity manageable emotionally and provide people with private space.[1133]

Arthur Roberts, *Exploring Heaven*

All the deep designs of God will be unfolded in their events; then the wisdom of his marvellous contrivances in his hidden, intricate, and inexplicable works will appear, the ends being obtained; then God's glory will more abundantly appear in his works, his works being perfect. This will cause a great accession of happiness to the saints who behold it; then God will fully have glorified himself, and glorified his Son, and his elect; then he will see that all is very good, and will rejoice in his own works, which will be the joy of all heaven. God will rest and be refreshed; and thenceforward will the inhabitants keep an eternal sabbath, such an one as all foregoing sabbaths were but shadows of.[1134]

Jonathan Edwards, "Miscellaneous Observations"

We now have perfect peace with God, of whose love for us we no longer doubt, as we may have often done when on earth. We also have peace with ourselves, for those unruly passions which formerly disturbed our peace, no longer exist in our glorified bodies. We enjoy perfect peace with our neighbor; for conflicting interest, envies, and jealousies, which gave rise to dissensions and enmities, have not found and never will find their way into Heaven. We also have peace from the devil, who no longer, "goeth about like a roaring lion, seeking whom he may devour." He has found no admittance into the kingdom of peace. We also have peace from our past. For the sins which so often made us tremble, are washed away in the blood of Jesus, and are, therefore, no longer a source of trouble. The remembrance of them rather intensifies our love for the God of mercy, and therefore increases our happiness. We now, also, have peace from our future. That awful future was formerly shrouded in impenetrable darkness, and often filled us with gloomy foreboding.[1135]

Father J. Boudreau, *The Happiness of Heaven*

There is no contradiction in the statements that the saints of God rest in Glory, and that they are actively employed. The rest of the people of God is not the rest of inactivity. Inaction would be no rest for those who are all on fire with love to Christ, and who have intense longings to know more of Him, of His Person and of His work.[1136]

Judson Palmer, "The Child of God between Death and the Resurrection"

There is a strong *connection* between the future and the present. The prospect of future rest should lead to present activity. According to Paul, it is because of heaven that our life on earth matters. For the

Christian's calling is a heavenly calling; it comes from heaven, and it reaches out towards heaven. So that all aspects of our lives, not only those that are customarily referred to as being "spiritual," but the social and cultural as well, have significance because they are woven in as part of the divine calling which will end for the believer in heaven. So heaven is not an excuse for taking it easy, it is a reason for renewed effort.

The most basic reason that Paul gives for holding to this strong connection between the future and the present is that because of the certainty of Christ's public, final vanquishing of sin the labour of a Christian is not "in vain." Our lives on earth, despite the seeming randomness of what befalls us, the nasty surprises, the setbacks and tragedies, is purposive. It is not necessary to forsake the earth to find purpose. The work of the Christian, whether it is thought of in terms of the building of his own character, or as the work of the church in the world, or the wider cultural and social responsibilities of the Christian, is not futile. The fruit of such living does not die and rot at death. If in this life only we have hope in Christ we are of all men most miserable, Paul says (1 Corinthians 15:19); what folly it would be to live as if there is heaven to come when there is not! But the fact of the matter is that Christ *has* risen from the dead, he will vanquish death, and hence the activity of the Christian is not "in vain," it will not be frustrated.[1137]

Paul Helm, *The Last Things*

Heaven will offer much-needed rest to the weary (Revelation 14:13). . . . But rest renews us, revitalizes us to become active again. Heaven will offer refreshing activity, productive and unthwarted—like Adam and Eve's work in Eden before sin brought the curse on the ground.[1138]

Randy Alcorn, *The Law of Rewards*

What feels better than putting your head on your pillow after a hard day's work? (How about what it will feel like after a hard *life's* work?)

It's good to sit and have a glass of iced tea, feel the sun on your face, or tilt back in your recliner and close your eyes. It's good to have nothing to do but read a good book or take your dog for a walk or listen to your favorite music and tell God how grateful you are for his kindness. Rest is good, so good that God built it into his creation and his law.[1139]

Randy Alcorn, *We Shall See God*

If our lives on the New Earth will be restful, will we need to sleep? Some people argue that we won't sleep because we'll have perfect bodies. But the same argument would apply to eating—yet we know we'll eat. Adam and Eve were created perfect, but did they sleep? Presumably. If so, *sleep cannot be an imperfection.* It's a matter of God's design for the rhythm of life.[1140]

Randy Alcorn, *Heaven*

Resurrection of the Universe

Dear brothers and sisters, we want you to know what will happen to the believers who have died so you will not grieve like people who have no hope. For since we believe that Jesus died and was raised to life again, we also believe that when Jesus returns, God will bring back with him the believers who have died. We tell you this directly from the Lord: We who are still living when the Lord returns will not meet him ahead of those who have died. For the Lord himself will come down from heaven with a commanding shout, with the voice of the archangel, and with the trumpet call of God. First, the Christians who have died will rise from their graves. Then, together with them, we who are still alive and remain on the earth will be caught up in the clouds to meet the Lord in the air. Then we will be with the Lord forever. So encourage each other with these words.

PAUL, 1 THESSALONIANS 4:13-18, NLT

Don't be so surprised! Indeed, the time is coming when all the dead in their graves will hear the voice of God's Son, and they will rise again. Those who have done good will rise to experience eternal life, and those who have continued in evil will rise to experience judgment.

JESUS, JOHN 5:28-29, NLT

If Christ has not been raised, your faith is futile; you are still in your sins. . . . [And] we are to be pitied more than all men.

PAUL, 1 CORINTHIANS 15:17, 19

Against its will, all creation was subjected to God's curse. But with eager hope, the creation looks forward to the day when it will join God's children in glorious freedom from death and decay. For we know that all creation has been groaning as in the pains of childbirth right up to the present time.

PAUL, ROMANS 8:20-22, NLT

Just as death came into the world through a man, now the resurrection from the dead has begun through another man. Just as everyone dies because we all belong to Adam, everyone who belongs to Christ will be given new life. But there is an order to this resurrection: Christ was raised as the first of the harvest; then all who belong to Christ will be raised when he comes back.

PAUL, 1 CORINTHIANS 15:21-23, NLT

He was supreme in the beginning and—leading the resurrection parade—he is supreme in the end.

From beginning to end he's there, towering far above
everything, everyone. So spacious is he, so roomy,
that everything of God finds its proper place in him
without crowding. Not only that, but all the broken
and dislocated pieces of the universe—people and
things, animals and atoms—get properly fixed and
fit together in vibrant harmonies, all because of his
death, his blood that poured down from the cross.

PAUL, COLOSSIANS 1:18-20, *THE MESSAGE*

I shall rise from the dead. . . . I shall see the Son of God, the Sun of
Glory, and shine myself as that sun shines. I shall be united to the
Ancient of Days, to God Himself, who had no morning, never began.
. . . No man ever saw God and lived. And yet, I shall not live till I see
God; and when I have seen him, I shall never die.[1141]

John Donne, *The Works of John Donne*

Since our creation we have been gouged by many things; we have
been spilled upon, burnt by hot wax, water-stained and repainted in
garish colors. Our hinges are loose, the drawers do not slide like they
used to and one of our edges has been stripped of its molding. When
such antique pieces get restored and refinished, they are not fundamentally altered; rather, they are renewed to what they have always
been, despite the wear and tear.[1142]

Daniel Brown, *What the Bible Reveals about Heaven*

Our Lord has written the promise of the resurrection not in books
alone, but in every leaf in spring-time.[1143]

Martin Luther, *Watchwords for the Warfare of Life*

Now human nature is deficient in a twofold manner: in one way
because it has not yet obtained its ultimate perfection, and in a second way because it has already receded from its ultimate perfection.

Human nature is deficient in the first way in children, and in the second way in the aged. And therefore in each of these, human nature will be brought back by the resurrection to the state of its ultimate perfection, which is in the state of youth, toward which the movement of growth is terminated, and from which the movement of degeneration begins.[1144]

Thomas Aquinas, *Summa Theologica: Supplementum*

The whole chapter [1 Corinthians 15] echoes and alludes to Genesis 1–3. It is a theology of new creation, not of the abandonment of creation. The heart of the chapter is an exposition of the two different types of bodies, the present one and the future one. This is where all sorts of problems have arisen.

Several popular translations, notably the Revised Standard Version and its offshoots, translate Paul's key phrases as "a physical body" and "a spiritual body." Simply in terms of the Greek words Paul uses, this cannot be correct. The technical arguments are overwhelming and conclusive. The contrast is between the present body, corruptible, decaying, and doomed to die, and the future body, incorruptible, undecaying, never to die again. The key adjectives, which are quoted endlessly in discussions of this topic, do not refer to a physical body and a nonphysical one, which is how people in our culture are bound to hear the words *physical* and *spiritual.* . . .

Paul declares that "flesh and blood cannot inherit God's kingdom." He doesn't mean that physicality will be abolished. "Flesh and blood" is a technical term for that which is corruptible, transient, heading for death. The contrast, again, is not between what we call physical and what we call nonphysical but between *corruptible physicality,* on the one hand, and *incorruptible physicality,* on the other.

. . . For Paul, the bodily resurrection does not leave us saying, "So that's all right; we shall go, at the last, to join Jesus in a nonbodily, Platonic heaven," but, "So, then, since the person you are and the world God has made will be gloriously reaffirmed in God's eventual future, you must be steadfast, immovable, always abounding in the Lord's work, because you know that in the Lord your labour is not in vain." Belief in the bodily resurrection includes the belief that what is done in the present in the body, by the power of the Spirit, will be reaffirmed in the eventual future, in ways at which we can presently only guess.[1145]

N. T. Wright, *Surprised by Hope*

The kingdom of God . . . does not mean merely the salvation of certain individuals nor even the salvation of a chosen group of people. It means nothing less than the complete renewal of the entire cosmos, culminating in the new heaven and the new earth.[1146]

Anthony Hoekema, *The Bible and the Future*

God defines himself . . . as "the God of Abraham, Isaac and Jacob."

That those long-deceased fathers of the nation were no more than piles of bleached bones when God defined himself with respect to them was unthinkable; to define himself in terms of heaps of remains would be so demeaning for God as to represent an impossible contradiction of his nature. Only if these great figures continued to live before him, and were the continuing objects of his sovereign care, sustenance and loving affirmation, could such an identification have any congruence. "He is not the God of the dead, but of the living, for to him all are alive" (Luke 20:38).

What Jesus provides here is a significant and unchallengeable proof of the survival of death if we affirm the revealed character of God.[1147]

Bruce Milne, *The Message of Heaven and Hell*

The physicality of the resurrection is emphasized by Jesus himself in his drawing attention to the wounds still visible in his body and even, in Luke's account, in his sharing a meal with the disciples. They must grasp that this is not a matter of a "spirit appearance," but the utterly unprecedented, unique, world-transforming, heaven-anticipating, sovereign action of the Creator in the first installment of remaking the world.[1148]

Bruce Milne, *The Message of Heaven and Hell*

We need to banish from our minds anticipations of heaven in terms of a "spiritual" order "away beyond the blue." The Bible's final promise in both Testaments is of a "new heaven *and earth*" (Isaiah 65:17; 66:22; 2 Peter 3:13; Revelation 21:1, 5). The essential movement at the end is accordingly not so much a "taking up" into the heavens above but a "coming down" of the glorified Son of Man, who will be viewed as "coming," i.e. "coming to us." In Revelation 21:2 the New Jerusalem, the eternal home of the saints, is seen as "coming down out of heaven from God." Thus the prospect is of new bodies (not no-bodies!). The Jesus who says, "Touch me and see; a ghost does not have flesh and bones, as you see I have" (Luke 24:39); who "showed them his hands and his side" (John 20:20); who said, "Put your finger here; see my hands. Reach out your hand and put it into my side" (John 20:27)—this is the Jesus who draws back the curtain on the heavenly life and shows us what it will be like: embodied![1149]

Bruce Milne, *The Message of Heaven and Hell*

The human body itself then is part of the *imago Dei,* for it is the vehicle through which we can effectively acquire the limited self-subsistent power we must have to be truly in the image and likeness of God. In creating human beings in his likeness so that we could govern in his manner, God gave us a measure of *independent power.* Without such power, we absolutely could not resemble God in the close manner he intended, nor could we be God's co-workers. *The locus or depository of this necessary power is the human body.* This explains, in theological terms, why we have a body at all. *That body is our primary area of power, freedom, and—therefore—responsibility.*[1150]

Dallas Willard, *The Spirit of the Disciplines*

The world in which Christianity arose affirmed the immortality of the soul, a cornerstone of Greek philosophy. Platonic arguments for the soul's innate immortality have influenced views about life after death from Gnosticism to the New Age movement today. The soul's immortality was a central tenet in Kant's philosophy and this was echoed in the triad of Protestant liberalism—the fatherhood of God, the brotherhood of man, and the immortality of the soul.

But biblical faith has always insisted on something very different. God's ultimate purpose for all his human creatures, for the lost as well as for the redeemed (see John 5:29; Acts 24:15), is not an eternal, incorporeal existence but rather the resurrection of the body. This concept has been offensive to human reason from the beginning, as Paul found out when he preached about Jesus and the Resurrection to the philosophers of Mars Hill (see Acts 17:22-34).

Yet belief in the bodily resurrection is so basic that it was included in the Apostles' Creed. . . .

What will our resurrection bodies be like? This question was asked in 1 Corinthians 15:35. God does not give us a complete answer, but we do know that our new, glorified bodies will be imperishable. No more cancer, no more drownings, no more holocausts.

Our bodies will also be spiritual (Greek, *pneumatikos*). This word does not mean nonphysical, but rather bodies "transformed by and adapted to the new world of God's Spirit" (George E. Ladd). They also will be recognizable, but, like Jesus' risen body, so utterly transformed that we shall be aware of the differences as well as the sameness.

Most Christians believe that between death and the resurrection we shall indeed live in God's presence in conscious awareness of the Lord and others who have gone before us. This is wonderful, but it is not the end of the journey. In some ways, it is only the prelude to the main event that will begin in earnest on "that great getting-up morning" and that will include the new heavens and the new earth, the marriage banquet of the Lamb, the defanging of Satan, and the abolition of sin and sorrow forever.[1151]

Timothy George, "Good Question"

"Some day you will read in the papers that Dwight Moody is dead," the great evangelist exclaimed one hot Sunday in August 1899 to a New York City crowd. "Don't you believe a word of it! At that moment I shall be more alive than I am now. . . . I was born of the flesh in 1837; I was born of the Spirit in 1855. That which is born of the flesh may die. That which is born of the Spirit shall live forever."

Four months later, exhausted from years of preaching and labor, Dwight Moody was dying. Early in the morning of December 22, Moody's son Will was startled by his father's voice from the bed across the room: "Earth recedes, heaven opens before me!"

Will hurried to his father's side. "This is no dream, Will. It is beautiful. . . . If this is death, it is sweet. God is calling me and I must go. Don't call me back!"

A few hours later Moody revived to find his wife and family gathered around him. He said to his wife, "I went to the gate of heaven. Why, it is so wonderful, and I saw the children (Irene and Dwight, who had died in childhood)." Within hours the man who had stirred two nations for Christ took a few final breaths and then entered the gate of heaven.[1152]

Douglas Connelly, *Angels Around Us*

I have been dying for twenty years, now I am going to live.[1153]

James Drummond Burns, *Memoir and Remains*

How different is the epitaph on the tomb of Jesus! It is neither written in gold nor cut in stone. It is spoken by the mouth of an angel and is the exact reverse of what is put on all other tombs: "He is not here; for he is risen, as he said" (Matthew 28:6, [KJV]).[1154]

Billy Graham, *World Aflame*

On the third day the friends of Christ coming at daybreak to the place found the grave empty and the stone rolled away. In varying ways they realized the new wonder; but even they hardly realized that the world had died in the night. What they were looking at was the first day of a new creation, with a new heaven and a new earth; and in a semblance of the gardener God walked again in the garden, in the cool not of the evening but the dawn.[1155]

G. K. Chesterton, *The Everlasting Man*

On the one hand there will be those believers who at Christ's coming will already have died. On the other hand, there will be the survivors, children of God who will still be living on earth. What the apostle is saying, then, amounts to this: "Don't worry about your dear ones in the Lord, who have already died. In no sense at all will they suffer any disadvantage when Jesus returns. On the contrary, those who are still alive on earth will have to wait a moment until the souls of those who died have re-inhabited their bodies. In that moment of waiting the survivors will be changed in the twinkling of an eye. Then *together*, as one large multitude, those who formerly constituted the two groups will go forth to meet the Lord."[1156]

William Hendriksen, *The Bible on the Life Hereafter*

According to the Scriptures, the body is not less real than the soul; God created man in his totality, as both body and soul. Nor is the body inferior to the soul, or nonessential to man's true existence; if this were not so, the Second Person of the Trinity could never have assumed a genuine human nature with a genuine human body. In biblical thought the body is not a tomb for the soul but a temple of the Holy Spirit; man is not complete apart from the body. Therefore the future blessedness of the believer is not merely the continued existence of his soul, but includes as its richest aspect the resurrection of this body. That resurrection will be for believers a transition to glory, in which our bodies shall become like the glorious body of Christ (Philippians 3:21).[1157]

Anthony Hoekema, *The Bible and the Future*

We read in 1 Corinthians 15:23: "Christ [is] the firstfruits; afterward they that are Christ's at his coming." The term "firstfruits" is used of a harvest; the first sheaf garnered out of the field at the time of the harvest promises more of the same to follow. When Christ was raised from the dead, physically, He was the firstfruits of resurrection. It was a public notice that there was a great harvest of more of the same to follow. It is the promise of our resurrection.[1158]

J. Dwight Pentecost, *Things Which Become Sound Doctrine*

The resurrection is an exploding flare announcing to all sincere seekers that it is safe to believe. Safe to believe in ultimate justice. Safe to believe in eternal bodies. Safe to believe in heaven as our estate and the earth as its porch. Safe to believe in a time when questions won't keep us awake and pain won't keep us down. Safe to believe in open graves and endless days and genuine praise.[1159]

Max Lucado, *When Christ Comes*

Paul says, even if we were to suppose that believers survive the death of the body in some disembodied form, death would still have gained the victory, for death would still reign over their bodies, and this *cannot* be. Death occurs because of sin, and so if death is not reversed in resurrection it will follow that sin has triumphed. But sin cannot triumph if Christ has conquered sin, as indeed he has (2 Timothy 1:10). So it follows then that there *must* be the resurrection of the body. And only when this takes place will it become apparent in the most public and visible way possible that Christ has redeemed his people by triumphing over death. For when this corruptible shall have put on incorruption, and this mortal shall have put on immortality, *then* shall be brought to pass the saying that is written, "O death, where is thy sting? O grave, where is thy victory?" (1 Corinthians 15:55 [KJV]). At that time God will give his people public and final victory through Christ.[1160]

Paul Helm, *The Last Things*

[Referring to 1 Corinthians 15:] Thus, "*Christ died* [his body was subjected to the destructive forces of death] . . . *he was buried* [as a continuing embodied person he was laid in the tomb] . . . *he was raised on the third day*," as an embodied person at a datable moment in time (vv. 3-4, my italics). His body participated in that supernatural act of renewal. Accordingly, "He appeared to Peter" (v. 5). As this reanimated, embodied person he was encountered in a form which was registered by human eyes, at specific occasions in space and time. In other words, the resurrection of Jesus, the epicenter of the Christian faith (vv. 3a, 11), was a *bodily event.*

For the Hebrew consciousness, with their strong doctrine of the Creatorhood of God (Genesis 1:1), resurrection *could only mean a physical event*. Earl Ellis notes, "It is very unlikely that the earliest Palestinian Christians could conceive of any distinction between resurrection, and physical grave-emptying resurrection. To them an *anastasis* (resurrection) without an empty grave would have been about as meaningful as a square circle." Hence the "new thing" which the apostles preached was not so much the miracle of bodily resurrection; they and the great majority of their Jewish contemporaries already believed in that as part of the apocalyptic conclusion of history. The "new thing" was the occurrence of a specific event of resurrection *in the midst of history*—the end without the other accompaniments of the end.[1161]

Bruce Milne, *The Message of Heaven and Hell*

[Referring to 1 Corinthians 15:] [Paul] sees his own meeting with the risen Jesus as part of the evidence. "He appeared to me also" (v. 8). "You can check all this out for yourselves," he is saying when he notes that most of the five hundred who had met the risen Jesus on one celebrated occasion were still around (v. 6). . . . Paul is saying, in effect, "The witnesses are there to be questioned."[1162]

C. H. Dodd, "The Appearances of the Risen Christ"

The dead will be raised with the self-same bodies, and none other, although with different qualities.

Westminster Confession of Faith

That the disciples had experiences in which they believed they met Jesus risen from the dead is as incontrovertible as the fact that they saw him hanging on the cross on Good Friday.[1163]

G. R. Beasley-Murray, *The Resurrection of Jesus Christ*

Not simply a freakish oddity, a meteor fallen from some alien sky, *the resurrection cannot be isolated.* Specifically, it sets in motion two irresistible forces. The first is the future resurrection of the whole people of Christ, and the second is the eventual defeat of death.[1164]

Bruce Milne, *The Message of Heaven and Hell*

The return of Jesus to life by resurrection (Acts 1:3; 10:41) marked a crucial stage in the grand scheme for the rescue of mankind. It was the initiation of a new creation of immortal human beings, the restoration of the ideal which God had envisaged from the beginning. Mankind makes another new start in Jesus. With the resurrection of the one man, Jesus, to endless life, the prospect of the same destiny is open to all who follow in Jesus' steps.

The failure of the divided Church is that it has ceased to bear the Message of deliverance onwards to its great climax. Uncertain about where it is going, it cannot speak to the world with conviction. Something has happened to cast a smoke screen across the path which leads to the goal.[1165]

Anthony Buzzard, *Our Fathers Who Aren't in Heaven*

Both the transfigured body of Jesus and of the saved proceed from the earthly body of our present humanity and are linked with it. The fact of bodily resurrection proves this. For if there were no link between the heavenly and the present body, why should there be an opening of the graves and the raising of the earthly body? What would be the point of Easter in the story of Jesus?

Thus man's body—both at its beginning in Paradise and later in the whole setting of the history of salvation—is linked with the image of God, and with the nobility of man. During the course of history sin has succeeded in marring it, but not in fundamentally destroying it. Therefore there is hope also for the body of man.

Scripture bears clear witness to the eternal link between likeness to Christ and the transfiguration of the body. It teaches that also in the ages to come the image of God through Christ will shine out from their transfigured bodies. "For our citizenship is in heaven; whence also we wait for a Saviour, the Lord Jesus Christ: who shall fashion anew the *body* of our humiliation, that it may be *conformed* to the *body* of His glory" (Philippians [3:20-21, ASV (emphasis added)]). . . . "And as we have borne the image of the earthly (Adam), we shall also bear the image of the heavenly (Christ)" (1 Corinthians 15:49 [ASV]).

Man's body reflects something of the image of God only because the body is the home of man's spirit, and because the spirit which lives in the human body was created in the image of God.[1166]

Erich Sauer, *The King of the Earth*

We may hope that the resurrection of the body means also the resurrection of what may be called our "greater body"; the general fabric of our earthly life with its affections and relationships. But only on a condition; not a condition arbitrarily laid down by God, but one necessarily inherent in the character of Heaven: nothing can enter there which cannot become heavenly.[1167]

C. S. Lewis, *The Four Loves*

God, the Artificer of marvellous and unspeakable power, shall with marvellous and unspeakable rapidity restore our body, using up the whole material of which it originally consisted.[1168]

Augustine, *The Works of Aurelius Augustine*

If the blueprints for our glorified bodies are in the DNA, then it would stand to reason that our bodies will be resurrected at the optimal stage of development determined by our DNA.[1169]

Hank Hanegraaff, *Resurrection*

If the earth and heaven are renewed, why should we doubt that man, on account of whom heaven and earth were made, can be renewed? If the transgressor be reserved for punishment, why should not the just be kept for glory? If the worm of sins does not die, how shall the flesh of the just perish? For the resurrection, as the very form of the word shows, is this, that what has fallen should rise again, that which has died should come to life again.[1170]

Ambrose, *The Two Books on the Decease of His Brother Satyrus*

It is manifest that the happiness of the saints will increase in extent after the resurrection, because their happiness will then be not only in the soul but also in the body. Moreover, the soul's happiness also will increase in extent, seeing that the soul will rejoice not only in its own good, but also in that of the body. We may also say that the soul's happiness will increase in intensity. . . . If, then, there be removed from the body all those things wherein it hampers the soul's action, the soul will be simply more perfect while existing in such a body than when separated therefrom. Now the more perfect a thing is in being, the more perfectly is it able to operate: wherefore the operation of the soul united to such a body will be more perfect than the operation of the separated soul. But the glorified body will be a body of this description, being altogether subject to the spirit. Therefore, since beatitude consists in an operation, the soul's happiness after its reunion with the body will be more perfect than before. For just as the soul separated from a corruptible body is able to operate more perfectly than when united thereto, so after it has been united to a glorified body, its operation will be more perfect than while it was separated. Now every imperfect thing desires its perfection. Hence the separated soul naturally desires reunion with the body, and on account of this desire which proceeds from the soul's imperfection, its operation whereby it is borne towards God is less intense. . . . The soul united to a glorified body is more like to God than when separated therefrom, in so far as when united it has more perfect being. For the more perfect a thing is the more it is like to God.[1171]

Thomas Aquinas, *Summa Theologica: Supplementum*

The hope of heaven is a beacon toward which confidently we stride on our earthly journey. We see a Light ahead, beyond the vale of death, and we follow that Light; although what it beckons us to find at the horizon of our earthly time remains a mystery. Intimations of heaven are imprinted in our minds and engraved in our cultures. These dreams and visions mold the psyche and offer opportunities to seek and find the good, the true, and the beautiful. Our hopes for an afterlife are expressed in stories etched on cave walls and enshrined in art and literature. The resurrection of Jesus Christ assures us that such ancient and enduring visions, even crudely articulated ones, derive from our Creator and Redeemer.[1172]

Arthur Roberts, *Exploring Heaven*

If the resurrection body were nonmaterial or nonphysical, the devil would have won a great victory, since God would then have been compelled to change human beings with physical bodies such as he had created into creatures of a different sort, without physical bodies (like the angels). Then it would indeed seem that matter had become intrinsically evil so that it had to be banished. And then, in a sense, the Greek philosophers would have been proved right. But matter is not evil; it is part of God's good creation. Therefore the goal of God's redemption is the resurrection of the physical body, and the creation of a new earth on which his redeemed people can live and serve God forever with glorified bodies. Thus the universe will not be destroyed but renewed, and God will win the victory.[1173]

Anthony Hoekema, *The Bible and the Future*

A radio preacher, speaking about a Christian woman whose Christian husband had died, said, "Little did she know that when she hugged her husband that morning, she would never hug him again."

Though the preacher's words were well intentioned, they were not true. He could have said, "She'd never again hug her husband in this life," or better, "She would not be able to hug her husband again until the next world." Because of the coming resurrection of the dead, we *will* be able to hug each other again—on the New Earth.[1174]

Randy Alcorn, *Heaven*

Why does the creation wait eagerly for our resurrection? For one simple but critically important reason: *As mankind goes, so goes all of creation*. Thus, just as all creation was spoiled through our rebellion, the deliverance of all creation hinges on our deliverance. The glorification of the universe hinges on the glorification of a redeemed human race. The destiny of all creation rides on our coattails.

What possible effect could our redemption have on galaxies that are billions of light years away? The same effect that our fall had on them. Adam and Eve's sin did not merely create a personal catastrophe or a local, Edenic catastrophe; it was a catastrophe of cosmic—not just global—proportions.[1175]

Randy Alcorn, *Heaven*

Of Americans who believe in a resurrection of the dead, two-thirds believe they will not have bodies after the Resurrection. But this is self-contradictory. A nonphysical resurrection is like a sunless sunrise. There's no such thing. Resurrection by its very definition means that we will have bodies. If we didn't have bodies, we wouldn't be resurrected![1176]

Randy Alcorn, *We Shall See God*

Understanding that our peak doesn't come in this life should radically change our view of deteriorating health, which otherwise would produce discouragement, regret, anger, envy, and resentment. Elderly people could envy and resent the young for what they can do. People handicapped from birth could envy and resent others for what they can do. But when the elderly and handicapped recognize that their experiences on the New Earth will be far better than the best anyone else is experiencing here and now, it brings anticipation, contentment, consolation, and the ability to fully rejoice in the activities of the young and healthy, without envy or regret.

People without Christ can only look back to when they were at their best, never to regain it. Memories are all they have, and even those memories fade. But elderly or bedridden Christians don't look back to the peak of their prowess. They look *forward* to it.

When we Christians sit in wheelchairs or lie in beds or feel our bodies shutting down, let's remind ourselves, "I haven't passed my peak. I haven't yet come close to it. The strongest and healthiest I've ever felt is a faint suggestion of what I'll be in my resurrected body on the New Earth."

This isn't wishful thinking. This is the explicit promise of God. It is as true as John 3:16 and everything else the Bible tells us.[1177]

Randy Alcorn, *Heaven*

Rewards and Treasures

Do not store up for yourselves treasures on earth, where moth and rust destroy, and where thieves break in and steal. But store up for yourselves treasures in heaven, where moth and rust do not destroy, and where thieves do not break in and steal. For where your treasure is, there your heart will be also.

JESUS, MATTHEW 6:19-21

If you have not been trustworthy with someone else's property, who will give you property of your own?

JESUS, LUKE 16:12

I have fought the good fight, I have finished the race, I have kept the faith. Now there is in store for me the crown of righteousness, which the Lord, the righteous

Judge, will award to me on that day—and not only to me, but also to all who have longed for his appearing.

PAUL, 2 TIMOTHY 4:7-8

If any man builds on this foundation [Christ] using gold, silver, costly stones, wood, hay or straw, his work will be shown for what it is, because the Day will bring it to light. It will be revealed with fire, and the fire will test the quality of each man's work. If what he has built survives, he will receive his reward. If it is burned up, he will suffer loss; he himself will be saved, but only as one escaping through the flames.

PAUL, 1 CORINTHIANS 3:12-15

Whatever you do, work at it with all your heart, as working for the Lord, not for men, since you know that you will receive an inheritance from the Lord as a reward. It is the Lord Christ you are serving.

PAUL, COLOSSIANS 3:23-24

When the Chief Shepherd appears, you will receive the crown of glory that will never fade away.

PETER, 1 PETER 5:4

Blessed are you who hunger now, for you will be satisfied. Blessed are you who weep now, for you will laugh. Blessed are you when men hate you, when they exclude you and insult you. . . . Rejoice in that day and leap for joy, because great is your reward in heaven.

JESUS, LUKE 6:21-23

One thing I do: Forgetting what is behind and straining toward what is ahead, I press on toward the goal to win the prize for which God has called me heavenward in Christ Jesus.

PAUL, PHILIPPIANS 3:13-14

Be faithful, even to the point of death, and I will give you the crown of life.

JESUS, REVELATION 2:10

To him who overcomes, I will give the right to sit with me on my throne, just as I overcame and sat down with my Father on his throne.

JESUS, REVELATION 3:21

The Lord will reward everyone for whatever good he does, whether he is slave or free.

PAUL, EPHESIANS 6:8

Rejoice and be glad, because great is your reward in heaven.

JESUS, MATTHEW 5:12

Do not be afraid, little flock, for your Father has been pleased to give you the kingdom.

JESUS, LUKE 12:32

See, your Savior comes! See, his reward is with him, and his recompense accompanies him.

ISAIAH 62:11

Behold, I am coming soon! My reward is with me, and
I will give to everyone according to what he has done.

JESUS, REVELATION 22:12

The sweet air grew suddenly sweeter. A brightness flashed behind
them. All turned. Tirian turned last because he was afraid. There
stood his heart's desire, huge and real, the golden Lion, Aslan himself,
and already the others were kneeling in a circle round his forepaws
and burying their hands and faces in his mane as he stooped his great
head to touch them with his tongue. Then he fixed his eyes upon
Tirian, and Tirian came near, trembling, and flung himself at the
Lion's feet, and the Lion kissed him and said, "Well done."[1178]

C. S. Lewis, *The Last Battle*

The world is poor because her fortune is buried in the sky and all her
treasure maps are of earth.[1179]

Calvin Miller, *The Finale*

Heaven is not like this world, where the mere accident of birth, or
the smile of fortune, instead of moral worth, generally determines a
man's position in society, as well as the amount of natural happiness
he shall enjoy. . . . How different all this is, when there is question of
Heaven! For, howsoever poor and ignorant we may now be, we may
reasonably aspire to a very high degree of glory, and to the exquisite
delights which come from a more intimate union with God. Howsoever insignificant we may be and however low our position in this
world, we may aspire to move in the highest society in Heaven.[1180]

Father J. Boudreau, *The Happiness of Heaven*

We are certain that when the mists of death are cleared away, the
whole city will stand visible and proud. Our inheritance is as sure as
morning.[1181]

Calvin Miller

If heaven had a daily newspaper, the headlines would read quite differently than our earthly tabloids.

HEAVEN'S HEADLINES:
Keeping You Informed about Significant Events on Earth
Kathy S.* Changes 10,000th Diaper
Rod K.* Mows Neighbor's Grass
Tony P.* Gets Saved; Starts Tithing
Max M.* Delivers Brownies to Enemy
Dan B.* Changes Tire for Stranded Motorist
Gayle H.* Takes Meal to Sick Person
Unnamed Widow Puts Last Two Coins in Treasury Box
(*Last names are omitted until rewards are handed out in heaven.)[1182]

Kent Crockett, *Making Today Count for Eternity*

Remember that in your lifetime you received your good things, but now you are in agony.

What startles me most in this startling story [see Luke 16:19-31] is one phrase: *your good things.* Actually, what startles me is one word: *your.* There is in store for us, all of us, good things: your good things. That part is fixed. What we have a role in deciding is whether or not we seek to receive all those good things in this lifetime—*Father, give me my inheritance* [see Luke 15:11-31]—or whether we are willing, for the sake of something bigger, to store up our treasure in heaven.[1183]

Mark Buchanan, *Things Unseen*

The doctrine of rewards and punishments after the resurrection, seems to carry such superior force in it, especially upon those who believe the gospel, that it is no wonder the New Testament more frequently refers to this great day of resurrection, and the Apostle derives the chief part of his consolations or terrors from it.[1184]

Isaac Watts, *The World to Come*

Notice how the rewarding is put in terms of what they were deprived of:

> Eating of the tree of life (Revelation 2:7)
> Not being hurt by the second death (2:11)
> Eating of the hidden manna (2:17)
> Given a white stone (2:17)—whereas in real life the black stone was the decision to have them executed!
> Clad in white robes (3:4; 6:11)—the symbol of victory, whereas on earth their ignominious exits were cast in the form of seeming defeat! . . .

Their rewards were not described as consolation prizes for those who met premature death, but were a celestial recovery of lost benefits.[1185]

John Gilmore, *Probing Heaven*

We are often pressed with the reality of eternity only when a loved one dies. Or when we grow old and begin to realize that most of life has passed and we note with regret the little we have done for eternity, the little we will take with us there, and the short time left to do much of significance for heaven's sake. Most of us live as though this world is where we are rewarded, and happiness, satisfaction, fulfillment, and prosperity not only can be ours here and now but should be.[1186]

Joseph Stowell, *Eternity*

The small will be great. The forgotten will be remembered. The unnoticed will be crowned and the faithful will be honored.[1187]

Max Lucado, *When Christ Comes*

Your day is coming. What the world has overlooked, your Father has remembered, and sooner than you can imagine, you will be blessed by him.[1188]

Max Lucado, *When Christ Comes*

On the one hand the whole basis of heaven is free, unmerited grace. On the other hand there are differences, and these differences are described as rewards (Luke 6:35). Can this be consistent? Some have been so impressed by the testimony of the Protestant Reformation to salvation by divine grace through faith alone that they have difficulty in making room for any idea of reward. To their way of thinking "reward" suggests "merit" and, as they quite correctly insist, the very idea of personal merit is excluded from heaven.

But the works of the saints do not merit the reward. For the holiness of the saints is itself the product of the work of Christ and of the sanctifying grace of the Spirit. So the believer cannot boast of himself (Romans 3:27) only of Christ (Galatians 6:14). For he does not have anything that he has not received (1 Corinthians 4:7).[1189]

Paul Helm, *The Last Things*

During the sixteenth and seventeenth centuries, the best available Greek manuscripts of 2 Peter 3:10 read that "the earth and all of its works will be *burned up*." This is how every translation of that period, including the King James Version, rendered this verse. It is easy to see how whole generations of Christians learned from their Bibles to expect a future fire that would annihilate the entire world.

However, scholars have since discovered older, more reliable Greek manuscripts, and these texts say that rather than burning up, "the earth and all of its works will be *found*." Instead of being destroyed, this term "found" implies that the quality of our works will be "laid bare," discovered for all to see. Much like gold passing through a smelting furnace, the good that we do will be purified while our less noble efforts will slough off. Read this way, Peter's vision of a coming conflagration seems to be a purging rather than annihilating fire.[1190]

Michael Wittmer, *Heaven Is a Place on Earth*

According to the Scriptures, we shall all enjoy unending progress and ceaseless growth. It might be said that our initial rewards will constitute our capital assets at the start and that, thenceforth, the constant returns on our increasing investment will enhance our happiness and usefulness continually, forevermore.

It stands to reason, though, that those who start ahead at the beginning will enjoy a priceless advantage throughout the ensuing ages of eternity.[1191]

E. X. Heatherley, *Our Heavenly Home*

Unless there be such a state [of rewards and punishments], it will certainly follow, that God, in fact, maintains no moral government over the world of mankind. For, otherwise, it is apparent, that there is no such thing as rewarding or punishing mankind, according to any visible rule, or indeed, according to any order or method whatsoever . . . if God maintains a moral government over mankind, then there must be rewards and punishments.[1192]

Paul Helm, *The Last Things*

If a person comes to heaven solely through divine grace, how can there be rewards there?

There is no doubt that heaven is the last stage, the crown of Christ's work. That anyone is in heaven is the result of God's free and unmerited mercy and grace.

All the redeemed are equally redeemed. No-one will be able to say, nor will he have the least desire to say, that he is more, or less, dependent on divine grace for his final redemption than is someone else. For each member of the church, death is swallowed up in victory (1 Corinthians 15:54). All the redeemed have the prospect of being like Christ because they will see him as he is (1 John 3:2). There is, therefore, about heaven a fundamental and essential equality in the status of those who are there because the standing of each of them is due completely to divine grace, God's free and unmerited favour to them as sinners. . . .

The thought of rewards and of differences in heaven might conjure up the idea that in heaven there could be envy of those who are better placed. But a moment's thought will show the absurdity of this.[1193]

Paul Helm, *The Last Things*

When God has made us meek and humble and lowly and reverent and pure, then we shall become fit to be promoted to this high calling of being priests and kings for Christ unto God in glory, and even here on Earth in the day that is coming.[1194]

Charles Spurgeon, "The Heavenly Singers and Their Song," Sermon 2321

The rewards God promises us are treasures too, and he expects us to want them. Christ offers us the incredible opportunity to trade temporary goods and currency for eternal rewards. By putting our money and possessions in his treasury while we're still on earth, we assure ourselves of vastly greater eternal rewards in heaven.[1195]

Randy Alcorn, *The Law of Rewards*

Not only is heavenly treasure not subject to thieves and moths, not only will the heavenly money belt not wear out, but there is "a treasure in heaven that will not be exhausted." This means not only that these heavenly treasures are safe and indestructible, as Matthew 6 suggests, but that they are also *inexhaustible*. That is, they can be *used* in heaven without ever being *used up*.[1196]

Randy Alcorn, *The Law of Rewards*

The law of rewards, which God has built into the universe, requires that every act of kindness and obedience be rewarded. But not only will there be rewards in heaven for the cup of water given on earth, those rewards *will never disappear*. The act of kindness will be remembered forever and its reward will always last. Hence, eternal rewards are not only rewards we'll receive in eternity, but rewards that are themselves eternal, imperishable, and inexhaustible (1 Peter 1:4).[1197]

Randy Alcorn, *The Law of Rewards*

When heaven fills our thoughts, we will never look at earthly money and possessions the same way. We will view them as kingdom capital—perishable instruments that can be used here and now to make an eternal difference in the home world, where we'll live forever.[1198]

Randy Alcorn, *The Law of Rewards*

The five-hundred-year-old play *Everyman* is a picture of all people. As Everyman faces Death, he looks among his friends for a companion. Only one friend would accompany him on the journey through death to final judgment. His name? "Good Deeds."

Some balk at such a picture. Yet it's explicitly biblical: "Then I heard a voice from heaven say, 'Write: Blessed are the dead who die in the Lord from now on.' 'Yes,' says the Spirit, 'they will rest from their labor, for their deeds will follow them'" (Revelation 14:13).[1199]

Randy Alcorn, *The Law of Rewards*

Prosperity theology gets it right that God rewards faithfulness but gets it wrong when it comes to the location and timing of rewards. It assumes rewards are here and now, while Scripture teaches us that the greatest rewards will be not here and now but then and there.[1200]

Randy Alcorn, *The Law of Rewards*

Whenever we speak of rewards, particularly because we speak of them so rarely, it's easy to confuse God's work and man's. Many mistakenly believe that heaven is our reward for doing good things. This is absolutely not the case. Our presence in heaven is in no sense a reward for our works, but a gift freely given by God in response to faith, which is itself God's gift (Romans 6:23; Ephesians 2:8-9; Titus 3:5).[1201]

Randy Alcorn, *The Law of Rewards*

If we do a compassionate act that goes unrewarded by others in this life, God will pay us back in the next life. This gives us an extra incentive to help the helpless. Not only do they need our help, not only does it please God, but he is eager to reward us for it![1202]

Randy Alcorn, *The Law of Rewards*

Why does God reward us? Because he is pleased by what we've done. A child who wants to be rewarded by his parents realizes they will be pleased by his good deeds. Hence, his desire for reward is not mercenary—it is inseparable from his love for his parents and his desire for their approval.[1203]

Randy Alcorn, *The Law of Rewards*

Selfishness is when we pursue gain at the expense of others. But God doesn't have a limited number of treasures to distribute. When you store up treasures for yourself in heaven, it doesn't reduce the treasures available to others. In fact, it's by serving God and others that we store up heavenly treasures. This is God's law of rewards. Everyone gains; no one loses.[1204]

Randy Alcorn, *The Law of Rewards*

It's by giving up various pleasures, possessions, and power now that we obtain them in the next world. So, it's not only virtuous for us to make sacrifices for the needy now; it's also *wise*.[1205]

Randy Alcorn, *Heaven*

"Welcome, travelers," said the girl. "We meet again. You are about to enter the city. Present to us your gifts for the King."

"Gifts?" Malaiki asked.

"Yes. The stones you picked up in the riverbeds."

My heart pounded. I put down my worn sack, just over half full. Though I'd often tried before, for the first time in daylight I managed to open it.

I pulled out a stone. It glimmered in the sunlight.

"It's gold!" I said. I reached back into the sack. "Silver! A ruby. Look—two diamonds. An emerald! And this one . . . I've never seen anything like it!"

I was vaguely aware of the others shouting. I looked to see them rifling through their bags, holding up precious stones in the rosy sunlight.

I reached farther into my bag and found what I'd thought were some light stones. I pulled them out and stared at them.

"They're not stones at all," I said. "They're just crumpled balls of straw."

I turned the bag upside down. One last gem fell out, a small one. The rest was straw and stubble.

The girl in black picked up my stones and straw and placed them on a grate connected to a long pole. She held it over the blaze. The fire immediately consumed the straw, while it burned off impurities from the gold and silver and gems. They glowed with an otherworldly beauty, and I stared at them, breathlessly, held captive by their glow.

. . . For the next hour we all watched Shad go through the rest of his sacks. He stopped to laugh and dance a jig. Then he stood still, and solemnly handed each stone, one by one, to the king's envoy. She nodded her approval and put them on a large grate. It took two warriors to help her swing the pole out over the fire. The old man's eyes watered as he watched the straw burn away and the precious metals glow in the fire.

I stared at all those stones. How could one old man have carried them all on our journey? In his own strength it would have been impossible—of course, that was it. He'd carried them with the strength of another.

"Thuros, like Earth, is the womb of Charis," whispered a familiar voice beside me. "Choice and consequences. What is done in one world has profound effects on the next."

As I nodded at Marcus, a warrior carrying the fine tools of an artisan stepped forward. He went to the grates where the stones were cooling. He picked up gold and jewels from each grate and masterfully forged them together into crowns of stunning beauty. Then he handed them to my companions, one by one.

"You will cast these at the King's feet," said the girl in black. "And sometimes you will wear them. The King and all the citizens of Charis will be forever reminded of your faithful service. You will remember the meaning of every stone, and so will he. Elyon's book says, 'A scroll of remembrance was written in his presence concerning those who feared the King and honored his name.' All your works are recorded here. Every cup of cold water given in his name."

. . . I remembered then the words spoken by the girl in black when she first told us to pick up stones by night. "In the morning, you will be both glad and sad."

The long night was over and morning was here at last. I looked at the stones I'd picked up, knowing they were my tribute to the King. Seeing them, I'd never felt so glad.

Then I thought about all the stones within my reach, all those I could have picked up, but didn't.

I'd never felt so sad.[1206]

Nick Seagrave, in *Edge of Eternity*, by Randy Alcorn

"I feel like I'm drinking from the Source of the Stream. Does this mean I'll feel no more longing?" The King—the Source—replies, "You will have the sweet longing of desire that can be fulfilled and shall be, again and again and again. [Heaven] is not the absence of longing but its fulfillment. Heaven is not the absence of itches; it is the satisfying scratch for every itch."[1207]

Li Quan and the King, in *Safely Home*, by Randy Alcorn

Sinners No More, Forever Righteous

The Son of Man will send out his angels, and they
will weed out of his kingdom everything that causes
sin and all who do evil. They will throw them into the
fiery furnace. . . . Then the righteous will shine like
the sun in the kingdom of their Father.

JESUS, MATTHEW 13:41-43

Just as through the disobedience of the one man the
many were made sinners, so also through the obedience of the one man the many will be made righteous.

PAUL, ROMANS 5:19

For our sake he made him to be sin who knew no sin,
so that in him we might become the righteousness
of God.

PAUL, 2 CORINTHIANS 5:21, ESV

You have come to Mount Zion, to the heavenly Jerusalem, the city of the living God. You have come to thousands upon thousands of angels in joyful assembly, to the church of the firstborn, whose names are written in heaven. You have come to God, the judge of all men, to the spirits of righteous men made perfect.

HEBREWS 12:22-23

Nothing impure will ever enter [the New Jerusalem], nor will anyone who does what is shameful or deceitful, but only those whose names are written in the Lamb's book of life.

JOHN, REVELATION 21:27

Let wrath deserved be written on the door of hell,
*   But the free gift of grace on the gate of heaven.*
I know that my sufferings are the result of my sinning,
*   but in heaven both shall cease.*[1208]

The Valley of Vision: A Collection of Puritan Prayers and Devotions

I must frankly confess that of all my expectations of heaven, I will cheerfully renounce ten thousand things if I can but know that I shall have perfect holiness. If I may become like Jesus Christ—pure and perfect—I cannot understand how any other joy can be denied me. If we shall have that, surely we shall have everything.[1209]

Charles Spurgeon, "The Hope that Purifies," Sermon 3235

While Scripture places a value upon the ability of a person to act in an unconstrained or uncoerced way, it places a greater value upon the individual acting in accordance with the truth, in accordance with what is right. "Freedom" in Scripture is not the freedom that an amoral individual has to do what he wants to do; it is the service of

God. It is this freedom, in contrast to the bondage to sin, that Christ promised to his followers (John 8:32-36). So however "free"—politically, financially or in other ways—a person may be, if his uncoerced choices are sinful then that person is not free but is in bondage.

The freedom of heaven, then, is the freedom from sin; not that the believer just happens to be free from sin, but that he is so constituted or reconstituted that he *cannot* sin. He does not want to sin, and he does not want to want to sin.[1210]

Paul Helm, *The Last Things*

Divorced people know what alienation is all about. But the gravest alienation that there is, is the divorce between God and man because of sin. If we are not reconciled to God in this life, we will certainly not have a chance of reconciliation in the next (Hebrews 9:27).[1211]

Jill Briscoe, *Heaven and Hell*

You remember the story of the three wonders in heaven. The first wonder was that we should see so many there we did not expect to see. The second was that we should miss so many we did expect to see there. But the third wonder would be the greatest wonder of all— to see ourselves there.[1212]

Charles Spurgeon, "The Glory of Grace," Sermon 2763

Sin is the rejection of authority. Man concentrates on himself, staggering feverishly round his own axis. It reaches its peak in self-deification. It rejects God's leadership and makes an idol of man's vital instincts while ignoring the true God. Hence it also ignores the fountain of life. This means that in its real essence it is denial of life, disintegration and destruction, spiritual and psychic "death." No wonder that it leads to bodily death as well. "The wages of sin is death" (Romans 6:23).

The death of the body is thus not merely a natural event, but has to be understood ethically. The sinless man need not die. Death is judgment. It is both the *essence* of sin and its necessary *consequence*.[1213]

Erich Sauer, *The King of the Earth*

What does contradict our nobility as men is *sin*, not redemption. Man should be ashamed of *sin*, not of repentance or of a change of heart.[1214]

Erich Sauer, *The King of the Earth*

Purgatory arose to resolve a problem created by Catholic soteriology. It was meant to honor the holiness of God. Now the rationale for purgatory, in public views, is not because there is a strong commitment to God's holiness, but because people look for and want a place to atone for their sins and to have an opportunity to unlive the life they lived on earth.

. . . Purgatory strikes a responsive chord. A person will believe in purgatory rather than hell, because he is not convinced of the need of eternal exaction against iniquity and he is not convinced he is "that wicked."

This approach, however, means man must reshape God.[1215]

John Gilmore, *Probing Heaven*

We are fully redeemed in that the work was finished on the Cross, and there is nothing more that Christ needs to do or that we can do. Yet we have not yet experienced the fullness of our redemption. We still carry the weight of sin. A common cold or a bout with the flu reminds us that the effects of our fallenness are still with us.[1216]

Joseph Stowell, *Eternity*

Rationalism and relativism leave no room for a righteous God and the reality of heaven. We were left to ourselves without God and an eternal home. Like children left at home alone, the results have been devastating.[1217]

Joseph Stowell, *Eternity*

Will we be free to sin in heaven? . . . If we answer no, we seem to lack something: free will. If we answer yes, we lack something else: moral perfection. The Heavenly question thus lands us squarely into an earthly and present issue concerning the nature of freedom and of morality and may help us to puncture one of modernity's most pervasive and destructive illusions: the association of freedom with rebellion and of obedience with unfreedom.[1218]

Peter Kreeft, *Everything You Ever Wanted to Know about Heaven*

We sin because we see sin as a bargain. We unconsciously calculate that it's worth it, that it pays, that "justice is *not* more profitable than injustice." Sin seems to be simply a choice between alternative lifestyles on earth. But if we recognize that all sin is Hellish, if we see sin as Hell wearing an earthly mask, we will fly to the Father in fear.[1219]

Peter Kreeft, *Everything You Ever Wanted to Know about Heaven*

It is not sin that attracts men and women, but it is sin that fills our relations with control and suspicion. It is not sin that makes music, but it is sin that fills our songs with vanity and lust. It is not sin that makes us construct cities and towers, but it is sin that makes those towers symbols of pride and power. It is not sin that calls human beings to live and love, to make music and art, to work and create, to plant and harvest, to play and dance. But it is sin that undercuts and perverts them all.

Sin does not create things. It has no originality, no creativity, no being in itself. Sin lives off that which is good. It is a parasite, feeding greedily on the goodness of what God has made.[1220]

Paul Marshall, *Heaven Is Not My Home*

Søren Kierkegaard told a parable about a rich man riding in a lighted carriage driven by a peasant who sat behind the horse in the cold and dark outside. Precisely because he sat near the artificial light inside, the rich man missed the panorama of stars outside, a view gloriously manifest to the peasant. In modern times, it seems, as science casts more light on the created world, its shadows further obscure the invisible world beyond.[1221]

Philip Yancey, *Rumors of Another World*

Imaginary evil is romantic and varied; real evil is gloomy, monotonous, barren, boring. Imaginary good is boring; real good is always new, marvelous, intoxicating.[1222]

Simone Weil, *Gravity and Grace*

The sins which so often made us tremble, are washed away in the blood of Jesus, and are, therefore, no longer a source of trouble. The remembrance of them rather intensifies our love for the God of mercy, and therefore increases our happiness.[1223]

Father J. Boudreau, *The Happiness of Heaven*

When Christ's followers rise, they shall leave the old Adam behind them. Blessed day! One of the happiest aspects of Heaven will be freedom from the tendency to sin, a total death to that old nature which has been our plague and woe.[1224]

Charles Spurgeon, "The First Resurrection," Sermon 391

We may say that sin and evil always have the character of a caricature—that is, of a distorted image that nevertheless embodies certain recognizable features. A human being after the fall, though a travesty of humanity, is still a human being, not an animal. A humanistic school is still a school. A broken relationship is still a relationship. Muddled thinking is still thinking. In each case, what something in fallen creation "still is" points to the enduring goodness of creation— that is to say, to the faithfulness of God in upholding the created order despite the ravages of sin. Creation will not be suppressed in any final sense.[1225]

Albert Wolters, *Creation Regained*

Some theologians have called the curbing of sin and its effects God's "common grace." Through God's goodness to all men and women, believers and unbelievers alike, God's faithfulness to creation still bears fruit in humankind's personal, societal, and cultural lives.

"Common grace" is thus distinguished from God's "special grace" to his people, whereby sin is not only curbed but forgiven and atoned for, making possible true and genuine renewal from within. . . . God never lets go of his creatures, even in the face of apostasy, unbelief, and perversion.[1226]

Albert Wolters, *Creation Regained*

No evil angels are permitted to infest heaven as they do this world, but they are kept forever at a distance by that great gulf which is between them and the glorious world of love. And among all the company of the saints, there are no unlovely persons. There are no false professors or hypocrites there; none that pretend to be saints, and yet are of an unchristian and hateful spirit or behavior, as is often the case in this world. . . .

There are spots on the sun; and so there are many men that are most amiable and worthy to be loved, who yet are not without some things that are offensive and unlovely. Often there is in good men some defect of disposition or character or conduct that mars the excellence of what otherwise would seem most amiable; and even the very best of men, are, on earth, imperfect. But it is not so in heaven. There shall be no pollution or deformity or offensive defect of any kind, seen in any person or thing; but every one shall be perfectly pure, and perfectly lovely in heaven.[1227]

Jonathan Edwards, *Heaven: A World of Love*

There shall be no such thing as fickleness and unfaithfulness in heaven, to molest and disturb the friendship of that blessed society.[1228]

Jonathan Edwards, *Heaven: A World of Love*

To enter heaven as we are, and for heaven to remain heaven in the process, is a moral impossibility. Nothing that defiles can enter heaven (Revelation 21:27) and so the idea that death marks a natural and inevitable transition to the bliss of heaven, a bliss which awaits us all, is a deep and deadly mistake. Heaven is made possible only by the work of Christ and by personal union with him through faith.[1229]

Paul Helm, *The Last Things*

"Many shall come from the east and west—and shall sit down with Abraham, Isaac, and Jacob in the kingdom of heaven." (Matthew 8:11)

If we were in the presence of a stern judge, or of a king clothed in awful majesty, we should not dare to sit down.

But there will be nothing to make believers afraid in the kingdom of heaven. Though the sins of their lives "were as scarlet, they shall be made white as snow; and though red like crimson, they shall be as wool." Their sins will be "remembered no more"; "sought for, and not found"; "blotted out as a thick cloud"; "cast behind God's back"; "plunged in the depths of the sea."

Once joined to Christ by faith, they are complete in the sight of God the Father, and even the perfect angels shall see no spot in them. Surely they may well sit down; and feel at home![1230]

J. C. Ryle, *The Upper Room*

Christ promises on the New Earth, "There will be no more death or mourning or crying or pain, for the old order of things has passed away" (Revelation 21:4). Since "the wages of sin is death" (Romans 6:23), the promise of no more death is a promise of *no more sin.* Those who will never die can never sin, since sinners always die. Sin causes mourning, crying, and pain. If those will never occur again, then *sin* can never occur again.[1231]

Randy Alcorn, *Heaven*

The inability to sin doesn't inherently violate free will. My inability to be God, an angel, a rabbit, or a flower is not a violation of my free will. It's the simple reality of my nature. The new nature that'll be ours in Heaven—the righteousness of Christ—is a nature that cannot sin, any more than a diamond can be soft or blue can be red. God cannot sin, yet no being has greater free choice than God does.[1232]

Randy Alcorn, *Heaven*

We won't sin in Heaven for the same reason God doesn't: He cannot sin. Our eternal inability to sin has been purchased by Christ's blood. Our Savior purchased our perfection *for all time.*[1233]

Randy Alcorn, *TouchPoints: Heaven*

Someone once asked me, "If we're sinless, will we still be human?" Although sin is part of us now, it's not essential to our humanity. In fact, it's *foreign* to it. It's what twists us and keeps us from being what we once were—and what we one day will be.

Our greatest deliverance in Heaven will be from ourselves. Our deceit, corruption, self-righteousness, self-sufficiency, hypocrisy—all will be gone forever. And we will never stop praising God for the miracle of his grace![1234]

Randy Alcorn, *We Shall See God*

"Won't it be boring to be good all the time?" someone asked. Note the assumption: sin is exciting and righteousness is boring. We've fallen for the devil's lie. His most basic strategy, the same one he employed with Adam and Eve, is to make us believe that sin brings fulfillment. However, in reality, sin robs us of fulfillment. Sin doesn't make life interesting; it makes life empty. Sin doesn't create adventure; it blunts it. Sin doesn't expand life; it shrinks it. Sin's emptiness inevitably leads to boredom. When there's fulfillment, when there's beauty, when we see God as he truly is—an endless reservoir of fascination—boredom becomes impossible.[1235]

Randy Alcorn, *Heaven*

Will we be tempted to turn our backs on Christ? No. What would tempt us? Innocence is the absence of something (sin), while righteousness is the presence of something (God's holiness). God will never withdraw from us his holiness; therefore we cannot sin.

We'll *never* forget the ugliness of sin. People who've experienced severe burns aren't tempted to walk into a bonfire. Having known death and life, we who will experience life will never want to go back to death. We'll never be deceived into thinking God is withholding something good from us or that sin is in our best interests.[1236]

Randy Alcorn, *Heaven*

Thinking Heavenward

Show me, O LORD, my life's end and the number of my days; let me know how fleeting is my life. You have made my days a mere handbreadth; the span of my years is as nothing before you. Each man's life is but a breath.

DAVID, PSALM 39:4-5

Since you have been raised to new life with Christ, set your sights on the realities of heaven, where Christ sits in the place of honor at God's right hand. Think about the things of heaven, not the things of earth. For you died to this life, and your real life is hidden with Christ in God. And when Christ, who is your life, is revealed to the whole world, you will share in all his glory.

PAUL, COLOSSIANS 3:1-4, NLT

Don't you know that friendship with the world is hatred toward God? Anyone who chooses to be a friend of the world becomes an enemy of God.

JAMES 4:4

Resolved, to endeavor to obtain for myself as much happiness, in the other world, as I possibly can.[1237]

Jonathan Edwards, *The Resolutions of Jonathan Edwards*

All men seek happiness. This is without exception. Whatever different means they employ, they all tend to this end.[1238]

Blaise Pascal, *Pensées*

If that other world is once admitted, how can it, except by sensual or bustling pre-occupations, be kept in the background of our minds? How can the rest of Christianity—what is this "rest"? —be disentangled from it? How can we untwine this idea, if once admitted, from our present experience, in which, even before we believed, so many things at least *looked* like "bright shoots of everlastingness"?[1239]

C. S. Lewis, *Letters to Malcolm: Chiefly on Prayer*

If we insist on keeping Hell (or even earth) we shall not see Heaven: if we accept Heaven we shall not be able to retain even the smallest and most intimate souvenirs of Hell.[1240]

C. S. Lewis, *The Great Divorce*

Heaven is full of answers to prayers for which no one ever bothered to ask![1241]

Billy Graham, *Till Armageddon: A Perspective on Suffering*

And storied windows richly dight,
Casting a dim religious light,
There let the pealing organ blow,
To the full-voiced choir below,
In service high, and anthems clear
As may, with sweetness, through mine ear
Dissolve me into ecstasies,
And bring all Heaven before mine eyes.[1242]

John Milton, *Il Penseroso*

Pippin: "I didn't think it would end this way . . ."

Gandalf: "End? No, the journey doesn't end here. Death is just another path . . . one that we all must take. The grey rain-curtain of this world rolls back, and all change to silver glass . . . and then you see it."

Pippin: "What? Gandalf? See what?"

Gandalf: "White shores . . . and beyond. The far green country under a swift sunrise."

Pippin: "Well, that isn't so bad."

Gandalf: "No . . . no, it isn't."[1243]

Philippa Boyens and Fran Walsh, *Lord of the Rings: The Return of the King*

A heavenly mind is a joyful mind: this is the nearest and truest way to live a life of comfort. . . . A heart in heaven will be a most excellent preservative against temptations, a powerful means to kill thy corruptions.[1244]

Richard Baxter

A little faith will bring your soul to heaven: a great faith will bring heaven to your soul.[1245]

Charles Spurgeon

Heaven lifts your eyes off your own daily struggles and frees you to see and meet the needs of others.[1246]

Larry Dick, *A Taste of Heaven*

Amy Carmichael writes of little joys, like flowers springing up by the path unnoticed except by those who are looking for them. . . . Little things, like a quietly sinking sun, a friendly dog, a ready smile. We sang a little song in kindergarten which I've never forgotten: "The world is so full of a number of things / I'm sure we should all be as happy as kings Simple, but such a devastating rebuke to the complaining heart. I am impressed with the joy that is ours in Christ, so that heaven above and earth below become brighter and fairer.[1247]

Jim Elliot, in a letter to his wife, Elisabeth

Above, beneath, around, within, without, everywhere it is heaven. I breathe heaven, I drink heaven, I feel heaven, I think heaven. Everything is heaven. Oh, "what must it be to be there?" To be there is to be with Christ.[1248]

Charles Spurgeon, "Fellowship with Christ," Sermon 2572

Does anyone honestly think that the idea of heaven that lies behind the church's myriad stories of faith and daring, endurance and sacrifice, is nothing more than pillowy clouds, plinky music, and pudgy angels?[1249]

Mark Buchanan, *Things Unseen*

The first thing Paul claims is that trouble in this life is nothing compared with the glory in the next life. What we will know and what we will be and what we will have in heaven make anything and everything on earth as light as a cotton spore and as brief as a shooting star.

Light and momentary troubles? *But Paul, didn't you just tell us that you are persecuted, perplexed, struck down, and all day, every day, given over to death? Didn't you say earlier that you've been so over-whelmed that you feel under the sentence of death? Paul, your life has been a chronicle of suffering. Aren't these things terror and tragedy?*

No. They're light and momentary troubles.[1250]

Mark Buchanan, *Things Unseen*

Here is the meat of it: There is nothing that you experience—good or bad—in this world that either has more substance or is longer in duration than the glory of heaven.

. . . Look at anything around you—the chair you sit in, the walls around you, the piano or desk against the wall. Solid. But a hundred years from now? A thousand years?

Rubble and dust. Likewise, the heartache, the pain, or the stress you suffer seems so all-consuming and all-defining now. So unmovable and permanent. But it's passing away. It is light and momentary.

In the Greek, the word for light is *elaphros.* It means easy to bear. The death of my father is easy to bear? Only if I compare it to what's coming. Everything hinges on our willingness to fix our eyes not on what is seen, but on what is unseen. It hinges on our being heavenly-minded.[1251]

Mark Buchanan, *Things Unseen*

You that are poor, and think yourself despised by your neighbors and little cared for among men, do not much concern yourselves for this. Do not care much for the friendship of the world; but seek heaven, where there is no such thing as contempt, and where none are despised, but all are highly esteemed and honored, and dearly beloved by all. You who think you have met with many abuses, and much poor treatment from others, do not be concerned about it. Do not hate them for it, but set your heart on heaven, that world of love, and press toward that better country, where all is kindness and holy affection.[1252]

Jonathan Edwards, *Heaven: A World of Love*

We have today almost lost the ability that many of our forefathers had to profit spiritually from meditation on the prospect of death. As a consequence, we are impoverished not only in the way we die but also in the way we live.[1253]

Chuck McGowen, *Let's Talk about Heaven*

Otherworldliness is escapism only if there is no other world. If there is, it is worldliness that is escapism.[1254]

Peter Kreeft, *Heaven: The Heart's Greatest Longing*

There is the danger that the redeemed one will become so occupied with the anticipation of his own experience of glory that the supreme glorification of the Godhead is lost. Our occupation in the eternal state will not be with our position or glory, but with God Himself.[1255]

J. Dwight Pentecost, *Things to Come*

Surely, if we do not get to heaven the fault will be all our own. Let us arise and lay hold on the hand that is held out to us from heaven.

. . . The prison doors are set wide open; let us go forth and be free. The lifeboat is alongside; let us embark into it and be safe. The bread of life is before us; let us eat and live. . . . Have we a good hope of going to heaven, a hope that is Scriptural, reasonable, and will bear investigation? Then let us not be afraid to meditate often on the subject of "heaven," and to rejoice in the prospect of good things to come.[1256]

J. C. Ryle, *Heaven*

It's fascinating that the most important, most strategic, most enduring place in the universe gets so little attention. The moon and Mars get more press than heaven. Yet heaven is of unrivaled significance. When we stretch our view of life to embrace its reality, all of life is wonderfully rearranged.[1257]

Joseph Stowell, *Eternity*

Our generation, while admitting that heaven is real, has ceased to embrace its relevance and is paying dearly for the loss.[1258]

Joseph Stowell, *Eternity*

Heaven must become the target of our hearts. It's what we are meant to aim for.[1259]

Joseph Stowell, *Eternity*

A person may sit in church regularly and even read his Bible daily. But that doesn't mean he's heavenly minded. . . . To be heavenly minded means to live a life of faith in things not seen (Hebrews 11:1). It means to live for the world to come, not this present world. It means to see all of life from an eternal perspective. It means to live every day and weigh every decision in the light of eternity. It means to live for that which is timeless, not temporal; to live for that which is spiritual, not tangible; to live for that which is invisible, not visible.[1260]

Steven J. Lawson, *Heaven Help Us!*

It is the Christian soldier who is ever awake and on his guard, that is only fit for every sudden appointment to new stations and services, he is more prepared for any post of danger or hazardous enterprise, and better furnished to sustain the roughest assaults. We shall be less shocked at sudden afflictions here on earth, if our souls keep heaven in view, and are ready winged for immortality. When we are fit to die we are fit to live also, and to do better service for God in whichever of his worlds he shall please to appoint our station. My business, O Father, and my joy, is to do thy will among the sons of mortality, or among the spirits of the blest on high.[1261]

Isaac Watts, *The World to Come*

The apocalypse is not given for drafting intricate eschatological charts, but for pointing our lives unto godliness.[1262]

Steven J. Lawson, *Heaven Help Us!*

Discomfort? You've been told your mistakes will be revealed. You've been told your secrets will be made known. Books will be opened, and names will be read. You know God is holy. You know you are not.

Denial might be more accurate.

Consequently, you opt not to think about it. Why consider what you can't explain? If he comes, fine. If not, fine. But I'm going to bed. I have to work tomorrow.

. . . Disappointment?

Who would feel disappointment at the thought of Christ's coming? A mother-to-be might—she wants to hold her baby. An engaged couple might—they want to be married. A soldier stationed overseas might—he wants to go home before he goes home.[1263]

Max Lucado, *When Christ Comes*

And yet I joy, as storm on storm awakes;
Not that I love the uproar or the gloom;
But in each tempest over earth that breaks,
I count one fewer outburst yet to come.

No groan creation heaves is heaved in vain,
Nor e'er shall be repeated; it is done.
Once heaved, it never shall be heaved again;
Earth's pangs and throes are lessening one by one.

So falls the stroke of sorrow, and so springs
Strange joy and comfort from the very grief,
Even to the weariest sufferer; so brings
Each heavy burden still its own relief.

One cross the less remains for me to bear;
Already borne is that of yesterday;
That of to-day shall no to-morrow share;
To-morrow's with itself, shall pass away.

That which is added to the troubled past
Is taken from the future, whose sad store

Grows less and less each day, till soon the last
Dull wave of woe shall break upon our shore.

The storm that yesterday ploughed up the sea
Is buried now beneath its level blue;
One storm the fewer now remains for me,
Ere sky and earth are made for ever new.[1264]

Horatius Bonar, "Life's Storms Are Passing"

Biology is destiny, concludes the one who looks down. The prospects are bleak, for according to psychologists our impulses include a natural urge to murder our fathers and mothers, at least an occasional tendency to laziness and idleness, a penchant for cruelty and vulgarity.

Eternity is destiny, concludes the one who looks up. Our genes may indeed contain predispositions toward bestial instincts, but we hear a call to rise above them.[1265]

Philip Yancey, *Rumors of Another World*

We must face today as children of tomorrow. We must meet the uncertainties of this world with the certainty of the world to come. To the pure in heart nothing really bad can happen. He may die, but what is death to a Christian? Not death but sin should be our great fear. Without doubt the heavens being on fire shall be dissolved, and the earth and the works that are therein shall be burned up. Sooner or later that will come. But what of it? Do not we, according to His promise, look for new heavens and a new earth, wherein dwelleth righteousness?[1266]

A. W. Tozer, *Of God and Men*

Hope is one of the Theological virtues. This means that a continual looking forward to the eternal world is not (as some modern people think) a form of escapism or wishful thinking, but one of the things a Christian is meant to do. It does not mean that we are to leave the present world as it is. If you read history, you will find that the

Christians who did most for the present world were just those who thought most of the next. The Apostles themselves, who set on foot the conversion of the Roman Empire, the great men who built up the Middle Ages, the English Evangelicals who abolished the Slave Trade, all left their mark on Earth, precisely because their minds were occupied with Heaven. It is since Christians have largely ceased to think of the other world that they have become so ineffective in this. Aim at Heaven and you will get earth "thrown in": aim at earth and you will get neither.[1267]

C. S. Lewis, *Mere Christianity*

Always he that is best bred, and that is most in the bosom of God, and that so acts for him here; he is the man that will be best able to enjoy most of God in the kingdom of heaven.[1268]

John Bunyan, "The Resurrection of the Dead, and Eternal Judgment"

If we could only see far enough we would see earth's failures changed into Heaven's triumphs, earth's discords changed into Heaven's harmonies.[1269]

James Campbell, *Heaven Opened*

I don't lose heart. I made a decision a long time ago: My hope lies elsewhere. I accept that—after I've eaten well and exercised often, after I've flossed and scrubbed and groomed and scoured, after I've cleaned the dirt from under my fingernails and clipped the hair bristling out my ears—I am still outwardly wasting away. I live by a great *nevertheless. Nevertheless,* though I die, yet I shall live. *Nevertheless,* though the stall is empty and the fig tree does not blossom, yet will I trust. *Nevertheless,* though He slay me, yet shall I worship.

I have staked everything on being renewed inwardly day by day.

. . . What is it that renews us inwardly and daily?

One thing above all: being heavenly-minded.

Inwardly we are being renewed day by day. For our light and momentary troubles are achieving for us an eternal weight of glory that far outweighs them all. This is one of the most remarkable declarations in the Bible. Paul is claiming two things here, both staggering in their implications.[1270]

Mark Buchanan, *Things Unseen*

Women sometimes have the problem of trying to judge by artificial light how a dress will look by daylight. That is very much like the problem of all of us: to dress our souls not for the electric lights of the present world but for the daylight of the next. The good dress is the one that will face that light. For that light will last longer.[1271]

C. S. Lewis, "The World's Last Night"

One obvious reason why many of us do not reflect on heaven nearly as much as we should is that we are too preoccupied with this present world. We are surrounded by what we can see and hear, touch, taste, and smell. If I take a coin in my hand and hold it close to my eye, it will block out the sun. . . . Now the sun is bigger than a coin, but because the coin is close it blocks from my sight something incomparably greater. . . . The very closeness of this world blocks out the infinitely vaster prospect of the glorious world which is to come.[1272]

Edward Donnelly, *Biblical Teaching on the Doctrines of Heaven and Hell*

Let's not get too settled in, too satisfied with the good things down here on earth. They are only the tinkling sounds of the orchestra warming up. The real song is about to break into a heavenly symphony, and its prelude is only a few moments away.[1273]

Joni Eareckson Tada, *Heaven: Your Real Home*

On hearing it said of Francis Thompson, author of *The Hound of Heaven*, that the great tragedy of his life was that he never felt at home, a colleague of Thompson responded, "Our great tragedy is that we do!" Attempts to transform this life into heaven have failed abysmally; from the utopian efforts of the early nineteenth century to calamitous cults like the Branch Davidians and Heaven's Gate, to the contemporary "health and prosperity" movement, such attempts have either undervalued heaven or overvalued earth—or both. How foolish—and sad—to confuse the two![1274]

Larry Dixon, *Heaven: Thinking Now about Forever*

Be acquainted with this heavenly work, and thou wilt, in some degree, be acquainted with God; thy joys will be spiritual, prevalent and lasting, according to the nature of their blessed object; thou wilt have comfort in life and death. When thou hast neither wealth, nor health, nor the pleasures of this world, yet wilt thou have comfort. Without the presence or help of any friend, without a minister, without a book, when all means are denied thee, or taken from thee, yet mayst thou have vigorous, real comfort. Thy graces will be mighty, active and victorious; and the daily joy which is thus drawn from heaven will be thy strength. . . . Men's threatenings will be no terror to thee, nor the honors of this world any strong enticement; temptations will be more harmless, as having lost their strength; and afflictions less grievous, as having lost their sting; and every mercy will be better known and relished. It is now, under God, in thy own choice, whether thou wilt live this blessed life or not. . . . O man, what hast thou to mind but God and heaven? Art thou not almost out of this world already? Dost thou not look every day, when one disease or another will release thy soul? Does not the grave wait to be thine house, and worms to feed upon thy face and heart? . . . Where, then, should thy heart be now but in heaven? Didst thou know what a dreadful thing it is to have a doubt of heaven when a man is dying, it would raise thee up. And what else but doubt can that man then do, that never seriously thought of heaven before.

Some there be that say, "It is not worth so much time and trouble to think of the greatness of the joys above; if we can make sure they are ours, we know they are great." But as these men obey not the command of God, which requires them to have their "conversation in heaven, and to set their affections on things above;" so they wilfully make their own lives miserable, by refusing the delights which God hath set before them. And if this were all, it were a small matter: but see what abundance of other mischiefs follow the neglect of these heavenly delights. This neglect will damp, if not destroy, their love to God—will make it unpleasant to them to think or speak of God, or engage in his service—it tends to pervert their judgment concerning the ways and ordinances of God—it makes them sensual and voluptuous—it leaves them under the power of every affliction and temptation, and is a preparative to total apostacy—it will also make them fearful and unwilling to die; for who would go to a God or a place he hath no delight in? . . . God is willing you should daily walk with him, and draw consolations from the everlasting fountain: if you are unwilling, even bear the loss; and, when you are dying, seek for comfort where you can get it, and see whether fleshly delights will remain with you. Then conscience will remember, in spite of you, that you were once persuaded to a way for more excellent pleasures—pleasures that would have followed you through death, and have lasted to eternity.

As for you, whose hearts God hath weaned from all things here below, I hope you will value this heavenly life, and take one walk every day in the New Jerusalem. God is your love and your desire; you would fain be more acquainted with your Savior; and I know it is your grief that your hearts are not nearer to him, and that they do not more feelingly love him and delight in him. O try this life of meditation on your heavenly rest! Here is the mount on which the fluctuating ark of your souls may rest. Let the world see, by your heavenly lives, that religion is something more than opinions and disputes, or a task of outward duties.[1275]

Richard Baxter, *The Saints' Everlasting Rest*

Always remember whither you are going; that you are preparing for everlasting rest and joy.[1276]

Richard Baxter, *The Practical Works of Richard Baxter*

The life of a Christian is wondrously ruled in this world, by the consideration and meditation of the life of another world.[1277]

Richard Sibbes, *The Pilgrim's Progress and Traditions in Puritan Meditation*

What business so ever we have in the world . . . our main business is in heaven.[1278]

John Preston

Let your life on earth be a conversation in heaven.[1279]

Richard Baxter, *The Practical Works of Richard Baxter*

Nothing can deservedly be taken into account as among the causes of our happiness that does not somehow or other regard both that everlasting life and this civil life below.[1280]

John Milton, *An Introduction to the Prose and Poetical Works of John Milton*

Narratives appeal to our imagination in a way that the abstractions of theology do not. . . . The chief reason for investing the time to understand and value this deeply Christian [story-telling] literature is that it reawakens our longing for Home and strengthens our hearts, minds, and souls for the rigors of the journey while preparing us for the joys along the way: those foretastes of heaven vouchsafed to us even now.[1281]

Wayne Martindale, *Journey to the Celestial City*

Set your hope fully on the grace that will be brought to you at the revelation of Jesus Christ (1 Peter 1:13). This is a commanded obsession. Fixate fully! Rivet your soul on the grace that you will receive when Christ returns. Tolerate no distractions. Entertain no diversions. Don't let your mind be swayed. Devote every ounce of mental and spiritual and emotional energy to concentrating and contemplating on the grace that is to come. What grace is that? It is the grace of the heavenly inheritance.[1282]

Sam Storms, *The Hope of Glory*

A contemplative focus on heaven enables us to respond appropriately to the injustices of this life. Essential to heavenly joy is witnessing the vindication of righteousness and the judgment of evil. Only from our anticipation of the new perspective of heaven, from which we, one day, will look back and evaluate what now seems senseless, can we be empowered to endure this world in all its ugliness and moral deformity.[1283]

Sam Storms, *The Hope of Glory*

Secular optimists are merely wishful thinkers. Discovering the present payoffs of optimism, they conduct seminars and write books on thinking positively. Sometimes they capitalize on optimism by becoming rich and famous. But then what happens? They eventually get old or sick, and when they die, if they haven't trusted Christ, they go to Hell forever. Their optimism is an illusion, for it fails to take eternity into account.

The only proper foundation for optimism is the redemptive work of Jesus Christ. Any other foundation is sand, not rock. It will not bear the weight of eternity.[1284]

Randy Alcorn, *We Shall See God*

Life becomes different when we realize that death is a turnstile, not a wall, and that our funerals will mark a small end and a great beginning.[1285]

Randy Alcorn, *50 Days of Heaven*

Anticipating Heaven doesn't eliminate pain, but it does lessen it and put it in perspective. Meditating on Heaven is a great pain reliever. Suffering and death are temporary conditions—they are but a gateway to eternal life of unending joy.[1286]

Randy Alcorn, *We Shall See God*

Setting our minds on Heaven is the key to liberated, non-legalistic holy living. Why? Because instead of just denying ourselves something—sin—we focus on what is far better, what is outrageously eternally better. Legalism is self-congratulatory: "Look what I've sacrificed." Heaven-mindedness is Christ-centered. . . . In fact, Paul argues that legalism itself is worldliness (Colossians 2:20-23), and since we don't belong to this world, we shouldn't be captured by legalism. A life that is centered on the here and now—even if an attempt to be holy—is self-centered. A life centered on the then and there, Heaven, is God-centered.

Randy Alcorn, unpublished notes

He will be ready for us to come—we should be ready to go.

Randy Alcorn, unpublished notes

When we see him with our resurrected eyes, we will realize that all our lives, as we went down every dead-end street pursuing what we thought we wanted, it was really him we were searching for, longing for.

Randy Alcorn, notes

Perhaps you're afraid of becoming "so heavenly minded you're of no earthly good." There's another one of Satan's myths. On the contrary, most of us are so earthly-minded we are of no heavenly or earthly good.[1287]

Randy Alcorn, *In Light of Eternity*

If you're a Christian suffering with great pains and losses, Jesus says, "Be of good cheer" (John 16:33, NKJV). The new house is nearly ready for you. Moving day is coming. The dark winter is about to be magically transformed into spring. One day soon you will be home—for the first time. Until then, I encourage you to meditate on the Bible's truths about Heaven. May your imagination soar and your heart rejoice.[1288]

Randy Alcorn, *Heaven*

In the truest sense, Christian pilgrims have the best of both worlds. We have joy whenever this world reminds us of the next, and we take solace whenever it does not.[1289]

Randy Alcorn, *Money, Possessions, and Eternity*

Time and Process in Heaven

With the Lord a day is like a thousand years, and
a thousand years are like a day.

PETER, 2 PETER 3:8

They [the martyrs in Heaven] called out in a loud
voice, "How long, Sovereign Lord, holy and true,
until you judge the inhabitants of the earth?" . . .
And they were told to wait a little longer.

JOHN, REVELATION 6:10-11

There was silence in heaven for about half an hour.

JOHN, REVELATION 8:1

On either side of the river [in the New Jerusalem, on the New Earth], the tree of life with its twelve kinds of fruit, yielding its fruit each month. The leaves of the tree were for the healing of the nations.

JOHN, REVELATION 22:2, ESV

"With the Lord a day is like a thousand years." . . . That rate of comparison yields the approximate ratio of one second of our time equaling four days to God. In other words, the intensity of time for God means that what passes us by as a mere moment has the potential to be teased out in the presence of God so that all its features and ingredients are minutely exposed.[1290]

Bruce Milne, *The Message of Heaven and Hell*

A favorite assumption is that heaven is absolute timelessness.

Timelessness presents problems. Timelessness, for instance, does away with music. . . . Music, of course, requires timing. Other recreations do, too. The games of tennis and golf, as well as other sports, cannot be played well without coordination, which requires timing.

. . . The tree of life will bear twelve kinds of fruit "every month." Of all the things said to be eliminated from heaven, time is not one of them.[1291]

John Gilmore, *Probing Heaven*

Our nostalgia for Eden is not just for another time, but for another kind of time. Time in Eden was the pool in which we swam. Time is now the river that sweeps us away. . . . We long in both directions; we feel both nostalgia and hope, fallen from the heights and on the upward road, exiles from Eden and apprentices to heaven.[1292]

Peter Kreeft, *Everything You Ever Wanted to Know about Heaven*

Time is the mould of our created human existence. Sin led to the fact that we have no time, and that we spend a hurried existence between past and future. But the consummation as the glorification of existence will not mean that we are taken out of time and delivered from time, but that time as the form of our glorified existence will also be fulfilled and glorified. Consummation means to live again in the succession of past, present, and future, but in such a way that the past moves along with us as a blessing and the future radiates through the present so that we strive without restlessness and rest without idleness, and so that, though always progressing, we are always at our destination.[1293]

Hendrikus Berkhof, *Christ the Meaning of History*

Clock time (*chronos* in Greek) is not the only kind of time. We live in *kairos*: lived time, or life-time. *Kairos* is time *for* something, time relative to human purpose. There is never enough time for anything, enough *kairos*, because *kairos* is bounded by *chronos* here on earth. But not in Heaven. After death there will be all the time in the world—more than all the time in the world—to learn, to savor, to sink totally into the meaning of everything.

At the moment of death, according to very widespread testimony, your whole lifetime often flashes before you in vivid detail, in perfect order, and in a single instant. All your *kairos* does not take a single minute of *chronos*, for the boundary, the *chronos*-limit, is removed. An infinitely small unit of *chronos* (the instant in which your lifetime flashes by) is in fact enormous. For it is *kairos* measured not by *chronos* but by eternity.[1294]

Peter Kreeft, *Everything You Ever Wanted to Know about Heaven*

Eternity perfects time. Just as Heaven's space is more truly a place than earth's, so Heaven's time is more truly time, more timely.[1295]

Peter Kreeft, *Everything You Ever Wanted to Know about Heaven*

Time matters; it was part of the original good creation. Though it may well itself be transformed in ways we cannot at present even begin to imagine, we should not allow ourselves to be seduced by the language of eternity (as in the phrase "eternal life," which in the New Testament regularly refers not to a nontemporal future existence but to "the life of the coming age") into imagining, as one old song puts it, that "time shall be no more." No: "the old field of space, time, matter and the senses is to be weeded, dug, and sown for a new crop. We may be tired of that old field: God is not."[1296]

N. T. Wright, *Surprised by Hope*

Though time will be endless we will not waste time there. Anything that develops relationships, of course, is never a waste of time in God's eyes.[1297]

Larry Dick, *A Taste of Heaven*

In Heaven every event is remembered forever. It becomes one of the billions of pictures in God's museum—rather, God's zoo, for they are alive there, not dead—open to inspection with no deadlines and with total understanding.

Our lives are a picture, and death is the frame. In Heaven we get off the picture and see it as it truly was. But time's *was* is eternity's *is*. All past times are present, all dead times are alive in eternity. Memory dimly foreshadows this; that is why it is so magically charming.

Perhaps this also helps to explain why memory is so selective, why we remember some events and not others.[1298]

Peter Kreeft, *Everything You Ever Wanted to Know about Heaven*

The most horrible lifetime on earth, seen from the viewpoint of Heaven, will look like only one bad cold.[1299]

Peter Kreeft, *Everything You Ever Wanted to Know about Heaven*

Hearts on earth say in the course of a joyful experience, "I don't want this ever to end." But it invariably does. The hearts of those in heaven say, "I want this to go on forever." And it will. There can be no better news than this.[1300]

J. I. Packer, *Concise Theology*

When we've been there ten thousand years,
Bright shining as the sun,
We've no less days to sing God's praise
Than when we've first begun.[1301]

John Newton, "Amazing Grace"

Although a popular hymn speaks of the time "when the trumpet of the Lord shall sound and time shall be no more," Scripture does not give support to that idea. Certainly the heavenly city that receives its light from the glory of God (Revelation 21:23) will never experience darkness or night: "There shall be no night there" (Revelation 21:25, [KJV]). But this does not mean that heaven will be a place where time is unknown, or where things cannot be done one after another. Indeed, all the pictures of heavenly worship in the book of Revelation include words that are spoken one after another in coherent sentences, and actions (such as falling down before God's throne and casting crowns before his throne) that involve a sequence of events. When we read that "the kings of the earth . . . shall bring into it the glory and honor of the nations" (Revelation 21:24-26), we see another activity that involves a sequence of events, one happening after another. And certainly that is the clear implication of the fact that the tree of life has twelve kinds of fruit, "yielding its fruit *each month*" (Revelation 22:2).

. . . Since we are finite creatures, we might also expect that we will always live in a succession of moments. Just as we will never attain to God's omniscience or omnipresence, so we shall never attain to God's eternity in the sense of seeing all time equally vividly and not living in a succession of moments or being limited by time.

As finite creatures, we will rather live in a succession of moments that will never end.[1302]

Wayne Grudem, *Systematic Theology*

Space has dimensions. It can be measured. It has directions: forward, backward, sideways, upward, downward. It has nearness and farness. To move in it from one point to another involves a going and a coming. When the Bible speaks of angels visiting this earth it indicates a coming *from* somewhere in the heavens *to* some place here on earth. Such movement from and to incurs succession: in other words, it takes *time*.[1303]

J. Sidlow Baxter, *The Other Side of Death*

To those in eternity, time may be like a book on our library bookshelf. If we choose, we can pick up and browse through it at random. We can enter the time sequence found in the book at any place we desire, follow it through for as long as we like, and then lay it down to reenter (in consciousness) the time sequence in which we normally live. In similar fashion those in eternity may select some period of history which they would like to live through and step back into that time, living out its events, though invisibly. This, of course, is pure speculation.[1304]

Ray C. Stedman, *Authentic Christianity*

Without the Curse time is no longer an enemy but a friend. It will never work against you. You won't run out of it. You'll want more and have more. No fear of losing a loved one, losing your health, or losing your mind.

Randy Alcorn, unpublished notes

Eternity is much more than either endless time or the end of time. It is the transformation of time. Time is, time dies and rises again in resurrection glory.

Randy Alcorn, unpublished notes

One writer says of Heaven, "It is certainly justifiable to abandon the scheme of time and space and to put in its place a divine simultaneity." This has a high-sounding resonance, but what does it mean? That we can be a thousand places at once, doing ten thousand different things? Those are the Creator's attributes, not the creature's. There's no evidence that we could be several places at once. The promise of Heaven is not that we will become infinite—that would be to become inhuman. It's that we'll be far better finite humans than we have ever been.[1305]

Randy Alcorn, *Heaven*

At the end of each day I'll have the same amount of time left as I did the day before. The things I didn't learn that day, the people I didn't see, the things I was unable to do—I can still learn, see, or do the next day. Places won't crumble, people won't die, and neither will I.[1306]

Randy Alcorn, *Heaven*

Many people believe that there will be no such thing as time on New Earth. They point to this verse, written by Peter: "A day is like a thousand years to the Lord, and a thousand years is like a day" (2 Peter 3:8).

But notice it says "to the Lord." It doesn't say "to human beings." Why? Because God has always existed (he is unlimited or infinite). But we had a beginning (we are limited or finite). He will always be the Creator, and we will always be creatures. God made us as physical and spiritual creatures to live in space and time.

Many people remember the phrase "time shall be no more" and think it's from the Bible. It's actually from an old hymn. That there is time in Heaven is made clear many places in the Bible:

We're told "there was silence throughout heaven for about half an hour" (Revelation 8:1).

Beings in Heaven relate to events as they happen on Earth, right down to rejoicing the moment a sinner on Earth repents (Luke 15:7).

People in Heaven ask God "how long"; then they are told by God to "wait a little longer" (Revelation 6:10-11). These words refer to lengths of time. . . .

When we have conversations in Heaven, they will have a beginning, a middle, and an end. All the words won't be spoken at once! (How weird would that be?) This means that we'll experience time in Heaven.

Some people get nervous or even scared about living forever. The idea of time going on and on bothers them. But that's because right now we are capable of getting tired and bored. So it naturally seems as if time that goes on forever would be boring. But the things that make us fearful of living forever will be completely gone. Once we're with the Lord, we'll be really excited to learn things about God and from God in a great new universe.

Time will always be our friend, never our enemy. We won't wish that time would slow down (like when we're having a great time laughing with family and friends at a pizza party) or speed up (like when we're waiting to ask Mom a question and she's on the phone). We won't be bored, and we won't have to stop doing what we love. Time in Heaven will always flow just right—it won't seem too long or too short![1307]

Randy Alcorn, *Heaven for Kids*

Paul spoke of Heaven in terms of "the coming ages" (Ephesians 2:7). He speaks not just of a future age but of ages (plural).

God's people in Heaven "serve him day and night in his temple" (Revelation 7:15).

The tree of life on the New Earth will be "yielding its fruit every month" (Revelation 22:2). There are days and months both in the present and eternal Heaven.

God says, "The new heavens and the new earth that I make will endure before me. . . . From one New Moon to another and from one Sabbath to another, all mankind will come and bow down before me" (Isaiah 66:22-23). New Moons and Sabbaths require moon, sun, and time.

The book of Revelation shows the present Heaven's inhabitants operating within time. The descriptions of worship include successive actions, such as falling down at God's throne and casting crowns before him (Revelation 4:10). There's a sequence of events; things occur one after another, not all at once.

The inhabitants of Heaven sing (Revelation 5:9-12). Music in Heaven requires time. Meter, tempo, and rests are all essential components of music, and each is time-related. Certain notes are held longer than others. Songs have a beginning, middle, and end. That means they take place in time.

. . . To say we'll exist outside of time is like saying we'll know everything. It confuses eternity with infinity. We'll live for eternity as finite beings. God can accommodate to us by putting himself into time, but we can't accommodate to him by becoming timeless. It's not in us to do so because we're not God.

. . . Will we still live in chronological sequence, where one word, step, or event follows the previous and is followed by the next? The Bible's answer is yes.[1308]

Randy Alcorn, *Heaven*

For too long we've allowed an unbiblical assumption ("there will be no time in Heaven") to obscure overwhelming biblical revelation to the contrary. This has served Satan's purposes of dehumanizing Heaven and divorcing it from the existence we know. Since we cannot desire what we can't imagine, this misunderstanding has robbed us of desire for Heaven.[1309]

Randy Alcorn, *Heaven*

Even though I believe we'll live in time, God is certainly capable of bending time and opening doors in time's fabric for us. Perhaps we'll be able to travel back and stand alongside angels in the invisible realm, seeing events as they happened on Earth. Maybe we'll learn the lessons of God's providence through direct observation. Can you imagine being there as Jesus preached the Sermon on the Mount? Perhaps you will be.

Want to see the crossing of the Red Sea? Want to be there when Daniel's three friends emerge from the fiery furnace? It would be simple for God to open the door to the past.

Because God is not limited by time, he may choose to show us past events as if they were presently happening. We may be able to study history from a front-row seat. Perhaps we'll have opportunity to see the lives of our spiritual and physical ancestors lived out on Earth.

Usually we're not able to see God's immediate responses to our prayers, but in Heaven God may permit us to see what happened in the spiritual realm as a result of his answers to our prayers. In the Old Testament an angel comes to the prophet Daniel and tells him what happened as the result of his prayers: "As soon as you began to pray, an answer was given, which I have come to tell you" (Daniel 9:23).

Will God show us in Heaven what almost happened to us on Earth? Will he take us back to see what would have happened if we'd made other choices? Perhaps. Will the father whose son had cerebral palsy see what would have happened if he'd followed his temptation to desert his family? Would this not fill his heart with gratitude to God for his sovereign grace?

Will I see how missing the exit on the freeway last night saved me from a crash? Will I learn how getting delayed in the grocery store last week saved my wife from a fatal accident? How many times have we whined and groaned about the very circumstances God used to save us? How many times have we prayed that God would make us Christlike, then begged him to take from us the very things he sent to make us Christlike? How many times has God heard our cries when we imagined he didn't? How many times has he said no to our prayers when saying yes would have harmed us and robbed us of good?[1310]

Randy Alcorn, *Heaven*

Uniting of Heaven and Earth

I saw a new heaven and a new earth, for the first
heaven and the first earth had passed away. . . . I saw
the Holy City, the new Jerusalem, coming down out
of heaven from God, prepared as a bride beautifully
dressed for her husband. And I heard a loud voice
from the throne saying, "Now the dwelling of God
is with men, and he will live with them. They will be
his people, and God himself will be with them and be
their God."

JOHN, REVELATION 21:1-3

After my body has decayed,
    yet in my body I will see God!
I will see him for myself.
      Yes, I will see him with my own eyes.
      I am overwhelmed at the thought!

JOB 19:26-27, NLT

When Revelation 21:1 and 2 Peter 3:10 say that the present earth and heavens will "pass away," it does not have to mean that they go out of existence, but may mean that there will be such a change in them that their present condition passes away. We might say, "The caterpillar passes away, and the butterfly emerges." There is a real passing away, and there is a real continuity, a real connection.[1311]

John Piper, *Future Grace*

In light of what we have been saying about the earthly creation and man's task of subduing and developing it, those purified works on the earth must surely include the products of human culture. There is no reason to doubt that they will be transfigured and transformed by their liberation from the curse, but they will be in essential continuity with our experience now—just as our resurrected bodies, though glorified, will still be bodies. . . . Perhaps the most fitting symbol of the development of creation from the primordial past to the eschatological future is the fact that the Bible begins with the garden and ends with a city—a city filled with "the glory and the honor of the nations."[1312]

Albert Wolters, *Creation Regained*

Wrong will be right, when Aslan comes in sight,
At the sound of his roar, sorrows will be no more,
When he bares his teeth, winter meets its death,
And when he shakes his mane, we shall have spring again.[1313]

Mr. Beaver, in *The Lion, the Witch and the Wardrobe,* by C. S. Lewis

Notions of heaven which see our future destiny as a "going up" to a distant, purely spiritual realm somewhere in the blue yonder . . . appear to need correction. Heaven is not so much a new world "up there" as a new world "down here." This is the element of validity in the dream of a millennial kingdom of Jesus here on earth. The doubtful dispensationalist schematic to which it is commonly tied should not blind us to the validity of the instinct to see God and his purposes vindicated in some real sense within this very world in which these purposes have been challenged by the incursion of evil.[1314]

Bruce Milne, *The Message of Heaven and Hell*

Since where God dwells, there heaven is, we conclude that in the life to come heaven and earth will no longer be separated, as they are now, but will be merged. Believers will therefore continue to be in heaven as they continue to live on the new earth.[1315]

Anthony Hoekema, *The Bible and the Future*

Since God will make the new earth his dwelling place, and since where God dwells there heaven is, we shall then continue to be in heaven while we are on the new earth. For heaven and earth will then no longer be separated as they are now, but they will be one. But to leave the new earth out of consideration when we think of the final state of believers is greatly to impoverish biblical teaching about the life to come.[1316]

Peter Toon, *Heaven and Hell: A Biblical and Theological Overview*

In physical strength and material size man is a mere nothing, even in comparison with the earth, which itself is scarcely even a speck of dust in the universe; in spiritual strength, in morality and intelligence, he ranks, at least at present, far beneath the angels of heaven, those mighty heroes, the executors of the Divine good pleasure (Psalm 103:21; cf. Psalm 8:3-6).

But what exalts him *above* all these creations is his calling to be united in an eternal fellowship of life and nature with Christ, the Son of the Highest.[1317]

Erich Sauer, *The King of the Earth*

Christians can be proheaven without being antiearth. The biblical heaven is not antimatter, but for restored and revised matter. Those committed to a biblical heaven do not despise the physical world. Because of the biblical vision of a new heaven and new earth, there is no cause to reject the anthropocentric over the theocentric models, for properly understood, they show two sides of the same reality, two orientations which are not incompatible. Therefore, for the Christian, the choice is not between heaven and earth, but the dual prochoice of heaven and earth in renewal.[1318]

John Gilmore, *Probing Heaven*

Jews were accustomed to thinking of heaven ahead, not heaven now. But Jesus relentlessly stressed the here-nowness of heaven (Matthew 6:33; 11:12; 12:28; Mark 10:15; Luke 12:31; 11:19ff). The arrival of the kingdom in Christ, however, did not rule out a future expression of it. In Jesus' arrival is heaven's extension. Heaven is where Jesus is. Where Jesus reigns, heaven resides.[1319]

John Gilmore, *Probing Heaven*

We are in the kingdom, and yet we look forward to its full manifestation; we share its blessings and yet await its total victory; we thank God for having brought us into the kingdom of the Son he loves, and yet we continue to pray, "Thy kingdom come."[1320]

Anthony Hoekema, *The Bible and the Future*

Ethically, the righteous children of God should never feel comfortable in this world of sin. The daily news reports of robbery, rape, murder, and their consequent cover-ups should remind us to cry out, as Christ taught us, for God's heavenly kingdom of righteousness to come quickly to this earth. However, no matter how evil this world becomes, we must never forget that *ontologically* we belong here. We were made from the earth so that we might live here forever. In this ontological, though not ethical sense, we're already home.[1321]

Michael Wittmer, *Heaven Is a Place on Earth*

The favourite Jewish figure of speech regarding the "labor pains of the Messiah" is apposite. They form the transition between this world and that of the future. The pains are a part of this world. They seem to stand in sharp contrast with the new world. Yet, they do not prove the absence of the future world, but precisely its hidden presence. The new world does not fall into the old like a bomb, nor does it take the place of the old which is destroyed, but it is born through the old in which it had been active. Although it is active, it is hidden to the extent that it can come into existence only through an unshackling, a redemption, and a great intervention. . . . We expect a new earth in the sense of a renewed one; this earth, but completely renewed. This world moves toward its end, but only because there it will meet its goal.[1322]

Hendrikus Berkhof, *Christ the Meaning of History*

Christians often talk about living with God "in heaven" forever, but in fact the biblical teaching is richer than that: it tells us that there will be new heavens and a new earth—an entirely renewed creation—and we will live with God there. . . . There will also be a new kind of unification of heaven and earth. . . . There will be a joining of heaven and earth in this new creation.[1323]

Wayne Grudem, *Systematic Theology*

Eternal heaven will be different from the heaven where God now dwells. . . . God will renovate the heavens and the earth, merging His heaven with a new universe for a perfect dwelling-place that will be our home forever. In other words, heaven, the realm where God dwells, will expand to encompass the entire universe of creation, which will be fashioned into a perfect and glorious domain fit for the glory of heaven. The apostle Peter described this as the hope of every redeemed person: "We, according to his promise, look for new heavens and a new earth, wherein dwelleth righteousness" (2 Peter 3:13, KJV). . . .

John writes, "I, John saw the holy city, new Jerusalem, coming down from God out of heaven, prepared as a bride adorned for her husband" (Revelation 21:2).

As John watches (Revelation 21), an entire city, magnificent in its glory, descends whole from heaven and becomes a part of the new earth. Heaven and earth are now one. The heavenly realm has moved its capital city intact to the new earth. Pay special attention to the key terms in this verse:

"*Prepared*" seems to imply that New Jerusalem had already been made ready before the creation of the new heavens and new earth. John does not say he saw the city being created. When he laid eyes on it, it was complete already. In other words, it was brought to the new earth from another place. Where is this place?

"*Coming down from God out of heaven*" indicates that the city—already complete and thoroughly furnished—descended to the new earth from the heavenly realm. . . . This occurs immediately after the new heaven and earth are created. New Jerusalem, the capital city of the eternal realm, descends right before John's eyes, out of the very realm of God, where it has already been "prepared." Who "prepared" it? Evidently this incredible heavenly city is precisely what our Lord spoke of when He told His disciples that He was going away to "prepare a place" for them (John 14:3). Now at the unveiling of the new heavens and new earth, the city is finally prepared and ready.

"*As a bride adorned for her husband.*" This speaks of the glory of this unimaginable city. Just think, when our Lord fashioned the material universe at the beginning of time, He did it in seven days. He has been working on heaven for nearly two millennia. What a wonder it must be! The surpassing glory of this city is too rich to express in words.[1324]

John MacArthur, *The Glory of Heaven*

"The earth will be full of the knowledge of the LORD as the waters cover the sea" (Isaiah 11:9). Heaven and earth will be as one; the new heavens and earth will be the dwelling place of man with God as well as of God with man. Then, in the mystery of God's grace, there will be what our souls will have longed for: heaven on earth. The dwelling of God will be with men and he will live with them (Revelation 21:3); a heavenly earth and an earthly heaven![1325]

Chuck McGowen, *Let's Talk about Heaven*

At the hour of death all becomes faith. Faith in God, who knows every fiber of our being and loves us in spite of our sins, is the narrow gate which connects this world with the next.[1326]

Henri Nouwen

If God annihilated the present cosmos, Satan would have won a great victory. He would have succeeded in so corrupting the cosmos that God would have had to completely do away with it. But Satan did not win such a victory. On the contrary, Satan has been decisively defeated. God will reveal the full dimensions of that defeat when he shall renew this very earth on which Satan deceived mankind and finally banish from it all the results of Satan's evil machinations.[1327]

Anthony Hoekema, *The Bible and the Future*

I saw a dying cosmos hold out its weak right arm, longing for a transfusion, a cure for its cancerous chasm. I saw the Woodsman, holding what appeared to be a tiny lump of coal, the same size as the blue-green marble he'd held before. The Woodsman squeezed his hand and the world around me darkened. Just as I felt I would scream from unbearable pressure, the crushed world emerged from his grip a diamond. I gasped air in relief.

I saw a new world, once more a life-filled blue-green, the old black coal delivered from its curse and pain and shame, wondrously remade.

It looked so easy for the Woodsman to shape all this with his hands. But then I saw his scars . . . and remembered it was not.[1328]

Nick Seagrave, in *Edge of Eternity,* by Randy Alcorn

Incarnation is about God inhabiting space and time as a human being—the new heavens and New Earth are about God making space and time his *eternal* home. As Jesus is God incarnate, so the New Earth will be Heaven incarnate [in physical form].[1329]

Randy Alcorn, *Heaven*

We do not just say what we believe—we end up believing what we say. . . . It's hard for us to think accurately about the New Earth because we're so accustomed to speaking of Heaven as the opposite of Earth. It may be difficult to retrain ourselves, but we should do it. We must teach ourselves to embrace the principle of continuity of people and the earth in the coming resurrection that Scripture teaches.[1330]

Randy Alcorn, *Heaven*

The gospel is far greater than most of us imagine. It isn't just good news for us—it's good news for animals, plants, stars, and planets. It's good news for the sky above and the Earth below.[1331]

Randy Alcorn, *We Shall See God*

If Jesus will resurrect people and flowers, might he also resurrect a specific flower arrangement given to a sick person that prompted a spiritual turning point? Might he resurrect a song or book written to his glory? or a letter written to encourage a friend or stranger? or a blanket a grandmother made for her grandchild? or a child's finger painting? or a man's log cabin built for his pioneer family? or a photograph album lovingly assembled by a devoted mother? or a baseball bat that a man handcrafted for his grandson's eleventh birthday?

Some may think it silly or sentimental to suppose that nature, animals, paintings, books, or a baseball bat might be resurrected. It may appear to trivialize the coming resurrection. I would suggest that it does exactly the opposite: It *elevates* resurrection, emphasizing the power of Christ to radically renew mankind—and far more. God promises to resurrect not only humanity but also the creation that fell as a result of our sin. Because God will resurrect the earth itself, we know that the resurrection of the dead extends to things that are inanimate. Even some of the works of our hands, done to God's glory, will survive. I may be mistaken on the details, but Scripture is clear that in some form, at least, what's done on Earth to Christ's glory will survive. Our error has not been in overestimating the extent of God's redemption and resurrection but *underestimating* it.[1332]

Randy Alcorn, *Heaven*

The marriage of the God of Heaven with the people of Earth will also bring the marriage of Heaven and Earth. There will not be two universes—one the primary home of God and angels, the other the primary home of humanity. Nothing will separate us from God, and nothing will separate Earth and Heaven. Once God and mankind dwell together, there will be no difference between Heaven and Earth. Earth will become Heaven—and it will truly be Heaven on Earth. The New Earth will be God's locus, his dwelling place. This is why I do not hesitate to call the New Earth "Heaven," for where God makes his home is Heaven. The purpose of God will at last be achieved.[1333]

Randy Alcorn, *Heaven*

The "new heaven" in Revelation 21:1 apparently refers to exactly the same atmospheric *and* celestial heavens as "heavens" does in Genesis 1:1. It also corresponds to the "new heaven(s)" of Isaiah 65:17, Isaiah 66:22, and 2 Peter 3:13. . . .

The new heavens will surely be superior to the old heavens, which themselves are filled with untold billions of stars and perhaps trillions of planets. God's light casts the shadows we know as stars, the lesser lights that point to God's substance. As the source is greater than the tributary, God, the Light, is infinitely greater than those little light-bearers we know as stars.

The Bible's final two chapters make clear that every aspect of the new creation will be greater than the old. Just as the present Jerusalem isn't nearly as great as the New Jerusalem, no part of the present creation—including the earth and the celestial heavens—is as great as it will be in the new creation.

. . . Earth is the first domain of mankind's stewardship, but it is not the only domain. Because the whole universe fell under mankind's sin, we can conclude that the whole universe was intended to be under mankind's dominion. If so, then the entire new universe will be ours to travel to, inhabit, and rule—to God's glory.

Do I seriously believe the new heavens will include new galaxies, planets, moons, white dwarf stars, neutron stars, black holes, and quasars? Yes. The fact that they are part of the first universe and that God called them "very good," at least in their original forms, means they will be part of the resurrected universe. When I look at the Horsehead Nebula and ask myself what it's like there, I think that one day I'll know. Just as I believe this "self-same body"—as the Westminster Confession put it—will be raised and the "self-same" Earth will be raised, I believe the "self-same" Horsehead Nebula will be raised. Why? Because it is part of the present heavens, and therefore will be raised as part of the new heavens.

Will the new planets be mere ornaments, or does God intend for us to reach them one day? Even under the Curse, we've been able to explore the moon, and we have the technology to land on Mars. What will we be able to accomplish for God's glory when we have resurrected minds, unlimited resources, complete scientific cooperation, and no more death? Will the far edges of our galaxy be within reach? And what about other galaxies, which are plentiful as blades of grass in a meadow? I imagine we will expand the borders of righteous mankind's Christ-centered dominion, not as conquerors who seize what belongs to others, but as faithful stewards who will occupy and manage the full extent of God's physical creation.[1334]

Randy Alcorn, *Heaven*

It isn't merely an accommodation to our earthly familial structure . . . that God calls himself a father and us children. On the contrary, he created father-child relationships to display his relationship with us, just as he created human marriage to reveal the love relationship between Christ and his bride (Ephesians 5:25-32). God's plan is that there will be no more gulf between the spiritual and physical worlds. There will be one cosmos, one universe united under one Lord—forever. This is where history is headed. This is the unstoppable plan of God.

When God walked with Adam and Eve in the Garden, Earth was Heaven's backyard. The New Earth will be even more than that—it will be Heaven itself. And those who know Jesus will have the privilege of living there. What Spurgeon calls the thin partition between Earth and Heaven will be forever broken through.[1335]

Randy Alcorn, *We Shall See God*

God promises to make not only a New Earth but also "new heavens" (Isaiah 65:17; 66:22; 2 Peter 3:13). The Greek and Hebrew words translated "heavens" include the stars and planets and what we call outer space. Since God will resurrect the old Earth and the old Jerusalem, transforming both into the new, shouldn't we understand "new heavens" as an expression of his intention to resurrect galaxies, nebulae, stars, planets, and moons in a form as close to their original form as the earth will be to its original form and we will be to ours?

The stars of the heavens declare God's glory (Psalm 19:1), yet how vast and distant they are. God made countless billions of galaxies containing perhaps trillions of nebulae, planets, and moons. Not many in human history have seen more than a few thousand stars, and then only as dots in the sky. If the heavens declare God's glory now, and if we will spend eternity proclaiming God's glory, don't you think exploring the new heavens, and exercising dominion over them, will likely be part of God's plan?

As a twelve-year-old, I first viewed through a telescope the great galaxy of Andromeda, consisting of hundreds of billions of stars and untold numbers of planets, nearly three million light years from Earth. I was mesmerized. I also wept, not knowing why. I was overwhelmed by greatness on a cosmic scale and felt terribly small and alone. Years later I first heard the gospel. After I became a Christian, I found that gazing through the telescope became an act of delighted worship.

From the night I first saw Andromeda's galaxy, I've wanted to go there. I now think it's likely I will.

Many of us have taken pleasure traveling on this earth. What will it be like to travel both the New Earth and the new universe? People didn't venture across oceans and to outer space because of sin. They did so because God made us with the yearning to explore and the creativity to make that yearning a reality. Have you ever read about people who have taken amazing journeys and wished you had the time, money, courage, or health to do the same? In the new universe, none of those restraints will hold us back.

It's hard for me to believe God made countless cosmic wonders intending that no human eye would ever behold them and that no human should ever set foot on them. The biblical accounts link mankind so closely with the physical universe and link God's celestial heavens so closely with the manifestation of his glory that I believe he intends us to explore the new universe. The universe will be our backyard, a playground and university always beckoning us to come explore the greatness of our Lord—as one song puts it, the God of wonders beyond our galaxy.[1336]

Randy Alcorn, *Heaven*

Work in Heaven

The man with the two talents also came. "Master," he said, "you entrusted me with two talents; see, I have gained two more." His master replied, "Well done, good and faithful servant! You have been faithful with a few things; I will put you in charge of many things. Come and share your master's happiness!"

JESUS, MATTHEW 25:22-23

From the fruit of his lips a man is filled with good things as surely as the work of his hands rewards him.

SOLOMON, PROVERBS 12:14

Restrain your voice from weeping and your eyes from tears, for your work will be rewarded.

GOD, JEREMIAH 31:16

Whatever you do, work at it with all your heart,
as working for the Lord, not for men.

PAUL, COLOSSIANS 3:23

[A man who has cleansed himself] will be an instrument for noble purposes, made holy, useful to the Master and prepared to do any good work.

PAUL, 2 TIMOTHY 2:21

You call on a Father who judges each man's work impartially.

PETER, 1 PETER 1:17

I know your deeds, your hard work and your perseverance.

JESUS, REVELATION 2:2

No longer will there be any curse. The throne of God and of the Lamb will be in the city, and his servants will serve him.

JOHN, REVELATION 22:3

Beyond the grave is resurrection, judgment, acquittal,
dominion. . . .
And after judgment, peace and rest, life and service,
employment and enjoyment, for thine elect.
O God, keep me in this faith, and ever looking for
Christ's return.[1337]

The Valley of Vision: A Collection of Puritan Prayers and Devotions

May I be prepared for all the allotments
of this short, changing, uncertain life,
with a useful residence in it,
a comfortable journey through it,
a safe passage out of it. . . .
May I be increasingly prepared for
life's remaining duties,
the solemnities of a dying hour,
and the joys and the services that lie beyond the grave.[1338]

The Valley of Vision: A Collection of Puritan Prayers and Devotions

The work on the other side, whatever be its character, will be adapted to each one's special aptitude and powers. It will be the work he can do best; the work that will give the fullest play to all that is within him. The energy stored up in his nature, instead of being withdrawn at death will rather be set free to work on in higher forms of service.

. . . This throws some measure of relieving light upon the painful mystery of a life brought to a sudden close. . . . In the presence of such a tragedy we instinctively ask, Why this waste? Is all the training, discipline, and culture of this choice spirit to be lost? It cannot be; for in God's universe nothing is ever lost. No preparation is ever in vain. There is need up there for clear heads, warm hearts, and skilled hands. . . . If some kinds of work are over, others will begin; if some duties are laid down, others will be taken up. And any regret for labour missed down here, will be swallowed up in the joyful anticipation of the higher service that awaits every prepared and willing worker in the upper kingdom of the Father.[1339]

James Campbell, *Heaven Opened*

Imagine a working environment free from the restrictions of time, money, selfishness, greed, sickness, tiredness, laziness, pain, frustration and even mistakes. How incredibly satisfying and rewarding work will be in heaven, doing what you love doing with people who love you and all for the glory of God.[1340]

Larry Dick, *A Taste of Heaven*

In heaven human powers will be at full stretch. . . . In heaven there will be added responsibilities for the redeemed, for there they will be given the responsibility of using talents taken from those who on earth abused them (Matthew 13:12).[1341]

Paul Helm, *The Last Things*

Although based upon sufficiency rather than scarcity, the economy of heaven may involve some form of currency exchange even if goods are held in common and each works for the benefit of all. The cosmos is a huge place, and if under divine order human beings exercise stewardship over different parts of it with complementary skills, some accounting system for exchange of goods and services may be in order. Why shouldn't accountants and bookkeepers have a chance to use their skills? We remain creatures with limits to understanding, and some need for boundaries. . . . If angels can get along without a system of currency and do the work of God throughout the cosmos, maybe incoming human settlers can, too.[1342]

Arthur Roberts, *Exploring Heaven*

There will always be some new joy to discover, some place to visit or revisit, some new dish to create, a new flower to breed, a new song to sing, a new poem to write, a new golf club to try out, a new lesson to learn and then pass on to someone else, some person to know more deeply, something new in our relationship with God. And this stretching and growing will go on forever.

Imagine what we will accomplish after working a few million years without the limitations of sin! If you enjoy culture, technology, and the triumph of the human spirit, you are really going to feel at home on the new earth.[1343]

Michael Wittmer, *Heaven Is a Place on Earth*

We are active by nature. Action, therefore, both of mind and body, is a law of our being, which cannot be changed without radically changing, or rather destroying, our whole nature. Instead of destroying it, it follows that in Heaven we shall be far more active than we can possibly be here below. . . . The soul of Jesus Christ enjoyed the Beatific Vision, even while here on earth in mortal flesh. Was He, on that account, prevented from doing anything except contemplating the divine essence? He certainly was not. He labored and preached; He also drank and slept; He visited His friends and did a thousand other things.[1344]

Father J. Boudreau, *The Happiness of Heaven*

If it falls your lot to be a street sweeper, sweep streets like Michelangelo painted pictures, sweep streets like Beethoven composed music, sweep streets like Shakespeare wrote poetry. Sweep streets so well that all the hosts of heaven and earth will have to pause and say: Here lived a great street sweeper who did his job well.[1345]

Martin Luther King Jr., to students at Barratt Junior High School, Philadelphia, October 26, 1967

When earth's last picture is painted
    And the tubes are twisted and dried,
    When the oldest colours have faded
    And the youngest critic has died,
    We shall rest, and faith, we shall need it
    Lay down for an aeon or two,
    Till the Master of All Good Workmen
    Shall put us to work anew. . . .
No one will work for the fame.
    But each for the joy of the working,
    And each, in his separate star,
    Will draw the thing as he sees it.
    For the God of things as they are! [1346]

Rudyard Kipling, "When Earth's Last Picture Is Painted"

Heaven will be a place of rest but not retirement. We will have plenty of fascinating, fulfilling things to do and an eternity to do them. Work is not a curse (even though we feel that way most Monday mornings). Work is a blessing we will pursue even after this life. . . . You aren't just punching the clock to pay the rent. You are working to please your boss—your *real* boss, Jesus Christ (Colossians 3:23-24).[1347]

Douglas Connelly, *The Promise of Heaven*

Divine rest is not only a pattern of what our earthly life may become, but it is a prophecy of what our heavenly life shall surely be . . . unless, indeed, we suppose that the Christian's life on earth and his condition in heaven are two utterly different things, possessing no feature in common. The Bible presents a directly reverse notion to that. . . .

There is a basis of likeness between the Christian life on earth and the Christian life in heaven, so great as that the blessings which are predicated of the one belong to the other. Only here they are in blossom, sickly often, putting out very feeble shoots and tendrils; and yonder transplanted into their right soil, and in their native air with heaven's sun upon them, they burst into richer beauty, and bring forth fruits of immortal life. Heaven is the earthly life of a believer glorified and perfected. If here we by faith enter into the beginning of rest, yonder through death with faith, we shall enter into the perfection of it. . . .

Heaven will be for us, rest in work and work that is full of rest. Our Lord's heaven is not an idle heaven. Christ is gone up on high, having completed His work on earth, that He may carry on His work in heaven; and after the pattern and likeness of His glory and of His repose, shall be the repose and glory of the children that are with Him. . . .

The cataract foaming down from the hillside, when seen from half-way across the lake, seems to stand a silent, still, icy pillar. The divine work, because it is such work, is rest—tranquil in its energy, quiet in its intensity; because so mighty, therefore so still! That is God's heaven, Christ's heaven.

The heaven of all spiritual natures is not idleness. Man's delight is activity. The loving heart's delight is obedience. The saved heart's delight is grateful service. The joys of heaven are not the joys of passive contemplation, of dreamy remembrance, of perfect repose; but they are described thus, "They rest not day nor night." "His servants serve Him, and see His face."

Yes, my brother, heaven is perfect "rest." God be thanked for all the depth of unspeakable sweetness which lies in that one little word, to the ears of all the weary and the heavy laden. God be thanked, that the calm clouds which gather round the western setting sun, and stretch their unmoving loveliness in perfect repose, and are bathed through and through with unflashing and tranquil light, seem to us in our busy lives and in our hot strife like blessed prophets of our state when we, too, shall lie cradled near the everlasting, unsetting Sun, and drink in, in still beauty of perpetual contemplation, all the glory of His face, nor know any more wind and tempest, rain and change.

Rest in heaven—rest in God! Yes, but work in rest! Ah, that our hearts should grow up into an energy of love of which we know nothing here, and that our hands should be swift to do service, beyond all that could be rendered on earth—that, never wearying, we should for ever be honoured by having work that never becomes toil nor needs repose; that, ever resting, we should ever be blessed by doing service which is the expression of our loving hearts, and the offering of our grateful and greatened spirits, joyful to us and acceptable to God— that is the true conception of "the rest that remaineth for the people of God." Heaven is waiting for us—like God's, like Christ's—still in all its work, active in all its repose.

See to it, my friend, that your life be calm because your soul is fixed, trusting in Jesus, who alone gives rest here to the heavy laden. Then your death will be but the passing from one degree of tranquillity to another, and the calm face of the corpse, whence all the lines of sorrow and care have faded utterly away, will be but a poor emblem of the perfect stillness into which the spirit has gone. Faith is the gate to partaking in the rest of God on earth. Death with faith is the gate of entrance into the rest of God in heaven.[1348]

Alexander Maclaren, "Entrance into God's Rest"

They shall then [in Heaven] be more aware than they are now, of the great love that was manifested in Christ that He should lay down His life for them. And then will Christ open to their view the great fountain of love in His heart for them, beyond all that they ever saw before. . . . The sight of His love, for that very reason, will fill them with greater joy, admiration and love to Him.

. . . If any or all of them are at times sent on errands of duty or mercy to distant worlds, . . . or employed, as some suppose them to be, as ministering spirits to friends in this world, they are still led by the influence of love, to conduct themselves, in all their behavior, in such a manner as is well pleasing to God, and thus conducive to their own and others' happiness.[1349]

Jonathan Edwards, *Heaven: A World of Love*

As man was made for the knowledge and service of God so it is unthinkable that in heaven which is the culmination of God's saving purposes for his church, the new creation (2 Corinthians 5:17), the new heaven and earth (Revelation 21:1), man will be released from that which is the most basic aspect of his calling. For his calling, when renewed in heaven, is to know and to serve God. It is mistaken therefore to think of heaven as sheer self-indulgence and self-gratification, just as it is mistaken to think of it as motionless rest. Rather it is that sphere in which mankind will serve God, and will know him in a fuller and more elevated way than was possible at the first. . . .

There will be no prospect of boredom in heaven because of the ever-new powers of creativity that men and women will be able to exercise there. As Edwards suggests, there will be growth and increase in heaven. This is another reminder that heaven is not the habitation of spirits, but a city of people, people made in the image of God and for his service.[1350]

Paul Helm, *The Last Things*

Then shall I see—and hear—and know
All I desired, or wished below;
And every power find sweet employ,
In that eternal world of joy.[1351]

Isaac Watts, "Delight in the Worship of the Sabbath"

In heaven we will be permitted to finish many of those worthy tasks which we had dreamed to do while on earth but which neither time nor strength nor ability allowed us to achieve.[1352]

Wilbur Smith, *The Biblical Doctrine of Heaven*

The question of what happens to me after death is *not* the major, central, framing question that centuries of theological tradition have supposed. The New Testament, true to its Old Testament roots, regularly insists that the major, central, framing question is that of God's purpose of rescue and re-creation for the whole world, the entire cosmos. The destiny of individual human beings must be understood within that context—not simply in the sense that we are only part of a much larger picture but also in the sense that part of the whole point of being saved in the present is so that we can play a vital role (Paul speaks of this role in the shocking terms of being "fellow workers with God") within that larger picture and purpose. And that in turn makes us realize that the question of our own destiny, in terms of the alternatives of joy or woe, is probably the wrong way of looking at the whole question. The question ought to be, *How will God's new creation come?* and then, *How will we humans contribute to that renewal of creation and to the fresh projects that the creator God will launch in his new world?*[1353]

N. T. Wright, *Surprised by Hope*

I feel within me that future life. I am like a forest that has been razed; the new shoots are stronger and brighter. I shall most certainly rise toward the heavens the nearer my approach to the end, the plainer is the sound of immortal symphonies of worlds which invite me. For half a century I have been translating my thoughts into prose and verse: history, drama, philosophy, romance, tradition, satire, ode, and song; all of these I have tried. But I feel I haven't given utterance to the thousandth part of what lies within me. When I go to the grave I can say, as others have said, "My day's work is done." But I cannot say, "My life is done." My work will recommence the next morning. The tomb is not a blind alley; it is a thoroughfare. It closes upon the twilight, but opens upon the dawn.[1354]

Victor Hugo, "The Future Life"

Consider Christ's activities: working in a carpenter shop, walking the countryside, fishing, sailing, meeting people, talking, teaching, eating—doing his life's work. Even after his resurrection he moved from place to place, connecting with his disciples and continuing his work. (A preview of life after our resurrection.)[1355]

Randy Alcorn, *Heaven*

What kind of work will we do in Heaven? Maybe you'll build a cabinet with Joseph of Nazareth. Or with Jesus. Maybe you'll tend sheep with David, discuss medicine with Luke, sew with Dorcas, make clothes with Lydia, design a new tent with Paul or Priscilla, write a song with Isaac Watts, ride horses with John Wesley, or sing with Keith Green. Maybe you'll write a theology of the Trinity, bouncing your thoughts off Paul, John, Polycarp, Cyprian, Augustine, Calvin, Wesley . . . and even Jesus.

Our work will be joyful and fulfilling, giving glory to God. What could be better?[1356]

Randy Alcorn, *Heaven*

On the New Earth, God will give us renewed minds and marvelously constructed bodies. We'll be whole people, full of energy and vision. . . . What will it be like to perform a task, to build and create, knowing that what we're doing will last? What will it be like to be always gaining skill, so that our best work will always be ahead of us? Because our minds and bodies will never fade and because we will never lack resources or opportunity, our work won't degenerate. Buildings won't last for only fifty years, and books won't be in print for only twenty years. They'll last forever.[1357]

Randy Alcorn, *Heaven*

Worship and Music

The ransomed of the LORD will return. They will enter Zion with singing; everlasting joy will crown their heads. Gladness and joy will overtake them, and sorrow and sighing will flee away.

ISAIAH 35:10

Speak to one another with psalms, hymns and spiritual songs. Sing and make music in your heart to the Lord, always giving thanks to God the Father for everything, in the name of our Lord Jesus Christ.

PAUL, EPHESIANS 5:19-20

Since we are receiving a kingdom that cannot be shaken, let us be thankful, and so worship God acceptably with reverence and awe.

HEBREWS 12:28

I looked and heard the voice of many angels, numbering thousands upon thousands, and ten thousand times ten thousand. They encircled the throne and the living creatures and the elders. In a loud voice they sang:

"Worthy is the Lamb, who was slain,
to receive power and wealth and wisdom and strength
and honor and glory and praise!"

Then I heard every creature in heaven and on earth and under the earth and on the sea, and all that is in them, singing:

"To him who sits on the throne and to the Lamb
be praise and honor and glory and power,
              for ever and ever!"

The four living creatures said, "Amen," and the elders fell down and worshiped.

JOHN, REVELATION 5:11-14

I saw before me what seemed to be a glass sea mixed with fire. And on it stood all the people who had been victorious over the beast and his statue and the number representing his name. They were all holding harps that God had given them. And they were singing the song of Moses, the servant of God, and the song of the Lamb: "Great and marvelous are your works, O Lord God, the Almighty. Just and true are your ways, O King of the nations. Who will not fear you, Lord, and glorify your name? For you alone are holy. All nations will come and worship before you, for your righteous deeds have been revealed."

JOHN, REVELATION 15:2-4, NLT

Let everything that has breath praise the LORD.

PSALM 150:6

O may angels glorify him incessantly,
and, if possible, prostrate themselves lower
before the blessed king of heaven!
I long to bear a part with them in ceaseless praise;
But when I have done all I can to eternity
I shall not be able to offer more than
a small fraction of the homage
that the glorious God deserves.[1358]

The Valley of Vision: A Collection of Puritan Prayers and Devotions

Even announcing that we are going to preach about worship must start the wings of the seraphim in heaven to waving and the organs to playing, because heaven exists to worship God. The atmosphere and the very breezes that flow out of heaven are filled with divine worship.

The health of the world is worship. When intelligent, moral creatures are in tune in worship, we have the symphony of creation. But anywhere there is not worship, there is discord and broken strings. When all the full redeemed universe is back once more worshiping God in full voice, happily and willingly, then we will see the new creation—the new heaven and the new earth.

In the meantime you and I, belonging to another creation, are called upon to worship God. And it says, "He is thy Lord; and worship thou him" (Psalm 45:11 [KJV]).[1359]

A. W. Tozer, *Tozer on Worship and Entertainment*

Since heaven itself is God's temple, every place we go, everything we do, and every conversation we have will be an act of worship. This is worship as it was meant to be.[1360]

Tony Evans, *Tony Evans Speaks Out on Heaven and Hell*

How much there will be to talk about! What wondrous wisdom will appear in everything that we had to go through in the days of our flesh! We shall remember all the way by which we were led, and say, "Goodness and mercy followed me all the days of my life. In my sicknesses and pains, in my losses and crosses, in my poverty and tribulations, in my bereavement and separation, in every bitter cup I had to drink, in every burden I had to carry, in all these were perfect wisdom."[1361]

J. C. Ryle, *Heaven*

Worship in heaven is centered on the person of Jesus Christ. Without a personal relationship to Him, worship is meaningless and boring and so is the thought of serving Him forever. Those who don't know Him won't be there anyway. For the redeemed, this is what we have been waiting for, to see Christ and know Him forever.

What an incredible moment to finally meet Jesus face to face and hear Him say, "Well done."[1362]

Larry Dick, *A Taste of Heaven*

There is nothing unearthly or un-creational about worship. . . . It is not a time when we shed our human selves; it is a time when we are most fully human. . . . We touch the source of our lives, our hopes, and our salvation.[1363]

Paul Marshall, *Heaven Is Not My Home*

The most ecstatic orgasm ever experienced in a love-caressed marriage won't hold a candle to what touch and taste and smell and sight and sound will bring to "children of the resurrection," to persons sanctified and glorified by the Holy Spirit. I can imagine capacities for love expressions in a magnitude of self-fulfilling powers only hinted at by earthside joys of sex and companionship. . . . We worship. . . . What a thrill to be in the presence of God the creator and all the angels and inhabitants of heaven! To experience such unity with the Divine![1364]

Arthur Roberts, *Exploring Heaven*

Ibi vacabimus et videbimus, videbimus et amabimus, amabimus et laudabimus. Esse quod erit in fine sine fine. ["There we shall rest and we shall see, we shall see and we shall love, we shall love and we shall praise. Behold what shall be in the end without end."][1365]

Augustine, *The City of God*

No legitimate activity of life—whether in marriage, family, business, play, friendship, education, politics, etc.—escapes the claims of Christ's kingship. . . . Certainly those who live and reign with Christ forever will find the diversity and complexity of their worship of God not less, but richer, in the life to come. Every legitimate activity of new creaturely life will be included within the life of worship of God's people.[1366]

Cornelius Venema, *The Promise of the Future*

Music certainly is prominent in the descriptions of heaven in Revelation, and we might imagine that both musical and artistic activities would be done to the glory of God. Perhaps people will work at the whole range of investigation and development of the creation by technological, creative, and inventive means, thus exhibiting the full extent of their excellent creation in the image of God.[1367]

Wayne Grudem, *Systematic Theology*

> *In mansions of glory and endless delight,*
> *I'll ever adore Thee in heaven so bright;*
> *I'll sing with the glittering crown on my brow,*
> *If ever I loved Thee, my Jesus, 'tis now.*[1368]

William Featherston, "My Jesus I Love Thee"

How great shall be that felicity, which shall be tainted with no evil, which shall lack no good, and which shall afford leisure for the praises of God, who shall be all in all![1369]

Augustine, *The City of God*

When we begin to stand up to assume another posture of praise before His throne, we will receive another revelation that will send us to our knees again. Over and over and over we will learn of the mercies of our God. Again and again His wonders will be made known to us that we might sing His praises throughout all eternity.[1370]

Daniel Brown, *What the Bible Reveals about Heaven*

The best, most beautiful, and most perfect way that we have of expressing a sweet concord of mind to each other is by music.[1371]

Jonathan Edwards, *The Miscellanies*

One of the reasons we struggle with the idea of worship in heaven is that we find worship on earth so routine, so predictable. We gather with other believers and say we have come together to worship God, but if we are honest, we are focused far more on ourselves than on the Lord. We've fallen into the trap of thinking that we are the audience in worship and that the performers are the professionals up front. Nothing will kill the spirit of genuine worship more effectively than sitting in a comfortable seat, just watching the show. . . .

The only audience in worship is God. He is the one we are gathered to honor and praise and exalt. His character, his goodness, his grace and mercy and forgiveness are the focus of true worship. . . . Our single goal is to please our Audience. . . . The Audience we are striving to please is not impressed with the outward motions of worship. He is impressed with the attitude of our hearts before him and with the sacrifice we offer of our praise to him.[1372]

Douglas Connelly, *The Promise of Heaven*

What thrills me most about our heavenly praise is that it will be perfect. Many times I want to praise God with all my heart, but other thoughts crowd in and clutter my mind. Have you ever been praising

God when some evil or trivial thought entered your mind, or some nonsensical notion interrupted your praise? How discouraging to realize how earthbound we are! In heaven our praise will always come out of pure hearts with pure motives and no distractions.[1373]

John MacArthur, *Heaven: Selected Scriptures*

The sole justification for praising God is that God is praiseworthy. We do not praise God because it does us good, though no doubt it does. Nor do we praise Him because it does Him good, for in fact it does not. Praise is thus strictly ecstatic. . . . Praise is entirely directed upon God. It takes our attention entirely off ourself and concentrates it entirely upon Him.[1374]

E. L. Maskell, *Grace and Glory*

I don't know whether we'll have wristwatches on the New Earth, but if we do, we won't be looking at them during worship.

Randy Alcorn, unpublished notes

I love the ocean—the constant reassuring sound of the tide, the waves form a comforting backdrop. In Heaven, wherever we travel in the Holy City or to the far corners of the universe, the backdrop sound will be this—day and night the chant of the four living creatures who never, even for a moment, stop speaking the praise of God: "Holy, holy, holy is the Lord God Almighty, who was, and is, and is to come" (Revelation 4:8).

Randy Alcorn, notes

Music is transcendent—a bridge between this world and another. That's why people devote so much of themselves to it and gain such pleasure in it. . . . In Heaven God will unleash our creativity, not confine it. As a musical novice, I might compose something worthy of Bach. And what kind of music do you suppose Bach will compose?

It's God, not Satan, who made us to dance. If you believe that Satan invented dancing or that dancing is inherently sinful, you give Satan too much credit and God too little. God placed within us an instinctive physical response to music. As music is a means of worship, so is dancing. True, some dancing dishonors God, just as some eating, drinking, prayer, and religious activities dishonor God. Unfortunately, much dancing has become associated with immorality and immodesty. But, of course, that kind of dancing won't exist on the New Earth.[1375]

Randy Alcorn, *Heaven*

At times throughout the day, as I work in my office, I find myself on my knees thanking God for his goodness. When I eat a meal with my wife, talk with a friend, or take our dog for a walk, I worship God for his goodness. The world is full of praise-prompters—the New Earth will overflow with them. I've found great joy in moments where I've been lost in worship—many of them during church services—but they're too fleeting. If you've ever had a taste of true worship, you crave *more* of it, never less.[1376]

Randy Alcorn, *Heaven*

If someone rescued you and your family from terrible harm, especially at great cost to himself, no one would need to tell you, "Better say thank you." On your own, you would shower him with praise. Even more will you sing your Savior's praises and tell of his life-saving deeds.[1377]

Randy Alcorn, *Heaven*

We rejoined our comrades in the great camp of Charis, embracing and shedding tears and slapping each other on the back. Suddenly warriors around me turned toward the masses of untold millions gathered in Charis. The army began to sing, perhaps hundreds of thousands, perhaps a million.

"Elyon miriel o aeron galad, chara domina beth charis o aleathes celebron!"

I added my voice to theirs and sang the unchained praises of the King. Only for a moment did I hear my own voice, amazed to detect the increased intensity of the whole. One voice, even mine, made a measurable difference. But from then on I was lost in the choir, hardly hearing my voice and not needing to.

As we sang to the gathered throngs of Charis, the sheer power of their voices, *our* voices, nearly bowled me over.

Then suddenly the multitudes before us sang back to us and our voices were drowned by theirs. We who a moment earlier seemed the largest choir ever assembled now proved to be only the small worship ensemble that led the full choir of untold millions, now lost to themselves. We sang together in full voice, "To him who made the galaxies, who became the Lamb, who stretched out on the tree, who crossed the chasm, who returned the Lion! Forever!"

The song's harmonics reached out and grabbed my body and my soul. I became the music's willing captive.

I knew now that all my life I had caught occasional strains of the music of Charis. But it was elusive, more like an echo. All that clatter, all those competing sounds, all the CDs and sitcoms and ringing phones and blowing horns and nagging voices drowned out the real music. I'd spent my life humming the wrong tunes, dancing to the wrong beat, marching to the wrong anthem.

No longer—for at long last I heard, undiluted, the song for which I was made. And I not only heard the song, I sang it!

The galaxies and nebulae sang with us the royal song. It echoed off a trillion planets and reverberated in a quadrillion places in every nook and cranny of the universe. The song generated the light of a billion burning supernovae. It blotted out all lesser lights and brought a startling clarity to the way things really were. It didn't blind, it illuminated and I saw as never before.

At long last, things *were* as they appeared.

Our voices broke into thirty-two distinct parts, and instinctively I knew which of them I was made to sing. "We sing for joy at the work of your hands. . . . We stand in awe of you." It felt indescribably wonderful to be lost in something so much greater than myself.

There was no audience, I thought for a moment, for audience and orchestra and choir all blended into one great symphony, one grand cantata of rhapsodic melodies and powerful sustaining harmonies.

No, wait, there *was* an audience. An audience so vast and all-encompassing that for a moment I'd been no more aware of it than a fish is aware of water.

I looked at the great throne, and upon it sat the King . . . the Audience of One.

The smile of his approval swept through the choir like fire across dry wheat fields.

When we completed our song, the one on the throne stood and raised up his great arms and clapped his scarred hands together in thunderous applause, shaking ground and sky, jarring every corner of the cosmos. His applause went on and on, unstopping and unstoppable.

And in that moment I knew, with unwavering clarity, that the King's approval was all that mattered—and ever would.[1378]

Nick Seagrave, in *Edge of Eternity*, by Randy Alcorn

We were all made for a person and a place. Jesus is the person. Heaven is the place.

If you know Jesus, I'll be with you in that resurrected world. With the Lord we love and with the friends we cherish, we'll embark together on the ultimate adventure, in a spectacular new universe awaiting our exploration and dominion. Jesus will be the center of all things, and joy will be the air we breathe.

And right when we think "it doesn't get any better than this"— *it will*.[1379]

Randy Alcorn, *Heaven*

Notes

1. W. H. Griffith Thomas, cited by Charles Ferguson Ball, *Heaven* (Wheaton, IL: Victor Books, 1980), 9.
2. C. S. Lewis, *Letters to Malcolm* (New York: Harcourt, Brace and World, 1964), 124.
3. Charles H. Spurgeon, "Feeble Faith Appealing to a Strong Savior," Sermon 2881, March 19, 1876.
4. C. S. Lewis, *The Last Battle* (New York: HarperCollins, 2001), 742.
5. C. S. Lewis, *The Last Battle* (New York: Macmillan, 1956), 173.
6. Bruce Milne, *The Message of Heaven and Hell* (Downers Grove, IL: InterVarsity Press, 2002), 143.
7. Ibid., 197.
8. Daniel A. Brown, PhD, *What the Bible Reveals about Heaven* (Ventura, CA: Regal Books, 1999), 83.
9. Jonathan Edwards, *Heaven: A World of Love* (Amityville, NY: Calvary Press, 1999), 31.
10. Peter Kreeft, *Everything You Ever Wanted to Know about Heaven* (San Francisco: Ignatius Press, 1990), 29.
11. Larry R. Dick, *A Taste of Heaven* (Victoria, BC: Trafford Publishing, 2002), 140.
12. Steven J. Lawson, *Heaven Help Us!* (Colorado Springs: NavPress, 1995), 189.
13. Ibid., 194.
14. Arthur O. Roberts, *Exploring Heaven* (San Francisco: HarperSanFrancisco, 2003), 5.
15. Richard Baxter, *The Saints' Everlasting Rest* (Edinburgh: Waugh and Innes, 1824), 250.
16. Drake W. Whitchurch, *Waking from Earth* (Kearney, NE: Morris Publishing, 1999), 120–121.
17. George MacDonald, *The Heart of George MacDonald*, ed. Rolland Hein (Vancouver, BC: Regent College, 2004), 15.
18. Joni Eareckson Tada, quoted in Douglas J. Rumford, *What about Heaven and Hell?* (Carol Stream, IL: Tyndale House, 2000), 31.
19. Arthur O. Roberts, *Exploring Heaven* (San Francisco: HarperSanFrancisco, 1989), 139–140.
20. C. S. Lewis, *Miracles* (New York: Macmillan, 1947), 169.
21. T. S. Eliot, *T. S. Eliot: The Complete Poems and Plays* (London: Faber and Faber, 2004), last of "The Four Quartets."
22. Walton J. Brown, *Home at Last* (Washington, DC: Review and Herald Publishing, 1983), 81.
23. Edward Donnelly, *Biblical Teaching on the Doctrines of Heaven and Hell* (Edinburgh: Banner of Truth, 2001), 123.
24. E. J. Fortman, SJ, *Everlasting Life after Death* (New York: Alba House, 1976), 313.
25. Ray C. Stedman, "The City of Glory," a sermon, April 1990, http://www.pbc.org/messages /the-city-of-glory.

26. Randy Alcorn, *Heaven* (Carol Stream, IL: Tyndale House, 2004), 405.

27. Ibid., 413.

28. Randy Alcorn, *50 Days of Heaven* (Carol Stream, IL: Tyndale House, 2006), 257–258.

29. Randy Alcorn, *Money, Possessions, and Eternity* (Carol Stream, IL: Tyndale House, 2003), 115.

30. Randy Alcorn, *We Shall See God* (Carol Stream, IL: Tyndale House, 2011), 12.

31. Randy Alcorn, *Heaven* (Carol Stream, IL: Tyndale House, 2004), 277.

32. Ibid., 274.

33. Ibid., 416.

34. Ibid., 433.

35. Ibid., 303.

36. Ibid., 213.

37. Ibid., 215.

38. Charles H. Spurgeon, "Obtaining Promises," Sermon 435, February 16, 1862, as cited in Randy Alcorn, *We Shall See God* (Carol Stream, IL: Tyndale House, 2011), 238.

39. Charles H. Spurgeon, *Morning and Evening*, February 7 (morning).

40. James T. Jeremiah, *The Place Called Heaven* (Schaumburg, IL: Regular Baptist Press, 1991), 21.

41. Alister E. McGrath, *A Brief History of Heaven* (Oxford: Blackwell Publishing, 2003), 5.

42. Bruce Milne, *The Message of Heaven and Hell* (Downers Grove, IL: InterVarsity Press, 2002), 275.

43. Larry Dixon, *Heaven: Thinking Now about Forever* (Camp Hill, PA: Christian Publications, 2002), 65.

44. Mark Buchanan, *Things Unseen* (Sisters, OR: Multnomah Publishers, 2002), 29.

45. J. C. Ryle, *Heaven* (Ross-shire, UK: Christian Focus Publications, 2000), 21–23.

46. Edward Judson, *The Life of Adoniram Judson* (Philadelphia: American Baptist Publication Society, 1883), 539–540.

47. Colleen McDannell and Bernhard Lang, *Heaven: A History* (New York: Vintage Books, 1988), 307.

48. Charles H. Spurgeon, quoted in Paul Lee Tan, *Encyclopedia of 7700 Illustrations* (Garland, TX: Bible Communications, 1996).

49. Mark Buchanan, *Things Unseen* (Sisters, OR: Multnomah Publishers, 2002), 43.

50. Ibid., 49–53.

51. Steven J. Lawson, *Heaven Help Us!* (Colorado Springs: NavPress, 1995), 158.

52. Martin Luther, as cited in Randy Alcorn, *We Shall See God* (Carol Stream, IL: Tyndale House, 2011), 209.

53. Samuel Rutherford, quoted in Charles H. Spurgeon, *Morning and Evening*, January 17 (morning).

54. Mark Buchanan, *Things Unseen* (Sisters, OR: Multnomah Publishers, 2002), 30.

55. Frederick Buechner, *The Magnificent Defeat* (New York: Seabury Press, 1966), 1.

56. Jean Fleming, *The Homesick Heart* (Colorado Springs: NavPress, 1995), 17–18.

57. C. S. Lewis, *Till We Have Faces* (Grand Rapids, MI: Eerdmans, 1956), 74–76.

58. Jean Fleming, *The Homesick Heart* (Colorado Springs: NavPress, 1995), 24.

59. A. W. Tozer, *The Size of the Soul* (Harrisburg, PA: Christian Publications, 1992), 17–18.

60. Isak Dinesen, *Babette's Feast and Other Anecdotes of Destiny* (New York: Random House, 1986), 53.

61. C. S. Lewis, *Mere Christianity* (New York: Macmillan, 1960), 120.

62. John Baillie, *A Diary of Private Prayer* (New York: Charles Scribner's Sons, 1949), 53.

63. C. S. Lewis, *Mere Christianity* (New York: Macmillan, 1960), 119.

64. Dietrich Bonhoeffer, *Letters and Papers from Prison*, trans. Reginald H. Fuller (New York: Touchstone, 1971), 169.

65. Joni Eareckson Tada, *Heaven: Your Real Home* (Grand Rapids, MI: Zondervan, 1997), 68.

66. Blaise Pascal, *Pensées*, para. 398, 425, quoted in John Eldredge, *The Journey of Desire* (Nashville: Thomas Nelson, 2000), 12–13.

67. C. S. Lewis, *The Problem of Pain* (New York: Macmillan, 1962), 115.
68. A. W. Tozer and H. Verploegh, *The Quotable Tozer II* (Camp Hill, PA: WingSpread, 1997), 102.
69. G. K. Chesterton, *Orthodoxy* (Chicago: Thomas More Association, 1985), 99–100, chapter 5.
70. Cyprian, *Mortality*, chapter 26.
71. Charles H. Spurgeon, *Morning and Evening*, April 25 (morning).
72. Donald Bloesch, *Theological Notebook* (Colorado Springs: Helmers and Howard, 1989), 183.
73. C. S. Lewis, *The Problem of Pain* (New York: Macmillan, 1962), 43.
74. C. S. Lewis, *The Weight of Glory* (New York: HarperCollins, 2001), 37.
75. Mark Buchanan, *Things Unseen* (Sisters, OR: Multnomah Publishers, 2002), 49–50.
76. C. S. Lewis, *The Weight of Glory* (New York: HarperCollins, 2001), 41–42.
77. Claire Cloninger and Paul Smith, quoted in Gary Moon, *Homesick for Eden* (Ann Arbor, MI: Servant Publications, 1997), 39.
78. Thomas à Kempis, *The Imitation of Christ*, trans. F. A. Paley, book 2, chapter 1.
79. Joseph Bayly, *A Voice in the Wilderness* (Grand Rapids, MI: Zondervan, 2000), 256.
80. E. X. Heatherley, *Our Heavenly Home* (Austin, TX: Balcony Publishing, 2000), 13.
81. Randy Alcorn, *50 Days of Heaven* (Carol Stream, IL: Tyndale House, 2006), 113–114.
82. Randy Alcorn, *In Light of Eternity* (Colorado Springs: WaterBrook, 1984), 10–11.
83. Randy Alcorn, *TouchPoints: Heaven* (Carol Stream, IL: Tyndale House, 2008), 82–83.
84. Randy Alcorn, *Heaven* (Carol Stream, IL: Tyndale House, 2004), 78.
85. Ibid., 153.
86. Randy Alcorn, *We Shall See God* (Carol Stream, IL: Tyndale House, 2011), 45.
87. Randy Alcorn, *Heaven* (Carol Stream, IL: Tyndale House, 2004), 439.
88. Randy Alcorn, *We Shall See God* (Carol Stream, IL: Tyndale House, 2011), 85.
89. Arthur Bennett, ed., *The Valley of Vision* (Carlisle, PA: Banner of Truth, 2002), 370.
90. Ibid., 371.
91. Jonathan Edwards, *Heaven: A World of Love* (Amityville, NY: Calvary Press, 1999), 24.
92. Jonathan Edwards, *The Works of Jonathan Edwards: The Miscellanies* (New Haven, CT: Yale University Press, 1994), 341.
93. Charles H. Spurgeon, "God Rejoicing in the New Creation," Sermon 2211, July 5, 1891, as cited in Randy Alcorn, *We Shall See God* (Carol Stream, IL: Tyndale House, 2011), 151.
94. Peter Toon, *Heaven and Hell* (Nashville: Thomas Nelson, 1986), 204.
95. Father J. Boudreau, SJ, *The Happiness of Heaven* (Rockford, IL: TAN Books, 1984), 129–130.
96. Elizabeth Barrett Browning, *Aurora Leigh* (New York: C. J. Francis, 1857), 275.
97. Nicholas Berdyaev, *The Divine and the Human* (London: G. Bles, 1949), 139.
98. Arthur O. Roberts, *Exploring Heaven* (San Francisco: HarperSanFrancisco, 2003), 60.
99. C. S. Lewis, *Screwtape Proposes a Toast* (London: Collins, 1995), 99.
100. Gordon R. Lewis and Bruce A. Demarest, *Integrative Theology* (Grand Rapids, MI: Zondervan, 1996), 3:480–481.
101. Drake W. Whitchurch, *Waking from Earth* (Kearney, NE: Morris Publishing, 1999), 101.
102. Percy Bysshe Shelley, "Prometheus Unbound," in *The Poetical Works of Percy Bysshe Shelley* (Philadelphia: Crissy and Markley, 1847), 144.
103. C. S. Lewis, *The Weight of Glory* (Grand Rapids, MI: Eerdmans, 1949), 13.
104. N. T. Wright, *Surprised by Hope* (New York: HarperCollins, 2008), 222, 224.
105. A. W. Tozer, *Born after Midnight* (Camp Hill, PA: Christian Publications, 1992), 138.
106. James Montgomery, *The Poetical Works of Rogers, Campbell, J. Montgomery, Lamb, and Kirke White* (Philadelphia: Grigg and Elliot, 1843), 337.
107. Randy Alcorn, *We Shall See God* (Carol Stream, IL: Tyndale House, 2011), 11.
108. Randy Alcorn, *Heaven* (Carol Stream, IL: Tyndale House, 2004), 251.
109. Randy Alcorn, *Safely Home* (Carol Stream, IL: Tyndale House, 2001), 376–377.
110. Arthur Bennett, ed., *The Valley of Vision* (Carlisle, PA: Banner of Truth, 2002), 48.
111. Benjamin Calamy, *Sermons Preached upon Several Occasions by Benjamin Calamy* (London: Cambridge University Library, 1687), 495.

112. John Piper, "What Happens When You Die?" *Desiring God,* July 25, 1993, http://tinyurl.com/4y9kqjw.

113. Anthony A. Hoekema, "Heaven: Not Just an Eternal Day Off," *Christianity Today*, June 6, 2003, http://www.christianitytoday.com/ct/2003/122/54.0.html.

114. Charles H. Spurgeon, "A Prepared Place for a Prepared People," Sermon 2751, May 25, 1879, as cited in Randy Alcorn, *We Shall See God* (Carol Stream, IL: Tyndale House, 2011), 201.

115. Charles H. Spurgeon, "God Rejoicing in the New Creation," Sermon 2211, July 5, 1891, as cited in Randy Alcorn, *We Shall See God* (Carol Stream, IL: Tyndale House, 2011), 150.

116. R. A. Torrey, *Heaven or Hell* (New Kensington, PA: Whitaker House, 1985), 68.

117. Timothy George, "Heavenly Bodies," *Christianity Today*, February 2003, 84.

118. Augustine, *The City of God*, 22:19, 2; 22:20, 3 (PL 41:781.783).

119. N. T. Wright, *Surprised by Hope* (New York: HarperCollins, 2008), 43–44.

120. Charles H. Spurgeon, "The Resurrection of the Dead," Sermons 66–67, February 17, 1856.

121. Arthur O. Roberts, *Exploring Heaven* (San Francisco: HarperSanFrancisco, 2003), 37.

122. Isaac Watts, *The World to Come* (Morgan, PA: Soli Deo Gloria Publications, 1954 [1745]), 85.

123. John Piper, *Future Grace* (Sisters, OR: Multnomah Publishers, 1995), 374.

124. T. W. Hunt and Melana Hunt Monroe, *From Heaven's View* (Nashville: Broadman and Holman Publishers, 2002), 235.

125. Larry R. Dick, *A Taste of Heaven* (Victoria, BC: Trafford Publishing, 2002), 118.

126. Ibid., 49.

127. Father J. Boudreau, SJ, *The Happiness of Heaven* (Rockford, IL: TAN Books, 1984), 67–68.

128. Ibid., 87.

129. Jill Briscoe, *Heaven and Hell* (Wheaton, IL: Victor Books, 1990), 35–36.

130. Peter Kreeft, *Everything You Ever Wanted to Know about Heaven* (San Francisco: Ignatius Press, 1990), 93.

131. Arthur O. Roberts, *Exploring Heaven* (San Francisco: HarperSanFrancisco, 2003), 31.

132. N. T. Wright, *Surprised by Hope* (New York: HarperCollins, 2008), 159–161.

133. Charles H. Spurgeon, "Creation's Groans and the Saints' Sighs," Sermon 788, January 5, 1868, as cited in Randy Alcorn, *We Shall See God* (Carol Stream, IL: Tyndale House, 2011), 27–28.

134. Joni Eareckson Tada, *Heaven: Your Real Home* (Grand Rapids, MI: Zondervan, 1995), 53.

135. Wayne Grudem, *Systematic Theology* (Grand Rapids, MI: Zondervan, 1994), 1158–1164.

136. Charles Ferguson Ball, *Heaven* (Wheaton, IL: Victor Books, 1980), 38.

137. Thomas C. Oden, *Life in the Spirit*, vol. 3 of *Systematic Theology* (San Francisco: HarperSanFrancisco, 1992), 402.

138. J. Sidlow Baxter, *The Other Side of Death* (Grand Rapids, MI: Kregel Publications, 1987), 48–49.

139. Charles H. Spurgeon, "God Rejoicing in the New Creation," Sermon 2211, July 5, 1891, as cited in Randy Alcorn, *We Shall See God* (Carol Stream, IL: Tyndale House, 2011), 152.

140. Martin Luther, "Enemies of the Cross of Christ" (Sermon for the 23rd Sunday after Trinity), sections 31–35 in *Sermons of Martin Luther*. Ed. John Nicholas Lenker. Taken from *Sermons on Epistle Texts,* Vol. 8, 356–357. Reprinted Grand Rapids, MI: Baker Book House, 1983. Reproduction of *Luther's Epistle Sermons,* Vol. 3. Minneapolis: Luther Press, 1909.

141. Randy Alcorn, *Heaven* (Carol Stream, IL: Tyndale House, 2004), 256–257.

142. Ibid., 114.

143. Ibid., 295.

144. Randy Alcorn, *TouchPoints: Heaven* (Carol Stream, IL: Tyndale House, 2008), 86–87.

145. Peter Kreeft, *Everything You Ever Wanted to Know about Heaven* (San Francisco: Ignatius Press, 1990), 19–20.

146. Isaac Asimov, quoted in *Words from the Wise*, ed. Rosemary Jarski (New York: Skyhorse Publishing, 2007), 18.

147. Mark Twain, *The Adventures of Huckleberry Finn* (New York: Fawcett Columbine, 1996), 6.

148. Mark Buchanan, *Things Unseen* (Sisters, OR: Multnomah Publishers, 2002), 66–67.

149. John Eldredge, *The Journey of Desire* (Nashville: Nelson, 2000), 111.

150. Peter Rowland, *David Lloyd George* (New York: Macmillan, 1976), 13.

151. Richard Brooks, *The Doors of Heaven* (Ross-shire, UK: Christian Focus Publications, 1998), 80.

152. Peter Kreeft, *Everything You Ever Wanted to Know about Heaven* (San Francisco: Ignatius Press, 1990), 19.

153. Mark Buchanan, *Things Unseen* (Sisters, OR: Multnomah Publishers, 2002), 76.

154. Wayne Martindale, PhD, ed., *Journey to the Celestial City* (Chicago: Moody Press, 1995), 129–130.

155. Mart De Haan, *Been Thinking About* (Grand Rapids, MI: RBC Ministries, 2007), 50.

156. Wayne Martindale, PhD, ed., *Journey to the Celestial City* (Chicago: Moody Press, 1995), 21–22.

157. Randy Alcorn, *Heaven for Kids* (Carol Stream, IL: Tyndale House, 2006), xxiv–xxv.

158. Randy Alcorn, *Heaven* (Carol Stream, IL: Tyndale House, 2004), 443.

159. Randy Alcorn, *50 Days of Heaven* (Carol Stream, IL: Tyndale House, 2006), 238.

160. Randy Alcorn, *Heaven* (Carol Stream, IL: Tyndale House, 2004), 395.

161. Ibid.

162. Randy Alcorn, *TouchPoints: Heaven* (Carol Stream, IL: Tyndale House, 2008), xvi.

163. Randy Alcorn, *Heaven* (Carol Stream, IL: Tyndale House, 2004), 184.

164. Ibid., 187.

165. John Piper, *Desiring God* (Sisters, OR: Multnomah Publishers, 1996), 50.

166. Jonathan Edwards, *The Works of Jonathan Edwards: The Miscellanies* (New Haven, CT: Yale University Press, 1994), 105, 275–276.

167. Joseph M. Stowell, *Eternity* (Chicago, IL: Moody Press, 1995), 108.

168. Max Lucado, *When Christ Comes* (Nashville: W Publishing Group, 1999), 144, 148.

169. Annie Ross Cousin, *Immanuel's Land and Other Pieces (1876)* (Whitefish, MT: Kessinger, 2009), 7.

170. Edward Donnelly, *Biblical Teaching on the Doctrines of Heaven and Hell* (Edinburgh: Banner of Truth, 2001), 86; citation from Letter 21 in the Andrew Bonar edition of *Rutherford's Letters*.

171. Tony Evans, *Tony Evans Speaks Out on Heaven and Hell* (Chicago: Moody Press, 2000), 51.

172. Randy Alcorn, *50 Days of Heaven* (Carol Stream, IL: Tyndale House, 2006), 203–204.

173. Randy Alcorn, *We Shall See God* (Carol Stream, IL: Tyndale House, 2011), 253.

174. Randy Alcorn, *Heaven* (Carol Stream, IL: Tyndale House, 2004), 193.

175. Randy Alcorn, *We Shall See God* (Carol Stream, IL: Tyndale House, 2011), 252.

176. J. Vernon McGee, *Death of a Little Child* (Pasadena, CA: Thru the Bible Radio, July 1970), 20.

177. Larry R. Dick, *A Taste of Heaven* (Victoria, BC: Trafford Publishing, 2002), 98.

178. Charles H. Spurgeon, "Infant Salvation," Sermon 411, September 29, 1861, www.spurgeongems.org.

179. J. Sidlow Baxter, *The Other Side of Death* (Grand Rapids, MI: Kregel Publications, 1987), 65.

180. Charles H. Spurgeon, "Infant Salvation," Sermon 411, September 29, 1861, www.spurgeongems.org.

181. Isaac Watts, *The World to Come* (Morgan, PA: Soli Deo Gloria Publications, 1954; originally written in 1745), 111–112.

182. J. Vernon McGee, *Death of a Little Child* (Pasadena, CA: Thru the Bible Radio, July 1970), 10–11.

183. J. Sidlow Baxter, *The Other Side of Death* (Grand Rapids, MI: Kregel Publications, 1987), 64.

184. Charles H. Spurgeon, "Infant Salvation," Sermon 411, September 29, 1861, www.spurgeongems.org.

185. Ibid.

186. Randy Alcorn, *Heaven* (Carol Stream, IL: Tyndale House, 2004), 290.

187. Ibid., 341.

188. Ibid., 342.

189. G. K. Chesterton, cited by John Stott in *Christ the Liberator* (Downers Grove, IL: InterVarsity Press, 1971), 244.

190. John Hannah, "Hell," Sermon Illustrations, accessed September 15, 2011, http://www .sermonillustrations.com/a-z/h/hell.htm.

191. J. I. Packer, *Knowing God* (Downers Grove, IL: InterVarsity Press 1973), 127.

192. A. W. Tozer, *The Attributes of God, Volume 1: A Journey into the Father's Heart* (Camp Hill, PA: WingSpread, 2003), 190–191.

193. C. S. Lewis, The Chronicles of Narnia Series (New York: HarperCollins, 2001), 541.

194. C. S. Lewis, *Letters to Malcolm* (Boston: Houghton Mifflin Harcourt, 2002), 76.

195. A. J. Conyers, *The Eclipse of Heaven* (Downers Grove, IL: InterVarsity Press, 1992), 21.

196. Wayne Martindale, PhD, ed., *Journey to the Celestial City* (Chicago: Moody Press, 1995), 134.

197. A. W. Tozer, *The Attributes of God, Volume 1: A Journey into the Father's Heart* (Camp Hill, PA: Christian Publications, 1997), 138.

198. C. S. Lewis, *The Problem of Pain* (New York: Macmillan, 1962), 147.

199. Wayne Martindale, PhD, ed., *Journey to the Celestial City* (Chicago: Moody Press, 1995), 136.

200. Isaac Watts, *The World to Come* (Morgan, PA: Soli Deo Gloria Publications, 1954; originally written in 1745), 33.

201. C. J. Mahaney, "Loving the Church" (recorded message, Covenant Life Church, Gaithersburg, MD, n.d.).

202. Ron Rhodes, *Heaven: The Undiscovered Country* (Eugene, OR: Harvest House, 1960), 39–40.

203. Isaac Watts, *The World to Come* (Morgan, PA: Soli Deo Gloria Publications, 1954; originally written in 1745), 101–102.

204. Jonathan Edwards, *Heaven: A World of Love* (Amityville, NY: Calvary Press, 1999), 49.

205. Isaac Watts, *The World to Come* (Morgan, PA: Soli Deo Gloria Publications, 1954; originally written in 1745), 93.

206. Tony Evans, *Tony Evans Speaks Out on Heaven and Hell* (Chicago: Moody Press, 2000), 10.

207. Ibid., 6.

208. Jonathan Edwards, *Heaven: A World of Love* (Amityville, NY: Calvary Press, 1999), 53–54.

209. J. C. Ryle, *Heaven* (Ross-shire, UK: Christian Focus Publications, 2000), 43.

210. Ibid., 83.

211. C. S. Lewis, *The Great Divorce* (New York: Collier Books, 1946), 72. Also cited in Geisler, *Baker Encyclopedia of Christian Apologetics*, 311.

212. Drake W. Whitchurch, *Waking from Earth* (Kearney, NE: Morris Publishing, 1999), 155.

213. G. K. Chesterton, quoted in Philip Yancey, *Rumors of Another World* (Grand Rapids, MI: Zondervan, 2003), 78.

214. J. Sidlow Baxter, *The Other Side of Death* (Grand Rapids, MI: Kregel Publications, 1987), 9.

215. Paul Helm, *The Last Things* (Carlisle, PA: Banner of Truth, 1989), 44–45.

216. Randy Alcorn, *Heaven for Kids* (Carol Stream, IL: Tyndale House, 2006), 168–171.

217. Randy Alcorn, *We Shall See God* (Carol Stream, IL: Tyndale House, 2011), 230.

218. Randy Alcorn, *Heaven* (Carol Stream, IL: Tyndale House, 2004), 36.

219. Ibid.

220. Ibid., xx–xxi.

221. Randy Alcorn, *We Shall See God* (Carol Stream, IL: Tyndale House, 2011), 235.

222. Randy Alcorn, *Heaven* (Carol Stream, IL: Tyndale House, 2004), 25.

223. Ibid., 28.

224. Randy Alcorn, *In Light of Eternity* (Colorado Springs: WaterBrook, 1984), 74.

225. Randy Alcorn, "Death: Signing and Framing Your Life's Portrait," Eternal Perspective Ministries, December 30, 2009, http://www.epm.org/resources/2009/Dec/30/death-signing-and-framing-your-lifes-portrait.

226. Randy Alcorn, *The Law of Rewards* (Carol Stream, IL: Tyndale House, 2003), 41.

227. Ibid., 50.
228. Ibid., 70.
229. Randy Alcorn, *We Shall See God* (Carol Stream, IL: Tyndale House, 2011), 90.
230. C. S. Lewis, *Mere Christianity* (New York: Collier, 1960), 118.
231. Father J. Boudreau, SJ, *The Happiness of Heaven* (Rockford, IL: TAN Books, 1984), 25–26.
232. Dallas Willard, *The Divine Conspiracy* (New York: HarperCollins, 1998), 394.
233. Joni Eareckson Tada, *Heaven: Your Real Home* (Grand Rapids, MI: Zondervan, 1995), 39.
234. Bruce Milne, *The Message of Heaven and Hell* (Downers Grove, IL: InterVarsity Press, 2002), 194.
235. Colleen McDannell and Bernhard Lang, *Heaven: A History* (New York: Vintage Books, 1988), 280.
236. Peter Kreeft, *Everything You Ever Wanted to Know about Heaven* (San Francisco: Ignatius Press, 1990), 90.
237. Millard J. Erickson, *Christian Theology* (Grand Rapids, MI: Baker Book House, 1998), 1205.
238. Alister E. McGrath, *A Brief History of Heaven* (Malden, MA: Blackwell, 2003), 37–38.
239. Thomas Aquinas, *Summa Theologica*, supplementum, question 81, article 1.
240. Hank Hanegraaff, *Resurrection* (Nashville: Word, 2000), 133–134.
241. C. S. Lewis, *The Great Divorce* (New York: Macmillan, 1946), 29–30.
242. Jonathan Edwards, quoted in John Gerstner, *Jonathan Edwards on Heaven and Hell* (Grand Rapids, MI: Baker Book House, 1980), 39.
243. John Gilmore, *Probing Heaven* (Grand Rapids, MI: Baker Book House, 1991), 269.
244. Hendrikus Berkhof, *Christ the Meaning of History*, trans. Lambertus Buurman (Richmond, VA: John Knox, 1966), 190.
245. Peter Kreeft, Ronald Keith Tacelli, *Handbook of Christian Apologetics* (Downers Grove, IL: InterVarsity Press, 1994), 262.
246. Edward Thurneysen, quoted in J. A. Schep, *The Nature of the Resurrection Body* (Grand Rapids, MI: Eerdmans, 1964), 218–219.
247. W. Graham Scroggie, DD, *What about Heaven?* (London: Christian Literature Crusade, 1940), 36–37.
248. Amy Carmichael, *Thou Givest . . . They Gather*, quoted in *Images of Heaven,* comp. Lil Copan and Anna Trimiew (Wheaton, IL: Harold Shaw, 1996), 111.
249. Tony Evans, *Tony Evans Speaks Out on Heaven and Hell* (Chicago: Moody Press, 2000), 35–36.
250. Bruce Milne, *The Message of Heaven and Hell* (Downers Grove, IL: InterVarsity Press, 2002), 257.
251. Albert M. Wolters, *Creation Regained: Biblical Basics for a Reformational Worldview* (Grand Rapids, MI: Eerdmans, 1985), 40.
252. James M. Campbell, DD, *Heaven Opened* (New York: Revell, 1924), 135.
253. J. Sidlow Baxter, *The Other Side of Death* (Grand Rapids, MI: Kregel Publications, 1987), 63.
254. Charles H. Spurgeon, "Departed Saints Yet Living," Sermon 1863, October 4, 1885, as cited in Randy Alcorn, *We Shall See God* (Carol Stream, IL: Tyndale House, 2011), 35–36.
255. Abraham Kuyper, cited in Hendrikus Berkhof, *Christ the Meaning of History* (Richmond, VA: John Knox, 1966), 191.
256. Sam Storms, "Heaven: The Eternal Increase of Joy," *Decision* Magazine (Billy Graham Evangelistic Association, May 1, 2007), http://www.billygraham.org/articlepage.asp?articleid=810.
257. E. X. Heatherley, *Our Heavenly Home* (Austin, TX: Balcony Publishing, 2000), 87–90.
258. Ibid., 90–91.
259. John Calvin, *Commentary on the Book of the Prophet Isaiah*, Volume Four, Chapter 65, Verse 17 (Bellingham, WA: Logos Research Systems).
260. Methodius, *The Discourse on the Resurrection*, Part I, VIII–XI, *Ante-Nicene Fathers: Vol. 6*, http://www.newadvent.org/fathers/0625.htm.
261. Randy Alcorn, *50 Days of Heaven* (Carol Stream, IL: Tyndale House, 2006), 92.

262. Randy Alcorn, *Heaven* (Carol Stream, IL: Tyndale House, 2004), 115–116.

263. Randy Alcorn, *50 Days of Heaven* (Carol Stream, IL: Tyndale House, 2006), 115.

264. Randy Alcorn, *TouchPoints: Heaven* (Carol Stream, IL: Tyndale House, 2008), 117.

265. Randy Alcorn, *Heaven* (Carol Stream, IL: Tyndale House, 2004), 412.

266. Anthony A. Hoekema, "Heaven: Not Just an Eternal Day Off," *Christianity Today* (June 6, 2003), http://www.christianitytoday.com/ct/2003/122/54.0.html.

267. Arthur O. Roberts, *Exploring Heaven* (San Francisco: HarperSanFrancisco, 2003), 63–64.

268. Michael E. Wittmer, *Heaven Is a Place on Earth* (Grand Rapids, MI: Zondervan, 2004), 203.

269. C. S. Lewis, *The Great Divorce* (New York: Macmillan, 1946), 80.

270. Arthur O. Roberts, *Exploring Heaven* (San Francisco: HarperSanFrancisco, 2003), 148.

271. Paul Marshall with Lela Gilbert, *Heaven Is Not My Home* (Nashville: Word, 1998), 173.

272. Albert M. Wolters, *Creation Regained* (Grand Rapids, MI: Eerdmans, 1985), 63.

273. Ibid., 64.

274. Arthur O. Roberts, *Exploring Heaven* (San Francisco: HarperSanFrancisco, 1989), 148.

275. Albert M. Wolters, *Creation Regained* (Grand Rapids, MI: Eerdmans, 1985), 37.

276. Bruce Milne, *The Message of Heaven and Hell* (Downers Grove, IL: InterVarsity Press, 2002), 321–322.

277. Paul Marshall with Lela Gilbert, *Heaven Is Not My Home* (Nashville: Word, 1998), 32–33.

278. Cornelius P. Venema, *The Promise of the Future* (Trowbridge, UK: Banner of Truth, 2000), 481.

279. Ibid.

280. Paul Marshall with Lela Gilbert, *Heaven Is Not My Home* (Nashville: Word, 1998), 30.

281. Anthony A. Hoekema, "Heaven: Not Just an Eternal Day Off," *Christianity Today* (June 6, 2003), http://www.christianitytoday.com/ct/2003/122/54.0.html.

282. N. T. Wright, *Surprised by Hope* (New York: HarperCollins, 2008), 193.

283. Anthony A. Hoekema, "Heaven: Not Just an Eternal Day Off," *Christianity Today* (June 6, 2003), http://www.christianitytoday.com/ct/2003/122/54.0.html.

284. Randy Alcorn, *Heaven* (Carol Stream, IL: Tyndale House, 2004), 367.

285. Ibid., 368–369.

286. Ibid., 234.

287. Ibid., 427–428.

288. Randy Alcorn, *50 Days of Heaven* (Carol Stream, IL: Tyndale House, 2006), 214–215.

289. Randy Alcorn, *Heaven* (Carol Stream, IL: Tyndale House, 2004), 429–430.

290. Ibid., 254.

291. Ibid., 407.

292. Ibid., 400–401.

293. Ibid., 219.

294. John Calvin, *Commentary on Romans* (Romans 8:19-22), Christian Classics Ethereal Library, http://www.ccel.org/ccel/calvin/calcom38.all.html#xii.

295. Charles H. Spurgeon, "Creation's Groans and the Saints' Sighs," Sermon 788, January 5, 1868, as cited in Randy Alcorn, *We Shall See God* (Carol Stream, IL: Tyndale House, 2011), 20, 22.

296. Albert M. Wolters, *Creation Regained* (Grand Rapids, MI: Eerdmans, 1985), 58.

297. Steven J. Lawson, *Heaven Help Us!* (Colorado Springs: NavPress, 1995), 106.

298. Larry Crabb, quoted in Gary Moon, *Homesick for Eden* (Ann Arbor, MI: Servant Publications, 1997), 10.

299. Anthony A. Hoekema, *The Bible and the Future* (Grand Rapids, MI: Eerdmans, 1979), 275.

300. C. S. Lewis, *The Screwtape Letters*, rev. ed. (New York: Macmillan, 1982), 41–42.

301. Albert M. Wolters, *Creation Regained* (Grand Rapids, MI: Eerdmans, 1985), 71.

302. James M. Campbell, DD, *Heaven Opened* (New York: Revell, 1924), 131.

303. Peter Kreeft, *Everything You Ever Wanted to Know about Heaven* (San Francisco: Ignatius Press, 1990), 112.

304. Steven J. Lawson, *Heaven Help Us!* (Colorado Springs: NavPress, 1995), 166.

305. Albert M. Wolters, *Creation Regained* (Grand Rapids, MI: Eerdmans, 1985), 56.

306. Charles H. Spurgeon, "A Heavenly Pattern for Our Earthly Life," Sermon 1778, April 30, 1884, www.spurgeongems.org.

307. Dallas Willard, *The Spirit of the Disciplines* (New York: HarperCollins, 1988), 54.

308. Randy Alcorn, *Heaven* (Carol Stream, IL: Tyndale House, 2004), 281.

309. Ibid., 244–245.

310. Randy Alcorn, *We Shall See God* (Carol Stream, IL: Tyndale House, 2011), 268.

311. Randy Alcorn, *Heaven* (Carol Stream, IL: Tyndale House, 2004), 302.

312. Ibid., 120.

313. Ibid., 464.

314. Randy Alcorn, *50 Days of Heaven* (Carol Stream, IL: Tyndale House, 2006), 104.

315. Randy Alcorn, *We Shall See God* (Carol Stream, IL: Tyndale House, 2011), 181.

316. Randy Alcorn, *Heaven* (Carol Stream, IL: Tyndale House, 2004), 122–123.

317. Randy Alcorn, *If God Is Good . . .* (Colorado Springs: Multnomah Publishers, 2009), 299.

318. Arthur Bennett, ed., *The Valley of Vision* (Carlisle, PA: Banner of Truth, 2002), 221.

319. Ibid., 375.

320. Matthew Henry, *The Miscellaneous Works of the Rev. Matthew Henry*, "Directions for Daily Communication with God," third discourse.

321. Richard Baxter, "Lord, It Belongs Not to My Care" (1681), *Hymnal of the Protestant Episcopal Church*.

322. Jack MacArthur, *Exploring in the Next World* (Minneapolis: Dimension Books, 1967), 16.

323. C. S. Lewis, *The Lion, the Witch and the Wardrobe* (New York: Macmillan, 1950), 159–160.

324. Variously attributed to Henry Scott Holland and Henry Van Dyke; source uncertain.

325. George Sweeting and Donald Sweeting, "The Evangelist and the Agnostic," *Moody Monthly* (July/August 1989), 69.

326. Calvin Miller, *The Divine Symphony* (Minneapolis: Bethany House, 2000), 139.

327. Bruce Milne, *The Message of Heaven and Hell* (Downers Grove, IL: InterVarsity Press, 2002), 194.

328. John Richard Moreland, *A Blue Wave Breaking* (Dallas, TX: Kaleidograph Press, 1938).

329. John R. Rice, *Bible Facts about Heaven* (Murfreesboro, TN: Sword of the Lord Publishers, 1993), 38–39.

330. John Preston, quoted in Richard Brooks, *The Doors of Heaven* (Ross-shire, UK: Christian Focus Publications, 1998), 113.

331. Eberhard Bethge, *Dietrich Bonhoeffer: A Biography* (Minneapolis: Fortress Press, 2000), 927.

332. Charles H. Spurgeon, "The First Resurrection," Sermon 391, May 5, 1861, as cited in Randy Alcorn, *We Shall See God* (Carol Stream, IL: Tyndale House, 2011), 222–223.

333. John Donne, *The Sermons of John Donne*, vol. VII (Berkeley: University of California Press, 1954), 69.

334. Daniel A. Brown, PhD, *What the Bible Reveals about Heaven* (Ventura, CA: Regal Books, 1999), 25.

335. Ibid., 118.

336. Mark Buchanan, *Things Unseen* (Sisters, OR: Multnomah Publishers, 2002), 205.

337. James M. Campbell, DD, *Heaven Opened* (New York: Revell, 1924), 178.

338. Charles H. Spurgeon, "Why They Leave Us," Sermon 1892, March 21, 1886, as cited in Randy Alcorn, *We Shall See God* (Carol Stream, IL: Tyndale House, 2011), 8–9.

339. Henry Wadsworth Longfellow, as quoted in J. Sidlow Baxter, *The Other Side of Death* (Grand Rapids, MI: Kregel Publications, 1987), 12.

340. Tony Evans, *Tony Evans Speaks Out on Heaven and Hell* (Chicago: Moody Press, 2000), 7, 9.

341. Anthony A. Hoekema, *The Bible and the Future* (Grand Rapids, MI: Eerdmans, 1979), 85.

342. Ken Gire, *Instructive Moments with the Savior* (Grand Rapids, MI: Zondervan, 1992), 75.

343. Joseph Bayly, *When a Child Dies* (Chicago: Moody Press, 1966), 15.

344. Martyn Lloyd-Jones, cited in Ron Rhodes, *Heaven: The Undiscovered Country* (Eugene, OR: Harvest House, 2003), 12.

345. Max Lucado, *When Christ Comes* (Nashville: W Publishing Group, 1999), 68.
346. Ibid., 44.
347. Paul Helm, *The Last Things* (Carlisle, PA: Banner of Truth, 1989), 55–56.
348. C. S. Lewis, *Mere Christianity* (New York: Macmillan, 1972), 190.
349. Augustine, quoted in Colleen McDannell and Bernhard Lang, *Heaven: A History* (New York: Vintage Books, 1988), 60.
350. Augustine, *On the Christian Doctrine*, 1:32–33.
351. Douglas Connelly, *The Promise of Heaven* (Downers Grove, IL: InterVarsity Press, 2000), 27–29.
352. Daniel A. Brown, PhD, *What the Bible Reveals about Heaven* (Ventura, CA: Regal Books, 1999), 132.
353. Ibid., 223.
354. Joseph Bayly, *A Voice in the Wilderness* (Grand Rapids, MI: Zondervan, 2000), 263.
355. C. S. Lewis, *Letters to an American Lady* (Grand Rapids, MI: Eerdmans, 1967), 117.
356. Paul Helm, *The Last Things* (Carlisle, PA: Banner of Truth, 1989), 49–50.
357. Isaac Watts, *An Arrangement of the Psalms, Hymns, and Spiritual Songs of Isaac Watts* (Boston: Richardson and Lord, and Cummings and Hilliard, Cornhill, 1820), 627.
358. A. W. Tozer and D. E. Fessenden, *The Attributes of God, Volume 1: A Journey into the Father's Heart* (Camp Hill, PA: WingSpread, 2003), 190–191.
359. Harriet Beecher Stowe, *Uncle Tom's Cabin* (Boston: Houghton, Osgood, 1879), 485.
360. Randy Alcorn, "Death: Signing and Framing Your Life's Portrait," Eternal Perspective Ministries, December 30, 2009, http://www.epm.org/resources/2009/Dec/30/death-signing-and-framing-your-lifes-portrait.
361. Randy Alcorn, *We Shall See God* (Carol Stream, IL: Tyndale House, 2011), 4.
362. Randy Alcorn, *The Law of Rewards* (Carol Stream, IL: Tyndale House, 2003), 46.
363. Randy Alcorn, *50 Days of Heaven* (Carol Stream, IL: Tyndale House, 2006), 86.
364. Randy Alcorn, *Heaven* (Carol Stream, IL: Tyndale House, 2004), 111.
365. Randy Alcorn, *50 Days of Heaven* (Carol Stream, IL: Tyndale House, 2006), 267.
366. John Updike, "Pigeon Feathers," in *Pigeon Feathers and Other Stories* (New York: Fawcett Columbine, 1987), 135–138.
367. J. Sidlow Baxter, *The Other Side of Death* (Grand Rapids, MI: Kregel Publications, 1987), 53.
368. Colleen McDannell and Bernhard Lang, *Heaven: A History* (New York: Vintage Books, 1988), 351–352.
369. C. S. Lewis, *The Great Divorce* (New York: Collier Books, 1946), 68–69.
370. Augustine, *The City of God*, Book XXII, chapter 29.
371. E. X. Heatherley, *Our Heavenly Home* (Austin, TX: Balcony Publishing, 2000), 39–41.
372. Daniel A. Brown, PhD, *What the Bible Reveals about Heaven* (Ventura, CA: Regal Books, 1999), 189.
373. John Gilmore, *Probing Heaven* (Grand Rapids, MI: Baker Book House, 1991), 91–92.
374. Arthur O. Roberts, *Exploring Heaven* (San Francisco: HarperSanFrancisco, 2003), 13.
375. C. S. Lewis, *The Last Battle* (New York: HarperCollins, 1994), 211.
376. Wayne Grudem, *Systematic Theology* (Grand Rapids, MI: Zondervan, 1994), 1158–1164.
377. John Updike, *Telephone Poles and Other Poems* (New York: Alfred A. Knopf, 1963), 12.
378. Barry Morrow, *Heaven Observed* (Colorado Springs: NavPress, 2001), 231–232.
379. Colleen McDannell and Bernhard Lang, *Heaven: A History* (New York: Vintage Books, 1988), 352.
380. Steven J. Lawson, *Heaven Help Us!* (Colorado Springs: NavPress, 1995), 16.
381. C. S. Lewis, *The Silver Chair* (New York: Collier Books, 1970), 151–161.
382. C. S. Lewis, *The Problem of Pain* (New York: Macmillan, 1962), 144–148.
383. Paul Helm, *The Last Things* (Carlisle, PA: Banner of Truth, 1989), 10.
384. Wayne Grudem, *Systematic Theology* (Grand Rapids, MI: Zondervan, 1994), 1158–1164.
385. N. T. Wright, *Surprised by Hope* (New York: HarperCollins, 2008), 104.
386. Ibid., 153.

387. Isaac Watts, *The World to Come* (Morgan, PA: Soli Deo Gloria Publications, 1954; originally written in 1745), 78–79.

388. W. Graham Scroggie, DD, *What about Heaven?* (London: Christian Literature Crusade, 1940), 93–95.

389. Isaac Watts, *The World to Come* (Morgan, PA: Soli Deo Gloria Publications, 1954; originally written in 1745), 81.

390. Randy Alcorn, *Heaven* (Carol Stream, IL: Tyndale House, 2004), 464.

391. Randy Alcorn, *50 Days of Heaven* (Carol Stream, IL: Tyndale House, 2006), 40.

392. Randy Alcorn, *Heaven* (Carol Stream, IL: Tyndale House, 2004), 51.

393. Ibid., 59.

394. Randy Alcorn, *TouchPoints: Heaven* (Carol Stream, IL: Tyndale House, 2008), 13.

395. Randy Alcorn, *Heaven* (Carol Stream, IL: Tyndale House, 2004), 131.

396. Randy Alcorn, *We Shall See God* (Carol Stream, IL: Tyndale House, 2011), 44.

397. Randy Alcorn, *50 Days of Heaven* (Carol Stream, IL: Tyndale House, 2006), 111.

398. Randy Alcorn, *Heaven* (Carol Stream, IL: Tyndale House, 2004), 242.

399. Ibid., 7.

400. Ibid., 475–476.

401. Tertullian, *The Shows*, or *De Spectaculis*, 30, in *ANF*, 3:91; cited by Gregg Allison, *Historical Theology* (Grand Rapids, MI: Zondervan, 2011), 724.

402. Irenaeus, *Against Heresies*, 5.36, in *ANF*, 1:566–567. The text has been rendered clearer by Gregg Allison, *Historical Theology* (Grand Rapids, MI: Zondervan, 2011), 725–726.

403. John Piper, "Behold, I Make All Things New," April 26, 1992, www.desiringgod.org.

404. Origen, *First Principles*, 1.6.4, in *ANF*, 4:262.

405. Anthony A. Hoekema, *The Bible and the Future* (Grand Rapids, MI: Eerdmans, 1979), 73.

406. Herman Bavinck, *The Last Things* (Grand Rapids, MI: Baker Books, 1996), 155.

407. Anselm, *Why God Became Man*, 1.18, in Anselm, 295.

408. Thomas Aquinas, cited in Gregg R. Allison, *Historical Theology* (Grand Rapids, MI: Zondervan, 2011), 727.

409. John Calvin, *Commentaries on the Catholic Epistles*, ed. and trans., John Owen (reprinted, Grand Rapids, MI: Baker Book House, 2005), 420. Cited by Gregg R. Allison, *Historical Theology* (Grand Rapids, MI: Zondervan, 2011), 728.

410. William Ames (Amesius), *Medullas Theologiae (The Marrow of Theology)* (Amsterdam, 1634 [1628]), 31, in Heppe, 706. Cited by Gregg R. Allison, *Historical Theology* (Grand Rapids, MI: Zondervan, 2011), 729.

411. Jonathan Edwards, *The Works of Jonathan Edwards* (Banner of Truth, 1974), vol. 1, 534.

412. Charles Hodge, *Systematic Theology*, 3 vols. (Grand Rapids, MI: Eerdmans, 1946), 3:851–852.

413. Wayne Grudem, *Systematic Theology* (Grand Rapids, MI: Zondervan, 1994), 1158–1164.

414. Methodius, *The Discourse on the Resurrection*, Part I, VIII–X, quoted in A. Roberts, J. Donaldson, and A. C. Coxe, *The Ante-Nicene Fathers, Vol. VI : Translations of the Writings of the Fathers Down to AD 325* (365–366) (Oak Harbor: Logos Research Systems, 1997).

415. Ibid.

416. N. T. Wright, *Surprised by Hope* (New York: HarperCollins, 2008), 104–105.

417. Charles H. Spurgeon, "Creation's Groans and the Saints' Sighs," Sermon 788, January 5, 1868, as cited in Randy Alcorn, *We Shall See God* (Carol Stream, IL: Tyndale House, 2011), 14.

418. Randy Alcorn, *50 Days of Heaven* (Carol Stream, IL: Tyndale House, 2006), 61.

419. Ibid., 62–63.

420. Ibid., 110–111.

421. Richard Brooks, *The Doors of Heaven* (Ross-shire, UK: Christian Focus Publications, 1998), 78.

422. Larry R. Dick, *A Taste of Heaven* (Victoria, BC: Trafford Publishing, 2002), 107.

423. Drake W. Whitchurch, *Waking from Earth* (Kearney, NE: Morris Publishing, 1999), 113.

424. Douglas Connelly, *The Promise of Heaven* (Downers Grove, IL: InterVarsity Press, 2000), 109.

425. John Calvin, cited by Paul Marshall with Lela Gilbert, *Heaven Is Not My Home* (Nashville: Word, 1998), 164.

426. Randy Alcorn, *Heaven* (Carol Stream, IL: Tyndale House, 2004), 303–304.

427. Ibid., 305.

428. Randy Alcorn, *We Shall See God* (Carol Stream, IL: Tyndale House, 2011), 145–146.

429. Randy Alcorn, *Heaven* (Carol Stream, IL: Tyndale House, 2004), 295.

430. Ibid., 308.

431. Ibid., 297–298.

432. Ibid., 354.

433. Ibid., 292.

434. Ibid., 309.

435. Ibid., 453.

436. Ibid., 471–472.

437. A. W. Tozer, *Who Put Jesus on the Cross?* (Camp Hill, PA: Christian Publications, 1975), 85–86.

438. W. B. Hinson, cited in Ron Rhodes, *The Undiscovered Country* (Eugene, OR: Harvest House), 49.

439. Nathaniel Hawthorne, *The Old Manse* (Boston: Houghton, Mifflin, and Co., 1904), 72.

440. John Wesley, *Wesley Bicentennial* (Middletown, CT: Wesleyan University, 1904), 82.

441. A. W. Tozer and D. E. Fessenden, *The Attributes of God, Volume 1: A Journey into the Father's Heart* (Camp Hill, PA: WingSpread, 2003), 190–191.

442. John Bradford, *Writings of John Bradford* (Edinburgh: Banner of Truth, 1848, 1979), 1:267; cited by John Gilmore, *Probing Heaven* (Grand Rapids, MI: Baker Book House, 1991), 26–27.

443. Isaac Watts, *The World to Come* (Morgan, PA: Soli Deo Gloria Publications, 1954; originally written in 1745), 83.

444. Bruce Milne, *The Message of Heaven and Hell* (Downers Grove, IL: InterVarsity Press, 2002), 135.

445. Isaac Watts, *The World to Come* (Morgan, PA: Soli Deo Gloria Publications, 1954; originally written in 1745), 110.

446. John Gilmore, *Probing Heaven* (Grand Rapids, MI: Baker Book House, 1991), 15–16.

447. James M. Campbell, DD, *Heaven Opened* (New York: Revell, 1924), 149.

448. Seneca, cited in James M. Campbell, DD, *Heaven Opened* (New York: Revell, 1924), 179.

449. Daniel A. Brown, PhD, *What the Bible Reveals about Heaven* (Ventura, CA: Regal Books, 1999), 27.

450. Colleen McDannell and Bernhard Lang, *Heaven: A History* (New York: Vintage Books, 1988), 349.

451. James M. Campbell, DD, *Heaven Opened* (New York: Revell, 1924), 190.

452. Ivor Powell, *Heaven: My Father's Country* (Grand Rapids, MI: Kregel Publications, 1995), 6–7.

453. John Piper, *Future Grace* (Sisters, OR: Multnomah Publishers, 1995), 370.

454. Joseph M. Stowell, *Eternity* (Chicago: Moody Press, 1995), 103.

455. W. Graham Scroggie, DD, *What about Heaven?* (London: Christian Literature Crusade, 1940), 24.

456. Ibid., 87.

457. Mark Buchanan, *Things Unseen* (Sisters, OR: Multnomah Publishers, 2002), 46.

458. Ibid., 211.

459. Bruce Milne, *The Message of Heaven and Hell* (Downers Grove, IL: InterVarsity Press, 2002), 272.

460. J. Sidlow Baxter, *The Other Side of Death* (Grand Rapids, MI: Kregel Publications, 1987), 52.

461. Dallas Willard, *The Divine Conspiracy* (San Francisco: HarperSanFrancisco, 1998), 376.

462. Charles H. Spurgeon, "Fallen Asleep," Sermon 2659, www.spurgeongems.org.

463. Ibid.

464. Daniel A. Brown, PhD, *What the Bible Reveals about Heaven* (Ventura, CA: Regal Books, 1999), 30.

465. Ibid., 121–122.

466. Hank Hanegraaff, *Resurrection* (Nashville: Word Publishing, 2000), 126–127.

467. Norman L. Geisler, *Baker Encyclopedia of Christian Apologetics* (Grand Rapids, MI: Baker Book House, 1999), 643.

468. Horatius Bonar, "The God of Grace" (Sermon #34), *Fifty-Two Sermons* (Grand Rapids, MI: Baker Book House, 1954), 285.

469. Randy Alcorn, *Heaven* (Carol Stream, IL: Tyndale House, 2004), 9.

470. Randy Alcorn, *50 Days of Heaven* (Carol Stream, IL: Tyndale House, 2006), 118–119.

471. Randy Alcorn, *Heaven* (Carol Stream, IL: Tyndale House, 2004), xxi.

472. Ibid., 432.

473. Ibid., 433.

474. Ibid., 434.

475. Joseph M. Stowell, *Eternity* (Chicago: Moody Press, 1995), 142.

476. Barry Morrow, *Heaven Observed* (Colorado Springs: NavPress, 2001), 332.

477. C. S. Lewis, *The Problem of Pain* (New York: Macmillan, 1962), 147.

478. John Gilmore, *Probing Heaven* (Grand Rapids, MI: Baker Book House, 1991), 262.

479. Ibid., 264.

480. Richard J. Mouw, *When the Kings Come Marching In* (Grand Rapids, MI: Eerdmans, 1983), 47–48.

481. Cornelius P. Venema, *The Promise of the Future* (Trowbridge, UK: Banner of Truth, 2000), 481.

482. Jonathan Edwards, quoted in John Gerstner, *Jonathan Edwards on Heaven and Hell* (Grand Rapids, MI: Baker Book House, 1980), 21–22.

483. Richard J. Mouw, *When the Kings Come Marching In* (Grand Rapids, MI: Eerdmans, 1983), 55–56.

484. Ibid., 63.

485. N. T. Wright, *Surprised by Hope* (New York: HarperCollins, 2008), 258, 259.

486. C. S. Lewis, *The Problem of Pain* (New York: Simon and Schuster, 1996), 134–135.

487. Randy Alcorn, *Heaven* (Carol Stream, IL: Tyndale House, 2004), 362.

488. Ibid.

489. Ibid., 368–369.

490. Ibid., 380.

491. Ibid., 365.

492. Randy Alcorn, *TouchPoints: Heaven* (Carol Stream, IL: Tyndale House, 2008), 120.

493. Randy Alcorn, *Heaven* (Carol Stream, IL: Tyndale House, 2004), 354.

494. Larry R. Dick, *A Taste of Heaven* (Victoria, BC: Trafford Publishing, 2002), 138.

495. Peter Kreeft, *Everything You Ever Wanted to Know about Heaven* (San Francisco: Ignatius Press, 1990), 53–54.

496. T. W. Hunt and Melana Hunt Monroe, *From Heaven's View* (Nashville: Broadman and Holman Publishers, 2002), 239.

497. Father J. Boudreau, SJ, *The Happiness of Heaven* (Rockford, IL: TAN Books, 1984), 142.

498. J. C. Ryle, *Heaven* (Ross-shire, UK: Christian Focus Publications, 2000), 36–37.

499. Larry R. Dick, *A Taste of Heaven* (Victoria, BC: Trafford Publishing, 2002), 158.

500. Arthur O. Roberts, *Exploring Heaven* (San Francisco: HarperSanFrancisco, 2003), 47.

501. Tony Evans, *Tony Evans Speaks Out on Heaven and Hell* (Chicago: Moody Press, 2000), 35–36.

502. Charles H. Spurgeon, "Heaven and Hell," Sermons 39–40, September 4, 1855, as cited in Randy Alcorn, *We Shall See God* (Carol Stream, IL: Tyndale House, 2011), 99–100.

503. Richard Baxter, *The Practical Works of Richard Baxter* (Grand Rapids, MI: Baker Book House, 1981), 97.

504. Dr. Steven Waterhouse, *Not by Bread Alone* (Amarillo, TX: Westcliff Press, 2000), 107.

505. Jonathan Edwards, *Heaven: A World of Love* (Amityville, NY: Calvary Press, 1999), 18.

506. Ibid.

507. John Greenleaf Whittier, *The Complete Poetical Works of John Greenleaf Whittier* (New York: Houghton Mifflin Company, 1894), 401.

508. Charles H. Spurgeon, "Heaven and Hell," Sermons 39–40, September 4, 1855, www .spurgeongems.org.

509. Jonathan Edwards, *Heaven: A World of Love* (Amityville, NY: Calvary Press, 1999), 32.

510. J. Paterson-Smyth, *The Gospel of the Hereafter* (New York: Revell, 1910), 98–99, 105, 220– 221.

511. R. A. Torrey, *Heaven or Hell* (New Kensington, PA: Whitaker House, 1985), 71.

512. J. C. Ryle, *Heaven* (Ross-shire, UK: Christian Focus Publications, 2000), 34–35.

513. Harriet Beecher Stowe, *The Minister's Wooing* (New York: Derby and Jackson, 1859). Reproduced in W. Robertson Nicoll, *Reunion in Eternity* (New York: George H. Doran, 1919), 239.

514. Jonathan Edwards, *Heaven: A World of Love* (Amityville, NY: Calvary Press, 1999), 25.

515. Ibid., 27.

516. Ibid., 34–35.

517. Ibid., 39–40.

518. Jonathan Edwards, *The Works of Jonathan Edwards: The Miscellanies*, Volume 13. Edited by Thomas A. Schafer (New Haven, CT: Yale University Press, 1994), no. 198, 336–337.

519. Randy Alcorn, *Heaven* (Carol Stream, IL: Tyndale House, 2004), 342.

520. Ibid., 353–354.

521. Ibid., 360.

522. Randy Alcorn, *50 Days of Heaven* (Carol Stream, IL: Tyndale House, 2006), 210.

523. C. S. Lewis, *Miracles* (New York: Macmillan, 1947), 160.

524. Peter Kreeft, *Everything You Ever Wanted to Know about Heaven* (San Francisco: Ignatius Press, 1990), 117–120.

525. Ibid., 127–128.

526. John Gilmore, *Probing Heaven* (Grand Rapids, MI: Baker Book House, 1991), 225–227.

527. Peter Kreeft, *Everything You Ever Wanted to Know about Heaven* (San Francisco: Ignatius Press, 1990), 128.

528. Bruce Milne, *The Message of Heaven and Hell* (Downers Grove, IL: InterVarsity Press, 2002), 137.

529. Peter Kreeft, *Everything You Ever Wanted to Know about Heaven* (San Francisco: Ignatius Press, 1990), 130–132.

530. Larry R. Dick, *A Taste of Heaven* (Victoria, BC: Trafford Publishing, 2002), 98.

531. C. S. Lewis, *Miracles* (New York: HarperCollins, 2001), 261.

532. Randy Alcorn, *Heaven* (Carol Stream, IL: Tyndale House, 2004), 38.

533. Ibid., 287.

534. Randy Alcorn, *Deadline* (Sisters, OR: Multnomah Publishers, 1994), 238.

535. Arthur Bennett, ed., *The Valley of Vision* (Carlisle, PA: Banner of Truth, 2002), 23.

536. Richard Brooks, *The Doors of Heaven* (Ross-shire, UK: Christian Focus Publications, 1998), 62.

537. James M. Campbell, DD, *Heaven Opened* (New York: Revell, 1924), 159.

538. Jonathan Edwards, *Heaven: A World of Love* (Amityville, NY: Calvary Press, 1999), 17.

539. Paul Helm, *The Last Things* (Carlisle, PA: Banner of Truth, 1989), 101.

540. Richard Baxter, *The Saints' Everlasting Rest*, http://www.ccel.org/ccel/baxter/saints_rest.iii .XV.html.

541. Charles H. Spurgeon, *Morning and Evening: Daily Readings* (1869), August 3, morning.

542. John Bradford, *Writings of John Bradford* (Edinburgh: Banner of Truth, 1848, 1979), vol. 1:267.

543. Steven J. Lawson, *Heaven Help Us!* (Colorado Springs: NavPress, 1995), 42.

544. Martyn Lloyd-Jones, *Great Doctrines of the Bible* (Wheaton, IL: Crossway Books, 2003), part 3, 247–248.

545. Paul Helm, *The Last Things* (Carlisle, PA: Banner of Truth, 1989), 138.

546. Charles H. Spurgeon, *Morning and Evening: Daily Readings* (1869), August 3, a.m.

547. T. W. Hunt and Melana Hunt Monroe, *From Heaven's View* (Nashville: Broadman and Holman Publishers, 2002), 22.

548. Ray Stedman, *Authentic Christianity* (Waco, TX: Word Books, 1975), chapter 9.

549. Steven J. Lawson, *Heaven Help Us!* (Colorado Springs: NavPress, 1995), 23.

550. Randy Alcorn, *Heaven* (Carol Stream, IL: Tyndale House, 2004), 295.

551. Randy Alcorn, *50 Days of Heaven* (Carol Stream, IL: Tyndale House, 2006), 118.

552. Randy Alcorn, *Heaven* (Carol Stream, IL: Tyndale House, 2004), 293.

553. Randy Alcorn, *TouchPoints: Heaven* (Carol Stream, IL: Tyndale House, 2008), 83–84.

554. A. W. Tozer, *The Knowledge of the Holy* (San Francisco: Harper and Row, 1961), 121–122.

555. Jonathan Edwards, *The Sermons of Jonathan Edwards: A Reader*, eds., Wilson H. Kimnach, Kenneth P. Minkema, and Douglas A. Sweeney (New Haven, CT: Yale University Press, 1999), 74–75.

556. Joseph Pearce, *Literary Giants, Literary Catholics* (San Francisco: Ignatius Press, 2005), 210.

557. Robert W. Oliver, *John Owen: His Life and Times* (Darlington, UK: Evangelical Press, 2002), 36–37.

558. Charles H. Spurgeon, "The Heaven of Heaven," Sermon 824, August 9, 1868, as cited in Randy Alcorn, *We Shall See God* (Carol Stream, IL: Tyndale House, 2011), 61.

559. Jonathan Edwards, *Heaven: A World of Love* (Amityville, NY: Calvary Press, 1999), 47.

560. Anthony A. Hoekema, *The Bible and the Future* (Grand Rapids, MI: Eerdmans, 1979), 45.

561. Thomas Aquinas, *Summa contra Gentiles*, Book II (Notre Dame–London: University of Notre Dame Press, 1995), translated by James F. Anderson, 1–34.

562. Daniel A. Brown, PhD, *What the Bible Reveals about Heaven* (Ventura, CA: Regal Books, 1999), 42.

563. Samuel Rutherford, *Letters of Samuel Rutherford* (Edinburgh and London: Oliphant Anderson and Ferrier, 1891), 511.

564. A. W. Tozer, *The Attributes of God* (Camp Hill, PA: Christian Publications, 1997), 129.

565. Jonathan Edwards, "The Christian Pilgrim," sermon preached in 1733, quoted in Alister E. McGrath, *A Brief History of Heaven* (Malden, MA: Blackwell, 2003), 115.

566. C. S. Lewis, cited in Dr. Chuck McGowen, *Let's Talk about Heaven* (Phoenix, AZ: ACW Press, 2001), 49.

567. Jonathan Edwards, *Heaven: A World of Love* (Amityville, NY: Calvary Press, 1999), 23.

568. Peter Kreeft, *Everything You Ever Wanted to Know about Heaven* (San Francisco: Ignatius Press, 1990), 40.

569. Steven J. Lawson, *Heaven Help Us!* (Colorado Springs: NavPress, 1995), 87.

570. Wayne Grudem, *Systematic Theology* (Grand Rapids, MI: Zondervan, 1994), 1164.

571. Steven J. Lawson, *Heaven Help Us!* (Colorado Springs: NavPress, 1995), 134.

572. T. W. Hunt and Melana Hunt Monroe, *From Heaven's View* (Nashville: Broadman and Holman Publishers, 2002), 235.

573. Ulrich E. Simon, *Heaven in the Christian Tradition* (London: Wyman and Sons Limited, 1958), 52–53.

574. Sam Storms, "Heaven: The Eternal Increase of Joy," *Decision* Magazine (Billy Graham Evangelistic Association, May 1, 2007), http://www.billygraham.org/articlepage.asp?articleid=810.

575. Bruce Milne, *The Message of Heaven and Hell* (Downers Grove, IL: InterVarsity Press, 2002), 327.

576. Julian of Norwich, cited by Barry Morrow, *Heaven Observed* (Colorado Springs: NavPress, 2001), 9.

577. Charles H. Spurgeon, "Departed Saints Yet Living," Sermon 1863, October 4, 1885, www.spurgeongems.org.

578. Augustine, "Of the Eternal Felicity of the City of God, and of the Perpetual Sabbath," in *The City of God,* Book 22, chapter 30, trans., Marcus Dods. Taken from the *Nicene and Post-Nicene Fathers,* First Series, ed., Philip Schaff (Peabody, MA: Hendrickson, 1999). Reprint of the American Edition, Vol. 2, *St. Augustine's City of God and Christian Doctrine.* Originally published by Christian Literature, 1887.

579. Jonathan Edwards, *Heaven: A World of Love* (Amityville, NY: Calvary Press, 1999), 12–13.

580. Augustine, *The City of God,* Book XX (Nicene and Post-Nicene Fathers, First Series: Vol. II), ch. XXIX.

581. Drake W. Whitchurch, *Waking from Earth* (Kearney, NE: Morris Publishing, 1999), 119.

582. Bruce Milne, *The Message of Heaven and Hell* (Downers Grove, IL: InterVarsity Press, 2002), 314.

583. J. C. Ryle, *Heaven* (Ross-shire, UK: Christian Focus Publications, 2000), 59–61.

584. Bruce Milne, *The Message of Heaven and Hell* (Downers Grove, IL: InterVarsity Press, 2002), 325.

585. Charles H. Spurgeon, "The Heaven of Heaven," Sermon 824, August 9, 1868, www.spurgeongems.org.

586. Ibid.

587. Joni Eareckson Tada, *Heaven: Your Real Home* (Grand Rapids, MI: Zondervan, 2001), 47.

588. Jonathan Edwards, *Heaven: A World of Love* (Amityville, NY: Calvary Press, 1999), 29.

589. John MacArthur's Bible Studies, *Heaven: Selected Scriptures* (Panorama City, CA: Word of Grace Communications, 1988), 89–90.

590. A. W. Tozer, *The Attributes of God, Volume 1: A Journey into the Father's Heart* (Camp Hill, PA: WingSpread, 2003), 55–57.

591. Randy Alcorn, *We Shall See God* (Carol Stream, IL: Tyndale House, 2011), 209.

592. Randy Alcorn, *Heaven* (Carol Stream, IL: Tyndale House, 2004), 27.

593. Ibid., 183–184.

594. Ibid., 171.

595. Ibid., 182.

596. Randy Alcorn, *Edge of Eternity* (Colorado Springs: WaterBrook, 1998), 317.

597. Randy Alcorn, *Heaven* (Carol Stream, IL: Tyndale House, 2004), 165.

598. Ibid., 181.

599. Ibid., 190.

600. J. Sidlow Baxter, *The Other Side of Death* (Grand Rapids, MI: Kregel Publications, 1987), 57–58.

601. Randy Alcorn, *50 Days of Heaven* (Carol Stream, IL: Tyndale House, 2006), 49–50.

602. Ibid., 50–52.

603. Ibid., 50.

604. Donald Grey Barnhouse, *Revelation* (Grand Rapids, MI: Zondervan, 1985), 269.

605. Martin Luther, *The Familiar Discourses of Dr. Martin Luther,* trans., H. Bell; ed., Joseph Kerby (Oxford University, 1818), 406.

606. J. I. Packer, *Knowing God* (Downers Grove, IL: InterVarsity Press, 1973), 125.

607. Arthur T. Pierson, *Many Infallible Proofs,* vol. 2 (Grand Rapids, MI: Zondervan, n.d.), 98.

608. A. W. Tozer, *The Knowledge of the Holy* (New York: Harper and Row, 1961), 95.

609. Charles H. Spurgeon, "The First Resurrection," Sermon 391, May 5, 1861, cited in Randy Alcorn, *We Shall See God* (Carol Stream, IL: Tyndale House, 2011), 225–226.

610. Ibid., 232–233.

611. Arthur T. Pierson, *Many Infallible Proofs,* vol. 2 (Grand Rapids, MI: Zondervan, n.d.), 90.

612. Dante Alighieri, "The Gate of Hell," from *The Inferno.*

613. St. Teresa of Avila, E. Allison Peers, Silverio (of St. Teresa), trans. and ed., *The Life of Teresa of Jesus* (New York: Random House, 1960), 275–276.

614. C. S. Lewis, *The Screwtape Letters* (New York: Macmillan, 1980), 65.

615. Isaac Watts, *The World to Come* (Morgan, PA: Soli Deo Gloria Publications, 1954; originally written in 1745), 93.

616. W. G. T. Shedd, *The Doctrine of Endless Punishment* (1885; repr., Edinburgh: Banner of Truth, 1986), 153.

617. Dorothy Leigh Sayers, *Introductory Papers on Dante* (London: Methuen, 1954), 44–45.

618. J. I. Packer, "Hell's Final Enigma," *Christianity Today* (April 22, 2002): 84.

619. J. I. Packer, *Your Father Loves You* (Harold Shaw Publishers, 1986), September 29.

620. Isaac Watts, *The World to Come* (Morgan, PA: Soli Deo Gloria Publications, 1954; originally written in 1745), 98.

621. C. S. Lewis, *The Problem of Pain* (New York: Macmillan, 1962), 128.

622. Paul Helm, *The Last Things* (Carlisle, PA: Banner of Truth, 1989), 112.

623. Richard Brooks, *The Doors of Heaven* (Ross-shire, UK: Christian Focus Publications, 1998), 167–168.

624. Tony Evans, *Tony Evans Speaks Out on Heaven and Hell* (Chicago: Moody Press, 2000), 16.

625. C. S. Lewis, *The Great Divorce* (New York: Collier Books, 1946), 7.

626. T. S. Eliot, *The Cocktail Party* (New York: Harcourt Brace and Co., 1950), 98.

627. John Milton, *Paradise Lost*, Book IV (London: John Bumpus, 1821), 101.

628. Isaac Watts, *The World to Come* (Morgan, PA: Soli Deo Gloria Publications, 1954; originally written in 1745), 10.

629. A. W. Tozer, *The Attributes of God* (Camp Hill, PA: Christian Publications, 1997), 192.

630. Ibid., 190–191.

631. Tony Evans, *Tony Evans Speaks Out on Heaven and Hell* (Chicago: Moody Press, 2000), 24–25.

632. Ibid., 25–26.

633. William Hendriksen, *The Bible on the Life Hereafter* (Grand Rapids, MI: Baker Book House, 1959), 81.

634. Peter Kreeft, *Everything You Ever Wanted to Know about Heaven* (San Francisco: Ignatius Press, 1990), 206.

635. Ibid., 213.

636. Ibid., 215.

637. Ibid., 221.

638. Ibid., 226–227.

639. Max Lucado, *When Christ Comes* (Nashville: W Publishing Group, 1999), 117.

640. Paul Helm, *The Last Things* (Carlisle, PA: Banner of Truth, 1989), 112.

641. Ibid., 113–115.

642. Ibid., 116–117.

643. Ibid., 127–128.

644. Harriet Beecher Stowe, *Uncle Tom's Cabin* (New York: Hurst and Company, 1901), 58–59.

645. E. J. Fortman, SJ, *Everlasting Life after Death* (New York: Alba House, 1976), 321.

646. George MacDonald, cited by Barry Morrow, *Heaven Observed* (Colorado Springs: NavPress, 2001), 232.

647. D. A. Carson, *How Long, O Lord?* (Grand Rapids, MI: Baker Academic, 2006), 92.

648. John H. Gerstner, *Jonathan Edwards on Heaven and Hell* (Grand Rapids, MI: Baker Book House, 1980), 58.

649. Ibid., 77–78.

650. "What Ever Happened to Hell?", pp. 114–115; Edward Donnelly, *Biblical Teaching on the Doctrines of Heaven and Hell* (Edinburgh: Banner of Truth Trust, 2001), 58.

651. E. X. Heatherley, *Our Heavenly Home* (Austin, TX: Balcony Publishing, 2000), 41.

652. Ibid., 104.

653. Paul Helm, *The Last Things* (Carlisle, PA: Banner of Truth, 1989), 109.

654. Ibid., 110.

655. Hank Hanegraaff, *Resurrection* (Nashville: Word Publishing, 2000), 83–84.

656. C. S. Lewis, *The Great Divorce* (New York: HarperCollins, 2001), 77–78.

657. Randy Alcorn, *Lord Foulgrin's Letters* (Sisters, OR: Multnomah Publishers, 1999), 29.

658. Randy Alcorn, *TouchPoints: Heaven* (Carol Stream, IL: Tyndale House, 2008), 113–114.

659. Randy Alcorn, *Money, Possessions, and Eternity* (Carol Stream, IL: Tyndale House, 2003), 112.

660. Randy Alcorn, *Heaven* (Carol Stream, IL: Tyndale House, 2004), 26–27.
661. Randy Alcorn, *We Shall See God* (Carol Stream, IL: Tyndale House, 2011), 235.
662. Randy Alcorn, *Heaven* (Carol Stream, IL: Tyndale House, 2004), 25.
663. Randy Alcorn, *We Shall See God* (Carol Stream, IL: Tyndale House, 2011), 74.
664. Randy Alcorn, *Heaven* (Carol Stream, IL: Tyndale House, 2004), 27–28.
665. Ibid., 25.
666. Ibid., 35.
667. Ibid., 28.
668. Ibid., 348.
669. Randy Alcorn, *We Shall See God* (Carol Stream, IL: Tyndale House, 2011), 44.
670. Randy Alcorn, *Deadline* (Sisters, OR: Multnomah Publishers, 1994), 338–345.
671. Donald A. Carson, *The Gospel according to John* (Grand Rapids, MI: Eerdmans, 1991), 489.
672. Charles H. Spurgeon, "Fallen Asleep," Sermon 2659, January 29, 1882, as cited in Randy Alcorn, *We Shall See God* (Carol Stream, IL: Tyndale House, 2011), 54.
673. C. S. Lewis, *The Problem of Pain* (New York: Macmillan, 1962), 147.
674. J. C. Ryle, *Heaven* (Ross-shire, UK: Christian Focus Publications, 2000), 10.
675. Bruce Milne, *The Message of Heaven and Hell* (Downers Grove, IL: InterVarsity Press, 2002), 273.
676. Ellen G. White, *The Great Controversy*, cited in Walton J. Brown, *Home at Last* (Washington, DC: Review and Herald Publishing, 1983), 8.
677. Mark Buchanan, *Things Unseen* (Sisters, OR: Multnomah Publishers, 2002), 74–75.
678. John Eldredge, *The Journey of Desire* (Nashville: Thomas Nelson, 2000), x.
679. John Milton, *Paradise Lost*, bk. 5, lines 574–576.
680. Paul Marshall with Lela Gilbert, *Heaven Is Not My Home* (Nashville: Word, 1998), 247, 249.
681. Philip Yancey, *Disappointment with God* (Grand Rapids, MI: Zondervan, 1988), 246.
682. Amy Carmichael, cited in *Promises of Heaven* (Wheaton, IL: Harold Shaw Publishers, 1997), 39.
683. Randy Alcorn, *Heaven* (Carol Stream, IL: Tyndale House, 2004), 333–334.
684. Ibid., 456.
685. Ibid., 334–335.
686. Ibid., 335.
687. Randy Alcorn, *Dominion* (Colorado Springs: WaterBrook, 1996), 98–99.
688. Randy Alcorn, *The Law of Rewards* (Carol Stream, IL: Tyndale House, 2003), 80.
689. Randy Alcorn, *Dominion* (Colorado Springs: WaterBrook, 1996), 307–308.
690. Randy Alcorn, *Heaven* (Carol Stream, IL: Tyndale House, 2004), 157.
691. Randy Alcorn, *Safely Home* (Carol Stream, IL: Tyndale House, 2001) 391–392.
692. Arthur Bennett, ed., *The Valley of Vision* (Carlisle, PA: Banner of Truth, 2002), 40–41.
693. Ibid., 143.
694. Thomas Boston, *Human Nature in Its Fourfold State*, http://www.gracegems.org/28/human_nature11.htm.
695. Bruce Milne, *The Message of Heaven and Hell* (Downers Grove, IL: InterVarsity Press, 2002), 191.
696. Ibid., 198.
697. Abraham Kuyper, *Abraham Kuyper: A Centennial Reader*, Bratt James, ed. (Grand Rapids, MI: Eerdmans, 1998), 488.
698. Bruce Milne, *The Message of Heaven and Hell* (Downers Grove, IL: InterVarsity Press, 2002), 198.
699. A. W. Tozer and H. Verploegh, *The Quotable Tozer II* (Camp Hill, PA: WingSpread, 1997), 102.
700. A. W. Tozer, *The Knowledge of the Holy* (San Francisco: Harper and Row, 1961), 89.
701. J. I. Packer, *Your Father Loves You* (Colorado Springs: Harold Shaw Publishers, 1986), x.
702. Charles H. Spurgeon, "Bringing the King Back," Sermon 808, http://www.spurgeongems.org/vols13-15/chs808.pdf.

703. Charles H. Spurgeon, *Spurgeon at His Best* (Grand Rapids, MI: Baker Book House, 1988) 96.

704. T. H. L. Parker, *John Calvin: A Biography* (Philadelphia: The Westminster Press, 1975), 155.

705. Steven J. Lawson, *Heaven Help Us!* (Colorado Springs: NavPress, 1995), 76.

706. John Bunyan, *The Pilgrim's Progress*, Part II.

707. Peter Toon, *Heaven and Hell* (Nashville: Thomas Nelson, 1986), 205.

708. C. S. Lewis, *Letters of C. S. Lewis to Arthur Greeves,* February 22, 1944.

709. Wayne Grudem, *Systematic Theology* (Grand Rapids, MI: Zondervan, 1994), 1158–1164.

710. Erich Sauer, *The King of the Earth* (Grand Rapids, MI: Eerdmans, 1962), 99–100.

711. Randy Alcorn, *Dominion* (Colorado Springs: WaterBrook, 1996), 90–91.

712. Randy Alcorn, *We Shall See God* (Carol Stream, IL: Tyndale House, 2011), 86.

713. Arthur Bennett, ed., *The Valley of Vision* (Carlisle, PA: Banner of Truth, 2002), 292–293.

714. C. S. Lewis, The Chronicles of Narnia Series (New York: HarperCollins, 2001), 744.

715. Father J. Boudreau, SJ, *The Happiness of Heaven* (Rockford, IL: TAN Books, 1984), 95–96.

716. Isaac Watts, "Psalm 92:1, Sweet Is the Work of God My King."

717. Father J. Boudreau, SJ, *The Happiness of Heaven* (Rockford, IL: TAN Books, 1984), 103–104.

718. Ibid., 124.

719. Jonathan Edwards, as quoted in Richard Brooks, *The Doors of Heaven* (Ross-shire, UK: Christian Focus Publications, 1998), 80–81.

720. Blaise Pascal, *Pensées*, para. 398, 425, quoted in John Eldredge, *The Journey of Desire* (Nashville: Thomas Nelson, 2000), 12–13.

721. St. Thomas Aquinas, *Summa Theologica.*

722. Ibid.

723. A. W. Tozer and H. Verploegh, *The Quotable Tozer II* (Camp Hill, PA: WingSpread, 1997), 103–104.

724. Charles H. Spurgeon, "God Rejoicing in the New Creation," Sermon 2211, July 5, 1891, as cited in Randy Alcorn, *We Shall See God* (Carol Stream, IL: Tyndale House, 2011), 156–157.

725. Paul Helm, *The Last Things* (Carlisle, PA: Banner of Truth, 1989), 131.

726. George R. Beasley-Murray, *The Book of Revelation* (Oliphant, 1974), 350.

727. Jonathan Edwards, *Heaven: A World of Love* (Amityville, NY: Calvary Press, 1999), 41.

728. John Gilmore, *Probing Heaven* (Grand Rapids, MI: Baker Book House, 1991), 251, 255.

729. Ibid., 329.

730. Richard Baxter, *The Saints' Everlasting Rest*, http://www.ccel.org/ccel/baxter/saints_rest.iii .XV.html.

731. Peter Kreeft, *Everything You Ever Wanted to Know about Heaven* (San Francisco: Ignatius Press, 1990), 198.

732. Steven J. Lawson, *Heaven Help Us!* (Colorado Springs: NavPress, 1995), 25.

733. George MacDonald and Rolland Hein, *The Heart of George MacDonald* (Oxford: Regent College Publishing, 2004), 13.

734. T. W. Hunt and Melana Hunt Monroe, *From Heaven's View* (Nashville: Broadman and Holman, 2002), 231–232.

735. Martin Luther, cited by Randy Alcorn, *Heaven* (Carol Stream, IL: Tyndale House, 2004), 407.

736. C. S. Lewis, *Letters to Malcolm* (New York: Harcourt Brace Jovanovich, 1963), 92–93.

737. C. S. Lewis, *The Last Battle* (New York: Collier, 1956), 179.

738. Charles H. Spurgeon, "God Rejoicing in the New Creation," Sermon 2211, July 5, 1891, www.spurgeongems.org.

739. John Gilmore, *Probing Heaven* (Grand Rapids, MI: Baker Book House, 1991), 248.

740. Ibid., 251.

741. Charles H. Spurgeon, "The Sympathy of the Two Worlds," Sermon 203, July 4, 1858, www.spurgeongems.org.

742. Douglas Connelly, *The Promise of Heaven* (Downers Grove, IL: InterVarsity Press, 2000), 116.

743. Cyprian, *Treatise VII: On the Morality*, quoted in *A Glimpse of Heaven* (New York: Howard Books, 2007), xiii.

744. E. J. Fortman, SJ, *Everlasting Life after Death* (New York: Alba House, 1976), 309.

745. Jonathan Edwards, *Heaven: A World of Love* (Amityville, NY: Calvary Press, 1999), 21.

746. Ibid., 35–36.

747. Ibid., 36.

748. Sam Storms, "Heaven: The Eternal Increase of Joy," *Decision* Magazine (Billy Graham Evangelistic Association, May 1, 2007), http://www.billygraham.org/articlepage.asp?articleid=810.

749. Ibid.

750. Ibid.

751. Ibid.

752. Sarah K. Bolton, *Famous Men of Science* (London: Hodder and Stoughton, 1893), 18.

753. A. W. Tozer, *Who Put Jesus on the Cross?* (Camp Hill, PA: WingSpread, 1996), 132–134.

754. Randy Alcorn, *We Shall See God* (Carol Stream, IL: Tyndale House, 2011), 153–154.

755. Randy Alcorn, *50 Days of Heaven* (Carol Stream, IL: Tyndale House, 2006), 233–234.

756. Randy Alcorn, *The Law of Rewards* (Carol Stream, IL: Tyndale House, 2003), 94.

757. Randy Alcorn, *Heaven* (Carol Stream, IL: Tyndale House, 2004), 170.

758. Randy Alcorn, *50 Days of Heaven* (Carol Stream, IL: Tyndale House, 2006), 138.

759. Paul Helm, *The Last Things* (Carlisle, PA: Banner of Truth, 1989), 112.

760. Daniel A. Brown, PhD, *What the Bible Reveals about Heaven* (Ventura, CA: Regal Books, 1999), 170.

761. Isaac Watts, *The World to Come* (Morgan, PA: Soli Deo Gloria Publications, 1954; originally written in 1745), 93.

762. Bruce Milne, *The Message of Heaven and Hell* (Downers Grove, IL: InterVarsity Press, 2002), 299.

763. Ibid., 300.

764. John Gilmore, *Probing Heaven* (Grand Rapids, MI: Baker Book House, 1991), 317.

765. Thomas Ice and Timothy J. Demy, *What the Bible Says about Heaven and Eternity* (Grand Rapids, MI: Kregel Publications, 2000), 43.

766. Larry R. Dick, *A Taste of Heaven* (Victoria, BC: Trafford Publishing, 2002), 160.

767. Max Lucado, *When Christ Comes* (Nashville: W Publishing Group, 1999), 102.

768. Paul Helm, *The Last Things* (Carlisle, PA: Banner of Truth, 1989), 59.

769. Ibid., 65–66.

770. John Wesley, *The Nature of Salvation* (Minneapolis: Bethany House, 1987), 135.

771. Paul Helm, *The Last Things* (Carlisle, PA: Banner of Truth, 1989), 70.

772. Ibid., 78.

773. R. T. Kendall, *When God Says "Well Done!"* (Scotland: Christian Focus Publications, 1993), 13.

774. Paul Helm, *The Last Things* (Carlisle, PA: Banner of Truth, 1989), 62.

775. Ibid., 71.

776. Jonathan Edwards, "Observations on the Scriptures," #27, *Miscellaneous Observations on Important Theological Subjects*, vol. 8 (London: James Black and Son, 1817).

777. Jonathan Edwards, *The Works of Jonathan Edwards* (Edinburgh: Banner of Truth, reprinted 1992), 883–884.

778. James Ussher, *A Body of Divinity* (Birmingham, AL: Solid Ground Christian Books, 2007), 408.

779. Randy Alcorn, *The Law of Rewards* (Carol Stream, IL: Tyndale House, 2003), 60.

780. Randy Alcorn, *Money, Possessions, and Eternity* (Carol Stream, IL: Tyndale House, 2003), 148.

781. Ibid., 149–150.

782. Randy Alcorn, *Heaven* (Carol Stream, IL: Tyndale House, 2004), 347.

783. Bruce Milne, *The Message of Heaven and Hell* (Downers Grove, IL: InterVarsity Press, 2002), 111.

784. Richard Mouw, *When the Kings Come Marching In* (Grand Rapids, MI: Eerdmans, 1983), 30.

785. Anthony A. Hoekema, *The Bible and the Future* (Grand Rapids, MI: Eerdmans, 1979), 133.

786. Anthony F. Buzzard, *Our Fathers Who Aren't in Heaven* (McDonough, GA: Atlanta Bible College and Restoration Fellowship, 1999), 78.

787. Herman Ridderbos, *Paul and Jesus*, trans., David H. Freeman (Philadelphia, PA: Presbyterian and Reformed, 1958), 77.

788. Anthony A. Hoekema, *The Bible and the Future* (Grand Rapids, MI: Eerdmans, 1979), 33.

789. Max Lucado, *When Christ Comes* (Nashville: W Publishing Group, 1999), 82–83.

790. Anthony F. Buzzard, *Our Fathers Who Aren't in Heaven* (McDonough, GA: Atlanta Bible College and Restoration Fellowship, 1999), 27.

791. Ibid., 54.

792. Ibid., 62.

793. N. T. Wright, *Surprised by Hope* (New York: HarperCollins, 2008).

794. Anthony F. Buzzard, *Our Fathers Who Aren't in Heaven* (McDonough, GA: Atlanta Bible College and Restoration Fellowship, 1999), 100.

795. George Ladd, *A Theology of the New Testament* (Grand Rapids, MI: Eerdmans, 1974), 48.

796. Anthony F. Buzzard, *Our Fathers Who Aren't in Heaven* (McDonough, GA: Atlanta Bible College and Restoration Fellowship, 1999), 147.

797. Ibid., 237.

798. James Ussher, *A Body of Divinity* (Birmingham, AL: Solid Ground Christian Books, 2007), 407.

799. Randy Alcorn, *Heaven* (Carol Stream, IL: Tyndale House, 2004), 212–213.

800. Ibid., 222.

801. W. Graham Scroggie, DD, *What about Heaven?* (London: Christian Literature Crusade, 1940), 75.

802. Father J. Boudreau, SJ, *The Happiness of Heaven* (Rockford, IL: TAN Books, 1984), 122.

803. St. Teresa of Avila, *The Life of Teresa of Jesus: The Autobiography of St. Teresa of Avila,* trans., Edgar A. Peers (New York: Random House, 1960), 335.

804. John Gilmore, *Probing Heaven* (Grand Rapids, MI: Baker Book House, 1991), 287.

805. Ibid., 319.

806. William Hendriksen, *The Bible on the Life Hereafter* (Grand Rapids, MI: Baker Book House, 1959), 75–76.

807. Don Baker, *Heaven: A Glimpse of Your Future Home* (Portland, OR: Multnomah Publishers, 1983).

808. Ivor Powell, *Heaven: My Father's Country* (Grand Rapids, MI: Kregel Publications, 1995), 86.

809. Walton J. Brown, *Home at Last* (Washington, DC: Review and Herald Publishing, 1983), 78.

810. Wayne Grudem, *Systematic Theology* (Grand Rapids, MI: Zondervan Publishing House, 1994), 1158–1164.

811. Ibid., 1162.

812. Francis Schaeffer, *Art and the Bible* (Downers Grove, IL: InterVarsity Press, 1973), 61.

813. Father J. Boudreau, SJ, *The Happiness of Heaven* (Rockford, IL: TAN Books, 1984), 120–122.

814. Philip Melanchthon, cited by W. Robertson Nicoll, *Reunion in Eternity* (New York: George H. Doran, 1919), 117–118.

815. Peter Kreeft, *Everything You Ever Wanted to Know about Heaven* (San Francisco: Ignatius Press, 1990), 28.

816. Judson B. Palmer, "The Child of God between Death and the Resurrection," http://bibleteacher.org/cogbda.htm.

817. E. J. Fortman, SJ, *Everlasting Life after Death* (New York: Alba House, 1976), 316.

818. St. Jerome, *The Principal Works of St. Jerome* (Canterbury: W. H. Fremantle, 1892).

819. C. S. Lewis, *God in the Dock* (Grand Rapids, MI: Eerdmans, 1970), 216.

820. Randy Alcorn, *Heaven* (Carol Stream, IL: Tyndale House, 2004), 320.

821. Randy Alcorn, *TouchPoints: Heaven* (Carol Stream, IL: Tyndale House, 2008), 124.

822. Randy Alcorn, *Heaven* (Carol Stream, IL: Tyndale House, 2004), 305.

823. Randy Alcorn, *50 Days of Heaven* (Carol Stream, IL: Tyndale House, 2006), 184–185.

824. Randy Alcorn, *Heaven* (Carol Stream, IL: Tyndale House, 2004), 322–323.

825. Ibid., 310.

826. Ibid., 324–325.

827. Ibid., 325–326.

828. Arthur Bennett, ed., *The Valley of Vision* (Carlisle, PA: Banner of Truth, 2002), 373.

829. Drake W. Whitchurch, *Waking from Earth* (Kearney, NE: Morris Publishing, 1999), 129.

830. Steven J. Lawson, *Heaven Help Us!* (Colorado Springs: NavPress, 1995), 192.

831. James M. Campbell, DD, *Heaven Opened* (New York: Revell, 1924), 143.

832. George MacDonald, "A Voice," in *Sir Gibbie* (New York: A. L. Burt, n.d. [First published in London: Hurst and Blackett, 1880]), http://www.ccel.org/ccel/macdonald/sirgibbie.xxviii .html. (NOTE: Bethany House republished *Sir Gibbie* under the title *The Baronet's Song*, abridging the book and modernizing the language from the hard-to-read Scottish dialect. This passage was not included in the abridgement, so Dr. Richard Leonard created the updated version; chapter 27, 188–192.)

833. William Barclay, *The Apostles' Creed* (Louisville: Westminster John Knox Press, 2005), 305.

834. St. Bede, a sermon preached on All Saint's Day ca. 710, cited by William Jennings Bryan, ed., *The World's Famous Orations* (New York: Funk and Wagnalls, 1906).

835. J. C. Ryle, *Heaven* (Ross-shire, UK: Christian Focus Publications, 2000), 84.

836. Cicero, *De Amicitia*, XXIII.

837. C. S. Lewis, *The Four Loves* (New York: Harcourt Brace Jovanovich, 1960), 190–191.

838. Dr. Chuck McGowen, *Let's Talk about Heaven* (Phoenix, AZ: ACW Press, 2001), 82.

839. W. Graham Scroggie, DD, *What about Heaven?* (London: Christian Literature Crusade, 1940), 93–94.

840. Randy Alcorn, *Heaven* (Carol Stream, IL: Tyndale House, 2004), 337.

841. Randy Alcorn, *50 Days of Heaven* (Carol Stream, IL: Tyndale House, 2006), 203–204.

842. Ibid., 203.

843. Randy Alcorn, *Heaven* (Carol Stream, IL: Tyndale House, 2006), 350–351.

844. Ibid., 340.

845. Randy Alcorn, *Heaven* (Carol Stream, IL: Tyndale House, 2004), 290.

846. Randy Alcorn, *Heaven* (Carol Stream, IL: Tyndale House, 2006), 372–373.

847. C. S. Lewis, The Chronicles of Narnia Series (New York: HarperCollins, 2001), 758.

848. Anthony A. Hoekema, *The Bible and the Future* (Grand Rapids, MI: Eerdmans, 1979), 274.

849. Paul Marshall with Lela Gilbert, *Heaven Is Not My Home* (Nashville: Word, 1998), 11.

850. Anthony F. Buzzard, *Our Fathers Who Aren't in Heaven* (McDonough, GA: Atlanta Bible College and Restoration Fellowship, 1999), 41–45.

851. Bruce Milne, *The Message of Heaven and Hell* (Downers Grove, IL: InterVarsity Press, 2002), 273.

852. Anthony A. Hoekema, *The Bible and the Future* (Grand Rapids, MI: Eerdmans, 1979), 276.

853. Steven J. Lawson, *Heaven Help Us!* (Colorado Springs: NavPress, 1995), 142.

854. Ibid., 148–149.

855. Ralph Waldo Emerson, "Nature," *Addresses and Lectures*, 1849.

856. R. C. H. Lenski, *The Interpretation of St. Paul's Epistle to the Romans* (Minneapolis: Augsburg Publishing House, 1936), 538.

857. Steven J. Lawson, *Heaven Help Us!* (Colorado Springs: NavPress, 1995), 156.

858. Michael E. Wittmer, *Heaven Is a Place on Earth* (Grand Rapids, MI: Zondervan, 2004), 16–17, 205.

859. Ibid., 74.

860. Greg K. Beale, "The Eschatological Conception of New Testament Theology," *Eschatology in Bible and Theology*, eds., Kent E. Brower and Mark W. Elliott (Downers Grove, IL: InterVarsity Press, 1997), 21–22.

861. John Gilmore, *Probing Heaven* (Grand Rapids, MI: Baker Book House, 1991), 86–87.

862. E. J. Fortman, SJ, *Everlasting Life after Death* (New York: Alba House, 1976), 310.

863. Anthony A. Hoekema, *The Bible and the Future* (Grand Rapids, MI: Eerdmans, 1979), 280.

864. E. J. Fortman, SJ, *Everlasting Life after Death* (New York: Alba House, 1976), 311.

865. J. A. Schep, *The Nature of the Resurrection Body* (Grand Rapids, MI: Eerdmans, 1964), 218–219.

866. Irenaeus, *Against Heresies.* Book V, Chapter XXXVI:1, quoted in A. Roberts, J. Donaldson, and A. C. Coxe, *The Ante-Nicene Fathers Vol. I: Translations of the Writings of the Fathers down to AD 325* (Oak Harbor, WA: Logos Research Systems, 1997), 566–567.

867. Henry Alford, *Greek New Testament*, Vol. I, 35, 36, emphasis added.

868. C. S. Lewis, *Letters to Malcolm* (New York: Harcourt Brace Jovanovich, 1963), 84.

869. C. S. Lewis, *The Last Battle* (New York: Macmillan, 1956), 161–162.

870. Ibid., 181.

871. A. A. Hodge, *Evangelical Theology* (Edinburgh: Banner of Truth, 1976), 399–402.

872. C. S. Lewis, *Letters to Malcolm* (New York: Harcourt Brace Jovanovich, 1963), 121–122.

873. Charles H. Spurgeon, "Heavenly Rest," Sermon 133, May 24, 1857, www.spurgeongems.org.

874. Anthony F. Buzzard, *Our Fathers Who Aren't in Heaven* (McDonough, GA: Atlanta Bible College and Restoration Fellowship, 1999), 77.

875. John Calvin, *Commentary on the Book of the Prophet Isaiah*, Volume Four, Chapter 65, Verse 22.

876. Anselm, *Why the God-Man?* (LaSalle, IL: Open Court Publishing, 1951), 217.

877. N. T. Wright, *Surprised by Hope* (New York: HarperCollins, 2008), 18.

878. Randy Alcorn, *Heaven* (Carol Stream, IL: Tyndale House, 2004), 45.

879. Ibid., 81.

880. Randy Alcorn, *TouchPoints: Heaven* (Carol Stream, IL: Tyndale House, 2008), 191.

881. Randy Alcorn, *Heaven* (Carol Stream, IL: Tyndale House, 2004), 157.

882. Randy Alcorn, *50 Days of Heaven* (Carol Stream, IL: Tyndale House, 2006), 110.

883. Randy Alcorn, *In Light of Eternity* (Colorado Springs: WaterBrook, 1999), 31–32.

884. Randy Alcorn, *Heaven* (Carol Stream, IL: Tyndale House, 2004), 248.

885. Ibid., 269.

886. Augustine, *Confessions,* trans., H. Chadwick (Oxford: Oxford Press, 1991), 257.

887. Anthony A. Hoekema, "Heaven: Not Just an Eternal Day Off," *Christianity Today* (June 6, 2003).

888. Larry R. Dick, *A Taste of Heaven* (Victoria, BC: Trafford Publishing, 2002), 81.

889. Steven J. Lawson, *Heaven Help Us!* (Colorado Springs: NavPress, 1995), 127–128.

890. D. L. Moody, *Heaven: Where It Is, Its Inhabitants, and How to Get There* (New York: Revell, 1880), 29.

891. Tony Evans, *Tony Evans Speaks Out on Heaven and Hell* (Chicago: Moody Press, 2000), 32.

892. John Gilmore, *Probing Heaven* (Grand Rapids, MI: Baker Book House, 1991), 115.

893. F. B. Meyer, as quoted in Douglas Connelly, *The Promise of Heaven* (Downers Grove, IL: InterVarsity Press, 2000), 122–123.

894. William Hendriksen, *More than Conquerers* (Grand Rapids, MI: Baker, 1961), 249.

895. Larry R. Dick, *A Taste of Heaven* (Victoria, BC: Trafford Publishing, 2002), 3.

896. Steven J. Lawson, *Heaven Help Us!* (Colorado Springs: NavPress, 1995), 131, 132.

897. Arthur O. Roberts, *Exploring Heaven* (San Francisco: HarperSanFrancisco, 2003), 73.

898. Frederick Buechner, quoted in *A Little Bit of Heaven* (Tulsa, OK: Honor Books, 1995), 118.

899. J. Sidlow Baxter, *The Other Side of Death* (Grand Rapids, MI: Kregel Publications, 1987), 46–47.

900. E. J. Fortman, SJ, *Everlasting Life after Death* (New York: Alba House, 1976), 318.

901. Isaac Watts, *The World to Come* (Morgan, PA: Soli Deo Gloria Publications, 1954; originally written in 1745), 158–159.

902. Richard Baxter, *The Saints' Everlasting Rest*, http://www.ccel.org/ccel/baxter/saints_rest.iii.XV.html.

903. A. W. Tozer, *The Tozer Pulpit, Volume One* (Camp Hill, PA: WingSpread, 1994), 147–148.

904. Charles H. Spurgeon, "Creation's Groans and the Saints' Sighs," Sermon 788, January 5, 1868, www.spurgeongems.org.

905. Randy Alcorn, *Heaven* (Carol Stream, IL: Tyndale House, 2004), 247–249.

906. Ibid., 258–260.

907. Ibid., 444–445.

908. Ibid., 243.

909. Randy Alcorn, *50 Days of Heaven* (Carol Stream, IL: Tyndale House, 2006), 166.

910. Randy Alcorn, *Heaven* (Carol Stream, IL: Tyndale House, 2004), 78.

911. Randy Alcorn, *TouchPoints: Heaven* (Carol Stream, IL: Tyndale House, 2008), 142.

912. Randy Alcorn, *Heaven* (Carol Stream, IL: Tyndale House, 2004), 253.

913. Ibid., 417.

914. Ibid., 260.

915. John Milton, cited by James M. Campbell, *Heaven Opened* (New York: Revell, 1924), 75.

916. Arthur Bennett, ed., *The Valley of Vision* (Carlisle, PA: Banner of Truth, 2002), 213.

917. Richard Baxter, *The Saints' Everlasting Rest* (Edinburgh: Waugh and Innes, 1824), 32.

918. René Pache, *The Future Life* (Chicago: Moody Press, 1971), 68.

919. Alister E. McGrath, *A Brief History of Heaven* (Malden, MA: Blackwell, 2003), 40.

920. James M. Campbell, DD, *Heaven Opened* (New York: Revell, 1924), 151.

921. William Hendriksen, *The Bible on the Life Hereafter* (Grand Rapids, MI: Baker Book House, 1959), 55.

922. John R. Rice, *Bible Facts about Heaven* (Murfreesboro, TN: Sword of the Lord Publishers, 1993), 35.

923. Spiros Zodhiates, *Life after Death* (Chattanooga, TN: AMG Publishers, 1977), 108.

924. J. C. Ryle, *Holiness* (Welwyn, UK: Evangelical Press, 1985), 40.

925. Alister E. McGrath, *A Brief History of Heaven* (Oxford: Blackwell Publishing, 2003), 70 (describing the viewpoint of C. S. Lewis and J. R. R. Tolkien).

926. J. Sidlow Baxter, *The Other Side of Death* (Grand Rapids, MI: Kregel Publications, 1987), 56.

927. Ibid., 104–105.

928. Ibid., 58–59.

929. Dr. Steven Waterhouse, *Not by Bread Alone* (Amarillo, TX: Westcliff Press, 2000), 103.

930. J. Sidlow Baxter, *The Other Side of Death* (Grand Rapids, MI: Kregel Publications, 1987), 60.

931. Ibid., 61–62.

932. Charles H. Spurgeon, "Creation's Groans and the Saints' Sighs," Sermon 788, January 5, 1868, www.spurgeongems.org.

933. John Owen, *The Works of John Owen*, vol. 1:269.

934. John Bunyan, *The Pilgrim's Progress* (New York: Grosset and Dunlap Publishers, n.d.), 180.

935. Randy Alcorn, *Heaven* (Carol Stream, IL: Tyndale House, 2004), 63.

936. Ibid., 56.

937. Randy Alcorn, *TouchPoints: Heaven* (Carol Stream, IL: Tyndale House, 2008), 30–31.

938. Randy Alcorn, *50 Days of Heaven* (Carol Stream, IL: Tyndale House, 2006), 35–36.

939. Randy Alcorn, *Heaven* (Carol Stream, IL: Tyndale House, 2004), 73.

940. Ibid., 111.

941. John Wesley, cited in Ron Rhodes, *Heaven: The Undiscovered Country* (Eugene, OR: Harvest House), Introduction.

942. Charles Ferguson Ball, *Heaven* (Wheaton, IL: Victor Books, 1980), 111.

943. John R. Rice, *Bible Facts about Heaven* (Murfreesboro, TN: Sword of the Lord Publishers, 1993), 54–57.

944. Isaac Watts, *The World to Come* (Morgan, PA: Soli Deo Gloria Publications, 1954; originally written in 1745), 92–93.

945. Erich Sauer, *The King of the Earth* (Grand Rapids, MI: Eerdmans, 1962), 99.

946. John Gilmore, *Probing Heaven* (Grand Rapids, MI: Baker Book House, 1991), 135.

947. Arthur Bennett, ed., *The Valley of Vision* (Carlisle, PA: Banner of Truth, 2002), "Divine Support."

948. Ibid., "Morning Dedication."

949. Ibid., "In Prayer."

950. Peter Kreeft, *Everything You Ever Wanted to Know about Heaven* (San Francisco: Ignatius Press, 1990), 20.

951. Ibid., 246.
952. Spiros Zodhiates, *Life after Death* (Chattanooga, TN: AMG Publishers, 1977), 191, 217–219.
953. Richard Brooks, *The Doors of Heaven* (Ross-shire, UK: Christian Focus Publications, 1998), 22.
954. Ivor Powell, *Heaven: My Father's Country* (Grand Rapids, MI: Kregel Publications, 1995), 66.
955. Paul Helm, *The Last Things* (Carlisle, PA: Banner of Truth, 1989), 89.
956. Randy Alcorn, *Heaven* (Carol Stream, IL: Tyndale House, 2004), 23.
957. Randy Alcorn, *We Shall See God* (Carol Stream, IL: Tyndale House, 2011), 91.
958. John Wesley, "The General Deliverance," *Sermons on Several Occasions*, vol. 1 (London, 1825), 131.
959. Peter Kreeft, *Everything You Ever Wanted to Know about Heaven* (San Francisco: Ignatius Press, 1990), 45.
960. Ibid., 45–46.
961. C. S. Lewis, *The Problem of Pain* (New York: Macmillan, 1962), 139–141.
962. Niki Behrikis Shanahan, *There Is Eternal Life for Animals* (Tyngsborough, MA: Pete Publishing, 2002), 4–5.
963. Steve Wohlberg, *Will My Pet Go to Heaven?* (Enumclaw, WA: WinePress Publishing, 2002), 63–64.
964. R. C. H. Lenski, *The Interpretation of St. Paul's Epistle to the Romans* (Minneapolis: Augsburg Publishing House, 1936), 534.
965. Gary R. Habermas and J. P. Moreland, *Beyond Death* (Wheaton, IL: Crossway, 1998), 106.
966. Steve Wohlberg, *Will My Pet Go to Heaven?* (Enumclaw, WA: WinePress Publishing, 2002), 49.
967. Joni Eareckson Tada, *Holiness in Hidden Places* (Nashville: J. Countryman, 1999), 133.
968. John Piper, *Future Grace* (Sisters, OR: Multnomah Publishers, 1995), 381–382.
969. C. S. Lewis, *The Great Divorce* (New York: Macmillan, 1946), 107–108.
970. Steve Wohlberg, *Will My Pet Go to Heaven?* (Enumclaw, WA: WinePress Publishing, 2002), 57.
971. John Wesley, "The General Deliverance, Sermon 60," with comments by Randy Alcorn, at Eternal Perspective Ministries, http://www.epm.org/articles/wesleysermon.html.
972. Randy Alcorn, *Heaven* (Carol Stream, IL: Tyndale House, 2004), 387.
973. Ibid., 384.
974. Ibid., 383.
975. Ibid., 388–389.
976. Ibid., 391–392.
977. Randy Alcorn, *50 Days of Heaven* (Carol Stream, IL: Tyndale House, 2006), 160–161.
978. Ibid., 154–155.
979. Randy Alcorn, *Heaven* (Carol Stream, IL: Tyndale House, 2004), 400.
980. Ibid., 379.
981. Ibid., 385.
982. Randy Alcorn, *50 Days of Heaven* (Carol Stream, IL: Tyndale House, 2006), 156–157.
983. Randy Alcorn, *Heaven* (Carol Stream, IL: Tyndale House, 2004), 384–385.
984. Randy Alcorn, *TouchPoints: Heaven* (Carol Stream, IL: Tyndale House, 2008), 82.
985. Aristides, *Apology*, 15.
986. Arthur Bennett, ed., *The Valley of Vision* (Carlisle, PA: Banner of Truth, 2002), 387.
987. Jim Elliot, cited by Elisabeth Elliot, *Through Gates of Splendor* (Carol Stream, IL: Tyndale, 1986), 172.
988. Richard Brooks, *The Doors of Heaven* (Ross-shire, UK: Christian Focus Publications, 1998), 64.
989. Ibid., 87.
990. Bruce Milne, *The Message of Heaven and Hell* (Downers Grove, IL: InterVarsity Press, 2002), 263.

991. David Chilton, *Paradise Restored* (Ft. Worth, TX: Dominion Press, 1987), 51.

992. Joni Eareckson Tada, *Heaven: Your Real Home* (Grand Rapids, MI: Zondervan, 1995), 110.

993. Joseph M. Stowell, *Eternity* (Chicago: Moody Press, 1995), 59.

994. A. J. Conyers, *The Eclipse of Heaven* (Downers Grove, IL: InterVarsity Press 1992), 58.

995. Joseph M. Stowell, *Eternity* (Chicago: Moody Press, 1995), 68.

996. Ibid., 88.

997. Ibid., 191.

998. A. W. Tozer, "The World to Come," in *Of God and Men* (Harrisburg, PA: Christian Publications, 1960), 127, 129–130.

999. Charles H. Spurgeon, *Morning and Evening: Daily Readings* (1869) March 10, evening.

1000. John Bunyan, cited by Bruce Milne, *The Message of Heaven and Hell* (Downers Grove, IL: InterVarsity Press, 2002), 282.

1001. Joni Eareckson Tada, *Heaven: Your Real Home* (Grand Rapids, MI: Zondervan, 1995), 112.

1002. Wayne Martindale, PhD, ed., *Journey to the Celestial City* (Chicago: Moody Press, 1995), 75.

1003. Randy Alcorn, *The Law of Rewards* (Carol Stream, IL: Tyndale House, 2003), 37.

1004. Randy Alcorn, *Money, Possessions, and Eternity* (Carol Stream, IL: Tyndale House, 2003), 134.

1005. Ibid., 159.

1006. Randy Alcorn, *50 Days of Heaven* (Carol Stream, IL: Tyndale House, 2006), 270.

1007. Randy Alcorn, *Heaven* (Carol Stream, IL: Tyndale House, 2004), 472.

1008. Thomas Aquinas, *Summa Theologica*, quoted in Craig Brian Larson and Brian Lowery, *1001 Quotations That Connect* (Grand Rapids, MI: Zondervan, 2009), quotation 602.

1009. Arthur O. Roberts, *Exploring Heaven* (San Francisco: HarperSanFrancisco, 2003), 46.

1010. Paul Marshall with Lela Gilbert, *Heaven Is Not My Home* (Nashville: Word Publishing, 1998), 106–107.

1011. H. A. Williams, *True Resurrection* (New York: Holt, Rinehart, Winston, 1972), 36, quoted in Arthur O. Roberts, *Exploring Heaven* (San Francisco: HarperSanFrancisco, 1989), 119.

1012. Ivor Powell, *Heaven: My Father's Country* (Grand Rapids, MI: Kregel Publications, 1995), 91.

1013. C. S. Lewis, *The Joyful Christian* (New York: Simon and Schuster, 1996), 228.

1014. *Chariots of Fire,* directed by Hugh Hudson (Warner Bros., 1981).

1015. Mart De Haan, *Been Thinking About* (Grand Rapids, MI: RBC Ministries, 2007).

1016. Charles H. Spurgeon, *Morning and Evening*, December 19 (evening), as cited in Randy Alcorn, *We Shall See God* (Carol Stream, IL: Tyndale House, 2011), 167–168.

1017. Randy Alcorn, *We Shall See God* (Carol Stream, IL: Tyndale House, 2011), 169–170.

1018. Randy Alcorn, *Heaven* (Carol Stream, IL: Tyndale House, 2004), 410–411.

1019. Ibid., 413.

1020. Ibid., 411.

1021. Ibid., 395.

1022. Randy Alcorn, *50 Days of Heaven* (Carol Stream, IL: Tyndale House, 2006), 120.

1023. Ibid., 115.

1024. Arthur Bennett, ed., *The Valley of Vision* (Carlisle, PA: Banner of Truth, 2002), 25.

1025. Jonathan Edwards, cited in Ola Elizabeth Winslow, *Jonathan Edwards: Basic Writings* (New York: New American Library, 1966), 142.

1026. J. C. Ryle, "Home at Last," as quoted in John MacArthur, *The Glory of Heaven* (Wheaton, IL: Crossway Books, 1998), 259.

1027. C. S. Lewis, *Mere Christianity* (San Francisco: HarperCollins, 2001), 74.

1028. Drake W. Whitchurch, *Waking from Earth* (Kearney, NE: Morris Publishing, 1999), 131, 132.

1029. Paul Helm, *The Last Things* (Carlisle, PA: Banner of Truth, 1989), 84.

1030. Father J. Boudreau, SJ, *The Happiness of Heaven* (Rockford, IL: TAN Books, 1984), 195–196.

1031. Steven J. Lawson, *Heaven Help Us!* (Colorado Springs: NavPress, 1995), 173.

1032. Alan Hirsch, *The Forgotten Ways* (Grand Rapids, MI: Baker Books, 2006), 111.

1033. John Knox, quoted in Bruce Milne, *The Message of Heaven and Hell* (Downers Grove, IL: InterVarsity Press, 2002), 73.

1034. Dr. Chuck McGowen, *Let's Talk about Heaven* (Phoenix, AZ: ACW Press, 2001), 95.

1035. Mark Buchanan, *Things Unseen* (Sisters, OR: Multnomah Publishers, 2002), 23.

1036. Helen Keller, cited by Philip Yancey, *Rumors of Another World* (Grand Rapids, MI: Zondervan, 2003), 59.

1037. Jonathan Edwards, *Heaven: A World of Love* (Amityville, NY: Calvary Press, 1999), 58–59.

1038. Charles H. Spurgeon, "Creation's Groans and the Saints' Sighs," Sermon 788, January 5, 1868, as cited in Randy Alcorn, *We Shall See God* (Carol Stream, IL: Tyndale House, 2011), 16.

1039. Tony Evans, *Tony Evans Speaks Out on Heaven and Hell* (Chicago: Moody Press, 2000), 37.

1040. Charles H. Spurgeon, *Metropolitan Tabernacle Pulpit* (1887; reprint, London: Banner of Truth, 1969), 14:419–420.

1041. Ivor Powell, *Heaven: My Father's Country* (Grand Rapids, MI: Kregel Publications, 1995), 73.

1042. Joseph M. Stowell, *Eternity* (Chicago: Moody Press, 1995), 58.

1043. Isaac Watts, *The World to Come* (Morgan, PA: Soli Deo Gloria Publications, 1954; originally written in 1745), 122–123.

1044. Chaim Potok, *The Chosen* (New York: Random House, 1967), 217.

1045. Dallas Willard, *The Divine Conspiracy* (San Francisco: HarperSanFrancisco, 1998), 398.

1046. Mark Buchanan, *Things Unseen* (Sisters, OR: Multnomah Publishers, 2002), 151.

1047. Thomas à Kempis, cited in Dr. Chuck McGowen, *Let's Talk about Heaven* (Phoenix, AZ: ACW Press, 2001), 135.

1048. Ray C. Stedman, *Authentic Christianity* (Waco, TX: Word Books, 1975), 143–144.

1049. Barry Morrow, *Heaven Observed* (Colorado Springs: NavPress, 2001), 258.

1050. Isaac Watts, *The World to Come* (Morgan, PA: Soli Deo Gloria Publications, 1954; originally written in 1745), 134.

1051. John Gilmore, *Probing Heaven* (Grand Rapids, MI: Baker Book House, 1991), 104.

1052. Charles H. Spurgeon, "The Hope Laid Up in Heaven," Sermon 1438, October 13, 1878, www.spurgeongems.org.

1053. E. X. Heatherley, *Our Heavenly Home* (Austin, TX: Balcony Publishing, 2000), 97.

1054. C. S. Lewis, *The Weight of Glory* (New York: HarperCollins, 2001), 45–46.

1055. Randy Alcorn, *Heaven* (Carol Stream, IL: Tyndale House, 2004), 453, 454–455.

1056. Randy Alcorn, *The Law of Rewards* (Carol Stream, IL: Tyndale House, 2003), 69.

1057. Randy Alcorn, "Death: Signing and Framing Your Life's Portrait," unpublished sermon manuscript.

1058. Randy Alcorn, *The Law of Rewards* (Carol Stream, IL: Tyndale House, 2003), 71–72.

1059. Randy Alcorn, *Money, Possessions, and Eternity* (Carol Stream, IL: Tyndale House, 2003), 161.

1060. Randy Alcorn, *The Treasure Principle* (Sisters, OR: Multnomah, 2001), 41, 59.

1061. Randy Alcorn, *Heaven* (Carol Stream, IL: Tyndale House, 2004), 455.

1062. N. T. Wright, *Surprised by Hope* (New York: HarperCollins, 2008), 93.

1063. Ibid., 100–101.

1064. Mark Buchanan, *Things Unseen* (Sisters, OR: Multnomah Publishers, 2002), 87.

1065. C. S. Lewis, *The Problem of Pain* (New York: Macmillan, 1962), 118–119 (emphasis in original).

1066. John Piper, "What Happens When You Die?" *Fresh Words,* July 25, 1993, www.desiringgod.org.

1067. Anthony A. Hoekema, *The Bible and the Future* (Grand Rapids, MI: Eerdmans, 1979), 275.

1068. Albert M. Wolters, *Creation Regained* (Grand Rapids, MI: Eerdmans, 1985), 58–59.

1069. Augustine, cited by Robert Llewelyn, *The Joy of the Saints* (Springfield, IL: Templegate Publishers, 1989), 125.

1070. Albert M. Wolters, *Creation Regained* (Grand Rapids, MI: Eerdmans, 1985), 51.

1071. Ibid., 57–58.

1072. Dorothy L. Sayers, "The Greatest Drama Ever Staged," in *The Whimsical Christian* (New York: Collier Macmillan, 1987), 12.

1073. John Stott, *The Cross of Christ*, adapted by Randy Alcorn, *90 Days of God's Goodness* (Sisters, OR: Multnomah Publishers, 2011), 85.

1074. Joseph Conrad, *Notes on Life and Letters*, J. H. Stape, ed. (Cambridge, UK: Cambridge University Press, 2004), 58.

1075. Bruce Milne, *The Message of Heaven and Hell* (Downers Grove, IL: InterVarsity Press, 2002), 323.

1076. W. Hendriksen, ThD, *More than Conquerors* (Grand Rapids, MI: Baker Book House, 1961), 253.

1077. Bruce Milne, *The Message of Heaven and Hell* (Downers Grove, IL: InterVarsity Press, 2002), 326.

1078. James M. Campbell, DD, *Heaven Opened* (New York: Revell, 1924), 129.

1079. Erich Sauer, *The King of the Earth* (Grand Rapids, MI: Eerdmans, 1962), 98.

1080. Anthony A. Hoekema, *The Bible and the Future* (Grand Rapids, MI: Eerdmans, 1979), 11.

1081. Ibid., 21.

1082. Max Lucado, *When Christ Comes* (Nashville: W Publishing Group, 1999), 109.

1083. Paul Marshall with Lela Gilbert, *Heaven Is Not My Home* (Nashville: Word Publishing, 1998), 33, 38.

1084. N. T. Wright, *Surprised by Hope* (New York: HarperCollins, 2008), 211–212.

1085. Albert M. Wolters, *Creation Regained* (Grand Rapids, MI: Eerdmans, 1985), 58.

1086. Ibid., 59–60.

1087. Ibid., 62.

1088. Erich Sauer, *The King of the Earth* (Grand Rapids, MI: Eerdmans, 1962), 97.

1089. E. J. Fortman, SJ, *Everlasting Life after Death* (New York: Alba House, 1976), 304–305.

1090. Randy Alcorn, *Heaven* (Carol Stream, IL: Tyndale House, 2004), 5.

1091. Randy Alcorn, *TouchPoints: Heaven* (Carol Stream, IL: Tyndale House, 2008), 15.

1092. Randy Alcorn, *Heaven* (Carol Stream, IL: Tyndale House, 2004), 81.

1093. Ibid., 89.

1094. Randy Alcorn, *We Shall See God* (Carol Stream, IL: Tyndale House, 2011), 45.

1095. Irenaeus, *Against Heresies*, 5:32, 1 (SC 153:396–399).

1096. Larry R. Dick, *A Taste of Heaven* (Victoria, BC: Trafford Publishing, 2002), 171–172.

1097. Arthur O. Roberts, *Exploring Heaven* (San Francisco: HarperSanFrancisco, 2003), 52.

1098. Richard Baxter, *The Saints' Everlasting Rest* (Grand Rapids, MI: Baker Book House, 1978), 17.

1099. Anthony F. Buzzard, *Our Fathers Who Aren't in Heaven* (McDonough, GA: Atlanta Bible College and Restoration Fellowship, 1999), 92.

1100. Dallas Willard, *The Spirit of the Disciplines* (New York: HarperCollins, 1988), 48.

1101. A. B. Caneday, "Veiled Glory," cited in John Piper, Justin Taylor, and Paul Kjoss Helseth, *Beyond the Bounds* (Wheaton, IL: Crossway, 2003), 163.

1102. Arthur O. Roberts, *Exploring Heaven* (San Francisco: HarperSanFrancisco, 2003), 67.

1103. N. T. Wright, *Surprised by Hope* (New York: HarperCollins, 2008), 161–162.

1104. Dallas Willard, *The Divine Conspiracy* (San Francisco: HarperSanFrancisco, 1998), 378.

1105. Jonathan Edwards, "The End for Which God Created the World," *The Works of Jonathan Edwards* (Edinburgh: Banner of Truth, 1974), 2:210.

1106. Bruce Milne, *The Message of Heaven and Hell* (Downers Grove, IL: InterVarsity Press, 2002), 326.

1107. Erich Sauer, *The King of the Earth* (Grand Rapids, MI: Eerdmans, 1962), 80–81.

1108. Wilbur M. Smith, *The Biblical Doctrine of Heaven* (Chicago: Moody Press, 1968), 220–221.

1109. Charles H. Spurgeon, *Morning and Evening*, May 14 morning.

1110. Jonathan Edwards, *Heaven: A World of Love* (Amityville, NY: Calvary Press, 1999), 25–26.

1111. Ibid., 24.

1112. Wayne Grudem, *Systematic Theology* (Grand Rapids, MI: Zondervan, 1994), 1158–1164.

1113. Randy Alcorn, *Heaven* (Carol Stream, IL: Tyndale House, 2004), 224.

1114. Ibid., 208.

1115. Ibid., 216–217.

1116. Ibid., 211–212.

1117. Ibid., 215.

1118. Ibid., 223.

1119. Randy Alcorn, *50 Days of Heaven* (Carol Stream, IL: Tyndale House, 2006), 126.

1120. Randy Alcorn, *We Shall See God* (Carol Stream, IL: Tyndale House, 2011), 294–295.

1121. Arthur Bennett, ed., *The Valley of Vision* (Carlisle, PA: Banner of Truth, 2002).

1122. Richard Brooks, *The Doors of Heaven* (Ross-shire, UK: Christian Focus Publications, 1998), 90.

1123. J. C. Ryle, *The Upper Room* (Carlisle, PA: Banner of Truth), 91. Quoted in Richard Brooks, *The Doors of Heaven* (Ross-shire, UK: Christian Focus Publications, 1998), 92.

1124. Richard Baxter, cited by Richard Brooks, *The Doors of Heaven* (Ross-shire, UK: Christian Focus Publications, 1998), 98.

1125. Colleen McDannell and Bernhard Lang, *Heaven: A History* (New York: Vintage Books, 1988), 287.

1126. Isaac Watts, 1707, "The Hope of Heaven Our Support under Trials on Earth."

1127. John R. Rice, *Bible Facts about Heaven* (Murfreesboro, TN: Sword of the Lord Publishers, 1993), 45.

1128. Charles H. Spurgeon, *Feathers for Arrows* (New York: Sheldon and Company, 1870), 105.

1129. Larry R. Dick, *A Taste of Heaven* (Victoria, BC: Trafford Publishing, 2002), 107.

1130. Ibid., 122.

1131. Richard Baxter, "The Saints' Everlasting Rest," in *The Practical Works of Richard Baxter* (Grand Rapids, MI: Baker Book House, 1981), 39–40.

1132. Paul Helm, *The Last Things* (Carlisle, PA: Banner of Truth, 1989), 94.

1133. Arthur O. Roberts, *Exploring Heaven* (San Francisco: HarperSanFrancisco, 2003), 60.

1134. Jonathan Edwards, cited in John H. Gerstner, *Jonathan Edwards on Heaven and Hell* (Grand Rapids, MI: Baker Book House, 1980), 43–45.

1135. Father J. Boudreau, SJ, *The Happiness of Heaven* (Rockford, IL: TAN Books, 1984), 116–117.

1136. Judson B. Palmer, "The Child of God between Death and the Resurrection," bibleteacher.org.

1137. Paul Helm, *The Last Things* (Carlisle, PA: Banner of Truth, 1989), 141.

1138. Randy Alcorn, *The Law of Rewards* (Carol Stream, IL: Tyndale House, 2003), 57.

1139. Randy Alcorn, *We Shall See God* (Carol Stream, IL: Tyndale House, 2011), 82.

1140. Randy Alcorn, *Heaven* (Carol Stream, IL: Tyndale House, 2004), 318.

1141. John Donne, Henry Alford, ed., *The Works of John Donne* (London: Parker, 1839), 238.

1142. Daniel A. Brown, PhD, *What the Bible Reveals about Heaven* (Ventura, CA: Regal Books, Division of Gospel Light, 1999), 224.

1143. Martin Luther, *Watchwords for the Warfare of Life,* trans., Elizabeth Rundle Charles (New York: M. W. Dodd, 1869), 317.

1144. Thomas Aquinas, *Summa Theologica: Supplementum*, question 81, article 1.

1145. N. T. Wright, *Surprised by Hope* (New York: HarperCollins, 2008), 155.

1146. Anthony A. Hoekema, *The Bible and the Future* (Grand Rapids, MI: Eerdmans, 1979), 53.

1147. Bruce Milne, *The Message of Heaven and Hell* (Downers Grove, IL: InterVarsity Press, 2002), 133.

1148. Ibid., 198.

1149. Ibid.

1150. Dallas Willard, *The Spirit of the Disciplines* (New York: HarperCollins, 1988), 53.

1151. Timothy George, "Good Question," *Christianity Today* (February 2003), 80, 84.

1152. Douglas Connelly, *Angels Around Us: What the Bible Really Says* (Downers Grove, IL: InterVarsity Press, 1995), 92.

1153. James Burns, *Memoir and Remains of the Rev. James D. Burns, MA, of Hampstead* (London: J. Nisbet, 1869), 170.

1154. Billy Graham, *World Aflame* (New York: Doubleday, 1965), 108.

1155. G. K. Chesterton, *The Everlasting Man* (Radford, VA: Wilder Publications, 2008), 136.

1156. William Hendriksen, *The Bible on the Life Hereafter* (Grand Rapids, MI: Baker Book House, 1959), 183.

1157. Anthony A. Hoekema, *The Bible and the Future* (Grand Rapids, MI: Eerdmans, 1979), 91.

1158. J. Dwight Pentecost, *Things Which Become Sound Doctrine* (Grand Rapids, MI: Zondervan, 1965), 151.

1159. Max Lucado, *When Christ Comes* (Nashville: W Publishing Group, 1999), 26.

1160. Paul Helm, *The Last Things* (Carlisle, PA: Banner of Truth, 1989), 51–52.

1161. Bruce Milne, *The Message of Heaven and Hell* (Downers Grove, IL: InterVarsity Press, 2002), 246.

1162. C. H. Dodd, "The Appearances of the Risen Christ," in *More New Testament Studies* (Manchester, UK: University of Manchester Press, 1968), 128; cited in W. L. Craig, *The Son Rises* (Chicago: Moody Press, 1981), 94.

1163. G. R. Beasley-Murray, *The Resurrection of Jesus Christ* (UK: Oliphants, 1964), 16.

1164. Bruce Milne, *The Message of Heaven and Hell* (Downers Grove, IL: InterVarsity Press, 2002), 247.

1165. Anthony F. Buzzard, *Our Fathers Who Aren't in Heaven* (McDonough, GA: Atlanta Bible College and Restoration Fellowship, 1999), 28.

1166. Erich Sauer, *The King of the Earth* (Grand Rapids, MI: Eerdmans, 1962), 140.

1167. C. S. Lewis, *The Four Loves* (New York: Harcourt Brace Jovanovich, 1960), 187.

1168. Augustine, *The Works of Aurelius Augustine*, Vol IX (Edinburgh: T and T Clark, 1892), 237.

1169. Hank Hanegraaff, *Resurrection* (Nashville: Word, 2000), 133–134. This refers to the original intention God had for our DNA before the Fall. It should also be noted that saying our DNA comprises the blueprints for our glorified bodies is based on sanctified speculation—if this is the case, it would justify believing that those who die as infants and those who die in old age will be resurrected physically mature and perfect, as God had originally intended them to be.

1170. Ambrose, *The Two Books on the Decease of His Brother Satyrus*, Book II:87 (Nicene and Post-Nicene Fathers, Second Series: Vol. X).

1171. Thomas Aquinas, *Summa Theologica: Supplementum,* "Treatise on the Last Things," Question 93: Of the Happiness of the Saints and of Their Mansions, First, Second and Third Articles.

1172. Arthur O. Roberts, *Exploring Heaven* (San Francisco: HarperSanFrancisco, 2003), 76.

1173. Anthony A. Hoekema, *The Bible and the Future* (Grand Rapids, MI: Eerdmans, 1979), 249.

1174. Randy Alcorn, *Heaven* (Carol Stream, IL: Tyndale House, 2004), 130.

1175. Ibid., 122.

1176. Randy Alcorn, *We Shall See God* (Carol Stream, IL: Tyndale House, 2011), 29.

1177. Randy Alcorn, *Heaven* (Carol Stream, IL: Tyndale House, 2004), 439.

1178. C. S. Lewis, The Chronicles of Narnia Series (New York: HarperCollins, 2001), 747.

1179. Calvin Miller, *Singer Trilogy* (Downers Grove, IL: InterVarsity Press, 1990), 341.

1180. Father J. Boudreau, SJ, *The Happiness of Heaven* (Rockford, IL: TAN Books, 1984), 179–181.

1181. Calvin Miller, cited by Harold Shaw, *Promises of Heaven* (Carol Stream, IL: Harold Shaw Publishers, 1997), 73.

1182. Kent Crockett, *Making Today Count for Eternity* (Sisters, OR: Multnomah Publishers, 2001), 65.

1183. Mark Buchanan, *Things Unseen* (Sisters, OR: Multnomah Publishers, 2002), 188.

1184. Isaac Watts, *The World to Come* (Morgan, PA: Soli Deo Gloria Publications, 1954; originally written in 1745), 74.

1185. John Gilmore, *Probing Heaven* (Grand Rapids, MI: Baker Book House, 1991), 273.

1186. Joseph M. Stowell, *Eternity* (Chicago: Moody Press, 1995), 28.

1187. Max Lucado, *When Christ Comes* (Nashville: W Publishing Group, 1999), 67.

1188. Ibid., 74.

1189. Paul Helm, *The Last Things* (Carlisle, PA: Banner of Truth, 1989), 105–106.

1190. Michael E. Wittmer, *Heaven Is a Place on Earth* (Grand Rapids, MI: Zondervan, 2004), 202.

1191. E. X. Heatherley, *Our Heavenly Home* (Austin, TX: Balcony Publishing, 2000), 97.

1192. Paul Helm, *The Last Things* (Carlisle, PA: Banner of Truth, 1989), 102.

1193. Ibid., 104–106.

1194. Charles H. Spurgeon, "The Heavenly Singers and Their Song," Sermon 2321, July 14, 1889, as cited in Randy Alcorn, *We Shall See God* (Carol Stream, IL: Tyndale House, 2011), 291.

1195. Randy Alcorn, *The Law of Rewards* (Carol Stream, IL: Tyndale House, 2003), 21.

1196. Ibid., 27.

1197. Ibid., 27–28.

1198. Ibid., 59.

1199. Ibid., 67.

1200. Ibid., 89.

1201. Ibid., 95.

1202. Ibid., 102.

1203. Ibid., 106–107.

1204. Ibid., 117.

1205. Randy Alcorn, *Heaven* (Carol Stream, IL: Tyndale House, 2004), 420.

1206. Randy Alcorn, *Edge of Eternity* (Colorado Springs: WaterBrook, 1998), 293–297.

1207. Randy Alcorn, *Safely Home* (Carol Stream, IL: Tyndale House, 2001), 377.

1208. Arthur Bennett, ed., *The Valley of Vision* (Carlisle, PA: Banner of Truth, 2002), 13.

1209. Charles H. Spurgeon, *A Passion for Holiness in a Believer's Life* (Lynwood, WA: Emerald Books, 1999), 74.

1210. Paul Helm, *The Last Things* (Carlisle, PA: Banner of Truth, 1989), 92.

1211. Jill Briscoe, *Heaven and Hell* (Wheaton, IL: Victor Books, 1990), 43.

1212. Charles H. Spurgeon, "The Glory of Grace," Sermon 2763, http://www.spurgeongems.org.

1213. Erich Sauer, *The King of the Earth* (Grand Rapids, MI: Eerdmans, 1962), 121–122.

1214. Ibid., 123–124.

1215. John Gilmore, *Probing Heaven* (Grand Rapids, MI: Baker Book House, 1991), 140.

1216. Joseph M. Stowell, *Eternity* (Chicago: Moody Press, 1995), 69.

1217. Ibid., 120.

1218. Peter Kreeft, *Everything You Ever Wanted to Know about Heaven* (San Francisco: Ignatius Press, 1990), 39.

1219. Ibid., 233.

1220. Paul Marshall with Lela Gilbert, *Heaven Is Not My Home* (Nashville: Word Publishing, 1998), 32.

1221. Philip Yancey, *Rumors of Another World* (Grand Rapids, MI: Zondervan, 2003), 18.

1222. Simone Weil, *Gravity and Grace* (New York: Routledge, 2002), 70.

1223. Father J. Boudreau, SJ, *The Happiness of Heaven* (Rockford, IL: TAN Books, 1984), 117.

1224. Charles H. Spurgeon, "The First Resurrection," Sermon 391, May 5, 1861, as cited in Randy Alcorn, *We Shall See God* (Carol Stream, IL: Tyndale House, 2011), 223.

1225. Albert M. Wolters, *Creation Regained* (Grand Rapids, MI: Eerdmans, 1985), 48.

1226. Ibid., 50.

1227. Jonathan Edwards, *Heaven: A World of Love* (Amityville, NY: Calvary Press, 1999), 16.

1228. Ibid., 30.

1229. Paul Helm, *The Last Things* (Carlisle, PA: Banner of Truth, 1989), 89.

1230. J. C. Ryle, *The Upper Room* (London: Banner of Truth, 1970, originally published in 1888), 245.

1231. Randy Alcorn, *Heaven* (Carol Stream, IL: Tyndale House, 2004), 299.

1232. Ibid., 301.

1233. Randy Alcorn, *TouchPoints: Heaven* (Carol Stream, IL: Tyndale House, 2008), 170.

1234. Randy Alcorn, *We Shall See God* (Carol Stream, IL: Tyndale House, 2011), 268.

1235. Randy Alcorn, *Heaven* (Carol Stream, IL: Tyndale House, 2004), 394.

1236. Ibid., 301.

1237. Jonathan Edwards, *The Resolutions of Jonathan Edwards (1722–1723),* JonathanEdwards .com, http://www.jonathanedwards.com/text/Personal/resolut.htm; see also Stephen Nichols, ed., *Jonathan Edwards' Resolutions and Advice to Young Converts* (Phillipsburg, NJ: Presbyterian and Reformed, 2001).

1238. Blaise Pascal, *Pensées,* trans., W. F. Trotter, Christian Classics Ethereal Library, http://www.ccel.org/p/pascal/pensees/cache/pensees.pdf, section VII, article 425.

1239. C. S. Lewis, *Letters to Malcolm* (New York: Harcourt Brace Jovanovich, 1963), 120.

1240. C. S. Lewis, *The Great Divorce* (New York: Collier Books, 1946), 6.

1241. Billy Graham, *Till Armageddon: A Perspective on Suffering* (Nashville: W Publishing Group, 1981), 153.

1242. John Milton, in *Il Penseroso,* 1.159, cited in John Bartlett, *Bartlett's Familiar Quotations* (Boston, MA: Little, Brown, 1855, 1980), 278–279.

1243. Philippa Boyens and Fran Walsh, dialogue from Peter Jackson's film *The Return of the King.*

1244. Richard Baxter, cited in J. I. Packer, ed., *Alive to God* (Downers Grove, IL: InterVarsity Press, 1992), 167.

1245. Charles H. Spurgeon, cited by Jim Elliot in *Shadow of the Almighty,* by Elisabeth Elliot (Grand Rapids, MI: Zondervan, 1970), 83.

1246. Larry R. Dick, *A Taste of Heaven* (Victoria, BC: Trafford Publishing, 2002), 17.

1247. Elisabeth Elliot, *Shadow of the Almighty* (Grand Rapids, MI: Zondervan, 1958), 85.

1248. Charles H. Spurgeon, *Spurgeon at His Best* (Grand Rapids, MI: Baker Book House, 1988), 96.

1249. Mark Buchanan, *Things Unseen* (Sisters, OR: Multnomah Publishers, 2002), 71.

1250. Ibid., 182–183.

1251. Ibid.

1252. Jonathan Edwards, *Heaven: A World of Love* (Amityville, NY: Calvary Press, 1999), 57–58.

1253. Dr. Chuck McGowen, *Let's Talk about Heaven* (Phoenix, AZ: ACW Press, 2001), 96.

1254. Peter Kreeft, *Heaven: The Heart's Greatest Longing* (San Francisco: Ignatius Press, 1989), 164.

1255. J. Dwight Pentecost, *Things to Come* (Grand Rapids, MI: Zondervan, 1964), 582.

1256. J. C. Ryle, *Heaven* (Ross-shire, UK: Christian Focus Publications, 2000), 45–46.

1257. Joseph M. Stowell, *Eternity* (Chicago: Moody Press, 1995), 55.

1258. Ibid., 59.

1259. Ibid., 98.

1260. Steven J. Lawson, *Heaven Help Us!* (Colorado Springs: NavPress, 1995), 12.

1261. Isaac Watts, *The World to Come* (Morgan, PA: Soli Deo Gloria Publications, 1954; originally written in 1745), 158.

1262. Steven J. Lawson, *Heaven Help Us!* (Colorado Springs: NavPress, 1995), 173.

1263. Max Lucado, *When Christ Comes* (Nashville: W Publishing Group, 1999), xvi–xvii.

1264. Horatius Bonar, *Hymns of Faith and Hope* (New York: Carter and Bros., 1866), 76–77.

1265. Philip Yancey, *Rumors of Another World* (Grand Rapids, MI: Zondervan, 2003), 58.

1266. A. W. Tozer, *Of God and Men* (Harrisburg, PA: Christian Publications, 1960), 163.

1267. C. S. Lewis, *Mere Christianity* (New York: HarperCollins, 2001), 134.

1268. John Bunyan, "The Resurrection of the Dead, and Eternal Judgment," http://acacia.pair .com/Acacia.John.Bunyan/Sermons.Allegories/Resurrection.of.Dead/6.html.

1269. James M. Campbell, DD, *Heaven Opened* (New York: Revell, 1924), 193.

1270. Mark Buchanan, *Things Unseen* (Sisters, OR: Multnomah Publishers, 2002), 181.

1271. C. S. Lewis, "The World's Last Night," in *The World's Last Night and Other Essays* (New York: Harcourt Brace Jovanovich, 1952), 110, 113.

NOTES

1272. Edward Donnelly, *Biblical Teaching on the Doctrines of Heaven and Hell* (Edinburgh: Banner of Truth, 2001), 65.

1273. Joni Eareckson Tada, *Heaven: Your Real Home* (Grand Rapids, MI: Zondervan, 1995), 16.

1274. Larry Dixon, *Heaven: Thinking Now about Forever* (Camp Hill, PA: Christian Publications, 2002), 42.

1275. Richard Baxter, *The Saints' Everlasting Rest,* http://www.ccel.org/ccel/baxter/saints_rest.iii .XV.html.

1276. Richard Baxter, *The Practical Works of Richard Baxter, Vol. 1* (London: George Virtue, 1838), 77.

1277. Richard Sibbes, *The Pilgrim's Progress and Traditions in Puritan Meditation* (Boston, MA: Lamson, Wolffe and Company, 1966), 134.

1278. John Preston, cited by Wayne Martindale, PhD, ed., *Journey to the Celestial City* (Chicago: Moody Press, 1995), 59.

1279. Richard Baxter, *The Practical Works of Richard Baxter, Vol. 1* (London: George Virtue, 1838), 153.

1280. John Milton, *An Introduction to the Prose and Poetical Works of John Milton* (London: Macmillan, 1899), 34.

1281. Wayne Martindale, PhD, ed., *Journey to the Celestial City* (Chicago: Moody Press, 1995), 12.

1282. Sam Storms, *The Hope of Glory* (Wheaton, IL: Crossway Books, 2008), 33–34.

1283. Ibid., 34.

1284. Randy Alcorn, *We Shall See God* (Carol Stream, IL: Tyndale House, 2011), 159.

1285. Randy Alcorn, *50 Days of Heaven* (Carol Stream, IL: Tyndale House, 2006), 267.

1286. Randy Alcorn, *We Shall See God* (Carol Stream, IL: Tyndale House, 2011), 160.

1287. Randy Alcorn, *In Light of Eternity* (Colorado Springs: WaterBrook, 1984), 144.

1288. Randy Alcorn, *Heaven* (Carol Stream, IL: Tyndale House, 2004), 22.

1289. Randy Alcorn, *Money, Possessions, and Eternity* (Carol Stream, IL: Tyndale House, 2003), 464.

1290. Bruce Milne, *The Message of Heaven and Hell* (Downers Grove, IL: InterVarsity Press, 2002), 286–287.

1291. John Gilmore, *Probing Heaven* (Grand Rapids, MI: Baker Book House, 1991), 153, 155.

1292. Peter J. Kreeft, *Everything You Ever Wanted to Know about Heaven* (San Francisco: Harper and Row, 1982), 41, 45, 46.

1293. Hendrikus Berkhof, *Christ the Meaning of History,* trans., Lambertus Buurman (Richmond, VA: John Knox, 1966), 188.

1294. Peter Kreeft, *Everything You Ever Wanted to Know about Heaven* (San Francisco: Ignatius Press, 1990), 57.

1295. Ibid., 152.

1296. N. T. Wright, *Surprised by Hope* (New York: HarperCollins, 2008), 162–163.

1297. Larry R. Dick, *A Taste of Heaven* (Victoria, BC: Trafford Publishing, 2002), 109.

1298. Peter Kreeft, *Everything You Ever Wanted to Know about Heaven* (San Francisco: Ignatius Press, 1990), 188.

1299. Ibid., 203.

1300. J. I. Packer, *Concise Theology* (Carol Stream, IL: Tyndale House, 2001), 267.

1301. John Newton, "Amazing Grace," hymn in the public domain.

1302. Wayne Grudem, *Systematic Theology* (Grand Rapids, MI: Zondervan, 1994), 1158–1164.

1303. J. Sidlow Baxter, *The Other Side of Death* (Grand Rapids, MI: Kregel Publications, 1987), 215.

1304. Ray C. Stedman, *Authentic Christianity* (Waco, TX: Word Books, 1975), 141.

1305. Randy Alcorn, *Heaven* (Carol Stream, IL: Tyndale House, 2004), 257.

1306. Ibid., 310.

1307. Randy Alcorn, *Heaven for Kids* (Carol Stream, IL: Tyndale House, 2006), 63–66.

1308. Randy Alcorn, *Heaven* (Carol Stream, IL: Tyndale House, 2004), 267–268

1309. Ibid., 268.

1310. Ibid., 449–450.
1311. John Piper, *Future Grace* (Sisters, OR: Multnomah Publishers, 1995), 371, 376.
1312. Albert M. Wolters, *Creation Regained* (Grand Rapids, MI: Eerdmans, 1985), 41.
1313. C. S. Lewis, The Chronicles of Narnia Series (New York: HarperCollins, 2001), 146.
1314. Bruce Milne, *The Message of Heaven and Hell* (Downers Grove, IL: InterVarsity Press, 2002), 310.
1315. Anthony A. Hoekema, *The Bible and the Future* (Grand Rapids, MI: Eerdmans, 1979), 285.
1316. Peter Toon, *Heaven and Hell* (New York: Thomas Nelson, 1986), 144.
1317. Erich Sauer, *The King of the Earth* (Grand Rapids, MI: Eerdmans, 1962), 150.
1318. John Gilmore, *Probing Heaven* (Grand Rapids, MI: Baker Book House, 1991), 89.
1319. Ibid., 97.
1320. Anthony A. Hoekema, *The Bible and the Future* (Grand Rapids, MI: Eerdmans, 1979), 52.
1321. Michael E. Wittmer, *Heaven Is a Place on Earth* (Grand Rapids, MI: Zondervan, 2004), 75.
1322. Hendrikus Berkhof, *Christ the Meaning of History*, trans., Lambertus Buurman (Richmond, VA: John Knox, 1966), 181.
1323. Wayne Grudem, *Systematic Theology* (Grand Rapids, MI: Zondervan, 1994), 1158.
1324. John F. MacArthur, *The Glory of Heaven* (Wheaton, IL: Crossway Books, 1996), 89, 103–104.
1325. Dr. Chuck McGowen, *Let's Talk about Heaven* (Phoenix: ACW Press, 2001), 89.
1326. Henri Nouwen, cited in Joseph M. Champlin, *Behind Closed Doors* (Mahwah, NJ: Paulist Press, 1984), 44.
1327. Anthony A. Hoekema, *The Bible and the Future* (Grand Rapids, MI: Eerdmans, 1979), 281.
1328. Randy Alcorn, *Edge of Eternity* (Colorado Springs: WaterBrook, 1999), 311.
1329. Randy Alcorn, *Heaven* (Carol Stream, IL: Tyndale House, 2004), 45.
1330. Ibid., 130–131.
1331. Randy Alcorn, *We Shall See God* (Carol Stream, IL: Tyndale House, 2011), 287.
1332. Randy Alcorn, *Heaven* (Carol Stream, IL: Tyndale House, 2004), 129–130.
1333. Ibid., 177–178.
1334. Ibid., 262.
1335. Randy Alcorn, *We Shall See God* (Carol Stream, IL: Tyndale House, 2011), 126.
1336. Randy Alcorn, *Heaven* (Carol Stream, IL: Tyndale House, 2004), 447–448.
1337. Arthur Bennett, ed., *The Valley of Vision* (Carlisle, PA: Banner of Truth, 2002), 49.
1338. Ibid., 275.
1339. James M. Campbell, DD, *Heaven Opened* (New York: Revell, 1924), 123.
1340. Larry R. Dick, *A Taste of Heaven* (Victoria, BC: Trafford Publishing, 2002), 103.
1341. Paul Helm, *The Last Things* (Carlisle, PA: Banner of Truth, 1989), 94–95.
1342. Arthur O. Roberts, *Exploring Heaven* (San Francisco: HarperSanFrancisco, 2003), 63.
1343. Michael E. Wittmer, *Heaven Is a Place on Earth* (Grand Rapids, MI: Zondervan, 2004), 207.
1344. Father J. Boudreau, SJ, *The Happiness of Heaven* (Rockford, IL: TAN Books, 1984), 107–108.
1345. Martin Luther King Jr., to students at Barratt Junior High School, Philadelphia, October 26, 1967.
1346. Rudyard Kipling, "When Earth's Last Picture Is Painted."
1347. Douglas Connelly, *The Promise of Heaven* (Downers Grove, IL: InterVarsity Press, 2000), 104.
1348. Alexander Maclaren, "Entrance into God's Rest," *Maclaren's Expositions of Holy Scripture*, Vol. 10 (Grand Rapids, MI: Eerdmans, 1959), 320–323.
1349. Jonathan Edwards, *Heaven: A World of Love* (Amityville, NY: Calvary Press, 1999), 28, 38.
1350. Paul Helm, *The Last Things* (Carlisle, PA: Banner of Truth, 1989), 94–95.
1351. Isaac Watts, *Church Psalmody* (Boston: T. R. Marvin, 1864), 163.
1352. Wilbur M. Smith, *The Biblical Doctrine of Heaven* (Chicago: Moody Press, 1968), 195.
1353. N. T. Wright, *Surprised by Hope* (New York: HarperCollins, 2008), 181.

1354. Victor Hugo, "The Future Life," quoted by Dave Wilkinson, "And I Shall Dwell," sermon preached at Moorpark Presbyterian Church, February 18, 2001, "Sermons from Moorpark Presbyterian Church," Moorpark Presbyterian Church, http://www.mppres.org/sermons /2001/021801.htm.

1355. Randy Alcorn, *Heaven* (Carol Stream, IL: Tyndale House, 2004), 331–332.

1356. Ibid., 320–321.

1357. Ibid., 395, 398.

1358. Arthur Bennett, ed., *The Valley of Vision* (Carlisle, PA: Banner of Truth, 2002), 233.

1359. A. W. Tozer and J. L. Snyder, *Tozer on Worship and Entertainment* (Camp Hill, PA: WingSpread, 1997), 4.

1360. Tony Evans, *Tony Evans Speaks Out on Heaven and Hell* (Chicago: Moody Press, 2000), 42.

1361. J. C. Ryle, *Heaven* (Ross-shire, UK: Christian Focus Publications, 2000), 41–42.

1362. Larry R. Dick, *A Taste of Heaven* (Victoria, BC: Trafford Publishing, 2002), 201.

1363. Paul Marshall with Lela Gilbert, *Heaven Is Not My Home* (Nashville: Word Publishing, 1998), 189.

1364. Arthur O. Roberts, *Exploring Heaven* (San Francisco: HarperSanFrancisco, 2003), 49.

1365. Augustine, *The City of God*, The Modern Library series, translated by Marcus Dods (New York: Random House, 1950), 867.

1366. Cornelius P. Venema, *The Promise of the Future* (Trowbridge, UK: Banner of Truth, 2000), 478.

1367. Wayne Grudem, *Systematic Theology* (Grand Rapids, MI: Zondervan, 1994), 1158–1164.

1368. William Featherston, "My Jesus I Love Thee."

1369. Augustine, "Of the Eternal Felicity of the City of God, and of the Perpetual Sabbath," in *The City of God*, Book 22, chapter 30, trans., Marcus Dods. Taken from the Nicene and Post-Nicene Fathers, First Series, ed., Philip Schaff (Peabody, MA: Hendrickson, 1999). Reprint of the American Edition, Vol. 2, St. Augustine's *City of God* and *Christian Doctrine*. Originally published by Christian Literature, 1887.

1370. Daniel A. Brown, PhD, *What the Bible Reveals about Heaven* (Ventura, CA: Regal Books, Division of Gospel Light, 1999), 214.

1371. Jonathan Edwards, *The Works of Jonathan Edwards: The Miscellanies*, Volume 13, ed., Thomas A. Schafer (New Haven, CT: Yale University Press, 1994), no. 188, 331.

1372. Douglas Connelly, *The Promise of Heaven* (Downers Grove, IL: InterVarsity Press, 2000), 77.

1373. John MacArthur, *Heaven* *(Panorama City, CA: Word of Grace Communications, 1988), 98.

1374. E. L. Maskell, *Grace and Glory* (New York: Morehouse-Barlow, 1961), 68–69.

1375. Randy Alcorn, *Heaven* (Carol Stream, IL: Tyndale House, 2004), 404–405.

1376. Ibid., 190.

1377. Ibid., 189.

1378. Randy Alcorn, *Edge of Eternity* (Colorado Springs: WaterBrook, 1998), 312–313.

1379. Randy Alcorn, *Heaven* (Carol Stream, IL: Tyndale House, 2004), 473.

Index

A

Alcorn, Randy
  See quotations at end of each topic.
À Kempis, Thomas 25, 469
Alford, Henry 382
Alighieri, Dante 262
Ambrose 526
Ames, William (Amesius) 166
Anselm 165, 385
Aquinas, Thomas 91, 165, 237, 315, 453, 516, 526
Aristides 444
Augustine 41, 138, 148, 241, 242, 394, 480, 525, 611

B

Baillie, John 21
Baker, Don 354
Ball, Charles Ferguson 48, 419
Bavinck, Herman 165
Baxter, J. Sidlow 49, 69, 71, 81, 95, 147, 191, 253, 399, 411, 412, 578
Baxter, Richard 5, 208, 228, 318, 400, 494, 506, 509, 557, 567, 568
Bayly, Joseph 25, 137, 139
Beale, Greg 379
Beasley-Murray, G. R. 317, 523
Bede 366
Berdyaev, Nicholas 32
Berkhof, Hendrikus 92, 575, 587
Bloesch, Donald 23
Bonar, Horatius 194
Bonhoeffer, Dietrich 21, 133
Boston, Thomas 303
Boudreau, Father J. 32, 45, 88, 206, 314, 315, 352, 355, 464, 510, 534, 550, 599
Boyens, Philippa 557
Bradford, John 186, 229

Briscoe, Jill 45, 547
Brooks, Richard 56, 175, 227, 268, 425, 444, 445, 506
Brown, Daniel 3, 134, 139, 148, 188, 192, 193, 237, 332, 515, 612
Browning, Elizabeth Barrett 32
Brown, Walton 7, 354
Buchanan, Mark 15, 17, 18, 19, 24, 55, 56, 135, 190, 290, 465, 469, 479, 535, 558, 559, 565
Buechner, Frederick 19
Bunyan, John 306, 414, 449, 564
Burns, James Drummond 520
Buzzard, Anthony 343, 345, 346, 347, 376, 385, 495, 524

C

Calamy, Benjamin 39
Calvin, John 97, 119, 176, 385
Campbell, James 94, 122, 135, 188, 189, 227, 365, 409, 484, 564, 597
Caneday, A. B. 495
Carmichael, Amy 93, 291
Carson, D. A. 276, 288
Chesterton, G. K. 23, 74, 81, 520
Chilton, David 446
Cicero 366
Connelly, Douglas 139, 175, 321, 520, 600, 612
Conrad, Joseph 483
Conyers, A. J. 75, 447
Cousin, Annie Ross 64
Crockett, Kent 535
Cyprian 23, 321

D

De Haan, Mart 57, 455
Demarest, Bruce 33

Demy, Timothy J. 333
Dick, Larry 4, 44, 68, 175, 206, 207, 222, 334, 395, 397, 494, 508, 558, 576, 598, 610
Dinesen, Isak 20
Dixon, Larry 15, 566
Dodd, C. H. 523
Donne, John 134, 515
Donnelly, Edward 7, 64, 277, 565

E

Eareckson Tada, Joni 6, 21, 47, 89, 245, 432, 446, 449, 565
Edwards, Jonathan 4, 31, 62, 79, 80, 91, 166, 200, 208, 209, 210, 213, 214, 227, 235, 236, 238, 242, 246, 276, 277, 315, 317, 322, 336, 337, 463, 466, 497, 499, 510, 551, 556, 559, 602, 612
Eldredge, John 55, 290
Eliot, T. S. 7, 269
Elliot, Jim 558
Emerson, Ralph Waldo 378
Erickson, Millard 90
Evans, Tony 64, 79, 93, 136, 207, 269, 271, 396, 466, 609

F

Featherston, William 611
Fleming, Jean 19, 20
Fortman, E. J. 8, 276, 322, 356, 380, 381, 399, 488

G

Galilei, Galileo 324
Geisler, Norman 193
George, Timothy 41, 519
Gilmore, John 92, 149, 187, 198, 199, 221, 317, 318, 321, 333, 353, 380, 396, 422, 470, 536, 548, 574, 586
Gire, Ken 136
Graham, Billy 520, 556
Grudem, Wayne 48, 150, 154, 168, 239, 307, 354, 355, 500, 578, 587, 611

H

Habermas, Gary 432
Hanegraaff, Hank 91, 193, 278, 525
Hannah, John 74
Hawthorne, Nathaniel 185
Heatherley, E. X. 25, 96, 97, 148, 470, 538
Helm, Paul 81, 138, 140, 153, 228, 230, 268, 273, 274, 277, 278, 317, 332, 334, 335, 336, 426, 464, 509, 511, 522, 537, 538, 547, 552, 598, 602

Hendriksen, William 272, 353, 396, 409, 483, 521
Henry, Matthew 131
Hinson, W. B. 185
Hirsch, Alan 464
Hodge, A. A. 384
Hodge, Charles 167
Hoekema, Anthony 40, 103, 108, 110, 121, 136, 164, 237, 343, 344, 376, 377, 380, 395, 480, 484, 485, 517, 521, 527, 585, 586, 589
Hugo, Victor 604
Hunt, T. W. 44, 206, 230, 239, 319

I

Ice, Thomas 333
Irenaeus 164, 382, 494

J

Jeremiah, James 14
Jerome 356
Judson, Adoniram 16
Julian of Norwich 240

K

Keller, Helen 465
Kendall, R. T. 335
King, Martin Luther, Jr. 599
Kipling, Rudyard 599
Knox, John 465
Kreeft, Peter 4, 45, 54, 56, 90, 92, 122, 206, 220, 221, 222, 238, 272, 273, 318, 356, 423, 430, 549, 560, 574, 575, 576
Kuyper, Abraham 96, 304

L

Ladd, George 346
Lang, Bernhard 17, 90, 147, 151, 188, 507
Lawson, Steven J. 4, 18, 120, 122, 151, 229, 231, 238, 239, 306, 319, 365, 377, 378, 395, 398, 464, 561
Lenski, R. C. H. 378, 432
Lewis, C. S. 2, 3, 7, 19, 20, 21, 22, 23, 24, 33, 34, 75, 76, 80, 88, 91, 104, 121, 131, 138, 140, 148, 149, 152, 198, 202, 220, 223, 238, 263, 268, 269, 278, 289, 306, 313, 320, 357, 367, 376, 382, 383, 384, 431, 434, 454, 463, 471, 479, 525, 534, 556, 564, 565, 584
Lewis, Gordon 33
Liddell, Eric 454
Lloyd-Jones, Martyn 137, 229
Longfellow, Henry Wadsworth 136

Lucado, Max 63, 137, 273, 334, 344, 485, 522, 536, 562
Luther, Martin 18, 50, 260, 319, 515

M
MacArthur, Jack 131
MacArthur, John 246, 588, 613
Maclaren, Alexander 601
MacDonald, George 6, 276, 319, 365
Mahaney, C. J. 77
Marshall, Paul 104, 107, 108, 290, 376, 453, 485, 549, 610
Martindale, Wayne 57, 58, 75, 76, 449, 568
Maskell, E. L. 613
McDannell, Colleen 17, 90, 147, 151, 188, 507
McGee, J. Vernon 68, 70
McGowen, Chuck 367, 465, 560, 588
McGrath, Alister 15, 91, 409, 410
Melanchthon, Philip 355
Methodius 98, 169
Meyer, F. B. 396
Miller, Calvin 132, 534
Milne, Bruce 3, 15, 89, 93, 107, 132, 186, 190, 222, 240, 242, 243, 289, 303, 304, 333, 343, 376, 446, 483, 484, 497, 517, 518, 523, 524, 574, 585
Milton, John 269, 290, 408, 557, 568
Monroe, Melana Hunt 44, 206, 230, 239, 319
Montgomery, James 35
Moody, Dwight L. 132, 396
Moore, Thomas 313
Moreland, John Richard 132
Moreland, J. P. 432
Morrow, Barry 151, 198, 469
Mouw, Richard 199, 200, 201, 343

N
Newton, John 577
Nouwen, Henri 589

O
Oden, Thomas 48
Origen 164
Owen, John 414

P
Pache, René 408
Packer, J. I. 74, 260, 267, 305, 577
Palmer, Judson 356, 510
Pascal, Blaise 22, 315, 556
Paterson-Smyth, J. 211
Pentecost, J. Dwight 521, 560

Pierson, A. T. 260, 262
Piper, John 40, 43, 62, 164, 189, 433, 479, 584
Potok, Chaim 468
Powell, Ivor 189, 354, 425, 454, 467
Preston, John 133, 568

R
Rhodes, Ron 78
Rice, John 133, 410, 420, 508
Ridderbos, Herman 344
Roberts, Arthur 4, 6, 33, 43, 46, 103, 104, 106, 149, 207, 398, 453, 494, 495, 509, 527, 598, 610
Rutherford, Samuel 18, 237
Ryle, J. C. 16, 80, 207, 212, 243, 289, 366, 410, 506, 552, 560, 610

S
Sauer, Erich 307, 421, 484, 488, 498, 525, 547, 548, 585
Sayers, Dorothy 266, 482
Schaeffer, Francis 355
Schep, J. A. 381
Scroggie, W. Graham 93, 155, 189, 352, 367
Shakespeare 352
Shanahan, Niki Behrikis 431
Shedd, William 266
Shelley, Percy Bysshe 34
Sibbes, Richard 568
Simon, Ulrich 240
Smith, Wilbur 498, 603
Spurgeon, Charles 2, 14, 17, 23, 31, 40, 42, 47, 49, 68, 69, 71, 95, 120, 123, 134, 136, 171, 192, 200, 208, 210, 229, 230, 236, 241, 244, 245, 261, 262, 264, 265, 266, 288, 305, 316, 321, 384, 401, 413, 448, 455, 466, 467, 470, 499, 508, 539, 546, 547, 550, 557, 558
Stedman, Ray C. 8, 231, 469, 578
Storms, Sam 96, 240, 323, 569
Stott, John 483
Stowe, Harriet Beecher 141, 212, 275
Stowell, Joseph 63, 189, 198, 447, 467, 536, 548, 560, 561
Studd, C. T. 463

T
Tacelli, Ronald 92
Teresa of Avila 263, 353
Tertullian 164
Toon, Peter 32, 306, 585
Torrey, R. A. 41, 211, 260

Tozer, A. W. 20, 22, 34, 74, 76, 141, 184,
    185, 235, 237, 261, 270, 271, 304, 305,
    316, 325, 401, 448, 563, 609
Twain, Mark 54

U
Updike, John 147, 151
Ussher, James 337, 348

V
Venema, Cornelius 107, 199, 611

W
Walsh, Fran 557
Waterhouse, Steven 208, 412
Watts, Isaac 43, 70, 77, 78, 79, 120, 140,
    155, 156, 186, 187, 263, 268, 270, 314,
    332, 399, 421, 468, 470, 507, 535, 561,
    603
Weil, Simone 550

Wesley, John 185, 335, 419, 430, 435
Whitchurch, Drake 6, 33, 80, 175, 242, 364,
    464
White, Ellen G. 289
Whittier, John Greenleaf 209
Willard, Dallas 88, 123, 191, 468, 495, 497,
    518
Williams, H. A. 454
Wittmer, Michael 103, 379, 537, 586, 598
Wohlberg, Steve 431, 432, 434
Wolters, Albert 94, 105, 106, 120, 121, 122,
    480, 481, 486, 487, 550, 551, 584
Wright, N. T. 34, 42, 46, 109, 154, 155, 170,
    202, 346, 386, 478, 485, 496, 517, 603

Y
Yancey, Philip 291, 549, 563

Z
Zodhiates, Spiros 410, 425

About the Author

RANDY ALCORN is the founder of Eternal Perspective Ministries (EPM), a nonprofit ministry dedicated to teaching the principles of God's Word and assisting the church in ministering to unreached, unfed, unborn, uneducated, unreconciled, and unsupported people around the world. His ministry focus is communicating the strategic importance of using our earthly time, money, possessions, and opportunities to invest in need-meeting ministries that count for eternity. He accomplishes this by analyzing, teaching, and applying biblical truth.

Before starting EPM in 1990, Randy served as a pastor for fourteen years. He holds degrees in theology and biblical studies and has taught on the adjunct faculties of Multnomah University and Western Seminary in Portland, Oregon.

Randy is a *New York Times* bestselling author of more than forty books, including *Heaven, 50 Days of Heaven, We Shall See God, If God Is Good, Safely Home,* and *Courageous.* His books in print exceed 5 million and have been translated into more than thirty languages. Randy has written for many magazines, including EPM's quarterly issues-oriented magazine, *Eternal Perspectives.* He is active daily on Facebook and Twitter, and has been a guest on more than seven hundred radio, television, and online programs, including *Focus on the Family, FamilyLife Today, Revive Our Hearts, The Bible Answer Man,* and The Resurgence.

Randy resides in Gresham, Oregon, with his wife, Nanci. They have two married daughters and are the proud grandparents of five grandchildren. Randy enjoys hanging out with his family, biking, playing tennis, doing research, and reading.

Contact Eternal Perspective Ministries:
39085 Pioneer Blvd., Suite 206
Sandy, OR 97055
(503) 668-5200
www.epm.org

Follow Randy on
Facebook: www.facebook.com/randyalcorn
Twitter: www.twitter.com/randyalcorn
Blog: www.epm.org/blog

BOOKS BY RANDY ALCORN

FICTION

Deadline
Dominion
Deception
Edge of Eternity
Lord Foulgrin's Letters
The Ishbane Conspiracy
Safely Home
Courageous
The Chasm

NONFICTION

Heaven
Touchpoints: Heaven
50 Days of Heaven
In Light of Eternity
Managing God's Money
Money, Possessions, and Eternity
The Law of Rewards
ProLife Answers to ProChoice Arguments
Sexual Temptation: Guardrails for the Road to Purity
The Goodness of God
The Grace and Truth Paradox
The Purity Principle
The Treasure Principle
Why ProLife?
If God Is Good . . .
The Promise of Heaven
We Shall See God
90 Days of God's Goodness
Life Promises for Eternity
Eternal Perspectives

KIDS

Heaven for Kids
Wait until Then
Tell Me about Heaven

CP0143